THE BUILDING OF BRITISH SOCIAL ANTHROPOLOGY

STUDIES IN THE HISTORY
OF MODERN SCIENCE

Editors:

ROBERT S. COHEN, *Boston University*

ERWIN N. HIEBERT, *Harvard University*

EVERETT I. MENDELSOHN, *Harvard University*

VOLUME 8

IAN LANGHAM

History Department, University of Sydney, Australia

THE BUILDING OF BRITISH SOCIAL ANTHROPOLOGY

W. H. R. Rivers and his Cambridge Disciples in The Development of Kinship Studies, 1898–1931

D. REIDEL PUBLISHING COMPANY

DORDRECHT : HOLLAND / BOSTON : U.S.A.

LONDON : ENGLAND

Library of Congress Cataloging in Publication Data

CIP

Langham, Ian, 1942–
    The building of British social anthropology.

    (Studies in the history of modern science; v. 8)
    Bibliography: p.
    Includes indexes.
        1.   Rivers, W. H. R. (William Halse Rivers), 1864–1922.
    2.   Kinship–Study and teaching (Higher)–England–History.
    3.   Ethnology–Study and teaching (Higher)–England–History.
    I.   Title.   II.   Series.
    GN21.R53L36   306.8′3′071142   81–10638
    ISBN 90-277-1264-6   AACR2
    ISBN 90-277-1265-4 (pbk.)

Published by D. Reidel Publishing Company,
P.O. Box 17, 3300 AA Dordrecht, Holland.

Sold and distributed in the U.S.A. and Canada
by Kluwer Boston Inc.,
190 Old Derby Street, Hingham, MA 02043, U.S.A.

In all other countries, sold and distributed
by Kluwer Academic Publishers Group,
P.O. Box 322, 3300 AH Dordrecht, Holland.

D. Reidel Publishing Company is a member of the Kluwer Group.

Printed in The Netherlands

To Kathie,

*who understands better
than anyone else the
reasons for my
gratitude to her*

CONTENTS

LIST OF ILLUSTRATIONS

(Between Pages 192 and 193)

Lewis Henry Morgan, circa 1870.

Alfred W. Howitt.

Howitt with Lorimer Fison, Sale, Victoria, 1882.

W. Baldwin Spencer, circa 1905.

F. J. Gillen.

Members of the Torres Straits Expedition, 1898.

Rivers and Henry Head engaged in their experiments on the cutaneous nervous system, circa 1903.

John Layard engaged in fieldwork in the New Hebrides, circa 1915.

A. Bernard Deacon in the New Hebrides, circa 1926.

"Shell-shock Psychotherapists" at the Military Hospital, Maghull, 1915.

Brenda Seligman towards the end of her life.

Daisy Bates.

Daisy Bates and her Aboriginal charges, Peak Hill, Western Australia, 1908.

A. R. Radcliffe-Brown.

PREFACE

The nature of that transition to maturity [a transition involving "The acquisition of the sort of paradigm that identifies challenging puzzles, supplies clues to their solution, and guarantees that the truly clever practitioner will succeed"] deserves fuller discussion than it has received in this book, particularly from those concerned with the development of the contemporary social sciences. (Thomas S. Kuhn, 1969, Postscript to *The Structure of Scientific Revolutions.*)

The first two or three decades of the twentieth-century represents a shadowy period in the history of science. For most contemporary scientists, the period is a little too far away to be the subject of a first-hand oral tradition; while at the same time it is not sufficiently remote to have acquired the epic and oversimplified contour of history which has been transformed into mythology. Historians of science, by contrast, who want to free themselves from the mythology which is used to legitimize the present state of the discipline, are interested in discovering what really happened, and how it was regarded at the time. For them the nature of science in the early twentieth-century is obscured by what they regard as its proximity in time, and they are disturbed by a general lack of depth in scholarly work in the area, which makes it difficult to see the period in proper perspective. Moreover, by the beginning of the present century, most branches of science had progressed a goodly distance along the exponential curves which typically mark their rates of growth. This entails that the number of scientists involved in the various modern disciplines is so great that it is difficult for the historian to encompass the material and to sort out the grain from the chaff. Even Charles C. Gillispie's multi-volumed *Dictionary of Scientific Biography*, which gives a usefully documented encapsulation of the careers of a very large number of important figures from almost all eras in the history of science, breaks down badly in its coverage of all but the most eminent of twentieth-century scientists.

One scientist from this period, who has to some extent been lost in the crowd, is W. H. R. Rivers, who made substantial contributions to experimental physiology and neo-Freudian psychology, and who played a pivotal role in ushering the infant science of anthropology into the twentieth-century. More specifically, Rivers and his students laid the foundations for what was eventually to become known as British Social Anthropology.

xi

If one surveys the anthropological section of a large research library, a remarkable fact will become evident. In terms of quantity, but more particularly in terms of quality, the material written on contemporary aboriginal[1] societies over the past six or seven decades is vastly superior to that written previously. Such an observation has prompted a modern anthropologist, who is not prone to hyperbole, to speak of an "Ethnographic Revolution", perceived as comparable in importance to the Industrial Revolution which transformed the Western world in the century following Watt's development of the steam engine.[2] To be more specific, about seventy years ago the anthropological monograph or "ethnography", constituting a comprehensive (and usually single-volume) study of one particular society, first entered the picture and has served as the most clearly-defined unit of ethnological communication ever since. At about the same time as ethnographies made their appearance, a corresponding change became evident in the pre-existing specialist anthropology journals. The proportion of contributions by ethnological amateurs began to decline, and their place was gradually taken by articles written by professional anthropologists. And in both the monographs and the journals, the same trends were evident: an increasing reliance on intensive, personally-conducted fieldwork; a growing sympathy, and often empathy, with the people being investigated; a finer appreciation of the subtleties and complexities of preliterate life; a narrowing of objectives so that only one society is treated, rather the whole of "primitive culture"; a replacement of the typically late nineteenth-century attempt to demonstrate that societies have evolved over time with the concern for elucidating the factors which keep a society functioning synchronically; and the emergence of technical procedures resembling what Kuhn calls "puzzle-solutions" (the nature of which I shall discuss shortly). Consonant with these trends, the audience for the subject rapidly narrowed. No longer did the anthropologist aim at lay-people who had a prurient curiosity about "savages". Rather her/ his contributions were directed at professional colleagues, the fellow anthropologists who shared similar aptitudes, educational experiences and scientific value-systems.

In short, the discipline has found its own path to maturity, and the future historian who wishes to understand fully the process must compare it with a range of maturation processes exhibited by other disciplines.[3] One particular school, namely British Social Anthropology, has been prominent in the maturation of world anthropology. After originating at Cambridge and the London School of Economics in the early years of the twentieth-century, it rapidly made extensive inroads into academic anthropology throughout the

nations of the British Commonwealth (or British Empire as it then was).
During the second and fourth decades of the twentieth-century, it had a
significant impact upon the discipline in the United States, where it interacted
with the predominantly Boasian tradition of cultural anthropology, the
development of which had, in many respects, independently converged
with that of British Social Anthropology. The *Register of Members* of the
Association of Social Anthropologists of the Commonwealth, published in
1969, lists members attached to no less than seventy universities and ten
other teaching and/or research institutions, and residing in some twenty-two
countries in addition to England and Wales. On figures such as these, it would
seem no exaggeration to describe British Social Anthropology as certainly the
most widely dispersed, and arguably the most influential school of anthropology in the English-speaking world, over the past half-century. Jairus Banaji,
no friend of the school, has referred to its "quasi-hegemonic role within the
global spectrum of anthropological research".[4]

Apart from participating in the general trend towards maturation which I
have already mentioned, British Social Anthropology also had some distinctive features of its own. One was the specialized deployment of its triad of
crucially important theoretical concepts, namely "society", "function" and
"structure". By the first of these words British Social Anthropologists tended
to mean a self-contained, static and harmoniously operating group of aboriginal men and women,[5] bound together by ties of kinship, affinity and/or
economic interchange, and utilizing institutions of a religious, political and/
or legal nature. However, in pointing out that this use of the word was characteristic of British Social Anthropology, I do not wish to imply that the
underlying theoretical concept was totally unique to that discipline. On
the contrary, when a British anthropologist used the word "societies", his
meaning would have — especially after the early thirties — approximated
quite closely to that of an American anthropologist employing the term
"cultures". The fact that Americans like Margaret Mead, and people with
British backgrounds, such as Reo Fortune and Gregory Bateson, could function professionally either in the Boasian "cultural" milieu or in the company
of British Social Anthropologists, like Radcliffe-Brown and Malinowski,
provides a nice illustration of the convergence of the American and English
traditions. Indeed, this convergence, which had been aided and abetted by
Robert Lowie's appreciation of the contributions of Rivers and Radcliffe-
Brown, was furthered by Mead, Fortune and Bateson themselves, both intellectually and maritally.[6]

The second key term in British Social Anthropology was "function". Used

as a catch-cry by Malinowski, who once said light-heartedly that he had
christened the "Functionalist School" largely "out of my own sense of
irresponsibility", this word sums up better than any other the preoccupation
of British Social Anthropology with institutional consistency. Malinowski
tended to define function in terms of adaptation, stressing that all elements
of culture work "directly or indirectly for the satisfaction of human needs",
and deducing from this that all the manifold institutions of a society are "at
work, functioning, active, efficient".[7] For Malinowski, it was enough to ask
how a given cultural institution was related to other parts of the system.
Radcliffe-Brown, however, was interested in using the concept of function
to introduce the question of equilibrium and social order. Given any element
of the social system, Radcliffe-Brown's expansion of the question "What is
its function?" might be expressed as "How does it contribute to the workings
of the society as a whole?" His assumptions were, of course, that all living
societies *are* fundamentally harmonious, and that any operational element
within a society *does* contribute to the overall concordance. Such assumptions
point to the basic metaphor lying behind Radcliffe-Brown's theoretical
position — the analogy of society as an organism.

The third and final key word in British Social Anthropology is "structure".
Associated particularly with Radcliffe-Brown, who is often referred to as a
"structural-functionalist", and whose best known book is entitled *Structure
and Function in Primitive Society*, this term enables comparisons to be made
between different societies. Over the years, anthropologists have developed a
series of analytic tools which enable them to label the alternative ways in
which a particular society copes with the organizational problems which
confront it. For example, if descent is traced through the male line for some
purposes, the descent system is labelled "patrilineal" in that respect, if through
the female line, "matrilineal". If, after marriage, a couple normally resides
with the husband's relatives, the residential rule is said to be "patrilocal", if
with the wife's relatives, "matrilocal". For modern social anthropologists,
what might be termed the "structural situation" of a given society consists in
the combination of behavioural options employed by the society. That is,
if one says that a society has a patrilineal descent system and a matrilocal
residential rule, one will have specified part of its "structure". This use of
structure overlaps to some extent with that of French structuralists like
Claude Lévi-Strauss and Louis Dumont. However, the two usages should not
be conflated, since the French concept has a pedigree which includes not just
Radcliffe-Brown and Durkheim, but also thinkers like Marx and Hegel. For
this reason the concept, as used in the writings of the French structuralists, is

at once more politically oriented, more "idealistic" (in the philosophical sense) and has undertones of subjectivity which are absent in the British usage.

A second distinctive feature of British Social Anthropology is its exhaustive treatment of restricted social groups. To mention only four of the most prominent, Malinowski among the Trobrianders, Fortes among the Tallensi, Firth among the Tikopia and Evans-Pritchard among the Nuer; each worker in his day achieved a reputation for thorough ethnography within a circumscribed area. Before the discipline had developed, an anthropologist with zero or very superficial experience of an indigenous culture could write about it professionally with no qualms of conscience. After the ethnographic example of the early British Social Anthropologists, intensive and prolonged fieldwork conducted in the indigenous language became both the accepted norm, and the "rite of initiation"[8] into the anthropological fraternity. Indeed, the development of practical ethnographic skills constituted one of the most important signs and causes of the maturing of anthropology as a discipline, and complemented the growth of the theoretical and analytic procedures which are also discussed at length in this book.

A third distinguishing feature of British Social Anthropology was its close links with British imperialism. Almost all the influential fieldwork done by British Social Anthropologists was performed in what were or had been colonies of Mother England. One would only have to skim the issues of the journal *Africa* which were produced during the 1930s, to convince oneself that this imperial connection was in no way adventitious. Leading anthropologists like Malinowski made blatant (and, one gathers, successful) attempts to raise money for anthropological research by pushing anthropology as useful in colonial administration. In fact, the very bone and fibre of structural-functional theory and practice dovetails so neatly with the policy of indirect rule that to deny a causal connection between them would be to strain credibility past the breaking point. An anthropology with the avowed aim of uncovering the factors which kept societies in smoothly-functioning harmony, and a national colonial policy which imposed its will upon distant peoples by plugging into the indigenous political organization, could not have been innocent playmates. British Social Anthropologists who claim that their discipline has never been in any way linked to imperialism put one in mind of a woman who wears skin-tight gold lamé slacks and a leopard-skin blouse unbuttoned to the waist, who frequents a house illuminated by red lights, and who lets it be known that the reason she has been standing in the street for the past four hours is simply to catch a breath of night air.

One distinctive aspect of British Social Anthropology remains. I refer to the leading role the discipline has played in the enshrining of kinship studies as plausibly the focal element in modern anthropological theory. As the aim of this book is to outline the part played by the Cambridge school in this enshrining, I shall not preempt myself in the Preface. For the anthropologically uninitiated, however, it may be appropriate to include here a brief explanation and justification of the assertion that kinship theory is central to modern anthropology.

It is a common experience of young anthropologists that, before embarking upon their first field trip, they feel little or no interest in the subject of kinship, firstly because their own society does not normally stress the institutions pertaining thereto, and secondly because the analyses of the topic which they have encountered during their anthropological education, may have seemed repugnantly technical. However, it is probably almost equally as common that, in the course of their first piece of intensive fieldwork, young ethnographers will be struck by the fact that almost every social act seems to be conceptualized in terms of kinship relations. Let us imagine, for example, that upon observing a ritual, our investigator notices that specific people perform specific acts in relation to other people. Supposing she/he asks, "Why does that woman perform that particular action?" The typical answer will be of the form: "Because she is the father's sister [or some other specific relative] of the person who is the object of the action". Or, if one asks a particular person why he always goes hunting or fishing with the same group of young men, he might reply: "Because they are of my father's line". In fact, our observer could well be tempted to conclude that relationships which a Westerner would regard as economic or political or religious, are all conceptualized by non-Westernized indigenes in terms of kinship. Alternatively, to use an analogy which has been commonly deployed in British Social Anthropology, kinship is the thread which holds the social fabric together. Or, switching to a linguistic analogy which is not without currency in the discipline, kinship is the *idiom* through which all other types of relationship are expressed.[9]

In the preliterate society which they are observing, our fieldworkers are also likely to discover that people remember enormous genealogies extending back for many generations, and out to third or fourth cousins. And the way that their informants organize and classify their relatives will probably appear very involuted, so that they will more than likely conclude that the people possess "a very complex kinship system". The classic instance of such a people is provided by the Australian Aborigines, the various tribes of which, despite the rudimentary state of their material culture, have kinship systems which appear complicated enough to have served as the object of anthropological disputations extending back for nearly a century.

In actual fact, the assertion that non-Westernized indigenous societies differ from our own society in that the former are "kin-based", while the latter is not, represents a considerable oversimplification. For one thing, kinship relations are important in the everyday behaviour of Westerners in ways which we are scarcely conscious of. For another thing, there are considerable problems in sustaining the view that indigenous societies are, in any simple and straightforward sense, totally "kin-based". Consider for instance the example adduced in the penultimate paragraph about the woman who is said to perform a ritual action because she is "the father's sister" of the person who is the object of the action. It may well be that a *possible* translation of the locution which was actually used is "the father's sister". However, it is also likely that such a translation does not exhaust the full range of possible connotations, which may well include meanings which have no kin reference at all. So more critical and wide-ranging ethnography and analysis would be required before one could sensibly evaluate the notion of a "kin-based society".

Nonetheless, someone who has realized from first-hand experience that non-Westernized societies *appear* to be far more kinship-oriented than Westernized ones, is in a much better position to begin a career in social anthropology than someone who has not. For, however much it may require ultimate qualification, the assertion that indigenous societies are "kin-based" represents a *prima facie* plausible attempt to pin down the essential difference between "them" and "us". And social anthropologists who wish to travel swiftly to the theoretical and methodological centre of their discipline, could hardly do better than to use this assertion as their take-off point.

Because of considerations like these, social anthropology, as it has developed in the twentieth-century, has tended to place a great deal of emphasis on kinship, a fact which is reflected not only in the quantity of the material published but, more especially, in the pivotal significance of what has been published. An infant discipline aspiring to live up to its name and become a true "science of man", anthropology seized upon the task of accurately analysing and specifying kinship systems as a major means of advancing its claim to scientific status. And when the most recent fundamental reorientation in anthropological theory occurred, kinship studies led the way. Lévi-Strauss's 1949 book *Les Structures Elémentaires de la Parenté*, a monumental reinterpretation of previously-accepted work in kinship, ushered in the new "structuralist" approach to anthropology. Such considerations and occurrences have inspired a member of the rising generation of anthropologists to write: "Kinship is to anthropology what logic is to philosophy or the nude is to art; it is the basic discipline of the subject." [10] While this presupposes a particular view of philosophy, and of aesthetics, the message behind the rhetoric is clear. Kinship studies are germane to contemporary anthropological theory and practice in a way in which other topics are not.

Let me emphasize that my belief in this thesis regarding the central place of kinship in modern ethnology constituted the reason for pursuing the research which led to the present work. Although I realize that not all anthropologists would accept the thesis without argument, and some undoubtedly not even then, I have met very few who do not regard it as being *prima facie* plausible, or, at the very least, worthy of serious consideration. Since the present work itself constitutes a kind of historical justification of the thesis, I would ask the reader who has substantive reservations about it to suspend his judgement until he reaches the end of the book.

Now if one looks at nineteenth-century anthropological theory, kinship studies were certainly not focal. The greatest single work produced in British anthropology during the latter half of the nineteenth-century, E. B. Tylor's *Primitive Culture*, does not even mention kinship; and Tylor's other major book, *Researches into the Early History of Mankind*, includes a brief discussion of what was then known about certain aspects of kinship within a miscellaneous chapter entitled "Some Remarkable Customs". [11] As I shall argue in the first chapter, the fundamental concern of Tylor and of his younger contemporary, James Frazer, was the evolution of religious thought, a topic which was interpreted as having little relevance to kinship studies. Indeed, nineteenth-century anthropologists tended to regard religious thought as being as germane to non-Western mental processes as kinship is now widely believed to be for aboriginal social life. As Frazer expressed it:

... the religion of the savage does for him what philosophy and science essay to do for civilized man; it furnishes him with a general explanation of the processes of nature and his own being and destiny. Hence the life of the savage is saturated with it. By it he explains all events: on it he bases all his rules of conduct. He cannot separate it even in thought from the rest of his life: the distinction between religious and secular affairs, or between religion and morality, has no meaning for him. The progress of civilization tends to restrict the sphere of religion by substituting natural for supernatural agencies as the immediate basis of ethics. But the student of early thought and custom must remember that religion as an element of society, though it is slowly precipitated by civilization, is held in solution by savagery, colouring and being coloured by all the other elements with which it is blent. [12]

The switch of emphasis from the centrality of religious thought to the centrality of kinship is nicely illustrated by the 1912 edition of the *Notes and Queries on Anthropology*. This publication was prepared as an instruction booklet for intending anthropological observers, and accurately reflects the theoretical climate of the day. In sections under the general heading "Religion", Barbara Freire-Marreco, Research Fellow of Somerville College Oxford, and R. R. Marett, Reader in Social Anthropology at the University of Oxford, reveal the extent to which the new emphasis upon kinship and social organization was impinging upon the previous concern with the evolution of religious thought. Marreco, for example, summing up the previous twelve years' theoretical work in the anthropological study of religion, states that "above all, the religion of savages has been studied in its *social* aspect, in the very closest connection with social organization, social emotion and social action".[13] Even more interestingly, Marett's contributions reveal that, for this prominent anthropologist, the changeover was actually still taking place. Marett believes, like Frazer before him, that religious thought provides the medium through which preliterate man conceptualizes his life:

With uncivilized man, the magico-religious side of everything is always uppermost. When he is hunting, or fighting, or marrying, he is intensely keen on what he is about. What he is primarily about, however, is to control the process from first to last by magico-religious means ... It is precisely at its heart that every savage society is most dependent on magico-religious practices and beliefs, and it does not wear its heart on its sleeve.[14]

However, Marett is sceptical of the Tylorean/Frazerean view of aboriginal man as the constructor of an elaborate, rationally-conceived philosophy:

in a primitive society there is no such thing as a theology, or thought-out scheme of beliefs, at all; and ... , by putting questions that rest on the assumption that such a theology exists, the incautious observer may unawares extract from the native a sort of mock theology made on the spot, and divorced from the facts of his real life.[15]

In order that the study of magico-religious beliefs will not become thus divorced from the realities of life, Marett recommends an exhaustive investigation of social organization:

Thoroughness can be ensured only by working in the fullest attainable view of the social life as a whole, both *statically*, in all the complexities of its organization, including the kin-system, matrimonial and family arrangements, local divisions, sex distinctions, age-grades, and social ranks ... and also *dynamically* in its various activities, classifying these by reference to the various departments of the social organization. Such activities are the tribal law and government, the functions of tribes and families, including birth rites and burial rites ... Without this constant reference to the social conditions, the observer is certain to misrepresent the facts, by arranging them in an order that does not correspond to their real importance for the society concerned, but merely reflects some prejudice of his own . . . The real scheme of topics, then — and the only scheme which has scientific value — must be framed by the observer himself to suit the social conditions of the given tribe.[16]

So by 1912, the man who had succeeded Tylor at Oxford and who, like Tylor, had made aboriginal religion his area of special expertise, was recommending that this area should be approached through the intensive study of social organization. What more graphic illustration could we have of the process by which kinship and social organization were slowly dethroning religion from its central position in anthropological theory? The rise of kinship and social organization as the key topic in social anthropology did not, of course, mean that the study of preliterate religion simply withered on the vine. On the contrary, the *amount* of material produced on the latter topic has continued unabated down to the present day. What did change was the relative importance ascribed to the two topics, such that, for an ambitious young anthropologist who wished to stake out a claim to theoretical significance, it was no longer particularly prestigious to be involved with the study of religion. Rather, it became desirable *par excellence* to acquire a reputation for the ability to utilize kinship to illuminate social organization.

Here then we have an important problem in the history of anthropology — by what process did the study of kinship and social organization replace the evolution of religious thought as the central thread of anthropological theory? Now in an eclectic discipline like anthropology, in which there have been and are many competing schools, problems which are as clearly-defined and cover as much territory as this, are not easy to come by. In fact, many previous attempts to write the history of anthropology have foundered because the author has had no pegs, or unsuitable pegs, upon which to hang his analysis. Thus, for example, H. R. Hays's "informal history of social anthropology", *From Ape to Angel*, contains a large number of entertaining anecdotes, but possesses no central thread which might lend them structure and coherence. If the work were being judged simply as journalism, this defect might be forgivable, but unfortunately Hays's story-telling is shot-through with serious historical inaccuracies.

Marvin Harris's monumental *The Rise of Anthropological Theory*, by contrast, is a serious and scholarly work which utilizes a large number of analytic tools in evaluating the work of past anthropologists. Thus, for example, Harris distinguishes between nomothetic and idiographic approaches to the discipline, between materialistic and idealistic modes of explanation, between accounts which are synchronic and those which are diachronic, and between dialectical and non-dialectical styles of analysis. However, the purpose for which Harris employs such tools is simply to decide to what extent the great names in the history of anthropology have approximated to the theoretical position of Marvin Harris, who here appears as a thoroughly dogmatic non-dialectical materialist. Harris, in fact, effectively insists that, irrespective of their historical background, all past anthropologists should have attempted to produce diachronic, nomothetic accounts which place heavy emphasis upon the causative role of economic and technological factors. The perils of doctrinaire history of anthropology have never been so ponderously illustrated. Harris, in other words, has fallen foul of one particular variety of what Herbert Butterfield called "Whiggishness" — that most heinous of historical crimes in which the past is judged, not by reference to its own socio-intellectual context, but in terms of interests, values and/or concepts which belong to the present day.

Other examples of "Whiggish" accounts of the history of anthropology are firstly Adam Kuper's *Anthropologists and Anthropology: The British School 1922–1972*, which suffers from a paucity of archival research, and which never gets beyond the retrospective value-system of modern British Social Anthropology; and, secondly, Meyer Fortes's "Social Anthropology at Cambridge Since 1900", which bears all the marks of a bad inaugural address, being short on facts, long on sermonizing, very uncynical and "establishment" in its value judgements, and exhibiting a tendency to give somewhat jingoistic estimations of the past and likely future contributions of the school which the author had just become head of. Indeed, in his later work, *Kinship and the Social Order. The Legacy of Lewis Henry Morgan*, the first part of which represents a far more sophisticated and interesting contribution to the history of the discipline, Fortes makes some explicit avowals about his devotion to "Whiggishness". In one place he admits that he has been attempting to strip "the problem which lay at the heart of Morgan's researches" of its "historicist pretensions" and to restate it "in structural terms".[17] Unfortunately, however, the "historicist pretensions" to which Fortes is referring are the diachronic assumptions which are absolutely germane to the Morganian variety of social evolutionism. So much for real history! In another place, Fortes declares that modern anthropologists such as himself can only evaluate their predecessors "fruitfully for their own instruction if we judge them frankly by our own standards of theory and practice".[18] To such an avowal, someone who aspires to doing real history of anthropology can only reply, with as much vehemence as he can muster, that the principle which guides (and must guide) his own researchers is diametrically opposed to that espoused by Professor Fortes.

Far more suitable as a model for the historian of anthropology is the work of George W. Stocking Jr.[19] Carefully researched, meticulously documented and compactly expressed, Stocking's studies are often written with the express purpose of demolishing myths about the history of anthropology which are current among practising anthropologists. In other words, far from being bound by "Whiggishness", Stocking uses it constructively as something to react against, something to convert what might otherwise be merely an academic exercise into an argument which modern practitioners of the trade will find challenging. Thus, the history of anthropology is given life and purpose, instead of simply acting as a mythology which reinforces current preconceptions. One specific exmaple of Stocking's work which I found useful as a model for my own is his article "From Physics to Ethnology". Here Stocking gives an exemplary exposition of the way Franz Boas moved from the tough-nosed field of physics to the more humanistic regions of cultural anthropology. According to Stocking, Boas's shift of focus did not involve any sudden conversion.

On the contrary, his viewpoint developed slowly out of his family and cultural background, his work with physics and psychophysics, his geographical interests, his contact with German Romantic idealist and historicist traditions, and his work with Bastian, all in the context of his field experience. In short, it flowed from his total life experience.[20]

One would have to read the whole article quite closely to appreciate the sophistication and subtlety with which Stocking assembles these myriad components into a coherent argument. I would be the first to admit that my self-imposed task of doing for Rivers what Stocking had done for Boas, ultimately proved beyond me. But the fact that a detailed reconstruction of an equally interdisciplinary career had been achieved before, was a constant source of encouragement during my attempts to complete what proved to be the most difficult part of the entire project.

In telling the story of how the study of kinship (and by extension, of social organization) replaced the evolution of religious thought as the central thread of anthropological theory, I had originally intended to include an account of the history of American kinship studies. However, this proved too broad in scope, and the book now focuses upon English developments, and more specifically upon developments which proceeded from one British university. For this reason my discussion of the work of the pioneer American kinship theorist Lewis Henry Morgan is relatively superficial, and has been confined to the introductory first chapter.

The real subject of this book is what I shall call the "school"[21] of Cambridge Ethnology, in which the leading intellectual figure was W. H. R. Rivers. Following his introduction to anthropology in 1898, Rivers devised a methodology and a value system which were zealously guarded, propagated and institutionalized by his friend and colleague A. C. Haddon. The story is complicated somewhat by the fact that, circa 1910, Rivers converted to diffusionism, which for him involved a very different approach to the study of human culture. This change of direction resulted in the establishment of a second and distinct Rivers school. Although Rivers himself would not have admitted it, his conversion effectively undermined his earlier methodology and value system, and was to cause considerable friction between the proponents of his earlier and later approaches. While our fundamental interest is in the school of earlier Rivers, it will be necessary to look closely at the school of later Rivers, since the former acquired its distinctive character, partly by reacting against the latter.

The fundamental unit of conventional intellectual history is the author-*cum*-seminal work, and the basic form of interaction between units is an "influence", usually considered as an ethereal meeting of minds via the medium of the printed word. This book represents a conscious attempt to break with this tradition, and to write history of science in a more down-to-earth manner. In such an enterprise, I take the fundamental unit to be the school itself, and the basic form of interaction to be that occurring between members of the school. Hence, the type of influence regarded as important is no longer that which takes place between intellectual ivory towers, but rather the kind which involves teacher and pupil, or pupil and pupil, or teacher and teacher.[22] Considered from this point of view, factors such as the desire for mentor approval, and competition or co-operation with other members of the school, loom as crucial. Taking the teacher-pupil relationship, its importance lies not only in the obvious instructional interaction, but also in the pupil's dependence on the teacher for references, for obtaining a job, for having books published, for nomination to professional societies, and so forth. The asymmetry of this relationship does much to determine the shape and flavour of the "influence" of the teacher on the pupil, and sometimes vice-versa.

By defining the problematic in this way, I have very much determined the emphasis to be given to individual figures in the story. Using a different problematic, it would have been possible to argue that, for example, the true intellectual forebear of all students of kinship was Lewis Henry Morgan, whose work was successively "developed" by Lorimer Fison, Baldwin Spencer and Durkheim, a "tradition" which was eventually grafted (through the work of Radcliffe-Brown) onto a more-or-less separate "tradition" which had emanated from Rivers. Now while all historical schemas are, to some extent, arbitrary, it seems to me that, if the aim is to tell the story of how kinship studies came to the fore in *British* anthropology, cogent reasons can be given for preferring the schema given in this book to the one outlined above. The book itself will hopefully provide the requisite justification, but at this point let me say that I believe that, given the choice, anyone who will carefully go through the Haddon Collection with the aim of reconstructing the activities of the Cambridge school in regard to kinship studies, would opt for the alternative which has been adopted in the present work. Indeed, I honestly believe that the above definition of the problematic is not the direct result of a doctrinaire application of a preconceived theory of the history of science. Here as everywhere, no doubt, fact and theory interacted, but rather than emphasizing the role of a preconceived theory, I think it would actually be more accurate to represent my statement of the problematic as a *post hoc* justification of the impression gained from reading through the Haddon Collection after coming to it with a more-or-less open mind.

The correct label to characterize the style of history of science which I am attempting is a matter for debate. Early in the book, and especially in Chapter II, my concerns will seem basically psychological. However, this is because the person whose career I am trying to analyse left material which is more amenable to a psychological than to any other kind of interpretation. The real unit of the book as a whole is the Cambridge school itself, and although the total number of people involved is quite small, the fact that their activities were dominated by a collectively-held value system and methodology renders the word "psychological" inappropriate. While recognizing that the data adduced are not statistically significant, the label I would like to suggest as descriptive of my approach is "sociological". In this respect I am supported by Professor Kuhn:

Some of the principles deployed in my explanation of science are irreducibly sociological, at least at this time. In particular, confronted with the problem of theory-choice, the structure of my response runs roughly as follows: take a *group* of the ablest available people with the most appropriate motivation; train them in some science and in the specialties relevant to the choice at hand; imbue them with the value system, the ideology, current in their discipline (and to a great extent in other scientific fields as well); and finally, *let them make the choice*. If that technique does not account for scientific development as we know it, then no other will. There can be no set of rules of choice adequate to dictate desired *individual* behaviour in the concrete cases that scientists will meet in the course of their careers. Whatever scientific progress may be, we must account for it by examining the nature of the scientific group, discovering what it values, what it tolerates, and what it disdains. That position is intrinsically sociological . . .[23]

As may seem fitting for the application of my "sociological" approach to the Cambridge school of anthropology, a number of tools and methods have been borrowed from sociology. Now I realize that, in general, both historians and anthropologists detest what they regard as sociological "jargon". Nonetheless, for purposes of brevity, and because I am attempting an avowedly "sociological" approach, I have borrowed a number of tools and methods from what is, after all, anthropology's sister discipline. The first of these is the label "role-hybrid" with which, despite its embarrassingly psycho-scientistic aura, I have decided to tag Rivers. The second is the notion of "professionalization", which I have used in my account of Radcliffe-Brown. The third is what I have followed one of my protagonists in calling "the test case", which I regard as a sociological adaptation of the idea of the "crucial experiment", long deployed by scientists and historians of science. The fourth is the mode of institutional analysis which I have utilized in my presentation of the diffusion controversy. Finally, there is the distinctive pattern exhibited when a discipline matures as a science, against which can be measured the maturation process of disciplines which aspire to be scientific (but which have not necessarily attained that aim). The pattern of scientific maturation has been sketched out in the work of Thomas S. Kuhn.[24] According to Kuhn, the key feature of the developed sciences is what he calls "puzzle-solving". This is to be sharply distinguished from "problem-solving", which Kuhn regards as characteristic, not of science, but of philosophy. In *Conjectures and Refutations*, Karl Popper had claimed that the immediate intellectual ancestor of science was the critical discourse of the Presocratics. In the opening essay of *Criticism and the Growth of Knowledge*, Kuhn opines that the description of such discourse which Popper had given in *Conjectures and Refutations*, is "most apt" but then states that "what is described does not at all resemble science". Rather, continues Kuhn, what Popper describes is in "the tradition of claims, counterclaims and debates over fundamentals which, except perhaps during the Middle Ages, have characterized philosophy and much of social science ever since".[25] In this tradition, critical debate continues unceasingly, and it is exceedingly improbable that all the practitioners of the trade would ever agree that one correct answer to a problem has been achieved, or even that there is one unique answer which must be formulated in one particular fashion. (Indeed, some sceptics would maintain that the practitioners of such disciplines are incapable of agreeing about what the problem is, let alone about the solution!) However, as the various branches of knowledge develop, some of them undergo a "scientific revolution", adopt their first firm "paradigm", abandon "problem-solving" in favour of "puzzle-solving", and enter a period of "normal science". By the Hellenistic period, for example, astronomy, statics, and the geometrical part of optics had made the transition, which involved the renunciation of critical discourse, and the adoption of technical modes of solving "puzzles" with only one right answer, upon which all competent practitioners would agree. After the puzzle-solving which characterizes normal science has continued for a time, the usual pattern is that "anomalies" — puzzles for which the accepted technical procedures fail to work — begin to appear. Eventually, the anomalies build up to the point where a "crisis" is reached, and the discipline goes into a further phase of scientific revolution, in which rival paradigms compete during another period of critical discourse. The revolutionary phase finally ends when a new paradigm is established, and a further period of normal science begins. This will, in turn, be followed by more anomalies, another crisis, a further scientific revolution, and an ensuing period of normal-scientific puzzle-solving. And so on indefinitely — the development of science is a constant series of stops and starts, of critical free-for-all followed by the dogmatic technicalities of solving puzzles. Such, in brief, is the Kuhnian analysis of scientific development and anyone who wants a fuller exposition of it will find it in his famous book *The Structure of Scientific Revolutions*. But for our purposes, the most important part of the analysis is the description of how a discipline undergoes its first scientific revolution, acquires its first paradigm, and enters its first period of normal science. For it is this part of the analysis which I shall be using to illuminate the maturation process undergone by social anthropology. The appearance, in the school of earlier Rivers, of a common institutional locus, a shared set of values, an empirical methodology, and techniques which accurately mimicked scientific puzzle-solving, I have interpreted as indicators that British Social Anthropology was coming of age as a quasi-scientific enterprise.

Anthropologists reading this book will probably be struck by a number of apparent anomalies. For example, many of the episodes given lengthy treatment will be quite unfamiliar. Modern anthropologists are accustomed to thinking of Malinowski and Radcliffe-Brown as the founding fathers of British Social Anthropology,[26] and may be surprised to learn that a whole host of other people took part in the creation. My neglect of Malinowski will most likely be particularly annoying. After all, apart from his undoubted renown as an intensive fieldworker, his very first book was about the family among the Australian Aborigines, a topic which might seem germane to the subject under consideration. Nonetheless, it is my contention, for reasons given in Chapter V, that it is inappropriate to regard Malinowski as a member of the Rivers school and, hence, for purposes of this book, he can largely be ignored. Finally, very little is said about the relationship between anthropology and imperialism. This is not because I believe the relationship to have been unimportant for the history of British anthropology, but because, inasmuch as it is relevant to our story, it was about equally important for the two rival schools emanating from Rivers. For this reason, the subject of imperialism rarely entered into the disputes between the two schools, and has little relevance to the topic in hand.

The final point I wish to make about the content of this book is that this is a history which quite deliberately takes sides. There is a widespread opinion that historians should be not merely fair-minded and even-handed, but strictly "neutral" in their evaluation of personalities and controversies from the past. While I am all for fair-mindedness and even-handedness (not to mention motherhood and baseball!), the demand for "neutrality" is something which I cannot accept. In my view, it is imperative that if one has opinions about the rights and wrongs of an historical situation, the best thing to do is to be quite frank about the existence and nature of one's opinions and, where appropriate, to incorporate such opinions into one's analysis. Thus, this book takes sides in favour of earlier Rivers, of Deacon, and of Radcliffe-Brown's professional ability; and against later Rivers, Elliot Smith, Perry, and Radcliffe-Brown's personality and "professional" conduct. No doubt if the reader has different opinions, sympathies or intuitions, my account will seem biased. But I would rather run the risk of irritating some of my readers than try to pretend that I am a moral and emotional neuter.

It is an indication of the international significance of British Social Anthropology in general, and of the chosen topic in particular, that researching this book involved recourse to no less than eight manuscript collections in four different countries. In this regard, my thanks are due to Miss Pamplin and Dr Leedham-Green of the Cambridge University Library Manuscripts Room; Miss B. J. Kirkpatrick of the Royal Anthropological Institute Library; Mr Saville of the Library of the British Association for the Advancement of Science; the keeper of the Lothian Collection, Edinburgh; Dr J. William Hess of the Rockefeller Foundation Archives, New York; Professor Peter Lawrence of the Department of Anthropology, University of Sydney; the officials of the La Trobe Library, Melbourne; and the John S. Battye Library, Perth. I would also like to thank Mr Paul Jorion and Professor Edmund Leach of the Cambridge University Anthropology Department, who made some privately-held Deacon archives available to me.

Let me also take the opportunity of thanking the four people who were, at the time when I began my research, the only surviving former disciples of Rivers from his days as an anthropologist at Cambridge; namely W. E. Armstrong, T. T. Barnard, C. E. Fox and, especially, the late John Layard, whose recollections of Rivers and his work on kinship proved invaluable. I am similarly grateful for several fruitful discussions with the late A. P. Elkin, formerly Professor of Anthropology at the University of Sydney. Professor Elkin knew personally a number of people discussed in this book, and although he never met Rivers, became an early exponent of the Cambridge approach to anthropology through reading Rivers's published work. In addition, I would like to thank Dell Hymes, who kindly allowed me to attend a superbly informative course on the history of anthropology which he gave at the University of Pennsylvania in 1971; George Stocking of the University of Chicago, who pointed my neophytic footsteps in the direction of some critically important research material; and Derek Freeman and his Department at the Australian National University, whose comments on my treatment of Rivers and Radcliffe-Brown proved extremely pertinent and stimulating.

Any infelicities, errors or solecisms which this book may still contain should not be blamed on the four people who produced thoughtful criticisms of the penultimate typescript. To John Barnes, who is the proverbial scholar and gentleman, I owe a meticulous exploration of a number of technical points relating particularly to the specification of marriage-class systems. Meyer Fortes produced many marginal annotations which, although expressed in generally unsympathetic terms, embodied, as I can now see, long experience of kinship studies explored by a penetrating intellect. To George Stocking, who understood what I wanted to do, as well as where I had failed, I am grateful for a brief but nicely balanced critique. And, lastly, my sincere thanks are due to the anonymous person with the magnificently detailed understanding of kinship studies and their history, who taxed me with the most penetrating of referee's reports.

I am also very grateful to my friends and fellow tea drinkers from the Anthropology Department at the University of Sydney. Over the past four years their discussions have provided many valuable insights into what makes an Anthropology Department tick. Individuals whom I would especially like to single out for thanks are Michael Allen, who put it to me very gently that it was about time I published my doctoral research; Mary Patterson, who gave much needed technical advice on kinship; Jeremy Beckett and Tim Murray, whose knowledge of, and enthusiasm for, the history of anthropology prevented my own interest from lapsing; Peter White, for helpful suggestions about the practicalities of getting material into print; and finally Paul Alexander, Roland Fletcher, Richard Wright, Les Hiatt, Daryl Feil, John Clegg, Doug Miles, Chris Eipper and Marie de Lepervanche, for being themselves in both the personal and professional senses. I would also like to express my gratitude to Gary Nicholls, a former post-graduate student from the Department who convinced me by example of the need for taking a firm and committed line on the history of the discipline.

My thanks are likewise due to four charming people who performed routine but essential tasks in preparing this book for publication. Jane Benyon not only did a superb job of typing numerous early drafts of the manuscript, but also went far beyond the call of duty in taking a friendly and intelligent interest in the subject matter. Robyn Wood and Wilma Sharp had the frustrating task of assembling the final typescript from a tangled mass of original pages and added inserts, but performed it with their customary precision and efficiency. And Lorraine Garland has my warm thanks for making an elegant job of the diagrams.

In conclusion, allow me to record my gratitude to my mentors at Princeton University, where the doctoral dissertation upon which this book is based was conceived, largely researched, and the early chapters written. The idea for the project came to me during one of Martin Silverman's graduate anthropology seminars, and would never have got off the ground but for his friendly encouragement and criticism. Gerald Geison, who bore the main brunt of supervision, managed to express substantive reservations in an unfailingly sympathetic and helpful way. Charles C. Gillispie, who was called in as a dissertation reader at the last moment, produced some exceptionally well-considered comments, without which the present work would have been very much the poorer. And, finally, I would like to thank Thomas S. Kuhn, who apart from creating almost single-handedly the approach to the history of science which I have attempted to follow, also applied his awesome critical faculties to an early draft of the very troublesome second chapter, and subsequently produced a very thoughtful critique of the entire dissertation. Indeed, it seems to me that, since the epistemological debates in which philosophers of science like Popper, Lakatos and Feyerabend attacked, reacted against, and built upon Kuhn's insights into the development of the various branches of science, the nature of the history of science has changed appreciably. No longer is the discipline interested only in the objective empirical and theoretical achievements which give science its internal dynamic. It is now equally interested in the external factors which impinge directly upon the content of theories during periods of scientific revolution; in the socio-economic context which conditions not only value-systems, but also the processes by which science institutionalizes; in the career tactics of individual scientists, and the political strategies by which scientific groups advance their interests; in the ideology of science, and the rhetoric which is used to advance that ideology. No longer is it good enough to simply consider the objective face which science presents in its official publications; one must also consider who is doing the writing, the audience being aimed at, and the political or career-oriented purpose which the writer has in mind. The shift to this new type of problematic is still very much in process of happening, and the present work was researched and written in the early stages of the intellectual upheaval which gave rise to the shift. Consequently my book is a transitional one, with footholds in both the old internalist approach to the discipline, and the new concern with welding external and internal factors together. But I hope that the shortcomings of the present work will not deter those who wish to further explore the methods and intellectual basis of the new history of science.

IAN LANGHAM
University of Sydney,
November 1980

ACKNOWLEDGEMENTS

My thanks are due to Oxford University Press for permission to quote from
W. H. R. Rivers and Henry Head, "A Human Experiment in Nerve Division",
Brain 31 (1908), pp. 442, 443; Cambridge University Press for permission to
reprint a diagram from W. E. Armstrong, *Rossel Island* (Cambridge, 1928),
p. 248; Mrs. Katherin Grant Watson and the Hutchinson Publishing Group for
permission to quote from E. L. Grant Watson, *But To What Purpose* (Cresset
Press, London, 1946), pp. 83—85, 105, 106, 109, 110, 112, 113; Warren
R. Dawson and Jonathan Cape Ltd for permission to quote from Warren
R. Dawson (ed.), *Sir Grafton Elliot Smith, A Biographical Record By His
Colleagues* (London, 1938), pp. 51—53, 63—65, 178; Margaret Rishbeth
for permission to quote from the Haddon Collection; Penguin Books for
permission to quote from Robin Fox, *Kinship and Marriage* (Pelican, Har-
mondsworth, 1967), p. 260; Macmillan Publishers Ltd for permission to
quote from J. G. Frazer, *The Gorgon's Head and Other Literary Pieces*
(London, 1927), pp. 286, 287; the Geographical Association, for permission
to quote from J. L. Myres, "A Geographical View of the Historical Method in
Ethnology", *Geographical Teacher* 13 (1925—26); Cambridge University
Press for permission to quote firstly from T. S. Kuhn, "Reflections On My
Critics", in I. Lakatos and A. Musgrave (eds.), *Criticism and the Growth of
Knowledge* (Cambridge, 1974 reprint), pp. 237, 238; and secondly from
A. R. [Radcliffe] -Brown, *The Andaman Islanders* (Cambridge, 1922), p. 393;
John Wiley and Sons Inc., for permission to quote from William Coleman,
Biology in the Nineteenth Century (New York, London, Sydney, Toronto,
1971), pp. 165, 166; St. John's College for permission to quote from Frederic
Bartlett, "W. H. R. Rivers", *The Eagle* 62 (1968), p. 160; the Australian
National University for permission to quote from J. A. Barnes's Foreword to
L. R. Hiatt, *Kinship and Conflict* (Canberra, 1965), p. x; the Royal Anthro-
pological Institute for permission to quote from Barbara Freire-Marreco and
John Linton Myres (eds.), *Notes and Queries on Anthropology* (4th edn.,
London, 1912), pp. 252, 254, 255; The British Academy for permission to
quote from Raymond Firth, "Alfred Reginald Radcliffe-Brown 1881—1955",
Proceedings of the British Academy 42, 290, 296 (1956); Methuen and Co.
for permission to quote from W. J. Perry, *The Children of the Sun* (London,

(1923), pp. 476—479, 484, 485; Times Newspapers Limited for permission to quote from the anonymous review of C. E. Fox, *Threshold of the Pacific*, *Times Literary Supplement*, Thursday 11 June, 1925; the Rockefeller Foundation for permission to quote from their archives; and Encyclopaedia Britannica for permission to quote from Malinowski's article on "Anthropology", *Encyclopaedia Britannica* (13th ed., 1926).

The extracts from *Man*, the *Journal of the Royal Anthropological Institute* and the Royal Anthropological Institute Archives are quoted by permission of the Royal Anthropological Institute of Great Britain and Ireland; the extract from B. Malinowski, *Myth in Primitive Psychology* (London, 1926), pp. 92, 93, is quoted by courtesy of the Orthological Institute, London; and the extracts from Sol Tax with which I close the final chapter are reprinted from *Social Anthropology of North American Tribes*, F. Eggan (ed.), by permission of the University of Chicago Press. (Copyright 1937 by the University of Chicago. All rights reserved.)

CHAPTER I

PROLOGUE

A person brought up in Western society might be forgiven for regarding the subject of kinship as being of meagre interest. To be sure we Westerners do possess kith and kin, and there are social tendencies and moral obligations associated with having relatives. However, except during specific social occasions like weddings, such tendencies and obligations do not generally dominate our lives. Most of our conscious decisions and social acts are determined (or, at any rate, we *believe* them to be determined) by utilitarian considerations based upon an assessment of economic or other pragmatic factors.

When a social or cultural anthropologist first attempts to seriously study the workings of preliterate society, she/he will be struck by the observation that, in such societies, the wellsprings of social action would seem to be far more kinship-oriented than they are in the West. More specifically, values and imperatives deriving from one's perception of the identity and status of one's kinsmen, would seem to dominate aboriginal social behaviour. Ask a non-Westernized aboriginal why he performs almost any of the acts which make up his social life, and one will characteristically be rewarded by an answer which attributes his motivations to actual or perceived ties of blood or marriage.

In fact, of course, human motivations are complex, and an absolute contrast between the allegedly pragmatic behaviour of Westerns, the apparently kinship-dominated behaviour of preliterate people, cannot be rigidly sustained. More often than we realize, kinship values, which may not be consciously espoused, are important determinants of social action in the West.[1] And behaviour in preliterate communities, which may not appear, at first sight, to have any pragmatic or practical basis, will often be seen to have such a basis after more thoughtful consideration.[2] No doubt, the fledgling fieldworker's common experience of perceiving kinship as the mainspring of aboriginal social action, is partly explicable in terms of ethnocentrism. If a person from a culture in which kinship values are present, but normally unstressed, begins to observe a culture in which such values are highly stressed, one would expect such values to make an impression upon the observer.

Nonetheless, the contrast between the apparently pragmatic West and the apparently kinship-dominated non-West is useful as a first approximation.

1

And without doubt, the formulation of this first approximation constituted a major achievement in the history of anthropology. Right up until the mid-nineteenth century, Western scholars had failed to recognize that kinship can be regarded as the key to the different modes of operation of literate and preliterate societies. Only during the second half of the nineteenth century did this insight begin to force itself upon the consciousness of Western scholarship. Briefly, the sources of this new realization were two in number. The first was concerned with an historical reappraisal of the origins of Western civilization. In particular, Sir Henry Maine, eminent British lawyer and imperialist, discovered that the legal institutions of ancient Roman society had placed a very high priority on kinship values. The second depended upon the actual empirical observation of non-Western cultures. Deeply involved in this enterprise was the American businessman-solicitor Lewis Henry Morgan, now widely (and justly) recognized as the founding father of kinship studies. So novel were Morgan's investigations that, even though his direct effect on Cambridge anthropology seems to have been fairly minimal, he nonetheless could not be denied pride of place in the introductory prologue which constitutes this chapter.

LEWIS HENRY MORGAN

Morgan's accomplishments in founding kinship studies were formidable. He was the first to recognize that, in aboriginal societies, the modes by which kinsmen are designated are sufficiently consistent and rational as to collectively constitute "systems", which are worthy of scholarly analysis and comparative study. Following up the empirical consequences of this insight, he was the first to systematically collect kinship data from widely divergent societies. His initial major publication on the subject, the 1870 tome *Systems of Consanguinity and Affinity of the Human Family*, embodies an heroic attempt to collate and order this material and contains his now-famous distinction between classificatory and descriptive systems of relationship. His second substantial contribution, published in 1877, was *Ancient Society*. This more popular exposition attempts to weld his kinship data into a general account of the "natural . . . sequence of progress" by which mankind progressed from the state of "savagery", through "barbarism", to "civilization".

Let us now briefly review the historical facts relating to Morgan achievement.[3] In 1842 Morgan, having been admitted to the bar in New York State, found himself unable to begin practising as an attorney, due to a general depression in business. Therefore, having time on his hands, he joined a fraternal society called "The Gordian Knot", the members of which were associated with the Cayuga Academy in the town of Aurora. Initially, the activities of the society seem to have been mainly literary in nature, being based upon a common admiration for classical Greek mythology. In 1843 however, Morgan proposed, by way of cutting the Gordian Knot, that the society should cease to centre its meetings around ancient legends, but should instead model itself upon the organization of the Iroquois Indians. From these beginnings emerged a fraternity known as "The Order of the Iroquois", with separate "council fires", as Morgan calls them, named after the various Iroquois tribes and meeting in appropriately located towns scattered throughout the state. The rationale behind this reorganization was expressed by the pioneer anthropologist Henry Schoolcraft, who accepted an invitation to join the remodelled society. In an address to the members delivered during August 1845, Schoolcraft alleged that America's historical reliance upon the "noble fountains and crystal streams" of Europe, was misplaced. Rather the New World should cultivate an interpretation of its history more consonant with "the peculiarities of its own soil and climate". "And where", Schoolcraft asks, "when we survey the length and breadth of the land can a more suitable element for the work be found, than is furnished by the history and antiquities and institutions of the free, bold, wild, independent native hunter race? They are relatively to us what the ancient Pict and Celt were to Britain or the Teuton, Goth and Maygar were to continental Europe."[4] Hence, the society's newly-acquired interest in the customs of the Red Indian can be seen on one level as arising from the desire to forge an historical mythology appropriate to the United States. However, apart from these romantically nationalistic aspirations, the society also had a humanitarian basis. Early in the piece, a Seneca named Ely Parker had joined the society. In a speech to the Aurora branch, Parker told of the incursions made into Iroquois territory by white business corporations. Convinced by Parker of the urgency for preventing the despoilation of further Indian land, Morgan involved himself in legal negotiations with state and national authorities, making trips to Albany and Washington in 1846. At this time, Morgan and the members of his society also visited various reservations in New York State and attended Indian council meetings. With the intelligent and articulate Ely Parker as his prime informant, Morgan pursued the twin aims of familiarizing himself with the needs and aspirations of the Indians in regard to land rights and investigating the structure of the Iroquois League, which was to serve as the model for his own fraternity. Aided by Parker, who guided him past those aspects of Indian culture which would have been of interest to a white observer for unworthy ethnocentric reasons, Morgan came to the following conclusion about Iroquois social organization:

Their laws of descent are quite intricate . . . They follow the female line and as children always follow the mother, and the man never is allowed to marry in his own tribe, it follows that the father and the son are never of the same tribe.[5]

While this conclusion is central for understanding the Iroquois kinship system, Morgan did nothing with it for more than a decade. His *League of the Hode-no-sau-nee, or Iroquois*, for example, gives it only a brief mention. Following the publication of this book in January 1851, Morgan tells us that he "laid aside the Indian subject to devote my time to my profession".[6]

In 1856, however, Morgan attended the Albany meeting of the American Association for the Advancement of Science, and his interest in Indian social organization was rekindled. At the next annual meeting of the Association, Morgan read a paper on the laws of consanguinity and descent among the Iroquois. Considered by itself, he explained in the paper, the Iroquois kinship system is scarcely more than a curiosity. However, it was possible that similar systems existed among other North American tribes and, judging from reports by missionaries, may even be found as far away as Micronesia. Hence, the investigation of such systems might be useful as a means of demonstrating that the American Indians have all descended from a common stock, and for inferring the remoter origins of the race.[7] Hence, it would seem that the rekindling of Morgan's interest in kinship systems was connected with the contemporary debate about whether the different races of men had a single origin or whether they had arisen separately in different regions of the globe. Polygenists, like the Harvard naturalist Louis Agassiz, said that the American Indian (and the buffalo) were indigenous to the North American continent and arose there. Morgan, on the other hand, sided with the monogenists and was thereby motivated to look for evidence that the Indian had originated in places other than North America.

In 1858, Morgan, while inspecting some business interests he had acquired in Upper Michigan, obtained the kinship system of the Ojibwa tribe. To his mild surprise and considerable delight, he found the system to be virtually identical to that of the Iroquois. In the hope of discovering generalized kinship laws, he then prepared a lengthy kinship questionnaire. After testing it on the local Iroquois, he distributed it to missionaries and government agents on Indian reservations all over the United States. In a letter accompanying the questionnaire, he stated that the ultimate aim of the exercise was to decide whether the hypothesis of an Asiatic origin for the American Indian could be substantiated. From replies obtained by this means, and from personal investigations conducted in Kansas and Nebraska, Morgan ascertained that an Iroquois-style system prevailed over much of the country. Cheered by this result, Morgan sent one of his questionnaires to a missionary who was going to Southern India, with the request that it should be tried out on the Tamil system of relationship. The resulting reply left Morgan, as one biographer put it, "breathless and purple with excitement".[8] The Tamil system was substantially the same as that of the American Indians. Interpreting this discovery as a substantiation of his Asiatic homeland hypothesis, Morgan's ambitions soared, and he became determined to pursue his kinship investigations on a worldwide basis.

Morgan then contacted the physicist Joseph Henry, who was Secretary of the Smithsonian Institution. Beginning in 1860, the Smithsonian sent off Morgan's questionnaires to American consular officials all over the world, with instructions to distribute them to parties suitably acquainted with aboriginal races. The first major product of this kinship survey was a preliminary draft of *Systems of Consanguinity* . . . completed in 1865. This draft, having been submitted to the Smithsonian, was returned to Morgan after Henry pronounced it incomprehensible. Over the next year Morgan revised his draft and resubmitted it to Henry with the request that it should be published immediately, lest other writers anticipate his conclusions. However, Henry evidently still found Morgan's presentation unnecessarily opaque, for he did not comply. Morgan's response was to produce an hypothetical reconstruction of man's social history. Beginning with the state of sexual communism in the "primitive horde", Morgan detected fifteen stages in the development of the laws prohibiting incest, culminating with the modern monogamous family. For each of the types of cohabitation implied by this evolutionary scheme, Morgan deduced the expected terms of relationship and demonstrated that his empirically-discovered kinship systems corresponded to his theoretical prognostications.[9]

The most implausible feature of the scheme involved the relationship system of the Hawaiians. Because the only blood relationships specified by the Hawaiian terminology were those of parent, child, grandparent, grandchild, brother and sister, Morgan attempted to correlate the Hawaiian system (or, as he called it, the "Malayan" type of system) with his earliest stage in the development of the family. He postulated that the Hawaiian terminology had arisen from the now extinct "consanguine" form of the family, in which brothers and sisters had intermarried. Now, according to

Morgan, terminologies tended to lag behind the presently operative mode of cohabitation. Hence, he interpreted the actual form of the Hawaiian family as the stage which had evolved from the consanguine family. In this second or "Punaluan" stage of the family, a group of men was said to be conjointly married to a group of women. The composition of the groups was such that either the men were all brothers, or the women were all sisters. This account of the Hawaiians gave them a kinship terminology which was the most rudimentary extant, and a family structure which was as primitive as that of any other people. In view of the degree of cultural development exhibited by the Hawaiians in all other areas, their placement at the bottom of the scale in respect of kinship and social organization seemed an obvious anomaly.[10]

Despite this apparent fault, Morgan's developmental scheme was accorded a favourable reception by the American Academy of Arts and Sciences, and Morgan subsequently inserted a chapter expounding the evolution of the family into his draft of *Systems of Consanguinity* . . . Only then did Henry agree to publication.[11] Hence, it would seem that Morgan's evolutionary scheme originated as an attempt to render his monumental compilation of the world's kinship systems more comprehensible.

Apart from the chapter on the development of the family, the primary aim of *Systems of Consanguinity* . . . is classificatory rather than explanatory. However, by the time Morgan published *Ancient Society*, the explanatory objective had become dominant. In his second great work, Morgan's evolutionary account of the relationship between family structure and systems of relationship had been elaborated to include the development of material culture, types of subsistence, governmental structure and attitudes towards property.

From our point of view, Morgan's most important achievements were two in number. The first was his invention and deployment of the concept of social organization. For Morgan, "social organization" constituted the division of a people into gentes, phratries and tribes, groups which ultimately depended for their cohesion upon ties of kinship. This was to be contrasted with "political organization", which is based upon land and possessions. Under the first type of organization a "gentile" society was the result, in which power and authority were mediated through relations which were purely personal, being founded upon notions of consanguinity and affinity. Under the second type, a "political" society was manifest, in which the government dealt with persons through their impersonal relations to territory or property. For Morgan these two types of organization were essentially disparate. The former was characteristic of "ancient society", the latter of modern Western civilization.[12] To my knowledge, the first time Morgan employed the social organization concept in print was in some "Letters on the Iroquois", published in 1847 under the *nom de plume* "Skenendoah". Speaking of the Iroquois, Morgan wrote:

With the ties of kindred as its principle of union, the whole race was interwoven into one great family, composed of tribes in its first subdivision (for the nations were counterparts of each other); and the tribes themselves, in their subdivisions, composed of parts of many households.[13]

The earliest use of the actual term "social organization" appears, as far as I know, four years later in his book on the Iroquois.[14]

The second achievement on which I wish to focus is Morgan's distinction between classificatory and descriptive systems of relationship. Fundamentally, this distinction rested upon the observation that, among aboriginal peoples, individual relationship terms such as "father", "mother", "brother", "sister", "grandfather" and "grandmother", which in Western societies apply primarily to lineal relatives, are inclined to be extended so as to cover a wide range of non-lineal or "collateral" kinsmen. Whereas, for example, a European speaking an Indo-Germanic language would terminologically distinguish between his father and his paternal uncle, or between his brother and his mother's sister's son, or between his grandmother and his great aunt, an Iroquois would apply the words for father, brother and grandmother to his paternal uncles, his mother's sister's sons, and his great aunts, respectively. This process, which Morgan conceptualized as merging collateral lines into the lineal line, he labelled "classificatory", since he saw it as effectively classifying the members of a community into groups on the basis of purely social criteria. By merging various collateral kinsmen under the lineal term "brother" for example, an indigene could be regarded as creating a conceptual class of all the men in the tribe to whom he is obliged to relate in a fraternal fashion. For Morgan, such an approach was to be contrasted with that of the West, as typified by the Roman system of kinship nomenclature. On Morgan's account, such systems employed terms which are "descriptive" of real genetic relationship. In practice, of course, it is difficult for the distinction to be rigidly sustained. Some so-called "descriptive" terminologies have classificatory aspects and some allegedly "classificatory" terminologies are partially descriptive. Nonetheless, as a first approximation for bringing some order to the mass of kinship data which Morgan had unearthed, the distinction had its uses. And most significantly of all, it indicated that the mechanism of social cohesion could be seen as differing in traditional as opposed to modern societies. Specifically, the former type of society can be regarded as bound together by kinship ties, whereas, in the latter, such ties generally appear to be subservient to other factors.[15]

It must be realized that, in drawing the distinction between classificatory and descriptive systems of relationship, Morgan was exhibiting profound originality. As W. H. R. Rivers was to acknowledge in 1914:

I do not know of any discovery in the whole range of science, which can be more certainly put to the credit of one man than that of the classificatory system of relationship by Lewis Morgan. By this I mean, not merely that he was the first to point out clearly the existence of this mode of denoting relationship, but that it was he who collected the vast mass of material by which the essential characters of the system were demonstrated, and it was he who was first to recognize the great theoretical importance of his new discovery.[16]

Half a century after Morgan first made the distinction, Sir James Frazer stated that the classificatory system of relationship "may perhaps be described as the hall-mark of savagery, since it appears to be universally prevalent among savage tribes and universally absent among civilized peoples".[17]

Morgan believed that a classificatory terminology was an indication that sexual promiscuity was, or had once been, practised within the society now using the terms. The ethnocentric nature of this line of thought has been neatly expressed by the modern kinship theorist Robin Fox. On Fox's account, Morgan's mistake lay in taking the idiosyncratic system of kin classification employed by modern Western man as the standard by which all others are to be judged:

Taking our own rather peculiar system as the norm leads only to confusion. Thus, for example, we single out the male parent and give him a distinctive term "father". Consequently, in our system "begetter" and "father" are (ideally!) synonymous. Thus when Morgan found systems in which the father's brother, and perhaps the father's sister's son, were called by the same term, he translated this as "father", assumed it was synonymous with "begetter", and tried to work out tortuous reasons to account for ego's seeming inability to pin down who begat him. Clearly, because we were Christian monogamists we knew who our begetters were, whereas the poor benighted savages living in a state of promiscuity did not.[18]

Following Malinowski, among others, Fox then goes on to argue that it is certainly not true that people who employ classificatory systems do not know who their real fathers are:

All these systems have either a term for "begetter" (like the Roman *genitor* – as opposed to *pater*), or a pronominal system which allows ego to state that of the class of male relatives designated X which includes his own male parent, one of them is his *own* X.[19]

The evolutionary form of Morgan's anthropology undoubtedly had important scientific and quasi-scientific determinants during the second half of the nineteenth-century. However, the way in which Morgan applied this developmental scheme to the observed varieties of human cohabitation indicates that Victorian sexual morality also entered the picture. Placing primitive promiscuity at the bottom of the evolutionary scale and the monogamous family at the top, did not merely fulfil a scientific objective. It also managed to convey an unmistakable moral judgement. As Radcliffe-Brown was to express it, Morgan conceived social progress as "the steady material and moral improvement of mankind from crude stone implements and sexual promiscuity to the steam engines and monogamous marriage of Rochester, N.Y."[20]

Although Morgan had singlehandedly demonstrated that aboriginal kinship systems warranted serious scientific attention, British anthropologists generally failed to realize the magnitude of his achievement, or, inasmuch as they did realize it, failed to give Morgan due credit. A contemporary evaluation of Morgan's impact on late nineteenth-century British ethnology was provided by Frederick Engels. In the preface to the 1891 edition of his *Origin of the Family, Private Property and the State, in the Light of the Researches of Lewis H. Morgan*, Engels opined that

the English prehistoric school, which is tinged with chauvinism, continues to do its utmost to kill by silence the revolution Morgan's discoveries have made in conceptions of the history of primitive society, although it does not hesitate in the least to appropriate his results.[21]

Engels' allegation is supported by a perusal of the early editions of the *Notes and Queries on Anthropology*. This publication, conceived as an instructional handbook to facilitate the collection of ethnological data by amateurs, was prepared and successively revised by a panel of interested parties connected with the Royal Anthropological Institute and the Anthropology Section of the British Association for the Advancement of Science. As can be verified through the more lengthy process of perusing the relevant contemporary journals, the first three editions of the *Notes and Queries*, published between 1874 and 1899, provide a reasonably sensitive barometer of British anthropological thought during the final quarter of the nineteenth-century. The first edition does include a table of kinship terms borrowed (without acknowledgement) from Morgan's questionnaire. However, since it omits the explanatory remarks and instructions which he had carefully devised to render his table comprehensible to an amateur data-collector, one could hardly regard the inclusion as evidence of any real appreciation of Morgan's approach on the part of the editors. This observation is supported by the second and third editions of the *Notes and Queries*. In both editions the table itself has been left out entirely, and the only section at all relevant to kinship is a brief note pointing out a few of the difficulties inherent in ascertaining the relationship terminology of an alien culture. As a final indicator of the nature of Morgan's reception in England, we have some lengthy correspondence between Morgan and his Australian protégés Lorimer Fison and A. W. Howitt. These letters reveal that Morgan, Fison and Howitt uniformly perceived most of the major figures in British anthropology to be solidly hostile to Morgan's views.[22]

EARLY BRITISH WORK RELATING TO KINSHIP

While Morgan was battling with the technical intricacies of the world's relationship systems, a number of British writers were also demonstrating a certain amount of interest in topics relevant to kinship. In 1861, for example, Sir Henry Maine had published his *Ancient Law*. The primary aim of this book was to delineate what has been called "the natural history of law" — to demonstrate, in other words, that Western legal practices (and that term should here be given a meaning sufficiently broad as to include social and political institutions) are the product of a protracted historical development.[23] From the point of view of the history of anthropology, the most interesting feature of the book is the distinction he draws between societies which are ancient or "primitive" and those which are modern or "progressive". Through a close study of archaic law, Maine infers that in ancient times, society was not what it is assumed to be today, namely a collection of individuals. Rather it was, and was regarded as, an aggregation of families.[24] The force which Maine saw as binding the ancient family together was Patria Potestas, the authority of the father. According to the conservatively-inclined Maine, the dominance of this single type of authority gave early societies stability and cohesion, and ensured that kin relationships within the society were always traced through male links, or, to use the term which Maine borrows from ancient Roman usage, "Agnatically". This contrasts with modern society, where such relationships are customarily traced via links involving both sexes or, as the Romans expressed it, "Cognatically". If in ancient society, people had traced relationships through their mother (as well as through their father) they would then have been subject to two distinct Patriae Potestates (that of their mother's father as well as that of their own father). This situation would have constituted "a conflict of laws in the domestic forum", with the result that "the organization of primitive societies would have been confounded".[25] The dominance of Patria Potestas also allegedly provided the mechanism for a change in the law governing women. According to Maine, "Ancient Law subordinates the woman to her blood-relations, while a prime phenomenon of modern jurisprudence has been her subordination to her husband." The origins of this change can be seen in three forms of marriage which were practised in ancient Rome. In these types of marriage, the husband acquired certain rights over the person and property of his wife. These rights were acquired, not by virtue of his role as husband, but by virtue of him assuming the legal status of father. In other words, the wife was technically regarded as the daughter of her husband, and he acquired rights over her because she then became included in his Patria Potestas.[26]

To further highlight the differences between ancient and modern societies, Maine employed the dichotomy between "status" and "contract". In ancient societies, personal interactions are regulated by status, whereby "all the relations of Persons are summed up in the relations of Family". In modern societies, on the other hand, personal interactions are regulated by contract, which involves "the free agreement of Individuals".[27] It was the gradual development of this notion of contract, by which an individual was enabled to freely enter into agreements with strangers outside his family group, which provided the motive power for the evolution of legal institutions. Or, as Maine himself expressed it in his well-known aphorism: "the movement of the progressive societies has hitherto been a movement from Status to Contract".[28]

Although the book overtly deals with the history of legal institutions in ancient Rome, Maine obviously believed his analysis to have more general significance for the development of culture. It must be doubted, however, that Maine succeeded in making his study of *Ancient Law* sufficiently revelatory of the nature of non-literate tribal societies to render his book a contribution to anthropology in the modern sense. Maine's procedure in attempting to recover the rudiments of generalized pre-literate society from the surviving written records of the Roman judicial system, is reminiscent of a gold-miner who confines his activities to fossicking among the worked-out tailings of old diggings, instead of searching out a new seam. Gleams of gold may well turn up, but the big finds are unlikely to be made in such a locale.

In 1865, the Scottish lawyer John Ferguson McLennan produced a book entitled *Primitive Marriage: An Enquiry into the Origin of the Form of*

Capture in Marriage Ceremonies. Unlike Maine, who in *Ancient Law* had concentrated exclusively on surviving records of Western legal institutions, McLennan believed that there were two chief sources of information regarding the early history of human society. Not only could one study "the symbols employed by advanced nations in the constitution or exercise of civil rights".[29] One should also study contemporary tribal communities. As McLennan put it:

For the features of primitive life, we must look ... to [the tribes] of Central Africa, the wilds of America, the hills of India, and the islands of the Pacific; with some of whom we find marriage laws unknown, the family system undeveloped, and even the only acknowledged blood relationship that through mothers. These facts of today are, in a sense, the most ancient history.[30]

By investigating these two sources of information simultaneously, McLennan hoped to arrange social phenomena according to their antiquity and, hence, to reconstruct the stages of human advancement in their correct chronological order.

In the Preface McLennan described his book as "an exercise in scientific history". Just what he meant by "scientific history" may be gathered from the final sentences of the book, in which he implies that future researches into early human history will so advance the cause of naturalistic explanation that it will no longer seem appropriate to refer unsolved problems to miracles. The general type of naturalistic explanation favoured by McLennan, as with so many of his contemporaries, was of course social evolutionism. But what distinguished McLennan from his fellow social evolutionists was the tenacity with which he espoused one particular evolutionary scheme. In summary this scheme, argued with immediacy (although with little plausibility) in the pages of *Primitive Marriage*, ran as follows.

Faced with hostile neighbours and unaided by even the most rudimentary forms of technology, early tribes soon discovered that females were a liability in the struggle for social survival. Such communities were, therefore, compelled to resort to female infanticide. This, however, led to a shortage of potential wives, which forced the men to practise "exogamy", by taking spouses from outside their local community. (It was McLennan who coined the term "exogamy", and its contrary "endogamy".) Where the surrounding tribes were hostile, exogamy was feasible only if men adopted the custom of forcibly abducting their women. Thus arose the practice of "marriage-by-capture" which, according to McLennan, had rapidly developed into an institutionalized "system". For McLennan, the most convincing evidence for the allegedly widespread nature of marriage-by-capture in early society consisted in vestigial "symbols" of the system, which he detected in modern marriage ceremonies. To mention only one of the many examples cited by the Scottish barrister, the following custom had been observed amongst the Welsh until comparatively recent times:

On the morning of the wedding day, the bridegroom, accompanied with his friends on horseback, demands the bride. Her friends, who are likewise on horseback, give a positive refusal, upon which a mock scuffle ensues. The bride, mounted behind her nearest kinsman, is carried off and is pursued by the bridegroom and his friends, with loud shouts . . . When they have fatigued themselves and their horses, the bridegroom is suffered to overtake his bride. He leads her away in triumph, and the scene is concluded with feasting and festivity.[31]

As Morgan was to do later, McLennan made his scheme of social evolution rely heavily upon the postulate that sexual promiscuity had prevailed in the early stages of human society. McLennan believed that before society had adopted any form of marriage, general promiscuity had been the norm. However, in the context of a shortage of women due to female infanticide, two successive types of polyandrous marriage developed, which progressively placed limits upon the degree and type of promiscuity indulged in. In the first type of polyandry, each woman had several husbands who were not necessarily related to each other. In the second and later type, each woman had several husbands who were related as brothers. Following the train of thought established four years earlier by the Swiss judge J. J. Bachofen, in his book *Das Mutterrecht*, McLennan argued that the promiscuous aspects of the earliest stages of society made it impossible for male parentage to be established with any certainty, thereby ensuring that kinship was traced through females only. This, of course, applied with the fullest possible force for the stage of general promiscuity. It also applied for the first stage of polyandry, in which there was uncertainty, not only as to the particular identity of the father, but also as to the paternal bloodline. Only with the onset of the second stage of polyandry was it possible for kinship to be traced in the male line. For although there could still be no certainty as to the particular identity of the father, the paternal bloodline was clearly established.

Stated as briefly and as baldly as I have just done, McLennan's evolutionary schema can be seen for what it is — a rather crude piece of mythologizing which more accurately reflects the problems and preoccupations of Victorian England than the likely form of ancient society. Even at the time of its formulation, it was not regarded as particularly plausible, and towards the end of his life, McLennan, ailing and paranoid, was forced to defend it against a variety of opponents, including Morgan, Maine, John Lubbock, Herbert Spencer and even former Prime Minister Gladstone. Despite *prima facie* similarities between the accounts of social evolution produced by McLennan and Morgan, the former's prime target seems to have been the American. McLennan's response to *Systems of Consanguinity* ... was to label it "a wild dream, not to say nightmare of early institutions".[32] This hostility was apparently attributable to McLennan's distaste for the incestuous stages in the evolution of marriage postulated by Morgan. Savage promiscuity was all very well for the earliest stages of society, providing it could be gradually phased out without recourse to anything quite as disgusting as incest.

One of the major problems of McLennan's schema is that it relies so heavily on the gimmicky and imperfectly substantiated postulate of the widespread nature of marriage-by-capture in ancient times. In the Preface, McLennan attempts to turn the problem into a virtue by venturing to hope that the result of his investigation "may to some extent interest [the public] by its novelty". In one sense it would seem that this hope was realized. Although McLennan's full evolutionary scheme was acceptable to very few, the lightly-held cartoonist's stereotype of the caveman who bashes his future wife over the head and drags her off by the hair is still alive today, and constitutes the only survival of the marriage-by-capture hypothesis.

Unlike the conservative Maine, who was a successful lawyer and academic, and a fully accredited member of the Establishment, McLennan was a political liberal whose legal abilities were limited, who aspired to an academic career which never came to anything, and who is said to have been "unable to come to terms with the conventions of the society in which he lived".[33] These differences in station and attitude would seem to be reflected in the social theories of the two men. Maine's theory effectively legitimated patriarchal authority by allotting it a formative role in social evolution. McLennan's theory, on the other hand, was politically more daring. At a time when the subjection of women to men was the cultural norm, McLennan's theory suggested that, in the earliest period of human history, the physical dominance of males had led to a matrilineal rather than a patrilineal mode of tracing descent.

Although McLennan's forays into anthropological theory were by no means impressive, he did inspire one notable disciple, in the person of the Scottish classicist and biblical scholar, William Robertson Smith. In 1885, Robertson Smith published a book entitled *Kinship and Marriage in Early Arabia*, parts of which can still be read with profit by modern anthropologists.

In the early chapters, Robertson Smith develops the concept of the "kindred group", an entity which he rightly regards as being of considerable moment in Arabian society. All the members of such a group regard themselves as being of one blood, a belief which draws the group together and ensures that individual relationships within the group will be governed by communally-directed rights and obligations. As Robertson Smith himself expressed it:

Kinship . . . among the Arabs means a share in the common blood which is taken to flow in the veins of every member of a tribe — in one word, it is the tribal bond which knits men of the same group together and gives them common duties and responsibilities from which no member of the group can withdraw.[34]

Robertson Smith was fully aware that the attribution of such kinship bonds is not necessarily indicative of real genetic relationship, but may have occurred for purely social reasons.

However, despite the attaining of such important insights, the overall trend of the argument in Robertson Smith's book is disappointing. Time and again he will astutely remark upon some important fact about Arabian kinship, but will then proceed to expend his energies in attempting to demonstrate that it supports the views of McLennan. For example, in the first chapter he notes that, in some polygamous societies which trace descent in the male line, the children of one father may be subdivided into groups by the use of their mother's name. However, he does not go on to consider, in general terms, how social divisions can arise from the superimposition of one form of descent upon another. Instead, he simply assumes the use of the mother's name to be a vestigial relic of an earlier system of kinship through women, and, therefore, cites such usage as "proof" that McLennan's evolutionary scheme is correct.[35] Indeed, in the Preface, Robertson Smith goes so far as to claim that the "general result" of the whole book is that male kinship has been preceded by kinship through women only, and that his own reconstruction of social evolution "corresponds in the most striking manner" with that of McLennan.[36] In social anthropology, as in many other marginally scientific disciplines, it is often difficult for pioneers of specific areas to find suitable theoretical pegs to hang their facts upon. Nonetheless, the present writer feels bound to agree with E. L. Peters that, as regards Robertson Smith's work on kinship, the influence of McLennan was "an unmitigated misfortune".[37]

In evaluating Robertson Smith's study of Arabian kinship, it must also be realized that the book represented something of a diversion from the major goal of his career. For Robertson Smith's main interest was not in the evolution of kinship systems or marriage forms, but in a critical evaluation of the development of religion. As background to this, it is important to realize that during the 1880s, Robertson Smith had been dismissed from his Chair in Hebrew and Old Testament Exegesis at the Free Church College in Aberdeen. The issue leading to his dismissal had been that of Biblical criticism, with the governing church hierarchy regarding Robertson Smith's "advanced" views on this matter as heretical.[38] His most substantial and influential work, *Lectures on the Religion of the Semites*, was published in 1889. Taking up an idea which had been advanced by McLennan — that totemism represents an early form of animal worship — this book examines the social functions of ritualized feasting and sacrifice. Although the specific focus was sociological, in the sense that Robertson Smith was interested in overt ritual acts rather than private religious beliefs, the general perspective was evolutionary. As political organization developed, and loose aggregations of individuals fused into socially-defined groups, a matching hierarchy of gods appeared. The supreme deity of the Judaeo-Christian-Islamic tradition represented a personification of the notion of social unity, expressing the subordination of individual members of the community to the welfare of the social organism as a whole.

TYLOR AND FRAZER

As I have pointed out in the Preface, the dean of nineteenth-century English anthropology, E. B. Tylor, likewise subordinated the development of kinship to that of religion. In a book published in 1865, Tylor states that the rules governing marriage and social contact between kinsmen properly belong "to that interesting, but difficult and almost unworked subject, the Comparative Jurisprudence of the lower races".[39] His masterwork, *Primitive Culture*, published in 1871, does not so much as mention the topics of kinship and social organization, but addresses itself primarily to the evolution of religion. Only in his 1888 article "On a Method of Investigating the Development of Institutions, Applied to Laws of Marriage and Descent", does Tylor make any concerted attempt to analyse the facts relating to kinship. Tabulating a wide range of data, Tylor attempts to discover whether phenomena such as marriage-by-capture, cross-cousin marriage, and changes in line of descent are statistically correlated. However, even in this article, Tylor seems less interested in kinship as a subject in its own right, than as raw material for testing the efficacy of statistical methods in anthropology.[40]

The other major figure in late nineteenth-century anthropology, and the one best-known to the general public, was James Frazer. His interest in the subject seems to have been inspired by two sources. The first was Robertson Smith, with whom Frazer had become friendly as a young man. It was from Robertson Smith that Frazer took the idea of treating the religions of the world, not as received dogmas or heresies, but as subjects for comparative historical study.[41] The second major source was the work of Tylor, which, as Frazer tells us, "opened up a mental vista undreamed of by me before".[42] Here the crucial influence was *Primitive Culture*. As might have been expected if these influences were operative, Frazer's greatest contribution to the discipline was in the field of the evolution of religion. His most famous work, *The Golden Bough*, ostensibly set out to elucidate an ancient myth concerned with the rule of priestly succession in a sacred grove at Nemi, in the Alban hills of Italy. However, in the third edition, Frazer was to admit that this objective was merely an excuse for a more global task:

While nominally investigating a particular problem of ancient mythology, I have really been discussing questions of more general interest which concern the gradual evolution of human thought from savagery to civilization.

Or, as he expressed it in more poetic vein:

The cycle of *The Golden Bough* depicts, in its sinuous outline, in its play of alternate light and shadow, the long evolution by which the thoughts and efforts of man have passed through the successive stages of Magic, Religion and Science. It is, in some measure, an epic of humanity which, starting from magic, attains to science in its ripe age, and will find there, perhaps, its death.[43]

So the exposition of the myth of the priestly succession of Nemi was nothing more than a poetic device. The real thesis of the book was that civilization had been attained only because mankind had passed through the evolutionary stages of magic, religion and science.

In short then, the basic concern of Tylor and Frazer, the two most prominent representatives of late nineteenth-century British anthropology, was the evolution of religious thought. And the selection of this particular topic was by no means random. Whatever may have been the intentions of the natural scientists involved, the work of Lyell in geology, of Darwin in biology, and of Huxley in combatting critics of Darwin's theory, was collectively serving to undermine faith in active divine intervention, and was contributing to a diminution of the evangelical piety which had marked the early part of the century.[44] The tradition within which Tylor and Frazer were working can, in one very important sense, be contrasted with the tradition of natural theology. Whereas natural theologians like Paley had attempted to infer God's existence from evidences of design in nature, social evolutionists like Tylor and Frazer argued that the institutions of Western civilization, from the taking of a single wife to the worship of a single God, had attained their present form by purely natural means without recourse to divine intervention. For this reason, the work of Tylor and Frazer might aptly be described as "anti-natural theology", or perhaps more accurately, "natural anti-theology". "Theologians all to expose, Tis the *mission* of Primitive Man", Tylor once wrote in a piece of light-hearted doggerel.[45] For Tylor, this mission consisted of demonstrating that the social institutions of aboriginal peoples provided living evidence of former stages in the natural evolutionary development of Western culture.

But while their vessel of natural causation enabled them to steer past the Scylla of facile pietism, the social evolutionists also hoped that it would help them to avoid the Charybdis of purposeless atheism. This may be seen from the opening pages of *Primitive Culture*, where Tylor states the aim of the book as follows:

Keeping aside from considerations of extranatural interference and causeless spontaneity, let us take the existence of natural cause and effect as our starting point, and travel as far as it will bear us . . . Rudimentary as the science of culture still is, it would seem that even its most spontaneous and motiveless phenomena will be shown to come within the range of cause and effect as certainly as the facts of mechanics.

In an allusion to Paley's famous watch analogy, Frazer makes quite explicit the expected source of the "natural cause and effect" which he and Tylor saw as lying behind social evolution. Referring to the kinship systems of the Australian Aborigines, Frazer writes:

To suppose that they have originated through a series of undesigned coincidences . . . is to tax our credulity almost as heavily as it would be to suppose that the complex machinery of a watch has come together without human design by a mere fortuitous concourse of atoms . . .[46]

Using the watch analogy, Paley had inferred divine artifice from the observation of order in the natural world. Using the same analogy, Frazer infers human rationality from the observation of order in the social world. The arguments are structurally similar, but their conclusions are theologically antithetical. One aspires to make God a necessity. The other conspires to banish Him from the evolution of human culture. For Tylor and Frazer, divine teleology is to be replaced by a teleology based on human rationality.

Implicit in the anti-theological, pro-rational tone of the writings of the social evolutionists, there is the assumption that their enterprise possessed (or at least was capable of acquiring) genuine scientific status. However, it seems to me that neither Tylor nor Frazer should be credited with having pursued (or even with having attempted to pursue) a true science of man. The essential characteristic of a mature science, the presence of esoteric puzzle-solving techniques, is conspicuously absent. Certainly Tylor's paper on the application of statistical methods to anthropology could be taken as indicating that he wished to develop means of solving technical puzzles. However, in relation to his total body of work, this remained a solitary exercise, an obelisk in the desert and a tantalizing glimpse of what might have been accomplished. And consonant with the dearth of puzzle-solving, the primary audience and judge of the social evolutionist's work was not a small band of fellow specialists, but the intelligent layman, the man of letters, or the literary dilettante. Tylor's career exhibits some sort of transition in this regard. Early in the piece he tended to publish in the literary periodicals which had flowered during the seventies and eighties — the weeklies, the monthlies and the quarterlies. Later on, as he became more committed to the aim of making anthropology a science, the locus of his contributions shifted to the newer specialist journals, the appearance of which was itself an indication that the audience for anthropology was narrowing.[47]

In the case of Frazer, it is doubtful that he ever intended his work to be read by a restricted group of specialists. *The Golden Bough* was intended for, and was in fact received by, a very varied reading public. Even in his relatively esoteric contributions to the debate over the nature of Arunta totemism, Frazer was keen to reach the widest possible audience. Writing to Baldwin Spencer in 1898, Frazer opines that it would be a good idea to publish an article in one of the literary magazines in order to call attention to Spencer's forthcoming book. After all, says Frazer, the *Journal of the Anthropological Institute* "is read only by anthropologists".[48] Frazer's aims were, as one might expect knowing of his background in classics, at least partially aesthetic. To Edmund Leach we owe a scathing, but nonetheless accurate evaluation of the worth of *The Golden Bough* to a serious modern anthropologist. Leach demonstrates, by comparing a passage from Frazer's book with the original missionary's account on which it was based, that Frazer's aim was not to give a straightforward rendition of the ethnographic facts, nor even to transform the facts by subjecting them to a scientific theory, but, by altering a word here and there, to lend an atmosphere of romantic "savagery", to play upon the emotions, and to make the account sound more "literary".[49]

Finally, it should be mentioned that Tylor's avowed aim of "exposing theologians" was part of a broader program which involved passing judgement upon a whole spectrum of contemporary European social institutions. Tylor's notion of "survivals" was crucial to this. In demonstrating that some practices of Western civilization were akin to those of "savagery", and in labelling them "survivals", Tylor hoped to make it possible for modern Europeans to rise above what he regarded as unwholesome reminders of man's evolutionary history. *Primitive Culture* concludes with the famous passage in which Tylor avers that the science of culture is essentially a reformer's science.

As a result of his concern with the evolution of religion, Frazer became involved in a wide ranging controversy over the significance of some material relating to the Australian Aborigines. But the story of the impingement of Australian data upon British anthropology involves many more people than just Frazer and is sufficiently important for our story to warrant detailed treatment.

DATA FROM THE ANTIPODES

(a) *Introduction*

The kinship systems of the Australian Aborigines have long been considered one of the more remarkable of the phenomena which anthropology has brought to light. A people who possessed one of the most primitive technologies in the world, apparently utilized almost incredibly involuted methods of regulating marriage and descent. So labyrinthine, indeed, do the Australian kinship systems seem, that an authority on the subject recently admitted that the complexities of certain cases "have caused sinking feelings of incomprehension in many undergraduates — and if the truth be told, in their teachers as well".[50]

However, the main point about the Australian kinship systems is not simply that they seem complex, but that their apparent complexity is extremely systematic and symmetrical. Any Aboriginal born into a tribe automatically finds himself or herself placed in one particular division of the tribe, the overt function of the divisions being the regulation of marriage and descent. The number of such divisions is commonly two, four or eight per tribe. In cases where there are only two of these divisions, anthropologists usually refer to them as dual divisions or "moieties". In cases where there are four divisions, they were, for most of the period covered by this book, known as "classes", although "sections" is now the preferred term. In cases where there are eight divisions, they are generally called "subsections". I shall use the term "class" either as a generic label to cover sections *and* subsections or else, for reasons of literary variety, as a synonym for either "sections" *or* "subsections". In both four-class and eight-class kinship systems there will always be, as one of cleavages defining the boundaries of the classes, a dual division such that half of the classes fall on one side of the division, and half on the other side. Hence, the term "moiety" is applied, not only to systems with two kinship divisions, but also to systems possessing a large number of divisions. In the former usage, a moiety is not further subdivided. In the latter usage it is. Collectively, the two usages serve to underline the structural unity of the various types of Australian systems, since a matrilineal dual division, implicit or explicit, runs right across the whole continent and serves as the link which makes inter-system compatibility possible.

When, in a marriage-class sytem, the time comes for a young man to marry, his spouse will be taken from a specific class other than his own, and any resulting offspring will be placed in a third class. The most ingenious feature of this arrangement stems from the way the classes interlock and overlap. In both the Kariera and Arunta systems, the best-known cases of four-class and eight-class systems, respectively, this interlocking and overlapping entails that, for the male line, the systems will repeat themselves every second generation — a man being subject to the same rules for marriage and descent as was his paternal grandfather. For the female line, the Kariera and the Arunta systems differ. In the former case, the system will again repeat itself every second generation — a woman being placed in the same section as her maternal grandmother. In the latter case, a woman will find herself in the subsection to which her mother's mother's mother's mother had belonged, which means that the system is repeating itself every fourth generation.

Within this appearance of total rigidity, the systems are amazingly flexible. Despite the fact that there are many possible cases, the degree of compatibility between cases is considerable. If, for example, a member of a given tribe goes to live with a neighbouring tribe, it will generally be possible, by investigating genealogies, to find a common kinsman or ancestor, and thereby discover the correspondence which should obtain between the kinship systems of the man's home and adopted tribes. Even where one tribe has four classes and the other eight, the underlying structure is such that the two systems can normally be made to intermesh with little difficulty. The structural factor which promotes this compatibility and lends a fundamental unity to scores of kinship systems scattered over, literally, hundreds of tribes distributed throughout Australia, is the aforementioned dual division into matrilineal moieties. That is, in virtually all Australian kinship systems, descent through the woman travels by two separate routes which function like threads, drawing together the totality of the social fabric.

Having introduced the reader to Australian systems of relationship in a quasi-technical fashion, let me now briefly survey a brave attempt to deduce a spectrum of different types of kinship system from a limited number of social specifications. The purpose of introducing this material is to indicate, firstly, that the Australian systems are not as idiosyncratic as they may appear at first sight and, secondly, that they must not be regarded as intellectual exercises which are divorced from social reality. For, as the analysis demonstrates, the Australian systems lie within a range of theoretically-possible arrangements, and represent concrete solutions to problems of social taxonomy and organization. Having put the Australian systems into perspective in this way, we shall then be in a position to examine the methods by which particular systems can be more-exactly specified.

The Americal sociologist Harrison C. White is responsible for the most impressive attempt yet made to formulate a general theory of relationship systems.[51] Although White's analysis is sometimes ethnographically under-nourished,[52] and fails to cover even the full range of extant (let alone theoretically possible) kinship systems, it demonstrates a tenacity and a mathematical proficiency which are sorely needed in kinship studies. Beginning with a set of eight axioms which lay down the specifications of societies in which marriage and descent are regulated by exogamous clans, White systematically derives, describes and (where appropriate) produces diagrams for all kinship systems which not only satisfy these axioms, but also embody one of four common kinds of prescribed marriage. He then compares the ideal types so derived with ethnographic reality and demonstrates that a number of well-known kinship systems are instances of his ideal types. In this way, for example, he shows that the four-section system which is attributed to the Kariera tribe of Western Australia, arises from an eight-clan society in which pairs of clans exchange patrilateral or matrilateral cross-cousins.[53] Similarly, he demonstrates that the six-class arrangement generally attributed to the New Hebridean island of Ambrym, is one particular systematization which can arise from a six-clan society in which marriage between first cousins is forbidden, and wives are exchanged between pairs of clans.[54] And finally, we may note his derivation of the eight-subsection system of the Arunta as one possible product of a sixteen-clan society in which marriage involves an exchange of second cousins between pairs of clans.[55] From the work of White, and from extensions made to it by the social anthropologist J. A. Barnes, it now appears that there are actually six distinct kinds of four-class system,[56] fourteen kinds of six-class system,[57] and sixteen kinds of simple eight-class system.[58]

In the periods to be covered in this introductory chapter and in the book as a whole, the systematic perspective offered by White and Barnes was not yet available. The pioneer anthropologists who brought to light the various cases of marriage-class system were, therefore, forced to resort to more *ad hoc* means of ordering their data. This was, emphatically, not due to incompetence on their part. In view of the paucity of the analytical work which they had to draw upon, their method of approach was entirely appropriate. This method involved the selection of specific cases of marriage-class system, which were then regarded, in some sense as being "typical" of a range of similar systems. In this way, the previously-mentioned Kariera, Ambrym and Arunta systems were each singled out as exemplary of four-class, six-class and eight-class systems respectively. The precise details of how each of these systems came to be selected as exemplary were, to some extent, dependent upon historical accidents, such as when the system was discovered and by whom it was described. However, one should not infer from this that the selection process was an arbitrary one. In fact, the fundamental criteria used to make these selections were those of simplicity, clarity and elegance. Specifically, the questions which pulled most weight in deciding whether a particular kinship system should be regarded as prototypical of a range of systems were as follows: Firstly, could the system of relationship be neatly disentangled from other social artefacts (such as the totemic system)? Secondly, could the arrangements for marriage and descent be unambiguously specified as an ordered set of verbal rules? Thirdly, could the system be easily and elegantly figured in the modes of diagrammatic representation favoured at the time? In going through the historical material, therefore, these questions will furnish a set of criteria by which the various attempts to sort out the data can be rationally assessed.

Let us now embark on the technical question as to how the Kariera and Arunta systems may be precisely specified and figured. The Kariera system works in the following way. A tribe deploying the system is divided into four named sections which I shall call A, B, C and D. Every man and woman in the tribe will have been assigned at birth to one or other of these sections. Marriage and descent are regulated such that

(i)   a man from section A marries a woman from section B, and any resultant offspring will be placed in section D;

(ii)   a man from section B marries a woman from section A, and any resultant offspring will be placed in section C;

(iii) a man from section C marries a woman from section D, and any resultant offspring will be placed in section B;

(iv)   a man from section D marries a woman from section C, and any resultant offspring will be placed in section A.

If double horizontal lines are used to indicate marriage, and directed lines with arrowheads to indicate descent, all the above rules may be schematically summarized as follows: [59]

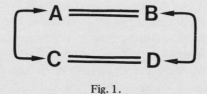

Fig. 1.

If it is desired to show exactly what happens for a man and a woman within each section, this schema may be drawn in more detail, using triangles to represent men, circles to represent women, and vertical brackets without arrowheads to represent siblingship.[60] Since in the Kariera system, the class of the offspring is determined only by the class of her/his mother,[61] the lines of descent will be drawn as emerging from the female partner in each marriage.

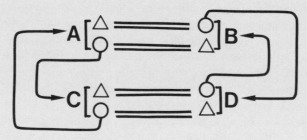

Fig. 2.

As may be seen from Figure 2 by following the lines which indicate descent and siblingship, if a man is in section A, his mother will be in section C, his mother's brother will be in section C and his mother's brother's daughter will be in section B. Likewise, his father will be in section D, his father's sister will be in section D and his father's sister's daughter will be in section B. In other words, for a man in section A, both his female cross-cousins, that is, his mother's brother's daughter and his father's sister's daughter, will be in section B, into which he is legally obliged to marry. Actually, for the normally functioning Kariera system, one's mother's brother's daughter *will be the same person* as one's father's sister's daughter. So the usual form of Kariera marriage is with the person who is one's cross-cousin twice over. It should be noted that, for the pair of marriages between Sections A and B and for the pair of marriages between sections C and D, each man may be regarded as obtaining a wife by giving his sister (real or classificatory) in exchange. Hence, anthropologists often refer to such an arrangement as "sister-exchange".[62]

The standard eight-section system, generally called the "Aranda" or "Arunta" system after a tribe in Central Australia which used it, may be specified in the following manner. A tribe deploying the system will be divided into eight named subsections which I shall call A1, A2, B1, B2, C1, C2, D1 and D2. Every man and woman in the tribe will have been assigned at birth to one or other of these subsections. Marriage and descent are regulated such that

(i)   a man from subsection A1 marries a woman from subsection B1, and any resultant offspring will be placed in subsection D2;

(ii) a man from subsection B1 marries a woman from subsection A1, and any resultant offspring will be placed in subsection C1;

(iii) a man from subsection A2 marries a woman from subsection B2, and any resultant offspring will be placed in subsection D1;

(iv) a man from subsection B2 marries a woman from subsection A2, and any resultant offspring will be placed in subsection C2;

(v)   a man from subsection C1 marries a woman from subsection D1, and any resultant offspring will be placed in subsection B1;

(vi) a man from subsection D1 marries a woman from subsection C1, and any resultant offspring will be placed in subsection A2;

(vii) a man from subsection C2 marries a woman from subsection D2, and any resultant offspring will be placed in subsection B2;

(viii) a man from subsection D2 marries a woman from subsection C2, and any resultant offspring will be placed in subsection A1.

Using the same conventions as previously, these criteria may be schematized as:

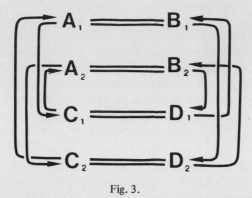

Fig. 3.

Or, using the same conventions as in Figure 2, plus the knowledge that the Arunta system resembles the Kariera one in that the class of the children is determined matrilineally,[63] Figure 3 may be drawn in more detail as follows:

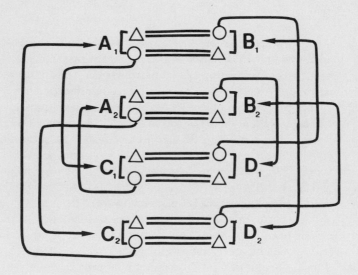

Fig. 4.

The typical form of marriage for an Arunta male is with a variety of "second cousin", namely the mother's mother's brother's daughter's daughter. That this particular relative is in the appropriate subsection, may be seen from Figure 4 via the laborious process of tracing around the relevant lines indicating descent, siblingship and marriage. If, for example, the male in question is in subsection A1, his mother will be in C2, his mother's mother will be in A2, his mother's mother's brother will be in A2, his mother's mother's brother's daughter will be in D1 and his mother's mother's brother's daughter's daughter will be in B1 — the subsection from which A1 males take their spouses. And the symmetry of the system is such that a similar tracing process will reveal that, for any male in any of the other subsections, the mother's mother's brother's daughter's daughter will be placed in the subsection from which he must take a wife. One may also note that, like the Kariera, the Arunta practice sister-exchange, males in A1, for example, exchanging sisters with males in B1.

In order that the cyclic nature of the Arunta system be made manifest, the system may be redrawn after the manner of J. A. Barnes as follows: [64]

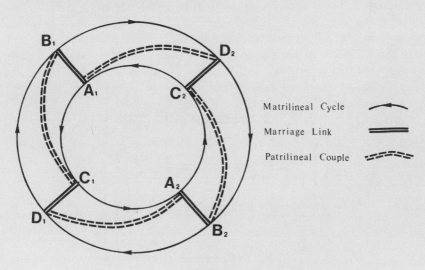

Fig. 5.

As Figure 5 illustrates, the system embodies two matrilineal cycles, B1 → D2 → B2 → D1 → B1 and A1 → C1 → A2 → C2 → A1, each with a periodicity of four generations. Similarly, Figure 5 shows that the system includes four patrilineal couples, B1 → C1 → B1, D1 → A2 → D1, B2 → C2 → B2 and D2 → A1 → D2, each with a periodicity of two generations. Finally, we may use Barnes's notion of "affinal periodicity" to give a measure of the way in which spouses circulate around the system. If we take as a unit in the cycle, the link between a man and his wife's brother (or alternatively between a man and his sister's husband; or between a woman and her husband's sister, or her brother's wife), the affinal periodicity is defined as the number of links in the cycle. In the case of the Arunta system, this periodicity is two. Using Barnes's shorthand for denoting matrilineal periodicity, patrilineal periodicity and affinal periodicity, the Arunta system may be briefly specified as a "422" arrangement.

Such then is the Arunta system, which White's analysis shows to be one particular product of a sixteen-clan society practising marriage based on second-cousin exchange. Another eight-class system in which marriage with the second cousin is similarly practised, was first reported by Howitt for the Warramunga,[65] and later by Webb for the Murngin.[66] The society on which this system is based is not covered by White's analysis since, in addition to allowing marriage with the mother's mother's brother's daughter's daughter, the system also allows marriage with the mother's brother's daughter and with the father's sister's daughter. The Warramunga system may be schematically represented as follows:

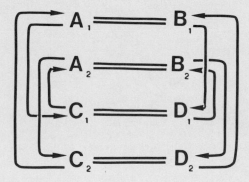

Fig. 6.

Or, when a circular diagram is deployed in the manner of Barnes,[67] the Warramunga system appears as follows:

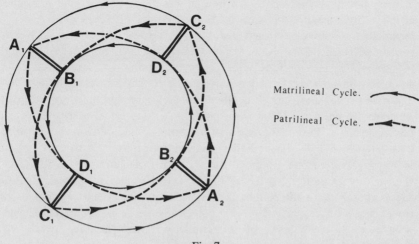

Matrilineal Cycle.

Patrilineal Cycle.

Fig. 7.

As can be seen from Figure 7, the Warramunga system is 442.

In a passage which I quoted earlier in the chapter, James Frazer attributed the origin of the Australian kinship systems to a feat of intellectual ingenuity, presumably by some prehistoric aboriginal genius. As faith in "primitive rationality" declined, such explanations became unfashionable and recent opinion now favours the view that the Australian systems have grown up via a process of natural social selection, rather than through intellectual deliberation. Recent work has also tended to indicate that the systems are not as complex as they look or, alternatively, that their complexities are of a different kind than was once believed. Lévi-Strauss' revaluation of the Australian data implies that one should apprehend kinship in the way that the Aborigines themselves are postulated to. More specifically, one should think about marriage in terms of "sister-exchange" and in terms of rules-of-thumb, like the following (which would work for the Kariera and Arunta tribes, although not for the Warramunga): "a man should marry into the same class as did his grandfather". If one conceptualizes kinship in this way, the suggestion is that the systems are much easier to learn and apply than if one attempts to remember them via a complete set of necessary and sufficient verbal regulations.[68]

(b) Early Work Among the Kamilaroi

The intricacies of the Australian data were first noticed during the former half of the nineteenth-century when it was reported that the Kamilaroi people, who inhabited an area to the northwest of Sydney, possessed a remarkable system of marriage regulation. The Kamilaroi were known to be subdivided into four groups which (using McLennan's terminology) were "exogamous", since persons were generally required to marry *outside* the group to which they themselves belonged. The tribe, as a whole, was "endogamous", however, since members of any given group were normally expected to marry *inside* the tribe and, in fact, to select a spouse from a particular one of the other three groups. Around the middle of the century, a settler named T. E. Lance added that, although a man is thereby limited to marriage within one group, he has some sort of marriage tie with all the women of that group.[69] In 1853, the Reverend W. Ridley, whose attention had been drawn to the Kamilaroi system by Lance,[70] sent a paper to Dr Hodgkin, Vice President of the Ethnological Society in London, describing what he called the "classes" of the Kamilaroi.[71] Now the term "classes", as deployed in logic, does not suggest hierarchical displacement. However, the term also has a more common connotation which is far from neutral in respect of social stratification. For this reason, the use of the term tended to impose the hierarchical assumptions of British culture upon the essentially-egalitarian social organization of the Australian Aborigines.[72] As such, the term represented a misnomer and eventually came to be little used in comparison with the hierarchically-neutral term "sections". Ridley's paper is also of interest because, on his account it *was* sometimes possible for a man of one particular class to marry a woman from that same class.[73]

In 1869, Morgan had received, in reply to his questionnaire, a letter from the Reverend Lorimer Fison, a Wesleyan missionary then stationed in Fiji. Fison provided a competent description of the relationship systems of the Fijians and the Tongans and Morgan was able to include them in a supplement to his *Systems of Consanguinity* ... In 1871, Fison moved to Australia and soon came into contact with Lance and Ridley. From Lance he learned that the justification given for the irregular marriages which sometimes took place among the Kamilaroi, was that the people concerned were from different totems. Seeing this as an indication that Kamilaroi marriage regulations were based not merely upon marriage-classes, but also upon totemic subdivisions of the classes, Fison asked Ridley, who was about to start on a journey into the outback, to make further enquiries. The official purpose of Ridley's journey was to make philological investigations requested by the Colonial Secretary of New South Wales on behalf of Professor Max Mueller of Oxford.[74] However, Ridley also managed to collect a good deal of information relating to aboriginal marriage regulation.[75] On Ridley's account, men belonging to one of the classes were named "Ippai" and women "Ippata", men of a second class were named "Murri" and women "Mata", men of a third class were named "Kubbi" and women "Kapota", and men of the fourth and final class were named "Kumbo" and women "Buta". Ridley also ascertained that, if one disregards marriages which are regulated by totems, the following rules are strictly enforced:

(1)   An Ippai may marry only a Kapota.
(2)   A Murri may marry only a Buta.
(3)   A Kubbi may marry only an Ippata.
(4)   A Kumbo may marry only a Mata.

When children result from a marriage, the following laws of descent are observed:

(1)   The children of Ippai and Kapota are all Murri or Mata.
(2)   The children of Murri and Buta are all Ippai or Ippata.
(3)   The children of Kubbi and Ippata are all Kumbo or Buta.
(4)   The children of Kumbo and Mata are all Kubbi or Kapota.

In Ridley's opinion, the above rules prevail over a large portion of New South Wales and Queensland, and "probably with some variations over all parts of Australia".[76]

Now, recognizing that Ippata is simply the feminine form of Ippai, Mata the feminine form of Murri, and so forth, these rules may be summarized schematically as follows:

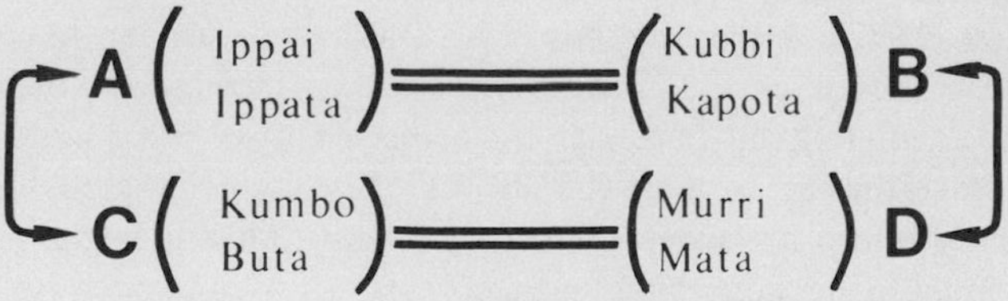

Fig. 8.

Hence, as may be seen by comparing this schema with Figure 1, the Kamilaroi system of marriage and descent is identical to that which was later singled out as the standard type of a four-class system. And, in fact, during the four decades following Ridley's description of the Kamilaroi system, it did function as a norm in much the same way as the Kariera system has for the past sixty years.

However, as Ridley himself recognized, the above rules did not, in the case of the Kamilaroi, constitute the whole story. Marriages *could* sometimes take place *within* classes and Lance had been correct in observing that such irregular marriages were justified by totemic considerations. According to Ridley, the four classes of the Kamilaroi were subdivided into ten totemic groups. The purpose of these subdivisions is, he infers, to prevent the appearance of incest when people from the same class intermarry.[77]

Between May and August 1871, Fison sent Morgan three memoranda outlining Lance and Ridley's material on the Kamilaroi system for regulating marriage and descent. Ridley had alleged that there are three totemic subdivisions in the Ipai-Ippata class, two in the Murri-Mata class, three in the Kubbi-Kapota class and two in the Kumbo-Buta class. Fison, however, suggests that there must be an additional subdivision in the Murri-Mata class and one in the Kumbo-Buta class, thereby yielding a symmetrical system with three subdivisions in each class. Now on this hypothesis, the totemic subdivisions of the Ippai-Ippata class would be identical to those of the Kumbo-Buta class and those of the Murri-Mata class would be identical to those of the Kubbi-Kapota class. Hence, according to Fison, there are, in fact, only six totemic subdivisions, each of which occurs in two classes. Now, as I have argued in discussing Ridley, the Kamilaroi system can be regarded as a system of four marriage-classes, with additional complications arising from the superimposition of the totemic divisions. Fison, however, chooses to say that what we have is *six* classes, each containing four "names". On this interpretation, it is the totemic divisions which are regarded as the classes and the named groupings which are regarded as the superimposition.[78]

In March 1872, Morgan presented a paper on Australian kinship to the American Academy of the Arts and Sciences. Although he claimed to be simply amalgamating the material from Fison's three memoranda, Morgan actually did rather more than this. Specifically, he attempted to weld the Australian data into his own evolutionary scheme. Morgan begins his account of the Kamilaroi by describing their political structure, or as he prefers to call it, their "tribal" organization. He states that the Kamilaroi are divided into six "tribes", and lists the six totemic subdivisions described in Fison's memoranda. In a footnote, he compares this organization with the totemic groupings of the Seneca or Iroquois, which he had described in his 1851 book on *The League of the Iroquois*. However, he goes on to say that, among the

Kamilaroi, there are signs that an even more primitive type of organization is operative – an organization which is not fundamentally "tribal" or political, but sexual. In fact, in Morgan's view, the type of sexual cohabitation practised by the Kamilaroi comes closer to the base level of primitive promiscuity than does that of any other people. When a Kubbi meets any woman from the Ippata class, they address each other by a word which means "spouse". This is "but a step from promiscuous intercourse or the same thing, in reality, with a method". It provides "the first direct evidence of a condition of society which had previously been deduced from systems of consanguinity and affinity". The great interest attaching to the Kamilaroi people, says Morgan, centres in their retention of "a conjugal system more stupendous and extraordinary than any hitherto found in any nation of barbarians or in any other nation of savages". The stage of development of the Kamilaroi "seems much nearer to the primitive constitution of society than any organized form previously known".[79]

(c) *The Fison-Howitt Collaboration*

Fired by the task of investigating aboriginal social organization in the Morganian style, Fison advertised in the Australian newspapers for information and assistance and was rewarded by a response from A. W. Howitt, explorer, bushman, naturalist and public official. This was the beginning of a fruitful collaboration and friendship which lasted for three decades.[80]

The first major product of their collaboration was the 1880 publication *Kamilaroi and Kurnai*, which contains three contributions by Fison, two by Howitt and a "prefatory note" by Morgan. Dedicated to Morgan as a "token of esteem", the book owes a lot to the American lawyer. Not only are his definitions of the stages of the family and of the various types of kinship system adopted, but Fison in particular, makes a concerted effort to develop Morgan's account. As Morgan notes in his preface, Fison introduces the first chapter with a legend which might be taken to indicate that the original form of aboriginal cohabitation was promiscuously incestuous. Here then, we have Fison producing inferential evidence for the most rudimentary stage of the family postulated by Morgan – the "undivided commune", in which brothers and sisters intermarried. Moreover, in a later section entitled "Theory of the Kurnai System", Fison attempts to use Morgan's ideas to discover how the kinship system of the Kurnai tribe of eastern Victoria differs from that of the Kamilaroi. Analysing the Kurnai system in Morgan's terms, Fison finds it to be "more advanced" than the Kamilaroi system. However, the Kurnai are in no way technologically superior to other Australian tribes. Now on Morgan's account, which links the development of social organization with that of material culture, this state of affairs looks paradoxical. Fison thus feels obliged to offer an explanation: The area inhabited by the Kurnai tribe is cut off from the rest of Australia by high mountains. Hence, argues Fison, the Kurnai system must have developed, under circumstances of considerable isolation, as an offshoot of the evolutionary process which produced the Kamilaroi system as its lineal descendant. Although Fison does not explain how, he evidently believes that it was this isolation which made it possible for the kinship system to develop rapidly, while the tribe's material culture failed to make appreciable headway. Thus, according to Fison, the various manifestations of social evolution are not necessarily synchronized. Under exceptional circumstances, it is possible for one aspect of a social system to develop in independence from other aspects of the system.[81]

Another example of Fison's attempting to extend and improve Morgan's views may be found in the discussion of the Kamilaroi kinship system, which constitutes Fison's major theoretical contribution to the book. The core of his argument consists of a section which is structured like a geometry text, with "propositions" set out and then "proved" with a great show of mathematical rigour. These propositions embody Morgan's specifications of the second or "Turanian" stage in the development of kinship systems. In order that the "proof" may be accomplished, Fison invokes four "laws of marriage and descent", which he has abstracted from tables containing his empirical data on the Kamilaroi. Thus, Fison considers himself to be showing that Morgan's Turanian type of kinship system is the logical outcome of the Australian division into exogamous classes. The belief in primitive rationality, common to many writers in the late nineteenth-century, was never more strikingly presented. Fison then goes on to argue that each of the exogamous divisions of the Kamilaroi may be regarded as consisting of certain homogeneous groups. Taking each group as a unit, Fison demonstrates that the relations between group and group are precisely those which would arise and continue between individuals in modern Western society if marriages were contracted between first cousins, and continued during subsequent generations between pairs of their descendants (who would also be first cousins). In other words, Fison was employing the notion of first cousin marriage as a conceptual device for understanding the marriage regulations of the Kamilaroi.[82]

In a number of places throughout the book, Fison and Howitt take

Morgan's side in his disputes with several British authors, including and especially McLennan. For example, Fison attacks McLennan's assertion that Morgan's kinship terms are merely "modes of addressing people", with no social significance.[83] He also argues against McLennan's theory that exogamy and bride-capture resulted from the practice of "female infanticide", which produced a scarcity of women.[84] The main reason for Fison and Howitt's support of Morgan would seem to be that they saw him as a man who, like themselves, had arrived at his conclusions after real and sustained experience in the field. By contrast, McLennan's work would have had, in their view, an insufficient empirical basis. There are hints too that Fison regarded McLennan's conception of how the preliterate mind works as defective. Like Fison and Morgan, McLennan believed that aboriginal man is rational, but according to Fison, McLennan's "primitive rationality" was far too immediately inductive and empirical. In Fison's opinion, indigenes are the captives of past marriage arrangements and rules of descent, from which they continue to draw logical conclusions long after alterations in day-to-day conditions have made it impossible for these rules and arrangements to be applied in the real world. In other words, Fison believed, as did Morgan, that present kinship systems are likely to be fossilized relics of a stage in the development of the family which has long since passed.[85]

One reason for the consonance between Morgan's and Fison's views is that both men believed that the general trend of social evolution is towards the eventual triumph of individualism. Thus, Morgan implies that future American political institutions will represent the culmination of the liberty, equality and fraternity which he had detected among the Iroquois.[86] In a similar manner, Fison discerns in the various forms of Australian class system "what appears to be a steady progress towards the *individualizing of the individual*" [italics in original]. According to Fison, the end product of this process is "the civilized man with his personal rights and possessions, and his gospel of political economy teaching him that self-seeking on the part of the individual must result in the greatest good of the greatest number".[87] Without wishing to subscribe to the facile view that scientific work is inevitably influenced by the political or religious convictions of the scientists concerned, the evidence here would seem to suggest that the social theories of both Morgan and Fison reflect firmly-held beliefs about the role of the individual. In Morgan's case, such beliefs apparently derive from his political position (he was a staunch Republican). In Fison's case, they might be linked to his non-conformism and his evident espousal of a utilitarian social ethic.

Apart from its development of Morgan's position, *Kamilaroi and Kurnai*

is also notable for two other reasons. First, having mentioned the type of
Australian kinship system which involves two moieties, it goes on to suggest
that this type of system was the lineal ancestor of the four-class Kamilaroi
type.[88] Second, it presents an account of mother-in-law avoidance among the
Kurnai.[89] This practice is one of a number of customs which later assumed
prominence in discussions of the rights and obligations of kinsmen. As we
shall discover in subsequent chapters, the work of Rivers and Radcliffe-Brown
was instrumental in welding this latter topic into the theoretical framework
of British anthropology.

In a generally favourable review of Fison and Howitt's book in *The Academy*, E. B. Tylor stated that it confirms the scientific importance of Australian
marriage-customs, "if only they can be thoroughly understood and reduced
to a system". "This is not easy to do", he continues, "indeed the exceptions
and anomalies and variations of rule among different tribes make the study of
the subject in its whole difficulty a task for legal minds used to the problem
of contingent remainders".[90] With the problem conceived in these terms,
Tylor took a step towards solving it by inviting A. Macfarlane, Examiner
in Mathematics at the University of Edinburgh, to develop a systematic
notation capable of representing any consanguineous or affinal relationship.
The results of Macfarlane's researches were published in the *Journal of
the Anthropological Institute* in 1883. This work, however, was not to be
taken up by anthropologists until the 1920s, when, as we shall discover in a
later chapter, Radcliffe-Brown borrowed Macfarlane's notation without
acknowledgement.

If credit is to be allocated for *Kamilaroi and Kurnai*, the first great anthro-
pological work on the Australian Aborigines, it must go primarily to Fison.
It was he who initiated the correspondence with Morgan, who functioned on
Howitt's account as the "chief architect" of the book,[91] and who produced
its most impressive theoretical chapters. Over the next quarter of a century,
Fison and Howitt continued to make notable contributions to Australian
anthropology, culminating in Howitt's 1904 classic *The Native Tribes of
South-east Australia*. As the years progressed, Howitt's achievements came
to overshadow those of Fison. The 1880s in particular, were productive years
for the former explorer. Firstly, he distinguished "local" organization from
social organization.[92] This distinction, which later anthropologists found
fruitful, may be regarded as an adaption of the Morganian contrast between
political and social organization. Secondly, he advanced a theory to explain
the postulated development from Morgan's "undivided commune", through
the two-moiety to the four-class system. According to Howitt, the dual

division, which produced the two-moiety system, originated in a "reformatory movement" designed to prevent brothers from marrying their sisters. Similarly, the transition to a four-class system was the result of a "reformatory movement", which ruled out the possibility of intermarriage between parents (real or classificatory) and children. Letting A and B designate the classes produced by the original dual division, Howitt points out that, for a system which has segmented into four classes, "the old law 'A and B mutually intermarry and the child follows the mother's class' still underlies the new arrangements".[93] Thirdly, he did important work on the typology of Australian kinship systems. As typical of systems with two classes and matrilineal descent, he specified the system of the Barkinji tribe,[94] later substituting that of the Dieri;[95] as typical of systems with four classes, he specified that of the Kamilaroi;[96] and as typical of systems with eight classes, he specified that of the Warramunga.[97] Now a broader comparative knowledge would have revealed that marriage regulation in the latter system is more complex than in at least one other type of eight-class system (namely the 422 Arunta system). Specifically, the 442 Warramunga system allows marriage, not only with a form of second cousin, but also with certain forms of first cousin. Nonetheless, Howitt's account of the Warramunga system represents what is, to my knowledge, the first clear, published description of an eight-class marriage system. Fourthly, Howitt provides his reader with what are probably the first maps ever prepared to illustrate the distribution of the various types of kinship system over large areas of the Australian continent.[98] Finally, Howitt devised a schematic method of representing marriage-class systems, which soon became standard anthropological practice.[99] In 1904, Howitt was presented with an honourary doctorate by Cambridge University. Summing up the work of the two men in 1908, an eminent colleague wrote that, although it was Fison who first drew Howitt's attention to "the particular line of work that needed to be done in regard to our Australian tribes, . . . it was really Howitt who did the work."[100]

(d) Schulze and the Arunta

In 1891, an article describing the social organization of aboriginals belonging chiefly to the Arunta tribe of central Australia, was published by the Reverend Louis Schulze, a Lutheran missionary. On Schulze's account, the kinship system had eight classes.[101] Here then, was corroboration of Howitt's earlier description of an eight-class system among the Warramunga, who also inhabit central Australia. As with Howitt, the rules given by Schulze did not necessarily indicate what would now be defined as an Arunta system. However, Howitt's Warramunga system and Schulze's Arunta system depart from the norm in different ways. In the case of Schulze's data, it *is* possible to extract the standard Arunta system, but only by selecting out certain of the permitted marriages, and ignoring others. In Howitt's case, the marriage rules specify a system which is definitely of a different type. Over the next decade or two, as the social organization of tribes from central and northern Australia was progressively uncovered, a good deal of anthropological attention was focussed on the nature and significance of eight-class systems.

(e) *R. H. Mathews*

One person who was involved in these investigations was R. H. Mathews, a licensed surveyor who took up ethnology as a hobby and eventually succeeded in producing nearly two hundred papers on the subject. Of these, approximately one half deal with the social organization of the Australian Aborigines. Published in such widely distributed journals as the *Proceedings of the American Philosophical Society*, the *American Anthropologist*, the *Bulletin et Memoires de la Société d'Anthropologie de Paris*, the *Journal of the Anthropological Institute, Man* and *Folklore*, Mathew's articles were, and are, surprisingly little known.[102] Although many of his papers are repetitive, the amount of original material contained therein is still sufficient to entitle Mathews to a front ranking among the pioneers of Australian anthropology. The late A. P. Elkin, in his time the acknowledged expert on the details of Australian social organization, lists a total of eleven achievements of Mathews in this area.[103] For our purposes, Mathews's most important contributions were his investigations of eight-class systems, his work on the distribution of the various types of Australian social organization and his recognition of the significance of irregular marriages for questions of descent.

   In an article published in 1898, Mathews reproduces data supplied by an informant from northern Australia. These data give what is, to my knowledge, the first specification of what later came to be called the Arunta system. Using the word later popularized by Radcliffe-Brown, Mathews characterizes the system as consisting of eight named "sections". These sections may be arranged, according to Mathews, into two groups of four. "The sons of the women of one group", he writes, "marry the daughters of the women of the other group. Or, what amounts to the same thing, the men of group A marry the sisters of the men of their own generation in group B, and *vice-versa*." Mathews states that this eight-class system, with various modifications, is in force over the greater part of the Northern Territory.[104] In a string of eight further articles published in rapid succession over the next two years, Mathews cemented his claim to being the pioneer enumerator of the various cases of eight-class system.[105] The last article in the series maps the distribution of these cases, and suggests that they should be collectively known as "the Wombya organization", after the tribe in which the system was first reported.

Around the same time, Mathews also published a complete map of Australia showing the boundaries of the various types of kinship system, and the areas in which the customs of circumcision and splitting the male urethra were practised.[106] Far more detailed and comprehensive than anything previously produced, this map, although imperfectly acknowledged by Radcliffe-Brown, would most certainly have been utilized by the latter in his celebrated work on the distribution of Australian social organization.

Another contribution by Mathews was the recognition that irregular marriages can be useful for determining mode of descent. If in a standard marriage-class system the normal rules are followed, there is no point in asking whether descent with respect to the classes is through the male or the female. In all cases it appears to be through both. But if irregular marriages are also practised, it is possible, as Mathews realized, to infer whether a child owes its class membership to its father or to its mother.[107] However, Mathews did not clearly apprehend the full implications of this insight, an achievement which, as we shall discover in a later chapter, was reserved for Radcliffe-Brown.

Despite this important work, Mathews managed to antagonize a number of influential colleagues, including and especially Howitt. In 1907 he had an unpleasant little exchange with Howitt in the columns of *Nature*, in which he implied that Howitt had plagiarized him, and which ended with each man accusing the other of "personal animus".[108] Howitt's last publication, dictated from his deathbed in March 1908, consists of a "message to anthropologists" warning the anthropological world of the danger of accepting as pristine the currently observed marriage customs of most Australian tribes. According to Howitt, "some investigators" have failed to acknowledge that, among the Aborigines in the settled districts, it is very difficult to find informants "whose memory goes back to the time when the tribes were in their full vigour". Hence, there is a very real danger of forming "altogether fallacious views of [Aboriginal] marriage laws and customs". The only offending investigator named by Howitt is Mathews, who is said to have drawn "quite erroneous conclusions in some most important points".[109] A distribution list among Howitt's personal papers indicates that the message was sent to virtually all the prominent English periodicals and newspapers, all the anthropological journals in Europe and elsewhere, and to all the most eminent anthropologists in Europe and the United States.[110] Apart from the matter of treading on each others corns in regard to priority, the basic difference between Howitt and Mathews seems to have involved a point of theory. As Mathews expressed it:

Having studied the question of Australian sociology for many years, I am forced to the conviction that neither promiscuous intercourse of the sexes, nor what has been called "group-marriage", have ever existed among the social institutions of the aborigines of Australia. I am equally convinced that the divisions into cycles, phratries, sections and totems, have not been deliberately inaugurated with intent to prevent consanguineous marriages or counteract the supposed evil results of incest, but have been developed in accordance with the surrounding circumstances and conditions of life.[111]

This denial of primitive promiscuity, and the related denial that social institutions were consciously devised to prevent incestuous unions, puts Mathews very much out on a limb. Almost all the other major workers in the field, including Howitt, Morgan, Fison and Frazer, believed that human sexual relations had originally been promiscuous, and that the various class systems represented successful attempts to prohibit incest.

(f) *Spencer and Gillen*

The next chapter in the history of Australian anthropology was written by W. Baldwin Spencer and F. J. Gillen. Spencer had come to Australia in 1887 to take up the Chair of Biology at the University of Melbourne.[112] In 1894, being interested in some rare marsupials, he took part in a scientific expedition to central Australia.[113] Apart from furthering Spencer's zoological enquiries, the expedition also attempted some anthropological investigations, this part of the work being performed by a Dr E. C. Stirling. Stirling, who acknowledged his debt to Howitt and Fison, was unable to confirm Schulze's observation that the kinship system of the Arunta tribe contains eight classes. Rather, Stirling discerned only four classes which, from the data he gives, were evidently arranged in the standard Kamilaroi format.[114] Spencer, who edited the published reports of the expedition, would thus have been confronted with a central problem in the typology of the Australian kinship systems. While visiting Alice Springs during the expedition, Spencer also made the acquaintance of Gillen, an experienced bushman with a longstanding interest in the Aborigines. Late in 1896, Spencer returned to Alice Springs and set off with Gillen to investigate "the institutional and mental life" of the Arunta.[115] This fieldwork, continued over the following two years, resulted in Spencer and Gillen's *Native Tribes of Central Australia*. One contemporary tells us that the publication of this book in 1899 "instantly attracted such widespread attention that the book soon came to be regarded as the classical treatise on Australian ethnology".[116] Or, as R. R. Marett was to write, the work "took the scientific world by storm".[117] For the first time, competent investigators had painted a detailed portrait, not of the shattered remnants of cultures decimated by contact with civilization, but of societies which were functioning in much the same way as they had for thousands of years before the coming of the white man. In 1904, Spencer and Gillen published a sequel, *The Northern Tribes of Central Australia*, which confirmed the importance and accuracy of their first book, and consolidated their ethnographic reputation. *The Native Tribes of Central Australia* was dedicated to Howitt and Fison, "who laid the foundation of our knowledge of Australian anthropology". And indeed, the influence of the pioneering anthropologists is felt in a number of places throughout the volume. For example, Spencer and Gillen support the Fison—Howitt position in the controversy as to whether kinship terms are merely modes of address.[118] They use a variety of Howitt-like tables and diagrams to present their own kinship data.[119] The simpler the tribal organization, the more clearly do they detect evidence of what Fison and Howitt had called "group-marriage".[120] And like Fison and Howitt, they believe that the fundamental feature of Australian social organization is the division of the tribe into two exogamous moieties.[121]

Speaking of the Arunta kinship system, Spencer and Gillen mention that the southern part of the tribe contains four named classes, whilst the northernmost part contains eight. Hence, the accounts of Schulze and Stirling can be reconciled. There are no problems when a person from the southern Arunta attempts to marry someone from the northern Arunta. Although the southern Arunta possess only four named classes, each of these classes is, according to Spencer and Gillen, divided into two, so that both branches of the tribe function, for purposes of intermarriage, as eight-class systems.[122] Although typology is not their major concern, Spencer and Gillen do state that at least two important types of social organization are to be found in

central Australia — the first of these being exhibited by the Urabunna and
Dieri tribes, and the second by the Arunta tribe, among others.[123]

In an article in the 1900–1901 volume of his journal *Anneé Sociologique*,
the French sociologist Émile Durkheim took up an interesting point made in
Spencer and Gillen's *Native Tribes of Central Australia*. According to the
Australian ethnographers, people from the southern Arunta sometimes marry
into the neighbouring Urabunna tribe, which has two exogamous matrilineal
moieties. The problem is that the four classes of the southern Arunta are
normally grouped into two patrilineal moieties of two classes each, which
implies an incompatibility between the social organizations of the two tribes
in the mode of tracing descent. What happens, on Spencer and Gillen's
account, is that for purposes of dealing with the Urabunna, the southern
Arunta group their four classes, not into patrilineal moieties of two classes
each, but into two matrilineal moieties consisting of different pairs of the
same four classes. This somewhat difficult train of thought may be followed
using a schematic diagram:

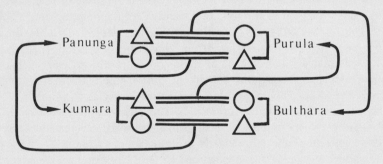

Fig. 9.

As can be seen from Figure 9, if a man is Panunga, his son will be Bulthara,
his son's son will be Panunga, his son's son's son will be Bulthara, and so on.
Likewise, if a man is Kumara, his son will be Purula, his son's son will be
Kumara, his son's son's son will be Purula, and so on. That is, patrilineal
descent travels along two separate closed paths, one involving the sections
Panunga and Bulthara, and the other involving the sections Kumara and
Purula.

Similarly from the diagram, if a woman is Panunga, her daughter will be
Kumara, her daughter's daughter will be Panunga, her daughter's daughter's
daughter will be Kumara, and so on. Likewise, if a woman is Bulthara, her

daughter will be Purula, her daughter's daughter will be Bulthara, her daughter's daughter's daughter will be Purula, and so on. That is, matrilineal descent also travels along two separate closed paths, one involving the sections Panunga and Kumara, and the other involving the sections Bulthara and Purula.

Normally the southern Arunta regard their four classes as grouped into the pairs Panunga-Bulthara and Kumara-Purula, each of which constitutes a patrilineal moiety. However, for purposes of arranging marriages with the Urabunna, the pairs are considered to be Panunga-Kumara and Bulthara-Purula, thereby yielding two matrilineal moieties. According to Durkheim, this flexibility in the southern Arunta system gives a clue to its evolutionary development, in that the normal, patrilineal grouping must be interpreted as a later modification of an earlier, matrilineal one.[124]

Following Baldwin Spencer's death in 1929, the Oxford University Press released, during a time of economic depression, not one but two commemorative volumes, the first entitled *Spencer's Last Journey*, and the second *Spencer's Scientific Correspondence*. Although one might think that the latter title, in particular, could have been interpreted as referring to Herbert Spencer, the achievements of the great ethnographer-biologist were evidently sufficiently well appreciated that any mention of his given name was deemed superfluous.

(g) *Arunta Totemism*

The topic which felt the greatest impact as a result of the publication of Spencer and Gillen's *Native Tribes of Central Australia* was the vexed problem of totemism; and the man primarily concerned was James Frazer. Two particular points impressed the Cambridge classicist greatly. First there was the revelation that the Arunta have no notion of the connection between sexual intercourse and conception, but believe instead in a continual reincarnation of mythical ancestors. Second there was Spencer and Gillen's account of Arunta totemism as uninherited and unrelated to marriage regulations, consisting mainly in the performance of "*intichiuma*" ceremonies, which Frazer interpreted as magical rites designed to ensure a plentiful supply of the various totemic plants and animals. Concluding that the Arunta are, with regard to their totemic beliefs, the most primitive people extant, Frazer attempted to demonstrate that Spencer and Gillen's material contained the key to the first beginnings of religion within the previous phase of magic. In the tradition of McLennan and Robertson Smith, Frazer used the new Arunta material to argue that the religious aspect of totemism was the original one, and had preceded the introduction of social measures controlling marriage. By this move, he was attacking the views of Sir John Lubbock and Herbert Spencer, who held that totemism began as a system of social regulations and that its superstitious aspects were a later accretion. In thus arguing for the religious and pre-religious nature of totemism, Frazer was careful to avoid the charge that he was reducing aboriginal thought to vague mysticism or metaphysical speculation. On the contrary, Frazer affirms his belief in "the simple, sensuous and concrete modes of thought of the savage".[125] By December 1900, Frazer had published the second edition of *The Golden Bough*, rewritten so that the new central Australian evidence could be seen as crucial to his account of the development of religious thought.

Once Frazer had promulgated his views on Arunta totemism, a storm of controversy and discussion broke loose and continued for a decade and a half. The people concerned included, not only Frazer and Baldwin Spencer, but also Howitt, Tylor, Andrew Lang, A. C. Haddon, Durkheim, Wilhelm Schmidt and Arnold Van Gennep. A whole chapter would be required to fill in the details of this debate, but since its relevance to our main theme is minimal, only a very brief discussion will be appropriate. Frazer seemed to regard his main antagonist as Lang,[126] who proposed a degenerationist rather than an evolutionary account of religion. According to Lang, the evidence from Australia was that many tribes believed in one supreme God, and phenomena such as the *intichiuma* rites could thus be explained as resulting from the degeneration of an originally monotheistic religion into nature-worship and magic. Hence, in Lang's view, the Arunta were far from being the most primitive tribe in Australia, and the *intichiuma* ceremonies told one little about the earliest stages of religion.

Inasmuch as the whole controversy impinges upon the subject of this book, it is largely as a negative influence. The discovery that Arunta totemism has nothing to do with regulating marriage and descent, tended to divert discussion away from the specification of social organization and lead back to more typically late nineteenth-century concerns with the evolution of religious thought. This enabled people like Frazer and Lang, whose technical ability was strictly limited, to hold the spotlight for longer than they otherwise would have done.

(h) *N. W. Thomas*

Before leaving this discussion of the impingement of Australian evidence upon British anthropology, let us mention N. W. Thomas's 1906 volume on *Kinship Organizations and Group Marriage in Australia*. Although published as part of the Cambridge Archeological and Ethnological Series, this book should not be regarded as a product of Cambridge ethnology. Nor, for that matter, did it constitute any sort of original contribution to Australian ethnography. Thomas was a marginal figure in relation to people like Frazer, Haddon and Rivers and, to my knowledge, had never visited the Antipodean continent. Radcliffe-Brown, admittedly a somewhat biased critic for reasons which will be outlined in Chapter VII, tells us that Thomas was in the habit of boasting that he had written his Australian book in a mere two weeks.[127] Undistinguished in conception and execution, the book is little more than a none-too-exhaustive compilation of other people's findings. At one point, Thomas produces some fairly detailed maps of Australian social organization, but was later accused by Mathews of plagiarizing them, a charge which may well be justified. The major influence on the book seems to have been Andrew Lang. Thomas writes that he considers himself to have been "more than fortunate in securing aid from Mr Lang in a subject which he has made his own".[128] Knowing of Lang's literary dilettanteism and general ineptitude in matters requiring technical proficiency, one would hardly be likely to let this comment inspire confidence in its author.

(i) *Conclusion*

The general attitude of the British school of social evolutionists to the data which had come to light on the Australian Aborigines, was perhaps best expressed by Frazer. It was a happy circumstance that Baldwin Spencer settled in Australia, averred Frazer because, as a biologist, he "was well prepared to grasp the significance of . . . archaic forms of plant, animal and human life, which the immemorial seclusion of that continent from the rest of the world has preserved as in a museum to satisfy the curiosity of later ages concerning the development of life on our planet." And Spencer's later acquaintance with the Arunta was doubly fortunate because that tribe, "dwelling in the most isolated region of the most isolated continent, have survived to our time as if on purpose to hold up to us a mirror of the life of man as it was in ages long before the dawn of history".[129] In other words, the Australian aborigines in general, and the Arunta in particular, were (to use Tylor's word) a gigantic "survival" of past human history. One also may speculate that Australian kinship material, from which such "archaic" practices as promiscuity and group-marriage could allegedly be inferred, tended to have a somewhat morbid fascination for a culture as bound down by repressive sexual mores as Victorian England. It still remained for the sexual aspects of the Australian data to be subjected to a disinterested methodology with genuinely scientific aims.

With regard to the typology of Australian marriage-class systems, the situation at the turn of the century may be briefly recapitulated as follows: A number of cases representing three major types had been isolated and labelled. The simplest of these cases, which Howitt called the "Barkinji" and later the "Dieri", and which for Spencer and Gillen was exemplified by the Urabunna and Dieri tribes, had two exogamous matrilineal moieties. Of intermediate complexity was the system with four exogamous classes, which was usually designated the "Kamilaroi type", after its oldest known example. The most complex case, which Mathews called the "Wombya organization", and which for Spencer and Gillen was exemplified by the Arunta tribe (among others), had eight exogamous classes. With three major types represented in this way, one important deficiency remained to be corrected. Kamilaroi social organization is less than perfect as an exemplar because its rules governing marriage and descent are inextricably entwined with an intricate totemic system. Such is manifestly not the case with the Arunta, in which the eight-class system has no connection with totemic *intichiuma* rites. By 1903, it had been observed by J. G. Withnell that the totemic systems of Western Australia tend to be quite separate from the four-class systems for regulating marriage and descent.[130] However, the advantages of this observation for the typology of Australian social organization were not to be realized until 1913. For, as we shall discover in a later chapter, that was the year in which Radcliffe-Brown successfully proposed the organization of the Kariera tribe as the paragon of a four-class system.

*   *   *   *   *

In this chapter, I have presented an account of the investigations into kinship which either did impinge, or might have impinged upon the work of Rivers and his disciples. Since the historical evidence regarding the nature and extent of these impingements is ambiguous, I have chosen to err on the side of being too comprehensive rather than too concise. In so doing, I may well have made it appear that the quantity of work done on kinship during the second half of the nineteenth-century was such that the topic represented a dominant preoccupation of the school of social evolutionism. However, the impression of sheer quantity is, to some extent, an artefact of gathering together work done in one particular subject area over a considerable period of time. For, while the total amount of work done on kinship by the social evolutionists was not inconsiderable, the resulting literature, when viewed as a body, was not yet sufficiently coherent or technical to justify the assertion that a British sub-discipline of kinship studies had emerged. Only Morgan's work showed this promise, but, as I have argued, it had little influence in England. Morgan's most productive disciples were Fison and Howitt, but their work was, in both the geographical and intellectual senses, a long way from the epicentre of British social evolutionism. The lack of recognition accorded to Morgan would seem to have been due to the presentation rather than to the substance of his work. Many years later, Robert Lowie was to complain of

Morgan's intolerable diffuseness, the pages and pages of irrelevant data, and the unsatisfactory tabulation by which relationships according to our system are translated into native languages, so that the connotation of any one native term can only be learned by a complete re-arrangement of the information as presented.[131]

Only by such means is it possible to explain why the extraordinary achievements of *Systems of Consanguinity* . . . did not have the impact they so richly deserved.

One important reason for the failure of kinship studies to establish itself was that, of all the anthropological topics considered by the social evolutionists, kinship was especially vulnerable to those sociocultural prejudices which the Victorian era found most troublesome. I refer in particular to the characteristically Victorian heavy-handedness about the repression and control of sex.[132] The neuroses of Victorian society being what they were, it was inevitable that topics such as "primitive promiscuity", the dominance (or otherwise) of paternal authority, the chronology of the occurrences of patriliny and matriliny, and the interpretation of aboriginal statements about the connection (or lack of it) between intercourse and conception, could not be debated in a rational and objective fashion.

Victorian attitudes to sexual control must also constitute part of the explanation for a remarkable fact about the people who were involved with studies relating to kinship during the nineteenth-century. As even the most causal reader of this chapter will have noticed, very many of the people so involved had legal interests and training. Now lawyers are taught, above all else, to be aware of the formalities which can regulate and control potentially disruptive aspects of society. In the context of Victorian culture, the sexual instinct was *par excellence*, a socially disruptive force, which needed to be contained and repressed. And a prime function of kinship institutions is to provide for such containment and repression. Is it any wonder then that so many of the people who busied themselves with kinship-related studies during the Victorian era, were lawyers? [133]

As I have argued in respect of Tylor and Frazer, the central concern of the late nineteenth-century social evolutionists was to expunge teleological assumptions from their accounts of social development, and to replace such assumptions by explanations of a naturalistic cast. Especially since 1858, when archaeological investigations at Brixham Cave in Devon had revealed an apparently very early stage of human culture,[134] British anthropologists had attempted to reconstruct the natural processes by which social institutions had come into being and ramified into their present forms. As George Stocking Jnr has pointed out, Tylor in particular saw his anthropological vocation as being "to fill the gap between Brixham Cave and European Civilization without introducing the hand of God".[135] Consider a number of the social evolutionary projects described in this chapter, such as Morgan's attempt to correlate the evolution of kinship with the development of the material conditions of existence, Maine's goal of writing a "natural history of law", and McLennan's exercise in producing "scientific history". Each of these examples falls within the ambit of the generalized naturalistic programme of which Tylor and Frazer were the leading anthropological exponents in Britain.

It should also be remarked that Tylor and Frazer exhibit a special interest in one particular aspect of social evolution, namely the development of religious ideas. The reason behind their special interest would seem to be that the social evolutionary programme was carried out in the context of a widespread Victorian critique and revaluation of the role of divine teleology. Since theological (or more correctly, anti-theological) motives were the driving force of the programme, it is hardly surprising that the evolution of religious thought itself was subjected to the most searching scrutiny.

This concentration upon religion resulted in the production of a considerable amount of written material on the subject, constituting, in the case of the Tylorean and Frazerean corpora, by far the most detailed treatment of any single topic. However, the real point about the significance of the topic of religion in nineteenth-century anthropological evolutionism does not concern the *quanity* of literature produced. Rather, it concerns the centrality attributed to the topic. As Frazer asserted in a passage which I have quoted more fully in the Preface, religion permeates the entire social and intellectual life of the aboriginal, and determines his conduct in all situations. It provides him with "a general explanation of the processes of nature", and defines his place and destiny in the natural order. In fact, so thoroughly is religion said to infiltrate the mental processes and outward behaviour of the aboriginal, that he is allegedly incapable, "even in thought", of separating it from other aspects of his life. Even allowing for exaggeration arising from Frazer's literary hyperbole, and for the fact that the passage in question comes from a tribute to Robertson Smith, who had shared Frazer's interest in comparative religious studies, the message seems clear. Religion was at the very centre of Frazer's anthropology. It provided Frazer, and the other social evolutionists whose focus was anthropological, with the subject matter, the aetiology, and the framework for their reconstructions of the development of aboriginal thought and culture.

With religion thus monopolizing the theoretical spotlight, it was difficult for even the most spectacular kinship material to force its way to the centre of the anthropological stage. By the beginning of the twentieth-century, the most salient facts about Australian Aboriginal social organization were widely known, and a number of the necessary steps had been made towards a suitable taxonomy for Australian kinship systems. However, in the hands of people like Frazer and Lang, important new material from central Australia was treated, not so much as raw kinship data, inherently interesting in their own right, but as fuel for the longstanding debate over the origins of religious thought.

CHAPTER II

RIVERS, SEVERED NERVES AND GENEALOGIES

William Halse Rivers Rivers was the man who, more than any other, diverted the attention of British anthropologists from the evolution of religious thought to the synchronic functionings of single societies. This he did primarily by making kinship studies central to anthropological theory and practice. Rivers is, thus, the missing link in the quasi-historical account of the emergence of British Social Anthropology given in Ian Jarvie's *The Revolution in Anthropology*. Jarvie makes it sound as though Malinowski, with no help from anyone else, was reacting directly against the work of Frazer. In fact, Rivers and his colleagues A. C. Haddon and C. G. Seligman, were decisive in bringing about the change-over from nineteenth-century style social evolutionism to twentieth-century style structural-functionalism. A number of the major points generally associated with the names of Malinowski and Radcliffe-Brown can be clearly found and repeatedly stated in the work of Rivers, and much of what remains of the alleged Malinowski—Radcliffe-Brown contribution can be interpreted as a direct reaction against certain aspects of the teachings of their distinguished predecessor.[1]

From about 1906 until about 1930, eight years after his death, Rivers' work was probably the most talked-about in academic anthropology.[2] Long before Malinowski's influence was felt, Rivers was hailed as the apostle of the new approach to fieldwork, and as the greatest ethnographer who had ever lived.[3] Long before Radcliffe-Brown became interested in kinship studies, Rivers was acknowledged as the reigning champion in the difficult task of unravelling the intricacies of indigenous social organization. From about 1910 onwards, Rivers, as we shall discover in Chapter IV, became one of the leading figures in a new and contentious approach to anthropology — that of extreme diffusionism. But most of all, Rivers was renowned for giving the confused and infant science of man a method — the genealogical method which will be discussed in the latter part of this chapter.

Although I do not wish to allow biographical material primacy of place at this juncture, there is one fact about Rivers's life which we must note at the outset. As a physician, experimental psychologist, anthropologist, ethnologist, psychiatrist and prospective parliamentarian, Rivers had one of the most extraordinarily varied and changeable careers in the whole history of western science. If I may be forgiven for introducing a term which will sound to many of my readers like pseudo-scientific jargon, Rivers represents an extreme example of what the sociologists Joseph Ben David and Randall Collins would call a "role -hybrid".[4]

The process of "role-hybridization" may be defined as one in which an individual, in moving from one profession or academic field to another, simultaneously relinquishes some of the attitudes and behaviours appropriate to the old role, and adapts some of the methods and techniques of the old role to the materials of the new one. The role-hybrid most commonly moves from an academic field which is regarded as "harder" or more scientific, to one which is regarded as "softer" or less scientific. This is precisely what Rivers did, not once, but a number of times.

After beginning his career in 1887 as a ship's surgeon, followed by a brief period of private medical practice and a number of appointments as resident physician at various British hospitals, Rivers moved into academia via experimental psychology. At that time, the field was a "hard" discipline, in the sense of placing great value on empirical and theoretical rigour. In 1898, Rivers went as an experimental psychologist on the famous expedition to the Torres Straits between Australia and New Guinea, which event inspired what might be called the "anthropological" period of his career. Associated with the careful deployment of genealogies as a tool for elucidating indigenous social organization, this phase of Rivers's career is discussed at length in this chapter. One should note that it was pursued concurrently with further investigations by Rivers into experimental psychology. From about 1910 onwards, Rivers ceased his work as an experimental psychologist and entered the "ethnological" phase of his career, in which he speculated about the role of diffusion in the development of human culture. Then, following psychiatric analyses of shell-shocked soldiers during the First World War, Rivers's interests again shifted in the direction of a "softer" discipline. At a time when Freud's views were regarded as anathema by the great bulk of the British medical and scientific establishment, Rivers produced several substantial works advancing a quasi-Freudian interpretation of psychological illness. Were it not for his premature death in 1922, it seems likely that he would have pursued a further vocation, this time in politics, for not long previously, he had been nominated as a candidate for the University of London seat in the British Parliament. Summing up Rivers's total career in science, his friend C. G. Seligman wrote, "perhaps no man has ever approached the investigation of the human mind by so many routes".[5] From my knowledge of the history of science, this assessment carries only a slight trace of exaggeration.

Nonetheless, there is one respect in which Rivers differs from the classical type of role-hybrid described by Ben David and Collins. While not totally ruling out shifts in intellectual interest which are detached from financial or vocational considerations, these writers apparently consider the predominant factor determining the switching of roles to be the state of the job market. That is, for Ben David and Collins, ambition and economic necessity would seem to constitute the major motivations for role hybridization. However, Rivers was described by a close friend as "the least ambitious man I have ever met".[6] Moreover, quite early in his scientific career, Rivers was elected to a fellowship at St John's College Cambridge, an honour which apparently afforded him whatever prestige he desired and a sufficiently comfortable living. Hence, Rivers's role changes could not have been motivated by ambition or economic factors. Rather, the shape of his scientific career seems to have been largely conditioned by the development of his own personality within the changing socio-intellectual climate of the late nineteenth and early twentieth centuries. Especially during the early part of his life, Rivers was evidently the prototype of the shy, objectively ratiocinative intellectual, being introverted, reticent and unemotional. At this time, his political views tended towards conservatism. As one might be inclined to predict for some-one born in the middle of the Victorian era and having a clergyman for a father and two sisters who never married, Rivers seems to have been the victim of severe sexual repression, and this problem seems to have been compounded by what one of his close friends interpreted as Rivers's own tendencies towards homosexuality.[7] As sexual mores emerged slowly from the Victorian era, it would seem that Rivers's imperfect recognition of these tendencies became increasingly perspicuous. At the same time, his commit-ment to the efficacy of objective rational thought weakened. He seems to have become both more willing to allow the importance of subjective emotion in the behaviour of himself and others, and considerably more extroverted. Someone who knew him well during the latter period of his life, has described him as being "in obvious conflict ... with the Establishment (both army, medical and otherwise)",[8] a characterization which would certainly have been inappropriate for the younger Rivers. During the war, these develop-ments seem to have been strongly reinforced by his psycho-analytic inves-tigations, through which he became intensely involved with the repatriated servicemen who were his patients. In order, for example, that he would be able to empathize more fully with aviators whose nerve had failed them, Rivers, who was then approaching his mid-fifties, went on numerous flights, "looping the loop" and "performing other trying evolutions in the air".[9] The emotional involvement between Rivers and the men he treated was evidently mutual. As one account records:

Many of them simply worshipped him. He too became attached to them, would spend holidays with them or invite them to stay with him in his College rooms, and thus got to know them through and through.[10]

Two of the patients with whom he became friendly at this time were those future men of letters, Siegfried Sasson and Robert Graves, both of whom later acknowledged their debt to him.[11] Following his war experiences, the shyness and reticence which had hitherto marked his personal relations, were no longer in evidence. As one close friend was to state, through the attainment of a "more sympathetic insight into the mental life of his fellows, [Rivers] became another and a far happier man. Diffidence gave place to confidence, hesitation to certainty, reticence to outspokenness, a somewhat laboured literary style to one remarkable for its ease and charm." In the period between 1916 and his death, "intuition was less controlled by intellectual doubt" and "inspiration brought with it the usual accompaniment of emotional conviction".[12] In a similar vein, another close friend informs us that Rivers "was no longer wholly absorbed in his own thoughts — he was scarcely ever that — but was taking a keen interest in other people and in the ordinary affairs of life".[13] Arnold Bennett, who was introduced to Rivers by Sassoon, has left some amusing recollections of his friendship with Rivers, including his charmingly contemporary description of the latter as a "really great swell".[14] Whereas before the war he had shunned all administrative tasks, Rivers now involved himself with a multitude of committees, a number of which had evidently been set up to ameliorate the physical and mental health of the working man.[15] These new concerns were indicative of a shift towards the political left, as was further evidenced by the Labour Party's endorsement of him as a parliamentary candidate. His pedagogic role at St John's College was also deeply affected by the changes in his personality. In 1919 he assumed the position of Praelector of Natural Science Studies and, through the media of formal lectures and informal discussions in his rooms, dispensed counsel and guidance to the students of the College. From all accounts, he must have been outstandingly successful in this task, for his charges paid tribute to his "fascinating personality", his "boundless enthusiasm" and, above all, his sympathy. Indeed, as one friend wrote, it was not sufficient to say that Rivers was sympathetic. Rather, he exhibited "a sort of power of getting into another man's life and treating it as if it were his own".[16]

While the biographical accounts of Rivers make much of his war experience as a prime cause of the personality changes described above, it seems to me probable that this experience merely set the seal on developments in Rivers's personality, which had been taking place in a more or less continuous fashion, at least since the turn of the century. Although this hypothesis is based upon evidence relating only to one individual, it does tally with a more general conclusion which seems to be finding favour among modern historians of the First World War. The conclusion to which I am referring is that the war did not, by itself, cause the social and intellectual changes which were widely noticed and commented upon after 1918. Rather, it only accentuated pre-existing developments. Thus, for example, Arthur Marwick argues that what E. L. Woodward called the "scorching" effect of the war on the minds of British intellectuals, is best interpreted as the end-product of a "serious attack on Victorianism" which "began in the 1890s and developed under the leadership of Shaw, Wells, Davidson, Fry and many others in the Edwardian period".[17]

Before ceasing this introductory biographical sketch, there is one important point which should be made about the nature of Rivers's thought processes. As Rivers himself states on a number of occasions, his conscious cerebrations were almost wholly devoid of visual imagery, although he remembered being capable of visualization as a child and still experienced it while dreaming. According to Rivers, the loss of his childhood capacity to picture could be understood as part of the process by which he had become especially interested in abstract matters, and had, therefore, devoted less attention and interest to the concrete world. One of the major motivations of much of Rivers's scientific work seems to have been to understand mental processes based on visualization, a type of thought which he himself was apparently no longer able to consciously perform.[18]

The sea changes in Rivers's personality and career were not, of course, totally unique to him. A number of his scientific contemporaries, including Henry Head, Grafton Elliot Smith and several colleagues from the Torres Straits expedition, were to experience shifts of vocational interest and/or personality, some of which were quite similar to those undergone by Rivers. So obviously, there must have been broad socio-cultural factors which helped to determine these changes. Nonetheless, in the rest of this chapter, and to some extent in the two chapters which follow, I have found it convenient to focus on the unfolding of Rivers's personality. This is not because I am committed to "psycho-history", in the sense of believing individual psychological development to be aetiologically prior to socio-cultural determinants. On the contrary, it is because I believe that the extant sources on Rivers lend themselves far more readily to a psychological than to a sociological interpretation.

THE BACKGROUND IN EXPERIMENTAL PSYCHOLOGY

In 1891, Rivers became a house physician at the National Hospital for the Paralyzed and Epileptic in London. There he assisted Victor Horsley in the latter's pioneering excursions into neuro-surgery and made the acquaintance of the neurologists Hughlings Jackson and Henry Head.[19] While the practical experience with Horsley and the contact with Jackson's evolutionary account of the nervous system were both, doubtless, important, the association with Head was even more crucial to Rivers's intellectual development. For some years previously, Head had been working in Germany with the physiologist Ewald Hering, and returned to England as an ethusiastic exponent of Hering's work on vision. As Head himself tells us, Rivers avidly absorbed from him Hering's views on colour vision and the nature of vital processes.[20] Under these circumstances, "Rivers's interest became more definitely fixed on the border line between neurology and psychology".[21] The upshot of these influences was an exhaustive survey performed by Rivers of previous work on the psychology and physiology of vision, which was eventually published as a massive article.[22] More than two decades after its publication, this article was described as "still ... the most accurate and careful account of the whole subject in the English language", being of speoial value for its "unsurpassed critical account of the principal theories of colour vision" and for its detailed discussion of Hering's views.[23]

The most striking feature of the presentation of Hering's theory of colour vision contained in the article, is Rivers's endorsement of Hering's substitution of a physiological for a psychological explanation of the optical phenomenon known as "colour contrast". If a small patch of grey paper is placed on a green surface, it appears through contrast to be tinged with the complementary colour to green, namely pink. Previous investigators had attempted to explain this phenomenon psychologically, in terms of a perceptual illusion. Hering, however, offered a purely physiological account, invoking metabolic processes postulated to take place in the retina of the observer. Apparently then, the aspect of Hering's work which had most impressed Rivers, was the tackling of a problem involving the mind-body interaction in an objective, non-mentalistic fashion.

Beginning from this apparent demonstration of allegiance to scientific objectivity, one of the most striking trends throughout Rivers's career is the increasing intrusion of subjective or introspective elements into his scientific work. Following the 1898 expedition to the Torres Straits, which I shall be explicitly discussing later in the chapter, this trend was already apparent. Discussing the investigations on experimental psychology which he had performed during the expedition, Rivers remarked with what one can only interpret as a touch of regret, that owing to the limitations under which the experiments had been performed, the introspective element of psychological experimentation was almost entirely lacking.[24] This felt deficiency, however, was soon remedied by a remarkable series of experiments which Rivers performed on his friend Henry Head. In 1901, Head and his colleague James Sherren had determined to make a systematic study of nerve injuries among patients attending the London Hospital where Head was a physician and Sherren a surgeon. However, Rivers who, we are told, had "acted as their guide and counsellor" from "the early days of their research", and whose interests lay in placing the psychophysical aspect of the work on a sounder basis, "was impressed with the insecurity of this side of the investigation", since it seemed "unwise to demand any but the simplest introspection from patients".[25] Introspection, he decided, could only be made a legitimate topic for scientific enquiry if the subject under investigation was a trained observer, sufficiently discriminative to realize if his introspection was being prejudiced by external irrelevancies or molded by the form of the experimenter's questions, and sufficiently dedicated to lead a life of detachment throughout the entire course of the tests. It was in the belief that he could fulfil these requirements, that Head himself volunteered to act as Rivers's experimental guinea-pig.

The theoretical background against which the experiments were set, may be briefly sketched as follows.[26] In 1884, Magnus Blix had described the presence of "heat- and cold-spots" on the skin — minute areas which are peculiarly sensitive either to heat or to cold. This led to the conception of punctate sensibility, according to which the skin is endowed with sensitive spots, each of which reacts to a specific stimulus. It was postulated that there were spots not only for heat and cold, but also for pressure and pain. To this mechanism were attributed all the sensory impulses arising from stimuli applied to the skin.

Rivers and Head, while not questioning the existence of the sensitive spots, maintained that punctate sensibility alone could not account for all the impulses of cutaneous origin which reach the central nervous system. For one thing, when all the heat- and cold-spots have been marked out on normal skin, considerable areas remain between the spots. These areas, although incapable of reacting to thermal stimuli of a punctate nature, respond readily to such stimuli providing they are applied over an area of some extent. It was primarily in an attempt to explicate the sensory mechanism of the skin that the Rivers–Head experiments were performed.

One particular characteristic of Head's mental life seemed, to Rivers and Head, to be worthy of special comment. In sharp contrast to those of Rivers, Head's cerebral processes were apparently based upon visual images to an extraordinary degree. According to the two experimenters, Head was able to conceptualize numbers, the days of the week and abstract ideas such as virtue and cowardice, only by associating them with images in varying tones of black and white. He evidently had no power of cognizing scents or tactile sensations directly and could recall musical sounds only by picturing notes or by associating the sounds with "words which are clearly visualized". (Although no examples are given, this presumably means pictorially-conceived words like "flash", "coruscate" or "glow".) Thus, Rivers and Head suggest that the latter should be regarded as a strong visualizer, who has come to rely on pictorial images to such a degree that his other modes of sensory recall have virtually ceased to function. Now it seemed to the two co-workers that this feature of Head's mental processes would hinder his attempted introspective analyses of the predominantly tactile, cutaneous sensations to which he was to be subjected in the experiment. However, they further believed that, once having been performed, these analyses would yield insights of widespread generality, since "the majority of persons in this country seem to belong to the group of those who depend on visual images, and approximate, at any rate as far as somatic sensations are concerned, to the condition of [Head]".[27]

On 25th April, 1903, Head submitted to a surgical operation in which the radial and external cutaneous nerves[28] supplying his left forearm were severed in the region of the elbow, small portions of the nerves excised, and the ends reunited with silk sutures. The immediate result of the operation was that an extensive area of Head's forearm and the back of his hand became insensitive to all forms of cutaneous stimuli.[29] Then, over the next five and a half years, as the nerve fibres at the points of severance regenerated, Rivers studied the recovery process by a battery of intensive tests on the changing sensibility of the affected area.

So that the petty distractions of a busy life should not interfere with Head's introspective analysis, it was resolved that the tests should be performed in the quiet of Rivers's rooms in St John's College, Cambridge. In the normal course of events, Head would travel from the London Hospital to Cambridge on Saturday, having first spent several hours in the outpatients' ward. Then, after Head has rested on Saturday evening, Rivers would perform the greater part of the tests on Sunday morning. Throughout the tests, every effort was made to ensure that Head was relaxed, unfatigued and free from emotional harassments.[30]

Since Head was simultaneously collaborator and experimental subject, extensive precautions were taken to guard against the possibility of preconceived ideas influencing his subjective appreciation of what he was perceiving:

No questions were asked until the termination of a series of tests; for we found it was scarcely possible . . . to ask even simple questions without giving a suggestion either for or against the right answer . . . The clinking of the ice against the glass, the removal of the kettle from the hob, tended to prejudice his answers . . . [Rivers] was therefore particularly careful to make all his preparations beforehand; the iced tubes were filled and jugs of hot and cold water ranged within easy reach of his hand, so that water of the temperature required might be mixed silently.[31]

Moreover, although before each series of tests, the collaborators would discuss their plan of action, and frequently commit it to paper, Rivers was careful to vary this order to such an extent during the actual testing that Head was unable to guess what was coming next.[32]

As his arm began to recuperate from the effects of the operation, Head noticed that the first gradual recovery of the various forms of cutaneous sensation was associated with the reappearance of isolated spots, which were sensitive to heat, cold and pressure. However, the spaces between the spots initially remained insensitive, a fact which made it possible to demonstrate experimentally that these spots had quite a high threshold, the heat-spots responding only to temperatures above $36°C$, the cold-spots responding only to temperatures below $27°C$ and the "pain-spots" on the back of the hand responding only to pressures above about 70 grams per square millimeter. Moreover, once this threshold was exceeded, the sensation evoked was more unpleasant and was usually perceived as "more painful" than the sensation which followed the application of an equal stimulus to Head's other, normal arm. Finally, although the spots themselves were quite definitely localized, Head, who sat through the tests with his eyes closed, was unable to gain any exact appreciation of the locus of stimulation. On the contrary, the sensations evoked radiated widely, and Head tended to refer them to places remote from the actual point of stimulation.

Hence, the first stage of the recovery process, which Head and Rivers dubbed "protopathic", from the Middle Greek word *protopathes*, meaning "first affected", seemed to be marked by an "all-or-nothing" aspect — either, as in the case of the application of minor degrees of heat and cold, the spots did not respond at all to stimulation, or else, once the threshold had been passed, their responses seemed inordinate, with respect to normal standards of intensity and perceived area of distribution. In short, the spots alone seemed incapable of producing sensations which were accurately localized and graduated in proportion to the intensity of the applied stimulus.[33]

Having identified this initial phase in the process of recovery, Rivers and Head now detected a second phase. As the areas between the spots started to regain their sensitivity, Head observed that his skin was becoming sensitive to temperatures *between* 26°C and 37°C and that the back of the hand was responding to pressure as low as 12 grams per square millimeter. Moreover, he could now distinguish degrees of temperature and was able to locate the point of stimulation with increasing accuracy. Finally, he could now recognize when two compass points were simultaneously applied to the skin, which had been possible during the protopathic stage of recovery only for extremely wide separation distances of the compass points. In returning to normal sensibility then, Head's forearm seemed to have undergone a second stage of recovery, which was peculiarly associated with the localization and discrimination of cutaneous stimuli.[34] This stage the experimenters labelled "epicritic", from the Greek *epikritikos*, determinative.

Hence, Rivers and Head were postulating that the skin is endowed with not one but two sensory mechanisms, which blend in a complex fashion to produce normal sensibility. As they themselves expressed it:

... Blix, when he discovered the heat- and cold-spots, thought that the impulses arising in these specific organs passed unchanged through the nervous system to underlie all sensations of heat and cold. But we have been able to show that the process is one of much greater complexity. Under normal conditions there are no "protopathic" or "epicritic sensations". These terms may be justly applied to two anatomically distinct peripheral systems, or to the sensibility with which the skin becomes endowed by the preponderating activity of one or other nervous mechanism ... But sensations must be described solely by their specific qualities, and not by these names which apply to the peripheral physiological level only ... Both protopathic and epicritic end-organs may be stimulated by heat applied to the skin and the resulting impulses will travel by separate peripheral paths to the spinal cord. There they become united and pass on, as a single isolated group, to underlie, in the highest centres, specific sensations of heat.[35]

Apart from this process of blending or fusion, there is another important way in which the protopathic and epicritic mechanisms interact, namely the suppression of the former by the latter. As the experiment on Head's arm had shown, one characteristic reaction of protopathic sensibility, that of referring pain to a source distant from the point of stimulation, is permanently abolished by the return of epicritic sensibility.[36]

From control experiments performed on the unimpaired portions of Head's anatomy, Rivers concluded that there is one part of the skin of the human male in which protopathic sensibility normally reigns supreme, uninhibited by epicritic impulses. Interestingly enough, this part happens to be the glans penis.[37] With regard to internal anatomy, there is also a specific region supplied by the protopathic but not the epicritic system. One notes, again with interest in view of Rivers's reputed sexual proclivities, that this region was that of the lower alimentary canal. From experiments performed on the bypassed colon of operated patients, Rivers, Head and Sherren concluded that the large intestine in particular, and the viscera in general, are incapable of appreciating light touch, insensitive to minor degrees of heat and cold, and frequently given to referring drastic sensations to parts of the body other than the stimulated regions.[38]

Although one might well have guessed it from their use of the assumption that protopathic nerve fibres regenerate more rapidly than epicritic ones,[39] and from the knowledge that Rivers had been influenced by Hughling Jackson's notion that damage to an organism's nervous system reveals previous stages of its evolutionary history,[40] it is only in the final two sentences of their lengthy account that Rivers and Head choose to reveal that their theory is, in fact, an evolutionary one:

We believe that the essential elements exposed by our analysis owe their origin to the developmental history of the nervous system. They reveal the means by which an imperfect organism has struggled towards improved functions and psychical unity.[41]

Or, as Rivers expressed the idea more specifically in his later book, *Instinct and the Unconscious*, "the manifestations of protopathic sensibility which are suppressed belong to a crude form of nervous system which has been superseded by a later and more efficient mechanism".[42]

As outlined above, the protopathic-epicritic dichotomy made its first official appearance as a restricted and technical component of the Rivers–Head theory of the cutaneous nervous system. In this theory it was defined in terms of the distinction between indiscriminate, "all-or-nothing" reactions and graduated, accurately localized responses. However, in certain of Rivers's other works, and especially in those written during his psycho-analytic period, Rivers exhibits a tendency to use the words "protopathic" and "epicritic" in ways which reveal that other, related distinctions were involved as well. In particular, Rivers associated protopathicity with the emotions, with subjectivity, and with "concrete" forms of cognition. By using the word "concrete" in this context, Rivers was attempting to specify modes of thought which do not proceed by purely abstract and rational means, but depend upon such mental processes as visual imagery, or the ostensive apprehension of particular instances of a general phenomenon. Furthermore, he associates epicritic processes with lack of emotion, with objectivity, and with abstract modes of thought which function without recourse to visualization or ostensive procedures.[43] Hence, the protopathic-epicritic dichotomy should be seen as having a rather flexible content, in which a cluster of related distinctions are employed, or not employed as the situation warrants. Defining the dichotomy in these terms should not be regarded as a ploy to create a tool of analysis sufficiently expansible to handle all contingencies, but rather as an attempt to recreate the distinction which Rivers himself actually employed and to use it in as flexible or as precise a fashion as he himself was wont to do.

Before using the protopathic-epicritic dichotomy to illuminate the motivations underlying Rivers's work in anthropology, let me first place this dichotomy in a broader scientific and cultural context.

With regard to its scientific background, let us consider the Rivers–Head concept of "protopathicity" in relation to the discipline of physiology. Since the 1870s, many physiologists had considered the heartbeat to follow an "all-or-nothing" rule. This opinion was based on the observation that the heart muscle either contracts as fully as it is capable of doing, or else does not contract at all. Under the influence of the Cambridge school of physiology the "all-or-none" law was extended first to skeletal muscle and later to motor nerve fibres.[44] Now both Rivers and Head had institutional ties with this school. Head had received his education in medicine from the leading figures in Cambridge physiology. One of these was W. H. Gaskell, who had done important work on the heartbeat and to whom Head had dedicated a book.[45] Rivers had first been invited to lecture at Cambridge by the founder of the school, Sir Michael Foster, who had also worked on the heartbeat.[46] Hence, if the Rivers–Head concept of protopathicity is to be seen in its physiological context, it must be seen in relation to the Cambridge school.

With regard to the broader cultural background, it is certainly true that more research is needed in this area of Victorian and Edwardian studies. Nonetheless, several passages encountered in general reading suggest that the protopathic-epicritic distinction of Rivers and Head, and its physiological analogues, are merely the formalized tip of a much larger iceberg. To take a specifically anthropological example, a missionary writing about the Australian Aborigines during the 1850s averred that

The general character of the blacks is this: in forethought, and what phrenologists call "concentrativeness", they are very deficient; in mental acumen, and in quickness of sight and hearing, they surpass most white people.[47]

Here we have the attribution of visual and auditory acuity to people who would have been regarded as biologically more primitive than Europeans, and the contrast of these capabilities with the "civilized" talent for abstract, discriminative thought.

A further example is provided by one W. S. Lilly, writing in 1885:

... wherein lies the chief difference between civilized man and animals, human and other, beneath him in the scale of being? Is it not in the power of perceiving the ideal? ... the condition of advance in the scale of being is ... emancipation from the tyranny of the senses: ... The true law of progress is to "Move upwards, working out the beast, And let the ape and tiger die".[48]

Far from "working out the beast", a major psychological motivation behind Rivers' anthropological work was, as will now be argued, to bring this fearsome creature to the light of day.

Following up some clues provided in a brief but suggestive article by Jonathan Miller,[49] let us see how Rivers's distinction between protopathic and epicritic can be employed as a tool for analyzing his own personality. My purpose in employing this device will be to throw light on the changing shape of Rivers's scientific career. Beginning at the level of personal psychology, it seems clear that there was a rigid split in Rivers's psyche.[50] On the one hand, there were the indiscriminately emotional and subjective components, which Rivers associated with "concrete" modes of thought, as defined above. On the other hand, there were the rational, objective and discriminative components, which he associated with abstract mentation, divorced from visual imagery and ostensive enumeration. Let us call the former group of components the "protopathic" side of Rivers's psyche, and the latter group the "epicritic" side. From the biographical material we have, it would seem that, especially during the early part of his life, the protopathic aspects of Rivers's personality were very much suppressed by his epicritic faculties. As I have already mentioned, the young Rivers tended to be objective, unemotional and ratiocinative, and, inasmuch as this was possible for a person who had several stints as a practising doctor, led a life which was divorced from the down-to-earth realities of everyday life. Corresponding to this, his fascination with the protopathic manifestations of the human mind, evidently present even during the early period of his career, seems to have been kept under strictly epicritic control. Thus, when he encountered phenomena which he suspected of having protopathic significance, Rivers tended to subject them to rigorous scientific treatment. A revealing and amusing illustration of this is provided by some work done by Rivers and Head on the "pilomotor reflex" (erection of hairs). This topic, which had previously been investigated within the Cambridge school of physiology,[51] was tackled by Rivers and Head as part of their larger investigation into the regeneration of the cutaneous nervous system. While engaged on experiments which demonstrated that the pilomotor reflex is enhanced when sensibility is in the protopathic stage, and that "this excessive response is inhibited on the return of epicritic impulses", Head and Rivers discovered that the thrill evoked by aesthetic pleasure "is accompanied by the erection of hairs". In Head's case, "it started in the region of the neck and spread rapidly down the arms, over the trunk, the thighs and the outer aspect of the legs". If he sat with his arms bared to the shoulder in a carefully warmed room, Head, who was himself a poet of some distinction,[52] could bring on the reflex by reading aloud a favourite poem. After a time "he would call out that the thrill was beginning, and shortly afterwards the long hairs on both forearms were seen to be erected ... " However, the general pilomotor reflex was found to be "no greater over the highly protopathic area than elsewhere on the arms".[53] The image of a man reading a poem to evoke aesthetic pleasure while a close friend meticulously studies the erection of the hairs on his arm may seem ludicrous. However, it provides a neat encapsulation of Rivers's desire to subject possibly protopathic phenomena to the discipline of rigorous investigation.

Rivers's and Head's work on the regeneration of the cutaneous nervous system also provides evidence of what one might call Rivers's desire for "grounding", a desire which was prominent throughout his anthropological and ethnological periods. The evidence is implicit in the notion of fusion invoked to account for the interaction of the protopathic and epicritic elements of the nervous system. Through being fused with protopathic functions, epicritic processes may be regarded as "grounded" in them. That is, because the protopathic nervous mechanism is phylogenetically prior to the epicritic one, their fusion is not a process of balanced equality. Rather, one should consider the epicritic mechanism as scaffolding recently erected on the protopathic bedrock. If one wished to make a leap to the level of personal psychology, one could say that what the theory expresses is Rivers's probably-subconscious desire to ground the abstract, ordered, discriminative aspects of his personality in the more "concrete", more emotional, more chaotic aspects which lurked, in the heavily Freudian but, nonetheless, expressive phrase which Jonathan Miller has applied specifically to Rivers, like a "dog beneath the skin".

As his personality developed, as he became less wedded to the efficacy of purely rational thought, as he increasingly came to terms with his own subjective emotions, as he became more involved with matters which concerned ordinary people, Rivers' scientific work changed accordingly. More and more he attempted to bring subjectivity, emotionality and problems of human import under the aegis of his scientific concern. In fact, all his role hybridizations, from experimental psychologist, to kinship-centred anthropologist, to diffusionistic ethnologist, to quasi-Freudian psychiatrist, to prospective socialist, may be seen in terms of the gradual emergence of his repressed protopathic interests, and their subjection to conscious analytic scrutiny.

Armed with this insight into the development of Rivers' thought, let us now look closely at his work in anthropology.

THE ORIGINS AND EARLY PRESENTATION OF THE GENEALOGICAL METHOD

In 1888, Alfred Cort Haddon, then Professor of Zoology at the Royal College of Science in Dublin, went on an expedition to the Torres Straits. A biographer of Haddon was later to describe this event as "the turning point of his life".[54] Before Haddon's departure, James Frazer, who at that stage was not personally acquainted with the Dublin biologist, wrote to Haddon asking him to collect information about totemism.[55] The primary purpose of Haddon's expedition, however, was to investigate the biology of coral reefs and he, therefore, refrained from making any promises to Frazer. However, after arriving in the Torres Straits, Haddon found himself more intrigued by native folklore than plankton and devoted much of his time to collecting anthropological data. Becoming convinced of the urgency for recording such material before it vanished forever, Haddon returned to England determined to organize a further expedition, consisting of people with a sufficiently wide range of talents to investigate all aspects of native life in the Torres Straits.[56] Eventually resigning his Chair at Dublin, Haddon channelled all his energies into furthering the study of preliterate society.

Presumably because he had done his undergraduate degree there, and because of the presence of Frazer, Haddon's activities centred upon Cambridge.

Indeed, on one level, his organization of the second expedition to the Torres Straits may be regarded as symptomatic of his desire to establish anthropology as a scientifically respectable discipline at Cambridge and to secure his own role therein. Whilst Haddon was getting his team together, Frazer offered constant advice and encouragement, and the redoubtable Mrs Frazer assisted in the preparation of equipment suitable for recording native speech.[57] At one stage it was even suggested that Frazer should personally take part in the expedition,[58] but the thought of leaving his armchair at Cambridge evidently proved too much, for he did not go.

Haddon's first choice for the new expedition fell on Rivers, who was at that time lecturer in experimental psychology at Cambridge. Rivers at first declined the invitation, but changed his mind when C. S. Myers and William McDougall, who had been his two best students, committed themselves to go. The other members of the expedition were a pathologist named C. G. Seligman, who volunteered his services; a young Cambridge graduate named Anthony Wilkin, who was asked to accompany the expedition as photographer and a primary school teacher named Sidney Ray, who had already made a study of two Torres Straits languages on the basis of missionary publications and data supplied by Haddon.

The expedition, which finally took place between April and October 1898, occasioned among its members a profound awakening of anthropological interest in preliterate humanity. Myers, a talented musician whose major previous concern had been with psychological problems relating to auditory response, became particularly interested in indigenous music as a result of the expedition. McDougall, after returning to Cambridge, was at first inclined to devote his career to field anthropology. Although he eventually decided to continue as a psychologist, and acquired considerable eminence in that field, he nonetheless managed to co-author an ethnographical work on *The Pagan Tribes of Borneo*, write a best-selling *Introduction to Social Psychology* and produce a book, widely read by anthropologists, on *The Group Mind*. Seligman began the expedition by examining native medicine and surgery, and performing clinical observations on the diseases of natives. However, he soon became involved in the psychometric investigations of his colleagues, and this interest blossomed into more specifically ethnological concerns. Later he was to become the first lecturer and then the first professor of ethnology at the University of London. In 1904 he married and his wife Brenda, whose work will be mentioned later in the book, became a prominent advocate of Rivers's anthropological methods. Wilkin, who had already had some archeological and ethnographic experience in Egypt and northern Africa, developed more specific interests in the Torres Straits relating to material culture, land tenure and inheritance. Ray used the expedition to consolidate and extend his knowledge of Melanesian languages and thereafter became the acknowledged British authority on the languages of Western Oceania. For Haddon, the expedition reinforced his previous experience in the Torres Straits and encouraged him in his subsequent endeavours to establish anthropology at Cambridge.[59]

It is as part of these changing career patterns and developing fascination with preliterate man that we must view Rivers's conversion to anthropology and his invention of the genealogical method. For both during the expedition, and for a considerable number of years after it, there was a marked tendency for the core of the Torres Strait investigators to function as a solidary group. They had been together in Melanesia in 1898. They had taken British anthropology out of its "armchair" phase and placed it on a sound empirical basis. They had seen and questioned "savage" man in his own habitat and subjected him to carefully conducted psychometric and anthropometric tests. They had provided the model for future British anthropologists to copy. And this view of the Torres Straits expedition was not confined to Haddon and his team. Their peers in the English anthropological fraternity thoroughly concurred. For example, in 1916 Sir Arthur Keith stated in an address to the Royal Anthropological Institute, that the expedition had engendered "the most progressive and profitable movement in the history of British anthropology". In fact, the Torres Straits expedition rapidly became the cornerstone of the mythical charter which grew up around social anthropology in Britain. After the death of Anthony Wilkin in 1901, at the age of twenty-three, his memory was perpetuated at Cambridge by the creation of a special studentship for the pursuit of anthropological fieldwork. Administered by Haddon and Rivers, the Anthony Wilkin Studentship was deliberately used as a means of perpetuating what they took to be the ethnographic tradition of the 1898 expedition. Even in matters which were not strictly anthropological, the Torres Strait investigators tended to act as a group. For example, Rivers was not the only one to do psychiatric work on shell-shocked soliders during the war. Myers, McDougall and Seligman, who like Rivers were medically qualified, were similarly employed and there is evidence that all four men were cheered by the belief that they were thereby making a contribution to the real world, rather than engaging in purely academic pursuits. But, of the network of solidary relationships which bound the expedition members together, the strongest was that between Haddon and Rivers. Three years after Rivers's death, Haddon was to say:

One of the things of which I am most proud in a somewhat long life is that I was the means of seducing Rivers from the path of virtue ... (for psychology was then a chaste science) ... into that of Anthropology.[60]

Moreover, Haddon is said to have been in the habit of stating that his "claim to fame" was that he had induced Rivers to accompany him on the Torres Straits expedition.[61]

Before 1898 Rivers had shown very little interest in anthropology. In fact, on being offered the extensive anthropological library collected by his uncle James Hunt, who had been the first president of the Anthropological Society back in the 1860s, Rivers had refused on the grounds that such books would be of no use to him.[62] Prior to the expedition, Rivers was evidently somewhat discontented and unhappy with his life at Cambridge, experiencing periods of depression and nervous anxiety. He returned from the Antipodes however, "set up in health and full of mental vigour".[63] The intellectual basis of this change and the intellectual basis of Haddon's admiration for Rivers's anthropological work, was the latter's invention of the genealogical method.

Let us now consider what is known about the genesis of the genealogical method. A number of accounts corroborate the fact that Rivers, in the course of performing some comparative experimental studies on such sensory phenomena as visual acuity, colour vision and spatial perception, began collecting genealogies in an attempt to discover whether certain talents or disabilities were hereditary.[64] Although we have no direct indication of the source of this interest in the inheritance of sensory aptitudes, there can be little doubt that Rivers was influenced here by the work of Francis Galton. For, as we shall see shortly, Rivers's early presentation of the genealogical method certainly had a Galtonian aura about it. Whatever his motivation, we have it on the authority of his close friend Henry Head, that Rivers' first genealogical table was, in fact, drawn up during some experiments on colour vision.[65]

The earliest mention of Rivers's interest in orally transmitted genealogies, contained in the private journal which Haddon kept during the 1898 expedition, occurs as part of an entry dated Tuesday August 16th, which was made on location at Murray Island. Revealingly enough, the entry begins,

Our friends and acquaintances would often be very much amused if they could see us at some of our occupations and I am afraid these would sometimes give occasion to the enemy to blaspheme – so trivial would they appear. Every now and then we run one thing hard – for example one week we were mad on cat's-cradle [the string trick] – at least Rivers, Ray and I were – McDougall soon feel a victim and even Myers eventually succumbed.

Haddon then goes on to reveal that he and his colleagues were not satisfied simply with being able to perform the various forms of string trick. In order to record their manipulations, they invented a system of nomenclature, and felt very proud of themselves whenever they managed to successfully schematize the steps required to produce a particular string figure. "But", Haddon continues, in the passage which immediately precedes the reference to Rivers's work on genealogies, "I can imagine that some people would think we are demented — or at least wasting our time." [66]

Now for Haddon himself, the investigation of cat's-cradles was certainly not to be regarded as a waste of time. In fact, there is some evidence to suggest that he had been seriously interested in the phenomenon since the 1888 expedition.[67] And eventually cat's-cradles were to become his pet obsession — his trademark as an anthropologist. String figures played an important role both in the field and in the appearances he made to publicize ethnology at home. As a means of winning the confidence of his informants, Haddon found string tricks unequalled, for as his daughter Kathleen wrote, "who could suspect of guile a man who sits among the children playing with a piece of string?" [68] As a means of entertaining Western audiences and of rapidly convincing them that some aspects of "savage" culture were both clever and intricate, Haddon also relied heavily on his facility with string puzzles.[69] In 1906, he contributed an introduction and many data to Caroline Jayne's lavish *String Figures*, and, with enthusiastic encouragement and assistance from her father, Kathleen Haddon was to write two books on the subject. Thus for Haddon, whom Andrew Lang dubbed "our champion cat's-cradler",[70] string figures grew to be far more than just a gimmick. And for Rivers, who followed Haddon in performing string tricks for the entertainment of European audiences,[71] cat's-cradles acquired important theoretical significance. Specifically, Rivers saw them as throwing light on protopathic, as opposed to epicritic, mental processes. As he explained in 1907, string figures are divisible into two kinds. The first kind is such that a person with a considerable capacity for visualization could foresee the effects of the various finger movements and deliberately plan the end result. The second kind is so complicated that no one, no matter how pictorial his imagination, could possibly visualize that the final manipulations will produce a coherent pattern out of apparent chaos. This latter type of string figure, "if not arrived at by random manipulations, which is very improbable", must have been discovered by someone operating with a definite abstract idea in his mind. Now according to Rivers, the mental processes involved in producing the second type are "of a higher order" than those employed in producing the first type, "where the player merely proceeds from one concrete image to another". Hence, the interest of string figures of type one, of which the Papuan variety constitute prime examples, is that they provide insight into mental processes of people who have highly developed visual imaginations, "as is probably the case in most races of low culture".[72]

One should not be too quick to conclude that the juxtaposition of cat's-cradles and genealogies in Haddon's journal necessarily indicated that he and his colleagues at first regarded the latter phenomenon as a mere curiosity. Certainly, the journal depicts the Torres Straits investigators as realizing that Europeans with no interest in anthropological matters, would have regarded cat's-cradles as trivial and beneath their dignity. However, one suspects that this realization added piquancy to their attempts to investigate genealogies in a systematic and careful manner.

But, whatever the atmosphere in which the collection of genealogies originated, it rapidly became obvious, as Rivers extended his investigations to Mabuiag and Haddon tried his hand at genealogical compilation on Sabai, that the Torres Straits genealogies went back for an extraordinary number of generations, were apparently very accurate, and had great social importance for the people who used them. Haddon's work on Sabai, in which he completed a genealogical census of the island before midday,[73] seemed to indicate that the technique provided an incredibly rapid means of exposing the fundamental specifications and workings of a preliterate society. Hence, Haddon and Rivers, believing with many of their contemporaries that Western civilization was in the process of obliterating all such societies, came to regard the collection of genealogies as the key to obtaining important data over wide areas in the shortest possible time.

Thus, in the context of Haddon and Rivers' desire to establish anthropology on a scientific basis, and to create an institutional niche for the discipline at Cambridge University, the two men began, after their return to England, to publicize the utility of "the genealogical method" for ethnographic purposes. The first formal manifestation of this activity was an account of the new method by Rivers in a paper read to the Anthropology Section of the British Association in September 1899. Only a brief summary of this paper has survived. However, the summary does contain an indication that Rivers was already fitting genealogies into his still unexpressed protopathic-epicritic dichotomy. Specifically, Rivers states that the method provides a means of investigating kinship systems entirely by "concrete" examples, without any recourse to "abstract" terms of relationship derived from European sources.[74] So, as he was later to suggest for Papuan cat's-cradles, genealogies provide an insight into the protopathic workings of the indigenous mind.

The following year, having been elected a fellow of the Anthropological Institute [75] and a member of its governing council, [76] Rivers delivered a lecture to the Institute in which the relationship between orally transmitted genealogies and the abstract-concrete dichotomy was spelled out in considerably more detail:

All who have experience of the savage mind must have experienced the difficulty of eliciting information on abstract questions, while, on the other hand, there seems to be hardly any limit to the number of concrete facts which can be remembered. The memory of the savage for names is as highly developed as in any European, and far more so than in those Europeans who are accustomed to abstract thinking. The great value of the genealogical method is that it enables one to study abstract problems, on which the savage's ideas are vague, by means of concrete facts, of which he is a master. It is a means of utilizing the store of information which the extraordinary memory for detail of the savage has enabled him to accumulate. [77]

However, this lecture, which is entitled "A Genealogical Method of Collecting Social and Vital Statistics", is of interest for reasons additional to its portrayal of genealogies as a means of gaining insight into the abstract via the concrete. As the title suggests, it also presents the genealogical method as a tool for extracting statistical information from indigenous societies.

After discussing the technique he developed while collecting genealogies in the Torres Straits, Rivers presents his reasons for believing that they do, in fact, embody an accurate record of descent. On Murray Island, for example, where the natives would recount genealogies to Rivers only in the strictest privacy, "nearly every detail of these genealogies was obtained from two or more independent sources, with the result that different accounts corroborated one another to an extent which forms the best guarantee of the truthfulness and accuracy of the memory of the natives." [78] Now it so happens that, in many indigenous societies, anyone with whom a given person has a social relationship is regarded as a kinsman, whether in fact he is or not. So, for example, just because one man calls another "mother's brother", it does not necessarily follow that the kinship term reflects actual biological relationship. It could simply mean that the two people are linked by a series of social obligations and privileges which customarily exist between a man and his mother's brother. This fact, which tends to make genealogies biologically misleading, was evidently unknown to Rivers at this stage. Nor in the case of Mabuiag, where he was able to collect genealogies going back a considerable number of generations, does he consider the possibility that a widely-shared

ancestor mythology might have resulted in the more remote parts of the
genealogies representing a record of something other than strict biological
descent.

Hence, believing in their literal, genetic accuracy, Rivers promotes his
genealogies as a means of uncovering firstly, "social statistics", under which
title he includes the kinship system, and marriage customs such as polygamy,
the levirate [79] and sister-exchange and, secondly, "vital statistics", including
such topics as the average size of families, the proportion of the sexes and the
relative fertility of marriages contracted with partners coming from inside and
outside each island community. Only in the case of the determination of the
kinship system which, even at this early stage, he seems to regard as a problem
with a clearly-defined solution which is either right or wrong, does he give us
any hint that one's ultimate aim should be other than statistical.

Seen within the context of late nineteenth-century anthropology, this
promotion of statistical quantification is hardly surprising. For a number of
years, Francis Galton had been emphasizing the importance of quantification
and the efficacy of statistical analyses in a number of fields, of which anthropology was one of the most prominent.[80] In the 1889 paper which I
mentioned in the first chapter, E. B. Tylor, unquestionably the leading figure
in British anthropology at the time, had acknowledged the existence of
Galton's approach and underscored its fashionability by developing his own
statistically-oriented "method of adhesions", and applying it to the laws of
marriage and descent. Hence, the idiom in which Rivers's early account of the
genealogical method is expressed, may be interpreted on one level as a means
of decking out his novel approach in a garb which the members of the Royal
Anthropological Institute would find familiar and congenial.

By 1904, however, when Rivers's first major attempt to use the genealogical method to elucidate the sociology of a preliterate community was
published in Volume 5 of the *Reports of the Cambridge Anthropological
Expedition to Torres Straits*, his emphasis had changed somewhat. While one
of the major purposes of his chapter on "The Regulation of Marriage" is to
extract statistics relating to the frequency of such practices as brother-sister
exchange, polygamy and the levirate, and while he still wants to claim that, in
general, his genealogies are accurate, Rivers mentions elsewhere that inaccuracies can arise because of the practice of adoption. However, instead of drawing
the moral that, to the extent that these inaccuracies occur, they will vitiate
the usefulness of genealogies as an anthropological tool, he goes on to say:

A child adopted into a family became . . . so completely a member of the new family for all social purposes, that any such mistakes, if they have occurred, do not impair the value of genealogies in the investigation of social customs. The case is different if one wishes to use the genealogies as a means of collecting statistics on such subjects as the fertility of different kinds of marriage etc., and I do not like to guarantee the accuracy of the genealogies in this respect, though I believe any errors from this source to be relatively few in number.[81]

So as well as weakening his claims to the efficacy of the genealogical method as a tool for collecting vital statistics, Rivers has also recognized that inaccuracies themselves can have social import. Thus, instead of thinking of himself as doing "social statistics", Rivers has moved in the direction of using his genealogies as a means of investigating what he has now, significantly enough, begun to call the "social organization" of the tribe. In this new enterprise, biological reality takes second place to social reality and the attempt to find out how many people are doing various things is replaced by a concern to discover the functional interrelations between the things which are being done.

Hence, after a brief flirtation with sociological statistics, Rivers crossed into the territory of social anthropology. The former field deals with individual phenomena reiterated n times, the latter with human behaviour produced, not by the idiosyncracies of individual people, but by virtue of their membership of a social group. The difference is profound, but in my account of Rivers's intellectual development, I do not wish to make much of it. The reason is as follows. Rivers's excursion into statistical sociology was an abberration – a temporary borrowing of an approach to data developed by someone else. Prior to this Rivers's mode of scientific explanation had been that of experimental psychology. Here one should not be misled by the popular modern connotation of "psychology" as the study of individual psyches. In the evolutionary school of experimental psychology of which Rivers was a member, the aim was not to expose the individual traits of a single experimental subject. Rather, it was to arrive at general conclusions about the phylogeny of human sensory equipment. Thus, Rivers was little interested in the individual peculiarities of the process by which Head's arm recovered from its artificial injury. He was, on the other hand, vitally concerned with those aspects of the recovery process which (as he believed) originated from the fact that the whole of mankind had undergone evolutionary development. When the types of scientific explanation being aimed at are judged according to their degree of concern with individual (as opposed to group) phenomena, there is no essential difference between a Rivers-style experimental psychologist doing experiments on the sensory response of an individual subject, and a social anthropologist questioning an informant about his line of descent. Both investigators are attempting to rise above idiosyncratic features, which they regard as irrelevant, and fix on those characteristics which exist by virtue of the fact that the subject belongs to a wider group, meaning, in the first case, the human race, and in the second case, the informant's society. In this regard, one should not forget that Rivers continued, apparently without conflict, to pursue experimental psychology even after his invention of the genealogical method. As I shall argue later in the book, the only real discontinuity in his career came with his conversion to diffusionistic ethnology, an event which simultaneously marked a decline in the standard of his investigations into kinship and the end of his work in experimental psychology. These events are not well characterized in terms of the distinction between individual and group modes of thought, and their exposition and explanation must wait until the next two chapters.

THE SIGNIFICANCE OF GENEALOGIES IN RIVERS'S THOUGHT

Having outlined the major facts relating to the origin and early presentation of the genealogical method, let us now attempt, in speculative fashion, to place the more salient of these facts in the context of Rivers's intellectual and personal development.

Specifically, let us see whether we can use the protopathic-epicritic distinction to illuminate the initial phase of Rivers's anthropological career. In so doing, I hope that my account will not be seen, to use the words of one of this book's referees, as investing the distinction with "a kind of teleological determinative role". My intention is not to write about psychology as though it were physics. Rather, it is to use a "binary opposition" to illuminate the changing complex of attitudes, beliefs and practices exhibited by a creative and versatile scientist. No doubt, when judged by the literary standards of vintage Lévi-Strauss, the following pages will seem coldly cerebral and stilted. But in attempting to characterize a single phase of one scientist's career, and in placing a high priority on clarity and concision, I fould that an expansive style was beyond me and that, when I grabbed hard at the essentials, the nuances tended to slip through my fingers. In such circumstances, one can only hope that readers who find the next few pages dry and sterile will skip ahead to greener pastures.

In the ensuing discussion, I shall concentrate on the following four features of the early history of the genealogical method: the emergence of Rivers's fascination with indigenes; his focussing on a phenomenon which, for him, represented the aboriginal mode of "rendering the abstract concrete"; his belief that this phenomenon can be used to make ethnography more objective and more "scientific"; and his developing realization that the phenomenon should be used primarily for elucidating social organization. After each of these topics has been considered in turn, I shall then speculate about how the second, third and fourth features were blended in Rivers's thought.

(a) *The Emergence of Rivers's Fascination with Indigenous Man*

It is my contention that the key to understanding Rivers's developing fascination with aborigines is contained within the theoretical assumptions which underlay his collaborative experiment with Head. Surely, it cannot be coincidental that this fascination apparently arose conjointly with the protopathic-epicritic distinction. For, although this distinction was not then explicitly formulated, it was evidently incipient in Rivers's thought during or shortly after the Torres Straits expedition. Upon discovering, during his experiments on colour vision, that the islanders had trouble in distinguishing blue from black, and that their colour vocabulary included no word for "blue", Rivers chose to interpret these facts as meaning that a "primitive confusion" was involved, and that there was an "indefiniteness" in the native concept of blue.[82] Thus, Rivers was already linking the "primitive" state with lack of definiteness and, by implication, the "advanced" state with precision.

As additional evidence for the contention that Rivers and Head can hardly be said to have "discovered" the protopathic-epicritic distinction during the course of the experiment on Head's arm, we may cite the fact that later investigators who repeated the experiment, did not perceive the recovery process as occurring in two clearly-defined stages.[83] In other words, despite all the precautions taken to ensure that Head's introspective analysis was uninfluenced by preconceived ideas, in fact the distinction must have been lurking in the back of his mind all through the experiment, and must have influenced both what Head thought he was perceiving, and the interpretation which Rivers and Head placed on their results.

Whether or not the protopathic-epicritic dichotomy was initially triggered by Rivers's first face-to-face encounter with "savages", my basic hypothesis is that this fundamental dichotomy was incipiently present probably during, and certainly shortly after, the Torres Straits expedition, and that it is to this distinction that we must turn in order to understand the emergence of

Rivers's fascination with aboriginal man. For, as I have already argued, Rivers's concepts of "protopathic" and "epicritic" had a far more generalized content than one might gather from the technically restricted definitions given in the paper describing the experiment on Head's arm. Rivers's concept of the protopathic embraced the emotions, subjectivity and "concrete" modes of thought. His concept of the epicritic embraced emotionless objectivity and abstractly rational forms of cognition. With "protopathic" and "epicritic" interpreted in this broad fashion, Rivers's fascination with aboriginal man may be described as arising from his desire to uncover the protopathic elements in humanity — to see beneath the epicritic veneer to "the dog beneath the skin".

(b) *Genealogies as a Means of Rendering Abstractions Concrete*

Rivers's particular focussing on genealogies, as a phenomenon which represented for him the indigenous method of "rendering the abstract concrete", may be interpreted as an attempt to discover how men in whom the protopathic is relatively close to the surface, manage to handle thought processes which for men like Rivers are performed epicritically; to find out how preliterate man manages to "ground" the abstract in the concrete.

As I mentioned earlier, Rivers believed that "concrete" thought relies upon mental processes like visual imagery and ostensive enumeration. In the case of genealogies, Rivers evidently thought that ostensive enumeration is operative. For according to Rivers, it is only by remembering the proper names of specific people that preliterate man is able to come to grips with abstract terms of relationship. Or, in other words, Rivers saw little point in an aboriginal attempting to clothe his genealogical tree in the foliage of abstract relationship terms until after the trunk had been defined in a concretely ostensive fashion. In consonance with this attitude, Rivers recommended that the collection of genealogies should proceed in two clearly defined stages.[84] First, the ethnographer should compile a family tree consisting of the proper names of his informant's ancestors and relatives. Then he should direct the informant's attention to one proper name after another, asking on each occasion for the abstract term of relationship by which the informant customarily addresses that person. Rivers believed that, by following this procedure, the ethnographer can mimic the thought processes through which indigenes apprehend abstract ideas via concrete facts.

Whether the talent for ostensive enumeration which Rivers discerned among preliterate people, was mirrored by any corresponding ability (or lack thereof) in his own cognitive range, is unclear. However, we do know that the other example of concrete mental process which Rivers invoked on behalf of "savages", namely visualization, was notably absent from Rivers's own intellectual armory. For, as I said previously, the mature Rivers had apparently lost his childhood capacity for visualization and experienced visual imagery only when dreaming. This state of affairs he saw as contrasting sharply with that obtaining among preliterate people. According to Rivers, indigenes were capable of visualizing with special intensity, and depended very heavily on this mode of cognition. Furthermore, he considered that the reliance of aborigines on visual forms of thought fully agreed with "their almost excluisve interest in the concrete, with the high degree of development of their powers of observation, and with the accuracy and fullness of memory of the more concrete events of their lives." [85]

In support of his belief in the dependence of indigenes on visual thought forms, Rivers cited an experience he had had shortly after his arrival in the Torres Straits:

On Murray Island, where I gained my first acquaintance with savage people, courts were held by a British official in collaboration with the native chiefs, at which disputes were settled and offences punished. On the first occasion on which I attended these courts an old woman gave a vigorous and animated account of her experience in relation to the case. As she gave her evidence she looked first in one direction and then in another with a keenness and directness which showed beyond doubt that every detail of the occurrences she was describing was being enacted before her eyes. I have never seen a European show by his or her demeanor with any approach to the behaviour of this old woman, how closely knowledge and memory depended on sensory imagery.[86]

The vividness of this recollection, written fully two decades after the Torres Straits expedition, reveals the depth of Rivers's interest in the thought processes of people who are strong visualizers — an interest we have already detected in his endorsement of Head as a particularly suitable subject for the nerve-division experiment. It may not be too fanciful to regard this interest as symptomatic of Rivers's desire to recapture a world which was now almost closed to him, a more protopathic world, fleetingly visible in the dim memories of childhood and the tantalizing phantasms of dreams.

(c) *Genealogies as a Means of Advancing Ethnography's Claims to Scientific Status*

Let us now consider Rivers's belief that the deployment of the genealogical method makes anthropological fieldwork yield results which are less random, more objective and, in that sense, more scientific. In his introduction to *The History of Melanesian Society*, Rivers refers to systems of relationship as "bodies of dry fact the accuracy of which, especially when collected by the genealogical method, is about as incapable of being influenced by bias, conscious or otherwise, as any subject that can be imagined". This emphasis on the efficacy of genealogies as an objective tool for rendering ethnography more scientific may be interpreted on the psychological level as Rivers's way of ensuring that his subjectively-generated fascinations were curbed rather than indulged. Or to put the same point in different words, Rivers's pursuit of a method which he saw as scientific, can be read as a statement of his intention to control his own protopathic urges by means of his epicritic faculties. If Rivers had allowed his fascination with things protopathic to have free rein, he would presumably have centred his anthropology upon topics like witchcraft and taboo, which to most Westerners positively reek of "savagery". In fact, he did *not* do this, but concentrated on native genealogies which, from the vantage point of modern Western man, tend to seem as dry as dust and twice as boring. This could indicate that, during the early period of his career, Rivers's epicritic functions were functioning like a set of blinkers in that they prevented his attention from straying to phenomena which are more grossly protopathic than genealogies.

(d) *Genealogies as the Key to Social Organization*

With regard to Rivers's developing realization that the genealogical method should be used primarily as a tool for elucidating social organization, one would undoubtedly have to say that part of its explanation lies in the straight-forward empirical observation that genealogical information has great social importance in preliterate societies. However, one must also realize that, by fixing upon social organization, Rivers was confining his attention to an aspect of primitive life in which epicritic order had been successful in suppressing the less structured features of the protopathic state. Hence, on the theoretical as well as the empirical level, focussing on genealogies as a means of illumi-nating social organization in general, rather than as a means of extracting statistics about exotic oddments like the levirate and polygamy, may be seen as part of the wider movement in which anthropology was shifting from the study of features of native life which had, for unworthy psychological or Eurocentric reasons, attracted the curiosity of Westerners, to features which really were important to the natives themselves.

(e) *Abstractness, Concreteness and the Scientific Uses of Genealogies*

Finally, let us consider the relationship of the second feature to the third and fourth features. More specifically, what does Rivers's endorsement of the genealogical processes by which the epicritic is grounded in the protopathic, have to do with his commitment to using genealogies as a means of subjecting his fieldwork, and the content of his anthropological theories, to epicritic control? One can explore the connection using the notions of fusion and suppression which figure in the Rivers—Head theory of the cutaneous nervous system. These notions imply that there are two types of interaction between the protopathic and epicritic mechanisms. One of these types involves a coalescence in which the epicritic impulses are fused in the protopathic ones. The other type involves the epicritic mechanism suppressing some of the more indiscriminate impulses generated by the protopathic system. Now, although these two types of interaction differ in that one is complementary, the other inhibitory, on Rivers's account they have no trouble in proceeding together. Normal sensibility, in fact, results from both cutaneous mechanisms blending continuously by means of the two kinds of interaction.

Let us now utilize these theoretical ideas of Rivers for the characterization of his own anthropological investigations. With regard to fieldwork, one could describe Rivers's reliance on genealogies in the following terms. Having singled out a phenomenon which, for him, represented the aborigines' way of fusing an epicritic superstructure onto a protopathic foundation, Rivers used it to suppress his own tendencies to dwell on the more grossly protopathic manifestations of indigenous life. With regard to Rivers's emphasis upon social organization in his theoretical pronouncements and his belief that genealogies provide the key thereto, the notions of suppression and fusion may be similarly employed. In Rivers's view, the genealogy-producing fusion process, through which the abstract is grounded in the concrete, also enables the aboriginal to suppress protopathic anarchy and usher in the epicritic order which constitutes social organization. That is, the relationship between an abstract kinship system and the prevailing social order, which the civilized intellectual can appreciate entirely on the epicritic level and by rational means, is apprehended by preliterate man via a dual-level process. This process entails first grounding the kinship system in concrete genealogical fact, then using genealogies to ascend to the epicritically-ordered level of life in society. Hence, the fusion and suppression concepts help us to understand the rationale behind Rivers's belief in the theoretical centrality of social organization and the role of genealogies in elucidating the nature of this centrality.

THE GENEALOGICAL METHOD IN ACTION

Among Rivers's papers which survive at Cambridge, is an undated little piece of nonsense verse written by C. E. Fox, a missionary from the island of San Cristoval. Rivers had met Fox during his 1908 expedition to Melanesia and the latter had acted as interpreter for the genealogical investigations conducted by Rivers amongst natives travelling on the missionary vessel *Southern Cross*. The two men had developed a close friendship, Fox later visiting Cambridge and staying in Rivers's rooms at St John's College.[87] Fox was also to write an ethnological work about San Cristoval of which, as we shall learn later in the book, Rivers thought very highly. Entitled "Anthropological Thoughts", the verse depicts Rivers as having just alighted from the *Southern Cross*. Notebook in hand, the ethnographer plies a female native with questions about the kinship system of her tribe:

> "Now how", said he, "if I may ask
> About your cousin's mother
> Would she attempt the simple task
> Of speaking of your brother?
>
> Ah, yes, just so, but if she were
> Your mother's uncle's sister
> How would your cousin's sister's aunt
> Address her when she kissed her?
>
> Yes, that's a point I meant to add
> Your nephew's cousin's father
> If he an uncle's sister had
> (And neither of the two were mad)
> Would he respect her rather?
>
> But if your father's cousin's niece
> (*His* brother's cousin's mother)
> Were married to your father's son
> Would he be called your brother?
>
> Indeed, now this if it be so
> Is *very* interesting
> And really should not be I think
> The subject of your jesting.
>
> For if your mother's father's son
> Were nephew to your mother
> I really cannot understand
> Why she should call him brother.

Alas, alas, for just before
The doctor's mind could grip her
A shout of laughter issued from
The cabin of the Skipper.[88]

But however ridiculous Rivers's interest in native systems of consanguinity and affinity would have seemed to uninformed Europeans like the captain of a missionary boat, and however much Rivers's friends teased him about it, the fact remains that his early work on kinship represeents a milestone in the history of modern anthropology.

For, during the first decade of the twentieth century, Rivers made no less than three sustained attempts to use the genealogical method to elucidate the social organization of a preliterate community. The first two of these attempts arose out his fieldwork in the Torres Straits and are described in the fifth and sixth volumes of the *Reports of the Cambridge Anthropological Expedition to Torres Straits*, published in 1904 and 1908 respectively. The third attempt is based on fieldwork done in the Nilgiri Hills of Southern India during 1902, and reported in his 1906 book on *The Todas*.

To take the Torres Straits volumes first, it must be remarked that Rivers's contributions to Volume 5, in which he deals with the sociology of the Western Islands in general, and of Mabuiag in particular, are of a considerably higher standard than those of Volume 6, which attempt a similar task for Murray Island and the eastern regions of the Straits. There would seem to be three major reasons for this: Firstly, since it was on Murray Island that he first began collecting genealogies, he was not fully alert to the pitfalls involved. Specifically, he did not realize how widespread the custom of adoption was until near the end of his stay there and, consequently, his genealogies are defective in that they do not always distinguish between real and adoptive parentage.[89] Secondly, it was not until arriving at Mabuiag that he discovered the remarkable duties and privileges connected with kinship ties.[90] Hence, the section on the functions of kin in the Murray Island volume is superficial and inadequate. Thirdly, it would seem that Rivers never did get to the bottom of the complex system of social organization on Murray Island. As he describes it, it consisted of four types of grouping:

firstly a grouping in villages, of especial importance in connection with marriage; secondly a grouping in districts; thirdly a dual division into two groups, called the *Beizam le* and the *Zagareb le*; and lastly a grouping of people who are named after certain animals.[91]

While he does attempt some speculations as to how these different groupings are related to one another, the matter is, as he himself admits, "far from easy to understand."[92]

The major chapters which are contributed by Rivers and are common to both volumes, are those on genealogies, kinship and the regulation of marriage. In each case the chapter on genealogies which, with its accompanying genealogical tables, provides the empirical material on which the other two chapters are based, appears near the beginning of the book. In each case too, the chapter on the regulation of marriage is placed in such a way as to indicate that it was seen as part of a larger exposition of what Rivers's friend John L. Myres was later to designate "The Life History of the Individual in Society".[93] In Volume 5, the chapter in question is immediately preceded by chapters on "Birth and Childhood Customs", "Women's Puberty Customs", "Initiation" and "Courtship and Marriage", and is immediately followed by a chapter on "Funeral Ceremonies". The approach implied by this setting-out may be labelled "ontogenetic", since it attempts to elucidate the nature of the society as a whole by focusing on the stages gone through by a single individual within that society.

But for our purposes, the most interesting of the three chapters is, in both cases, the one on kinship, supplemented where necessary by Rivers's 1907 article, "On the Origin of the Classificatory System of Relationships". Upon examining the kinship systems of both Mabuiag and Murray Islands, Rivers has no hesitation in labelling them "classificatory", basing his decision on the ten "indicative features" which Morgan had used to define this type of system.[94] However, for Mabuiag Island he notes that the system differs in one respect from many versions of the classificatory system, in that it fails to differentiate between the children of the father's brother and those of the mother's brother, and that the name given to these relatives is also given to the children of the father's sister and to those of the mother's sister; or to put it in modern anthropological shorthand, the system fails to distinguish between cross- and parallel-cousins. In the next generation up, "there are still distinct terms of father's brother, mother's brother, father's sister and mother's sister, but there are definite signs that these distinctions are becoming blurred and that the people are on their way to giving the same name to the relationships of father's sister and mother's sister, and possibly even to those of father's brother and mother's brother".[95] On Murray Island, on the other hand, cross- and parallel-cousins *are* differentiated, as in a normal classificatory system. However, the distinction between father's sister and mother's sister, which had constituted one of Morgan's ten indicative features, is not just tending to become blurred, as on Mabuiag Island, but is definitely

lacking. Rivers regarded these departures from the typical form of the classificatory system as being of considerable theoretical interest, since they imply
important corrections to Morgan's theory.

As I stated in the first chapter, Morgan had supposed the so-called "Malayan" kinship system of Hawaii, which does not make any of the usual classificatory distinctions between father's brother and mother's brother, between
father's sister and mother's sister or between the children of these various kin,
to be the most primitive form of classificatory system. Moreover, Morgan had
inferred, from this system, the prior existence of what he postulated to be
the most primitive form of human familial arrangement – the "Consanguine
Family", in which brothers and sisters were thought to have intermarried.
Now as Rivers pointed out, if the inhabitants of Mabuiag were to cease
differentiating between the father's sister and mother's sister, as had already
been done on Murray Island, and if they were to further blur the distinction
between father's brother and mother's brother, their system would closely
approach the "Malayan" system.[96]

When Rivers turns to the Australian systems, on the other hand, which were
generally acknowledged to be associated with a very primitive form of social
organization, he finds the distinction between the above-mentioned types of
kin to be made almost universally. Only in the case of the social systems of
the Kurnai tribe, which most anthropologists would have considered as
representing a relatively late stage in the evolution of Australian society, had
the distinction between cross- and parallel-cousins been dropped.[97]

Hence, Rivers concludes that Morgan's "Malayan" system represents, not
a poorly articulated predecessor of the developed form of the classificatory
system, but a late modification and simplification of the latter system – a
conclusion which is in consonance with the supposition that it is hardly likely
that a very primitive kinship system would be found in close association with
a culture as advanced as that of the Hawaiians.[98] The Malayan system having
been thus displaced from the bottom of the evolutionary scale, Morgan's
inferential argument for the previous existence of the "Consanguine Family"
was rendered invalid and Rivers, therefore, proceeded to argue that the
"Punaluan Family", which according to Morgan had evolved out of the
Consanguine Family, could in fact have given rise to the typical form of the
classificatory system. Assuming an idealized Punaluan family, in which there
are two exogamous sections or moieties united in group-marriage, such that
all the sexually active males of one group are the husbands of all the child-
bearing women of the other group, Rivers deduced that, within each moiety,
it would be natural to distinguish between four categories of people; the

sexually active men, the child-bearing women, the elders and the children. Hence, for any given child assumed to belong to the moiety of his mother, the total community would be seen as divided into eight separate categories:

In his own moiety there would be a group of child-bearing women to whom he would give a name which was the origin of that we now translate as "mother". Secondly, there would be the active men of his own moiety to whom he would give a name which later came to denote a relationship which we translate "mother's brother". Thirdly there would be a group of children to whom names would be given which later came to mean "brother" and "sister". Lastly there would be the group of elders whose names would have been the origin of the terms translated "grandfather" and "grandmother". In the other moiety there would be four corresponding groups; men to whom the child would give the name which we now translate "father"; the group whom he would call by the name which came to mean "father's sister"; the children of the moiety to whom he would give a name which later came to denote the children of the mother's brother and father's sister; and lastly there would be the group of elders who would probably receive the same names as the elders of his own moiety.[99]

Thus, the major terms which are to be found in the classificatory system could have arisen from the Punaluan form of family organization.

There are a number of interesting things about the above demonstration, not the least of which is the fact that Rivers is, here, making a form of social organization become his theoretical ground-zero and using it to deduce an abstract system of kinship. However, the point on which I wish to focus is the implication that, in its origins, the classificatory system expressed relations, not so much of consanguinity and affinity, as of social status.[100] The child who refers to all the active men in his opposite moiety as "father", is doing so not primarily because he associates the group of men in general or one man in particular with paternity, but because he is linked to each man in the group by a network of "fatherly" duties and privileges defined by the social system.

Now in this 1907 account, Rivers goes on to say that classificatory systems, once having taken shape, tend more and more to express ties of consanguinity and affinity, rather than of social status. However, in an earlier work, Rivers had already produced a specific discussion of the social functions of certain kinsmen. His ground-breaking treatment of this topic, which his first, tentative ethnographic investigations had revealed to be of crucial importance for the workings of indigenous societies, occurs in the 1904 volume of the *Torres Straits Reports*.[101] Focussing on the special functions of the mother's brother in Mabuiag society, Rivers mentions such matters as the power of the maternal uncle to stop his nephew from fighting, the prominent role of the former in the latter's initiation and marriage ceremonies, and the special privileges possessed by the latter in relation to the former's personal belongings.

With regard to this final function, Rivers at one point considers a diffusionistic explanation, suggesting that it was probably introduced by the semi-legendary hero Kwoiam, who was said to have migrated from Australia sometime in the distant past.[102] However, for his general account, Rivers employs an explanation which marches straight out of the nineteenth-century. "The close relations between a man and his mother's brother which exist in Mabuiag", says Rivers, "may . . . be regarded as a survival of a state of society which has now disappeared, viz. that of maternal descent",[103] in which the mother's brother would have been regarded as closer kin than the real father.

Rivers similarly considered the special role of the brother-in-law, which includes the performance of important duties connected with funeral ceremonies and of certain menial tasks relating to fishing expeditions. Rivers's explanation of this kinsman's role likewise has a decidedly nineteenth-century ring to it:

The essential feature of the various customs connected with the relationship of brother-in-law . . . is that an individual could demand certain services of anyone who stood to him in this relation. The whole group of customs is strongly suggestive of a survival of a condition of society in which a man was closely associated with and had to render service to the family of his wife.[104]

It was while he was working amongst the Todas that a new and different kind of explanation for the special role of the paternal uncle occurred to him. As he describes this happening in his 1907 article on "The Marriage of Cousins in India":

Among this people, who reckon descent in the male line, the orthodox marriage is between the children of brother and sister, so that a boy should marry the daughter either of his maternal uncle or of his paternal aunt. The mother's brother takes a leading place in much of the ceremonial connected with the chief events of childhood, and if I had been ignorant of the origin of the uncle-nephew regulation elsewhere, and had sought for an explanation of the relation in the character of the social organization of the people as it is at the present time, I should naturally have found it in the marriage regulation to which I have referred.[105]

Here we have Rivers teetering on the great divide between the nineteenth-century tradition of explanation in terms of survivals and what can now be seen as the typically twentieth-century form of explanation in terms of the presently-functioning social order. As the rest of the article makes plain, however, here Rivers was not about to cross this particular divide. Certainly he goes on to endorse cross-cousin marriage as the probable explanation of the special role of the mother's brother among the Todas. But he never renounces his claim that, among many of the other societies where there are special customs relating to the mother's brother, these customs represent a survival of a previously existing condition of matrilineal descent. Even more significantly, though, Rivers suggests that cross-cousin marriage is itself a survival − a survival of "an old dual organization of society which has not completely disappeared".[106] Hence, on Rivers's account, the special relation between a nephew and his maternal uncle is always a survival; albeit, a survival which is sometimes transmitted via the presently operative custom of cross-cousin marriage. Nonetheless, the entertaining of explanations in terms of "the character of the social organization . . . as it is at the present time", turned out to be a crucially important innovation. For, as we shall learn in a later chapter, it was Rivers's pupil Radcliffe-Brown who, with a certain amount of help from Durkheim, passed through the gateway which Rivers had opened, and explored the new territory beyond. And it was Radcliffe-Brown who, together with Malinowski, was to claim this new territory in the name of British Social Anthropology.

As my final example of the early development of the genealogical method, I would now like to consider what was meant as its most impressive achievement − the description of the kinship system in *The Todas*, a book which was expressly intended as a demonstration of the efficacy of scientific method in anthropology [107] and in which Rivers promotes the genealogical method as "by far my most valuable instrument of inquiry".[108] In fixing upon the Todas as a suitable field of study, Rivers knowingly chose a society for which an extensive literature had already accumulated. However, as he explains in his Introduction:

A review of the literature . . . showed me that there were certain subjects about which our information was of the scantiest. This was especially the case in matters connected with the social organization. Little was known of the system of kinship, and it was not known whether there was any definite system of exogamy. The Todas furnish one of the best existing examples of the custom of polyandry, but scarcely anything was known about the various social regulations which must be associated with such a practice.[109]

As Rivers did not neglect to point out, one previous writer had, in fact, gone so far as to state that it is possible to find only "inextricable confusion in Toda ideas as to relationship".[110] Here then, on Rivers's own account, was a kinship problem of the first magnitude, the solution of which would, by implication, constitute a veritable anthropological coup.

Another factor which led Rivers to choose the Todas was the manageable size of the community. The 1891 Census of India had shown that the total number of Todas was only about 700. Thus, in collecting his data, Rivers was able to proceed in a thorough and systematic fashion. Just how thorough and systematic he was, may be seen from the genealogical charts which are appended to his book. Here Rivers attempted to list every individual in the community, and fell short of the Census total by only sixty-nine persons. And, as R. L. Rooksby points out, the discrepancy is probably explicable in the hypothesis that all the people missed were young children.[111]

In proceeding with his analysis of the Toda system of relationship, Rivers first designates it as "classificatory", then goes on to describe in some detail a number of special features, of which he singles out the following three as the "most characteristic":[112]

(1) the use of the same terms for mother's brother and father-in-law, on the one hand, and for father's sister and mother-in-law, on the other. As he quite plausibly points out, this feature "is a natural consequence of the regulation which ordains that the proper marriage is one with the daughter either of his mother's brother or father's sister";

(2) the marked development of vocative forms of the kinship terms, so that the group of terms used when speaking *to* relatives and in exclamations, is different from the group used when speaking *of* relatives;

(3) the marked development of distinctions according to age, such that there are different terms for members of the family and the clan depending on whether these members are older, younger or of the same age as the speaker.

Evaluating the worth of this specification of the Toda kinship system is a difficult task for the historian of anthropology. After all, one who has never done any fieldwork among the Todas can hardly be expected to comment with authority on the accuracy of the factual material involved. More than this, however, one feels the need for something which does not at present exist — a universally accepted taxonomy of the world's kinship systems, against which Rivers's specification could be judged, allowing for the state of anthropological knowledge during the early years of the twentieth century. Recognizing these difficulties, let us turn to two authorities, one a man who attempted a re-evaluation of Rivers's account of Toda kinship on the basis of personal investigations in the field, the other a currently respected introductory work in kinship theory and method.

The first of these authorities is M. B. Emeneau who, as a result of fieldwork among the Todas during the mid-thirties, concluded that this people are divided, not merely in patrilineal clans, as Rivers had stated, but also into matrilineal "sibs", which cut across the clans to produce a meshed system of double descent. Apart from this oversight, however, Emeneau finds Rivers's account correct in almost every detail. Agreeing with Rivers that the system is essentially classificatory, Emeneau goes on to locate it more accurately as one of the "Dakota-Iroquois" type, and states that the "salient points" of this type of system are, indeed, those stressed by Rivers. Prominent among these points are the second and third of the "most characteristic" features singled out by Rivers — the special development of vocative forms of kinship terms and of distinctions according to age.[113]

The second of these authorities is the book *Kinship and Social Organization* by Ira R. Buchler and Henry A. Selby. In an attempt to find the common denominator of the Toda system and forty other kinship systems which had been reported by various authorities as belonging to the "Iroquois" type, Buchler and Selby fix upon the following four "threshold variables" as constituting "the minimal criteria by virtue of which we will call a system Iroquois":[114]

(1) The same term is used for the father's sister's son as for the mother's brother's son.

(2) The same term is used for the father's sister's daughter as for the mother's brother's daughter.

(3) The same term is used for the father's brother's daughter as for the sister.

(4) The same term is used for the mother's sister's son as for the brother.

When one checks back to Rivers's chapter on Toda kinship, one finds each of these criteria clearly stated.[115] The last two criteria are, in fact, covered respectively by the fourth and eighth of Morgan's ten indicative features of the classificatory system.[116] The four criteria taken together imply a clear distinction between cross- and parallel-cousins, a distinction which is, of course, essential in a society possessing a marriage regulation which ordains that the proper form of marriage is between cross-cousins. Now, since it was from this very same marriage regulation that Rivers deduced the first of his "most characteristic" features, I think we may safely conclude that, whether we accept the allocation of the Toda system to the "Iroquois" group, *à la* Buchler and Selby, or to the "Dakota-Iroquois" group, *à la* Emeneau, Rivers's characterization of the Toda system was not only accurate and tolerably complete, but also tended to stress such features as really are important.

However, in comparison with the descriptions of some of the Australian marriage-class systems previously furnished by people like Howitt and Spencer, Rivers's account of Toda kinship was lacking in one important respect. As I have mentioned in the first chapter, the rules governing marriage and descent in many of the Australian tribes can be stated as a complete set of necessary and sufficient conditions. For this reason, the Australian data justify *par excellence* the use of the word "system" in the term "kinship system". Measured against the Australian material, Rivers's description of the kinship system of the Todas looks somewhat amorphous. The features of the Toda system, which Rivers labels "most characteristic", certainly could not be interpreted as a set of necessary and sufficient specifications. The problem here, of course, is in the system itself, rather than in Rivers's presentation of it. Nonetheless, in view of the formidable reputation Rivers was to acquire as an analyst of kinship systems, and in view of the apparently neat and unambiguous nature of the Australian marriage-classes, it is surprising that Rivers made no substantial contributions to Australian kinship theory. In fact, his only excursion into the field of Australian social organization was an indiscriminately laudatory review of N. W. Thomas's *Kinship Organizations and Group Marriage in Australia*.[117] The fact that Rivers's most definitive contribution to the art of specifying kinship systems involved the Todas, may be likened to the situation which would obtain if a chemist with the reputation of a Lavoisier, produced as his most definitive theoretical contribution to his discipline, an exposition of the chemistry of, let us say, leather tanning. Not that the chemistry involved would be trivial; rather there would seem to be other topics which would be of more fundamental theoretical importance because of their greater manageability.

What cannot be doubted, however, is that the Toda episode provided a victory for Rivers and his genealogical method at the level of propaganda. For, paradoxical as it may seem, Rivers, a scholar of considerable intellectual integrity and political naivete, had struck exactly the right posture to ensure that his somewhat ambiguous account of Toda society would be accepted as a vindication of the new approach to anthropology. In a review of *The Todas*, published in *Nature*, the educationist, sportsman and anthropological writer A. E. Crawley hailed the book as "a remarkable achievement", the significance of which would seem to reside in its exploration of method. "The social sciences are at a disadvantage", writes Crawley, in that they cannot match the exactitude of the physical and mathematical sciences. However, Rivers's book presents proof that "anthropology is attaining such exactness as the nature of the subject allows". This is a notable step forward, avers Crawley, "as anyone may see who compares the present monograph with the earlier accounts of the Todas". Rivers had carried out the testing of evidence "in the most pertinacious and patient manner", and has employed a method which is "new enough in its application to deserve the epithet original". The book is, Crawley concludes, "a monument of industry and care", and represents an achievement "of which Cambridge and the new anthropology may be proud".[118]

*   *   *   *   *

As Raymond Firth has said, Rivers was

a very complex person, much more emotional than he appeared on the surface . . . [and] his thinking about scientific matters, while intellectually rigorous within his chosen framework, owed more to deep emotional elements in the choice of this framework than he himself recognized.[119]

It is my hope that, in presenting Rivers's invention and deployment of the genealogical method as emerging from the same bundle of psycho-intellectual traits which nourished his work in experimental psychology, I have done justice to the complexity and emotionality of the man. Whatever the real story behind Rivers's intellectual peregrinations, I cannot imagine that the underlying *psychological* factors could have been any *less* complex than the ones here depicted. Certainly socio-cultural determinants must have been operative as well, but any historian is a prisoner of his sources, and the surviving sources on Rivers seem to me more amenable to a psychological than to any other kind of interpretation.

In concluding this chapter, several issues need to be discussed. The first concerns the extent to which Rivers's work on kinship was inspired by previous scholars, including and especially Morgan. Here the historical evidence, which I have presented comprehensively within the first two chapters, is somewhat ambiguous. Personally, I favour the view that Rivers arrived at his techniques and insights independently of all earlier students of kinship. When he embarked on the Torres Straits expedition in 1898, Rivers was a narrowly-educated experimental psychologist. Haddon tells us that, before arriving at Murray Island, Rivers had "absolutely no interest in the subject of genealogy".[120] Moreover, the accounts of how Rivers acquired his fascination for the subject make it transparently clear that he started collecting genealogies because he thought they would help him to interpret the results of his psychological experiments. In all the accounts of the expedition, which include Haddon's day-by-day journal, there is no suggestion that Rivers, or any other of the expedition members who were drawn into his genealogical enquiries, possessed any prior knowledge of Morgan's work on the subject. It is true that *after* the Torres Straits expedition, Rivers utilized at least some of Morgan's writings on kinship. His deployment of Morgan's ten "indicative features" of the classificatory system, for example, which occurs in the 1904 volume of the expedition's *Report*, could hardly have been done without close attention to a brief but technically difficult passage from *Systems of Consanguinity* . . . [121] However, it would be difficult to prove that Rivers's reading of the book went much deeper than this. His personal copy of Morgan's epic survey, now held in the St John's College library, is in mint condition, being neither annotated nor otherwise marked. It is true that Rivers's 1907 article "On the Origin of the Classificatory System of Relationships" refers repeatedly to Morgan and his evolutionary scheme. However, as will have been obvious from my discussion of the article, this is not a case of a disciple slavishly following in the footsteps of the master. On the contrary, Rivers uses the article to criticize Morgan's account and to suggest several important amendments to his scheme. It is also true that, in the passage which I have quoted in Chapter I, Rivers paid tribute to Morgan for his originality in discovering and describing the classificatory system of relationship. However, while this does represent an acknowledgement of Morgan's priority, Rivers does not go on to say, here or anywhere else, that Morgan's achievement inspired his own work, or contributed substantially to his understanding of kinship. Now there is nothing to suggest that Rivers was ever anything other than fulsome and frank in acknowledging his debts to his intellectual predecessors. Hence, without in any way wishing to denigrate Morgan's considerable achievements, I think I am justified in concluding that Rivers's kinship investigations were not heavily indebted to the American lawyer.

It might be argued, as an anonymous referee to the present work has done, that whether or not Rivers was directly influenced by Morgan, the genealogical method, in fact, represented little more than a modification of Morgan's use of questionnaires. What Rivers effectively did, it is alleged, was simply to add concrete names of actual persons to such abstract questions as "What is the term or relationship for your (for example) mother's mother's brother's son's son?" Now it would have to be admitted that, for someone who knew and understood Morgan's approach, the advantages of Rivers's widely trumpeted method might have seemed fairly minimal. The addition of concrete names to the questioning procedure no doubt avoided some degree of confusion, and helped to ensure that one was getting an answer to the question being asked. Also the recording of results in the form of chronologically-connected genealogies might be seen as focussing attention more clearly upon important questions like descent and succession. But, in general, there was nothing in Rivers's method which could not be duplicated by the patient application and intelligent interpretation of Morgan's procedure.

This train of thought, however, ignores the fact that the reception and influence of scientific discoveries is determined, not merely by their objective content, but also by the historical context into which they are launched. In the development of British Social Anthropology, it was of little practical consequence that Morgan had developed a method of extracting kinship data before Rivers. For, as I have argued, Morgan's work had been widely ignored or unappreciated by British anthropologists. What did matter was that Rivers had developed his method in the course of an expedition which was seen as demonstrating the inadequacy of "armchair" anthropology. What did matter, in the context of a national scientific tradition which valued first-hand experience above all else, was that the method was not to be pursued by proxy, but involved direct participant observation. What did matter was the fact that the method was promoted as a means of systematizing an ill-defined subject area and giving it a firm empirical basis. What did matter was that the inventor and leading exponent of the method was a respected scientist attached to a famous university, a man of undoubted achievements in a more tough-nosed discipline who was now applying his technical skills and value judgements to an area which aspired to the status of a science. What did matter, in terms of the confidence and power with which Rivers expounded his programme, was the fact that he had an intellectual rationale to justify the genealogical method. Specifically, Rivers regarded his method as duplicating what he interpreted as the aboriginal mode of approaching abstractions only via concrete examples. And, as I have argued, this rationale was reinforced by psychological factors which were deeply rooted in Rivers's personality. Hence, there were a whole host of reasons, most of them independent of objective scientific achievements, why the investigations of Rivers, rather than the previous exploits of Morgan, were crucial for the early development of kinship studies in British anthropology.

A further issue which needs to be raised in bringing this chapter to a close, concerns the ambiguity of Rivers's contributions to kinship studies. On the one hand we have the narrowly scientific (and sometimes scientistic) approach which permeates most of his work in this area. Rivers, we should note carefully, was to tell one of his younger disciples that he would like to be remembered by an epitaph on his tombstone reading "He Made Ethnology A Science".[122] And during the phase of his career in which he invented and used the genealogical method, this concern dominated his actions and his thinking. To come up with a method which would present a reliable means of extracting objective data, to use the method to decipher the intricacies of aboriginal social organization, to specify exactly and classify the different varieties of kinship system, to define one's theoretical terms in such a way as to avoid confusion,[123] these are the aims which form the central thread of Rivers's attempt to convert the study of human society into a science.

However, beneath these narrowly technical and scientistic concerns, there is sometimes detectable a broader and more humanistic approach. We have already noted Rivers's interest in the social obligations connecting kinsmen and his suggestion, in an article published in 1907, that a particular instance of these obligations might be explained by "the character of the social organization of the people as it is at the present time". As we shall find out in a later chapter, this approach was, under the aegis of Radcliffe-Brown in particular, to facilitate a more organic and more comprehensive account of the workings of aboriginal society. A further example of the humanism which lay hidden beneath Rivers's scientific exterior is provided by his Indian field-work. In his book on *The Todas* Rivers is insistent about the scientific utility of the genealogical method for yielding a comprehensible and accurate reconstruction of a complex social event:

An account of a Toda funeral, . . . with its many *dramatis personae*, would probably have baffled my powers of comprehension if I had not had my book of genealogies for reference . . . The method had the further advantage that it afforded me the means of checking the accounts which I was given. An informant inclined to be careless soon found that I had the means of checking his narrative on many points; and some of the people, not knowing the source of my information, credited me with more knowledge than I really possessed, and were in consequence extremely careful . . . not to tell me anything of which they were not absolutely certain.[124]

However, as he also points out, the advantages of his method are not confined to its narrowly scientific utility:

The chief actors in the ceremony were always mentioned by name; and whenever a name occurred, I looked up the clan and family of the person in question and noticed his relationship to other persons who had taken part in the ceremony. The actors in the ceremony were thus real people to me as well as to my informants, and the account of the ceremony proceeded with the maximum of interest and the minimum of fatigue both to myself and to my informants.[125]

And when it actually came to writing up one particular Toda funeral, the insights acquired through genealogies were used, not to further the complexities of the theoretical analysis, but to enhance the human aspects of the ceremony. "The Funeral of Sinerani", published in the magazine of St John's College in 1903,[126] is remarkable for its vivid evocation of an event which meant a lot to the people who participated in it.

Looking back to the first decade of the twentieth-century, Rivers's attempts to develop and publicize a method for elucidating those aspects of indigenous society which promote order and discrimination, must be accorded a considerable measure of success. Thanks to Rivers, the establishment of a new discipline as the kinship-oriented study of aboriginal social organization would have seemed an imminent possibility. However, as events were to turn out, this "kinship revolution" was delayed for over twenty years, and was finally brought about, not by Rivers himself, but by people who regarded themselves as disciples of the "earlier Rivers" we have just been considering. The story of what transpired in the interim, of why Rivers failed to complete the theoretical reorientation he had begun in so promising a fashion, will be told in the next two chapters.

CHAPTER III

RIVERS AND AMBRYM

The kinship system of Ambrym, an island in the New Hebrides, has for the past half-century been regarded by the *cognoscenti* as one of the more interesting examples of extant social organization. As we shall discover in Chapter VI, considerable excitement was generated among anthropologists by Bernard Deacon's 1927 postulate that Ambrym possessed an elegant and complicated form of closed kinship system embodying six marriage-sections. More lately, the marriage-section interpretation of the Ambrym system has been strongly challenged,[1] raising an anthropological problem of the first magnitude which has, from my reading of the evidence, not yet been satisfactorily resolved.

Whether the marriage-section interpretation withstands this recent challenge or not, it seems indisputable that, for a competent kinship specialist of the Cambridge school during the first three or four decades of the present century, the Ambrym data was such that a marriage-section interpretation would have been mandatory. For the deciphering of kinship systems in a particular way and employing particular kinds of data had reached a sufficient stage of elaboration to accurately mimic scientific puzzle-solving. And the solution to a puzzle having as its elements the Ambrym regulations governing marriage and descent, and the Ambrym type of kinship terms, was the postulation of a six-section marriage system. Certainly up until the early thirties, when this book breaks off the story, no anthropologist, and especially no Cambridge anthropologist, seriously challenged the validity of Deacon's hypothesis. For this reason, I shall henceforth refer, without qualification or apology, to the "discovery" and to the "existence" of the Ambrym six-section system.

A detailed account of Deacon's unravelling of the Ambrym system will be given in Chapter VI, but at this point let me outline a specification of the system which will make plain its structural similarities and differences in relation to the Australian marriage class systems. Assuming that the society is divided into six sections — A, B, C, D, E and F — and that every Ambrymese is assigned at birth to one or other of these sections, marriage and descent will be regulated so that

(i)   a man from section A marries a woman from section B and any
       resultant offspring will be placed in section F;
(ii)   a man from section B marries a woman from section A and any
       resultant offspring will be placed in section C;
(iii) a man from section C marries a woman from section D and any
       resultant offspring will be placed in section B;
(iv)   a man from section D marries a woman from section C and any
       resultant offspring will be placed in section E;
(v)   a man from section E marries a woman from section F and any
       resultant offspring will be placed in section D;
(vi)   a man from section F marries a woman from section E and any
       resultant offspring will be placed in section A.

Using the same conventions as in Chapter I, these criteria may be schematically summarized as

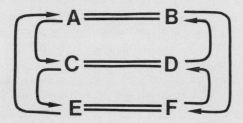

Fig. 10.

When Figure 10 is compared with Figures 1 and 3 in Chapter I, the structural
similarities between the Ambrym, Kariera and Arunta systems are highlighted.
However, these abbreviated schematic representations also obscure an important difference between the Ambrym system on the one hand, and the two
Australian systems on the other. Amongst the Kariera and the Arunta, the
class of the child is determined by the class of the mother. On Ambrym, by
contrast, the class of the child is determined by the class of the father. When,
using the same conventions as in Chapter I, the schematic summary is drawn
in more detail, the patri-determination of the class of the children may be
indicated by making the directed descent lines emerge from the symbols
which represent the males:

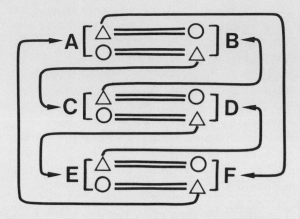

Fig. 11.

The typical form of marriage for an Ambrymese male is with the mother's brother's daughter's daughter or the mother's father's sister's daughter. That these particular relatives are in the appropriate section may be seen from Figure 11 via the process of tracing around the relevant lines indicating descent, siblingship and marriage. If, for example, the male in question is in section A, his mother will be in section E, his mother's brother will be in E, his mother's brother's daughter will be in D, and his mother's brother's daughter's daughter will be in B, the section from which A males take their spouses. Likewise, a similar tracing process reveals that A's mother's father's sister's daughter will also be in section B. And the symmetry of the system is such that, for any male in any of the other sections, the mother's brother's daughter's daughter and the mother's father's sister's daughter will be placed in the section from which he must take a wife. One may also note that, like the Kariera and the Arunta, the Ambrymese practise sister-exchange, males in A, for example, exchanging sisters with males in B.

In order for the cyclic nature of the Ambrym system to be made manifest, the system may be redrawn after the manner of Barnes as in Figure 12 on the next page. As Figure 12 illustrates, the system embodies two matrilineal cycles, A → C → E → A and B → F → D → B, each with a periodicity of three generations. Similarly, Figure 12 shows that the system includes three patrilineal couples, A → F → A, C → B → C and E → D → E, each with a periodicity of two generations. Finally, the affinal periodicity of the system is manifestly two generations. The Ambrym system can, therefore, be briefly specified as 322.

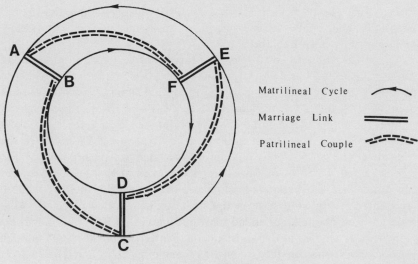

Matrilineal Cycle

Marriage Link

Patrilineal Couple

Fig. 12.

Such then is the Ambrym system, which White's analysis shows to be one particular product of a six-clan society which forbids marriage between first cousins, and exchanges wives between pairs of clans. Let us now see what Rivers made of the data which could have led him to it.

THE ENIGMA

Rivers's unfortunate encounter with the Ambrym system began during his 1914 expedition to the New Hebrides, when he spent about two months at a Presbyterian Mission Training School on the island of Tangoa at the southern end of Espiritu Santo. Here, under the auspices of the Principal, the Reverend Fred Bowie, Rivers spent a considerable period of time collecting genealogies and details of social organization from students at the school, who had come from various islands in the New Hebrides. Among these students was an older native named William Temar, who had originally lived in an area at the west end of Ambrym named Craig's Cove. At first, Rivers attempted to obtain ethnological information from Temar via the medium of English, but with the arrival of Fred Bowie's brother William, this became unnecessary, as the latter had lived on Ambrym for a number of years and spoke a number of Ambrymese dialects familiar to Temar. Favoured by this stroke of good luck,

Rivers made use of William Bowie's linguistic talents to question Temar intensively, and rapidly became convinced that Temar was an exceptionally intelligent and perceptive informant.[2]

There were at least two reasons why Rivers was particularly interested in Ambrym. The first was a purely pragmatic one. In 1913 the island had been devastated by a volcanic eruption and most of its inhabitants who had not been killed by the direct or indirect effects of the catastrophe had migrated to numerous other islands in the New Hebrides area. Hence, it seemed likely that if any record of Ambrym culture was to be preserved for posterity, the requisite ethnographic work would have to be done as soon as possible.[3] The second reason arose out of Rivers's previous work in Melanesia. Rivers had concluded that the culture of Pentecost Island, which adjoins Ambrym, represented a very early stage in the evolution of Melanesian society. What little he knew about Ambrym led him to suppose that its society might exhibit features whose previous existence on Pentecost could only be inferred from survivals; that, in fact, it might resemble a purer form of Pentecost society, uncomplicated by later developments.[4] Elsewhere, Rivers states his belief that, in a still earlier stage of cultural evolution than that represented by Pentecost, Melanesian systems of relationship may have resembled, in richness of terminology and degree of structural simplicity, the systems of Australia. In the same passage, he goes on to say that precursors of the Pentecost system may yet be found "in Ambrym or Malikolo or some other part of Melanesia".[5]

So it is possible that, at this early juncture, Rivers did suspect that the Ambrym kinship system was of the marriage-section type, analogous to the Australian variety. Had he steadfastly entertained this suspicion, and subjected it to a careful theoretical analysis, the history of British anthropology may have been considerably shortened. The discovery of a new type of marriage-section system, which would have represented the first new type discovered for many years, and the first ever discovered outside the Australian continent, would have greatly increased the status of the type of technical puzzle-solving which attempts to isolate and specify kinship systems. Moreover, since the possibility of culture contact between Australia and Melanesia was being seriously considered at this time, such a discovery would almost certainly have sparked a close comparative study of the various types of marriage-section system, thereby promoting the structural-functional study of social organization, and helping to bring to early fruition the "kinship revolution" which Rivers's work on the genealogical method had been instrumental in setting in motion.

As things turned out, however, Rivers totally failed to see that a closed six-section system could be inferred from the Ambrym data. Now, when it is remembered that Rivers's special forte was reputed to be unravelling the intricate details of kinship systems from relationship terminology, his failure in respect of the Ambrym system must be regarded as constituting a major enigma in the history of British Social Anthropology. Indeed, Bernard Deacon, after discovering the Ambrym six-section system some five years subsequent to Rivers's death, wrote in the letter in which he announced his find to Haddon, "What I *cannot* understand is how Rivers *missed* this marriage-class system in Ambrym"[6] [Deacon's emphases]. The aim of the present chapter will be to solve this enigma, to discover why Rivers failed to see that the kinship terminology of Ambrym can be neatly explained on the supposition that the island's society is organized into a system of six marriage-classes.

RADCLIFFE-BROWN'S EXPLANATION

As our starting point we may take the explanation offered by Radcliffe-Brown in 1929:

I think that probably the reason why Rivers failed to get at the Ambrym system was because he had never quite rid himself of the misconceptions that cluster round the use of the terms matrilineal and patrilineal, or mother-right and father-right. These misconceptions have created a lot of confusion not only in theory but also in fieldwork. Rivers explains (*Journal* XLV, 229) that on his theories he expected to find in Ambrym a matrilineal dual division. In this he was right, for it was there in the *batutun* of Deacon.[7] His first enquiries showed him the existence of patrilineal local clans. He thereupon gave up looking for the matrilineal dual division, because, perhaps unconsciously, he assumed that the two forms of organization could not exist in the same people. Consequently, when he did find traces of the social importance of matrilineal kinship he regarded them as survivals from an earlier form of social organization. He affords, therefore, another example of how the old confusions about patriliny and matriliny can mislead an able fieldworker.

It is worthwhile trying to make the nature of this confusion a little more clear. The late Sidney Hartland used to write about tribes where kinship is traced through females only. On any description of kinship that is at all satisfactory there are no such tribes ... In every society of which we have any knowledge kinship is traced through both males and females. A person is kin to his sister's children as to his brother's children, to his father's brother as well as his mother's brother. Kinship, as the saying goes, is always bilateral.[8]

According to Radcliffe-Brown then, who regarded marriage-classes as arising from the intersection of patrilineally-determined social divisions with matrilineally-determined ones, the solution was quite simple. Rivers had not detected the marriage-classes because, having failed to clear away the old confusions which accompanied the use of words like mother-right and father-right, he had assumed that it is impossible for matrilineal and patrilineal kinship ties to exist simultaneously in the same society. Even at first sight this explanation looks deficient. For one thing Rivers had, in the years before his investigation of Ambrym society, taken considerable pains to redefine the terminology of kinship analysis so that such misconceptions could be avoided.[9] More particularly, however, in his 1910 article on "The Father's Sister in Oceania", Rivers had criticized Bishop Codrington for speaking of a child as not being "of the same kin" as his father, and for using the word "kinship" to refer only to common membership of a descent group. Having demonstrated that, in various sections of Oceania where descent is traced matrilineally, the father's sister is honoured and obeyed above all other relatives, Rivers suggests that a man should be regarded as kin not only to the members of his mother's (and hence his own) social group, but also to the members of the social group of his father.[10] In other words, Rivers was arguing for precisely the same point as Radcliffe-Brown — that kinship is bilateral.

While I do not deny either that Rivers missed the matrilineal dual division on Ambrym or that this oversight would have made a marriage-class inter-pretation difficult, what I am disputing is the claim that these facts provide a sufficient explanation of Rivers's failure to detect a six-section system on the island.

AN ALTERNATIVE EXPLANATION

Let us now consider a different explanation, which takes cognisance of, but does not rely exclusively upon Rivers's failure to realize that Ambrym society is divided into matrilineal moieties. Rivers had recognized that the social organization of the island embodies a particular form of kinship grouping, which the natives referred to as the "*vantinbul*", and which as we now know, corresponds to what anthropologists call marriage-sections. However, as T. T. Barnard has pointed out, certain information supplied to Rivers by William Temar led the former to misconstrue the nature of this grouping.[11]

Firstly, as will be explained below, Rivers got the criteria for membership of a *vantinbul* wrong. Secondly, from Temar's account of his own village of

Sulol, Rivers apparently gained the impression that it was normal for a village to possess more than two *vantinbul*. Unfortunately, however, Sulol was not a typical village, as it represented a coalescence of the remnants of at least three former villages.[12]

In December 1916, Temar died of dysentery, and from that time on, Rivers obtained further Ambrym information by corresponding, through William Bowie, with a teacher at the Tangoa Training School named Lau,[13] who hailed from Lonwolwol, a village close to Sulol in western Ambrym. Early in 1917, Bowie, responding to an early draft of what Rivers intended as a book on Ambrym, commented that Lau and the other Ambrym men at the mission disagreed entirely with Temar's account of the *vantinbul*. According to Temar, a *vantinbul* was composed of people who trace relationship to one another in the male line, plus the sister's son. On the contrary, wrote Bowie, "The *vantinbul* are all those who call one another brother and sister, including the father's father and his brothers and sisters and the son's children".[14] In other words, each *vantinbul* is made up of people who belong to alternate generations in the male line, and the sister's son is certainly excluded. Lonwolwol contains only two *vantinbul*, and assuming the village to be a patrilineal group containing all a man's descendants in the male line, it follows that the members of one *vantinbul* will be separated from the members of the second *vantinbul* by an odd number of generations. Now one can deduce from Figure 11 that the members of any given marriage-section belong to alternate generations in the male line, comprising, to use Bowie's words, "all those who call one another brother and sister, including the father's father and his brothers and sisters and the son's children". One can also see that for any two sections which together form a patrilineal couple, each section will be made up of people separated by one, or some other odd number of generations, from the people in the other section. (For example, a man in A will have his father, his son and his son's son's son in section F.) Thus, as might be guessed, what Bowie was calling a *vantinbul* is identical to what was later isolated as a section within the postulated six-section system. And the pairs of *vantinbul* which comprise a typical village like Lonwolwol correspond to the patrilineal couples of the system. In its simplest form then, a six-section system could be composed of three exogamous villages, which exchange sisters for wives in such a way as to form a closed circular connubium.[15]

Rivers, however, having been informed of the necessary corrections to Temar's data, seems to have made no attempt to alter his account of the *vantinbul*, and evidently failed to realize that Lau's material implies a class interpretation of the Ambrym system.[16] Hence, we must conclude that the deficiencies of Temar as an informant which led to Rivers's misconceptions about the *vantinbul* cannot provide a satisfactory solution to our problem.

In fact, it is only when Rivers's Ambrym analysis is viewed against the background of his previous work on the history of Melanesian society that one can begin to assemble the elements of a complete explanation.

(a) *The Puzzle of Pentecost*

The seeds of Rivers's failure to pin down the Ambrym kinship system were sown in 1908 when Rivers visited the northern end of Pentecost, an island in the New Hebrides group immediately to the north of Ambrym. "When I recorded the system of this island", writes Rivers, "I found it to have so bizarre and complex a character that I could hardly believe at first it could be other than the result of a ludicrous misunderstanding between myself and my seemingly intelligent and trustworthy informants. Nevertheless, the records obtained from two independent witnesses, and based on separate pedigrees, agreed in details so improbable that I felt confident that the whole construction could not be so mad as it seemed."[17]

One of the things that immediately struck Rivers about the Pentecost system was that it tended to place relatives separated by two generations in the same category. The wife's mother, for example, was designated by the same kinship term as the daughter. The hypothesis which Rivers at first formulated in order to explain this merging of alternate generations was one which, as subsequent events would show, he would have done well to pursue – that Pentecost possessed a social institution resembling the marriage-classes of the Australian Aborigines.[18] That Rivers did not find this hypothesis fruitful seems, at first sight, surprising. Rivers had remembered from his reading of N. W. Thomas's 1906 book, *Kinship Organizations and Group Marriage in Australia*, that the kinship system of the Dieri tribe of Australia also possessed this feature of merging alternate generations, and since both the Pentecost and Dieri systems were organized on the basis of a dual division with matrilineal descent, the possibility of demonstrating a connection between Melanesian and Australian social organization naturally suggested itself to him.[19] Moreover, as it is so easy for us to see with the benefit of hindsight, he was in possession of information from which it might easily have been inferred that Pentecost possessed some kind of six-section system. As he records in Volume I of *The History of Melanesian Society*:

According to John Pantutun there are also subdivisions of the moieties of such a kind that a man of one subdivision is not free to marry any other woman of the other moiety, but must take one of a given subdivision. Thus he said that each moiety had three subdivisions which we may call A, B and C in one moiety and D, E and F in the other. It was said that a man of A had to marry a woman of D, a man of B a woman of E, and a man of C a woman of F, while men of D, E and F divisions could not marry women of A, B, and C respectively, but a man of the F division must marry a woman of A, and so on.[20]

These data, plus the existence of certain other forbidden marriages, seemed to Rivers "to point to some very important modification of the dual organization", and led him to suggest that "there is social grouping which crosses the grouping into moieties and that this secondary grouping has the effect of preventing marriage with certain kin, even though these belong to the moiety into which a man has to marry".[21]

Here then, one might imagine, were all the ingredients for a successful analysis of the Pentecost system in terms of six marriage-classes. Even though an examination of the only Pentecost genealogy which he then possessed did not seem to confirm the details about subdivision of moieties supplied by John Pantutun,[22] Rivers did not immediately abandon the hope that some sort of matrimonial class-system might still be found on Pentecost. It is true that, in the second volume of *The History of Melanesian Society*, he suggests that Pantutun, who was not a native of Pentecost, must have misunderstood the mechanism for regulating marriage within the moieties. However, even then his conclusion is *not* that Pentecost does not possess a marriage-class system, but that, on the contrary, the misunderstanding itself may have obscured resemblances between Pentecost social organization and the matrimonial classes of Australia.[23] Hence the fact that Rivers ultimately abandoned his attempt to discover a system of marriage-classes on Pentecost certainly warrants an explanation.

(b) *The Stacked Deck*

The reason which Rivers himself advanced as decisive in his abandonment of the search for Pentecost marriage-classes was as follows: After analyzing terms of relationship, he had concluded that a permissible form of marriage for Pentecost Islanders was with the wife of the mother's brother. Now, as he correctly observes, "In all forms of the Australian matrimonial classes, whether fourfold or eightfold, marriage with the wife of the mother's brother is quite impossible." (One may see this by consulting Figures 2 and 4 in Chapter I. For a male in section A of the Kariera system, his mother's brother's wife will be in section D and will, therefore, be ineligible as a marriage partner. For a male in section A1 of the Arunta system, his mother's brother's wife will be in section D2, and will likewise be unavailable for purposes of marriage.) Describing the prohibition of marriages between contiguous generations as "the essence" of class systems, Rivers draws the conclusion that, where marriage with the wife of the mother's brother is permitted, "any attempt at derivation from matrimonial classes similar to those of Australia breaks down entirely".[24]

However, as may be gathered from an article written in 1928 by Brenda Seligman, a keen disciple of Rivers and the wife of Torres Straits expedition member C. G. Seligman, this does not tell the whole story. Utilizing Deacon's Ambrym analysis, Mrs Seligman demonstrates that Pentecost social organization, when interpreted as a 166 type system with six matrimonial classes, turns out to have a number of peculiar features in addition to the one mentioned above.[25]

In an attempt to spotlight the aspects of Pentecost social organization which may have contributed to Rivers's failure to discern the six-section structure detected by Seligman, let us compare her interpretation with the marriage-class systems of Australia and Ambrym.

Firstly, one may note the odd role played by patrilineal descent in the Pentecost system. It has already been mentioned that Radcliffe-Brown regarded marriage-classes as arising from the intersection of patrilineal social divisions with matrilineal ones, and there is some evidence that Rivers himself would not have been averse to this point of view. In a passage which has been quoted previously,[26] Rivers suggests that the Pentecost system may involve a social grouping (called the "*verana*") which meshes with the matrilineally-determined division into moieties, thereby prohibiting marriage with some members of the moiety from which a man is obliged to choose his spouse. However, because Rivers was unable to determine the exact nature of the *verana*, he did not pursue this notion any further.

Seligman, after re-examination of Rivers's results, concluded that the *verana* is, in fact, a patrilineal grouping, but one of a very unusual kind, in that it includes only two generations in the direct male line — that is, each *verana* is made up of a man and his son.[27] The effect of the *verana* grouping on marriage regulations is that a man is barred from taking a wife from the marriage-group of his father. But this is not the only prohibition restricting the choice of a marriage partner. A further injunction prevents both men and women from marrying into the moiety of their mother. This result Seligman expresses (somewhat oddly, I think) by saying that the Pentecost system operated by invoking criteria of descent which are asymmetrical in the sense that men recognize both patrilineal and matrilineal descent as a "bar" to marriage, while women recognize only matrilineal descent.

Asymmetry of this kind is quite foreign to the other types of class system, and when one considers that Rivers was initially looking for a class system, must be allowed to have played a part in his failure to pin down the real nature of the *verana*, and to obtain a satisfactory specification of the Pentecost system.

In order to further our comparison of Seligman's interpretation of the Pentecost system with the exemplary cases of marriage-class system illustrated in Figures 2, 4 and 11, let us represent the former schematically:

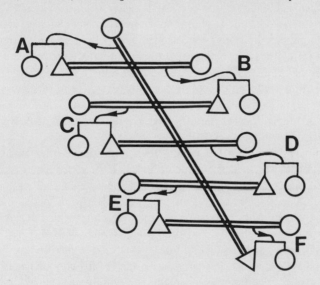

Fig. 13. Seligman's interpretation of Pentecost social organization as a six-section system. (Male descent line only is depicted.)

As can be seen from the above figure, the illustrated groupings cannot be the only factor regulating marriage. Otherwise marriage would be permissible between a father and his daughter. (For example, the daughter of a man from section A will be placed in section B, from which A may take a future spouse.) Moreover, a man would be able to marry both a girl and her mother,

something which, in fact, never occurs on Pentecost and, according to Seli-
man, rarely occurs anywhere else. Having noted this difficulty, Mrs Seligman
explains it away by saying that the first type of marriage is ruled out by "the
ordinary family rules of incest", the second type by an "almost universal
regulaton", which apparently operates quite independently of the groupings.
By way of contrast, the Australian and Ambrym systems do not need to
invoke additional *ad hoc* postulates to prohibit these two kinds of marriage,
which, as can easily be seen from the appropriate figures, are disallowed by
the arrangement of the classes themselves.[28] Thus, if Rivers was expecting a
class-system in which widely tabooed alliances such as parent-child incest
are automatically ruled out, the evidence suggests that he would have been
unable to extract it from the Pentecost data.

A comparison of the relevant figures also makes it clear that the practice
of sister-exchange figures prominently in each of the exemplary cases of
marriage-class system, but is absent in Pentecost. Now there is some direct
evidence to indicate that this particular anomaly would have materially added
to Rivers's difficulties in deciphering the structure of the Pentecost system. In
a passage which I have already mentioned in another context,[29] Rivers implies
that, since John Pantutun's account rules out the custom of sister-exchange,
it probably represents a misconstrual of the evidence and may, thereby, have
concealed affinities between the marriage regulations of Pentecost and those
of Australia.

In summary then, Mrs Seligman's interpretation of the Pentecost data
represents what can, at best, be described as a very peculiar instance of a
marriage-class system. Not only does it fail to separate contiguous generations
and to forbid incestuous unions automatically, it also disallows the custom
of sister-exchange, and invokes an oddly asymmetrical rule of descent.
Consequently, one is hardly surprised that Rivers, who did not have the
benefit of Deacon's analysis behind him, was unable to discern any six-section
structure to the Pentecost system, and completed his stay on the island with
the details of the terminology remaining "wholly inexplicable".[30] Later,
Rivers was to console himself with the observation that the complexities of
Pentecost kinship "have become as great as human beings are likely to be able
to endure".[31] He was also to recount, evidently with well-founded sympathy,
the story of a native New Hebridean who, having settled on Pentecost, found
himself quite unable to understand the local system of relationship.[32] So
although he would have had no way of knowing it, when Rivers undertook
the task of deciphering Pentecost social organization, the cards were well
and truly stacked against him. In Rivers's case, Pentecost did not signify the

liberating gift of the Spirit, but constituted one step towards something resembling his own personal Calvary.

(c) *The Theory of Anomalous Marriages*

Rivers was aware that in most types of classificatory system, members of different generations are terminologically distinguished[33] (for example, the term for mother will generally be different from the term for sister). Hence, he regarded as anomalous "kinship correspondences", in which people from separate generations are terminologically merged (an example of a kinship correspondence would be a word which means both nephew and father). For Rivers, such correspondences are subdivisible into two groups, the first group involving mergings between adjacent generations, the second involving mergings between "alternate" generations, that is between people who are two generations apart.[34]

After leaving Pentecost and journeying to the Banks Islands, Rivers decided that the first group of correspondences could be accounted for in terms of a type of marriage which was common to both areas, namely marriage with the wife of the mother's brother. By thus attempting to explain oddities of kinship terminology as survivals of past marriage practices, Rivers was following the lead of the German jurist and ethnologist Joseph Kohler. In fact, Kohler's 1897 essay "Zur Urgeschichte der Ehe" actually invoked marriage with the mother's brother's wife to explain the kinship system of one particular tribe.[35] Using a form of argument which is reminiscent of Kohler's, Rivers claimed that the fact that a Pentecost Islander calls his cross-cousin by the same term as his father can be explained by the following diagram.[36]

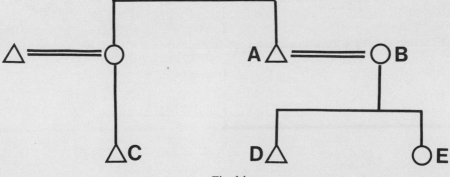

Fig. 14.

If C marries B, the wife (or widow) of his mother's brother A, then he will stand to D and E, not merely in the consanguineous relationship of cross-cousin, but also in the socially-defined role of father. Hence, one can see why D and E will address C by a term which means both cross-cousin and father.

Although he had thereby given an account of the first group of correspondences in terms of a marriage between adjacent generations, Rivers tells us that it did not immediately occur to him that the second group may be explicable in terms of a marriage between people who are two generations apart. Indeed, as he hastens to add, "The idea of a society in which marriages between those having the status of grand-parents and grand-children were habitual, must have seemed so unlikely that, if it entered my mind at all, it must have been at once dismissed." [37] It was only later that his informant John Pantutun, in the course of making an unfavourable comparison between Pentecost and his own island, happened to remark that Pentecost is a place where people marry their granddaughters. "I saw at once", says Rivers, "that he had given me a possible explanation of the peculiar features of the system of the island." [38]

Having by this time forgotten the details of Pentecost kinship terminology, Rivers deliberately refrained from making immediate reference to his field-notes but, instead, set out to construct an hypothetical system for a society practising marriage with the classificatory granddaughter. After performing this task, Rivers compared his results with the terms recorded in the field and, finding a very close agreement, concluded that this apparently implausible form of marriage provided the correct explanation for the second group of Pentecost anomalies. The mechanism of the explanation may be illustrated as follows: [39]

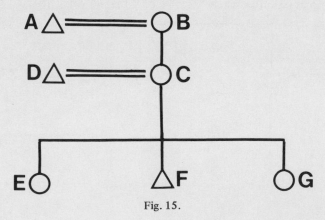

Fig. 15.

The diagram shows that, if E marries A, which could occur if B died, or if polygamy were practised, F, who had previously been related to A only as his daughter's son, would now become also his wife's brother. Similarly C, who before the marriage had been related to A only as his daughter, would acquire the role of his wife's mother, whilst D, A's daughter's husband, would become his wife's father. And, in fact, on Pentecost, the daughter's children are called by the same term as the wife's siblings, the daughter is called by the same term as the wife's mother, and the daughter's husband is called by the same term as the wife's father. It has been assumed for the sake of simplicity that a man marries his own granddaughter, but the conclusions would follow equally well if the preferred spouse were the granddaughter of the brother, where brother is used in either the classificatory or descriptive sense. After working out the implications of the clue provided by Pantutun, Rivers did not have the opportunity to return to Pentecost and was able to discuss the matter with only one inhabitant of the island. This man, whom Rivers describes as "not a very good informant", stated explicitly that marriage with the granddaughter of the brother can and actually does occur, while marriage with one's own granddaughter is strictly debarred. Since the former part of this statement could not be confirmed by a white missionary informant, Rivers concluded that such marriages might not be practised in present-day Pentecost, but that they must nevertheless have been customary in the past. This being the case, terminological mergings of people in alternate generations should be regarded as survivals of this former social condition.[40]

Upon arriving back in England, Rivers's conclusions were reinforced by the discovery that A. W. Howitt had previously recorded marriage with the brother's granddaughter among the Australian Dieri tribe which, as I have mentioned previously, uses a system of kinship terminology possessing anomalous correspondences similar to those of Pentecost.[41]

During the early part of the 1908 expedition, Rivers had visited Viti Levu, an island in the Fiji group, and had discovered the existence of terminological correspondences involving alternate generations. Once having concocted his explanation of the Pentecost system, Rivers decided that the Fijian correspondences should be accounted for in a similar fashion, but there was a problem in that patrilineal descent prevailed on Viti Levu, whereas his Pentecost explanation had been based on the premise of matrilineal descent. For some time, Rivers attempted to explain the peculiarities of Viti Levu by assuming that the system had originally resembled that of Pentecost, but had subsequently undergone a transition in its mode of tracing descent. Not being successful in this endeavour, he tells us that "for more than two years I failed

to see an obvious alternative explanation, although I returned to the subject
again and again".[42]

Eventually, a clue was provided by an analysis of the Buin system of
Bougainville, which had been performed by the German ethnologist Richard
Thurnwald. As with Viti Levu, Buin kinship terminology merges the elder
brother with the father's father, but because descent is still matrilineal on
Buin, Rivers concluded that his earlier attempts at explanation had been
misdirected. Having been forced to seek a fresh approach, he soon realized
that the above correspondence and several other apparently anomalous
aspects of the Buin and Viti Levu systems could be accounted for on the
supposition that marriage with the wife of the father's father was, or had
been, practised in both areas.[43]

Hence, one can see that, largely through the failure of other modes of explanation, Rivers was becoming deeply committed to accounting for kinship
anomalies in terms of marriages between people of alternate generations.
Once he had reached this stage, the apparent implausibility of such unions did
not appear to worry him. The American linguistic anthropologist Edward
Sapir, responding to *Kinship and Social Organization*, wrote to Rivers in
February 1917:

I did think some of the inferential applications of kinship nomenclature that you make
were a bit far-fetched, particularly where it was a question of intermarriage between
individuals two generations removed. It seemed to me that in such extreme forms of
marriage one would have to have direct evidence. Inferential evidence derived from the
facts of nomenclature seem to be too untrustworthy a guide.[44]

Rivers, however, had already forearmed himself against such criticism:

The marriage of a man with a woman belonging to a generation two generations senior to
his own may seem in the highest degree improbable, but this improbability becomes
much less when we consider the nature of the classificatory system of relationship.
Where this system exists, the difference of age between those who call one another by
the same terms as grandparent or grandchild may be very slight. It may even be possible,
though it probably rarely happens, that a man be actually older than a woman two
generations above him whom he classes with his own grandmother.[45]

Although at this point, Rivers might have been credited with having
provided some sort of "explanation" for a number of Oceanic kinship anomalies, it is apparent that he himself was dissatisfied with the *ad hoc* nature of
his account. He, therefore, became strongly committed to seeking a unifying
scheme to connect the three rather peculiar forms of marriage he had invoked.
In an undated and unpublished rough draft of a paper in which he endeavours

"to lay bare the mechanism which underlies the production of scientific and literary work in myself", Rivers gives the following account of his quest for unification:

One May term I was engaged on trying to discover the meaning of a number of peculiar forms of marriage which occur or were formerly practised in Melanesia. The whole set of marriages with their accompanying conditions formed a confused tangle of facts and processes, the meaning of which I wholly failed to see. Morning after morning I awoke with my head full of their complexities and the days were spent in . . . work by means of which little features of one island were brought into relation with those of another, and the scheme became clearer, but still there failed completely to be any central thought which would bind them all together. At length I got into such a state that I hardly slept at all. I woke so early so often that my short hours of sleep were having a serious effect on my health. I decided to go home to Ramsgate for a few days and following my usual custom of never travelling by land when it is possible to go by sea, I went to London one evening, slept the night there and took the river steamer . . . in the morning. The journey had the favourable effect on me that sea or river always has in allowing me to live without thinking [cogitating] and I had a quiet and more or less somnolent day with the minimum of mental activity of any kind. I went to bed very early and woke the next morning with the solution of my difficulty . . . The solution in question was that various forms of marriage were the results of a former state of dominance of the old men and monopoly of the younger women.[46]

Let us now consider a more detailed version of Rivers's solution. Its initial postulate is that marriage with the brother's granddaughter had its origins in an extreme form of gerontocracy, in which the old men dominated the society to such an extent that they would have been able to monopolize all the young women for purposes of marriage. From this it follows that the young men would not have been able to find wives in their own generation, but would have been obliged to wait around and marry cast-offs whom the elders had decided to give away.

Assuming matrilineal descent and a division of society into two exogamous moieties, let us consider the status of those young men to whom an old man would be permitted to donate a wife. His own son, his daughter's son and his brother's son would automatically be ruled out, since they belong to his wife's moiety. His son's son and his sister's son, on the other hand, would be eligible spouses, since they belong to the same moiety as himself. Hence, it must have become customary for those old men who were disposing of their wives to supply the son's son and the sister's son, thus bringing into being the other two forms of marriage which Rivers had invoked in explanation of Melanesian kinship anomalies, namely marriage with the wife of the mother's brother and with the wife of the father's father.[47]

This represented Rivers's basic scheme, and I shall henceforth refer to it as his "theory of anomalous marriages". However, for the Buin system, William James Perry, a young Cambridge disciple of Rivers who was later to assume prominence as an extreme diffusionist, had demonstrated that Thurnwald's results implied the existence of cross-cousin marriage. Hence, Rivers set himself the task of expanding his scheme to take into account the co-existence of marriage to the father's father's wife with marriage to the cross-cousin. As before, Rivers assumed that the monopoly of the young women by the old men could lead to the custom of donating superfluous wives to the sister's son and, hence, to the practice of marrying the mother's brother's wife. In addition, Rivers supposed that, as is the case in many indigenous societies, the sister's son would have acquired great social importance, such that he could demand anything he wished from his mother's brother. Hence, it could transpire that a man might feel obliged to give, not his wife, but his more nubile daughter to his sister's son, thereby transforming marriage with the mother's brother's wife into cross-cousin marriage.[48]

Rivers summarizes his own estimate of his achievement in the following words:

... it has been shown that four forms of marriage, which are either actually present in Melanesia or the presence of which can be inferred from the systems of relationship, are all to be explained as the result of the monopoly of young women by the old men. The beauty of the scheme which has been advanced is that the explanations suggested for the four forms of marriage form a coherent whole.[49]

The weakest part of the whole argument was that Rivers could find no direct evidence for the past or present existence of a Melanesian gerontocracy. However, in a paper presented to the Australian meeting of the British Association in 1914, Rivers attempted to minimize this deficiency by pointing out that, among the Australian Aborigines, the old men do control the society and their hegemony is often accompanied by a monopoly of the young women. Moreover, the evidence seemed to indicate that each of the three peculiar marriages which Rivers had postulated for Melanesia, either were or had once been customary in particular Australian tribes. It had long been known from Howitt's work that the Dieri practise marriage with the granddaughter of the brother. A recent book by Baldwin Spencer had shown that, in the Kakadu tribe of the Northern Territory, men transfer their wives to their sister's sons; while in many tribes the systems of relationship indicate that marriage with the wife of the father's father was once orthodox.[50] In other words, Rivers was pointing to data which seemed to indicate that there are tribes inhabiting a land mass geographically adjacent to Melanesia, which practise or once practised the requisite forms of marriage, and which also possess a gerontocracy. From Rivers's point of view, it must have seemed as if the postulates of his theory which at first sight appear quite implausible, had been empirically confirmed.

Meyer Fortes has suggested that Rivers's obsessive attempts to present marriage rules as the key to kinship relations "derived both from Morgan and from his Australian data".[51] However, as I hope the foregoing account has made clear, Rivers's theory of anomalous marriages had other and more immediate sources. To be sure, there was an input of Australian data, but this was in the nature of apparent confirmations of specific hypotheses, and did not involve the transference of some ill-defined but reputedly pervasive mode of approach. Moreover, Morgan's work, considered as a disembodied intellectual influence, does not seem to have played any part at all. Rather, the real story, which is both more concrete and more interesting, may be summarized as follows. After his humbling encounter with the complex and atypical Pentecost system, Rivers underwent several intellectually harrowing years grappling with the intricacies of Melanesian social organization. Eventually, through a number of occurrences, some of which must have appeared to him as fortuitous coincidences and some as flashes of insight, there emerged his theory of anomalous marriages in which kinship anomalies were explained in terms of unions between different generations. The formulation of the basic theory was followed by a subsidiary elaboration which succeeded in incorporating cross-cousin marriage into the framework of intergenerational unions, thereby lending an air of final plausibility to the whole approach.

(d) *Ambrym and Anomalous Marriages*

When we turn to Rivers's attempted theoretical analysis of the Ambrym system we find not the slightest hint that he was looking for a marriage-class system on the island. Indeed, what he was hoping to find was a functioning gerontocracy, and a consequent "condition of society . . . less complicated by later changes than in Northern Pentecost".[52]

A rough, unpublished typescript entitled "Marriage with the wives of the grandfather and uncle",[53] written after "a recent visit to the New Hebrides", probably represents the earliest surviving presentation of his Ambrym material, and seems to be nothing more nor less than an attempt to test the theory of anomalous marriages expounded in *The History of Melanesian Society*.

Rivers begins by asserting that Ambrym provides direct evidence for marriage with the wife of the father's father, a practice which he had previously inferred from Thurnwald's results for Buin and his own analysis of Viti Levu. Moreover, he notes that the Ambrym version of this marriage is accompanied by the very same features of kinship terminology which had led him to make the original inference.

He then goes on to discuss the presence or absence of various other forms of marriage on Ambrym. Although "some of the terms of relationship might be held to indicate the former existence of the cross-cousin marriage",[54] there is no direct or indirect evidence for marriage with the granddaughter of the brother or with the mother's brother's wife, the two forms of marriage which had figured so prominently in his explanation of the Pentecost system. Now, since he believed marriage with the granddaughter of the brother to be the most primitive of these three major forms of anomalous marriage, and since he states in the typescript that marriage with the wife of the father's father should be regarded as later than that with the wife of the mother's brother, we may take it that he had already abandoned the view that the Ambrym social order represented an earlier version of Pentecost society.

Marriage with the daughter of the sister's son, a form of alliance between alternate generations which had not been recorded elsewhere, is found to be practised on Ambrym, but Rivers is unable at this stage to see how it might be used to explain any terminological correspondences.[55] The typescript concludes, apparently as an afterthought, by mentioning seven "orthodox" forms of Ambrym marriage, in which the people being married are either of the same generation or are, at most, one generation apart. Although Rivers was obviously not aware of the fact, six out of these seven marriages would be consonant with a standard marriage-class system with six sections.

An even more striking demonstration of Rivers's failure to perceive the secret that lay hidden in his own data, is provided by an undated sheaf of hand-written pages entitled "Ambrim Relationship".[56] One of the pages lists, under the heading "Ambrim eccentric correspondences", no less than nineteen terminological juxtapositions, all of which would tally perfectly with a six-section system. As one might guess, however, what Rivers attempts to do with these correspondences is to explain them in terms of anomalous marriages. Although the rough and incomplete form of the notes make the extent to which he succeeds in this endeavour difficult to evaluate exactly, it is, nonetheless, apparent that he does manage to explain a number of correspondences by recourse to three anomalous unions – marriage with the wife of the father's father, with the daughter of the sister's son, and with the daughter of the daughter's daughter.[57]

The invocation of this last form of marriage, which would involve an alliance between people three generations apart, stretches plausibility past the breaking point. The reason for such an aberration lies, I suggest, not only in Rivers's desire to explain terminological correspondences between people who are separated by three generations, but also in his ambition to devise a second theory of anomalous marriages; to construct a scheme whereby the postulation of one peculiar marriage would bring it and two apparently disparate but almost equally peculiar marriages under the one rationale. Certainly, one of the pages contains the cryptic notation "marriage to daughter's daughter's daughter would explain two marriages otherwise unexplicable", and we can imagine Rivers playing with the idea that some form of super-powered gerontocracy might have given rise to a system in which the old men monopolized the young women right down to the third generation.

(e) *The Lapse into Particularism*

When we come to Rivers's final statement on Ambrym, a lengthy, hand-corrected typescript which seems to have been intended for publication in book form, we find that he has decisively rejected the notion that marriage with the daughter's daughter's daughter is, or even could have been, an orthodox form of alliance. Indeed, he now sees the Ambrym system as illustrating "how easily one might fall into serious error in inferring peculiar forms of marriage from the terminology of relationship". The fact that the mother is classed with the sister's daughter's daughter should not lead one to infer that a man marries or once married his great-granddaughter. Rather, this terminological correspondence "is almost certainly a secondary consequence of the marriage of a man with the daughter's daughter of his father's sister, the son's wife of a man being classed with his mother as a result of marriage with the father's mother".[58] Lest the logic of these final two sentences be deemed opaque, let us illustrate it by means of the sort of diagram which Rivers himself would have employed. The marriage of a man with the daughter's daughter of his father's sister may be depicted as follows:

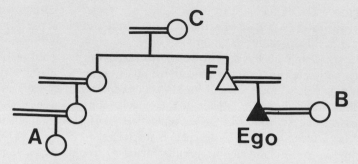

Fig. 16. Note that A and B represent the same person.

Now, because marriage with the father's mother is also sometimes practised, B and C could be the same person (although in this case they are not) and will, thus, be terminologically merged. But since B is the same person as A, A will be classed with C. Hence, for ego's father F, his mother C and his sister's granddaughter A will be the subject of a correspondence in nomenclature. Thus, a terminological juxtaposition of people who are three generations apart, has been explained, not in terms of one exceedingly anomalous marriage involving people separated by three generations, but as a "secondary consequence" of two somewhat less anomalous marriages, one between people who belong to adjacent generations, the other between people of alternate generations.

Apart from providing a further illustration of the mental gymnastics required by Rivers's approach, this passage, which relinquishes the aim of achieving a unified theory of anomalous marriages for Ambrym, may be taken as epitomizing the tone of Rivers's final account of the island's social organization. Unable to see a way of explaining Ambrym kinship correspondences which is at once systematic, comprehensive and plausible, Rivers lapses into a dull particularism, making only a few far-fetched and somewhat half-hearted attempts to suggest that given terms of relationship may have originated in certain marriage forms.[59] Nevertheless, Rivers's final typescript contains numerous facts which we, with the benefit of Deacon's analysis, can easily interpret as providing strong support for the six-section theory of Ambrym social organization.[60]

*   *   *   *   *

It has been the main burden of this chapter to argue that Rivers's failure to realize the implications of his Ambrym data has a long and rather tortuous history. Although at the time he began his investigations into Pentecost social organization, he was amenable to marriage-class interpretations, the intractable nature of this system prevented him from perceiving any six-section structure therein. He therefore resorted to explaining its eccentricities in terms of particular forms of anomalous marriages, an approach which was reinforced by the chance remark of a native informant, by the later discovery that some of the implausible social conditions he had postulated were instantiated among the Australian Aborigines and by his invention, as if by revelation, of a scheme which appeared to unify various forms of anomalous marriage into a "coherent whole".

Consequently, by the time Rivers came to consider the Ambrym material, explanations in terms of marriage classes were far from his thoughts. His typescript on "Marriage with the wives of grandfather and uncle" seems to be less concerned with the Ambrym system *per se* than with using it to support the theory of anomalous marriages which he had previously developed for Pentecost, Buin and Viti Levu. While his hand-written papers on "Ambrim Relationship" do reveal a desire to develop a similar theory for Ambrym, by the time he had written up his detailed notes for publication, this project had been discarded as implausible. So, despite the wealth of evidence he unwitting possessed in support of the marriage-class interpretation, Rivers's final work on Ambrym social organization tapers off into a disappointing particularism. Although he would not have admitted to it, it would seem that Rivers had effectively abandoned all hope of finding a functioning, inter-locking relationship "system" for the island. Such an abandonment was tantamount to relinquishing the genealogically-oriented, kinship-centred, puzzle-solving programme which had dominated his anthropological work since the Torres Straits expedition.

CHAPTER IV

RIVERS AND DIFFUSIONISM

The events described in the last chapter ran parallel to, and to some extent interacted with, the emergence and consolidation of Rivers's "ethnological" period. For it was while he was engaged in writing up the results of his 1908 expedition to Melanesia, that Rivers first became convinced of the crucial importance of diffusion in the development of human culture.

Briefly, an ethnologist who subscribes to diffusionism might be expected to proceed as follows. Confronted with a given cultural feature, he would evince little interest in its ongoing function in the community, or in its place within the social structure, or in its relationship to the techno-economic base. Nor would he attempt to reconstruct the history of its successive development. Rather, he would look for evidence that the feature had been transmitted by "diffusion", either through the actual migration of peoples or via trade routes. Thus, a diffusionist, asked to explain say, an Australian boomerang, would be less concerned with its function as a weapon, or with its role as a preserver of the socio-economic differentiation between men and women, or with its evolution from various forms of throwing-stick, than with the possibility that, at some specific time, it had been introduced into Australia by some specific race. In some historical instances, the diffusionist programme seems beyond reproach. For example, the spread of Christianity into the south Pacific (a process to which Rivers was a first hand witness) constitutes a clear case of cultural diffusion taking place during a specific historical period. And framing questions in the diffusionist mode does not, in this instance, exclude other illuminating approaches of a non-diffusionist kind. However, for some enthusiasts (and the modern writer of diffusionistic best-sellers Thor Heyerdahl should be numbered among them), the diffusionist postulate can act as an *idée fixe*, shutting out other modes of explanation which could be complementary, or more apposite in the circumstances. In the most extreme form of diffusionist programme, sometimes called "hyper-diffusionism", the attempt is made to trace virtually every cultural feature of worth back to one particular civilization.

It is well known that, between about 1910 and his death in 1922, Rivers increasingly carried out his ethnological investigations in conjunction with a former student named William James Perry, and the famous neuro-anatomist

Grafton Elliot Smith, thereby forming the school of British diffusionism. What is not so well appreciated is the personal and intellectual basis of this rather unlikely three-way collaboration. Why did Rivers and Elliot Smith, well-known and respected in their original fields of scientific expertise, choose to enter controversial new territory in company with the obscure Perry? What were the crucial steps in the assemblage of the extreme version of diffusionism which emerged from their labours? Who was the leader of the school? Questions such as these have, to my knowledge, never before been clearly posed or satisfactorily answered, and it will be the aim of this chapter to make a start along these lines. By giving an account of Rivers's conversion and developing commitment to diffusionism, I shall attempt, firstly, to put the puzzle-solving minutae of the last chapter into a broader context and, secondly, to set the stage for the conflict which followed Rivers's death. This conflict was between people who saw themselves as carrying on the work of Rivers the diffusionist, and people who regarded themselves as disciples of or collaborators with the Rivers whose main emphasis had been on the use of the genealogical method as a tool for elucidating social organization.

THE CONVERSION TO DIFFUSIONISM ACCORDING TO RIVERS

Rivers's endorsement of diffusionism represented a major shift in his personal and intellectual life. In his autobiographically revealing psychological work *Conflict and Dream*, which represents the published version of a course of lectures first delivered in 1920–1921, Rivers writes:

In some of us older people the educative influence of the last ten years has been so great that we should hardly recognize ourselves if brought face to face [with our former selves].[1]

Now while, in applying this statement to himself, Rivers would certainly have wished to include the "educative influence" of his work on psycho-neurotic soldiers, there can be little doubt that a further crucial factor in the lack of recognition would have been his prior adoption of the diffusionistic approach to anthropology.

The first public statement of what Rivers himself referred to as his "conversion" to diffusionism, was given in his well-known Presidential Address to the Anthropological Section of the British Association for the Advancement of Science in 1911.[2] This account may be fleshed out by reference to Rivers's two volume work on *The History of Melanesian Society*, which provides a unique record of his shift in point of view, since it begins as a work on the evolution of social structure, and abruptly shifts to a diffusionistic tack partway through the second volume. In the Presidential Address, Rivers explains how, during his 1908 expedition to Melanesia, he had spent much of his time doing ethnographical survey work, in which he used the genealogical method to collect terms of relationship for the various islands visited. Then, as we have seen in the last chapter, he began constructing a theoretical edifice on the premise that the kinship "correspondences" of each island could be explained in terms of the habitual practice, whether in the past or the present, of a limited number of anomalous forms of marriage. These anomalous marriages were, in turn, explained and placed in a definite sequence by the postulate that a state of "gerontocracy", or dominance of the society by the elders, accompanied by matrilineal descent and a division of the society into exogamous moieties, had once been widely distributed throughout Melanesia. Up to this point, Rivers informs us, his work "was of a purely evolutionary character, and only served to strengthen me in my previous standpoint".

However, he then began a linguistic comparison of the actual kinship terms themselves, and concluded that "these fell into two main classes: one class generally diffused throughout Oceania, while the terms of the other class differed very considerably in different cultural regions". In addition to being widely spread, the terms of the first class denoted relationships which, on the basis of his evolutionary reconstruction of changing marriage forms, he would have expected to have suffered appreciable changes in status. The terms of the second class, on the other hand, denoted relationships for which no marked adjustments in status would seem to have occurred. On his own account, it was these observations which led Rivers to the postulate of wide-spread cultural diffusion:

From these facts I inferred that at the time of the most primitive stage of Melanesian society of which I had evidence, there had been great linguistic diversity which had been transformed into the relative uniformity now found in Melanesia by the incoming of a people from without, through whose influence the change I had traced had taken place, and from whose language the generally diffused terms of relationship had been borrowed. It was through the combined study of social forms and of language that I was led to see that the change I had traced was not a spontaneous evolution, but one which had taken place under the influence of the blending of peoples. The combined morphological and linguistic study of systems of relationship had led me to recognize that a definite course of social development had taken place in an aboriginal society under the influence of an immigrant people.[3]

Proceeding to the study of the secret societies which abound in Melanesia,

Rivers concluded that these societies had arisen where the immigrant culture was not dominant enough to alter the indigenous mode of social organization; that, in fact, these institutions had originated in the desire of the immigrants to practise their rituals in secret. Hence, for Rivers, the interaction of two cultures was not a process to be likened to a mechanical mixture, in which all aspects of the resultant culture had originally belonged to one or other of the contributing cultures. As with his earlier theory of the interaction of protopathic and epicritic modes of sensibility, suppression was not the only process in operation, but fusion played an important role as well.

From additional investigations, Rivers decided that the immigrant people had arrived in at least two major streams. The first of these had practised kava drinking and had succeeded in penetrating the area very widely. The second stream was distinguished by the practice of betel-chewing and had propagated itself only through the more northerly regions of Melanesia. Rivers also detected traces of two additional cultural migrations, the first preceding the above two streams, the second postdating them and emanating from Polynesia.

Thus, Rivers convinced himself that Melanesian society was a complex product of the impingement of three or four migratory cultures upon an aboriginal people. This conclusion having been reached, it was a short step to decide that the classical British approach to anthropology, in which one endeavoured to construct evolutionary sequences for various institutions or beliefs, was liable to yield misleading results if the ethnological histories of the societies involved had not been reconstructed beforehand.

For example, the Melanesian concept of *mana*, an impersonalized force which was thought to lend supernatural efficacy to persons or objects, had recently been suggested as a precursor of the animism which, according to Tylor, had constituted the earliest stage of religion. However, in Rivers's view, such speculation was worthless, since his analysis of the history of Melanesian society had revealed the concept of *mana* to have been introduced to Melanesia by an immigrant people whose religion had already reached an advanced stage of animism.[4]

Lest there be any misunderstanding, I should point out that Rivers was not rejecting the evolutionary approach outright. Rather, the main point of his 1911 address was that, if an anthropologist is going to embark upon evolutionary speculations, he must first subject the societies involved to ethnological analysis. The main exception to this rule is provided by social institutions like marriage customs, which are so deeply interwoven with the structure of society that they can change only with great slowness. In fact,

such institutions exhibit such a relatively high degree of stability that the
reconstruction of their evolutionary development can furnish a useful guide
to the temporal ordering of the various components into which a given
culture has been analyzed. This belief in the comparative permanence of
social structure was the decisive factor in persuading Rivers not to recast the
early evolutionary sections of *The History of Melanesian Society*.[5]

From the above account, one might gather that Rivers's conversion to
diffusionism was the result of nothing more nor less than a careful study
of his empirical data. He simply looked closely at the facts and saw that
Melanesian society must be a heterogeneous blend of diverse cultures. However, one suspects that only Rivers would have read the particular meaning
he did into the facts he cites. Consider, for example, the linguistic analysis of
relationship terms which first convinced him of the complexity of Melanesian
culture. To this writer at any rate, it is far from obvious that the terms fall
into two clearly-defined categories, the members of one being much more
diverse than members of the other. For one thing, Rivers seems to have been
unaware of the problem of "alternating sounds", which can result in an
anthropological observer perceiving the same sound (or what his informants
would regard as the same sound) differently on different occasions.[6] His
orthographical naivety may be illustrated by the following extract from *The
History of Melanesian Society*:

For scientific purposes it is of the utmost importance that the actual sound shall be
expressed, for such differences as those between kw, pw and mbw may be of definite
ethnological significance.[7]

In other words, Rivers seriously believed that an ethnographer should be able
to document distinctions between similarly articulated sounds so accurately
that the variations would function like tags for the identification of past
diffusionistic influences. Now if the diversities detected by Rivers were
recorded on the basis of an assumption like that, many of them may well
have been artefacts arising from the unavoidable indeterminacies of cross-
cultural observation and amplified by the unrecognized limitations of his
orthography. Indeed, Rivers had been forewarned against such naivete by
Sidney Ray, the linguistic expert from the Torres Straits expedition. Writing
to Rivers in March 1911, Ray averred, apparently in response to an assertion
by Rivers similar to that quoted above:

I quite agree with what you say about the b and mb sounds. What I meant to imply in
my note is that in an initial mb or nd, the nasal was likely to be missed, either by a
European listener or by a European speaker.[8]

In contrast with Rivers's unduly optimistic assessments of the accuracy of his phonetic recording, there are a number of other occasions when, being anxious to convince the reader of the affinity between two apparently disparate terms, Rivers is quick to allege the existence of a suitable Melanesian sound-shift.[9] Such ruses only point up his failure to provide exact criteria for evaluating the precise degree of diversity or uniformity exhibited by a given collection of words. One also wonders how much validity there can be in a comparison between a large number of terms, collected under diverse circumstances over a huge area and transcribed by a variety of observers who undoubtedly would not have possessed uniform notions about orthography.

As a result of the above considerations, one is forced to the conclusion that, in order to explain Rivers's conversion to diffusionism, it will be necessary to look further than the empirical data presented by Rivers himself. But before proceeding with the explanation, let us first review the ethnographic occurrences which preceded the emergence of his diffusionistic tendencies.

THE 1908 EXPEDITION TO MELANESIA

Rivers's second expedition to the south Pacific, carried out during the greater part of 1908, began as might have been expected for someone who was renowned as the inventor of the genealogical method and the leading exponent of kinship studies. Having been awarded a grant "to make detailed sociological studies in the Pacific, and more particularly to study mother-right communities in the Solomon Islands and to trace the details of the transition from mother-right to father-right", Rivers broke his voyage *en route* in the Hawaiian islands.[10] There he found, still functioning precisely as it had decades before, the simple classificatory terminology which Morgan had pronounced the most primitive form of kinship system in existence. Although, as we have seen in Chapter II, Rivers did not accept this particular Morganian pronouncement as valid, the persistence of the Hawaiian system struck Rivers as a remarkable example of the stability and resilience of the kinship component of social structure. "The Hawaiians", he wrote, "have lost nearly the whole of their old culture, and present from the point of view of the anthropologist a most depressing picture of the results of a century of contact with civilization, and yet in the midst of the general wreckage there has persisted almost untouched the old system of kinship, which, so far as we can tell, is as it was fifty or a hundred years ago".[11] After leaving Hawaii, Rivers travelled to Savage Island, Tonga, Samoa, Fiji, the New Hebrides and the Solomons, in each place

indulging his talent for collecting an extraordinary amount of kinship data
in a minimum of time. Summing up this phase of the expedition, Haddon,
who had been keeping the home fires burning in Cambridge, wrote: "All this
work has been accomplished by the genealogical method, without which he
could have done nothing in the time to which he would have attached any
value." [12]

However, unbeknown to Haddon, the threads of Rivers's own personal
contribution to a kinship-centred anthropology were already beginning to
unravel. Whilst in Fiji, Rivers had first recorded the puzzling and troublesome
Viti Levu terminological correspondences involving alternate generations.
And on his trip through the New Hebrides, he had become embroiled in the
complexities of the Pentecost system. As outlined in Chapter III, these events
were instrumental in sowing the seeds for his disastrous encounter with the
Ambrym system six years later.

But another episode, crucial for Rivers's personal and intellectual life, was
about to take place. In May 1908, Rivers wrote to Haddon that he would
shortly settle down in a definite locality, probably Rubiana (Roviana) in the
Solomon Islands, where he would make "an exhaustive study of the natives".
For this endeavour, he would be assisted by "Dr A. M. Hocart of Exeter
College Oxford, and Mr G. C. Wheeler . . . of the University of London", both
of whom had already joined him.[13] Of these two gentlemen, the one who
turned out to be more important for anthropology in general, and for our
story in particular, was Arthur Maurice Hocart. A shy retiring bachelor,
Hocart had come to anthropology via classics and experimental psychology.
Despite Rivers's original plan, Wheeler was to pursue fieldwork on the islands
of the Bougainville Straits, while Rivers and Hocart journeyed together to the
Western British Solomons. For three months Rivers and his younger colleague
worked cooperatively on Eddystone Island. Then, after Rivers had left for
a time, the two again joined forces in a tour around Vella Lavella. Hocart
next proceeded alone to Roviana and stayed there for six weeks, finishing up
his Solomon Island sojourn by making several return visits to Eddystone
Island.[14] Later Rivers was to claim that their joint investigations on Eddystone
Island constituted the first "intensive" fieldwork done in British anthropology. By modern standards, their Eddystone ethnography could hardly be
described as intensive. For one thing, three months would now be regarded
as excessively brief, and for another, their investigations were done through
interpreters using Pidgin English of a most rudimentary kind.[15] Nonetheless,
for other reasons, the experience would seem to have been a memorable one
for the two ethnographers. As Hocart was to write to Rivers in 1912:

From what I hear ... they are doing their best to spoil our Solomons ... I met a Fijian in Suva who started talking Roviana; he told me my cook and brother was dead. A nice boy he was, and a precocious dandy, and eager to come to Fiji. I seriously thought of fatiguing him to have flute duets with him and keep a memorial of heathen Roviana but the financial difficulty was great besides possible legal ones.[16]

The exact interpretation which should be put on this oblique reference to the 1908 expedition is, admittedly, problematical. But whatever the correct nuance, there can be no doubt that, from Rivers's point of view, the expedition and its aftermath was of considerable personal import. Time and again in his later writings, and especially when he is waxing autobiographical, Rivers refers to incidents which took place during or shortly after the 1908 expedition. Rather than giving an account of these incidents immediately, let us instead proceed to offer an explanation of Rivers's conversion to diffusionism, invoking the more salient of the aforementioned incidents whenever it seems appropriate for furthering the explanation.

AN EXPLANATION OF RIVERS'S CONVERSION TO DIFFUSIONISM

From among the entangled series of personal and intellectual changes which constituted Rivers's conversion to diffusionism, it is possible to discern four separate tendencies exhibited by the Cambridge anthropologist.

(a) *Espousal of an Empiricist Ideology*

The first thing to note is Rivers's growing emphasis on the value of empirical evidence in ethnology, and his correlated downplaying of the importance of deductive thought. As the 1911 Presidential Address makes abundantly clear, when Rivers talks about the old evolutionary school of anthropology, the concept it brings to his mind above all is that of unwarranted *a priori* speculation. On the other hand, when he talks about diffusionism, the key word is "analysis", by which he means a careful examination of the observational evidence.

In rejecting an evolutionary hypothesis on empirical grounds, Rivers was not alone among contemporary scientists. For during this period, the life-sciences as a whole were undergoing a crisis in which extensive experimental evidence was being produced in an attempt to refute Dawin's theory of natural selection. In 1909 for example, Paul Kammerer had been awarded the

coveted Sommering Prize for experiments which apparently demonstrated the
Lamarckian hypothesis that acquired reproductive behaviour in salamanders
is inherited.[17] A few years earlier, a German biologist had opined:

... we [anti-Darwinians] are now standing by the death-bed of Darwinism, and making
ready to send the friends of the patient a little money to ensure a decent burial of the
remains.[18]

Summing up the state of Darwinism in 1907, Vernon L. Kellog wrote:

... a major part of the current published output of general biological discussions,
theoretical treatises, addresses, and brochures dealing with the great evolutionary problems, is distinctly anti-Darwinian in character ... The fair truth is that the Darwinian
selection theories, considered with regard to their claimed capacity to be an independently sufficient mechanical explanation of descent, stand today seriously discredited
in the biological world.[19]

Kellog then goes on to list a number of leading exponents of the life-sciences,
including von Sachs, Delage, Haacke, Kassowitz, Cope, Haberlandt, Henslow,
Goette, Wolff, Driesch, Packard, Morgan, Jaeckel, Steinmann, Korschinsky
and de Vries, who are to be counted as anti-Darwinians.[20] As historian of
science William Coleman has written:

Young men trained during the 1880s in the varieties of Darwinism soon expressed dissatisfaction with the principal objective set before them, the reconstruction by means of
comparative anatomy, embryology and palaeontology of the evolutionary history of
plants and animals. It was now much more important, they held, to attempt to analyse
the process of change than to seek probably unattainable detail regarding the products
of change. The only method truly suited to this new goal was experimental analysis of
plant and animal breeding behaviour and of the disposition among the offspring of
heritable traits. Such work promised to answer the outstanding questions of evolutionary
theory ... In the book of biology in 1900 was written a persuasive word: experiment ...
Experimental physiology had established a model approach ... [to vital processes] ...
and that approach — experiment — offered little encouragement to the traditional historian of life.[21]

Now, although such connections as existed between the behavioural and the
life-sciences were undoubtedly neither simple nor direct, the simultaneously
occurring rejections of evolutionary speculation on experimental grounds
could hardly have been totally unrelated.

Another area of science which reflected the empiricist aspect of the diffusionist attack on Tylorean evolutionism was the controversy over the so-called
"nature-nurture" problem. Francis Galton had formulated the problem in
terms of the relative efficacy of nature (genetic endowment) and nurture

(environmental factors) in determining particular aptitudes, and had come down heavily on the side of nature. "Nature", said Galton, "is far stronger than Nurture within the limited range that I have been careful to assign to the latter".[22] In his *English Men of Science* (1874), Galton had argued that it is genetic endowment which is responsible for ability across a range of scientific areas and that environmental factors tend merely to select out the specific area in which the ability is to take root.[23] Following Galton's death in 1911, biologists tended to take a less sanguine attitude to the possibility of the problem being solved through the postulation of a simple formula expressing the relative potency of genetic and environmental factors.[24] This state of affairs seems to have been echoed by ethnology, in that the new school of diffusionists tended to identify the belief that one can easily specify hereditary mental abilities with the old speculative school of evolutionists, and to regard this belief as unduly optimistic. Thus, in a 1915 review of Rivers's *History of Melanesian Society*, Hocart, who was at that stage a stronger diffusionist than Rivers, criticized the book on the grounds that Rivers, whom Hocart regarded as still somewhat tied to evolutionism, had assumed that it is sensible to speculate about differences in modes of thought between indigenes and civilized folk. "As a matter of fact", writes Hocart,

psychology has hardly begun to distinguish between the processes of thought, which are racial, and the material, which depends entirely upon circumstances . . . The author gives us nowhere a psychological sketch of each race, so that we might know on what grounds he assigns them certain "modes" of thought rather than others. It is all the more necessary as he is dealing with races probably as different from one another as we are from them. By "modes of thought" he presumably means ideas, the objects of thought; what they think, not the processes of thought. But how can you tell what a people thinks about until you know who they are, what their traditions and environment is? And these are precisely the things we have set out to seek.[25]

Thus, for Hocart, as for many post-Galtonian biologists, the attempt to specify natural genetic endowment was premature in the absence of a satisfactory determination of nurture.

No doubt there were many other areas of science, in addition to Darwinian and neo-Galtonian biology, in which attitudes to experiment ran somewhat parallel to those involved in the diffusionistic assault on anthropological evolutionism. However, it is beyond the scope of the present chapter to delineate the broader scientific context in any more detail than has already been provided.

More immediately relevant to the central thread of this book, is the fact that Rivers's downplaying of the importance of rational, deductive thought

came shortly after his traumatic struggles with the kinship systems of Pentecost, Buin and Viti Levu, in which rational procedures had failed to uncover
a marriage-class system on Pentecost and to concoct a scheme to unify the
various types of anomalous marriage allegedly found in the three regions. As
I have related in the preceding chapter, Rivers eventually hit upon such a
scheme only after renouncing concentrated thought and giving free rein to
his subconscious. Which brings us to the second tendency in Rivers's conversion to diffusionism.

(b) *Emphasis on the Role of the Personal Unconscious*

During the late nineteenth and early twentieth centuries, unconscious thought
first came to be accorded a role in creative scientific work. Two episodes in
particular were well known and widely discussed. In 1865, Friedrich August
von Kekulé, Professor of Chemistry in Ghent, who had been struggling with
problems of atomic arrangements in organic chemistry, dozed off by the fire
with visions of atoms dancing before his mind's eye. In a dream he saw long
structures entwining and undulating in snakelike movements. Then one of the
structures, which had become a snake, seized hold of its own tail, and spun
mockingly. Kekulé awoke, with the structure of the closed carbon chain
firmly implanted in his mind.[26] In 1908, the French mathematician Henri
Poincaré gave a lecture at the *Societé de Psychologie* in Paris, in which he
described the conceptual processes by which he had arrived at his theory of
the Fuchsian functions. On no less than four separate occasions during the
formulation of his theory, alleged Poincaré, solutions to perplexing problems
in the theory had come to him only after he had ceased to consciously cogi-
tate on them.[27] These two episodes, widely celebrated in the folklore of early
twentieth-century science, presumably formed an important part of the background to Rivers's beliefs about the utility of unconscious mental processes
in his own creative endeavours.

In the crucially important period following the 1908 expedition, Rivers
gradually became more aware of the positive role played in his own scientific
work by unconscious thought, and in particular by the unconscious thought
which takes place during sleep or the semi-comatose state. The unpublished
autobiographical paper quoted in Chapter III, in which Rivers describes how
his unifying scheme for anomalous marriages came to him immediately after
waking, also contains the following passage:

In an early stage of my work on the analysis of Melanesian culture I had already reached the opinion that the institutions of Melanesia were to be explained by the settlement of an immigrant people among an aboriginal population. I awoke one night suddenly with my heart beating wildly and with the idea which, as far as I know, had never even remotely crossed my mind before — that the two kinds of house found in Temotu [an island in the Santa Cruz group] was the work of two different peoples. And since the *mandwai* or club-house corresponded to the *gamal* of the Banks Islands, this must have been the form of house introduced by the immigrants who founded the institution of the club-house, while the round house must have belonged to the aborigines. Though I now know that this idea gives too simple an expression of the facts, I believe it to be correct in the main and I do not think that there can be any doubt that it was due to an action of the constructive imagination which took place in sleep.[28]

Thus, what Rivers regarded as an important step in the assembly of his diffusionistic theory of Melanesian society, also came to him at a moment of awakening.

Moreover, the aforementioned paper strongly supports the hypothesis that the role of the personal unconscious first dawned upon Rivers at precisely the period when he was shifting his theoretical position in the direction of diffusionism:

... it is only during the last few years, since my return from Melanesia in 1908, that I have become aware of the essential and vital part played in all my best mental activity by the work of the early morning ....[29]

When read in the context of the whole paper, it is evident that, by "the work of the early morning", Rivers meant cogitation performed "in the early hours of the morning between waking and rising". Such cogitation, he writes, "has already been in progress when I awake and certainly it is usually in full swing before I attain that distinctive awareness of my surroundings which would entitle me to say that I am fully awake".[30]

Now it happens to be a fact that Rivers regarded sleep as a process in which the more developed mental functions are successively put out of action as the sleep becomes deeper.[31] Hence, if one accepts that the first tendency indicates Rivers's developing realization of the scientific importance of his concrete (as opposed to abstract) modes of cognition, both tendencies may be regarded as symptoms of the same cause — the emergence of the protopathic in Rivers's thought. That is to say, the period in which Rivers was converting to diffusionism may be regarded as a period in which he was becoming increasingly aware of the positive role played by the protopathic in its fusion with the epicritic or, if you like, as a period in which Rivers was discovering the dog beneath his own skin.

(c) *Emphasis on the Role of the Collective Unconscious*

The third tendency to be considered is Rivers's growing conviction that the unconscious plays a vital role in most of the collective activities of human life and that conscious, rational thought is much less important for these activities than he had previously believed. This conviction dovetails nicely with the typically diffusionist assumption that cultural features are unlikely to have been invented independently in different societies.

Two episodes from the 1908 expedition, which made a big enough impression on Rivers for him to have used them illustratively in later writings, may have contributed to the development of this conviction. The first one, which Rivers describes as having greatly "excited my wonder", is recounted in his book *Instinct and the Unconscious*:

When in the Solomons in 1908 with Mr A. M. Hocart we spent some time in a schooner visiting different parts of the island of Vella Lavella. Whenever we were going ashore five of the crew would row us in the whale-boat, four rowing and the fifth taking the steer-oar. As soon as we announced our intention to go ashore, five of the crew would at once separate from the rest and man the boat; one would go to the steer-oar and the others to the four thwarts. Never once was there any sign of disagreement or doubt which of the ship's company should man the boat, nor was there ever any hesitation who should take the steer-oar, though, at any rate according to our ideas, the coxswain had a far easier and more interesting task than the rest. It is possible that there was some understanding by which the members of the crew arranged who should undertake the different kinds of work, but we could discover no evidence whatever of any such arrangement.[32]

The explanation of such incidents lies, according to Rivers, in the instinctive or unconscious process of intuition.

The second episode is described in an article entitled "The Primitive Conception of Death" and must have constituted an eerie and unforgettable experience for Rivers and his companion Hocart.

During the course of the work of the Percy Sladen Trust Expedition to the Solomon Islands, we obtained in the island of Eddystone a long account of the destination of man after death. We were told that he stays in the neighbourhood of the place where he died for a certain time until the spirits arrive in their canoes from a distant island inhabited by the dead to fetch the ghost to his new home. On one occasion we were present in a house packed tightly with people, who heard the swish of the paddles of the ghostly visitors, and the sound of their footsteps as they landed on the beach, while for several hours the house was filled with strange whistling sounds, which all around us firmly believed to be the voices of the ghostly visitors come to fetch the man who had lately died.[33]

Since Rivers and Hocart evidently did not themselves hear the swish of the paddles or the sound of the footsteps, they presumably interpreted the incident as a graphic demonstration of the power of the irrational among groups of preliterate people.

Perhaps Rivers's clearest statement of the observational difficulties encountered if one pursues one's fieldwork on the assumption that rational motives determine social behaviour, is to be found in his 1916 article entitled "Sociology and Psychology":

There is no more depressing and apparently hopeless task than that of trying to discover why people perform rites and ceremonies and conform to the social customs of their community . . . Directly one approaches the underlying meaning of rite or custom . . . one meets only with uncertainty and vagueness unless, as frequently happens, the people are wholly satisfied with the fact that they are acting as their fathers had done before them. Thus, it would seem as if the people have never attempted to justify their social actions by the search for motives and meanings. When explanations are offered, they come from persons who have been in contact with external influences, and the motives assigned by such persons for social actions bear only too clearly the signs of this influence. They are merely the results of a rationalizing process used to explain actions whose sources lie beyond the scope of reason.[34]

Rivers then proceeds to make it clear that this downgrading of the importance of intellectual processes in the determination of social behaviour has a wider currency than his own writings and extends to Europeans as well as to indigenes.[35] To back up these contentions, he refers the reader to Graham Wallas's *Human Nature in Politics*, first published in 1908. In this widely read book, reprinted in 1910 and 1920, Wallas had attempted to make two major points. As Wallas himself expresses them:

My first point was the danger, for all human activities, but especially for the working of democracy, of the "intellectualist" assumption, "that every human action is the result of an intellectual process, by which a man first thinks of some end which he desires, and then calculates the means by which that end can be attained" . . . My second point was the need for substituting for that assumption a conscious and systematic effort of thought.[36]

The relationship of Wallas's first point to the three tendencies already outlined in this chapter, should be obvious. Someone who was "intellectualist" in the sense defined by Wallas, would tend to place considerable emphasis on the efficacy of rational planning and might be expected to play down the role of unconscious or irrational motivations in human behaviour, whether personal or collective. Wallas's second point may, at first sight, seem reminiscent of Rivers in his prediffusionistic days, when the latter's epicritic faculties were firmly suppressing his protopathic tendencies. However, a more informed opinion would be that this point, too, is strikingly similar to much of Rivers's later writings. What Wallas is suggesting is that the scientist must simultaneously recognize that conscious rational thought does not determine all human behaviour and yet hold fast to his scientific goal of accounting for such behaviour in a methodically self-aware fashion. This indeed is what Rivers wants also. Immediately after his conversion to diffusionism, Rivers was concerned to emphasize his new sensitivity to protopathic phenomena by arguing for what was, in effect, Wallas's first point. In his subsequent work it is evident that Rivers does not wish to relinquish scientific methods of inquiry altogether, but simply wants to cast his scientific net more widely, so that protopathic phenomena will be included both in what is explained, and in the method of arriving at the explanation. Thus, in his psychological work *Conflict and Dream*, Rivers, who had come to believe that conventional methods of psychoanalysis result in the establishment of a complex and special relationship between the psychologist and his patient, argues that one must take account of the activity of the analyst in the process of analysis.[37] By so doing, Rivers thinks he is being not less, but more thoroughly scientific. In other words, Rivers would have endorsed the second of Wallas's points as heartily as he did the first. Assuming that the contributions of Rivers and Wallas were not related by anything so simple as a "direct intellectual influence", the mutual similarities suggest that the work of the two men must have emerged from the same socio-cultural ethos. The specification of this ethos would be a worthwhile contribution to the cultural history of the early twentieth-century. However, it unfortunately falls outside both the scope of this book, and the present knowledge of the writer.

In Chapter II it has been argued that by focussing upon social organization as his special area of study in anthropology, Rivers was confining his attention to an aspect of primitive life in which the epicritic forces of order had been successful in suppressing the less graduated and less discriminative tendencies of the protopathic state. If it occurred to Rivers before 1908 to ask whether epicritic features were governed by the processes of conscious or of unconscious thought, I have little doubt that he would have opted without hesitation for the former alternative. However, with the arrival of his conviction that the sources of social behaviour "lie beyond the scope of reason", an elaboration of the basic protopathic-epicritic dichotomy was necessary. This he attempts in his 1920 book *Instinct and the Unconscious*, where he introduces a distinction between two kinds of instinctive behaviour. The first kind, to which he applies the term "protopathic", since he sees it as possessing an "all-or-none" character, is concerned primarily with the welfare of the individual, and may be regarded as opposed to social forces of control. The second kind, which he labels "epicritic" because of its association with graduated and discriminative forms of activity, is especially associated with collective needs.[38]

Subsequently, he employs the concept of "suggestion" which, as he carefully points out, "belongs to a category of mental process widely different from cognition, association, imagination, volition and other concepts derived from the study of conscious mental states". Suggestion is, in fact, a "process" or "mechanism" of the unconscious and may be defined as "that aspect of the gregarious instinct whereby the mind of one member of a group of animals or human beings acts upon another or others unwittingly, to produce in both or all a common content or a content so similar that both or all act with complete harmony towards some common end".[39]

With the development of social or collective forms of life,

it became necessary to adjust behaviour to that of other members of a group, [and] the original "all or none" reactions had to be modified in the direction of discrimination and graduation. The presence in man of both suggestion and intelligence shows that the early protopathic forms of instinctive behaviour were modified in two directions, one leading towards intelligence and the other towards suggestion and intuition. In men the former has become, or perhaps more correctly may be gradually becoming, the more important, but suggestion still remains as a factor of the greatest potency in determining human behaviour, especially under certain conditions.[40]

All this may be summarized diagrammatically as follows:

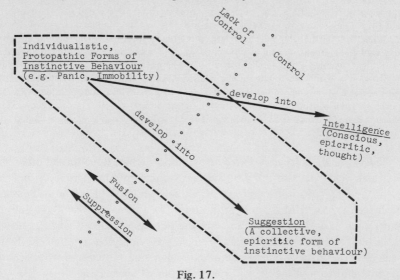

Fig. 17.

The forms of behaviour enclosed within the dashed figure, being instinctual, were regarded by Rivers as determined by unconscious thought processes. Hence, it can be seen that, in effect, Rivers split the epicritic half of his original protopathic-epicritic dichotomy into two branches, so that it now applied to unconscious as well as to conscious behaviour. This enabled him to continue to think of social organization in terms of the dichotomy, while maintaining his new emphasis on the importance of unconscious thought. The move may also be seen as Rivers's response to a controversy, which was flourishing circa 1920, about the nature of instinct.

(d) *Ethnographic Empathy*

The fourth and final tendency exhibited in Rivers's conversion to diffusionism may be characterized by the statement that, during and after the 1908 expedition, Rivers seems to have empathized more effectively with the subjects of his anthropological investigations than he had done previously.[41]

One particular incident from this expedition may be taken as illustrating the new sense of identification he apparently felt towards his informants. As Rivers describes it:

I was travelling on a boat with four inhabitants of Niue or Savage Island, and took the opportunity of enquiring into their social organization. At the end of the sitting they said they would like now to examine me about my customs, and using my own concrete methods, one of the first questions was directed to discover what I should do with a sovereign if I earned one. In response to my somewhat lame answers, they asked me point-blank whether I should share it with my parents and brothers and sisters. When I replied that I would not usually, and certainly not necessarily do so, and that it was not our general custom, they found my reply so amusing that it was long before they left off laughing. Their attitude towards my individualism was of exactly the same order as that which we adopt towards such a custom as the couvade, in which a man goes to bed when his wife has a child . . .[42]

This willingness to allow the ethnographical tables to be turned on himself indicates what one might designate as a new interchangeability between anthropologist and informant, an interchangeability which is also illustrated by his essay on "History and Ethnology". In this essay Rivers imagines the experience of a Melanesian who tests the principles which Rivers had used to assemble the history of Melanesian society by applying them to the British Isles. (Not surprisingly, the hypothetical Melanesian succeeds in reconstructing the actual history of the British Isles with almost uncanny accuracy.)[43]

This fourth tendency, it may be noted, harmonizes well with the previous three. If one interprets the first tendency as a signal of Rivers's realization of the importance of the concrete in his own scientific work, then, in view of what has already been said in the second chapter about his belief regarding the role of the concrete in preliterate thought, it is not surprising that we find him identifying more closely with his informants.

As well as being more aware of the similarities between himself and his informants, Rivers also seems to have become more sensitive to the differences. In particular, his downplaying of *a priori* deduction can be seen as a statement of his intention not to attribute modes of thought appropriate to the conscious deliberations of a European intellectual to indigenes. As he argues in his address on "The Place of Evolution in Sociology", because indigenes classify the world in different ways to us, "general evolutionary speculations based on *our own concepts* must have a very insecure basis"[44] (my emphasis).

It would have been surprising if the simultaneous occurrence of the second and third tendencies had not enhanced Rivers's empathy with the subjects of his investigations. For Rivers, at the same time as he was becoming aware of the importance of a particular type of unconscious mental process in his own scientific activities, was also discovering the role of unconscious factors in the social behaviour of preliterate communities.

*   *   *   *   *

Having described and explained Rivers's conversion to diffusionism, a process which, if my account is correct, took place mainly as a result of factors which were internal to Rivers's intellectual and psychological development, I shall now attempt to delineate the growth of Rivers's commitment to diffusionism after his conversion. Unlike the conversion itself, this developing commitment was intimately bound up with his intellectual and personal relationships to two men — Grafton Elliot Smith and William James Perry.

THE RIVERS–ELLIOT SMITH COLLABORATION

(a) *Biographical Background I*

Elliot Smith and Rivers had been closely associated since 1896, the year in which Elliot Smith arrived in Cambridge and made the necessary arrangements to enter St John's College. Having previously completed his Doctorate of Medicine in anatomy at the University of Sydney and published a number of highly regarded papers on anatomical subjects, Elliot Smith commenced work at Cambridge in close proximity to the anatomist Professor Alexander Macalister,[45] who had been Rivers's tutor at the time of the latter's admission to St John's in 1893.[46] Shortly after coming to Cambridge, Elliot Smith wrote that he was working most of the time in the physiological laboratory, and that W. H. Gaskell and J. N. Langley, two prominent members of the Cambridge school of physiology, were frequently visitors to his part of the laboratory.[47] Now, as previously mentioned, Rivers had originally come to Cambridge at the invitation of Sir Michael Foster, the founder of the Cambridge school of physiology, in order to deliver some lectures on the physiology of the sense-organs; and in 1897 he was to take up the newly-established Lectureship in Physiological and Experimental Psychology at that University.[48] Moreover, Henry Head, who had been Rivers's friend and collaborator in experimental psychology since 1891, was a pupil of Foster, Gaskell and Langley.[49] Hence, one may be sure that, during the periods in which their scientific world-views were taking shape, Rivers and Elliot Smith were exposed to similar social and intellectual environments.

The dawn of the twentieth-century found both Rivers and Elliot Smith in Egypt, the former following up the psycho-physiological aspect of his Torres Straits investigations by performing experiments on the colour vision of the natives of Upper Egypt, the latter having been appointed Professor of Anatomy in the Government School of Medicine in Cairo. By Elliot Smith's own account, it was Rivers who, in 1900, was responsible for his initial introduction to anthropology. Rivers achieved this by calling Elliot Smith's attention to the fact that some of the skulls of predynastic Egyptians unearthed during archeological investigations, contained dessicated brains which were sufficiently well preserved to allow their structure to be studied.[50]

Over the next decade Elliot Smith performed investigations on multitudinous remains of the earliest inhabitants of Egypt, with the aim of classifying them anatomically, reconstructing their history and correlating it with that of mankind in other parts of the world. His initial conclusion from these Egyptian investigations was that, around 3000 BC, Egypt had been invaded by an alien race with distinctive somatological traits. Having reached this conclusion, Elliot Smith then attempted to trace the movements of the race from archaeological evidence.

At the meeting of the Royal Anthropological Institute on 8th February 1910, at which Elliot Smith's election as an ordinary fellow of the Institute was announced, a paper on dolmens was presented by A. L. Lewis.[51] According to W. J. Perry, Lewis's inability to account for the facts evoked Elliot Smith's immediate reaction. Being conversant with the structure and history of Egyptian tombs and sepulchral monuments through his study of human remains, Elliot Smith instantly put forward the hypothesis that the rudely carved megaliths of Western Europe and the coastal areas surrounding the Mediterranean represent, "not primitive stages in the evolution of architecture, but simply crude, unskilled copies of the earlier, more finished monuments of the Pyramid Age in Egypt".[52]

In May 1911, Elliot Smith, having expressed this hypothesis in the manuscript of a book to be entitled *The Ancient Egyptians*, posted the manuscript to the publishers, then set off for Cambridge, where he was to serve as an examiner for the Natural Science Tripos. To let Elliot Smith continue the story:

When I reached Cambridge and called upon my friend the late Dr W. H. R. Rivers to give him an account of what I had just done, he told me that my first incursion into ethnology was a flagrant defiance of all the current doctrines of that branch of study, and would draw down upon my head the most bitter opposition – a prediction that was amply fulfilled. However, he reassured me by telling me that he was actually engaged (at the moment when I disturbed his work) on the task of writing his Presidential Address for the Anthropological Section of the British Association, in which he was making a full and frank recantation of his former acceptance of the orthodox ethnological doctrines . . .

But on the same day . . . I had another experience of a very different nature that was destined to have far-reaching consequences, although at the time it was very disconcerting. The most important scientific result set forth in the manuscript I had posted that morning was the definition of the traits of the aliens who made their way into Egypt about 3000 BC. When I entered the examination room in Cambridge, what was my surprise to see an example of this type, which had been chosen by my fellow-examiner, Professor E. Barclay-Smith, to test the candidates' knowledge of racial peculiarities! Filled with curiosity, I consulted the Museum catalogue to discover from which of the geographical areas of the Ancient East enumerated in this book the specimen had come; but to my intense amazement I learned that it came from the Chatham Islands, near New Zealand, in the South Pacific, about as far distant from the Ancient East as was possible. For a time I was in some doubt whether or not I should recall the manuscript of this book, for the discovery of this skull seemed to destroy the very foundations of the argument set forth in it. However, further examination of the available craniological material revealed the widespread distribution of what in this book I have called 'Giza traits' not only in Polynesia, but also in the Malay Archipelago and at certain places on the southern Asiatic littoral. This seemed, in fact, to afford evidence of far-reaching movements of people in many respects analogous to those of the Mediterranean and Erythraean Seas discussed in this book. But even more startling was the discovery that crania revealing the same distinctive traits were by no means rare on the Pacific Coast of

Central and South America. The facts were so definite and their vast significance so unmistakable that I searched for evidence on the cultural side in corroboration of the only inference one was justified in drawing from the somatological facts. Again, as in the Mediterranean area, the peculiar distribution of megalithic monuments in India, Eastern Asia, Oceania and America provided justification for the working hypothesis. Hence four months later (September 1911) at the meeting of the British Association ... I provoked the first of many onslaughts predicted by Dr Rivers by claiming that the sporadic distribution of megalithic monuments, west and east of Egypt, as far as the British Isles on one side, and as Japan and America on the other, was due to the influence, directly or indirectly, of Egyptian civilization.[53]

If Rivers's 1911 Presidential Address and Elliot Smith's concurrent paper on the diffusion of Egyptian culture suggested a budding collaboration, the next meeting of the British Association demonstrated that their alliance had blossomed considerably. This time it was Elliot Smith's turn to give the Presidential Address and Rivers's turn to support it. Elliot Smith opens by referring to the address of his immediate predecessor as "deeply instructive", and states that Rivers's account of his conversion to a diffusionistic outlook "first brought home to me the fact, which I had not clearly realized until then, that in my own experience, working in a very different domain of anthropology on the opposite side of the world, I had passed through phases precisely analogous to those described so graphically by Dr Rivers". More specifically, Elliot Smith too had begun his investigations into the history of a people by seeking evidence of evolution, but "gradually came to realize that the facts of racial admixture and the blending of cultures were far more obtrusive and significant".[54]

In two papers which were scheduled so as to immediately follow Elliot Smith's address, Rivers took up the cudgels on behalf of diffusionism. The distribution of megaliths had suggested that the art of constructing them must have spread by sea, and this presented a problem since, in many parts of Oceania, the indigenes do not possess vessels capable of making long voyages across the open ocean. Rivers's solution to this problem was to argue that it is quite possible for useful arts, such as canoe-building, to disappear or to survive only in a degenerate form. In his second paper, Rivers produced additional arguments for the occurrence of degeneration, this time in the field of art. According to Rivers, "conventionalization", the process by which naturalistic representations degenerate into geometric patterns due to factors such as inexactitude in copying, "has played a large part in the history of art". However, so far as can be judged from the brief summary which has survived, the main point of the paper was that, in order to explain the many variations displayed by the process, one must invoke the interaction of cultures possessing different forms of artistic expression. In other words, degeneration, necessary as a prop to diffusionism in some instances, cannot replace diffusionism as a general explanatory mechanism.[55]

At subsequent sittings of the 1912 meeting of the British Association, and at the 1913, 1914 and 1915 meetings, Elliot Smith presented further papers relating to the diffusion hypothesis, and introduced discussions on megalithic monuments (1912), and the influence of ancient Egyptian civilization on the world's culture (1915).[56] His biographer Warren Dawson tells us that, at these meetings, Elliot Smith "provoked the attacks of orthodox anthropology" and "always looked back with intense delight and amusement upon the (sometimes very heated) discussions that arose out of his remarks".[57]

We have no record of the role played by Rivers in these debates, but we do know that, at all the meetings concerned, Rivers read papers which lent support to the diffusionist position.[58] Moreover, Rivers is known to have shared Elliot Smith's conviction of the special importance of megaliths for the diffusionist position. An unpublished typescript from Rivers's papers which is corrected in his handwriting states that "it is around these monuments that there will be fought the first decisive battle between those who advocate the independent origins of human culture and those who believe in the vast part which has been taken in the history of this culture by the wanderings of peoples".[59] Finally, Elliot Smith was later to acknowledge that Rivers played a very important role in obtaining a hearing for his ethnological "heresies".[60]

It was during the meeting of the British Association in Australia in 1914, that Elliot Smith made the discovery which has subsequently been described as the "cornerstone" of his diffusionistic edifice.[61] While visiting the museum of his old medical school at the University of Sydney, Elliot Smith noticed that two of the exhibits were mummies from the Torres Straits, and took the opportunity of examining one of them. A detailed account of what followed has been provided by the zoologist D. M. S. Watson, who was present at the moment of revelation:

As neither the Museum Director nor I had much knowledge of how they were made, Elliot Smith told us that the methods were entirely unlike those known in Egypt: and that, if I remember rightly, the Torres Straits mummies were smoke-dried, whilst the essential process in Egyptian mummification was a long steeping of the body in a solution of natron, a naturally-occurring sodium carbonate.

The mummy we examined was the body of an adult man, shrunken but well preserved, lashed down at full length to a ladder-like framework of poles.

As soon as we took it out of the museum case, Elliot Smith pointed out to us that all the finger- and toe-nails were carefully tied on with a binding of thread, and with obvious excitement told us that this was a custom found in Egyptian mummies of a definite date, and that it there had the definite function of keeping the nails attached during the long soaking. He said immediately that he could not imagine that this would be necessary in the case of the Torres Straits mummies, the process there being such that it was unlikely to result in the loss of the nails.

He then, very characteristically, told us that in Egyptian mummies of the period to which he had referred it was the custom to remove the brain and viscera, the latter usually through a slit cut in the left flank. An immediate examination showed that both operations had been performed on the Torres Straits mummy. There was a hole in the occiput through which the brain had been removed, and a slit cut through the body-wall of the flank.

Elliot Smith pointed out that these removals (i.e. the brain and the viscera) would have facilitated the preservation of the body of the Torres Straits man as they did those of the Egyptians, but he called attention to the curious fact that the abdominal viscera had been removed through an artificial incision in the perineum, a difficult operation, and not as might have been expected by a large incision in the mid-line (of the ventral surface of the body).

He then told us of later developments of mummification in Egypt, especially of the fact that in order to restore the semblance of life to the mummy it became the practice to stuff it superficially, often with mud introduced below the skin through a series of short slits cut in definite positions, for example on the shoulders and above the knees and in other places he described to us. The Torres Straits mummy proved to have cuts through the skin in all, or at any rate in a large number, of the places where the stuffing incisions had been made by the Egyptian mummifiers some twenty-five centuries before, but these slits in the Torres Straits mummy were functionless: no attempt whatever had been made to pad out the body. They were merely clean cuts through the skin of no functional significance.

The whole examination was most dramatic: the immediate discovery on the Torres Straits mummy of custom after custom of the Egyptian mummifiers, as they were described to us by Elliot Smith, made a vivid impression on my mind, and the whole picture remains in my memory.

It was, I think, at lunch after the morning's work, but perhaps later in the day, that Elliot Smith developed to me his interpretation of the facts we had seen. He pointed out that the preservation of a human body was so long, difficult and gruesome a process that no people would undertake it unless they were driven by precise and definite religious beliefs which made it necessary to preserve a man's body in the form it had in life in order that his soul should have a habitation. Furthermore, the idea that it was possible to preserve a body permanently could only have arisen from the observation of the accidental preservation of bodies by desiccation through burial in hot dry sand; and that as a matter of historical record the earliest known mummies are Egyptian; that in Egypt predynastic men, buried in shallow graves in the sand, without coffins, were in fact well preserved; and that the basis of Egyptian religion lies in the power of the soul to reinhabit its body and to survive only as long as it can do so. As none of the conditions which led to the discovery of mummification by the Egyptians exists in Torres Straits, it is evident that the art of mummification could not have arisen there but must have been introduced either by a migration of the actual people who inhabit that region or by some spread of culture.[62]

It has not been recorded whether Rivers was a witness to these events, but undoubtedly his interest would have been immediately aroused by the knowledge that the mummies came from the Torres Straits, and it is certain that he was deeply impressed on learning of Elliot Smith's interpretation. In fact, Haddon was later to date Rivers's enthusiastic support of the diffusion doctrine from the time of his acceptance of the main principles enunciated in *The Migrations of Early Culture*,[63] the 1915 book in which Elliot Smith expounds the implications of his examination of the Torres Straits mummy. Certainly in his review of this book, and elsewhere, Rivers discusses Elliot Smith's investigations of the mummy in such a way as to indicate that he regarded them as furnishing crucial evidence for the diffusionist hypothesis.[64] In a note to Rivers, dated 25th October 1915, Perry writes: "I have heard about your Torres Mummies. E. S. is in great fettle about it . . . Isn't it splendid? . . . Things are going magnificently . . ."[65]

Elliot Smith himself nominates the date at which Rivers "went the whole way with me in recognizing the initiative of Egypt in the creation of civilization" as 1918, the year in which Rivers learned from his missionary friend, the Rev. C. E. Fox, of the resemblance between the mortuary customs of modern San Cristoval, an island in the Solomon group, and those of ancient Egypt.[66] In August 1918, Rivers received from Fox a letter containing "the first account of the burial customs of the chiefly clan and their worship of the sun and the serpent". Following this, Elliot Smith tells us, Rivers "gave up his hospital work and asked me to go to the Lake District with him to devote a week to the undisturbed discussion of the new evidence".[67]

No doubt Rivers's championing of the diffusionist cause occasioned a certain amount of annoyance to people who regarded Elliot Smith as a controversial personality, with even more controversial views on anthropology. Presumably the Tyloreans, whose fundamentally evolutionary view of anthropology was being attacked, would have been the group primarily offended, and it may at first have seemed as if Elliot Smith was acting as the spokesman for the new, empirically-oriented school of Cambridge anthropology, in opposition to the views of the older "armchair anthropologists" of Oxford. But, by the time of the 1914 meeting of the British Association in Australia, there were some hints of dissension within the Cambridge school itself. Haddon, who was far from averse to the diffusionistic approach when it was employed in a careful and limited fashion, had apparently come to view Rivers's conjectures about widespread cultural diffusion and his particular preoccupation with megaliths with some degree of disfavour.[68] In fact, the travel arrangements for the voyage to Australia might just have been related to the potential split between Haddon and Rivers. Haddon and his daughter Kathleen took a boat which went through the Suez Canal, while Rivers made the longer trip around the Cape of Good Hope. It is probably a coincidence, but the even more diffusionistically-oriented Graebner was also on the latter boat. So too was John Layard, a young Cambridge graduate whose fate was to be tragically entwined with Rivers's subsequent career.[69]

The general tone of Elliot Smith's attitude to his opponents may be recaptured by the following extract from a note he wrote to Haddon in March 1915, presumably in reference to a review Haddon was writing of *The Migrations of Early Culture*:

I have an overwhelming mass of data relating to the mummy-megalithic problem, the meaning and significance of which is as clear as daylight. The difficulty is to squeeze it all into a reasonable compass. Perhaps in the end I shall drop a 15 inch shell into the camp of the "proper" people and use the rest of my ammunition to pick off any heads that expose themselves after the explosion.[70]

While the militaristic idiom is appropriate to 1915, the sentiments expressed are, to put it mildly, contrary to the normal canons of polite scientific discourse.

In general, the character of the intellectual relationship between Rivers and Elliot Smith seems to have been such that the latter influenced the former much more strongly than the other way around. Certainly Rivers first arrived at his diffusionistic outlook without Elliot Smith's assistance. Certainly Elliot Smith does acknowledge that, in 1911, Rivers helped to convince him that the transmission of culture took place, not merely through the spread of ideas, but also via actual racial migrations.[71] And certainly it was mainly through Rivers's influence that Elliot Smith first developed an interest in psychology during the Great War.[72] However, the fundamental initiative for the more conjectural aspects of the Rivers-Elliot Smith collaboration seems to have emanated from Elliot Smith. In a rough draft of a review of A. A. Goldenweiser's 1922 textbook *Early Civilization*, Haddon wrote, "It is incorrect to describe Elliot Smith as a 'follower' of Rivers; if anything, the reverse is nearer the mark."[73]

We have then some awkward facts to explain. Why did Rivers, who by 1910 had established himself as one of the world's most eminent anthropologists, the proponent of an ethnological method whose implications were only beginning to be explored, abruptly switch his theoretical focus and proceed to yoke himself to a bombastic controversialist whose views, while respected in the field of cerebral anatomy, were regarded with mounting distaste by a considerable segment of the anthropological community? [74]

Even more paradoxically, how did it come about that, towards the end of his life, Rivers was not only prepared to accept Elliot Smith's most outlandish postulate — that the direct influence of ancient Egypt had permeated to the farthest reaches of the South Pacific — but, if Elliot Smith is to be believed, actually regarded C. E. Fox's *Threshold of the Pacific*, which allegedly substantiates this postulate, as "one of the most important, if not *the* most important, pieces of fieldwork that has ever been done in social anthropology", and counted as his "chief anxiety" the thought that his own ill-health might prevent him from arranging for Fox's book to be published? [75]

(b) *Personal Predilections*

As a preliminary observation, one should note that both Elliot Smith and Rivers were members of St John's College Cambridge, a fact which, from Rivers's point of view at any rate, was far from inconsequential. Rivers in fact dedicated his *magnum opus*, *The History of Melanesian Society*, "to the society of St John's College, Cambridge, to whose fellowship this book is largely due".

Secondly, it should be remarked that both Rivers and Elliot Smith seem to have held puritanical views with regard to sex. This comes out in both the ethnological and psychological work of the two men. In contrast to the nineteenth-century writers who seem to have obtained a kind of vicarious thrill by postulating a state of original sexual promiscuity, Rivers concluded from his analysis of Melanesian society that, in the earliest state of society he was able to infer, "there could have been no question of general promiscuity". [76] Similarly, Elliot Smith was of the opinion that

man is by nature a kindly and considerate creature, with an instinctive tendency to monogamy and the formation of a happy family group bound together by mutual affection and consideration. This is the basis of all social organization. The old theories of primitive promiscuity and lack of all sexual restraint are now shown to be devoid of any foundation and to be the very reverse of the truth. [77]

In the field of psychology, both men felt that Freud had placed far too much emphasis on the role of the sex instinct, Elliot Smith objecting vigorously to what he termed "the new Science of Sexology". [78] As a substitute for the sexually-oriented libido, Rivers put forward the instinct for self-preservation as the fundamental psychological drive,[79] a move which calls to mind Elliot Smith's hypothesis that the desire to find an elixir of life constitutes "one of the basic psychological principles upon which civilization is founded".[80] In this connection, one may also take note of Rivers's postulate that the primary cause of the then rapid depopulation of Melanesia was the loss of *joie de vivre* among its people.[81]

Thirdly, by the time of their ethnological collaboration, both Rivers and Elliot Smith were firmly convinced that the quantitative collection and analysis of human parameters was not a sufficient scientific end in itself. To be sure, Rivers had initially presented the genealogical method as a tool for collecting "social and vital statistics", but the general trend of his attitude towards the use of mathematics in science is aptly summed up by C. S. Myer's observation that "Rivers's interests did not lie in the collection of masses of heterogeneous data, in obtaining blurred averages from vast numbers of individuals, in concocting mathematical devices, or in applying mathematical formulae to the numerical data thus accumulated."[82] Likewise Elliot Smith, who approached the study of man from anatomy and was thus initially interested in physical anthropology, had registered his antipathy towards investigations of "the bone-measuring variety",[83] and was to speak of rescuing physical anthropology from "the thraldom of the anthropometrists".[84]

Fourthly, both men saw the scientific study of man as a field of vast scope and importance, and sought to develop institutions to further this vision. Elliot Smith tells us that in 1916, when Rivers "had come to regard ethnology as his real *métier*", the latter became particularly concerned that the Royal Anthropological Institute "should be made as strong and influential as possible and its journals instruments of much wider ethnological propaganda than they were".[85] This account is not inconsistent with the knowledge that, by 1916, Elliot Smith himself had become convinced that the existing anthropological journals, whether published in Britain or overseas, were inadequate to the task of providing a forum in which heterodox views could be aired. Consequently, Elliot Smith considered founding a new journal but abandoned the project after Rivers advised against it, apparently on the grounds that such reform should come from within, rather than from outside the Institute.[86] However, toward the end of 1916, Rivers had evidently become skeptical as to whether it was feasible to strengthen the Institute so as to make it capable of performing a broader function. Specifically, Rivers had his doubts about the competence of the Institute's governing Council, since a large percentage of its members were totally unknown as anthropologists.[87]

(c) *Biographical Background II*

Between 1917 and 1919, Rivers and Elliot Smith had little to do with the
Institute, both being deeply involved with psychiatric work in military
hospitals. T. H. Pear, a psychologist who was a colleague of Elliot Smith and
Rivers, has recorded the manner in which the latter had taken up this work.
Elliot Smith sent an "imperative" telegram to Rivers at Cambridge, which
"ordered" him to come to the Maghull psychiatric hospital, near Liverpool.
To let Pear continue the story:

With what seemed to me a jack-in-the-box leap [Rivers] arrived with large suitcases,
prepared for a long stay. Perhaps this marked the beginning of a deliberate attempt to
change himself from introvert to extrovert: he told me that he had decided that his
cloistered life at Cambridge, interrupted by visits to simple people in the Pacific, as
unlike ordinary persons as many university dons are, must cease . . .

Almost before he had unpacked, Rivers paid me an honour which I shall never forget.
He said he would like to be regarded as a student who had been away from books for a
long time (the outbreak of war had found him for the second time visting Melanesia) and
wanted to catch up. Would I direct his reading for the next few weeks, and on afternoon
walks – Cambridge fashion – discuss it? His first desire was to grasp what Freud meant
by the Unconscious, which Rivers thought was the most important contribution to
psychology for a long time.[88]

The flavour and content of the Elliot Smith-Rivers collaborations at this time
may be gauged from the following description by Pear:

In the evenings, these two anthropologists would talk, like priests, of mysteries. Gradually I pieced together the jigsaw of their references; 'the mother's brother', stone seats,
megaliths, rags hung on trees, dragons, cranial deformation, circumcision, mummification
and other heterogeneous items in the 'bag of tricks'. They made world-maps showing the
routes of the voyagers and the location of their alleged attractions; gold, pearls and
purple. One day I handed Elliot Smith the Christmas Number of the *Illustrated London
News*, remarking that its maps showing the routes taken by the Queen's presents of
chocolate to the troops in the Dominions and Colonies suggested an identity with the
'bag of tricks' maps. Elliot Smith twinkled [sic] as he said, 'All out for loot!'[89]

During this period, Elliot Smith transferred the bulk of his ethnological
activities to Manchester, where he played a vigorous role in the activities of
the John Rylands Library, the Manchester Literary and Philosophical Society
and the Manchester Egyptian and Oriental Society.[90] Aided by a widespread
Mancunian enthusiasm for things Egyptian, Elliot Smith, Perry, Rivers and
others who sympathized with the extreme diffusionist position, such as Dr
J. Wilfrid Jackson and A. Mingana, all made contributions to the journals

associated with these institutions. The University of Manchester, where Elliot
Smith had held the Chair of Anatomy since 1909, inaugurated a series of
ethnological works by the publication of his *Migrations of Early Culture*,
subsequent titles in the series being authored by Jackson, Perry and W. R.
Dawson, who was later to write a sympathetic biographical account of Elliot
Smith.

In 1919, Elliot Smith's connections with Manchester were severed when,
attracted by the prospect of creating a huge interdisciplinary medical school,
he accepted the Chair of Anatomy at University College London. With the aid
of generous benefactions from the Rockefeller Foundation, Elliot Smith set
about creating an Institute of Anatomy in which many aspects of the study
of man were blended. Apart from pursuing traditional areas of medicine such
as comparative anatomy, neurology, embryology and cytology, the new
Institute also became involved with radiography, forensic medicine and the
statistical analysis of health, diet and disease. Even more surprising was the
appointment of Dr Charles Singer to a position in the history of medicine.
But the most controversial innovation of all was Elliot Smith's establishment
of a Readership in Cultural Anthropology, tenable in the Department of
Anatomy. H. A. Harris, one of Elliot Smith's proteges in anatomy at University
College, tells us that there is little doubt that Elliot Smith intended to import
Rivers to fill this position. However, Rivers was apparently unwilling to leave
Cambridge, and the post was offered to Perry, who eventually took up the
appointment in 1923.[91]

Elliot Smith's reorganization of anatomy at University College must be
seen on one level as an attempt to reinstate anatomy to a place of importance
in British medicine. During the last decade of the nineteenth-century and the
first two decades of the twentieth, anatomy in England had been eclipsed by
the rapid expansion of physiology and the younger allied discipline biochemistry. Academic positions for young anatomists were almost impossible to
find, and where there was a Professor of Anatomy, he frequently found himself relegated to performing bureaucratic tasks within the medical school.[92]
In this context, Harris describes Elliot Smith as "the man who survived and
dispelled the period of anatomical nihilism".[93] Be this as it may, the description which Harris gives of a typical day at the Department of Anatomy hardly
bespeaks a high-powered research institution:

Imagine the callers at Gower Street. At one moment Sir Henry Wellcome wanted Elliot
Smith to unwrap a mummy which he had purchased in Egypt, or a Salvation Army
Officer from the West Coast of Africa asked why albinos and twins were drowned at

birth by the eugenically minded natives. At another moment a zealous missionary sought information on polygamy, or a goldminer demanded data on the association of pearls and cowrie shells. Resident magistrates and anthropologists from all parts of the Empire came in and stayed for months on study leave. Parcels of real and fictitious human remains, fossils, mummies and primitive tools were always arriving — with many a fantastic story. It was a never-ending procession of sleuths from Scotland Yard, phrenologists, Seventh Day Adventists, wealthy Americans and poor creatures who wished to leave their bodies to the Anatomical Institute for dissection on condition that Elliot Smith would "experiment on their brains". What a bedlam it was at times.[94]

A knowledge of Elliot Smith's activities at University College helps one to understand what he had in mind for the Royal Anthropological Institute. Both reorganizations, one actual and one merely projected, may be seen as aspects of the same desire — to create and institutionalize a field which he later came to call "Human Biology". That is, to pursue an integrated study of *homo sapiens*, his cultural as well as his biological attributes, his history, behaviour and beliefs.[95]

In 1921, while Elliot Smith was engaged in revamping anatomy at University College, Rivers was elected President of the Royal Anthropological Institute for the period 1921–1922, an event which evidently revived their plans for making the Institute an instrument of "ethnological propaganda" and the springboard for a comprehensive approach to anthropology. Rivers's Presidential Address, entitled "The Unity of Anthropology", emphasizes the inter-relatedness of ethnology and various other disciplines which attempt to study man in a scientific fashion, and discusses ways in which the Institute could help to bring about "a closer collaboration between the different branches of anthropology".[96] During the period of Rivers's Presidency, Elliot Smith assumed quite a prominent role, both in presenting papers to the Institute and in the discussion of other people's papers. Moreover the minutes of the meetings often mention Rivers and Elliot Smith as taking part in the same discussions.[97]

(d) *Shared Personal Tendencies*

While not wishing to minimize the importance of the aforementioned biographical factors in the growth of the relationship between Rivers and Elliot Smith, it seems to me even more significant that the two men shared a number of the tendencies which I previously invoked to explain Rivers's conversion to diffusionism.

With regard to the first tendency, it must be said that Elliot Smith, like Rivers subsequent to his ethnological conversion, tended to identify diffusionism with down-to-earth empiricism, and the theory of independent origins with unwarranted *a priori* speculation. In a review of Spencer and Gillen's *The Arunta*, Elliot Smith says that Spencer, who had reprinted the book after Gillen's death, has not modified the original theoretical standpoint, being still firmly opposed to admitting any external influences in Australia. However, this matters little, since the book has virtues independent of such "transcendental speculations in interpretation".[98] The basis of Elliot Smith's stance against such "transcendental speculations" seems to have been a verbal adherence to a scientific uniformitarianism. During September 1926, Elliot Smith wrote in a letter which represented part of a controversy with Sir Richard Temple over an alleged connection between Bhutan and Egypt:

> The chief value of this correspondence is that it reveals to the public the peculiar qualities of the opposition to the theory of cultural diffusion. The essence of our claim is that in ancient times knowledge was spread abroad in the same way that we know it to be happening today, which is revealed also in the written records of the past. We are trying to persuade the present generation of ethnologists to abandon the Cartesian Scholasticism into which it has recently lapsed and return to the common sense enunciated by Turgot in his famous discourse at the Sorbonne in 1750:
>> "All epochs are fastened together by a chain of causes and effects, linking the condition of the world to all the conditions that have gone before it".[99]

With regard to the second and third tendencies, one should note that, especially after his work with Rivers in psychiatric wards, Elliot Smith was sensitive to the importance of unconscious factors in human life. In his Introduction to Rivers's posthumously published book *Psychology and Ethnology*, Elliot Smith states that many lines of investigation point to the conclusion that "symbolism . . . is a process of vast importance in the history of human thought", being of special consequence in collective behaviour.

The final tendency, a genuine empathy for the subjects of one's ethnological investigations, is considerably more difficult to substantiate for Elliot Smith than for Rivers. For one thing, Elliot Smith, unlike Rivers, never did any real ethnological fieldwork. For another, he once stated that the most noteworthy advances in the civilization of ancient Egypt were made on the initiative of a ruling aristocracy, whose racial makeup contained relatively little Egyptian blood, while characterizing "real" Egyptians, that is, indigenes of peasant stock, as "simple-minded, unprogressive and extremely conservative".[100] However, while it is probably legitimate to interpret the first part of this statement as bespeaking an elitist attitude, the same is not necessarily true for the remainder of the assertion. In fact, Rivers himself, having acquired a genuine empathy for preliterate men, would still have regarded them as both "simple-minded", at least in the sense that Rivers believed them to use concrete rather than abstract modes of thought, and as "unprogressive and extremely conservative", especially in regard to such culturally-important matters as social organization and religion. With regard to the first part of Elliot Smith's statement, one should note that it was made in 1910, before the beginning of his intense friendship with Rivers. As the twentieth-century rolled on, Elliot Smith would seem to have acquired a less censorious attitude towards non-Europeans and the common man, thereby exhibiting a change of political heart similar to the one experienced by his friend. The main point of the Galton Lecture, which Elliot Smith delivered to the Eugenics Education Society in February 1924, is to emphasize the dominance of nurture over nature,[101] and ten years later he was appointed chairman of a committee whose purpose it was to investigate the fallacious use of the term "Aryan", with its implied associations of cultural accomplishments and inherent mental abilities.[102]

Thus, it can be seen that Rivers's progressive endorsement of the extreme version of diffusionism, and the growth of his intellectual rapport with its main practitioner, are explicable partly in terms of the fact that Elliot Smith shared a number of the tendencies which were instrumental in bringing about Rivers's conversion to a diffusionist outlook.

(e) Intellectual Correspondences

The other major consideration in the development of the Rivers—Elliot Smith collaboration was the way in which Elliot Smith's interpretation of the anatomy of the human brain dovetailed with Rivers's dichotomy between protopathic and epicritic. In fact, the former's scientific world-view can be regarded as a kind of neurological counterpart of this dichotomy. Since this is not the occasion for a detailed exposition of Elliot Smith's views on neurology, I shall content myself with a sketch containing just enough detail to bring out the affinities between the theoretical ideas of the two men.

In 1901, Elliot Smith coined the term "neopallium"[103] to delineate the part of the brain which has made possible the evolutionary triumphs and complex ethology of the mammals, and which finds its highest development in the human brain. The fundamental goal of most of his subsequent work, including his anatomical investigations into cerebral localization and the structure of the brain, his somatological investigations of fossil crania and his psychological investigations into shell-shock, has been characterized as the attainment of a "fuller understanding and interpretation of man's most distinctive attribute, his enormous neopallium".[104]

Elliot Smith believed that, in the evolutionary precursors of mammals, the brain had originally grown up around the terminations of the olfactory nerve, and the animal's behaviour would, therefore, have been determined, to a very large extent, by the impressions of smell. With the emergence of true mammals and the appearance of the neopallium, this dependence upon olfactory impressions was, at first, retained — being especially suited to a small land-grubbing animal in the search of nourishment and as a means of recognizing friends or enemies. Thus, the animal's mental life was governed by a "smell-brain", so that every object in the external world was judged primarily by its odour, the other senses playing only a subsidiary role.[105]

With the adoption by some mammals of an arboreal way of life, however, shortly before the dawn of the Tertiary period, the situation changed dramatically. The abandonment of terra firma lessened the utility of the organs of smell, and the requirements of life among the branches placed a premium on the development of touch, hearing and especially vision. Furthermore, survival in this new mode of life demanded agility, quick reflexes and precision of movement, the coordination of which was effected by an expansion of that part of the cortex which deals with motor control. Hence, "In the struggle for existence, . . . all arboreal mammals, such as Tree Shews, suffer a marked dimunition of their olfactory apparatus, and develop a considerable neopallium, in which relatively large areas are given up to visual, tactile, acoustic, kinaesthetic and motor functions".[106]

Near the end of the Cretaceous period, a further momentous evolutionary development occurred, marking the birth of the primates and the sprouting from the main mammalian trunk of the branch which was to culminate in *homo sapiens*. This development was associated with an enormous expansion and specialization of the visual cortex within the neopallium, so that "in the primitive Primate, vision entirely usurped the controlling place occupied by smell". The importance of this eventuality is not, however, exhausted by the observation that one sense had been substituted for another. Elliot Smith sees the growth of the visual cortex as being accompanied by an immense broadening of the sensory avenues by which the external world can affect the animal's thought processes. Instead of having their behavioural patterns dominated by olfactory sense-data, the early primates found themselves capable of correlating their ocular impressions with those of the other senses, as befits an animal which is required to perform visually guided activities of great agility.[107]

As Elliot Smith was to postulate in 1930, accompanying this change in the operation of the neopallium were interesting changes in cerebral anatomy. In non-arboreal mammals, an organ known as the lateral geniculate body receives a large proportion of the fibres which convey visual impulses from the eyes to the brain. However, only some of these impulses are transmitted from the lateral geniculate body to the neopallium. The rest are passed on to a lower centre in the hierarchy of neurological control, the mid-brain, from whence they proceed to the motor nuclei in the brain and spinal cord. In men and monkeys, however, almost all the visual fibres which enter the lateral geniculate body are routed directly into the neopallium, the only fibres not so routed being those responsible for the automatic and unconscious ocular reflexes which are so much more obtrusive in the majority of the lower animals. "This almost exclusively cortical connection of the pathway leading from the eyes", says Elliot Smith, "is a token of the fact that in man vision is brought into the full light of consciousness . . . Vision is the foundation of our intelligence and the chief source of our knowledge."[108]

In order to bring out the relevance of this theory to Rivers's scientific world-view, I should mention that Elliot Smith believed the thalamus (of which the lateral geniculate body is part) to possess the ability of conferring upon all non-olfactory sensory impulses "an affective quality which gives them a meaning and an influence in modifying behaviour".[109] In other words, the emotional content of experience, which determines whether one regards an impression as pleasant or unpleasant, and thereby influences one's subsequent behaviour, has its origin in the thalamus. The neopallium on the other hand, the organ of intelligence, permits "a fuller, more nicely discriminative appreciation of the environment".[110] The affective and cognitive aspects of the mind should not be regarded as essentially disparate, however. In fact, one of the features of the mind which most excited Elliot Smith's admiration, was its ability to integrate these aspects into a coherent and unified experience.[111]

As Rivers himself was to point out, citing some experimental work by Head and Gordon Holmes, the relation between the cerebral cortex (i.e., neopallium) and thalamus is very similar to that existing between protopathic and epicritic sensibility. Rivers assumes, like Elliot Smith, that the thalamus and cerebral cortex belong to widely-separated stages in the evolution of the nervous system, the former representing the dominant part of the brain of lower vertebrates, the latter developing far later. "When by injury, disease or operative procedure", says Rivers, "the cortex cerebri has been put out of action, stimulation of the skin produces sensations characterized by a peculiar quality such as would be produced by over-weight of the affective aspect of sensation, very similar to that shown by protopathic sensibility. Moreover, there is an absence of objective character very similar to that of this form of sensibility. When the cortex is in action, the affective over-response of the thalamus is largely suppressed under ordinary conditions, but the process of suppression does not come out so strongly, as in the case of the peripheral nervous system, because some of the primitive features which most need suppression have already suffered this fate. Thus, removal of cortical activity does not produce radiation and reference of localization because the suppression of these characters is still being maintained at the periphery".[112] Hence, as Rivers himself was aware, the work of Head and Holmes, which can be regarded as an attempt to test whether the anatomical theory of Elliot Smith is consonant with the Rivers—Head theory of the afferent nervous system, does indeed demonstrate that the former theory dovetails very neatly with the latter.

Finally, one should note that Elliot Smith's theory, which postulates a very important role for vision in the evolutionary drama which culminated in the human mind, could be expected to appeal to a man who believed that the thought patterns of "primitives" proceed by means of visual imagery. The fact that Elliot Smith, like Rivers's other close friend and collaborator Head, had an extraordinary visual memory,[113] and that Rivers himself did not, might not be entirely inconsequential from this point of view.

*   *   *   *   *

Summing up my account of the development of the Rivers—Elliot Smith collaboration, I would say that its apparently paradoxical aspects are explicable only in terms of a whole constellation of shared personal and intellectual predispositions, predispositions which were brought into conjunction at a period in both men's lives when mutual reinforcement was the end result.

THE RIVERS—PERRY COLLABORATION

(a) *Biographical Background*

The relationship between Rivers and W. J. Perry began after Perry, having come to Cambridge with the primary intention of studying mathematics, attended lectures by Rivers and Haddon and developed a compulsive interest in anthropology.[114] The earliest mention I have found of Perry in any of Rivers's correspondence occurs in a letter dated June 1910, when Rivers wrote to the Secretary of the Royal Anthropological Institute and informed him that he had asked "a man named Perry" to make inquiries about joining the Institute. Rivers then went on to state that he would be very glad to propose Perry for membership.[115] In *The History of Melanesian Society*, written between 1909 and 1914, Rivers includes Perry among the people thanked in the preface, acknowledging his gratitude for assistance in reading the proofs of the book, for "many valuable suggestions" and "for help in other ways".

The article which, to my knowledge, represents Perry's first published contribution to anthropology, appears in the 1914 volume of *Anthropos* and consists of an analysis of the genealogical tables collected by Richard Thurnwald in Buin.[116] After paying tribute to the importance of the genealogical method for anthropology, Perry discusses the shortcomings of Thurnwald's account and points out that most, if not all, of them could have been avoided if Thurnwald had followed Rivers's method more closely. Perry then mentions several kinds of anomalous marriage, including marriage with the cross-cousin, whose practice at Buin had been inferred by Rivers in *The History of Melanesian Society*. From an analysis of Thurnwald's data, Perry concludes that there is ample evidence for cross-cousin marriage at Buin, and that Rivers's theory of the origin of the practice (see Chapter III) is confirmed. Hence, Perry initially appears on the anthropological horizon as a disciple of Rivers, who lends support to Rivers's theory of anomalous marriage by employing the genealogical method.

By the time of the 1915 British Association meeting in Manchester, the Rivers—Perry and Rivers—Elliot Smith collaborations had consolidated into a *troika*, and it was at this meeting that Perry read his first paper in support of the diffusionist position.[117] One of the major difficulties confronting Rivers and Elliot Smith at this time was to find a convincing motive to explain the postulated migrations of culture. Earlier in 1915, Elliot Smith had sent Perry a map depicting the world-wide distribution of areas in which the presence of megalithic monuments had been demonstrated or inferred. At about the same time, he had informed Perry that a Mrs Zelia Nuttall had attributed the founders of the ancient American civilization with a special appreciation of pearls and precious metals. To let Rivers continue the story:

A chance examination of an economic atlas enabled Perry to combine these two items of information, for he saw that the distribution of pearl shell in the Pacific Ocean agreed so nearly with Elliot Smith's megalithic areas that the presence of pearls would provide a sufficient motive for the settlements in these regions. Further examination showed that, in inland areas, the chief motive for the megalithic settlements was supplied by the presence of gold and other forms of wealth.[118]

Hence, in his 1915 paper to the British Association, Perry put forward the hypothesis that the carriers of the megalithic culture were motivated by the desire for certain precious materials, of which gold and pearls were the most important.[119] In this way, Perry plugged what Rivers regarded as the largest lacuna in the diffusionist theory.

A further contribution by Perry, to which Rivers pays tribute,[120] was the removal of a stumbling block to the postulate that the megalithic civilization had permeated to the south Pacific. In proceeding from India to Oceania, the mariners who were reputed to have carried this civilization would have passed through the Indonesian archipelago. However, evidence of megaliths in this region was generally believed to be non-existent. On Rivers's suggestion,[121] Perry began to search Indonesian ethnographic records for other, less direct evidence of the passage of the megalithic culture-complex. The upshot of these investigations was Perry's 1918 work on *The Megalithic Culture of Indonesia*, dedicated to Rivers as "a token of affection and regard". In this book, Perry reported that, for certain islands of the archipelago, stone dolmens were indeed present, although their distribution was too limited for them to serve as confirmation of the diffusion hypothesis. On the other hand, he argued, the distribution of less ambitious types of stonework is correlated throughout Indonesia with a number of elements of culture which are linked elsewhere to the practice of erecting dolmens. Hence, he concluded that, in passing through Indonesia, the megalith-building aspect of the civilization had, for reasons special to the area, expended itself in stonework of considerably more modest proportions than in its original home, or in the islands farther to the east.

It would seem that, especially in the early days of their association, Rivers was the teacher and Perry the pupil in matters anthropological, the asymmetry of the relationship being mirrored by Perry's practice of addressing Rivers in letters as "Dear Uncle". In fact, in the preface to his huge work *The Children of the Sun*, published in 1923, Perry says of Rivers:

To him I owe everything as an anthropologist; and for ten years I had the benefit of his unceasing advice and sympathy, as well as, what is equally important, of his unsparing and unerring criticism. Those who have come under the kindly lash of his tongue will know what I mean.

But if Rivers was sometimes critical of Perry's ideas, and if in many respects the latter's work should be regarded as an appendage to that of the former, there is also evidence that the tail sometimes wagged the dog. In particular, it would seem that the end result of Perry putting forward a highly speculative conjecture was not always a decisive crushing of that conjecture by Rivers. On the contrary, Rivers sometimes seems to have been persuaded to swallow such conjectures himself, or to have come around to accepting them in a truncated form. According to Elliot Smith, Rivers remarked to him in 1915 that "Perry will make the broad generalizations and the big advance; my function is to move forward step by step and to consolidate the gains".[122] Although this may sound like undue modesty on the part of Rivers, it is supported by a letter which Perry wrote to him in May 1922. Having informed Rivers of his views on the nature of human thought during and following the inception of Egyptian civilization, views which were soon to be expounded in *The Children of the Sun*, Perry writes, "I think you will like it all right when you have got over the first shock of it".[123] Whether or not Rivers actually did like it we shall never know, as he died a week after receiving the letter. We do know, however, that Rivers had been intending to devote part of the summer vacation of 1922 to reading the manuscript of *The Children of the Sun*, and that he had hoped to clear away the discrepancies between his and Perry's interpretations of the evidence relating to social organization.[124]

The growth of the relationship between Rivers and Perry was, in its own way, even more remarkable than the Rivers–Elliot Smith *entente*, since Perry's views on ethnology were at least as outlandish as Elliot Smith's and, unlike the latter, Perry did not come to ethnology from a field of scientific endeavour to which he had already made significant and widely-acknowledged contributions. One way in which Perry indebted himself to Rivers was by doing translations from Dutch.[125] While Perry was at Cambridge, Rivers had persuaded him to learn the language so that the missionary journals of the Dutch East Indies could be used to test the hypothesis that the Indonesian archipelago had served as a route for cultural migrations.[126]

(b) *Intellectual Correspondences*

Whatever the value of Perry to Rivers as a translator, the most important intellectual bond between the two men was on the level of scientific theory.

While Elliot Smith's account of the structure and functions of the human brain can, as I have argued in this chapter, be interpreted as a kind of neurological analogue to the Rivers—Head theory of protopathic and epicritic sensibility, Perry's views on the development of human thought processes suggest a slightly warped ethnological counterpart to the same theory. Perry argues that the ancient Egyptians "derived their ideas in the first instance directly from facts of concrete experience and that these ideas had, in their inception, no element of speculation or of symbolism". The so-called "gods" of the earliest period of Egyptian civilization, for example, were actually men and the deeds for which they were reputed to be responsible, such as ensuring the fertility of the land, were not at first regarded as supernaturally achieved.[127]

Similarly, Perry believes the origin myths of Egypt to have been ultimately based on concrete human experience. The idea of a primordial ocean, from whence the land eventually emerged, was almost certainly founded on the Egyptian experience of the annual flooding of the Nile. When the archaic civilization diffused across the globe, however, its elements became detached from the experience through which they were originally derived and thus took on, to use Perry's phrase, "the appearance of speculation".[128] The notion of a primordial ocean, for example, was borrowed by the Indians of the eastern states of North America, who believed that their mythical ancestors dredged the earth up from the depths of pre-existent waters. Thus, while the Egyptian stories of creation are closely tied to their experiential sources, those of the tribes of North Eastern America appear fanciful and highly speculative, as one might expect on the assumption that they have been adapted by people who were ignorant of their empirical origins.[129]

Perry's attitude to the subsequent history of thought in ancient Egypt seems rather ambiguous. On the one hand, he says that "later developments in Egypt were parallel to those of the communities supposed to have derived their culture from Egypt",[130] and implies that, especially in the area of religion, thought became detached from its empirical basis and deteriorated into unwarranted speculation. On the other hand, he does quote a passage from Elliot Smith which assumes that the ancient Egyptians attributed symbolic content to water in order to interpret empirical knowledge acquired in the cultivation of cereals, and that this attribution may be regarded as an early instance of scientific theorization.[131] Moreover, Perry states that the creation myths of Sumer and Egypt, after originating in concrete experience, "have grown up by an orderly process of accretion of one idea to another, so that ultimately organized systems of thought have emerged". This state of affairs is to be contrasted with that of derivative cultures, which "invariably express their origins in terms of systems of ideas similar to those ultimately elaborated in the Ancient East", but in which these systems of ideas "are often . . . divorced from any facts of actual experience, and are not evidently part of an organized system of thought".[132]

The ambiguity of Perry's account of the development of Egyptian thought is marked by a related ambiguity in his use of the words "symbolic" and "speculative". At times he uses these words in a pejorative sense, as when he makes symbolic ideas mean simply ideas which are "detached from their original [empirical] context", and when he defines speculation as "reasoning on ideas the [empirical] origins of which are unknown".[133] At other times, however, especially when he couples these terms with the word "abstract", he means them to have laudatory connotations. Witness, for example, his account of how civilization progresses:

The growth of civilization is attained through the development of an organized system of thought, founded in the beginning on direct experience and consisting of empirical ideas concerning matters that interested early man. Once this process had begun, the original themes begin to influence one another, and to bring into existence fresh ideas, and thus ultimately to produce speculative and abstract thought.[134]

Such usages suggest that Perry believed that it is possible to develop a system of abstract thought which will complement rather than deny the concrete experience which preceded it.

The structural similarities between Perry's theory of the development of human thought and Rivers's scientific world-view are sufficiently striking to suggest that they constituted an important aspect of the intellectual relationship between the two men. As in the Rivers—Head theory of the afferent nervous system, Perry's theory rests on a dichotomy between two theoretical entities, one being concerned with mental processes arising from concrete experience of the real world, the other with mental processes which proceed by abstract means. When Perry is referring in laudatory terms to the branch of the dichotomy which deals with abstract thinking, there can be no doubt that the concept of order is involved, since "organized systems of thought" are the end result. Thus, like the protopathic-epicritic distinction, the division between concrete, empirical thought and abstract systems of thought relates to a contrast between cerebral processes which deal with raw, undifferentiated data, and ones which confer order and meaning upon such data. Moreover, although Perry is not particularly explicit on this point, it would seem that his organized conceptual systems are built up, not by rejecting or ignoring concrete empirical evidence, but by integrating it with abstract thought, an idea which fulfils an epistemological function similar to that performed by the notion of "fusion" in the Rivers–Head theory. Finally, one should note that, like the concept of the protopathic, Perry's notion of concrete thought seems to allocate a special place to visual imagery. At least Perry does quote James Henry Breasted to the effect that the earliest Egyptians "always thought in concrete terms and *in graphic forms*" [135] (my italics).

With regard to Perry's pejorative use of the word "speculative" in connection with the abstract branch of the dichotomy, two points are in order. Firstly this usage makes the dichotomy sound very like the distinction between unwarranted *a priori* speculation and careful empirical analysis which runs through Rivers's 1911 Presidential Address. Secondly, if I am correct in arguing that Perry's laudatory references to the abstract branch of the dichotomy imply a theory which is, in important respects, analogous to the protopathic-epicritic hypothesis, then the theory implied by the pejorative references may be likened to a version of this hypothesis, which would describe a pathological misfunctioning of the nervous system. People who are presented with a cultural heritage which had its origins in a firm basis of empirical fact, but who subsequently elaborate an unsystematic and unduly speculative conceptual superstructure, sound rather like a person in whom the epicritic functions of the nervous system have failed to fuse with the protopathic.

Thus it would seem that, as with Elliot Smith, the basis of Perry's intellectual relationship with Rivers was a structural parallelism between the scientific notions which both men found most exciting.

*   *   *   *   *

Before leaving the diffusionist trio of Rivers, Elliot Smith and Perry, I should like to mention two aspects of their collaboration which are problematical. The first is that, despite the endorsement by all three men of empiricism in anthropology, none made substantial contributions to anthropological fieldwork during the period of their collaboration. Rivers's most valuable field trips were to the Torres Straits and to the Todas, and those both occurred before his conversion to diffusionism. The most notable result of Rivers's 1914 expedition to Melanesia was his failure to grasp the kinship system of Ambrym, an island on which he never set foot. As I hope the preceding account has made clear, his great contribution to ethnographical method, the discovery of the efficacy of the collection and analysis of genealogies, was a product of his pre-diffusion days. Perry's only field trip, to the Pondo of South Africa, occurred in 1930,[136] some twenty years after he first took up the cudgels on behalf of diffusionism. Most striking of all, however, is Elliot Smith, who functioned as the chief spokesman for the British diffusionists without ever doing any anthropological fieldwork.

The second aspect is concerned with the fact that, despite the three men's repeated depictions of their ethnological work as "scientific", and their condemnation of unwarranted speculation in anthropology, they were themselves clearly guilty both of accepting assertions which were not amenable to scientific testing procedures, and of speculative flights of fancy. As one commentator has written in respect of the latter part of Rivers's career, "diffusionist speculation at last provided a key to his locked imagination, and he let himself go".[137] The reason that Rivers, while in fact accepting wildly implausible speculations as self-evident ethnological truths, never explicitly relinquished his attempt to create a true science of man, is contained in the following circumstance. His conversion to diffusionism and the subsequent deepening of his commitment to that creed, were less a matter of rational deliberation and free choice than of the interplay between the constants and the variables in his changing personality. The constant reiteration of his aim of giving anthropology scientific status was one of the constants, and its retention after his conversion may be interpreted as a signal of his unadmitted desire to keep the variables in check. These variables, as it has been a major task of this chapter to argue, included his more emphatic espousal of an empiricist ideology, his growing sensitivity to the importance of unconscious thought, his increasing empathy with indigenes, and his shift towards the political left.

On 4th June 1922, Rivers died unexpectedly following an operation to correct a twisted bowel, leaving as a legacy an ambiguous heritage for anthropology. On the one hand, there was "earlier Rivers", the Rivers of Chapter II: inventor, practitioner and publicist of the genealogical method, and reputedly skilful analyst of social organization. On the other hand, there was "later Rivers": the diffusionist Rivers of Chapters III and IV, who failed to unravel the mysteries of Ambrym social organization and lent his authority to implausible speculations about marriages between people several generations apart, and the penetration of the culture of ancient Egypt into the watery fastness of the south Pacific. The ensuing chapters will relate how, in the decade following his death, the ghost of Rivers, or rather, the twin apparitions of earlier and later Rivers, were to haunt the scientific study of man in England. These visitations took place on both the theoretical and institutional levels, and contained the key to the eventual rise to centrality of kinship studies in British anthropological theory.

CHAPTER V

THE DIFFUSION CONTROVERSY

On 15th June 1922, Elliot Smith wrote: "Rivers's death is a real catastrophe and compels me to make a new orientation in life, for it has upset so many plans that we were developing in common ... "[1] The passing of Rivers was indeed a watershed in the history of British anthropology, and we shall now consider its relation to a protracted and bitter debate between the supporters of extreme diffusionism and the opponents of that creed.

THE BROKEN REED

As I have pointed out in Chapter IV, the plans which Elliot Smith and Rivers had been developing in common, had included a scheme to re-organize the Royal Anthropological Institute. Following Rivers's demise, Elliot Smith abruptly abandoned this scheme, resigned his membership of the Institute[2] and ceased his active participation in its meetings. In sharp contrast to the period of Rivers's Presidency, Elliot Smith did not, from July 1922 until May 1927, present any papers to the Institute or participate in discussions of other people's papers.[3]

Having been informed that the Institute had been requested by the British Association to act as a central clearing house for the control and co-ordination of anthropological research and training in the British Empire, Elliot Smith registered his opposition to the idea, invoking the ghost of Rivers as the main authority for his arguments.[4] The provision of adequate teaching and research facilities in anthropology had indeed been a major concern of Rivers during the last decade of his life, says Elliot Smith. Rivers would have wanted to see the Institute tackling projects such as the correlation of anthropological teaching with history and psychology, and the publication of fieldwork like that of his missionary friend C. E. Fox. However, continues Elliot Smith, the Institute was not contemplating these projects, and its suitability for a wider role in anthropological research and teaching was very much in doubt. Ever since 1911, Rivers had repeatedly discussed the shortcomings of the Institute with Elliot Smith. As the latter relates:

The chief difficulty that troubled him was the inadequacy of the *Journal* and *Man* to provide a medium for publishing serious anthropological work of all kinds and especially for the publication of correspondence and of the freest possible discussion of conflicting views. So strongly did he feel the restraint which was imposed upon anthropology by the R.A.I.'s journals – the publication of so much rubbish, the refusal of important scientific work, and the elimination of frank and free discussion – that in 1914 he had made arrangements to start a new journal which it was his intention to call *The British Journal of Ethnology*. He went on with the preparations for this experiment in 1915 and 1916; and it was only the war-conditions in November 1916 that decided him to postpone the venture till after the war. The knowledge that he was to be made President determined him to wait and see whether he could do anything to remedy the state of affairs in the R.A.I.[5]

According to Elliot Smith, Rivers had been "intensely anxious" to increase the size and extend the influence of the Institute, but was continually thwarted in these aims by the group which Elliot Smith characterizes as "the British Museum party". Implying that this group was attempting to suppress the diffusionistic point of view, Elliot Smith states that "The reactionary and paralyzing influence of the British Museum must be got under control before anything can be done to use the Institute in the way proposed." For this reason, Elliot Smith regards the Institute in its present condition "as a broken reed", which does not warrant his support for its proposed expanded role in anthropological research and training.[6]

Discussing Elliot Smith's reaction with John L. Myres, Professor of Ancient History at Oxford, E. N. Fallaize, the Secretary of the Royal Anthropological Institute, put his finger on the root cause of Elliot Smith's hostility: "The trouble is that the British Museum does not accept Elliot Smith's views on Ethnology."[7]

Despite the lack of enthusiasm displayed by Elliot Smith, he was eventually persuaded to come to the first meeting of a Joint Committee formed to co-ordinate the Institute's efforts in anthropological research and teaching. At this meeting, it was resolved that Elliot Smith should prepare a memorandum on the relation of anthropology to the teaching of history and geography for consideration at the next meeting.[8] Exactly what else transpired is not recorded, but the day after the meeting Fallaize wrote to Myres:

It would be advisable . . . to say something to Elliot Smith as I pressed him to come and think he was rather cavalierly treated. It might be effective if we could suggest to him some practical way of giving effect to his memorandum when it has been drafted.[9]

Far from giving practical effect to the projected memorandum by Elliot Smith, the Joint Committee did not, in fact, stir themselves to do anything about the relation of anthropology to the teaching of history and geography until March 1925, nearly two years after the original suggestion. At this time, a memorandum on the subject was read, not by Elliot Smith, who had evidently failed to produce anything concrete, but by Myres. Myres's memorandum arrives at the conclusion that, where a student is being taught about non-Western societies, "it may well be that the general programme will have to be anthropological, and the geographical and (more especially) the historical commentary subsidiary".[10] This particular conclusion could hardly have been intended to please the extreme diffusionist school, who considered the "historical" approach to be the key to ethnology.

In the interim between the original suggestion to produce a memorandum and Myres's eventual compliance, there had been a string of incidents which indicated a breakdown in relations between Elliot Smith and the rest of the anthropological fraternity. The first of these involved a disagreement between Haddon and Elliot Smith over the interpretation of a Central American carving; the second, a dispute between Haddon, Perry and Elliot Smith over the psycho-cultural significance of pearls; the third, an exchange of letters between Elliot Smith and various members of the Royal Anthropological Institute in the correspondence section of *The Times*; and the fourth a jocular interchange between two anti-diffusionists. Let us now consider each of these incidents separately.

ELEPHANTS AND ETHNOLOGISTS

In June 1924, Haddon had published a review of Elliot Smith's book *Elephants and Ethnologists*.[11] Reviving a controversy which had begun some eight years before, Haddon pointed out that, in support of the contention that there had been extensive cultural diffusion between Central America and Asia, Elliot Smith had interpreted some carvings on a stela from Honduras as representing the heads of elephants. Other workers in the field, however, had interpreted them as the heads of macaws or tapirs. As the correctness of the interpretation was of considerable moment for the evaluation of the diffusionist theories, Haddon remarked that "it seems a great pity that Professor Elliot Smith did not give photographic reproductions of the carvings in question ... ; instead of these we are presented with woodcuts which are so indistinct as to be worthless as evidence." To lend weight to his hypothesis that the carvings represented an elephant rather than a macaw, Elliot Smith had reproduced, for purposes of comparison, pictures of two further carvings from the same area of Honduras, one admittedly depicting a macaw, and the other allegedly depicting an elephant. But, as Haddon commented, Elliot Smith "does not mention that the 'elephant's' head is placed upon a macaw's body, neither does he here refer to the avian nostril on the proboscidean's trunk, nor to the crest on the 'elephant's' head". While referring to Elliot Smith as an "acknowledged master" in neural anatomy, and conceding that the present evidence seems "overwhelmingly in favour" of some transmission of culture from South-Eastern Asia to Central America, the general tone of Haddon's criticisms, implying as they do some kind of presumably wilful manipulation of the evidence by Elliot Smith, can only be regarded as somewhat hostile to the extreme diffusionists. It is interesting to compare Haddon's version of this minor dispute with the one later given by Perry.

[This controversy] afforded the spectacle of a group of experts in Maya archeology firmly united in opposing the contention of Elliot Smith that a carving on the Stela was that of an elephant, but unable to agree whether it was an extinct mammoth, a macaw, a tortoise, a tapir or a squid! Truly a wonderful menagerie! [12]

PEARLS AS GIVERS OF LIFE

In an article in *Man*, published late in 1924, Haddon launched a further attack on the extreme diffusionists. [13] Perry's *Children of the Sun* had stated that "one of Elliot Smith's greatest services to knowledge has been his recognition of the *role* of man's search for 'life-giving' substances in the development of civilization", and that this is "one of the most important generalizations ever made in the study of human society". Limiting himself to discussing one of Perry's "life-giving substances", namely pearls, Haddon quotes Elliot Smith to the effect that, in many parts of the world, pearls have the reputation of being givers of life *par excellence*, a notion which, according to Elliot Smith, found literal expression in the ancient Persian word *margan* (from *mar* "giver", and *gan* "life"). Upon consulting a Professor of Arabic at Cambridge, says Haddon, he was informed that *marjan* means "coral", rather than "pearls", and that its Persian origin is doubtful. In addition, *mar* does not mean "giver"; "if one wanted to make wild etymological shots", said Haddon's authority, "one would rather connect it with the root *marg*, 'death', *murdan*, 'to die', though of course it has nothing to do with either". Moreover, in a compound Persian word meaning "life-giving", the word for "life" would come first, and the root of "give" last. Haddon then goes on the present further lingustic and historical evidence relating to pearls, not all of which strengthens the case against Elliot Smith and Perry, but which certainly conveys the impression that he is attempting to evaluate thoroughly a claim which he evidently feels had been advanced in a decidedly facile manner. Haddon must have been quite proud of this article, for a distribution list, which survives at Cambridge, indicates that he sent reprints of it to a wide circle of anthropologists and other interested parties, including Sidney Ray, Camilla Wedgwood, Alfred Kroeber and Robert Lowie, in addition to its main targets, Elliot Smith and Perry.[14]

Replying to Haddon in a personal letter, Elliot Smith assumes him to be the dupe of Captain T. A. Joyce, who was Deputy Keeper of the Department of Ethnology in the British Museum, and a Vice-President of the Royal Anthropological Institute:

I am very curious to see your attack on us in *Man*, and am very glad that you are coming out into the open in your opposition, though sorry you are acting as the cat's paw for Joyce and Co., which I think will be unfortunate for you . . . your attack will be excellent grist for our mill . . . As we have the heavy artillery your letter excites the pleasantest anticipations of an action which will settle the problem of pearls and pearl-shell for all time.[15]

Not satisfied with this salvo, Elliot Smith followed it up with another letter:

On thinking over the subject on which I wrote to you yesterday I realize that it was foolish of me to say that I was *glad* you were coming out into the open on the pearl controversy. For I realize how damaging such an exposure as you will force us to make will be to your reputation and we are certainly not anxious to see you put into a position such as Philip Henry Gosse occupied in zoology.

The evidence regarding pearls and pearl-shell is so abundant and incontrovertible that you can only make yourself look foolish if with your small B[ritish] M[useum] broom you try to sweep back the ocean! Don't think I am trying to dissuade you from your attack for personal reasons affecting us: but you are going to tempt us sorely and give us an opening for an offensive such as we hardly expected. But the first move is with you![16]

The reference to Philip Henry Gosse, a talented zoologist who for decades had opposed Darwin's evolutionary theory on fundamentalistic religious grounds, was apparently meant to be particularly cutting. In his earlier career in zoology Haddon had made use of Gosse's work on sea anemones, and had referred in print to the biological reactionary as a "friend and colleague".[17]

It is interesting to compare Elliot Smith's reaction to Haddon's article with that of William Ridgeway, Professor of Archaeology at Cambridge and an old friend of the Haddon—Rivers school of anthropology. In a letter written to Haddon in December 1924, Ridgeway remarks:

I have perused your Pearls in the Pacific with the keenest interest. It is a fine piece of work and quite convincing. It makes a fine opening of the ball against Elliot Smith and Perry.[18]

But if Haddon took the lead in the first dance, Perry was not far behind. In a reply to Haddon in *Man*,[19] Perry counter-quotes about the derivation of various words for "pearl", attempts to evade some of Haddon's objections by explaining that when he wrote "pearls" in *The Children of the Sun* he sometimes meant "pearl-shell", and points out some internal contradictions in the evidence adduced by Haddon. He also invokes a principle which, if accepted, would go a long way towards rendering his theories unfalsifiable. "Piecemeal objections", he says, "are often entirely beside the point: they are not objections, but simply minor details of local development that need explanation by local conditions". With Perry as the sole arbiter of what is and is not to be explained away as local development, awkward objections could always be avoided by declaring them "piecemeal". Which is no doubt as Perry intended.

In a rejoinder to Perry's reply, also published in *Man*, Haddon argues toward the following conclusion, which may be regarded as representing the last word in the controversy, in the metaphoric as well as the literal sense:

It is not at present my intention to enter into either a further discussion or a 'full discussion' of Mr. Perry's theories; indeed, it would almost require a syndicate to check his references and statements and to collect other evidence, for this would have to be a necessary prelude to satisfactory discussion. All writers are liable to slips, but careful students always bear in mind that the historical, as well as the scientific, method demands that among other matters, one should say exactly what one means, make as certain as possible of the data, quote correctly, consult the original sources at first hand, and that a clear distinction should be made between assumptions and definitely ascertained facts.[20]

A COVERT ATTACK AND ITS OVERWHELMING

While the "Pearls as Givers of Life" episode was still in progress, Elliot Smith, never one to let the initiative rest with the opposition, wrote a letter to the editor of *The Times*, stressing the need for anthropologically trained government advisers if currently pressing racial problems within the British Empire were to be solved. Citing the recent decision of the Australian Government to contribute towards the cost of establishing a Department of Anthropology at the University of Sydney as an example to be followed, Elliot Smith concluded that the present anthropology departments in British universities were inadequately equipped for the task at hand, and recommended that ampler provision be made for staffing. However, he concluded, the success of any scheme of anthropological teaching and research would depend upon the co-ordination of its various aspects by some central institution. These views were officially endorsed by *The Times*, in a leading article featured in the same issue.[21] While all this may sound very innocuous, the powers-that-were in the Royal Anthropological Institute thought otherwise. Fallaize interpreted Elliot Smith's action as a "covert attack on the Institute", and wrote:

I suspect Elliot Smith's letter to be the first step in a move to get something in the nature of an anthropological bureau at University College, and incidentally sidetrack the Institute.[22]

Specifically then, Fallaize was worried that Elliot Smith was attempting to usurp for University College the responsibilities which he felt to be the prerogative of the Institute's Joint Committee for anthropological research and training.

In an attempt to simultaneously capitalize on the publicity generated by Elliot Smith's letter, and to "overwhelm" Elliot Smith's "covert attack", Fallaize organized a series of letters to the editor of *The Times* by prominent members of the Institute,[23] including Myres, Joyce, C. G. Seligman, Sir Arthur Keith and Henry Balfour. The contribution of Balfour may be taken as typical. There can be little doubt, he asserts, that the Royal Anthropological Institute is the only institution which is capable of fulfilling the function of a centralized bureau.[24] In a private letter to Fallaize, Balfour makes the motivation for this assertion transparently clear: "I am glad you approved of my letter to *The Times*", he says, "We must prevent a job on the part of Elliot Smith and push the Institute's claims at all costs."[25] The contribution of Myres is probably the most forcefully stated. Several years ago, says Myres, the British Association for the Advancement of Science invited all universities, societies and other institutions engaged in anthropological work, to confer as to the best means of co-ordinating current projects via some central clearing-house in London. After careful consideration of all the alternatives, "a very representative committee . . . recommended unanimously that institutions concerned should put themselves in communication with the Royal Anthropological Institute as the obvious centre of reference and the only body with the necessary status, experience and equipment." The Institute accepted this recommendation, Myres continues, and established a Joint Committee for the purpose of implementing it. When deciding what further moves were desirable, "especially for those aspects of anthropological work which most closely border on historical and economic studies . . . , the joint committee naturally turned to Professor Elliot Smith . . . for advice and concrete proposals", and is presently awaiting "the report and recommendations which he was so good as to undertake to prepare nearly two years ago". Myres is here referring to Elliot Smith's projected memorandum on the relation of anthropology to the teaching of history and geography, which he was eventually forced to write himself. "Will Professor Elliot Smith now tell us all", Myres concludes, "what it is that he wants us to do?" [26]

JOY-RIDES OVER STONEHENGE

Shortly after the "covert attack" and its aftermath, a minor but amusing anti-diffusionist exchange occurred between Fallaize and O. G. S. Crawford, a pioneer of aerial archaeology who had been invited by the Royal Anthropological Institute to assist with a cartographical project. In a letter to Crawford, Fallaize first mentions a "Megalithic Committee", which had apparently been convened on the initiative of the extreme diffusionists by the Anthropological Section of the British Association. The purpose of this committee seems to have been to oversee the preparation of maps showing the distribution of megaliths. Fallaize then continues:

When the B[ritish] A[ssociation] Organizing Committee of Section H (Anthropology) met last month I was asked to consult you about two things: first of all whether you could give the Section a paper on archaeological investigation from the air; and secondly, whether there would be any chance of arranging for aeroplane joy rides over Stonehenge – for strictly scientific purposes of course – for selected members of the section.[27]

Crawford, who had previously attacked the extreme diffusionists in pieces written for the *Edinburgh Review*, [28] replied in a mock-serious tone, continuing the fantasy by outlining the arrangements which would have had to be made in order to organize such joy-rides. His letter concludes with the tongue-in-cheek disclaimer: "This . . . is for your consumption only of course: and needless to say is quite impersonal." [29]

A CAUSTIC REVIEW

But if these early disputes between the extreme diffusionists and the remainder of the anthropological establishment had jocular over-tones, the disputants' senses of humour were soon to evaporate. In June 1925, an anonymous review of C. E. Fox's *Threshold of the Pacific* appeared in *The Times Literary Supplement*. This constituted a savage attack on Rivers, Elliot Smith and Perry, who had all contributed towards getting Fox's material into print. While paying impressive tribute to the anthropological talents of Fox, the reviewer was critical of the influence of Rivers on Fox's field techniques:

The methods used by Dr Rivers in the field were excellent for rapid work, aiming at a survey of certain fundamental aspects of social organization. These methods consisted essentially in a collection of documents, such as genealogies, terminologies of kinship, plans, schematic outlines of ceremonies and in inquiring into native opinions. These methods, however, are not suited for real intensive work, for which Dr Fox had all the necessary ability and full opportunities; and he has unfortunately allowed himself to be fettered too much by the inappropriate "survey methods" which he received from his anthropological teacher. It is only the chapters on social organization, however, which have essentially suffered from the process. These have been made somewhat dry, abstract, remote from life, as if the writer had lived for twenty days instead of twenty years among Solomon Islanders, and then written them up twelve thousand miles away. We have kinship tables, clan lists, data about tabus and avoidances, anomalous marriages, all sorts of singular customs and exceptional rules – but the full-blooded reality of kinship life, the intimacy between parents and children, the small but extremely important facts of domestic existence, the habits of the hearth and of the household, are not given. All these facts, invisible for the ordinary anthropologically uneducated resident, entirely beyond the grasp of the survey ethnographer, a man with Dr Fox's qualifications and opportunities could well have given us.[30]

However, these criticisms were minor in comparison to the misgivings expressed by the review in relation to the treatment of Fox's manuscripts:

We are told in the preface by Professor Elliot Smith that "the present book has been prepared" from the manuscripts of the author. The first who took part in the process was Dr Rivers, who, as we are told, deeply influenced Dr Fox's results and observations, so that "the isolated worker in distant Melanesia was profoundly swayed by Dr Rivers's views, even in some cases where his own evidence came into conflict with them". Are we to conclude then that Dr Fox was made to sacrifice the evidence which he saw and recorded to the dictates of his distant friend and master? Presently we are told that Professor Elliot Smith and his colleague Mr Perry were busy altering parts of the manuscript. This must have been to a considerable extent since Professor Elliot Smith laments "that Dr Fox is so far away as to make discussion even by letter virtually impracticable. Hence I have felt obliged to leave certain of his statements in a form which I feel sure he would have agreed to modify had discussion been feasible." Again, are we to conclude that other statements are not left in the "form" given them by the author? Alterations have admittedly been made in the original manuscripts, yet there is not the slightest indication throughout the book what has been altered and in what manner or by whom.

As is well known, the three anthropologists who have been "preparing" the present book from the manuscripts are strong supporters of the hypothesis that all human culture arose in Egypt and thence spread over the world – a hypothesis by no means accepted by other students. So that when we find Egyptian influence directly "observed" in the Solomons or its existence forcibly suggested by other facts, we are in great doubt whether to attribute it to actually recorded facts or the subsequent "preparation" of them. When we are told in the description of certain burial customs that "the custom is rather to be connected with the Egyptian boat of the dead"; or when a native word *masitawa* is persuaded into the spelling *mastawa* (mastaba?); or where again the supreme being *Hatuibwari* is "indirectly" connected with the sun and "his" priests are all "children of the sun"; or when we are given detailed accounts of embalming, which is a practice now avowedly extinct in the Solomons, – we are in none of these cases able to find who is responsible for the statement, or whether the whole description of the facts has not been slightly readjusted to yield the Egyptogenic climax.

It is to be highly regretted in the interests of the book as well as in the interests of Professor Elliot Smith's hypothesis, and above all in the interests of science, that a manuscript of high ethnographic importance should have been submitted to any "preparation" other than that given it by the first-hand observer.[31]

Stung by this savage attack, Elliot Smith wrote an equally fiery reply to the editor of *The Times Literary Supplement*. Labelling the suggestion that Rivers, Perry and himself had meddled with Fox's manuscript, an "abominable accusation", Elliot Smith gives his version of the "preparation";

... no alterations whatever have been made in Dr Fox's manuscript, except the elimination of repetitions and redundancies, correcting inconsistencies of spelling (in every case adopting Dr Fox's most recent practice) and preparing the index. My references in the preface to Mr Perry's services related to proof-reading and indexing. No addition whatever has made to Dr Fox's text by Dr Rivers, Mr Perry or myself.

The passages quoted by your reviewer from my preface to Dr Fox's book were intended to make plain that *we refrained from altering* certain passages even where Dr Fox's facts seemed to us to be in conflict with the theoretical views he had adopted from Dr Rivers. But when your reviewer twists this plain statement so as to convert it into a confession that we did alter the rest he is only displaying casuistry which suggests a malicious falsehood. The spelling "*mastawa*" is Dr Fox's: the references to the "Egyptian boat of the dead" and to "the children of the sun" are also his, and we are innocent of any such "preparation" of the evidence as your reviewer charges against us".[32]

Since the whole issue boils down to that of personal veracity, continues Elliot Smith, "any serious enquirer who cares to test the rights and wrongs of the matter is at liberty to read the voluminous correspondence with Dr Fox, which covers the whole field of his book". That *The Times* has been used "for so disgraceful a method of representation" is a cause for regret, "but the review will serve a useful purpose if it opens the eyes of your readers to the reckless nature of the methods of attack that have been used against us for the past twelve months". "The fact that it has become necessary to misrepresent our view" before attacking it, concludes Elliot Smith, "is surely the strongest testimony of the strength of our argument."[33]

Not to be intimidated, the reviewer retaliated with a further letter to the *Literary Supplement*. Elliot Smith has complained, he said, about an alleged insinuation that Fox's manuscript had been tampered with. The reviewer then continues:

But I did not insinuate anything. I stated what I thought could be legitimately inferred from Professor Elliot Smith's own words. Besides references to "preparation", I had also in mind his statement that "it will, I am sure, be a satisfaction to Dr Fox to know that his book has been revised by the friend and colleague whom he is proud to call his master". (That is, Mr W. J. Perry.) And, as the preface to Dr Fox's book further states that Mr Perry "had just rendered a similar service in the case of Dr Rivers's *Social Organization*", I turned to that work to see what the "similar service" was. I there found it stated that Mr Perry "had done so much that his name ought to appear as part author". These passages left one uncertain as to the character and extent of the revision of Dr Fox's work. Hence my questions. If I went too far in concluding that alterations had been made in Dr Fox's manuscript, I am sorry; but in view of the phrases I have quoted, I do not think it was unreasonable to suppose that more was meant than the elimination of repetitions, correction of spellings, and preparing the index.[34]

The last word on the subject, which unfortunately did not get into print, was written by C. E. Fox to his reviewer. The blame for any deficiencies in the book, writes Fox with undue modesty, should be laid, not at the feet of the editors, but upon himself. Rivers, he states, "was incapable of altering evidence to prove a point", and the views of Elliot Smith must have functioned as an unconscious influence.[35] Moreover, Fox is quick to declare the genuineness of his agreement with Rivers, Elliot Smith and Perry, that many San Cristoval phenomena are best explained on the hypothesis that Egyptian influences had penetrated to the Solomon Islands. However, with regard to particular problems relating to the "preparation" of his material, Fox's account does little to exonerate the diffusionist trio. Specifically, a diagram of a San Cristoval "*heo*" or burial mound had appeared in the published book, presumably on the initiative of Perry, bearing an inscription which might have been taken to imply that "mastaba", the usual term for an Egyptian burial mound, was synonymous with "*heo*". "It is five years since I sent [Rivers] the manuscript", writes Fox, "and I am unable to be sure with that interval between." "And yet", he continues, "I feel sure I did not write the description of the *heo*, or write *mastaba*, which would seem to me begging the question, or say the bodies interred were mummified, since I have always known they were not." "That", Fox states with as much confidence as he could muster after a five-year interval, "was another's description." As for *mastawa*, "the similarity to *mastaba* is sure to be accidental". If, as Fox assumes, these things were written by Perry, then he is sure "it was with no intention of making the facts support his views, but simply to describe the *heo* as he believed I described it in the manuscript". "Or else", he concludes, with unconvincing humility, "I really did write it in a moment of aberration, anyhow the blame is mine."[36]

The identity of Fox's anonymous reviewer is not without interest for our story. As we shall discover shortly, the value placed by the reviewer on intensive fieldwork, and his obvious distaste for dry, abstract genealogical data, remote from "the full-blooded reality of kinship life", would have led many of the *cognoscenti* to suspect Malinowski. And, as is revealed by the editorial diary of *The Times* for 11 June 1925, Malinowski did in fact write the review.[37] That Elliot Smith knew or guessed the reviewer's identity is certain, for a year after the review appeared he complained to Haddon about "Malinowski's scurrilous review of Fox".[38] What is also known is that Haddon shared Malinowski's views on the role of Elliot Smith and Perrry in the preparation of Fox's manuscript for publication. In a letter to Radcliffe-Brown written during March 1927, Haddon states quite bluntly that there is "no doubt" that Smith and Perry "tampered" with Fox's book.[39] But, in view of the important role he was to assume in British Social Anthropology, and specifically in the diffusion controversy, let us now focus specifically on Malinowski and how his work relates to our story.

MALINOWSKI

For the supplementary volumes of the 1922 edition of the *Encyclopaedia Britannica*, the article on "Anthropology" had been written by Elliot Smith, and in true British diffusionist style, he had begun by attacking a statement of E. B. Tylor. When in 1926 a further supplement of the Encyclopaedia was produced, Elliot Smith's article had been replaced with one by Malinowski. The interest aroused by this action of Malinowski against the extreme diffusionists is indicated by a passage in Margaret Mead's autobiography. Mead relates that, on her way back to England following her first field expedition in Samoa, she and Reo Fortune eagerly left their ship at Adelaide to go to the University library and consult the latest supplement of the *Britannica*, so that they could read Malinowski's article for themselves.[40] Surprisingly perhaps for Malinowski, the tone of the article is relatively polite:

Whether the doctrines recently propounded by Professor Elliot Smith and Mr Perry about the universal spread of culture from Egypt will have to be classed with other discarded hypotheses or whether they contain a permanent contribution to the history of culture remains to be seen. Their use of anthropological data is unsatisfactory, and their argument really belongs to archeology, in which field their views have met with adverse criticism. One or two competent anthropologists, however, have given these theories their vigorous support (Rivers, C. E. Fox).

The real sting comes in Malinowski's footnotes to his second sentence above, where he lists a number of severe criticisms of the diffusionists by a wide range of authorities. His article, unlike that of Elliot Smith, also contains a sizeable section entitled "The Cultural Functions of Marriage and Family", which he refers to as "perhaps the most debated and most instructive of all anthropological problems". Hence, it might be thought that Malinowski, who at this stage would have been one of the most vocal opponents of later-Rivers style speculative diffusionism, was suggesting its replacement by an earlier-Rivers style kinship-centred approach to anthropology. In actual fact, Malinowski's work is much more peripheral to our story than this might suggest. Nonetheless, considering his prominence in British anthropology during the twenties and thirties, his changing attitude to the work of Rivers is important enough to warrant a fairly detailed discussion.

Early in his career Malinowski might have appeared to be shaping up as a straightforward disciple of Rivers. In a review in the 1910 volume of *Man*, which is signed "B.M." and probably represents Malinowski's first published contribution to anthropology, we read:

What is especially valuable in a book of first-hand information is a description as objective and full as possible of the facts. Every side and feature of native life should be described in as concrete terms as possible . . . On the other hand it is always good if the observer refrains from mixing his own theories with the related facts as much as possible. The book on the Todas, by Dr Rivers, stands as a model in both these methodological respects; as he is also the first who puts these two points as a basis of his methods of investigation.[41]

Malinowski's diaries, compiled while he was carrying out fieldwork in New Guinea between 1914 and 1918, contain many references to the work of Rivers, including the following entry for the 17th January 1915:

Reading Rivers, and ethnological theory in general, is invaluable, gives me an entirely different impulse to work and enables me to profit from my observations in an entirely different way . . . I went back home and read Rivers . . .[42]

In the entry for the next day he writes: "Read Rivers for a while . . . Problems of the Rivers type occur to me." [43] The diaries also reveal that Malinowski relied heavily on the 1912 edition of the *Notes and Queries on Anthropology*, for which the sections on anthropological method and kinship had been authored by Rivers. As James Urry has pointed out, "Natives of Mailu", Malinowski's first publication resulting from his investigations in the field, was divided into sections which are strikingly similar to those advocated by *Notes and Queries*, an influence which Malinowski acknowledges in the introduction to the article. [44]

On his own account, when Malinowski began his fieldwork he "still believed that by the 'genealogical method' you could obtain a foolproof knowledge of kinship systems in a couple of days or hours". And it was his ambition "to develop the principle of the 'genealogical method' into a wider and more ambitious scheme to be entitled the 'method of objective documentation'." [45] Writing to Haddon in May 1916, Malinowski sounds for all the world like a strict adherent of earlier Rivers, while possessing what Haddon would have regarded as suitable reservations about Rivers's later work:

Riverses [sic] method of strict concrete sociological analysis has been constantly in my mind and he is my patron saint in fieldwork – though I am afraid I shall commit a heresy with regard to his last book [*The History of Melanesian Society*], which is marvellous, inspiring, beautiful – but entirely unconvincing. [46]

In view of Malinowski's later claims to being the founding father and primary publicist of intensive ethnography, this acknowledgement of Rivers as his "patron saint in fieldwork" may seem uncharacteristically modest. Actually, as late as 1922, Malinowski, in advocating "intensive" field studies in preference to "survey" work, was allowing Rivers priority in both the terminology and the sentiments. [47] A concurrent discussion by Malinowski of the uses of a genealogy likewise indicates his debt to Rivers:

Its value as an instrument of research consists in that it allows the investigator to put questions which he formulates to himself *in abstracto*, but can put concretely to the native informant. As a document, its value consists in that it gives a number of authenticated data, presented in their natural grouping. [48]

However, the book in which this discussion occurs, the famous *Argonauts of the Western Pacific*, also contains strong hints of his later disillusionment with the collection of genealogies as an end in itself. Malinowski relates that he was at first unable to enter into detailed or explicit conversation with the natives. He continues:

I knew well that the best remedy for this was to collect concrete data, and accordingly I took a village census, wrote down genealogies, drew up plans and collected the terms of kinship. But all this remained dead material, which led no further into the understanding of real native mentality or behaviour.[49]

How does the ethnographer "evoke the real spirit of the natives", he asks, "the true picture of tribal life?" The secret is not in "the discovery of any marvellous short-cut leading to the desired results without any effort or trouble." Questionnaires of stereotyped methods are of little use for recording the phenomena which constitute "the real substance of the social fabric". Rather, the ethnographer must sometimes "put aside camera, notebook and pencil, and join in himself in what is going on". Or, as he eloquently expressed it in a later work:

The anthropologist must relinquish his comfortable position in the long chair on the verandah of the missionary compound, Government station, or planter's bungalow, where, armed with pencil and notebook and at times with a whisky and soda, he has been accustomed to collect statements from informants, write down stories, and fill out sheets of paper with savage texts. He must go out into the villages, and see the natives at work in gardens, on the beach, in the jungle; he must sail with them to distant sandbanks, and to foreign tribes, and observe them in fishing, trading and ceremonial overseas expeditions. Information must come to him full flavoured from his own observations, and not be squeezed out of reluctant informants as a trickle of talk.[50]

This famous passage, usually quoted as Malinowski's reaction to "armchair anthropologists" like Tylor and Frazer, was in fact directed against survey ethnographers like Rivers and Haddon.

As the twenties wore on, Malinowski began increasingly, as Raymond Firth has aptly said, "to react against Rivers's views and to measure himself against Rivers's reputation".[51] On one occasion, Malinowski is said to have remarked to Brenda Seligman, "Rivers is the Rider Haggard of anthropology, I shall be the Conrad."[52] While some measure of ambiguity always inheres in an analogical comparison such as this, two comments would seem to be in order. Firstly, it is clear from Malinowski's diaries that he was no admirer of Rider Haggard's novels and, secondly, one would have expected him to identify favourably with Conrad as another expatriate, Anglophilic, Polish intellectual.

In his previously-mentioned review of *The Threshold of the Pacific*, published in 1925, Malinowski had anonymously expressed the opinion that Rivers's methods, while useful for rapid survey work, were not suitable for intensive fieldwork, because they failed to capture "the full-blooded reality of kinship life". With the onset of the thirties, Malinowski's attitude to technical, formalized kinship investigations in the style of earlier Rivers, had crystallized into open hostility. Meyer Fortes, who was a student of Malinowski during this period, remembers that "Rivers was Malinowski's *bête noire*".[53] In an article for which the first section is provocatively headed "Must Kinship Be Dehumanized By Mock Algebra?", Malinowski confronted the school of earlier Rivers head on. Malinowski states that whenever he discusses kinship with people such as Brenda Seligman or Radcliffe-Brown, he is aware that mutual comprehension is somehow lacking. He confesses that there is not a single contemporary account of kinship in which he does not find himself "puzzled by some of this spuriously scientific and stilted mathematization of kinship facts and disappointed by the absence of those intimate data of family life, full-blooded descriptions of tribal and ceremonial activities . . . which alone make kinship a real fact to the reader". For Malinowski "kinship is a matter of flesh and blood, the result of sexual passion and maternal affection, of long and intimate daily life, and of a host of personal intimate interests". "Can all this be reduced to formulae, symbols, perhaps equations?", he asks. Is it sound, as Rivers assumed in the *History of Melanesian Society*, to hopefully anticipate the day when much of the description of indigenous social systems will resemble a work on mathematics, with the results expressed by symbols, or even in the form of equations? For Malinowski the answer is a resounding negative. The so-called "kinship systems" of peoples such as the Toda, Arunta and Melanesians, amount, he says, to "little more than incorrectly translated fragments of a vocabulary". Kinship studies, he alleges, are in an impasse due to the inheritance of false problems, such as the question of the origin and significance of classificatory systems of relationship. In a direct shot at Rivers, he refers to "the rage for the explanation of queer terms by anomalous marriages, which led to one or two half truths, but also to half a dozen capital errors and misconceptions". Malinowski says that there is a way around the impasse, and that this involves two steps. Firstly, the importance of the family, in which the initial notions of kinship germinate and are then "extended" to successively wider social groups, must be recognized. Secondly, "the functional method of anthropology", which consists "above all in the analysis of primitive institutions as they work at present, rather than in reconstructions of a hypothetical past", must be applied.[54]

Actually both these steps, or something very like them, had already been recommended by Rivers himself. The notion of kinship "extensions" had been prefigured in Rivers's section on Kinship in the fifth volume of the Torres Straits expedition *Reports*;[55] and a method which was broadly "functional" in Malinowski's sense, had been advocated by Rivers in his contributions to the fourth edition of the *Notes and Queries*.[56] The resemblance between the views of Malinowski and Rivers does not end here. Rivers's 1917 essay "On the Government of Subject Peoples" puts forward a number of points about the relationship between anthropology and colonial administration which are strikingly reminiscent of those later made by Malinowski during the 1930s.[57] These apparent echoes of Rivers in Malinowski's work, combined with the latter's admitted take-over of the former's advocacy of intensive fieldwork, might be taken as pointing to the conclusion that Malinowski was, in fact, a disciple of Rivers. This conclusion is prima facie supported by certain passages in the article dealing with the dehumanization of kinship by mock-algebra. Here Malinowski discusses "Rivers and his school", and includes himself among their number. Moreover, he refers to the members of this school as "the handful of us, the *enragés* or initiates of kinship," and later as "the inner ring". However, this seeming affirmation of loyalty to the school of earlier Rivers notwithstanding, Malinowski was definitely *not* a disciple of Rivers in the same sense as people like W. E. Armstrong, Bernard Deacon, T. T. Barnard, Brenda Seligman and Radcliffe-Brown. Certainly, if discipleship consists only in the transmission of intellectual influences from one scholar to another via the medium of the published word, then Malinowski was arguably a disciple of Rivers (and of a number of other anthropologists, including Frazer, Westermarck and C. G. Seligman). However, for the purposes of this book, I am assuming that membership of a scientific school involves the inheritance of a specific set of problems, approached on the basis of a number of shared assumptions and values, and tackled by a clearly-defined body of empirical and theoretical techniques. While these criteria would be most easily satisfied if the disciples received their professional training directly from the master himself – and under the auspices of a single educational institution, this condition is by no means essential. Malinowski's connections with Cambridge Ethnology were indeed rather tenuous, consisting mainly in the fact that C. G. Seligman, Malinowski's teacher at the London School of Economics, had been a member of the Torres Straits expedition, was a colleague and close friend of Rivers and Haddon, and was married to a devotee of Rivers's approach to kinship studies. However, this does not constitute my reason for excluding Malinowski from the Rivers school. The true disciples of early Rivers believed in the existence of "kinship systems", and devoted much of their energies to uncovering the specifications of the same. They regarded these "kinship systems" as embodying a series of rules regulating marriage and descent, each system being associated with a particular set of relationship terms, and carrying with it clearly defined rights and duties towards specific kinsmen and affines. As I hope is evident from my discussion of the context in which Malinowski lays claim to membership of the Rivers school, it was precisely the existence of "kinship systems" thus defined, and the scientific value of attempting to represent them in formalized symbolic fashion, that he was so vigorously disputing. In a later publication, Malinowski went so far as to say that he had sometimes been led to suspect that the "ill-omened kinship nomenclatures", a subject "widely over-discussed" and "often exaggerated in records of field-work", was "nothing but an avenue to anthropological insanity". Speaking of his own Trobriand corpus, he promised a future volume dealing with this aspect of kinship, in the fond hope that "by an overdose of terminological documentation and linguistic detail I can administer a cathartic cure to social anthropology".[58] Fortunately, this volume never materialized!

We shall return a little later to Malinowski and his subsequent role in the diffusion controversy, but for the present moment let me sum up by saying that, despite his early interest in, and apparent admiration for the genealogical method, Malinowski cannot be judged a member of the school of earlier Rivers. In fact, his mature work on kinship should be regarded as written more in opposition to the school of earlier Rivers than in sympathy with it. Being a fierce opponent of speculative diffusionism did not, in his case, entail a penchant for the formal analysis of kinship systems.

THE METHOD OF FLUELLEN

Early in 1925, a trenchant attack on Perry's work was launched by John L. Myres, who was at that time president of the Geographical Association in addition to being an active member of the Royal Anthropological Institute. In an article in *The Geographical Teacher*, Myres informed his readers that:

Since the publication of the late Dr Rivers's great *History of Melanesian Society* in 1914, hardly a season has passed without one or more fresh illustrations of the results which may be expected from the use of what is described by its exponents as the "historical method" in ethnology. To judge from their account of it, this is no mere supplement to existing methods of research; it is represented as superseding them all, as shattering their conclusions, and as furnishing a single simple key to all the mythologies, technologies and sociologies that flesh is heir to . . .[59]

After giving a sympathetic account of Rivers's exposition of the historical method, Myres notes that Rivers's serious applications of the method were confined to regions such as Melanesia, where its limitations were minimized.

With Perry, however, such restraint is, on Myres's account, entirely lacking. Although, for example, Perry admits to knowing little about the political organization of the Phoenician cities of Tyre and Sidon, he is ready to conclude that "what is known goes to link the Phoenicians still closer to the communities of the archaic civilization in Polynesia and elsewhere." The evidence on which this judgement is based is that, to quote Perry again, "Tyre and Sidon seem to have formed a dual grouping of cities with constant rivalry between them"; to which Myres responds, "how like Liverpool and Manchester!" [60]

Perry's use of the historical method is spurious, contends Myres, because "it relies mainly on the use of what the logic books call the 'method of agreement'. This method is as old as the hills; and you can draw by it almost any conclusion, provided you do not attempt proof." Its classical exponent, says Myres, is the character Fluellen from Shakespeare's *Henry V*, and offers the following quotation in which Fluellen "proves" the identity of the rivers of Monmouth and Macedon:

If you look in maps of the 'orld, I warrant, you shall find, in the comparisons between Macedon and Monmouth, that the situations look alike, is both alike. There is a river in Macedon, and there is also moreover a river at Monmouth — it is called Wye at Monmouth; but it is out of my prains what is the name of the other river; but tis all one, tis alike as my fingers is to my fingers, and there is salmons in both.

This discussion, claims Myres, would scarcely be noticed among contemporary illustrations of the "historical method". For Myres, however, Perry achieves the pinnacle of his absurdity in the following statement:

... it seems that all elements of thought, of whatever community, can ultimately be expressed in terms of the empirical experience of that, or some other community, so that human thought is ultimately anchored in human experience.

"Does this kind of thing really need showing?" asks Myres. "Or rather how is it possible to 'show' the truth of propositions so nearly devoid of meaning?" [61]

Unable to match Myres's mordant wit, Perry lapses into ill-humoured paranoia. "The claims advanced by Elliot Smith and myself", says Perry, "are being attacked on all sides". However, "anyone who ... reads the criticisms carefully will realize that all our critics feel it necessary to misrepresent our claims", and "Professor Myres has carried this process perhaps further than any other critic." Fixing on Myres's allegation that the extreme diffusionists have violated normal historical standards of accuracy and cogency, Perry attempts to show that, in Myres's own work on physical anthropology, the standards of accuracy and cogency leave much to be desired. [62] However, because the passages quoted from Myres have absolutely nothing to do with the content of the original criticisms, Perry's attempt to pour scorn on his critic comes out sounding oddly irrelevant, as Myres himself was quick to point out in a further reply.[63]

This minor but heated clash between Myres and Perry was perhaps best summed up by L. H. Dudley Buxton, later to be appointed Reader in Physical Anthropology at Oxford, who wrote to Haddon as follows:

In regard to Perry I don't like the tone of his reply or indeed of any of his work . . . [Myres] is very amusing. But it is wasting powder and shot. Perry told me he considered himself Daniel in the lion's den! Poor Daniel. His appalling ignorance combined with his entire lack of critical sense are such that no attacks appear to be worthwhile. Last night I – to amuse myself – proved by Perry's method that the archaic civilization and dual organization and matriliny survived in Oxford, and I feel that possibly the first does.[64]

HADDON'S REPLACEMENT AT CAMBRIDGE

In April 1926, with Haddon about to retire from his Readership, his pupil Winifred Hoernle voiced to her mentor what must have been a common fear around the halls of Cambridge ethnology: "Who is to take your place? . . . Elliot Smith must not be allowed to get too tight a grip."[65] Then, in the following month, after the new Readership had been formally established,[66] applications were invited for the job. Prominent amongst the members of a Committee appointed to consider the applicants were Haddon and his friend William Ridgeway, Professor of Classics at Cambridge.[67]

A total of four applications were received, including one from T. C. Hodson, the author of several ethnological works on India, and one from W. E. Armstrong, a talented analyst of kinship who had been a pupil of Rivers and whose work will be discussed in the next chapter. Two candidates were interviewed and it was unanimously decided to recommend the appointment of Hodson.[68] When asked, nearly half a century later, why in his opinion, Hodson had been successful, Armstrong replied that Hodson had acquired a reputation on the strength of his fieldwork in India, was "a good administrator and thoroughly mature". "I believe Haddon had me in mind", continued Armstrong, "but I was obviously too young, had nothing published at that time and, I believe, was over-ruled by Ridgeway".[69]

Certainly Hodson's expertise in Indian ethnography would have stood him in good stead. In March 1925, the Board of Archaeological and Anthropological Studies had, in response to Haddon's impending retirement, prepared a report which argued that anthropology is "not only an important, but an indispensable branch of knowledge, not merely for scholars, but for persons who in an Empire like ours were going to undertake – whether in the Consular Service, in India, or in the Crown Colonies – the work of administration." Referring to the recent spate of letters in *The Times* which, as just described, had been triggered by Elliot Smith's "covert attack" on the Royal Anthropological Institute, the report argued that there is general public recognition of "the scientific importance of anthropology and its practical value to the Empire".[70] The training of Indian Civil Service probationers had long been a function of the Cambridge School of Ethnology [71] and Hodson, who had wide experience as a public servant in India, and who had delivered a paper on a proposed Imperial Bureau of Ethnology as far back as 1911,[72] must have seemed the ideal man to give substance to the claims made in the report. India was the linchpin of British imperial trade, and Cambridge anthropology was not above depicting itself as capable of keeping the pin firmly in place.

But while it is apparent that the essential motivation behind Hodson's appointment was to further anthropology's claims to being an aid to imperialism, there can also be little doubt that Haddon's behaviour in respect of the appointment, was at least partly determined by the desire to ensure that Cambridge anthropology followed in the footsteps of earlier rather than later Rivers. Firstly, we have Armstrong's belief that, despite his (Armstrong's) inexperience and lack of publications, Haddon would have preferred to see the young kinship analyst as the new Reader. Secondly, we know that, at a time when it must have been evident that Hodson was a likely candidate for the job, Haddon went to the trouble of sending to Hodson a transcribed copy of the letter in which C. E. Fox reveals that someone, presumably Perry, had tampered with the manuscript of *The Threshold of the Pacific.*[73] Haddon's reason for doing this has not been preserved. However, one infers either that he was attempting to turn Hodson against the extreme diffusionists, or that he was sounding Hodson out to discover where he stood in relation to them. In either case, it seems clear that Haddon was anxious that, after his retirement, the hyperdiffusionists should not establish a foothold in Cambridge anthropology.

THE APOTHEOSIS OF FATHER SCHMIDT

A minor incident in the diffusion controversy during the mid-twenties revealed the extent to which the ghost of Rivers still haunted Elliot Smith's and

Haddon's perceptions of the issues involved. In September 1926, *The Times Literary Supplement* contained an anonymous review of Part I of *Volker and Kulturen* by the German diffusionists Schmidt and Koppers. This book provided a history of the science of ethnology, a statement of its methods, and an ethnological account of the structure and economic foundations of human societies. The review, which is very favourable and especially laudatory in regard to Schmidt, states that the book marks "a very great advance" in the science of ethnology. "It will have a deep influence on ethnological exposition and teaching" writes the reviewer, and one can expect that "the methods it lays down will become − doubtless developed and modified − the very bone and fibre of the science".[74]

Elliot Smith, who must have been perusing the pages of the *Literary Supplement* with mounting paranoia, read the review and wrote a letter of complaint to the editor. The review, Elliot Smith pointed out, had failed to mention Rivers, the "chief champion" of the historical method in British ethnology. In his capacity as Rivers's literary executor, Elliot Smith requested permission to point out the difference between the English and German diffusionists. The school of Dr Rivers, said Elliot Smith, does not disbelieve in social evolution. "Just as the biologist has to study both the development of new traits and the loss or modification of others, so we of the Rivers school regard society as an organic whole in which both progressive changes and degradation of culture are going on." Father Schmidt, on the other hand, in company with other members of the Graebner school, does not adopt an organic view of society. In particular, this school ignores degradation. The attitude of the German diffusionists "was shaped largely by the pre-war opposition on the part of German-speaking people to the British doctrine of Darwin". "It is important", Elliot Smith concludes, "that the glamour of quoting books written in the German language should not blind Englishmen to the fact that the true doctrine . . . was enunciated by my late friend, to whom the Cambridge School of Anthropology owes so much for its inspiration."[75]

The reason for this particular reference to the Cambridge School of Anthropology is revealed by a letter which Elliot Smith wrote to Haddon at the same time:

I suppose I can congratulate you on the splendid outburst in the Literary Supplement of *The Times* in justification of the historical method? At any rate I do not know anyone else who could write with such knowledge and fervour in support of Graebnerism. But I think you might have mentioned Rivers without weakening your indictment − and it would have strengthened your argument even though R[ivers] did not write in German! After all he was your colleague.[76]

Haddon's reply was brief and to the point:

I did not write the notice on *Volken and Kulturen* in the Times Literary Supplement. Nor have I any idea who wrote it. It is therefore somewhat rough on me for you to suppose I would in any way ignore the work or opinions of Rivers. I venture to think that few can appreciate him better than I do, and his death has been an irreparable loss to us in Cambridge – as indeed elsewhere – and what he has done can never be forgotten by those who knew him.[77]

This evoked something of an apology from Elliot Smith, although as might have been expected, Haddon's affirmation of loyalty to their mutual friend was fed straight into the databank of Elliot Smith's society for the protection of the memory of later Rivers:

I am sorry to have attributed the apotheosis of Father Schmidt in the Literary Supplement to you. But I am unfeignedly pleased at what you say of Rivers. Your actions and your opposition to those of us who are keeping alive the ideas that Rivers believed in lend themselves to those who are so active in their endeavours to destroy Rivers's influence and even, as in Malinowski's scurrilous review of Fox in the Literary Supplement last year, to besmirch his name. But I accept your assurance that you are not wittingly helping these people.[78]

ELLIOT SMITH, PERRY AND ANTHROPOLOGY AT UNIVERSITY COLLEGE

Shortly after Haddon and Elliot Smith had finished this minor tug-of-war with Rivers's dead body, negotiations concerning the financing of anthropology at University College London were commenced between Elliot Smith and the Rockefeller Foundation. A confidential statement by Elliot Smith of his plans for anthropology at University College reveals the extent to which he had come to regard himself and Perry as embattled guardians of the sacred flame, pitted against the ignorance and ineptitude of established anthropology:

In building up this scheme of work a new conception of anthropology is developing in this college, which I am convinced is the only way to rescue this subject from the disrepute into which it has fallen throughout the world, and the gross incompetence which is displayed in investigating its problems in most Universities. The subject has, however, now been put on a sound foundation of biological method and the cultural sides have been put on a sound psychological basis, so that the subject is being rescued from the two evils of scholasticism and stereotyped formalism, and made into a living subject in vital connection with the biological and psychological departments with which it is so intimately associated. It is of course inevitable that in rescuing a subject from the thralldom of dogmatic method of treatment, considerable feeling has been aroused amongst the upholders of the old conventions and it would be idle to pretend that what we are doing here is popular, but the question of rescuing anthropology from these destructive agencies was imperative, and there can be no doubt at all that any attempt to establish the strict discipline of science into the study of mankind, which is a matter of the utmost importance to every department of a University's work – scientific as well as humanistic – is a matter of the utmost urgency and importance. The very fanaticism of the attacks which have been made upon this experiment afford the most eloquent testimony that some Galileo was necessary in order to destroy the old dogmas.[79]

This parallel with Galileo was elaborated by Elliot Smith in a further communication with the Foundation, a communication remarkable for its bombastic exposition of the current state of the anthropological art:

As you no doubt are aware anthropology thoughout the world is in a deplorably inefficient state; and an effort to cleanse the Augean stables and to introduce into the study of mankind a definite aim and the strict discipline of the scientific method have provoked widespread misrepresentation and such malice as the Council of the Cardinals exhibited towards Galileo. In the history of science this has ever been the reaction against reform and Perry and I naturally refuse to bow the knee to the false gods that anthropologists have been worshiping since Tylor led them into the wilderness in 1871.[80] Of course we are heartened in this dispute, which unfortunately is bitter and unscrupulous, in the fact that *all* the students and graduates working at the subject in this country have made their choice and come to Perry, who is the Galileo of this movement, which within the next decade will effect as profound a reform in humanitarian studies as Galileo effected in physics. The study of human behaviour upon which he is engaged will be a great synthesis of biological, social, psychological and cultural facts with the only clear induction such data can justify.[81]

Such extravagant praise of Perry and his work is a feature not only of the letter from which the above quotation was extracted, but also of a second lengthy epistle which Elliot Smith wrote to the Rockefeller Foundation during this period. Indeed, one might be tempted to conclude from this pair of letters that, with regard to his perception of diffusionism and of Perry's role within it, Elliot Smith was suffering from delusions of grandeur. At one point he refers to Perry as "the great Humanist of the dawning era", and at another advances the opinion that Perry and his pupils will bring about "the most profound revolution ever effected in humanitarian studies". In case one should wonder how Perry will accomplish this, Elliot Smith has the answer:

The misunderstanding of Perry's work is due mainly to the very fact of the bigness of the idea, which hardly anyone has been able to grasp. By analysing the customs and beliefs of primitive peoples (and the ancient literatures of Egypt, Babylonia, Greece, India and

China) and comparing them with the folk-lore of the North American Indians and the peoples of Oceania and Indonesia, he has been able to establish the fact that the fundamental motive underlying all these customs and beliefs is the preservation of life and the restoration of youth, and is an expression of the fundamental biological instinct of self-preservation. Perry and his collaborators have carried this conception much further by showing that all the primitive systems of initiation are based on the idea of a new birth, which is modelled essentially upon the practice of mummification – the essence of all ritual is to confer upon the individual a new lease of life (and a new name to symbolize this new form of existence) in preparation for transference to the sky-world, which is the source of all life.

The conceptions expressed in these two simple statements have been found to apply in every part of the world – ancient and modern – and to supply the means of the interpretation of the most varied and complex incidents in social practice and belief, as well as the outstanding motives and symbolism in the world's literature, ancient and modern.[82]

Reading between the lines, it seems likely that Elliot Smith's absurdly overinflated prose was the result of desperation arising from the belief that his arch rival Malinowski had gained the upper hand with the Rockefeller Foundation. In the second of the aforementioned pair of letters, Elliot Smith implies that the Foundation has accepted the claim of the anti-diffusionists that Perry's work is of little value because of his never having done any fieldwork. "It is a curious fact", snorts Elliot Smith, "that the people who most frequently make this criticism of Perry are the worshippers of Sir James Frazer, who of course has never done a stroke of fieldwork."[83] Since Malinowski's admiration of Frazer was well known, this brickbat was undoubtedly aimed at the expatriate Pole. Elliot Smith's first letter contains a similar shot at Malinowski over the issue of fieldwork. In an implied reference to Malinowski's practice of parading his own intensive investigations in the Trobriands as a shining example for other anthropologists to follow, Elliot Smith writes:

The assumption that the sole method of studying mankind is to sit on a Melanesian island for a couple of years and listen to the gossip of the villagers is not our idea of humanitarian study.[84]

As part of his anti-Malinowski campaign, Elliot Smith also quoted at length from a memorandum drawn up by University College in 1921. In this document, it had been argued that the then current arrangement, in which ethnology was taught at the London School of Economics and physical anthropology at University College, entailed much unnecessary commuting by students. The solution proposed by the memorandum had been the establishment of an Institute of Ethnology at University College, so that the two branches of anthropology could carry on their teaching and research in close proximity.[85] Elliot Smith's reason for resurrecting this memorandum was apparently to advance the claims of University College as a centre for ethnological investigations, at the expense of the London School of Economics where, by 1927, Malinowski had become firmly entrenched.

In February 1927, the Rockefeller Foundation wrote to Elliot Smith advising him not to count on them providing any financial assistance for his anthropological projects at University College.[86] To this Elliot Smith replied expressing his deep disappointment and his amazement at the Laura Spelman Rockefeller Memorial's generosity towards "those who are wrecking anthropological study in this country". An annotation in the margin of Elliot Smith's letter by a Rockefeller Foundation official reveals that this latter phrase refers, as we might have expected, to Malinowski.[87] After some further correspondence regarding a truncated scheme to grant limited financial assitance for anthropology at University College, this too was rejected by the Rockefeller Foundation. In June 1927, Elliot Smith informed the Foundation that the rejection of this scheme had involved him with difficulties in meeting his moral obligations to Perry and others, and that he interpreted their action as implying a lack of confidence in himself.[88] To this the Foundation replied that no lack of confidence was intended, and pointed to their substantial recent endowments to the Department of Anatomy at University College. These endowments, the Foundation averred, "were based in a not inconsiderable degree upon your connection with the Department of Anatomy. Rather than lack of confidence, there is, I think, lack of agreement with you that nearly one half of the aid intended for help to the Departments of Anatomy, Pharmacology, Physiology and Biochemistry should have been given to Anthropology."[89]

ELLIOT SMITH EMBATTLED

Elliot Smith's quarrels with Malinowski and with anthropological opinion in the United States, spilled over into the public forum in 1928. In a slim work entitled *Culture: The Diffusion Controversy*, Elliot Smith put the case for diffusionism, and replies were lodged by Malinowski, Herbert Spinden of Harvard University's Peabody Museum and Alexander Goldenweiser, the American cultural anthropologist. As Rivers had done in his 1911 Presidential Address to the Anthropology Section of the British Association, Elliot Smith began by contrasting the diffusionist position with the theory (espoused, according to Elliot Smith, by the "vast majority" of contemporary anthropologists) that civilization had been independently invented at different places on the earth's surface. Presenting diffusionism as the embodiment of common-sense, Elliot Smith cited, as his prime supporting example, the case of the wooden match. If a European was travelling in some out-of-the-way country, and if he there discovered a wooden match, "he would inevitably conclude that the match afforded certain evidence of contact, direct or indirect, with someone who had benefitted by the English invention". If, on the other hand, our traveller was not an intelligent layman, but an orthodox anthropologist, "he would have to assume that so obvious a mechanism must have been invented independently by the uncultured people of the country where he had picked up the match".[90]

In his reply, Malinowski opened by pointing out that the diffusionist hypothesis, which Elliot Smith was presenting as the basis of a revolutionary new school of ethnology, was actually "as old as the Ten Lost Tribes fallacy". Those who support extreme diffusionism typically frame the problem in terms of whether it is diffusion or independent invention which has been the dominant factor in cultural progress. However, "as usually happens in the perpetration of scientific fallacies", the error has been introduced by the way the question has been framed. For, as clear as the distinction between diffusion and invention may appear, it cannot, in fact, be rigidly maintained. Elliot Smith has asked whether a wooden match found in use among a foreign tribe has been invented by them or diffused to them. "The answer", asserts Malinowski, "is *neither*". When, during the war, matches were in short supply, Melanesian natives quickly reverted to making fire by traditional methods. The match, having been presented as a *fait d'accompli* by Western traders, had not been creatively woven into the fabric of the indigenous society. It has simply been made available by a culture which had never succeeded in "diffusing" into Melanesia the science and technology which underlies the production of matches. Nor could Elliot Smith's match example be accepted as illustrating the impossibility of independent invention. For Malinowski had himself observed a native create "the counterpart of a wooden match by putting some kerosene on the end of a rubbing stick to make it flare up more easily".[91] "*Culture is not contagious!*", concluded Malinowski pugnaciously, "It has neither been invented nor diffused, but imposed by the natural conditions which drive man upon the path of progress with inexorable determinism."[92]

The American contributions to the book also reveal profound dissatisfaction with Elliot Smith's presentation of the diffusionist case. Spinden attempts to locate the British diffusionists within a tradition which he characterizes as the "romantic" school in anthropology. This school Spinden sees as invoking ill-substantiated hypotheses, and as inventing "variegated, stranger-than-fiction explanations".[93] Obviously not all such romantic theories can be true, says Spinden, because "they oppose each other and fall into riotous discord". The worst, in fact, are no better than "flights of childish adventure".[94] The late W. H. R. Rivers, writes Spinden, is "worthy of better remembrances for his early work".[95]

In a final and very brief contribution, Goldenweiser writes that, far from agreeing with Elliot Smith that the "vast majority" of anthropologists subscribe to the theory of independent invention, he has difficulty in thinking of "even a *single* anthropologist who holds such a view".[96] The "real issues", writes Goldenweiser, are whether independent invention ever does take place, if so, whether it is rare or frequent, and the extent to which the evidence can help to decide between independent invention and diffusion. But one reaches the end of Elliot Smith's contribution without having encountered any mention of these issues. Malinowski's reply, avers Goldenweiser, "raises the discussion to a higher level of fairness and realism".[97] For example, one can endorse Malinowski's rejection of the mechanical view of diffusion as the simple transfer of cultural artefacts from one place to another. And one can accept his depiction of cultural adaptation as a complex process in which diffusion and invention play complementary roles. However, Malinowski oversteps the mark by flatly declaring that "culture is not contagious". Clearly there are some instances which must be explained in terms of diffusion. Clearly, too, there are other instances in which independent invention must have occurred. But there are many other cases where it is either difficult or impossible to use the evidence to decide between independent invention on the one hand or diffusion on the other.[98] The trouble with the diffusion controversy as it is taking place in Britain, implies Goldenweiser, is that Elliot Smith's extremism has forced the opposition into an uncompromising position. Having been goaded by Elliot Smith's dogmatism, Malinowski too now shows signs of being unwilling to take the evidence as it comes — or to admit that the views of his opponents may contain a grain of truth.

THE RIVERS MEMORIAL FUND

At the same time that Elliot Smith's plans for anthropology at University College were being thwarted through lack of funds, the Royal Anthropological

Institute, discarded by Elliot Smith as a "broken reed", was actually having trouble disposing of one particular source of finance. I refer to the "Rivers Memorial Fund", which was originally collected in order to promote the type of investigations in which Rivers had been chiefly interested.[99] Although the Appeal for the fund had been circulated early in 1923 and the money had presumably been collected at that time, it was not put to good use for many years. In fact, at a Council meeting of the Institute in February 1928, attention was drawn to the fact that the amount received in response to the Rivers Memorial Appeal was still held by the Treasurer of the Fund, and had not even been handed over to the Institute in accordance with the instructions of the subscribers. And then it was not until November 1928 that the Institute's Secretary was able to report that the money had been received by the Treasurer of the Institute for investment in a trusty stock.[100] A Committee of Rivers's friends had been formed to administer the Fund as early as 1923. However, not until the early thirties, when Elliot Smith became an active member of the Committee, was the money utilized for the purpose for which it had been collected.[101] In view of this, one is tempted to conclude that the Committee's long impotence was wholly or partly due to the absence, and indeed hostility, of Elliot Smith, the closest of Rivers's friends over the latter part of his life, and by far the most dynamic.

THE JOINT COMMITTEE

(a) *The Multiple Appeals Fiasco*

If the above episode illustrated the ineffectualness of the Royal Anthropological Institute during the twenties, and if this ineffectualness was, in large measure, due to lack of co-operation on the part of Elliot Smith, a far more striking example of the same phenomenon was provided by one of the few projects seriously attempted by the previously-mentioned Joint Committee for the co-ordination of anthropological research and teaching. The account which follows may well strain the patience of the reader, but I can think of no more realistic means of demonstrating how the spoiling tactics of Elliot Smith rendered the potentially effective Joint Committee an object lesson in bumbling ineptitude. In October 1927, one of the objects of the Joint Committee was stated as raising £100,000 by public appeal "for the prosecution of research in anthropology, especially in the dependencies of the British Empire".[102] Nothing concrete was done about this project until July 1928, when following some correspondence in *The Times* about the value of anthropology, a special committee meeting was called to discuss what action should be taken to bring the Institute's appeal for funds before the public.[103] Discussing who should be invited to attend this meeting, E. N. Fallaize wrote to Myres:

... Malinowski and Perry and Hodson should be present to represent London and Cambridge ... Cambridge originally was represented by Haddon and London by Seligman, but no doubt it will be useful to have these other firebrands in, if only to keep them quiet.[104]

As it turned out, Perry was the only one of the "firebrands" who attended the meeting which resolved, among other things, to request Captain G. Pitt-Rivers, an old anthropological identity with a special interest in the evolution of material culture, to prepare a draft of the appeal for funds.[105] This draft having been produced, it was deemed unsatisfactory by Myres and Fallaize and the former therefore produced a revised version.[106] A copy of this version of the appeal was then sent to Elliot Smith for comment and signature. In a letter of reply to Pitt-Rivers, Elliot Smith first reveals his attitude to the Joint Committee:

At the outset I should like to make it clear that I have not been invited to attend any meeting of the Joint University Committee ... for more than 5 years. Hence it would be invidious of me to push in and volunteer information for which I have not been asked.[107]

Nonetheless, Elliot Smith was perfectly willing to offer some comments on Myres's draft. Although he claimed to find it "an admirable document" overall, Elliot Smith questioned the wisdom of any proposal which would enable the Royal Anthropological Institute to usurp the prerogative of the Universities by directing research, or by administering funds collected by public appeal. "It seems to me that that is not the business of the Institute at all", averred Elliot Smith, "and at a meeting of the Joint University Committee, I think in 1922, it was pointed out that no University could tolerate such an interference with its freedom".[108]

Following Pitt-Rivers, Myres had asserted in his version of the appeal that the aim of anthropology is "to discover the general laws" to which particular facts conform. Elliot Smith objected strenuously to this phrase, saying that it implied a claim which he could not endorse without exposing himself to derision, since on several recent occasions he had "called particular attention to the fact that this phrase, invented by Descartes two [sic] centuries ago, has been responsible for most of the confusion in anthropological doctrine". "So that", he continues, "if I were to put my signature to a document containing this phrase not only would I be stultifying a good deal of my recent writing, but also make myself supremely ridiculous".[109] Myres had also alleged that "no institution in Great Britain has at present any programme of ethnological exploration", to which Elliot Smith responded that University College did indeed have such a programme. Finally, in Elliot Smith's view, the appeal failed to present the strongest possible case because, while arguing for the value of anthropology in colonial administration, it did not mention the necessity for British Universities to co-operate with institutions which had recently been established in the various British dominions for anthropological research and training (i.e. in particular, the departments of Anthropology at Sydney and Capetown). In the light of these criticisms, Elliot Smith declined to add his signature to the appeal.[110]

Having disposed of this matter, Elliot Smith then took the opportunity of spelling out his perception of the relationship between University College and the Royal Anthropological Institute. Elliot Smith denies that he and his colleagues have been standing aloof from endeavours initiated by the Institute. On the contrary, he says, the Institute has neither invited him to participate in its activities nor informed him of its program. Moreover, "for several years Perry and myself, both in the technical journals and in the literary reviews, have been subjected to a vendetta of misinterpretation of a particularly glaring kind". The only conclusion he could draw was that his help was unwelcome and that anything he might do would be suppressed. "Under these circumstances", he says, "we thought that we could best serve the interests of anthropology by quietly going along with our work and paying no attention to the pin-pricks of the reviews and the only thinly-veiled antagonism of the authorities of the Royal Anthropological Institute." So as to avoid any possible misrepresentation of his motives or unnecessary friction, Elliot Smith relates, he resigned from the Institute in 1922 and only resumed his membership a year ago at the impassioned request of the President. By doing this he hoped to convince the powers-that-be of his willingness to co-operate. However, it seems that "the old suspicions still survive", and unless they can be allayed "there is no other alternative for us at University College than to plough a lonely furrow".[111]

Around the same time as Elliot Smith wrote to Pitt-Rivers, Sir Arthur Keith, a well-known anatomist who was also a prominent member of the Anthropological Institute, decided that the appeals of Pitt-Rivers and Myres had been aimed mainly at professional anthropologists. In an attempt to solicit the intelligent and hopefully moneyed layman, Keith wrote yet another version of the appeal.[112] Meanwhile, Myres had produced a shorter draft of his version. Deluged by appeals, Fallaize attempted to arrange a meeting between Keith, Myres and himself to decide upon a final version.[113] "As soon as we have agreed upon a form for the main appeal", wrote Fallaize to Myres, "we should arrange with individuals to follow it up with letters in support as I did before when we overwhelmed Elliot Smith's covert attack on the Institute in *The Times*." [114]

Whether the meeting between Fallaize, Keith and Myres ever transpired is uncertain, but we do know that Fallaize subsequently sent Keith's version of the appeal to a number of people, including Perry.[115] Perry's reaction was decidedly unfavourable and he produced a number of niggling criticisms. That these annoyed the hierarchy of the Anthropological Institute is obvious from the tone and quantity of the marginal comments added to Perry's letter, which appear from the handwritting to have been penned by Myres and Fallaize. The point about which Perry felt most strongly was that the appeal should not be addressed simply to those interested in colonial administration. "I don't agree", he says

that the chief object of anthropology is the study of native races. It is far wider in scope – it should be in the future one the master sciences. We need to study ourselves from the anthropological stand-point, let alone the native races. I think that it is an error in tactics to imply that anthropology is simply applied administration.

In the margin Fallaize has written "I agree; but can we at the present stage [subscribe?] to any investigation that [lacks?] appeal to the practical man and taxpayer?" [116]

Upon receiving the letter from Perry, Fallaize sent a copy of Keith's version of the appeal to Elliot Smith, mentioning that Perry had made a number of criticisms, but saying that he thought Perry's points could be accommodated without any essential modification. Fallaize also took the opportunity of waxing humble about the inaction of the Joint Committee:

It is a great pity that our Joint University Committee has been quiescent for so long until this summer. It must be three or four years since we have done anything at all. I am afraid the fault is mine . . . I hope, however, now that we have got going again, that we shall be able to pull things together a little.[117]

Elliot's Smith's reply has not been preserved, but early in November 1928 Fallaize wrote to Myres that in view of Elliot Smith's attitude, it would be wise to take no further notice of him. "It is hopeless to attempt to argue with him", says Fallaize, "and he seems so peaceably inclined just now that I should feel disposed to let sleeping dogs lie . . . "[118]

In the meantime, two further versions of the appeal had made their appearance. One, prepared by Myres and sent to Fallaize in October 1928, represented a *general* appeal, laying heavy stress on the value of anthropology in colonial administration and other practical applications.[119] The other, a *special* appeal advancing the particular views of the Institute, had apparently been prepared by combining the earlier drafts of Myres and Pitt-Rivers and emphasized the scientific as well as the practical worth of anthropology. This bifurcation of the appeal into special and general forms was probably intended as a concession to Perry's point about anthropology being more than simply applied administration, and there is some evidence that an effort was made to accommodate Elliot Smith's views as well. In deference to the latter's wishes, the special version of the appeal contained a passage about University College possessing a definite program of ethnological exploration. Responding to a draft of this version, C. G. Seligman, Professor of Ethnology at the London School of Economics, took exception to the singling-out of University College, saying "I think that you should add that the Anthropology Department of the School of Economics has a definite scheme for the exploration of the Anglo-Egyptian Sudan and has a highly qualified man working there at present."[120] Surprisingly, Elliot Smith, who had apparently been sent this latest version of the appeal despite Fallaize's earlier resolution to take no further notice of him, also objected to the reference to University College and suggested its deletion.[121] Hence, a modification of the special version of the appeal was produced, presumably by Fallaize or Myres, in which the University College passage had been dropped without, however, the addition of any reference to Seligman's program.[122]

Elliot Smith, apparently tired of being deluged with appeals emanating from the Royal Anthropological Institute, then produced his own version, written in his usual informal and vigorous style. This document represented an olive branch from Elliot Smith, since he unequivocally referred to the Royal Anthropological Institute as "the central clearing house for anthropological knowledge", and emphasized the need for British Universities to co-operate with the aforesaid body.[123] At the next meeting of the Joint Committee, Elliot Smith's version of the appeal was compared with the draft of the special appeal and it was unanimously agreed that the former was "more forcible and effective". It was decided, however, that providing Elliot Smith agreed, it would be best for the official appeal to take a more formal character and be followed by Elliot Smith's draft as a personal letter backing

Lewis Henry Morgan
(1818–1881), circa 1870,
when *Systems of
Consanguinity. . .* was
published (*University of
Rochester*).

Alfred W. Howitt
(1830–1908). Portrait by
William Strutt. Courtesy of
the *Dixson Library, Sydney*.

Howitt (on left) with Lorimer Fison (1832–1907),
Sale, Victoria, 1882.

W. Baldwin Spencer (1860–1929), circa
1905.

F. J. Gillen (1856–1912).

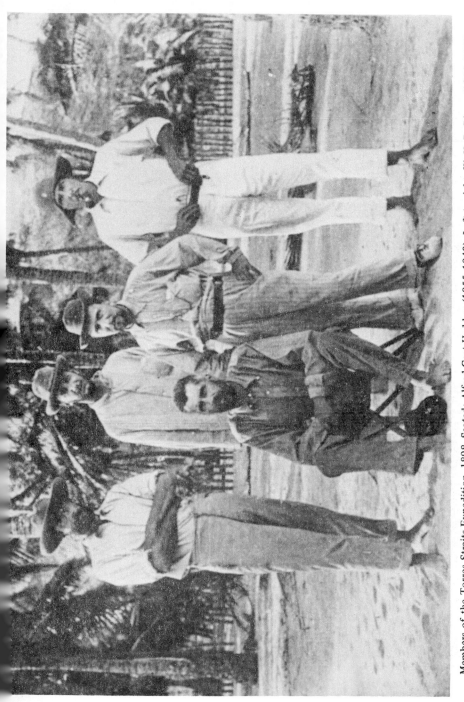

Members of the Torres Straits Expedition, 1898. Seated: Alfred Cort Haddon (1855–1940). Left to right: W. H. R. Rivers (1864–1922), C. G. Seligman, Sidney Ray and Anthony Wilkin. Absent: William McDougall and C. S. Myers (*University Museum of Archaeology and Ethnology, Cambridge*).

Rivers (right) and Henry Head (1861–1940) engaged in their experiments on the cutaneous nervous system. Taken in Rivers's rooms, St John's College, Cambridge, circa 1903 (*Psychology Department, University of Cambridge*).

John Layard (1892–1974) engaged in fieldwork in the New Hebrides, circa 1915.

A. Bernard Deacon (1903–1927) in the New Hebrides, circa 1926
(*Royal Anthropological Institute Photographic Collection*).

"Shell-shock Psychotherapists" at the Military Hospital, Maghull,
1915. Left to right: Dr William Brown, Rivers, Grafton Elliott
Smith (1871–1937).

Brenda Seligman (1882–1965) towards the end of her life (*Royal Anthropological Institute Photographic Collection*).

Daisy Bates (1863–1951). Portrait by Krischock.

Daisy Bates and some of her Aboriginal charges, Peak Hill, Western Australia, 1908.

A. R. Radcliffe-Brown (1881–1955). Reprinted by
courtesy of *Oceania*.

up the appeal.[124] Elliot Smith, however, had other ideas. Evincing sorrow that the Joint Committee had decided to issue its special appeal, which he described as "rather a damp squib", Elliot Smith averred that more harm than good might be done by publishing his document in support of the Institute's appeal. Hence, he concluded, "perhaps we can put our thing away for another occasion".[125]

Following this rebuff from Elliot Smith, negotiations with other people about a series of letters to back up the appeal continued for several months.[126] However, amazing though it may seem, none of these projected letters ever appeared in *The Times*. Nor, for that matter, did any version of the appeal itself.[127] Hence, the end-product of eighteen months of active correspondence, which produced no less than six versions of an appeal for funds, and involved at least eleven people, was precisely nothing. And, as I hope my account has made transparently clear, the primary cause of this debacle was friction between the extreme diffusionists and the rest of British anthropology.

(b) *International Co-operation*

A final example culled from the records of the Joint Committee for this period further demonstrates the extent to which Elliot Smith and Perry were out on a limb. During the late twenties, the ruling hierarchy of the Royal Anthropological Institute became concerned about the lack of official channels of communication between anthropologists of different countries. On making enquiries, it was discovered that an International Research Council already existed for the purpose of furthering international co-operation between scientists. However, anthropology was not one of the sciences represented on the Council. Fallaize therefore circulated to member institutions of the Joint Committee a letter requesting an expression of opinion as to whether it would be desirable for anthropology to ask for inclusion on the Council.[128] To this he received twenty-one definite replies, from representatives of all the important foci of anthropological and related studies in the British Isles. Of these replies, no less than twenty were in the affirmative, the lone veto coming from University College.[129] In his letter of reply, Elliot Smith simply says that he feels "no useful purpose would be served by making an application that is unlikely to lead to any result".[130] Perry's reply is equally succinct. He states that, having learned Elliot Smith's reason for answering in the negative, he can see no other course but to agree.[131] Hence, in this matter as in many others, the two diffusionists were thinking and acting as one, in what must have been a deliberate attempt to thwart their opponents.

*   *   *   *   *

An excellent, though hardly generous summation of the work of the Joint Committee was provided by Malinowski during the early thirties. In a "Report on the State of Anthropology and the Possibility of Its Development in England", Malinowski writes:

The Anthropological Institute Council started a Universities Research Committee (for the purpose of organizing anthropological research) in or about 1920. This Committee, so far, has achieved nothing, collected no money and arrived at no consensus of opinion. In spite of the superhuman efforts of Mr E. N. Fallaize, who is Secretary of that Committee, the Secretary of the Anthropology Section of the British Association, and the Secretary of the Anthropological Institute itself, nothing so far has been done.[132]

As I have argued, the prime reason for this inactivity was the hostility existing between the University College diffusionists and virtually everyone else in the world of British anthropology.

ROCKEFELLER MONEY

In October 1925, the Rockefeller Foundation, following a request from C. G. Seligman who was then President of the Royal Anthropological Institute, had awarded the Institute a grant of $17,500, payment being distributed over a period of five years.[133] In 1929, with the grant soon to expire, Fallaize wrote to the Foundation to ask whether it would be worthwhile for the Institute to make application for further assistance.[134] This request sparked a series of interesting exchanges between officials of the Rockefeller Foundation. One averred that the purposes which the Foundation had in mind in making the 1925 grant did not seem to have been fulfilled, and that "personal rivalries, not to say animosities, still seriously impede the progress of work among the British Anthropologists".[135] This impression was confirmed by Elton Mayo of the Harvard Business School, who was said to know the English anthropological scene most intimately.[136] The Foundation therefore wrote to Fallaize, asking for details of the purposes to which the proposed grant would be applied, and of the methods to be employed in administering the funds. From the tenor and direction of the requests, one gathers that the Rockefeller Foundation had heard about the inactivity of the Joint Committee:

Information indicating the ways in which the Institute endeavours to promote anthropological research would be of particular interest. If any committee would be charged with the responsibility for the allocation of the funds, would you kindly indicate the probable composition of this committee . . .[137]

Not having received a reply from Fallaize, the Rockefeller Foundation wrote again to the Institute, stating that they could not offer encouragement to the idea of making an application for a further grant.[138] At about this time A. M. Hocart, who had recently returned from Ceylon, got wind of what was going on, and wrote to Haddon expressing his generally sympathetic attitude to the extreme diffusionist cause. Hocart begins his letter by referring to the refusal of the Rockefeller Foundation to finance anthropology at University College in 1927:

Since coming to Oxford I have heard that a great Rockefeller opportunity was missed some three years ago owing to dissensions. I must say these dissensions made such a painful impression on me that I was almost glad to get away from England, so I am not surprised that they should have put off the Rockefeller people.

I do not want to go into the rights and wrongs. I can see both sides of the question, and I can see blame on both. But the Rockefeller people are back again and there is another chance. Whichever side refuses to sink differences which are largely personal, for the sake of a big scheme will have a lot on its conscience and will prove itself very small.

I will say this for the E. S. school, and that is that they are prepared to co-operate with people who differ from them . . . I get more encouragement from them though I am by no means an adherent and have been very critical as you will see in my review of the Children of the Sun. I think one can forgive a lot of bad manners, mistakes, and even excessive eagerness to bolster a weak argument, to people who can welcome co-operation from opponents. I have not found such a quality as well developed on the other side. I hope both will rise to the occasion and not let slip an opportunity to found a central institute for reconstituting the history of human thought.[139]

Apart from demonstrating the ambivalence of Hocart's loyalties in regard to Cambridge and University College, this letter also indicates that for Hocart there were two clearly defined sides, with Elliot Smith the leader of one and Haddon a prominent member of the other. Whether or not Hocart's letter inspired Haddon to do any bridge-building with Elliot Smith, and to thereby increase the Institute's chances of obtaining another Rockefeller Grant, is not recorded. However it is known that late in 1930, Sir William Beveridge, the Director of the London School of Economics, attempted to smooth things over with the Rockefeller Foundation. Stating that he knew the Foundation believed there to be "internecine strife" among British anthropologists, Beveridge explained the lack of harmony as due to friction with Elliot Smith, which had led to the latter's withdrawal from the Institute. However, according to Beveridge, the worst was now over, Elliot Smith having rejoined the Institute and become a Vice-President.[140]

Two additional occurrences may also have furthered the impression that British anthropology was now functioning harmoniously again. In 1929, Elliot Smith had acted as the official representative of the Royal Anthropological Institute at the Pan Pacific Science Congress in Java.[141] Secondly, circa 1930 the Proceedings of the Rivers Memorial Fund Committee were retrospectively written up in a manner which suggests that a deliberate attempt was being made to cover up the fact that absolutely nothing had been done about the Fund over the preceding eight years.[142] Moreover, the Proceedings for dates subsequent to 1930, which also just might have been written for the benefit of a passing Rockefeller official, can be interpreted as aiming to demonstrate on the one hand that projects were being embarked upon, and on the other that Elliot Smith was taking a prominent part in them.[143] In mid 1931, the Rockefeller Foundation grudgingly agreed to give a second grant to the Institute. However, the money was handed over according to a scheme involving a uniform taper over a six-year period, an arrangement which had, as one Rockefeller official remarked, "the advantage of providing a positive 'out' at the end of the term of the grant".[144]

Over the next few years, the Institute made a determined effort to prove that the rift with Elliot Smith had been bridged. The year 1931 saw the publication of a book called *Early Man, His Origin, Development and Culture*, which consisted of lectures delivered for the Institute, and included contributions by Elliot Smith and two of his former adversaries in Myres and Keith.[145] In January 1932, a Human Biology Research Committee was established by the Institute, with Elliot Smith as Chairman and chief organizer.[146] This move seems to have been specially designed to impress the Rockefeller Foundation, since the concept and the term "human biology" had apparently been invented by the Secretary of the Rockefeller Foundation in the course of some discussions with Elliot Smith.[147] In 1933, the Rockefeller Foundation made a grant to help the Institute stage the first meeting of the International Congress of Anthropological and Ethnological Sciences. In the material circulated by the Institute to publicize this event, Elliot Smith is prominently listed both as President of the Anatomy and Physical Anthropology Section, and as a member of the Executive Committee. It is also noticeable that the venues for the meeting are University College London, and the nearby Wellcome

Historical Medical Museum.[148] Hence, we may conclude that, by the early thirties at the latest, financial contingencies as exemplified by the problem of coaxing money from the Rockefeller Foundation in the context of an international economic crisis, had resulted in Elliot Smith being enthusiastically welcomed back into the anthropological fold.

*   *   *   *   *

In relation to the maturing of British Social Anthropology, there can be little doubt that the diffusion episode constituted a retrograde step. Whereas earlier Rivers had provided anthropology with a method, the mastery of which could be regarded as the rite of passage into the empirical side of the profession, later Rivers, Elliot Smith and Perry effectively took the discipline back a generation by invoking speculations which were at least as ill-substantiated as those of "armchair" anthropologists like Frazer and Tylor. For all their preaching about the virtues of common-sense empiricism, Elliot Smith and Perry made virtually no contributions to ethnographic data-collecting. With regard to theory, the work of the diffusionists similarly represented a step backwards. Whereas earlier Rivers had brought the hope that social anthropology would soon acquire technical modes of analysis and a cogent theoretical base, the hyperdiffusionists glorified in an *idée fixe* which was not amenable to formalized representation and which actually encouraged loose thinking. Indeed, Meyer Fortes refers to "Elliot Smith's unbending diffusionist commitment with its dogmas and doctrines that have more the marks of a mythological system than of objective scientific analysis".[149]

On the institutional front too, diffusionism must be judged a failure. Whereas Haddon and earlier Rivers had focussed, with a moderate degree of success, upon Cambridge University and the Royal Anthropological Institute as the main venues for promoting their kinship-centred anthropology, the diffusionists' attempts to institutionalize their approach came to nothing. Rivers failed to establish a journal in which diffusionist ideas could be aired, and in the months immediately preceding his death was apparently fighting a losing battle to change the nature of the Royal Anthropological Institute. The University College diffusionists, despite their self-aggrandizing claims, were not particularly successful in attracting students, and Elliot Smith proved singularly incapable of selling his grandiose diffusionistic plans to the Rockefeller Foundation. Indeed, the only tangible reminder of Elliot Smith's attempt to use Rockefeller money to promote hyperdiffusionism is the quasi-Egyptian architecture of the Medical School at University College.[150] Of all the people involved in the diffusion controversy during the 1920s, Elliot Smith looks less like a professional ethnologist than any of them. In fact, he never relinquished his primary vocation as an anatomist, and his excursions into diffusionistic ethnology resemble the outpourings of an over-enthusiastic amateur.

Summing up my account of the diffusion controversy, I would say that in many ways it looked like a case of bedevilment by the ghost of later Rivers. The two opposing sides were clearly defined and consisted of the remaining two extreme diffusionists, plus a few sympathizers, ranged against the balance of British anthropological opinion. Elliot Smith felt very strongly that the question at issue involved deciding who was applying the principles which Rivers had espoused in his later years. The role played by the ghost of earlier Rivers is not so easy to define. Haddon certainly saw the controversy as a morality play in which the sober, scientific precepts of earlier Rivers were threatened by the scurrilous and sometimes unprincipled outbursts of those who claimed to march under the banner of later Rivers. For Elliot Smith and Perry, it was not a case of earlier Rivers being diametrically opposed to later Rivers. Certainly they preferred Rivers's diffusionism to his work on social organization, but this was for them a matter of personal predilection rather than a conflict between good and bad scientific practice. In Elliot Smith's case, the forces of darkness were initially personified by the British Museum group, but as all sections of British anthropology joined in the attack on extreme diffusionism, Elliot Smith's perception of the enemy widened. The other people involved in the controversy, such as Fallaize, Myres, Seligman and Malinowski, had various motives and directed their barbs at different aspects of extreme diffusionism. For Fallaize, the whole affair unquestionably represented a frustration and an aggravation, increasing his secretarial work-load and rendering many of his efforts futile. However, there can be little doubt not only that he was firmly on the side of the opponents of extreme diffusionism, but also that, as the author of a respected article on "the Family",[151] he would have preferred a careful kinship-centred anthropology to speculations about cultural migrations. For Myres, the real incompetent was Perry, whose perversion of Rivers's historical method was best countered by satirical gibes. For Seligman and Malinowski, University College represented a rival to the London School of Economics for the largesse of anthropological benefactors. In Malinowski's case, there can be little doubt that Elliot Smith's ego provided a rival for his own, and that he found the empirically inexperienced Perry a perfect foil when presenting himself as the apostle of intensive fieldwork. However for Malinowski, the two surviving hyperdiffusionists were not the prime quarry. Rather Malinowski's target was Rivers, and his lingering reputation as the intellectual leader of British anthropology. Regarding Rivers as his *bête noire*, Malinowski was not concerned to take sides over the issue of earlier versus later Rivers. Rather he was as vehemently opposed to the narrowly technical concerns of the former, as he was to the speculative excesses of the latter.

For the Royal Anthropological Institute as a whole, their hostility to Elliot Smith and Perry was unquestionable. What is a little more controversial is the extent of their agreement regarding the positive alternative to extreme diffusionism. The general position of the Institute was perhaps best summed up by Myres, who said that what especially interested it was "the *sociological* aspect" (his emphasis) of anthropological data.[152] Just what Myres meant by this may be ascertained from the fourth edition of the *Notes and Queries on Anthropology*, of which Myres was a co-editor. This publication contains a major section entitled "Sociology", for which almost half the contributions were provided by Myres himself, and many of the remainder were due to Rivers. The topics covered by these contributions embrace anthropological method, including specifically the genealogical method, the life history of the individual in society, marriage and relations between the sexes, relationship terminology, economics of the social group, and politics – in other words, the kind of topics which are often captured under the general label "social organization". For the unlocking of such topics, the genealogical method was, in the first three decades of this century, widely regarded as the ethnographic key. Hence, if it is true that the Royal Anthropological Institute was primarily interested in one aspect of anthropology, and if this aspect is best described by the label "social organization", then the contributions of earlier Rivers would certainly have been germane to the Institute's position. In other words, from the standpoint of the Institute as a whole, which represented the main institutional locus of anthropological opposition to Elliot Smith and Perry, Haddon's perception of the diffusion controversy as a clash between the faithful disciples of earlier Rivers and the evil supporters of later Rivers, might not have been too wide of the mark. And, as we shall see in the next chapter, for Haddon and several other important members of the Cambridge school of ethnology, this interpretation was reinforced by an unlucky affair involving the Ambrym kinship system.

CHAPTER VI

AMBRYM – THE TEST CASE

The Torres Straits expedition of 1898 having been the direct inspiration for much subsequent fieldwork in British Social Anthropology, it was only natural that the locales for this fieldwork would emanate from the Torres Straits focal point. One major location for subsequent work was New Guinea itself, with Haddon, C. G. Seligman and the latter's pupil Malinowski acting as the prime movers for investigations in this area. The second major region of interest was Oceanic Melanesia, stretching south-east from New Guinea. Bishop R. H. Codrington had written a classic early account of *The Melanesians*, but in the first decades of the twentieth-century the pacesetter for the area was Rivers, whose penchant for long sea voyages, talent for performing anthropological surveys, preference for English-speaking informants and liking for the company of missionaries made him well-suited to probing the long fingers of the British Empire in the south Pacific.

As I have described in Chapter IV, Rivers's 1908 trip to Melanesia included what was, by his standards, intensive fieldwork with Hocart in the western Solomons.[1] But his most characteristic investigations were carried out during the voyages to and from the Solomons, on the missionary vessel *Southern Cross*. Apart from conducting rapid surveys on the various islands visited by the *Southern Cross*, Rivers had the benefit of captive informants, in the persons of the missionized natives who were using the boat to travel from one island to another. Moreover, for large portions of these voyages, Rivers had the co-operation of intelligent and sympathetic missionary interpreters in C. E. Fox and W. J. Durrad.[2] Rivers's *magnum opus*, the two volume *History of Melanesian Society*, is based on the survey-work he performed on the *Southern Cross*.

On the 1908 voyages to and from the Solomons, the *Southern Cross* had visited the New Hebrides, and it was to these islands that Rivers returned in 1914. After an abortive week on Atchin Island with John Layard, to be discussed later in the chapter, Rivers went to a mission station on the island of Tangoa and there devoted much of his energies to collecting material relating to the social organization of Ambrym. As we learned in Chapter III, much of Rivers's ethnological energies during the final years of his life were expended in an unsuccessful attempt to come to grips with the Ambrym kinship system, and his failure in this self-imposed task hung like a question mark over the activities of the Cambridge school of anthropology.

The other main theoretical thread in Rivers's later work on Melanesia was his attempt to support an extreme version of diffusionism. Much of *The History of Melanesian Society* is concerned with speculations about cultural migrations, but, as I mentioned in Chapter IV, it was not until 1918, when Rivers received an account of the mortuary customs of San Cristoval from C. E. Fox that his enthusiasm grossly exceeded his judgement. Reinforcing earlier suspicions aroused by Elliot Smith's investigations of the Torres Straits mummies, Fox's material finally convinced Rivers that the culture of Ancient Egypt had spread as far as the islands of the south Pacific. For someone interested in uncovering lingering survivals of ancient civilizations, the Pacific islands had a unique importance. As Rivers expressed it in his 1922 Presidential Address to the Royal Anthropological Institute:

The special point I wish to make in this address is that it is just because these islands of Oceania are so remote from regions which have been throughout human history the centres of civilization that they have preserved with so great fidelity the beliefs and customs of the ancient world. It is because of their remoteness and because they have not been reached by the many later influences which have obscured or obliterated the earlier cultures of Europe, India and Indonesia, that the conservatism of their people has preserved so many traces of the enterprise and hardihood which led voyagers from the early civilization of the Orient to undertake journeys of such vast extent. No one, whose interest in the past is so great that every possible clue to its understanding is of value, can ignore the possibility that these remote islands have preserved beliefs and practices which may serve to indicate the beliefs held by the peoples of ancient days.[3]

The specifically Egyptogenic aspect of Rivers's later diffusionism is not very important to our story, at least as a positive influence. Certainly in the work of two of Rivers's disciples, C. E. Fox and W. J. Perry, it provided a vital impetus. But in terms of the development of kinship theory, its positive role was very small. Far more important for our purposes are investigations by other members of the Cambridge school relating to the geographical area marked out for intensive empirical and theoretical work by Rivers himself. I refer to the islands of the New Hebrides group, and in particular to Ambrym.

One product of Cambridge anthropology who did field-work in the New Hebrides was C. B. Humphreys. In 1920 he was sent by Rivers to investigate the culture of Epi.[4] However, after arriving in the south Pacific, Humphreys learned from Fred Bowie, the head of the Tangoa mission school and Rivers's main contact in the New Hebrides, that it would not be possible to go to Epi, since the man upon whom Rivers was relying had died of blackwater fever.[5]

Moreover, as Bowie informed Rivers, the mission school had no Epi informants in residence.[6] Faced with this disruption of his plans, Humphreys
apparently went to stay with Bowie at Tangoa, developed and subsequently
abandoned a contingency plan to do the greater part of his field-work on
Eromanga,[7] and eventually put in four to five months on the island of Tanna
as his major effort in the field.[8] However, although in 1926 he succeeded in
publishing an ethnological monograph about the southern New Hebrides,
although the book was issued under the imprint of the Cambridge University
Press, and although it contains a number of genealogies and tables of relationship terms, Humphreys seems to have been well outside the mainstream
of the Rivers–Haddon school. Rarely referred to in subsequent writings of
the school, the monograph is generally quite superficial in its treatment of
kinship. Moreover Humphreys's "Introduction", while acknowledging some
sources of inspiration and practical assistance, pointedly does not mention
either Haddon or Rivers. Rather Humphreys states that "The division of the
material obtained into subject groups is that suggested by Malinowski, and his
plan of treatment of ethnological reports is followed throughout."[9] One also
gathers from the Introduction that Humphreys himself was very dissatisfied
with his own field-work. He describes his stay on Tanna as yielding "extremely
small returns, if judged by the results obtained in other remote parts of
the world".[10] In a letter to Haddon dated May 1922, Sir Geoffrey Butler,
Assistant Registrary for Research Studies at Cambridge, cites Humphreys as
an instance of a research student who did not "follow the ordinary line".[11]

More typical products of the Rivers–Haddon school, all of whom not
only did fieldwork in Melanesia, but also produced theoretical writings which
in some way bear on the Ambrym kinship system, are John Layard, W. E.
Armstrong, T. T. Barnard and A. Bernard Deacon. Their work is sufficiently
important to our story for us to devote the bulk of this chapter to them.

JOHN LAYARD (1892–1974)

As an undergraduate at Cambridge, Layard was drawn into ethnology via a
semi-formal group called the Heretics Society. Fired by humanistic, anti-
establishment and internationalistic sentiments, this Society, which met in
C. K. Ogden's room, apparently discussed issues, such as the psychological
basis of linguistics, which were later involved in Ogden's invention of "Basic
English".[12] Through the Cambridge "Heretics" Layard became involved in a
further Cambridge society, an "Anthropological Club" at which Rivers was a

frequent speaker. The young Layard rapidly came under the spell of what he later described as Rivers's "brilliance and charisma", and was elected to the position of secretary of the club.

In 1914, although Layard had had no formal training in anthropology, Haddon obtained money from the Percy Sladen Memorial Fund to subsidize Layard's passage to the antipodes for the Australian meeting of the British Association for the Advancement of Science. The arrangement was made for Layard to accompany Rivers on the S. S. *Euripides*, which went via the Cape of Good Hope, while Haddon and his daughter Kathleen took the shorter route via Suez on the S. S. *Orsova*. As I have mentioned in Chapter IV, the fact that Haddon and Rivers travelled in different boats may have had something to do with Haddon's disapproval of some of Rivers's more outlandish excursions into diffusionism. On the voyage out, Layard saw very little of Rivers, who was correcting the proofs of his soon-to-be-published *History of Melanesian Society*. While on the Indian Ocean, word came through of the outbreak of hostilities with Germany, the news being received with shock and disbelief by all on the boat.[13]

Following the British Association meeting, Haddon had planned to make a cruise along the coast of New Guinea in a naval gunboat, taking Layard along to assist in an ethnographic survey of the area. However, with the onset of war, the gunboat became unavailable, and Rivers decided, instead of immediately going back to a war-disrupted Cambridge, to carry out an anthropological expedition to Melanesia, his diffusionistic interests having recently been kindled by evidence, published by the Swiss ethnologist Felix Speiser, of a living megalithic culture in the northern New Hebrides.[14] At this stage Haddon advised Layard to accompany Rivers, since this would give the young student "the invaluable opportunity of practical tuition and supervision by the greatest field investigator of primitive sociology that there has ever been".[15] Hence, a flattered and delighted Layard found himself en route for Melanesia with the anthropologist whose work he most wished to emulate. As Layard understood it, the plan was for the two men to spend some three months together on fieldwork, with Rivers teaching the young student his methods and his general views on Melanesian society.

After arriving in the New Hebrides and speaking to the Resident Commissioner, Rivers decided to go to Atchin, one of the Small Islands off the north coast of Malekula, since the native culture there was alleged to be in its purest state. All attempts at evangelization had failed and an Irish trader had recently been driven from the the the island after a fracas with the natives. Having been deposited on Atchin by the Resident Commissioner's yacht, circa September

1914, Rivers and Layard found themselves the only white men on the island, surrounded by intensely hostile blacks. After an uneasy week living in a deserted building, Rivers was picked up by a missionary boat and taken to the island of Tangoa, where, as Layard later found out, he pursued ethnographic investigations in the relative comfort of a mission station. It was, in fact, at this place that Rivers obtained the data which led to his disastrous analysis of Ambrym, as outlined in Chapter III. Layard, who never ascertained whether or not Rivers had pre-arranged the arrival of the boat, was thus left by himself on Atchin, where he stayed for approximately one year. Apart from some brief visits to the neighbouring Small Island of Vao, where he enjoyed the hospitality of a Catholic priest, Layard's only contact with other white men during this period came with the two-monthly calls of an inter-island steamer. Hence, many months before Malinowski pitched his tent in the Trobriands,[16] Layard found himself in a situation where he had little option but to become deeply involved in Atchin society. Shifting to native quarters, he gained a good grasp of the vernacular, acted over a period of nine months as a kind of honorary "novice" at the young men's initiation ceremonies and, on occasion, danced with the natives dressed only in a penis wrapper. Discussing these matters with Layard more than half a century later, one could never doubt the profundity of his emotional involvement with and intellectual grasp of Atchin culture.

After returning to England to fight in the war, Layard suffered a serious nervous breakdown and was, for a time, visited daily by Rivers, who apparently felt guilty about his young charge and attempted to cure the latter's nervous condition by psychiatric means. This treatment of Layard seems to have been important in Rivers's own intellectual development, leading as it did to his interest in Freudian psychology, and more specifically to his work on shell-shocked soldiers. As far as Layard was concerned, the treatment was disastrous, since Rivers's desire to see Layard writing up his ethnological material conflicted sharply with his perception of Layard as a person suffering from nervous exhaustion and greatly in need of a rest.[17]

As Layard perceived the situation in later life, his psychiatric condition was badly mishandled by Rivers, and it was partly for this reason that Layard never succeeded in writing up his Atchin data in monographic form. His substantial *Stone Men of Malekula*, not published until 1942, was based on the mere three weeks he spent on Vao. Assuming that Vao possessed an unmixed form of the more complex Atchin culture, Layard intended this book merely as a ground-clearing operation for his projected *magnum opus* on Atchin. However, despite his production of an eight-hundred page typescript on kinship in the Small Island group, the Atchin book was never completed, and Layard's potentially great contribution to British Social Anthropology in general, and to kinship theory in particular, did not eventuate. Although *Stone Men of Malekula* does contain a great deal of interesting kinship material, including some ingenious diagrammatic methods of representing marriage-class systems, its late publication date, its limited circulation due to the Second World War, and its concern to demonstrate cultural diffusion, has minimized its influence.

For those members of the Rivers–Haddon school whose opinion counted during the late twenties and thirties, Layard was a man who had apparently done some intensive fieldwork, but who seemed unwilling or unable to write it up in publishable form and who, in any case, was tarred with the brush of diffusionism and had missed the big ethnographic coup that one might have expected of a Rivers's protégé – the discovery of the six-section system on Ambrym.

W. E. ARMSTRONG (1896–   )

As a Cambridge undergraduate taking the Moral Sciences Tripos with special subject Psychology, Wallace Armstrong was introduced to Rivers's work on experimental psychology by the former Torres Straits expedition member C. S. Myers and his colleague F. C. Bartlett. In his finals year, 1917–1918, Armstrong investigated the possibility of research in ethnology, and was given a year's postgraduate work under Haddon and Rivers. As Armstrong himself has written, Rivers's "fascinating work on relationship systems was a primary stimulus" at this time. In the autumn of 1919, when Armstrong left for New Guinea as Anthony Wilkin Student in Ethnology, Rivers was, to again use Armstrong's words, "undoubtedly . . . a principal inspiration", and it was Haddon and Rivers who directed his ethnographic attention to south-east Papua. The choice of Rossel Island as the specific venue for his fieldwork was actually suggested by Malinowski, whom Armstrong met in Australia, and possibly also by C. G. Seligman.[18] However, in the preface to his book on *Rossel Island*, Armstrong gives credit to Haddon for "fathering" the expedition, his debt to Seligman and Malinowski being described as "more indirect".

In his early investigations of Rossel Island culture, Armstrong, as befitting a pupil of Rivers, had devoted special attention to the system of relationships. However, in 1926, after Haddon had been replaced as Reader in Ethnology by T. C. Hodson under circumstances described in the previous chapter, Armstrong was not retained in his position as teacher in social anthropology and shifted his allegiances to economics. Whether for this reason, or simply because he had discovered an unusual system of currency on the island, Armstrong's major theoretical focus became the Rossel monetary system. Thus, his *Rossel Island* monograph, published by the Cambridge University Press in 1928, devotes relatively little space to kinship theory, and relegates his attempt to provide a general theory of the classificatory system of relationships to an appendix.

This appendix is, however, of considerable interest in the story of the development of kinship theory by the Rivers school. Starting with the initial aim of providing a theory of origin for the classificatory system he had detected on Rossel Island, Armstrong sketches out an hypothetical evolutionary relationship between three types of kinship system, each of which can be seen as utilizing the concept of a "classificatory relationship term" which Rivers had developed from Morgan's work (i.e., a relationship term whose meaning has been extended to all members of a clan of a given generation). These three types comprise what Armstrong calls "open-class systems" (i.e., systems possessing exogamous, unilineal classes, in which intermarriage between classes is governed by systematic rules, but in which the individual members of a given class can be from any generation); "closed class systems" (i.e., systems possessing a limited number of exogamous unilineal classes, in which intermarriage between classes is governed by systematic rules, and in which the individual members of any given class will either be in the same generation as each other, or separated by n times x generations, n being any integer from unity upwards, and x, the "interval of descent", an integer $\geqslant 2$ which is fixed for any particular closed class system); and "classificatory systems" (i.e., systems in which there are no classes, but intermarrying exogamous groups in which every member is related to every other member by every classificatory relationship consistent with exogamy and the sex of the members).

Assuming an open class system to be in operation, Armstrong asked what would happen if a type of marriage inconsistent with this kind of system became common, classificatory relationship terms being used throughout in the sense defined by Rivers. His answer is that either a closed class system or a classificatory system would result. Taking the former possibility first, and assuming a dual organization into matrilineal moieties, and a descent interval of two generations, Armstrong discerns a limited number of "solutions" to the problem created by the appearance of the new form of marriage. One of these solutions, which he calls Type A, involves marriage with the mother's brother's daughter and the father's sister's daughter. Now, as he acknowledges in a footnote, the four-class systems of the Australian Aborigines are of this type. If, on the other hand, a descent interval of three rather than two generations is assumed, the possible solutions will, as Armstrong points out, involve closed systems containing six classes.[19] To illustrate the forms of the six-class system which Armstrong regards as possible, three diagrams are produced.[20] In actual fact none of these three diagrams corresponds to the six-class system which may be regarded as functioning on Ambrym. His first diagram, which comes closest, invokes as its typical forms of marriage those with the mother's brother's daughter and father's sister's daughter, whereas the typical marriages for the Ambrym system are with the mother's brother's daughter's daughter, and the mother's father's sister's daughter. Moreover, the periodicity of Armstrong's hypothetical system is 362, whereas the periodicity of the Ambrym system is 322. Nonetheless, it is possible to represent the two systems diagrammatically in a way which makes them *appear* quite similar.[21] Hence, it may not be coincidental that, as we shall find out later in this chapter, Armstrong's star pupil Bernard Deacon was one of the codiscoverers of the Ambrym system.

The second possibility in Armstrong's postulated breakdown of class systems is that "classificatory systems" will result, although this does not mean that classificatory systems could not be formed by some other process. For the classificatory systems of Melanesia, however, Armstrong argues that one particular feature, the classing of mother's sister's children with father's brother's children, points strongly to the systems having had their origins in some form of class system. Moreover, the terminological merging of the words for wife and granddaughter on Pentecost, which, as we discovered in Chapter III, had been utilized by Rivers in his theory of anomalous marriages, Armstrong interprets as "additional and independent evidence of the former existence of a class system in Melanesia".[22]

Hence, a young student imbibing Armstrong's views on the phylogeny of class systems, might have expected to find survivals of a class system in Melanesia, which he would have interpreted as the original form of the various types of classificatory system which are presently common there. Moreover, he would also have been confronted with the specification of a possible six-class system, which, as we can now see with the benefit of hindsight, can be made to appear rather similar to the one eventually detected on Ambrym.

Despite his promising work on kinship theory, Armstrong was, as I have mentioned, not retained on the staff after Hodson succeeded to Haddon's

Readership in Ethnology, and his considerable talents were lost by Cambridge anthropology. Nonetheless, his enlargement of the tradition established by Rivers was, as we shall discover later in this chapter, to bear fruit in the work of his pupil Bernard Deacon.

T. T. BARNARD (1898–   )

Having taken an honours degree in Zoology at Oxford in 1921, Barnard went to Cambridge in October of that year with any thought of becoming an anthropologist far from his mind. However, while there he met Rivers and was persuaded by him to switch to social anthropology.[23] After Barnard had received one year's instruction in ethnology, which included attending Rivers's lectures on kinship,[24] it was decided that he and John Baker, a fellow student in Zoology at Oxford, should go to the New Hebrides. There it would be Barnard's task to fill certain gaps left by Rivers during his 1914 expedition. Specifically, Rivers recommended that Barnard should devote his time to one of three special areas — the southern Banks Islands, Pentecost, or northern Santo.[25] Barnard was to have spent June and July 1922 with Rivers, going through the latter's unpublished 1914 material. However, as Barnard recalled over half a century later: "[Rivers] died during the Whitsun weekend the very day before I was to start my intensive briefing and I went off to the New Hebrides knowing his earlier *History of Melanesian Society*, but in almost complete ignorance of his work on Ambrim".[26]

It would seem that the first of the three special areas selected by Rivers was the one decided upon, for there survives at Cambridge the following plan of action for Barnard in the southern Banks Islands, which Haddon evidently sketched out prior to his student's departure:

1 year — Expedition to the Banks Islands.
(first to Mota Lava — stay there about 6 weeks — then probably to Santa Maria, where there are some pagans. Coming back about June 1923.)[27]

If this sketch seems rather vague, it would also appear that the fieldwork which Barnard actually performed was neither very productive with regard to data collection, nor particularly intensive. During the late twenties Barnard stated that, on his return to England in 1923, he possessed "fairly full accounts of the social organization of the Banks Islands, of Efate (Vate), and of certain areas in Northern Santo, and some thirty incomplete kinship systems, with notes on the general social organization from other islands."[28] However, this probably gives a false impression of the extent of his empirical achievements since, in a recent personal communication, he readily acknowledges that his expedition yielded "very little original material".[29] In fact, to supplement his own data for purposes of writing his doctoral thesis, Barnard wrote to Elliot Smith, Rivers's literary executor, and obtained permission to see the latter's unpublished notes on the New Hebrides. These could not be located for three months, and when they were, Barnard found Rivers's handwriting barely legible.[30] After much laborious transcription, however, Barnard was able to extract valuable material therefrom. The full title of Barnard's thesis, completed in 1924, indicates the extent to which he relied on Rivers's data: "The Regulation of Marriage in the New Hebrides. From the original notes of the late Dr W. H. R. Rivers F. R. S. Edited, with additional material by T. T. Barnard." The first chapter, which deals with the island of Mota, where Haddon had stated that Barnard was to commence his fieldwork, contains the statement that, in terms of data, he has "nothing to add" to the accounts previously furnished by Rivers and Bishop Codrington. And if the volume of his ethnographic data-gathering apparently left something to be desired, it would also seem that he did not generally conduct his investigations in the vernacular. Certainly, the interrogations of his informants from Ambrym were all conducted in Pidgin English,[31] and in the brief preface to the thesis Barnard singles out for special thanks a missionary, "who for nearly two months acted as my interpreter in the Banks Islands".

At any rate, whatever the shortcomings of his fieldwork, Barnard's theoretical accomplishments in the thesis are considerable. Putting the limited data at his disposal to good advantage, Barnard makes a concerted effort to master, classify and map the myriad forms of marriage regulation in the New Hebrides. In doing this, he attempts to ensure that, unlike Perry or the later Rivers, any speculations he makes about the phylogeny or diffusion of social organization are modest in scope and, where not evidently warranted by the evidence at hand, expressed with suitable reservations.

For our purposes, the most interesting chapter of his thesis is the one dealing with Ambrym, in which is recorded the first discovery of the six-section system. Barnard relates that, since he was aware that Rivers and Layard had worked in the central New Hebrides, he had not thought it necessary to pay any special ethnographic attention to Ambrym. The information he did collect, comprising brief pedigrees from five Ambrym males,[32] "was obtained solely to elucidate problems connected with the distribution of relationship terms".[33]

Whilst Barnard was carrying out his fieldwork, the possible existence of a class system was first suggested to him by kinship correspondences from Ambrym and Malo similar to the Fijian ones which, as we discovered in Chapter III, Rivers had explained on the hypothesis that marriage with the grandmother had formerly taken place. Subsequently, Barnard's attention was redirected to the class system hypothesis by a man from the Big Namba people of northern Malekula. According to this informant, marriage for any individual Big Namba is regulated by the membership of an exogamous group to which all ego's brothers and sisters belong, his father and father's sister being attached to a second group, his mother and mother's brother to a third, and his mother's brother's children to a fourth. Now, as Barnard was well aware, these four conditions are satisfied by all the known class systems. However, the informant was very vague about the groups to which more distant relatives belonged, and stated with some hesitation that he thought his mother's father belonged to the same group as his father, which, as Barnard correctly observes, would mean that the groups could not correspond to matrimonial classes.[34]

Since the man was obviously unsure about the whole matter, Barnard did not question him further, hoping to obtain more reliable data from other informants. However, the only north-Malekulans he subsequently interrogated came from the other side of the island where marriage was regulated on different principles. Consequently, Barnard finished his fieldwork possessing no firm evidence in favour of the hypothesis that a class system existed in the New Hebrides. He was, nonetheless, "inclined to believe that some system of matrimonial classes had existed in the New Hebrides previous to the introduction of the matrilineal 'totemic' clans; and that traces of this system were still to be found in areas to which the clans have never penetrated."[35]

With specific regard to Ambrym, Barnard says that his information "was too fragmentary to allow any definite deductions", but he considered that "if a class system had previously existed in the New Hebrides it would be of the eight-class type such as is found among the Arunta".[36] Indeed, as he was to demonstrate in the thesis, the Ambrym system and the eight-class Arunta system do possess a number of features in common. However, upon returning to England and obtaining access to Rivers's Ambrym material and Bowie's corrections, Barnard concluded that the eight-class hypothesis could not be sustained. Nor for that matter was Rivers's own interpretation plausible. "It became clear", wrote Barnard,

that Rivers had got everything wrong. It was a classic example of an interrogator with firm preconceived ideas asking the wrong questions and misinterpreting the right answers when he got them. For a long time I could make nothing of it.[37]

Eventually, however, the fact that each *vantinbul* contained only alternate generations suggested to Barnard that some kind of class system might still be involved: "if not of eight classes perhaps of four, six, ten or twelve". Recalling this period of his research almost fifty years after the event, Barnard wrote

I have a vague memory of spending a cold weekend in front of a gas fire covering sheets of paper with hypothetical 4, 6, 8, 10 and 12 class systems and suddenly realizing that a six-class system was possible and could work in a relatively small isolated population and that all Bowie's corrections and the Ambrim men's statements fitted and could only fit a six-class system.[38]

The presentation of this important result in the thesis is somewhat tentative, with Barnard acknowledging that, even though the hypothesis of a six-class system harmonizes very well with the kinship correspondences recorded by Rivers, the problem remains "to prove that there are really six and only six classes" within each linguistically distinct district of the island. For the apparent class system "might conceivably be an illusion produced by the fact that each individual is intimately concerned with three villages and, hence, with six *vantinbul* and the six class system may only be relative to the individual and not comparable to the matrimonial classes of Australia". The resolution of this problem was made difficult by the inadequacies of Rivers's data, including his "conflicting evidence ... concerning the nature of the *vantinbul*", and the fact that he had not always recorded the villages of the people in his genealogies.[39] Hence, although Barnard had proved to his own satisfaction that a six-section system existed in Ambrym,[40] he continued in the thesis to refer to his "theory"[41] of Ambrym social organization, and even later did not attempt to claim it as anything more than a mere "deduction"[42] from incomplete data collected by previous investigators.

The communication of Barnard's conclusions about Ambrym to other members of the Rivers's school was far from complete, as we shall discover shortly when discussing Bernard Deacon. His thesis was never published, partly because Barnard felt the material needed redrafting and confirmation, and partly because the Cambridge University Press required a large subsidy which the recently-engaged Barnard could ill afford.[43] In fact, his only publications on Ambrym were brief contributions to the 1928 volume of *Man*, written after Deacon's rediscovery of the six-section system. As Barnard himself was to relate in 1954, R. and B. Lane, two subsequent workers on New Hebridean kinship, had complained that Barnard's work on Ambrym existed "only in footnotes".[44]

After eight years in Radcliffe-Brown's former chair of Social Anthropology at Capetown, Barnard dropped out of anthropology and is now generally forgotten by the profession — the discovery of the true nature of the Ambrym kinship system usually being attributed to the next disciple of Rivers whom we shall be discussing, Bernard Deacon.

A. BERNARD DEACON (1903–1927)

At first sight, the basic facts pertaining to the Bernard Deacon episode read like the plot of a second-rate romantic novel. After an exotic childhood in pre-revolutionary Russia, a sensitive and personable young man comes to England and distinguishes himself by an almost incredibly-brilliant high school and undergraduate career. Attracted to anthropology at Cambridge, he is awarded a fellowship to pursue intensive fieldwork on an apparently idyllic South Sea island. There he finds a dying culture, the people ravaged by disease and seduced by the trinkets of Western civilization. However, despite chronic bouts of melancholy and depression, he manages to win the confidence and friendship of the natives and complete some competent investigations. An eminent professor of anthropology, without having so much as met the young fieldworker, offers him a lectureship in his department. In the final weeks of his stay, the young man takes it upon himself to stray from the ethnographic plan laid down for him by his mentors, and proceeds to another island, for which, as he was later to claim, he had previously deduced that the social organization would be of great interest to anthropologists. There he convincingly demonstrates that the island possesses a complex, beautiful and symmetrical kinship system. Wasting no time he writes up his results and sends them off to several famous anthropologists, who hail his conclusions as being of considerable theoretical importance, and his method of presentation as superbly incisive. The young man is packing to leave the islands when he contracts a mysterious malady and, after a brief illness, dies. The official cause of death is given as blackwater fever, but there are persistent rumours, never settled, that he may have been poisoned by the missionaries with whom he was staying.[45] British anthropology widely mourns his passing, but two of the major theoretical schools within that discipline compete in the attempt to annex his work to their particular cause. After some delay, his effects are sent back to civilization by the missionaries, but his manuscripts are found on arrival to be in a very poor condition, and the field notes documenting his crucial theoretical discovery are missing. Eventually his surviving manuscripts are published as a substantial book — the index to this tome being prepared by the girl he had intended to marry, and the laborious task of editing being carried out by a young female colleague who likewise seems to have been performing a labour of love.

But if an outline of the story suggests a plot by Erich Segal, the fact of its truth and the fascination of its finer detail rescue it from banality. As an undergraduate at Cambridge, Deacon was placed in Class I of Part I of the Natural Science Tripos in 1923, and in Class I of the Medieval and Modern Languages Tripos the following year. He then proposed to enter the Foreign Office, but being too young to sit for the entrance examination, decided to while away a year by reading anthropology. It was then that he came under the influence of Haddon, who at first suggested that he should work for a Diploma of Anthropology, and later persuaded him to read for the Tripos.[46] His instructor in Social Anthropology was that erstwhile disciple of Rivers, W. E. Armstrong, whose lectures and evening conversation classes were to lay the foundation for Deacon's Ambrym triumph. In the letter in which he triumphantly announced his discovery of the six-section system to Haddon, Deacon locates the sources of his inspiration firmly within the Rivers school: " . . . the thing was to me a kind of crucial experiment at the end of a long train of ideas – beginning really in my first reading of Rivers and talks with Armstrong – I owe a great deal to him in social anthropology".[47] In a later letter to Haddon, he pays the following tribute to Armstrong: "On the theoretical side of social anthropology I found him very interesting and illuminating. He is extremely fair and unbiased, and a confirmed logician."[48]

Amongst the papers which were to survive Deacon's untimely death is a set of partially typed, partially handwritten notes on "Australian Social Organization".[49] The handwriting is definitely Deacon's, but the notes are undated, and the precise function for which they were written is unclear. They could well have been made on the basis of other people's lectures or published material. Alternatively, they could represent notes for lectures or papers which Deacon himself had been preparing. Since they contain no comparative references to Malekulan material, it seems certain that they were written in Cambridge before Deacon set off for the south Pacific. If so, it is likely that they embody material which was imparted to Deacon by Armstrong. This hypothesis is supported by the fact that the notes contain a species of kinship diagram which I have elsewhere encountered only in the appendix to Armstrong's book on *Rossell Island*. But the only safe inference that can be drawn is that the notes provide evidence of the milieu of ideas within which Deacon was operating shortly before his Malekulan fieldwork.[50]

The first thing which strikes one in respect of Deacon's notes on Australian

Social Organization is his use of circular digrams, similar to my Figure 5 in Chapter I, to represent the matrilineal and patrilineal cycles of the Arunta system. Already, it seems, Deacon was conceptualizing class-systems in terms of circular connubia in which maternal and paternal descent travel around well-defined paths connecting the classes. The second thing about the notes is that they clearly betray an interest, not just in the static structure of known class systems, but in the dynamic processes by which class systems change and evolve. One diagram, for example, attempts to depict a process of "interchange", by which the Dieri system may be transformed into the Arunta system. And a substantial portion of the notes is taken up with speculations about how the various kinds of known class system might be phylogenetically related.

These speculations tentatively explore three hypotheses relating to the evolution of the Australian systems. Firstly there is the suggestion, here attributed to Radcliffe-Brown, that the eight-class system resulted from the injunction that a man should marry his mother's mother's brother's daughter's daughter. This suggestion is rejected on the grounds that it could hardly provide a sufficient explanation for the origin of the eight-class system, since the same injunction could also have given rise to a four-class system.

Secondly, there is the suggestion that the evolution of the class systems can be explained in terms of a gradual tightening up of the rules prohibiting incest. The dual division prevents the marriage of brother and sister, but does not forbid the marriage of certain other close relatives. For example, in the Urabunna tribe, where descent within each moiety is matrilineal, a father could (in theory) marry his own daughter. Four-class systems like the Kamilaroi, as well as forbidding the marriage of brother and sister, additionally rule out marriages between alternate generations, including the case of a man with his daughter. However, they still allow marriage between cross-cousins. Eight-class systems like the Arunta, as well as prohibiting marriages between brother and sister, and between alternate generations, additionally forbid marriage between cross-cousins. In other words, through the extension of taboos on incest, primitive promiscuity developed into the dual division, the dual division developed into the four-class system, and the four-class system developed into the eight-class system.

Having briefly alluded to this causal theory, the notes proceed to discuss the third hypothesis, which is concerned, in a descriptive rather than causal fashion, with the process of "fissure", by which the dual division might develop either into a four-class system, or into an eight-class system. According to Deacon's notes:

It is obvious that the four-class system can be derived from the Dual Organization by a process of fissure; it is equally obvious that the eight-class system cannot be so derived from the four-class. The reason for this is that in the four-class system the moieties are symmetrical, or direct reflections of one another, in the method of tracing descent, [whereas] in the eight-class systems [the moieties] are in this respect "inverted reflections".

The notes then indulge in some rather ingenious speculations about how the dual organization might have undergone a "partial fissure" into a temporary "intermediate stage" of four-class system. In this intermediate stage, it is suggested, the method of tracing descent in one half of the system would be asymmetrical with the method of tracing descent in the other half. The argument then goes that the intermediate stage could subsequently undergo a further fissure, and thereby produce an eight-class system.

Although these three speculative hypotheses are not worked out in any great detail, the notes leave no doubt that, before his arrival in Malekula, Deacon had thought at some length about the different forms that class-systems can take, and about the phylogenetic ielationships which might connect the various known systems. One can hardly imagine a more relevant preparation for someone who was about to be confronted with the Ambrym data.

While still an undergraduate, Deacon wrote, and later published, a paper in which he correlated ghost societies and initiation cults from New Guinea with each other and with the Kakihan of Ceram, an Indonesian ghost society which Deacon took to represent the most complete survival of the original cult. While not so extreme in its diffusionism as to repel Haddon, who described it as "suggestive",[51] the article was nonetheless sufficiently diffusionistic to attract the attention of Elliot Smith, who marked Deacon down as a probable future contributor to his ethnological cause. However, in the surviving fragment of a letter to Haddon written on 8th September 1925, Deacon reveals a somewhat less than totally reverential attitude to Perry and his theories:

I must confess I find Perry interesting, in spite of a certain incapacity for seeing difficulties where they exist and an absence of give and take in argument. He intends returning shortly to the analysis of Indonesian cultures. I said I had been doing something of the same kind recently, and asked him whether he had tackled Ceram. He said he had not, but hoped to do so very soon, as there was a very interesting "Dual Organization" there – Patasiwa and Patalima (!)[52] Apparently initiation cults are shortly to be included in the kit of the "Children of the Sun". Hocart and he are working on them.[53]

In 1925, Deacon took a First in the Anthropological Tripos and Haddon suggested that the young ethnologist, who has been described as "extremely

Malekula-oriented" at this period of his career,[54] should carry out intensive fieldwork on Malekula, which, as Haddon said, "was known to possess a rich native culture concerning which scarcely anything had been published".[55] Deacon's ethnographic attention was directed to the locality of South West Bay, although the person to whose influence this occurrence should be attributed is in doubt, since both Haddon and Layard later wished to take the credit.[56]

Having been appointed to the Anthony Wilkin Studentship, Deacon sailed for the south Pacific on 1st October 1925. In a letter to Haddon, written on board ship and dated 25th October,[57] Deacon reveals that, like a true product of the Rivers–Haddon school, he counters the boredom of the long journey by becoming proficient at cat's cradles. He also discusses last-minute alterations to his paper on ghost societies and goes on to say that he imagines there would be some point in comparing the Indonesian nobility of Ceram with that of Micronesia. "Indeed", he writes, "the correspondence between the three-class social structure of Ceram and that of Micronesia may be less imaginary than it seems at first sight." Hence, it would appear that Deacon's early interest in social structure was intermingled with speculations about diffusion.

A letter to Armstrong, posted from Colombo and dated 4th November 1925, continues Deacon's speculations about the interrelationship of widely separated ghost societies and reveals that Deacon was having his doubts about how to treat cultural convergences from widely separated societies. After discussing a Tierra del Fuegian ghost society, Deacon writes:

What do you make of the whole thing? It seems to me to be remarkably similar to the sort of thing that goes on in parts of New Guinea . . . what does it mean? Ought the psychoanalysts to tackle it? I wish I could make up my mind about "convergences" of this kind. Are you to leave things to the "comfortable doctrine" of evolution? Transmission and evolution seem equally difficult.

Later in the letter, after again mentioning his dallying with cat's cradles, Deacon waxes apologetic: "This letter seems to contain very little pure Sociology or Social Organization as I suppose it should. I'm sorry. The next will."[58]

Upon arrival in the New Hebrides, Deacon was forced to spend nearly a forthnight at Vila on the island of Efate, waiting for a boat to Malekula. There he devoted his energies to making a general survey of the northern New Hebridean "grading system" used to rank people within the hierarchical social organization. Now in his paper on "Ceremonial and Descent in Ambrim",

Rivers had pointed out that, in the ceremonies connected with the Ambrym grading system, no part is taken by any of the people in the maternal line. This fact he correlated with the current system of descent, which he (incorrectly) believed to be purely patrilineal. Since he endorsed the then widely held view that matrilineal institutions are more archaic than patrilineal ones, and since he believed Ambrym to adjoin a region characterized by matrilineality, it was a short step to infer that Ambrym had originally been matrilineal but, having succumbed to patrilineality, was not acting as a source for the diffusion of patrilineal institutions, including the grading system. In accordance with this general scheme, Deacon concluded from his survey that "the dispersal centre for the whole grade system in New Hebrides was the East Malekula–West Ambrym area", and that this conclusion "harmonizes well with the distribution of patrilineal descent".[59] As one proceeds north from Malekula and Ambrym, both of which Deacon evidently regarded as patrilineal, one encounters, he points out, regions in which matrilineality becomes increasingly dominant. An interesting area to study, he writes, would be the island of Malo off the coast of Santo, where the influences of patrilineality and matrilineality are approximately equal. "I'd rather like to get up to West Santo before I leave and have a go at the systems of marriage regulation there", he says later in the letter. "I wish I could clear up the meaning of Rorsali's statement that every fourth generation the female descendants in the female line are sent back to the village from which their matrilineal group traces descent and married to sons of men of their group residing in that village."[60] Now since, according to one interpretation popular in Deacon's time, marriage-class systems were regarded as arising from the intermeshing of more or less equally stressed matrilineal and patrilineal systems of descent, and since it is a feature of the best known cases of eight-class systems that marriage arrangements for women repeat themselves every fourth generation, in regard to both the class and territory of eligible males,[61] we may infer that Deacon suspected the existence of a class system. In view of his later achievement in Ambrym, it is interesting to note that having apparently swallowed Rivers's conclusion that Ambrym institutions are patrilineal, Deacon evidently believed that the most promising place to look for a class system would be, not Ambrym, but the West Santo area, some eighty miles to the north-east.

Haddon's correspondence with Deacon while the young anthropologist was in the field, reveal the older man's style and persistence as a team co-ordinator. In a letter written during May 1926,[62] Haddon mentions that, having talked with Radcliffe-Brown, he expects the latter to offer Deacon a lectureship in Social Anthropology at the University of Sydney. One could do much worse than settle in Sydney and continue one's Melanesian researches, writes Haddon. Radcliffe-Brown will be devoting the next few years to his researches on the Australian Aborigines, and "proposes to leave Melanesia etc. to the lecturer". Haddon then reveals that Gregory Bateson, another product of Cambridge Ethnology, will soon be coming to Sydney preparatory to carrying out fieldwork in New Guinea. "He is an able man", writes Haddon, "and is very keen to do a piece of intensive fieldwork well up the Sepik. He will look out for you in Sydney when he arrives . . . on the chance that you may be there. Naturally, he will see A. R. Brown as soon as he gets there". What is more, Camilla Wedgwood, who had been the only person to obtain a First in the Cambridge Anthropological Tripos in 1924,[63] hopes to work in the Solomon Islands at about the same time. A further letter, written in August 1926,[64] continues Haddon's efforts to link Deacon into the network of connections making up the Rivers—Haddon school. Deacon having written about a New Hebridean secret society called the "Nalawan", Haddon suggests that Rivers's surviving notes may discuss this institution and advises Deacon to contact Rivers's former friend and colleague A. M. Hocart, whom Haddon believes to have custody of the notes. Haddon further mentions that he has been occupied in reading manuscripts of books produced by anthropologists of the Cambridge school, naming Gunnar Landtman's work on the Kiwai Papuans[65] and Armstrong's monograph on Rossell Island. "I hope you have got in touch with Professor A. Radcliffe-Brown", continues Haddon, "[because] he will be greatly interested in your results." Finally, Haddon concludes the letter by summarizing the results of the Anthropological Tripos for 1926. No less than five out of the thirteen students in the Tripos got Firsts. These five include Bateson, whose fieldwork is being financed by a St John's College scholarship; H. A. Stayt, who has been awarded a scholarship by Caius College; and, in the area of physical anthropology, L. S. B. Leakey, who is conducting an archaeological expedition to south-east Africa on another St John's scholarship. Thus, it can be seen that, just before Haddon's retirement, the Rivers—Haddon school was apparently thriving with Haddon himself actively forging and strengthening the links which held the school together.

After his arrival in Malekula, Deacon's vivid and eloquent letters home tell the story of his fieldwork and, in the account which follows, I shall rely heavily on direct quotations from his correspondence, most of which has never been published. An early letter from South West Bay reveals his ambivalent attitude towards the place and the people. The following passage would seem to lend substance to the romantic conception of his locale:

It is a magnificent setting for a play, a desolate, timeless paradise. But to the natives, of course, just their home: passing through a village at sundown they are cooking their evening meal (breadfruit) at their fires, the women separately, the men together in the clubhouse, the blue smoke curling up lazily through the overshadowing branches of some great banyan tree.[66]

However, the inhabitants of paradise had fallen on hard times:

It would be a wonderful world to live in, here, were it not that the natives are the last survivors of a dying people – dysentery, Spanish influenza, consumption, syphilis, yaws, elephantiasis, ulcers of all sorts, measles, whooping cough (fatal diseases here), opthalmia, tetanus – there is scarcely a strong man or woman among them ... The price these isolated races have paid for their isolation is a terrible susceptibility to diseases against which we have apparently inoculated ourselves – I mean measles and so on, tuberculosis, syphilis too. – "nous ne civilizons pas, nous syphilizons" as a Roman Catholic priest here said to me, with much truth.[67]

And, if the decimated state of the Malekulans was morally disturbing to a sensitive young member of the civilization which had brought about their decline, it also, as we learn from another letter, made his fieldwork very difficult:

I feel bitterly envious of Layard – he could follow through a whole ceremony, where I have to try and piece the whole thing together from descriptions, never sure that I am visualizing correctly. I have been here four months and not a single thing has taken place, except funerals, of which there have been about a dozen ... How can one hope to do any intensive work under such conditions?[68]

Moreover, life with the missionaries at South West Bay was far from idyllic for a conscientious fieldworker:

The missionary and his wife have been extremely hospitable and personally kind to me, but their attitude towards and treatment of my work, while I feel more acutely than they can possibly imagine, is bitterly hard to bear. That they should treat with amused superiority "little things [which] please little minds", is comprehensible; that they should be openly opposed to the spirit of it, natural. But that they should tell me the natives are deceiving me, that they are stuffing me with nonesense, that they tell the missionary's wife that they tell me lies, laugh at me behind my back, when I have tested by long and patient counter-checking and corroboration the essential trustworthiness, sympathy and interest and sincerity of the men with whom I have worked, and whom I know as friends, certainly as well as they will ever know them, this is disheartening beyond endurance. I can only be mute in [the] face of ignorance, and keep my thoughts to myself ... Here things are being lost forever, almost hour by hour, things I feel ... may be critical in the probing of the true history and development of mankind. Yet a missionary has been here *32* years, and had no interest to record, to preserve, to observe even. Such ignorance, prejudice, vulgarity – what a tragedy they are. I share them surely enough, and am blind. Yet I cannot believe I am vain in despising them – or pitying them – when I am forced to live with them. Humility is dishonourable toward them.[69]

Finally, the work itself did not seem to be fitting together, with disastrous results for Deacon's emotional attitude:

I have spent the morning in a dispersed desultory sort of way trying to piece together the work of the past four months and realizing again and again with a sort of wild panic how lamentably inadequate it is. At one or two points there has been a sudden vision of what the whole might be like, a sense of the movement of everything as marvellously living and an uncontrollable joy in it – and then suddenly there is this constantly searing, overwhelming depression, a sudden draining of intellect and will, by which alone it is possible to continue to live here.[70]

Circa July 1926 Deacon shifted his field of activities from South West Bay to Lambumbu on the west central coast of Malekula, and it seemed at first that the corner had been turned:

Everything has changed utterly and completely since I came up here away from S. W. Bay – I'm absurdly happy and hopefully fond, in some sudden and inexplicable way, of the natives – whether it is any better for anthropology – ridiculous word! – God only knows.[71]

However, after about three months at Lambumbu, Deacon's newly-found affection for the natives had tarnished somewhat:

The only privacy, the only remnant of Europe here, is thought. The publicity of native life is at times maddening . . . There is no white man here, nor does any steamer ever call. There are times of very great depression, especially if one is sick, since all the natives can do, with all the good will in the world, is to gather round and look at you, and, blessed moment, go. This sounds quite unlike the "sympathetic understanding" of the native that anthropologists say one should have. It seems to me fundamentally wrong to "approach" natives in any way, sympathetically or other.[72]

Furthermore, he had developed a deep pessimism about the very possibility of a science of man:

One of the most terrible things here is that you go living day after day with the same old impasses, never moving an inch further into or out of them, wondering in fact whether they really do exist or not . . . It is so different in physics and chemistry – there you have a vast structure of really beautiful theory, experimentally verified in enormous numbers of ways, and as undoubtedly true, I suppose, as anything of the kind that one can think of – so research has a great theoretical searchlight, there is coherence and direction. Here (in ethnology) it is all a mess – I suspect most ethnologists are bad historians, or bad psychologists, or bad romanticists.[73]

This pessimism also extended to his own investigations and to the viability of Rivers's views:

My own work I am in the most complete despair about – both quality and quantity. I am constantly trying to frame some general theory of New Hebrides culture; really it has been investigated pretty thoroughly by able men – Codrington, Rivers, Speiser, Layard, Barnard, Humphries [sic]. And surely if anywhere here's the chance for ethnology to show what it can arrive at in the way of theory. Rivers's theory I begin to find a hindrance. I was brought up on it at Cambridge, and now it cloys me. On every page I want to cry out, 'But there are so many other things!!!' and in lots of it I am very much puzzled to know what Rivers really thought about certain things – whether he was aware of particular difficulties, whether he regarded them as difficulties.[74]

But if Deacon was disillusioned with Rivers's approach to a general theory of New Hebridean culture, he could also see little future in one of the major alternatives:

I am very puzzled about "Psychology" and "Social Psychology" and depressed about my work, in consequence. It is at a stage when it should be mainly "psychological" – but I have no training in method – I don't know what one tackles, and how, what the nature of psychological problems and method are, as an experimental science – e.g. if you were set down to study the "social psychology" or something like that, of an English village, what do you do? Write a sort of novel?[75]

Listing such original discoveries as he had made to date, Deacon reveals that he has come around to thinking that the solution to his problems could lie in the diffusionistic reconstruction of cultural history:

I feel very grey at the moment about the possibility of making a coherent system of the New Hebrides – or Malekula. I have discovered perhaps four or five important new things. I mean signalling, geometrical figure drawing (amazingly intricate and ingenious), some secret societies with bull-roarer etc., a system of fertility magic connected with sacred pottery and certain mythical culture heroes, one or two interesting things about social organization. But what seems to me more and more important is to try and construct some outline of the cultural history of the New Hebrides . . . I must confess I don't share Malinowski's scorn for the historical people. I realize more and more that I have only the vaguest idea of what is meant by "sociology" and "social psychology" – at least as practical sciences in which research is to be done.[76]

The theories of previous British diffusionists could be corrected and modified, he suggested in one letter, if anthropologists would take the trouble to prepare a comprehensive "cyclopaedia of distributions". Were this done

One could refer to it immediately to check theories like Perry and Smith's, which slur over gaps and by selecting here and there distort the actual complexity. At present to check and correct them, you have to wade through practically the whole literature of ethnology and travel. I saw in Sydney a paper by Professor Griffith Taylor of Sydney University, about the diffusion of culture in the Pacific, in which there was a map of distributions in which, by using references of the type "occurs in the Northern New Hebrides", "is characteristic of the Melanesians" and so on, Malekula was lurid with serpent-cults, sun-mythology ... and goodness knows what.[77] Yet if there were a recognized cyclopaedia of distributions, no one would be able to do this kind of thing without being at once detected and exposed ... by reference to the maps etc. it would be possible at once to appraise the value of "diffusionist" theories.[78]

In a letter to Haddon, written from Lambumbu in October 1926, Deacon further details the decline of the New Hebridean people:

My best informant, Kukan, a fine old man, died of pneumonia following 'flu, a month ago, after I had doctored him as best I could for a week. At every turn it is "the men who knew are dead". Another thing is alcohol. This is sold freely by pretty well every French cutter, and a good many British cutters coming in, and consumed largely at the more important ceremonies ... The result is a general deterioration and falling to pieces of the old ceremonial. A man who is drunk cannot sing or dance or be properly dignified. But the most terrible thing to work against is the hopeless, fatalistic apathy of the people.[79]

Everyone has been led away by the glitter of civilization — rifles, gin, rum, watches, electric torches, condensed milk, tinned meat ... the price of cotton, the doings of traders, these are becoming more and more the principal interests of the natives.[80]

This sorry state of affairs necessitated a change of plans in his fieldwork:

I have decided that the best thing to do will be to get everything I can here in N.W. Malekula, and then try and make a couple or so of 2—3 months studies of other areas — Ambrym, and perhaps Pentecost, before they go altogether. Too many things are gone, everywhere, to make it profitable to stay long in a place and try intensive work.[81]

And later in the same letter:

I don't know what you think about having a shot at one or two other areas — say N.E. Ambrym, I think never touched, and then Oba. It seems to me it's a question of saving as much as you can here before it goes. What with depopulation, recruiting, and the gravitation of the natives to the big French settlement in Santo, to Vila, some to New Caledonia, intensive work is impossible.[82]

After leaving Lambumbu and arriving at Bushman's Bay on the east central coast of Malekula, Deacon apparently found a letter from Haddon waiting for him:

My S.W. Bay notes have reached Cambridge and Haddon says they're "wonderful". I confess it pleased me a little, somehow. It's absurd, because I think he's only gone through them quickly, and there are so many, so terribly many, gaps and faults and omissions, bitterly and acutely painful that he has not seen, and I am ashamed, it is all too loathsome, horrible — I have never understood and always hated this team-spirit and personal touch, it is so ugly, so irrelevant, marring things that are profoundly beautiful — and again and again I am bitterly ashamed.[83]

Since the above passage is followed by a heartrending lament about the tragedy of native life and death, we may conclude that it was written in a state of deep depression and could therefore be jaundiced. Nonetheless, it gives the lie to the notion of Deacon having any appreciable respect for Haddon's intellectual judgement, or at any rate for his prima facie intellectual judgement. In fact, I would venture to say that, from Deacon's point of view, his relationship with Haddon was certainly not that of admiration for a powerful intellect, but was primarily one of filial affection, even this being rendered ambivalent by the knowledge that the way to get on was to play the game as a member of Haddon's team. The lamenting outburst which follows the above passage bears quoting at length, as revealing Deacon's state of mind just before his departure for Ambrym:

I am terribly overstrained, my work seems all to be going to bits. There seems nothing here but Death — a man was dead in the village this morning, of dysentery . . . How many men I know have died? Paul and David and Kukan and Lagan and Manbogior, and Arbul, and Tota's father and many many more, terribly many. My notes read like the last confessions of dying men. They die so simply, so unassumingly, uncomprehendingly, and all with this tragic swiftness. In one village of 20, 9 died in one week. Men have become carelessly ironic about death. It's not like death in war or crisis — it is the final death, the death of a people, a race, and they know it more clearly than we do. I've got to collect skulls for Haddon: a man said to me one day 'Soon you (the white man) will be able to come and collect all our skulls — we won't bother you.' There is an utterly weary [aura?] about them — you cannot imagine how utterly suicidal the gloom of working in it sometimes becomes. A death is a relief almost from the tension . . . As for work, I despair and despair and despair again. Against this overwhelming, hopeless atmosphere it is almost insupportable to labour. It is difficult at times not to feel bitter, really it is a wretched atmosphere to do a first piece of work in, and takes quite 50% off the value of anything you do. "The men who knew are dead", is its eternal refrain. I have to piece together scraps that when Layard was here were a whole that could be seen and witnessed and gone through in actual experience.[84]

Leaving Bushman's Bay, Deacon went to the island of Ambrym, where he stayed for six weeks ending in mid-February 1927.[85] His next letter to Haddon contains the record of his big discovery:

I am really rather excited at the moment. I have found in Ambrym a system of marriage-classes, still in full working, of the type of those among the Central Australian tribes, though not exactly corresponding with any Australian system . . .

I have sent detailed notes on the system, the working out of it, confirmation of its relationship system and pedigrees, and its bearing on Rivers's work, to Professor Radcliffe-
Brown at Sydney. I am getting some typed copies of the notes done in Sydney, one of
which I have asked them to send you.

I think the whole thing is very important (excuse my swollen head). For me it clears
up a great deal, even here in Malekula. It bears, I think, on the general question of
anomalous marriages, dual organization, and Melanesian history. I have tried to sketch
out in the notes to Brown how it clears up problems, modifies Rivers's work, and so on.
To me it is like a sudden illumination. The day after I had got the final proof of the
thing I simply did nothing, just had an absolute rest, ate my best biscuits and tinned
peaches and felt nothing mattered now.[86]

The notes sent by Deacon to Radcliffe-Brown in Sydney, which were
eventually published as a paper on "The Regulation of Marriage in Ambrym"
in the *Journal of the Royal Anthropological Institute*, certainly provide
ample justification for Deacon's self-congratulatory tone. By any standards,
Deacon's paper makes intelligent and incisive use of crucially important
material. As an example of data collection and analysis performed in a few
weeks,[87] it is nothing short of extraordinary.

Deacon begins his paper by briefly recapitulating the three major types of
anomalous marriage which Rivers had invoked for Melanesia. One of these
types, marriage with the wife of the father's father, had been postulated
for Buin in the Solomons, and for Fiji. Now in both these places alternate
generations in the male line are classed together. The combination of this
kinship correspondence with patrilineal descent[88] and with marriage to the
father's father's wife suggested to Deacon, as a similar merging of alternate
generations on Pentecost Island had initially done to Rivers,[89] that "some
class-system of marriage" might be involved. "Personally," says Deacon, "I
am inclined to go further, and say that if classificatory F.F.W. marriage was
practised to such an extent as 'to give rise' to a definite relationship system,
then it must have been the accompaniment or rather the function, of a definite
system of marriage classes." Rivers's deduction of relationship systems from
certain types of marriage involves, argues Deacon, the assumption that the
marriages in question are, or were at one time, as firmly in force as are the
relationship systems. Such a situation, says Deacon, "I cannot conceive to be
possible without some system of marriage classes".[90]

Deacon then suggests that Rivers's interpretation of his informant's statement that Pentecost males marry their granddaughters, which, as we learnt
in Chapter III, was of fundamental importance in the assembling of his theory
of anomalous marriages, had been in error. "In North Pentecost", writes

Deacon, " . . . the mother's brother's children's children are classed as own grandchildren, so that the M.B.D.D., for example, is called 'granddaughter'. It does not seem to have occurred to Rivers that a man, in marrying his . . . 'daughter's daughter', might really be marrying his M.B.D.D."[91] This type of marriage, being between people one rather than two generations apart, is much more plausible than marriage with the daughter's daughter and, as Deacon goes on to demonstrate later in the paper, is indeed practised on Ambrym as an integral part of their kinship system.

Having thus briefly but convincingly undermined Rivers's theory of anomalous marriages, Deacon produces the evidence for his assertion that the Ambrym kinship system is of the marriage-class variety. As befitting a product of the Rivers school, Deacon had collected genealogies from each of the four linguistically distinct districts in the island. However, as Deacon himself recognizes, his surest evidence came from "the remarkably lucid exposition of the class-system by the natives themselves". A missionized informant from the Balap district stated that a man always married a woman of his father's mother's "line". He subsequently volunteered the information that a man must marry a woman of his mother's mother's "tribe", although not of her "line" in that "tribe". Deacon therefore devoted his energies to unravelling the meaning of "line" and "tribe". Employing genealogies, Deacon arrived at the following conclusions:

The population is divided into three 'tribes' called 'bwelem' at Balap, and 'bwulim' at Ranon. Descent in the bwelem is patrilineal – a man, his father, his father's father, son, son's son, and the children of all these, belong to his own bwelem . . . Each bwelem, however, is divided into two sides, or 'lines' such that a man, his father's father, his son's son (and sisters of all these) belong to his 'line', while his father, his son, and his son's son's son belong to his father's 'line', all in the same bwelem. This two-line structure causes the father's father to be called 'brother', etc. The three bwelem are referred to by a man as –

(1) 'My bwelem'
(2) 'My mother's bwelem'
(3) 'My mother's mother's bwelem'.

The mother's mother's mother, it was stated, 'came back' to a man's own bwelem, and to his own 'line' in that bwelem, and she is called 'sister'.[92]

Without any solicitation on his part, Deacon's Balap informants, on two separate occasions, gave diagrammatic expositions of the functioning of their kinship system. On the first occasion, the informant made an equilateral triangle with three stones, each of which was said to correspond to one bwelem (Figure 18). If a woman of A married a man from C, her daughter in

C would marry a man from B, and her daughter's daughter in B would marry a man from A again, this man coming from the daughter's daughter's mother's mother's father's "line". Representing men by large letters, women by small letters, and the two "lines" by the subscripts 1 and 2, Deacon translates this and some of the previous information about "lines" into the following diagram: (Figure 19)

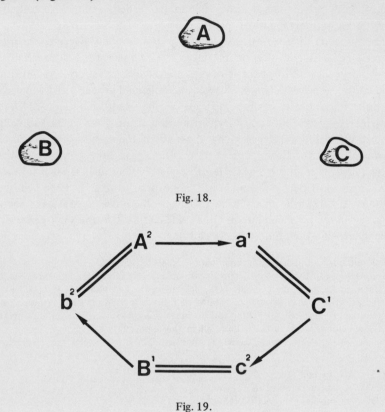

Fig. 18.

Fig. 19.

It should be noted that in Figure 19, which may be regarded as a reduced model of the total Balap system, the directed descent lines emerge from the symbols which represent males. This is a reflection of the fact that, in contrast to the matri-determination of class amongst the Kariera and Arunta, the class of Balap children is patri-determined. From Figure 19 one can also see why the *bwelem* are referred to as "my own, my mother's and my mother's mother's *bwelem*". If, for example, ego is considered to be a[1] in *bwelem* A, her mother will be in *bwelem* B and her mother's mother in *bwelem* C.

On the second occasion an informant drew three long marks (A^1, B^2, C^2), each representing a male in one of the three *bwelems*.[93] If these three marry, each union produces a boy and a girl, who are placed in the other "line" of each father's *bwelem*. Thus A^1 marries c^1 and has children A^2 and a^2; B^2 marries a^2 and has children B^1 and b^1; and C^2 marries b^1 and has children C^1 and c^1. Substituting the customary triangles and circles for the marks which Deacon's informant used to represent men and women we obtain the following diagram:

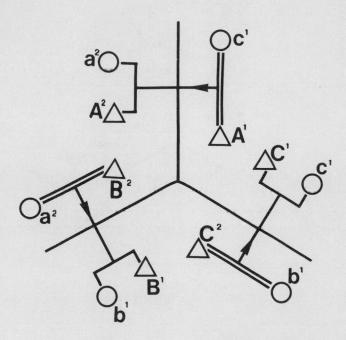

Fig. 20.   Females are indicated by small, males by large letters. Symbols which occur twice on the diagram, namely a^2, b^1 and c^1, represent the same person in both usages. The division between the two "lines" of the *bwelem* is indicated by the long strokes which come together at the centre of the figure.

Deacon's informant explained that the circulation of women around the triangle of the *bwelem* took place in two directions — clockwise and counterclockwise. One group, going around counterclockwise, he indicated by drawing lines from a^2 (as daughter) to a^2 (as spouse), from b^1 (as daughter) to b^1 (as spouse) and from c^1 (as daughter) to c^1 (as spouse). He then pointed out that there were men depicted, A^2, B^1 and C^1, who had no wives. But he described how A^2 would marry b^2, B^1 would marry c^2, and C^1 would marry a^1. This would result, he explained, in a second group of women "going round the other way". All this he depicted in a diagram similar to the following:

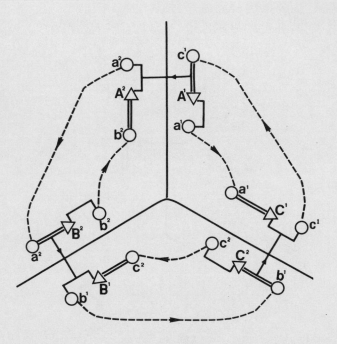

Fig. 21.   Dotted lines indicate the movement of women around the system.

Finally, the informant pointed out that the married couples[94] A^2, b^2; B^1, c^2; and C^1, a^1 would have children in "lines" of the original men, A^1, B^2 and C^2 respectively; that for example, the children of C^1 and a^1 would be siblings of C^2, and would therefore again marry, like C^2, a woman who was a sister of b^1. Although Deacon did not do so, redundancies may be eliminated, and the informant's total exposition of the Balap system elegantly summarized by the following circular diagram, which has been adapted from John Layard's exposition of six-section systems in *Stone Men of Malekula*.[95]

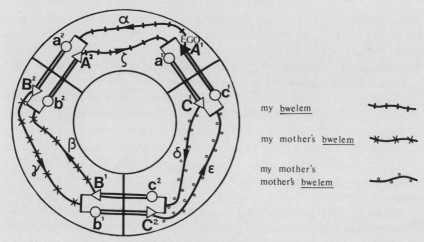

my <u>bwelem</u>

my mother's <u>bwelem</u>

my mother's
mother's <u>bwelem</u>

Fig. 22. α = "line" of man A^1, β = "line" of man B^1, γ = "line" of man B^2, δ = "line"
of man C^1, ϵ = "line" of man C^2, and ζ = "line" of man A^2.

In Figure 22, the repetitive, cyclic nature of the system has been expressed
by enclosing it in an annulus, which has been trisected by radial lines in such
a way that one *bwelem* falls within each trisection. The basic structure of
the Balap system may be illustrated by deploying a circular diagram in the
manner of Barnes. This diagram effectively represents a reduced version of
my Figure 22.

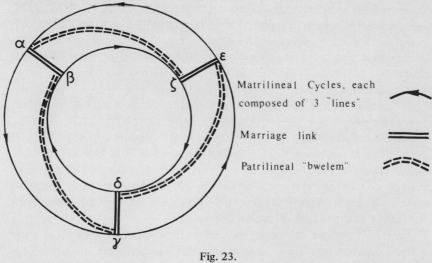

Matrilineal Cycles, each
composed of 3 "lines"

Marriage   link

Patrilineal "bwelem"

Fig. 23.

By comparing Figure 23 with Figure 12 in Chapter III, it can be seen that
the Balap system has the same basic structure as what was referred to in
Chapter III as the Ambrym system. Both systems, in short, have matrilineal
periodicities of three generations, patrilineal periodicities of two generations,
and an affinal periodicity of two.

Such then was the intricate system which emerged from the extraordinarily
detailed specifications offered by Deacon's informants. In a letter to Haddon
written just after his discovery of the system, Deacon states: "It is perfectly
clear that the natives (the intelligent ones) do conceive of the system as a
connected mechanism ... The way they could reason about relationships
from their diagrams was absolutely on a par with a good scientific exposition
in a lecture room." [96]

Comparing the actual kinship correspondences from Balap with those
deducible from the theoretically expounded system, Deacon found "complete
agreement". In those few cases where a slight divergence was present, the
informant anticipated Deacon's observation of the fact by pointing out that
some things were "not straight" about the terms actually used. " ... the
consciousness of this irregularity", writes Deacon, "besides being a great
tribute to the man's intelligence, is an additional proof of the correctness of
the system." [97]

For the district of Ranon in northern Ambrym, Deacon's work revealed
the society to be divided into three patrilineal *bwulim*, which resemble the
bwelem of Balap. Each *bwulim* is subdivided into two *wor*, similar to the
"lines" of Balap. However, in contrast to Balap, a further division is also
recognized. The society is regarded as being divided into two *batatun*, within
which descent is matrilineal. Each *batatun* is composed of one *wor* from each
of the three *bwulim*. The regulation governing marriage is that a man must
marry into his mother's mother's *bwulim*, but only to a woman who is not of
his own *batatun*.

In summary, the Ambrym system, as practised in the Ranon district, com-
prises three patrilineal divisions which intersect the two matrilineal divisions,
thereby producing six sub-divisions which are functionally equivalent to
Australian marriage-classes. The explicit recognition of matrilineal moieties,
which recalls a similar recognition amongst the Kariera and the Arunta,
further underlines the structural affinity of the Ambrym and Australian
systems, and was to make the Ranon version the most popular candidate for
the mantle of the "standard" six-section system.

Having completed his masterly presentation of the Ambrym kinship
system, Deacon indulges in a little speculation about the history of the

various types of kinship system in the area. Descent in the central New Hebrides had generally been described as patrilineal. However, in the northern New Hebrides, the system is a simple dual organization with matrilineal descent. Now, says Deacon, it is precisely in northern Ambrym, the portion of the central New Hebrides which is geographically closest to the matrilineal area, that descent is a combination of matriliny in the *batatun*, and patriliny in the *bwulim*. Deacon hypothesises that the northern islands originally possessed a dual organization with matrilineal descent of the type now practised in the *batatun*, but that with the advent of marriage with the wife of the mother's brother, this complex dual organization collapsed to a simpler variety. The father's sister's daughter's daughter marriage, however, persisted as a survival of the former system. The patrilineality of the Ambrym system Deacon regards as "probably a later, immigrant, influence".[98] After a few more speculations, the paper ends abruptly with the suggestion that, since it has been shown that many of Rivers's anomalous marriages can probably be derived from the Ranon class-system, Rivers's theory of Melanesian geron-tocracy will have to be modified.

THE RECEPTION OF DEACON'S DISCOVERY

While there can be no doubt that, if Deacon had lived, the Ambrym system would have been presented in a much more detailed and better documented form, the paper as it stands was sufficient to deeply impress almost all the central members of the Rivers–Haddon school. For Haddon, Deacon's conclusions about the Ambrym kinship system constituted "a discovery of great importance".[99] Brenda Seligman declared herself to be "frightfully interested ... in Deacon's paper and keen that it should be published as soon as possible". "It opens up an enormous number of points of vast theoretical interest", she writes, "and should attract a great deal of attention."[100] For Layard, Deacon's unveiling of the six-section system was a "sensational discovery",[101] "a landmark in the history of anthropology",[102] which demonstrated the "genius and determination" of the young fieldworker.[103] Barnard, who would have had a right to downgrade Deacon's achievement, allowed that "Deacon's discovery of the six section system must be accepted as a genuine discovery",[104] and referred to its "extreme interest and importance".[105] For Radcliffe-Brown, the discovery was "one of capital importance" for both sociological and ethnological theory.[106] It constituted, he averred, "one of the most important things that has been done in Melanesia for quite a long time", and was an indication of "really first-class fieldwork".[107] In fact, upon receiving Deacon's notes on Ambym marriage regulation, Radcliffe-Brown took the unusual step of advising the young anthropologist "to send a note of it as soon as possible to *Man*".[108] More than anything else that Deacon had done, it clearly revealed to Radcliffe-Brown the loss that anthropology had suffered by his early demise.[109]

But the most impressive tributes of all came in the form of work inspired by Deacon's paper. The lengthy and substantial discussion of kinship in Layard's book on Malekula was, as he himself acknowledged,[110] based upon Deacon's exposition of the six-section system. Indeed, Layard's kinship diagrams seem to have been devised in the first instance as a means of systematizing the diagrammatic expositions of the Ambrym kinship system given by Deacon's informants. Brenda Seligman, having been asked by Haddon to assist Camilla Wedgwood in preparing Deacon's Ambrym notes for publication, started to write some comments for an appendix, but became so fascinated that a full-length article on bilateral descent eventuated.[111] Her 1928 article on descent in Pentecost, which I utilized extensively in Chapter III, was also largely inspired by Deacon's Ambrym analysis. Radcliffe-Brown, eager to share some of the glory emanating from Deacon's discovery, wrote an article locating the Ambrym system as one variety of "a single general type of kinship organization . . . found over a large area of South India and Ceylon, over a great part, and perhaps the whole of Australia, and in certain parts of Melanesia." This article, which for some mysterious reason, was given the same title as Deacon's contribution, was, together with the above-mentioned article by Seligman on bilateral descent and an introductory note by Haddon, published in the same volume of the *Journal of the Royal Anthropological Institute* as the Deacon paper. Hence this edition of the *Journal* contains fifty concentrated pages by four different people discussing the technical specifications and significance of the Ambrym system, and as such may be regarded as a major product of the preoccupation of the Rivers's school with kinship theory. In fact, Haddon contrived to have the three articles specially bound together for distribution to people interested in Deacon's work.[112] Apparently responding to this emanation from Cambridge anthropology, the Swiss ethnologist Felix Speiser, whose discovery of a living megalithic culture in the northern New Hebrides had provided one of the major inspirations for the Rivers–Layard expedition, wrote to Haddon in April 1928:

I am reading with great interest the paper of Deacon on the six-class system in Ambrym.

It is a great discovery. But alas! I have such difficulties in understanding that sort of high mathematics ... in fact I CANNOT really understand it. if Deacon's other investigations are on the same level with this sample, his work will prove wonderfully rich.[113]

If a moral is to be drawn from this example of unconscious humor, it is that the technical proficiency demonstrated by the Rivers's school in analyzing the Ambrym system was impressing the older style, low-powered anthropologists at the same time as it was bemusing them. Within the school itself, the issue of technical proficiency was sometimes used as a weapon for scoring points from one's rivals. Brenda Seligman, for example, having received a printer's proof of the Ambrym paper of Deacon's which she and Camilla Wedgwood had jointly edited, wrote to Haddon "... I do not consider Deacon's paper fully corrected ... I don't know if Camilla has really been through it or not, but I see some things in it still that we both agreed to alter slightly, also there are some slips in the diagrams."[114] However, those who live by the sword risk injury by the sword. Radcliffe-Brown, writing to Haddon in January 1930, ventures the opinion that Brenda Seligman should not be given any hand in the editing of Deacon's notes on Malekula. "Her recent articles", he says, "show that she has thought herself into a regular muddle on the subject of Melanesian kinship. Only please don't let her know I say so."[115]

DEACON'S CLAIM TO FOREKNOWLEDGE

For Deacon himself, the six-section system was "by far the most important thing I have found out here",[116] and indeed, the "plum" of Melanesian ethnology.[117] But Deacon not only wanted credit for discovering the Ambrym system. He also claimed, on four separate occasions after the discovery, some kind of foreknowledge. The three most detailed versions of this claim are as follows:

In 1914 Rivers visited Ambrym,[118] and found that here also alternate generations in the male line were classed together as in Fiji and Buin. I determined, therefore, when I came out, to seek an opportunity of visiting Ambrym and going more deeply into the marriage regulations in that island.[119]

The discovery has for me a somewhat romantic history, beginning in the University Library at Cambridge and a discussion with Armstrong. The possibility of the existence of such a thing seemed to me so important, that I disobeyed "marching orders" and threw up my work in Malekula to come across here and search for it.[120]

. . . the thing was to me a kind of crucial experiment at the end of a long train of ideas —
beginning really in my first reading of Rivers and talks with Armstrong . . . Before I left
England I had determined to have a go at Ambrym, as a test-case, so the positive result
is to me hugely exciting.[121]

Hence Deacon apparently wished to claim that Ambrym was for him a
"test-case", in the sense that he was not only expecting to find something
important there, but that he was specifically looking for a marriage-class
system. Radcliffe-Brown, who was to make a similar contention regarding his
alleged discovery of the Kariera system,[122] was impressed by Deacon's claim,
and allows that the discovery was made "as the confirmation of an acute
reasoning that something of the sort should be there".[123] However, a perusal
of Deacon's pre-Ambrym correspondence, as already quoted in this chapter,
casts considerable doubt on the allegation that Deacon was expecting to find
a marriage-class system in Ambrym. Certainly he was on the lookout for a
marriage-class system in the New Hebrides, but he evidently expected to find
it in the Malo-West Santo area, rather than in Ambrym. His decision to pay
a quick visit to Ambrym seems to have been motivated by the realization that
intensive fieldwork was impossible anywhere in the New Hebrides, owing to
the decimated state of the natives and that his best plan would, therefore, be
to do a rapid general survey of Ambrym culture while there was still time.
Inasmuch as his immediately pre-Ambrym research interests had a focus, it
was apparently the reconstruction of cultural history, rather than the more
sociological task of determining the nature of kinship systems.

Such is the impression one gets from Deacon's early letters home. However, another interpretation is possible. It could have been that Deacon had
already learned of the Ambrym six-section system from Barnard's doctoral
thesis. On one occasion prior to his fieldwork on Ambrym, Deacon admits
that he had performed a "hurried reading" of the thesis.[124] Moreover, in
one of the two letters to Haddon in which he discusses his unravelling of the
six-section system, Deacon states that, if he remembers correctly, Barnard
suggested in his thesis that it was "just possible" that a marriage-class system
existed on Ambrym.[125] In the other letter to Haddon, Deacon writes that he
remembers Barnard suggesting "in his paper"[126] that "a six-class system
might be found on Ambrym", but goes on to say: "This means, I suppose,
that it had not been found. How both Rivers and Barnard missed it . . . I
cannot quite understand, because the older men explained the system to me
perfectly lucidly . . ."[127]

Barnard, at any rate, took an incredibly sporting view of the whole affair.
In a brief article in the 1928 volume of *Man*, Barnard acknowledges that "The

recent publication of the late Mr Deacon's paper on the regulation of marriage in Ambrym . . . has disclosed the existence of a unique type of social organization of extreme interest and importance."[128] Implying that he feels Rivers's work on the social organization of Ambrym to have been unduly neglected, he devotes much of the article to filling in the details of Rivers's contribution. He also mentions that, while working on his thesis, he had used Rivers's Ambrym data to "prove to my own satisfaction at least, that Ambrim society was an example of hitherto unsuspected class system with six classes". "Without further corroboration," continues Barnard, "I have hesitated to publish, in what must have been a very lengthy and circumlocutory form, my refutation of Rivers's published statements from a reconsideration of Rivers's own evidence. My theory has been known both to Dr Haddon and Mrs Seligman since the completion of my thesis, and I have made use of the Ambrim six-class system in my lectures both at Oxford and at Cape Town. The publication of Mr Deacon's admirable account of the regulation of marriage in Ambrim completely confirms my views."[129] In a personal communication with the author, Barnard writes that he was "very surprised" that Deacon seemed quite unaware of his previous Ambrym hypothesis. So also was Haddon, who, says Barnard, "was surprised that I had not briefed Deacon adequately before he left". "I saw Deacon fairly frequently at Cambridge", he continues, "but even a year or two after his death when Camilla Wedgwood was working on his material I couldn't remember how far our conversations had extended. He was entirely Malekula-oriented, and though he certainly had an opportunity of seeing my thesis, he presumably never read it – and that was no doubt my fault. Anyhow it was nice to have my deductions corroborated!"[130] In view of the nasty debates about priority which mar many areas in the history of science, Barnard certainly must be credited with remarkable restraint and good spirit. One can only conclude that he was imbued with loyalty to the Haddon team such as seems to have temporarily deserted Deacon during the blackest period of his fieldwork.

THE MISSING NOTES

After sending Radcliffe-Brown the notes which eventually became the 1927 paper on Ambrym marriage regulation, Deacon had also written the professor a letter giving some details of an analysis he had done of marriages in the Balap district of Ambrym.[131] From this Radcliffe-Brown concluded that "this work, which was the last he did . . . was probably the best of all," and implied that he was eagerly awaiting the recovery of the relevant field-notes.[132] However, despite Camilla Wedgwood keeping an eye out for them in the course of her systematic editing of all Deacon's surviving field-notes, the notes on Balap marriages were never located. Nor, for that matter, were the detailed field-notes and genealogies on which the 1927 paper must have been based. In a letter to Haddon written in 1931, Radcliffe-Brown states that, if he could have found the time, he would have personally gone to the New Hebrides to try and recover Beacon's Balap notes.[133] The disappearance of just these notes, which Deacon himself would presumably have valued above all his other work, is certainly a mystery, about which we can only speculate. One possibility is that, accidentally or otherwise, the notes were destroyed by the missionaries at South West Bay.[134] Another possibility is that the notes were sent to Radcliffe-Brown at Sydney, and that he destroyed them, either because they did not support his views on the significance of Ambrym marriage regulation, or because they contained something which he did not wish Deacon to get the credit for. Although this latter speculation will probably seem somewhat less gratuitous after the next chapter, such wanton hypothesizing is not the province of an historian of science, and I will, therefore, desist.

THE AFTERMATH

The body of Deacon had scarcely been laid in its sandy grave under the palm trees at South West Bay, when it evoked what I referred to in an earlier. chapter as "the twin apparitions of earlier and later Rivers". Replying to the letter from Deacon's mother in which she first informed him of Bernard's death, Haddon writes: "I regarded him as the best student I have had — In the relatively short time he had been in the field he fully realized the great promise of his year's work with me." Haddon goes on to say that he had hoped "that when [Deacon] had published his [Malekulan] results and had experience in teaching in Sydney that he eventually would become a Reader in Ethnology in this University and resuscitate the old traditions of our School, which promise to be in abeyance for a time."[135] I have no doubt that, by "the old traditions of our School", Haddon meant the brand of technical kinship theory which he associated with early Rivers, and which Deacon had so ably perpetuated in his paper on Ambrym. In saying that these traditions "promise to be in abeyance for a time", Haddon was undoubtedly referring to the pervasive influence of extreme diffusionism and possibly also to the non-retainment of W. E. Armstrong on the staff of the Cambridge Ethnology Department.

But if Haddon was upset by Deacon's death, so also was the rival camp. As I have already mentioned, Elliot Smith had been impressed by Deacon's first publication and, in fact, before Deacon set out for the antipodes, had given the young man a letter of introduction to his brother-in-law in Sydney, who was a director of a shipping line which plied the south Pacific.[136] Immediately upon hearing of Deacon's death from Haddon, Elliot Smith replied:

Your letter comes as a great shock: and in the great loss that has befallen us all I feel particular sympathy for you in losing the most promising of all the many men you have sent into the field. It is a desperate tragedy which comes as a great blow to our group also. Only yesterday I was talking with Layard and Perry of the extent to which our hopes for the future were bound up with Deacon.[137]

Elliot Smith and Perry also immediately wrote a letter of sympathy to Deacon's mother, in which, as Mrs Deacon told Haddon, they paid tribute to her son as a scholar and expressed "the hope they centred in him".[138] Mrs Deacon also informed Haddon that "a year or more ago", Elliot Smith had told her about "the new move in Anthropology", and remarked "I want to keep your son for Anthropology."[139]

Late in March 1927, John Layard, who had heard of Deacon's death from Elliot Smith, rang Haddon wanting to know what was going to be done about Deacon's manuscripts.[140] For several reasons Layard would have been the logical choice to edit Deacon's notes since, having more or less recovered from his nervous breakdown, he had, according to Haddon, "pretty well worked up his Malekula material", and had been entrusted by Elliot Smith with the task of whipping Rivers's Ambrym material into shape.[141] In a letter to Radcliffe-Brown, Haddon discusses Layard's enquiry:

Personally I do not see much of an objection to Layard editing some at least of Deacon's MS; but what I fear is that if Layard is working in conjunction with Elliot Smith, the latter may want to have his finger in the pie. To be quite candid, I do not trust the Elliot Smith–Perry combination – for it is most probable that Elliot Smith would turn the work over to Perry. There is reason to believe that they tampered with Fox's *Threshold of the Pacific* – in fact there is no doubt about it – and I do not want Deacon's stuff to come out under their patronage and tinctured with their particular views. What is to be published must be Deacon and nothing but Deacon. Elsewhere Elliot Smith and Perry can write what they like. If you care to entrust Layard with anything of Deacon's that you have, nothing should be published until some impartial third party has compared what Layard writes with what Deacon has written.[142]

In a postscript to the above letter, added a few days later, Haddon mentions that he has received the letters in which Mrs Deacon and Elliot Smith mention Elliot Smith's former ambitions for Bernard. Commenting on the remark of Elliot Smith about wanting to keep Bernard for Anthropology, Haddon writes, "considering that Deacon was my student this appears to me to be rather strange". Then, after quoting the section in which Elliot Smith talks about having discussed with Layard and Perry "the extent to which our hopes for the future were bound up with Deacon", Haddon states:

From this it is clear that Layard is working in conjunction with Elliot Smith and Perry. This may be all right if Rivers's and Layard's material is given as it stands and not tampered with to suit a particular view. In a recent letter to me (no date) but received about 6 weeks ago, Deacon says "I see Malinowski has been publishing and writing. I confess I don't quite follow some of his speculations. I never quite know how universal he intends his statements to be. Personally, I feel myself to be a disciple of Rivers (earlier Rivers) more than of any other ethnologist in so far as I have any theories at all. Malinowski and Smith-Perry seem to me two extremes." From what Elliot Smith once said to me, I suspected that he regarded Deacon as a member of his persuasion as he was particularly pleased with the "Kakihan Society" paper and it is also evident that he was trying to annex him. My strong opinion is that Deacon's material should be published as far as possible as he left it and only worked up sufficiently to make it coherent ... In any case I shall greatly value your opinion on the matter ... This P.S. somewhat modifies the letter which accompanies it.[143]

Replying to Haddon, Radcliffe-Brown writes:

In view of what you tell me I should feel very much disinclined to put the editing of Deacon's work in the hands of Layard. Even if Layard is quite recovered and could give full time and energy to the task, I think that there are two things that make him unsuitable. One is the very fact that he has worked in the same field and has I think missed some of the important things which Deacon discovered. The other is his relation to Elliot Smith and Perry, which you mention in your letter. I agree with you thoroughly in distrusting that school.[144]

Hence, Layard was denied the opportunity of editing Deacon's papers and the task was given to Camilla Wedgwood, a devoted pupil of Haddon and an ardent admirer of Bernard Deacon, who had managed to avoid any association with extreme diffusionism.

In the same letter, Radcliffe-Brown adds that he has "always deeply regretted the disagreement that arose between Rivers and myself when Elliot Smith got hold of him", and opines that "the phrase that you quote in your letter shows that it was the earlier Rivers of whom Deacon was a disciple, just as I am". Hence, Haddon and Radcliffe-Brown, the two senior members of the Cambridge school of anthropology, both saw the question as to what was to be done with the field-notes of the man who had made the most important new kinship discovery for decades, in terms of the distinction between the work of earlier and later Rivers. And there can be no doubt that their sympathies lay with the former rather than with the latter.

The question of the real nature of Rivers's influence upon Deacon will now be considered. Deacon's avowal of discipleship to "earlier Rivers" was, of course, made to Haddon, the guardian of the sacred Torres Straits flame and the person who would therefore have been most delighted to hear such an avowal. Moreover, it appears in the letter in which Deacon had just given notice of his technical proficiency in kinship theory, as evidenced by his deciphering of the Ambrym system. Now, if one discovers that one is good at something important, it is charitably modest, and may also be judicious, to locate an eminent predecessor whose work could be seen as foreshadowing one's own, irrespective of whether or not there has been any crucial or direct inspiration. However, if the concept of scientific discipleship is to have any meaning at all in the case of a person who arrived on the scene too late to meet the master, then Deacon *must* be regarded as a disciple of earlier Rivers. Deacon received his anthropological education in the institution where Rivers's initial value system had first been formulated and subsequently treasured and preserved by others. His two main teachers were Haddon and Armstrong — the former being a devoted propagandizer for the genealogical method, the latter being one of its more talented exponents. Deacon's tribute to Armstrong as "a confirmed logician" on the "theoretical side of social anthropology", a tribute paid in the context of the former's announcement of his Ambrym *coup*, may be taken as indicating the student's appreciation of his mentor's abilities as a kinship theorist. In addition to Deacon's use of genealogies for deciphering Ambrym social organization, the very task of specifying kinship systems in a complete and unambiguous fashion, has a decidedly "earlier Rivers" flavour to it. And even if Rivers himself had not been as proficient in this task as his reputation might have suggested, the fact remains that this reputation existed and constituted an important part of the legend which acted as a charter for the school of earlier Rivers.

The problem of deciding where Deacon really stood in relation to later Rivers and the extreme diffusionists, is rather more difficult. Certainly his early paper comparing Indonesia and New Guinea suggests an interest in, and a talent for, diffusionistic speculation. However, we must balance against this his somewhat scornful remark to Haddon about Perry's attempt to discern a dual organization in the Kakihan social structure. Deacon's theoretical pronouncements from the field are similarly ambiguous with regard to his position on Smith—Perry diffusionism. On the one hand, he does conclude, during a bout of disillusionment with his attempts at theorization, that his best plan of attack could be "to try and construct some outline of the cultural history of the New Hebrides", and confesses that he does not share "Malinowski's scorn for the historical people". On the other hand, he also speaks disparagingly of the careless diffusionism of Griffith Taylor and suggests the preparation of a "cyclopaedia of distributions" to check theories "like Perry and Smith's, which slur over gaps and . . . distort the actual complexity." Probably the safest conclusion would be that Deacon thought that diffusionistic reconstruction was an important and legitimate task for anthropology, but disapproved of some of the more outrageous hypotheses of Perry and Elliot Smith.

With specific regard to Rivers's later work, there can be little doubt that, as far as Deacon was concerned, this represented a negative influence. For one thing, there is his previously quoted statement from the field, that he is beginning to find Rivers's theory "a hindrance" and is puzzled about whether Rivers was aware of particular difficulties. For another, we have the revealing observation made by Ewan Corlette, a planter who had been friendly with Deacon on Malekula, about the nature of Rivers's influence in regard to Deacon's Ambrym discovery. Deacon was "immensely bucked up" by his unveiling of the six-section system, writes Corlette, "principally I fear because it enabled him to get one in on Rivers."[145] In particular, as I hope my discussion of Deacon's paper had made plain, it enabled Deacon to discredit Rivers's theories of Melanesian gerontocracy and anomalous marriages, and to reframe some of his speculations about the history of Melanesian social organization. In other words, Deacon was not only a disciple of earlier Rivers, but also an opponent of later Rivers.

Towards the end of 1927, Haddon read a paper to the Royal Anthropological Institute entitled "Notes on the Late A. B. Deacon's Investigations in Malekula". Layard, Wedgwood, Perry and Elliot Smith were present[146] and, after the meeting, the latter wrote a note to Haddon which contained the following passage:

What wonderful material Deacon collected! It is the most important thing the R.A.I. has got for many years. While you were presenting it I felt profoundly thankful that it had not passed through my hands: for people would have certainly accused me of faking such wonderful corroboration of our recent work. It is really magnifient, especially as it comes when you are in a phase so antagonistic to Perry and me that no one could accuse you of wanting to help us.[147]

Thus, five and a half years after Rivers's death, the ghost of later Rivers was still making mischief over the grave of a young man whose work should have offered it little real encouragement.

*   *   *   *   *

There were many senses in which the Ambrym kinship system functioned as a "test case" for the Rivers–Haddon school of anthropology. On the judgement of Deacon and Barnard, and of this historian of science, Ambrym provided a test of competence for the school's founder which he failed very badly. As I have argued in Chapter III, Rivers's unfortunate experience with the social organization of Pentecost Island, and his interrelated conversion to diffusionism, resulted in him developing a spurious approach to the study of kinship systems based upon the theory of anomalous marriages. This approach was reinforced by a series of unlucky accidents, with the result that Rivers's attempted analysis of his Ambrym data was doomed to failure from the outset.

The Ambrym affair was not the only issue to affect John Layard's standing amongst the anthropological fraternity. Always an individualist and a very original thinker, Layard was regarded by mainstream British Social Anthropology as a maverick. Moreover, during the early 1930s, there were still some question marks about his mental stability. Nonetheless, in a number of important ways, the Ambrym incident was crucial in the blighting of his anthropological career. On the judgement of the most influential members of the Cambridge school of anthropology, Layard had been weighed in the Ambrym balance and found wanting. Because he had worked in the same area as Deacon, but had missed the big empirical discovery, his fieldwork was judged inadequate, despite its undoubted intensiveness. Because Haddon and Radcliffe-Brown got the impression that he was associated with Elliot Smith and Perry, Layard was denied the task of editing Deacon's field-notes. And in losing out on this task to Camilla Wedgwood, Layard sustained other losses as well. For Deacon had copied out large portions of Layard's field-notes without labelling them as such and Wedgwood, assuming that they represented Deacon's rather than Layard's work, attributed them unhesitatingly to the former. Also, for whatever reasons, Wedgwood made a habit of inaccurately paraphrasing rather than quoting such material as Layard had then published about his Melanesian experience. So glaring were these misrepresentations that Haddon was eventually forced to concede Wedgwood's "editorial dishonesty", and to agree to Layard inserting a "Supplementary Preface" in Deacon's book, detailing some of the inaccuracies.[148]

On the evaluatory criteria elsewhere employed by Cambridge-trained anthropologists, Ambrym should have functioned as a test case for both Barnard and Armstrong, but for various ancillary reasons, did not. Following Deacon's Ambrym triumph, Armstrong should have been given more than simply a brief acknowledgement as Deacon's mentor in kinship theory. However, the replacement of Haddon by Hodson as Reader in Ethnology, and Armstrong's subsequent shift to the field of economics, rendered anything more tangible than a brief acknowledgement vocationally irrelevant. Barnard, of course, should have received at least some of the plaudits accorded to Deacon. He was, after all, the first person to suggest that Ambrym had a six-section system, and produced solid arguments to support this hypothesis. However, because his conclusions about Ambrym were presented in a tentative way, because they were not based on personally conducted fieldwork, because they had not been published, and finally because he chose not to press his own claims, Barnard's right to priority went largely unstated.

For Deacon, Ambrym was not a test case in the sense that he himself had implied. He did not, in other words, go to Ambrym with the expectation of finding a six-section system. Nonetheless, the Ambrym discovery was interpreted by Deacon's peers as a vindication of his intellectual capabilities. In particular, it reinforced the image of the young martyred hero, cut down before he could fulfil his great promise in anthropology. And, despite Deacon's ambiguous pronouncements on diffusionism, the supporters of a careful, kinship-centred anthropology hailed him as their own. Haddon was of the opinion that Deacon could have restored the Cambridge school to what he regarded as its former eminence. Radcliffe-Brown, without ever having met him, was convinced that Deacon would have made a worthy colleague at Sydney.[149] Now the evaluations of these two arbiters of anthropological achievement were based on differing aptitudes for kinship theory. Haddon, who apparently missed the significance of the structure of the Ambrym kinship system when first confronted with it in Barnard's thesis, was certainly not the equal of Radcliffe-Brown in matters of technical expertise. Nonetheless, both men agreed that Deacon's Ambrym discovery provided a vindication of the early approach to kinship devised by Rivers, and both relished the opportunity it provided of sniping at those infuriating people who, in their view, were attempting to use Rivers's later work for their own purposes.

Finally, for the Rivers–Haddon school as a whole, the Ambrym achievement provided a successful test. Not since the days of the almost legendary investigations into the social organization of the Australian Aborigines had a new type of marriage-class system been uncovered. Deacon had provided, not merely a case for employing the six-class interpretation as an intellectual exercise for anthropologists, but also evidence that the natives themselves conceptualized their kinship system in this way.

CHAPTER VII

RADCLIFFE-BROWN

Alfred Reginald Brown, who changed his surname by deed poll in April 1926 to Radcliffe-Brown, came to Cambridge as an undergraduate in 1901. At first, his main interest seems to have been in philosophy, where he was influenced by Whitehead, but he also studied experimental psychology under Rivers for several years. In 1904, when Rivers began teaching anthropology, Radcliffe-Brown became his first pupil in that subject. Radcliffe-Brown's other anthropological mentor at Cambridge was Haddon, whose influence at first seems to have been even more profound than that of Rivers. Hence, Radcliffe-Brown received his initial training in anthropology from the two founders of the Cambridge school of ethnology, in those heady days before the first flush of enthusiasm generated by the Torres Straits expedition had died down. All in all, Radcliffe-Brown's total undergraduate training in anthropology amounted to one year, which may not sound much to us but, by the standards of the day, would have been judged a fairly comprehensive introduction to the discipline.[1]

The nature of Radcliffe-Brown's subsequent career as an anthropological theoretician and fieldworker has, to a large extent, been obfuscated by the legend which he quite consciously and deliberately propagated about himself. Briefly, the legend runs as follows:

Having become interested in totemism in the early years of the twentieth-century, Radcliffe-Brown resolved to commence his attack on the problem by personal investigations among a primitive people who had no totemism, if such could be located. Upon learning of such a people in the Andaman Islands, in the Sea of Bengal, he went there and carried out some intensive fieldwork, utilizing the strictest and most scientific methods that the anthropology of the day could offer. As a result of this, he formulated a working hypothesis on totemism. On returning to England, he made a very thorough study of all the ethnographic literature relating to Australian totemism and social organization and found many unresolved problems and examples of confused thinking, especially in regard to the much-discussed phenomenon of Arunta totemism. Whilst being generally disappointed with Émile Durkheim's attempt to detect the origins of religion in Australian totemism, Radcliffe-Brown nonetheless adopted, from the Durkheimian school, the concept of "function" and the synchronic mode of explanation favoured by contributors to the *Année Sociologique*. Around this time, he also formed the surmise that a system of social organization similar to the one which he later dubbed "the Kariera system" might well exist, and that Western Australia would be a promising place to begin the search for it. Resolving to test this surmise and the previously-mentioned working hypothesis on totemism, he did fieldwork in Western Australia and was rewarded by the discovery of the Kariera system. Moreover, he gained the beginnings of a broad comparative knowledge of Australian totemism, which later enabled him to place the Arunta material in its proper context. Although his program was interrupted by the war, he eventually managed to spend eight years in Australia, and twenty years working on the classification and clarification of the varieties of Australian social organization and totemism. Despite having to rely for some of his data on the work of bumbling amateurs and notoriously muddled thinkers, by 1930 he had, with the aid of extensive data collected by himself and his disciples, produced the definitive work on Australian social organization.[2]

Before giving an account of Radcliffe-Brown's scientific career until 1931, and thereby separating the mixture of fact, falsehood and half-truth which make up this legend, let me make the point that Radcliffe-Brown was the first real professional in British anthropology. Now the criteria determining professionality in science may be schematized as follows: First, rigorous training by competent practitioners of the discipline. Second, earning one's living on the basis of one's contributions to the subject. Third, the propagation of one's scientific contributions and values by the training of pupils who will also make their living from the subject. In respect of social anthropology, it was usual that these contributions and values should be seen as furthering, not only the theoretical side of the discipline, but also intensive fieldwork, which came to function as a kind of rite-of-passage for entry into the profession. Fourth, the utilization or establishment of such institutions as are requisite for the satisfactory performance of the second and third criteria. Fifth and last, the production of scientific contributions which are sufficiently technical as to be comprehensible only to a group of fellow practitioners, which therefore functions as the exclusive judge and audience for one's work. Tylor, it is true, earned his living as a Reader and later as a Professor of Anthropology at Oxford over a long period, but his career fails to satisfy the first and fourth criteria, and could only be said to satisfy the third and fifth criteria by a considerable stretch of the imagination. Haddon and Rivers, although founding the Cambridge school of anthropology and training large numbers of pupils, also failed to satisfy the necessary set of conditions. Both fall short of the first criterion, and are decidedly suspect in regard to the second. Although holding academic positions in ethnology at Cambridge for a quarter of a century, Haddon was paid only the most meagre of salaries for his trouble. Rivers's living came from his being a Fellow of St John's College, an honour which was accorded to him in 1902 primarily on the basis of his work in experimental psychology. Many of Haddon's publications, moreover, fail to measure up to the fifth criterion. The career of Radcliffe-Brown, on the other hand, eminently satisfied all five criteria for professionality. Only as regards the actual performance of the ethnographic rite-of-passage does Radcliffe-Brown's career look at all deficient, but even here the deficiency is not fatal because, whatever the real nature of his fieldwork, Radcliffe-Brown certainly espoused and passed on to his pupils the *ideology* of intensive ethnography. What is more, as the following account will show, Radcliffe-Brown's own conception of himself as the first professional anthropologist did much to determine the shape and flavour of his contributions to the discipline.

THE ANDAMAN EMBARRASSMENT? 1906–1909

During the 1880s the interest of the Royal Anthropological Institute had been aroused by the publication in the *Journal* of a long article on the apparently very primitive inhabitants of the Andaman Islands.[3] The author of this piece, a penal officer named E. H. Man, had been aided in his first attempt to record the language of the Andamanese by Sir Richard Temple, Chief Commissioner of the Andaman and Nicobar Islands.[4] In a letter to Haddon dated 16th March 1906, Temple states that the Andamans and the Nicobars present "practically a clear field for the trained scientific student". Temple refers to his belief that the whole of South East Asia was originally populated by negritos, by far the purest remnants of which are allegedly found in the Andamans. He describes the population of the islands in the Bay of Bengal as "high and dry relics of very ancient times".[5] So in good Tylorean fashion, Temple was suggesting that the Andamanese warrant study because they represent survivals of the dim distant past.

Later in the same year, the Board of Anthropological Studies at Cambridge selected Radcliffe-Brown as the first Anthony Wilkin Student in Ethnology, thereby giving official and financial endorsement to his claim to being the first product of the new approach to anthropology arising out of the Torres

Straits expedition. The purpose of the Studentship was to fund a fieldtrip to the Andamans. Radcliffe-Brown arrived in the islands in August 1906, and spent two dry seasons of six months each doing fieldwork. Two letters written by Radcliffe-Brown to Haddon during the early part of the expedition reveal something of his aims and difficulties. A few days before landfall in the Andamans he wrote that he expected to spend only a month or two on Great Andaman. "This", he says, "should give me time to see all the natives individually, and to investigate them, since there are not more than 450 all told".[6] Hence, he obviously intended his work to involve what would now be regarded as little more than a brief survey. In actual fact, however, his field investigations appear to have been less superficial than his early statement of intentions indicated, since he eventually put in some eight and a half months on Great Andaman Island. Not all of this work involved what would now be called "social anthropology". He speaks in one letter about his "apparatus" having been delayed, which occurrence prevented him from performing the observations which he would otherwise have done.[7] This undoubtedly refers to anthropometric apparatus, used to determine physical parameters and establish a racial type. Such measurements later enabled him to conclude that physically the Andamanese are a very homogeneous race, exhibiting little variation from the norm. Some attempt was made to apply the genealogical method, but with little success. "I have not so far been able to collect genealogies", he writes after his first stumbling attempts at fieldwork. "The most intelligent native met could not remember such things, and I found that the woman to whom he recommended me as knowing all these things, died the day before yesterday."[8]

That he had considerable difficulties with the language is obvious. Some of the Great Andamanese spoke Hindustani, but he writes that as yet he had been unable to find a Hindustani-English interpreter. For this reason we find him, only about a week after arrival, expressing the desire (not to be fulfilled) to switch his fieldwork from the Andamans to the Nicobar Islands. Many of the coastal Nicobarese talk English, and most know Hindustani and Malay, he says. Besides which, friendly relations have currently been established with the Shom Pen — the inland tribe of Great Nicobar. The Shom Pen, he writes, represent a pure race which has been isolated for a long time by continual warfare with coastal tribes. They have retained their ancient manners and culture, and from what he hears of their marriage customs, taboos and so forth, they seem to be in "a most interesting stage of social progress". They have never been measured, but apparently represent "the original Indonesian stock in its purity, both physically and sociologically".[9]

Hence, it is obvious that Radcliffe-Brown embarked on his first fieldtrip with no great initial commitment to investigating the Andamanese. Inasmuch as he had a theoretical stance, one might describe it as vaguely Haddonesque — he was aiming to do a survey, to investigate a number of miscellaneous topics, of which genealogies was only one among a number of others, and he was very keen to find a primitive, racially pure type, with its sociology and physical characteristics untouched by intermixture with other cultures. Against this evidence, his later claim that he had specially chosen the Andamanese because they represented the rare case of a pre-totemic society, is not particularly believable.

Considering his apprenticeship under Rivers, the most surprising aspect of Radcliffe-Brown's investigation of the Andamanese was his total failure to come to grips with kinship problems. In a series of obscure footnotes to *The Andaman Islanders*, Radcliffe-Brown was later to admit that he had not fully unravelled the Andamanese system of relationship, and that some of his observations on the relationship system may have been in error.[10] Even more surprisingly, he was to confess that, although he had collected a number of genealogies from the natives, his "inexperience in the use of the genealogical method" and his consequent inability to surmount the obstacles with which he met, made this aspect of his investigations "a failure".[11] In fact, Radcliffe-Brown had little excuse for this failure, since, as well as being a pupil of Rivers, he had the benefit of a detailed list of Andamanese terms of relationship provided by Man.[12] Man's list was based on Morgan's kinship questionnaire, which had been included in the first edition of the *Notes and Queries*.

In 1908, Radcliffe-Brown ceased his fieldwork in the islands and went back to Cambridge to write up his Andaman material as a fellowship thesis for Trinity College. This thesis was never published as such, and I have not seen it, but on Radcliffe-Brown's own account his aims in writing it were to formulate hypotheses about the origins of cultural institutions and to provide hypothetical reconstructions of the details of culture history. By an investigation of physical characteristics, language and culture, he evidently attempted to provide a conjectural account of the history of the Andamanese in particular, and of the negritos in general.[13] The appendix on technology in the final, published work on *The Andaman Islanders* is, he tells us, an example of the approach taken in his fellowship thesis. This appendix uses data on the material culture of the Andamanese to try and reconstruct their racial and cultural history. As it stands in the 1922 book, it is full of qualifying terms like "possibly" and "probably", which indicate the extent to which he had lost faith in the viability of the historical approach in the interim between writing his thesis, and concocting his mature theory of Andamanese society.

At about the time he was writing up his thesis for Trinity College, Radcliffe-Brown became involved in what must have been for him (or, at any rate, *should* have been for him) a rather embarrassing controversy about Andamanese religion. In his first published contribution to anthropology, entitled "The Religion of the Andaman Islanders", Radcliffe-Brown makes some very cutting remarks about the work of E. H. Man. Radcliffe-Brown takes particular exception to Man's assertion that Andamanese religious notions should be interpreted as implying belief in a primitive All-Father God. He states that the only way to avoid such misinterpetations is to follow a strict method in observing and interpreting data. However, he says he cannot enter here into the question of methods.[14]

In a reply to Radcliffe-Brown, the German diffusionist and Roman Catholic priest Wilhelm Schmidt takes him to task for affirming the value of his strict methods, but refusing to say what they are. He regards Radcliffe-Brown's suggestion that Man may have "perhaps unwittingly" asked "leading questions" of the natives, as quite gratuitous. He remarks on the fact that, of all Man's data, Radcliffe-Brown has singled out the idea of a Supreme Being to cast discredit on, and implies that Radcliffe-Brown has his own personal prejudices which might tend to make him *dis*believe in a primitive All-Father.[15]

Stung by this attack, Radcliffe-Brown then retaliates in a most intemperate fashion, implying that Schmidt's criticism does not really warrant a reply. Since the question of method has been raised, however, he will take the opportunity to explain what he means by strict methods. This course of action is rendered especially suitable, he says, "because Father Schmidt's note is itself an example of the worst methods". Referring to his own "careful study" of Andamanese mythology, conducted "during a residence of several months among the Andamanese themselves", Radcliffe-Brown claims that Schmidt apparently disbelieves not only his arguments, but also his observations. Evidently, writes Radcliffe-Brown, Schmidt regards the earlier investigations of Man as "more reliable than mine". This matter, he remarks contemptuously "is one which it is very disagreable for me to discuss". Briefly, he explains the features of his own method upon which he most wishes to insist:

In my own interpretation I relied entirely on the comparison one with another of the different beliefs and customs to be found in the Andamans, explaining one belief by the light thrown on it by others. That is to say, I tried to understand the Andamanese mentality as a whole.

He then lists what he regards as the faults of Father Schmidt's methods. First, Schmidt is not seeking truth with an open mind, but is looking for support for a preformed theory. Second, he has no intimate knowledge of the people whose beliefs he would interpret. Third, his argument rests on suppositions concerning the former beliefs of the Andamanese, for which there is not, and never can be, any evidence. Radcliffe-Brown's conclusion bears quoting, as an example of the arrogance of the young scientific professional attacking entrenched amateurism:

I have replied at length to Father Schmidt's attack on me, because it brings out the fundamental disagreement that exists between those of us who are endeavouring, by an insistence on strict methods . . . to make ethnology a science fit to rank with the other sciences, and those writers who, by following such unjustifiable methods as those to be found in Father Schmidt's note, hinder the progress of our science. It is probably too late to hope that Father Schmidt will change his methods, but I have availed myself of this opportunity of showing what those methods are. We shall probably be justified in concluding that they are habitual with him, and therefore the whole of his work is rendered suspect. Theories elaborated on such a basis must be treated with the utmost scepticism, if indeed they are worthy of any attention at all.[16]

A few months later, a reply to Radcliffe-Brown appeared in the form of a letter by Andrew Lang. Employing a tone which is all the more effective for being gently chiding rather than argumentative, Lang attempts to correct what he obviously regards as Radcliffe-Brown's excessively harsh criticism of Schmidt and Man. Having admitted to himself being "greatly guilty of a theory of a primitive All-Father", Lang goes on to refer to his own "old-fashioned comparative ways", and to his "obsolete method of comparison". He then refers to one of Radcliffe-Brown's most unfair criticisms of Man:

As to [the ethical aspect of Pulaga, the God of the Andamanese], Mr Brown found no corroboration of Mr Man's statements. He therefore ventures to think that, perhaps unwittingly, Mr Man suggested to his informant that Pulaga was angry if one man wronged another, and the native of course agreed.

That, says Lang, "is cutting the knot with an axe". Finally, Lang makes a point which, whatever its objective validity, would have been very effective at the level of propaganda. Responding to Radcliffe-Brown's claim to having acquired more intimate knowledge of the Andamanese than Man, Lang mentions that the latter had "lived rather longer (namely 11 years) in this region than Mr. Brown did".[17]

Now, before evaluating this controversy, one must first acknowledge that Radcliffe-Brown was correct in arguing that Man's interpretation of

Andamanese religion was vitiated by his personal religious beliefs. In an obituary for Man, Temple was to admit that Man's "high sense of his own religion made it difficult for him to grasp the view of primitive savages".[18] Moreover, the motives of Schmidt and Lang in supporting Man were decidedly suspect. Schmidt's attempted reconstructions of cultural history were, as Marvin Harris has said, "dominated by the necessity of reconciling the findings of anthropology with scriptural precedent",[19] and there can be little doubt that he allowed his priestly vocation to intrude upon his ethnological theories. Lang, a literary dilettante whom W. E. Henley had dubbed "the divine amateur",[20] was somewhat notorious for his attempts to combat Tylor's evolutionary theory of religion by uncovering reputed evidences of monotheism among the most "primitive" peoples. In view of the strength of his case, then, it is significant that Radcliffe-Brown chose to assert the superiority of his own approach by reference to his allegedly "more scientific" methods, and that, when he was challenged as to just what these methods were, the best he could do was to make a lame reference to the necessity for comparing the various beliefs and customs of the Andamanese one with another, so that a comprehensive appreciation of Andamanese mental processes could be achieved. This earliest statement by Radcliffe-Brown of the efficacy of the scientific method in anthropology, therefore comes out sounding weak and insubstantial – an occurrence which should have been made doubly embarrassing for him by the fact that the person who fired the final arrow was Andrew Lang, whom Radcliffe-Brown regarded both as intellectually below par and as the adherent of an obsoletely amateurish approach to anthropology.

For this phase of his career at Cambridge, there exists a very memorable pen-portrait of Radcliffe-Brown by E. L. Grant Watson, about whom more will be said as the chapter unfolds.

Brown had a peculiar reputation at Trinity. In spite of his having passed all examinations with distinction, and being a Scholar and Fellow of the College, there were many of the erudite who looked on him with suspicion. He was too dramatic a personality to fit easily into the conservative life of a college. He often made wild statements. He was brilliantly informed on *all* subjects ... He was in fact a bit of a superman, and one who strove, more consistently than any other man I have met, to live consciously and according to a set plan, dictated by reason and will. It is true that he sometimes lapsed from his high standard, and was led by his inventive genius to fabricate the stories he told, and often it was not difficult to see this invention in process. This made the scholarly and conscientious distrustful of him, but I have every reason to believe that these extravagances which he allowed himself in talk, never once found their way into his published work.

I was advised by well-meaning friends that I would not be able to stand for a week Brown's overbearing manners. I was told he was a charlatan, and impossible, but despite such warnings I liked him, and had the good sense to recognise that in intelligence, experience and will-power he out-topped me in all directions.[21]

Grant-Watson contrasts Radcliffe-Brown's reception in the colleges of Cambridge with that which must have been accorded him on the islands where he had done his first fieldwork. There, says Watson, Radcliffe-Brown "had lived as a primitive autocrat, exercising a beneficent but completely authoritative sway over the simple Andamanese, who had not been in a position to criticize his grand gestures".[22]

The aspects of Radcliffe-Brown's personality which Grant Watson's account makes especially vivid, and upon which I would particularly like to focus, namely his egotism, aristocratic demeanour and desire to set himself apart from the common herd by the display of superior knowledge and insight, were evidently persistent traits throughout his life. Margaret Mead wrote, at a time when she was working under his direction, that "Brown identifies himself with every idea he has ever voiced and any disagreement, tacit or uttered, with his ideas he takes as a slap in the face . . . . "[23] In the early thirties, Ruth Benedict opined that Radcliffe-Brown seemed to her "impenetrably wrapped in his own conceit".[24] Amazingly enough, equally telling comments may also be found in obituaries written by colleagues after Radcliffe-Brown's death. A. P. Elkin, for example, speaks of his "air of academic superiority" and "somewhat exotic social pose".[25] Similarly, Raymond Firth has written that what pleased Radcliffe-Brown most during his Sydney years were

. . . the small informal gatherings at which he held forth on an amazing range of subjects, from Javanese dances, the theory of instincts, and the sociology of Herbert Spencer to the authorship of Shakespeare's plays. Here he sometimes displayed what one who knew him in his Cambridge days has referred to as his lack of power or of habit of distinguishing between first-hand and second-hand knowledge. This intellectual deafness was a reflex of his ego-centrism — all that he learned became an integral part of himself and was fitted into his own personality.[26]

Certainly during his student days in Cambridge, Radcliffe-Brown must have been a controversial character. Firth tells us that "among his more recondite interests at this time seems to have been hypnotism — which rumour has it, he practised at times with unfortunate results".[27] Whilst an undergraduate, Radcliffe-Brown, who at that time was nicknamed "Anarchy Brown" because of his political beliefs, used to tell his friends and colleagues that the famous

Anarchist philosopher Prince Peter Kropotkin was his neighbour in Birmingham. Radcliffe-Brown was apparently in the habit of claiming that, during his vacations from Cambridge, he would visit Kropotkin and the two would discuss Radcliffe-Brown's solutions to the deficiencies of contemporary England.[28]

But if Radcliffe-Brown was a poseur and a master of the art of intellectual oneupmanship, he played the game according to different rules depending on whether he was operating in the social or formally academic realms. His apparent fabrication of stories for dramatic social effect, for example, had no parallel in his published works, which tend to be factually reliable, closely argued, not particularly numerous, and expressed with remarkable concision. Rather, the form taken by his intellectual gamesmanship in the sphere of his scientific work involved a certain abusing of his status as the first professional in British anthropology. To use the scientific method as a weapon to browbeat his opponents, to create a false impression of his own empirical achievements by failing to explicitly acknowledge the full extent of the amateur observations on which his own edifice was in fact erected, and to take every opportunity of heaping scorn and abuse on previous theoretical work by amateurs, such were the tactics used by Radcliffe-Brown to advance his own career.

THE WEST AUSTRALIAN EXPEDITION 1910–1912

In 1909 Radcliffe-Brown had given a course of lectures on the Australian Aborigines at the London School of Economics. This had involved him in carrying out a survey of the existent literature on Australian social organization. During this exercise he was, no doubt, confronted with the necessity for coming to grips with the complex rules of marriage and descent in Australian tribes. The earliest published manifestation of this work was an article in the April 1910 issue of *Man*, in which Radcliffe-Brown endeavoured to correct some hazy thinking on the part of that prolific recorder of Australian marriage-class systems, R. H. Mathews. Mathews had argued that, in Australian tribes possessing eight marriage-classes, descent with respect to the classes was not patrilineal, as Spencer and Gillen had asserted, but matrilineal. Responding to this claim, Radcliffe-Brown pointed out that, provided only regular marriages are being considered, it is meaningless to speak about descent within the classes being either matrilineal or patrilineal, since descent proceeds, not through just the mother or just the father but through both parents. From a consideration of irregular marriages, however, the significance of which for questions of descent had first been recognized by Mathews himself, Radcliffe-Brown deduces, on the basis of Mathew's own Arunta data, that descent proceeds through the classes in the paternal line. Hence, Radcliffe-Brown was attempting to refute Mathew's conclusions about the Arunta by recourse to tools and materials supplied by the latter. Now Radcliffe-Brown's argument certainly must have *sounded* convincing in 1910 (although, as I pointed out in the first chapter, it is now generally accepted that in fact descent through the Arunta classes proceeds matrilineally). Moreover, it is my judgement that the early part of his article cleared away some of the fog which had accumulated around the problem of descent. However, Radcliffe-Brown then overstepped the mark by making this particular exercise the occasion for his first recorded claim to having discovered an anthropological "law". This "law" he states as follows:

Among the Arunta, when a man, instead of marrying into his regular class, enters into a marriage of Type II [a variety of irregular marriage], the children belong to the class to which they would have belonged if they had been his children by a regular marriage, and they do not belong to the class to which they would have belonged if they had been the offspring of their actual mother by a regular marriage.[29]

That a person with even a faint inkling of the content and methodology of the natural sciences could claim a statement of such low generality as a "law", seems to me incredible. We must assume, I think, that Radcliffe-Brown's ambition to promote himself as the prophet of what he later called "the natural science of society", and his elation at having apparently been able to clarify what he evidently regarded as the amateurish theoretical excursions of a previous worker in the field, led him into this extravagant absurdity.

Convinced of the importance of Australian social organization for anthropological theory, Radcliffe-Brown had, in November 1909, applied to the Board of Anthropological Studies at Cambridge for his second Anthony Wilkin Studentship in Ethnology. The investigation he wished to undertake, explained Radcliffe-Brown, was "a study in the Ethnology of Western Australia". This investigation would take place in three phases. First, "a general survey of the tribes in the neighbourhood of Perth and towards Coolgardie". Second, "a general survey of the coast tribes northward from Geraldton, tribes having four matrimonial classes". And finally "a detailed intensive study of one tribe or group of tribes, either north or south of Geraldton, that tribe to be selected which seems to promise the fullest and most valuable results".[30]

Presumably in reference to the stated intention of Radcliffe-Brown to pursue some intensive fieldwork among a single tribe or group of tribes, Rivers prepared a memo, which seems to have been intended for perusal by Haddon, Frazer and Ridgeway, who, together with Rivers himself, constituted a Committee which had been set up to direct the proposed expedition.[31] In this memo, Rivers advanced the proto-functionalist hypothesis that a satisfactory account of a subject like marriage-regulation can only be provided if the ethnographer undertakes a complete investigation of the total culture. Speaking as someone who had experience in such matters, Rivers further argued that this type of fieldwork is most satisfactorily and most economically performed, not in collaboration, but by a single investigator. Hence, he implies that if the expedition is going to consist of more people than just Radcliffe-Brown, then it will probably be desirable for them to split up and pursue their intensive investigations independently.

Whether this memo influenced the composition of the expedition I do not know, but a young zoologist named E. L. Grant Watson was eventually selected to accompany Radcliffe-Brown, it being understood that he would devote most of his energies to collecting zoological specimens and would assist Radcliffe-Brown with his anthropological investigations when called upon. Watson has left us a striking sketch of what it was like preparing for the expedition:

We spent several hours poring over maps of North-West Australia. Brown told me a good deal about primitive peoples, and lent me several books to read, including, of course, Spencer and Gillan [sic]. He expounded to me the principles of class-marriages. The more he talked with me the more I fell under his spell. There were times when he would pause from his eager, incisive speech; his eyes would be fixed on the distance, as a lion's eyes might be fixed on the distance, and he would seem to be dreaming some remote dream. He was beautiful to behold, and certainly surprisingly well informed.[32]

Watson introduced Radcliffe-Brown to his mother:

To her he was polite and charming, and both [she] and my stepfather fell under his sway. I saw a good deal of him during my remaining time in Cambridge, and discovered rather to my amazement how very much the reverse of polite and charming he could be towards those who failed to awake his interest. He was never vulgarly rude, but if he was not interested he did not pretend to be so. He made, in fact, no least effort towards people who seemed to him superfluous. They might talk to him, expecting an answer, but his eye would be fixed on the distance, and no reply would be forthcoming. This, I think, was all part of his system of using his time to the best advantage. No time should be wasted; everything should be done according to a conscious plan. The irrelevant should be ignored, and thoughts that might otherwise be squandered employed elsewhere. He expounded to me some of his philosophy. One must cultivate style. He dressed like a Paris *savant*, faultlessly. He aspired to be conscious of every gesture; had even thought out the best position in which to sleep. Not on the back, not wholly on the side, and not like a foetus. He pictured himself even in sleep. He read aloud to me sometimes, and I have never known any man read poetry better. . . . Sometimes, it is true, I found his astonishing versatility a bit trying, but he was always stimulating, and always my honesty had to acknowledge his superior achievement. He was gentle and very considerate towards those who fell within the sphere of his concern; for those who fell outside that sphere he had no regard whatsoever. I have never known a man be more ruthless, and can well understand the women who found cause to hate him, and who so often declared that he was "no gentleman".[33]

With this notable character sketch ringing in our ears, let me now introduce into the story one of the women who was to have good reason for declaring Radcliffe-Brown to be "no gentleman". As part of his survey of Australian ethnography, Radcliffe-Brown had read a chapter on social organization from the manuscript of a projected book on the Aborigines by one Daisy Bates. This chapter was entrusted to Radcliffe-Brown by Andrew Lang, who had been sent a copy of the complete work by Mrs Bates, with whom he had been corresponding. A remarkable Irish lady, Mrs Bates had emigrated to Australia at the turn of the century and lived in close proximity to the blacks for a decade — a life-style which gave her plenty of opportunity for indulging both her ample social conscience and her scientific curiosity about an apparently dying people.

Circa the beginning of 1910, Mrs Bates, having heard that an anthropological expedition to Western Australia was in the wind, had written to R. R. Marett of Oxford offering her assistance. Marett passed on her letter to Radcliffe-Brown, who replied gratefully accepting the offer. Radcliffe-Brown also mentioned that he had read her chapter on social organization and opined that she had "clearly got together a large amount of very valuable information, which will be of immense value to us in the work we propose to do".[34] Considering the form in which she had presented it, however, Radcliffe-Brown did not feel that publication was warranted without extensive revision, and possibly further empirical enquiries. He therefore suggested that she should shelve the question of publication until he came to Australia and discussed the matter with her at length. If she found herself willing to co-operate, he said, it was possible that her material might be published with the reports of the expedition, an eventuality which would ensure that she obtained "all the credit" which she "so richly deserved" for her labours.[35] Mrs Bates, evidently delighted at the prospect of taking part in an expedition led by a young professional anthropologist, devised a scheme which neatly expressed her conception of the future social and working relationship between the two kinship enthusiasts. Throughout the north of Western Australia she was regarded by the Aboriginals as a member of the Boorong marriage class. She therefore decided to place Radcliffe-Brown in the Paljeri class, in which event the natives would then consider him to be her son. This arrangement would facilitate their travels, since Aboriginal law deemed it right and proper for a woman to accompany her son anywhere.[36]

In a second letter, written to Mrs Bates around the middle of 1910, Radcliffe-Brown explained to her the usual schematic methods of representing class systems, and enclosed a copy of the article in which he had criticized Mathew's work. Speaking of the transpositions of section names which commonly occur in different districts of an area in which one major type of class system is in operation, Radcliffe-Brown wrote:

These changes interest me very greatly, and I should very much like to get at the cause of them. I should expect them to be connected with change of descent of the totems from the female to the male line.[37]

In order to see what Radcliffe-Brown might have meant by this, let us represent schematically two of the kinship systems which he outlined in his letter to Mrs Bates by way of illustrating such sectional transpositions.

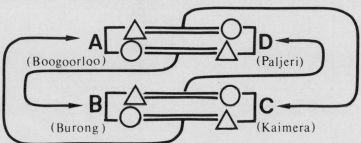

Fig. 24. Peak Hill kinship system.

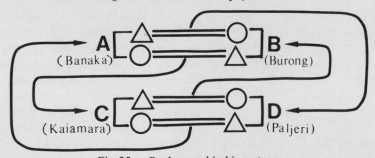

Fig. 25. Roebourne kinship system.

As can be seen by comparing the above schemata with Figure 1, the general structure of both kinship systems is identical to that which was later to be singled out as exemplary of four-section systems. Disregarding firstly the different names for section A, which may be interpreted as a minor regional variation, and secondly the variant spelling of the name for section C, the only significant dissimilarity between the Peak Hill and Roebourne systems lies in the fact that sections B, C and D have rotated their positions. Now let us assume that, in the Peak Hill district, there are two totems, M and N, which descend matrilineally; so that, for example, the totem of a person in section B will be the same as the totem of this person's mother, who is in section A. If totemic descent is represented by dashed lines, if the symbols representing people associated with totem M are drawn unshaded, and if the symbols representing people associated with totem N are drawn shaded, the relevant facts about kinship and totemism may be drawn on the one diagram as follows:

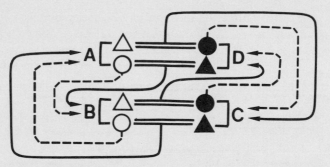

Fig. 26.   Peak Hill kinship system with matrilineal totemism.

Let us assume that totemic descent in the above type of system switches over from the matrilineal to the patrilineal mode. The resulting system would then look as in Figure 27 on the next page. What Radcliffe-Brown seems to have been postulating, is that the sectional arrangement of the Roebourne district represents an evolutionary transposition of a sectional arrangement like that of the Peak Hill district, and that the transposition was causally correlated with a change from matrilineal to patrilineal totemic descent. A perusal of Figures 24, 25, 26 and 27 reveals a possible rationale for such a correlation. With regard to totemic affiliation, A's relationship to B had been the same as C's relationship to D (Figure 26). Similarly, for the Peak Hill kinship system, A's relationship to B was, in respect of the sectional membership of mothers and their children, the same as C's relationship to D (Figure

Fig. 27.   Peak Hill kinship system with patrilineal totemism.

24). But if totemic descent altered in the way suggested, A's relationship to
C would have become the same as B's relationship to D (Figure 27). Similarly,
for the actual Roebourne system, A's relationship to C is, in respect of the
sectional affiliation of mothers and their children, the same as B's relationship
to D (Figure 25). Could not, therefore, the postulated change from the Peak
Hill to the Roebourne type of kinship system have represented an adjustment
in the structural relationships between the sections which was occasioned by
a similar adjustment accompanying a switchover in totemic descent? Whether
or not this speculative reconstruction accurately reproduces Radcliffe-Brown's
line of thought, this postulate of a change from matrilineal to patrilineal
totemic descent is itself evidence of his inheritance from nineteenth-century
anthropology. Since the postulate crops up in a number of his subsequent
letters and publications, we may conclude that it played an important heuristic role during the formative period of Radcliffe-Brown's work in Australian
social organization.

Reading between the lines, it seems likely that Radcliffe-Brown was led to
his consideration of the transposition of section names by a reading of Durkheim. In the 1900–1901 volume of the *Année Sociologique*, the French sociologist had published an article entitled "Sur le Totemisme". As I have stated
in Chapter I, Durkheim had here referred to the fact that, although the four
marriage-classes of the southern Arunta are currently grouped into patrilineal
moieties, the arrangement of the classes is such that, when the southern Arunta
come into contact with the Urabunna, it is possible for their class system to
mesh with the matrilineal system of the latter people. This Durkheim had
taken as indicating that the present southern Arunta system is a modification
of an older one, in which the sections had originally been grouped into matrilineal moieties. Hence, in suggesting that West Australian class systems with
transposed class names might be developmentally related, Radcliffe-Brown

might well have been enlarging upon Durkheim's suggestion regarding the history of the Arunta system. Certainly when expounding diagrammatic methods of representing class systems in his second letter to Mrs Bates, Radcliffe-Brown reveals that he takes the southern Arunta as his "starting point", and goes on to contrast the lack of totemic descent among the Arunta with the patrilineal form of totemic descent practised by another neighbouring tribe, the Warramunga. Moreover, at one point in the letter he presents, as the accepted opinion among ethnologists in general, the Durkheimian view that the word "totem" should be employed only when the animal or other object is regarded as in some sense "sacred" to a group of persons.[38] An article published by Durkheim in the 1903–1904 volume of the *Année Sociologique* may have been even more important in suggesting to Radcliffe-Brown the mechanism for the evolutionary transposition which he postulated in 1910. Entitled "Sur l'Organization Matrimoniale des Societés Australiennes", the article argues that the evolution of an eight-section system from a four-section system could have been caused by the tribe adopting the practice of transmitting the totem in the paternal rather than the maternal line.[39] Certainly when Radcliffe-Brown finally came to write up the results of his West Australian expedition, he refers to this Durkheimian article and reveals that he has taken it sufficiently seriously to have noted that his newly-collected data do not, in fact, support the argument which it advances.[40] Thus, I think we can safely conclude that Radcliffe-Brown had not only been reading Durkheim by 1910, but that one of his specifically technical interests in Australian social organization had been suggested by this source.

But if there were signs that Radcliffe-Brown had been influenced by the French sociologist, it was also obvious that he had acquired a further debt to the Cambridge school of ethnology. In an early but undated letter to Mrs Bates, Radcliffe-Brown had commented on her use of genealogies in the social organization chapter, saying that her account would have been improved if she had made out her genealogies in the form of a tree.[41] In a further undated communication, he went out of his way to compliment her as "the first student of Australian ethnology who has collected genealogies", and proferred some hints designed to make her genealogies more informative. Genealogies collected in the manner suggested, he states, "are more valuable perhaps to the student of ethnology than anything else you could give him".[42] While this evidence does not tally well with Radcliffe-Brown's later assertion that he "persuaded [Mrs Bates] to adopt the genealogical method in 1910",[43] it certainly demonstrates that he was in process of making amends for his earlier neglect of Rivers's most notable anthropological achievement.

Before leaving Radcliffe-Brown's early correspondence with Daisy Bates, I would like to mention that it also incorporates a statement of his principal ethnographic objectives as envisaged immediately before setting sail from England:

My chief aim in W[estern] A[ustralia] will be the thorough study of the classes and totemic systems. It is quite clear from your work that W[estern] A[ustralia] presents a large number of fascinating problems. (The N[orth] W[est] will probably give the key to the change from 4 to 8 classes).[44]

The letter containing the above passage concludes with Radcliffe-Brown observing that, if a way could be found, he would gladly give up his teaching in England and devote the next five or six years to solving some of the problems of Australian sociology.

A rather more detailed version of Radcliffe-Brown's perception of the situation was provided in a lengthy interview reported in a local newspaper shortly after his arrival in Western Australia in September 1910.[45] After predicating that, over the past decade, anthropology had "made good its claim to rank among the most important of the sciences", and that Cambridge University had taken a leading position in recent ethnological research, the interviewer reports that data from Australia loom large on the horizon of the anthropologist. By way of explaining why this should be so, Radcliffe-Brown is quoted as saying that the work of Spencer and Gillen in Central Australia had raised a number of problems and provided the occasion for a good deal of controversy in England, France and Germany. The specific points at issue in the controversy, states Radcliffe-Brown, relate principally to totemism, the importance of which lies in the fact that it probably represents "a stage of civilization through which all mankind has passed in its progress upwards from the lowest savagery to civilization". After this apparent endorsement of unilineal social evolution, Radcliffe-Brown briefly outlines his views on Australian marriage-class systems. The fact that some tribes have two exogamous classes, some four and some eight indicates, according to Radcliffe-Brown, a progressive development of social complexity. "The reason for these changing systems is obscure", he says, "and has occasioned a good deal of discussion in England. It points to a very complicated marriage system, and great interest centres on the origin of the system". The purpose of our expedition, he confides, is to attempt to throw light on some of these problems. Western Australia has been selected as the venue for the expedition by virtue of its being the only part of the continent where Aboriginal social organization has not yet been subjected to close scrutiny.

Thus, from the surviving evidence, one gathers that, before embarking on the expedition, Radcliffe-Brown's principal aims were to carry out a general survey of totemism and marriage regulation in Western Australia, followed by an intensive investigation of the same topics in a restricted area. With regard to totemism, the problems to be tackled had been specifically raised by Spencer and Gillen's work on the Arunta, but the solutions, considered in relation to the principles of unilineal social evolutionism, would hopefully yield some insights into the religious development of all mankind. In respect of marriage regulation the main objective seems to have been the provision of an explanation for certain changes from one type of system to another, including the transposition of class-names, which he thought might be connected with innovations in totemic descent, and the conversion of four-class to eight-class systems. Such changes Radcliffe-Brown evidently regarded as part of a progressive increase in complexity. At this stage he seems to have been aiming to provide a developmental account of social transformation rather than an exhaustive classification of the varieties of existent social organization, although, of course, a great deal of taxonomy would obviously be necessary in order to get the developmental account right, and to place Arunta totemism in a suitably broad context. Notable by its absence is any expressed intention of discovering a special or typical variety of four-class system.

Late in 1910 a wagon drawn by two horses set out from the small town of Sandstone on the upper Murchison River.[46] Its occupants were Radcliffe-Brown, Daisy Bates, Grant Watson, a Swede named Louis Olsen who had been engaged as cook, and two male Aborigines who had been persuaded to come along as interpreters. At first they headed eastwards into virgin bush, where a large corroboree involving some seven or eight tribes was about to be celebrated. Since leaving Perth, there had been friction between Radcliffe-Brown and Mrs Bates. Watson writes of the occurrence of "more than one of those symptomatic intervals when Brown's eyes had become fixed on distance and Mrs Bates had talked into the silence".[47]

After setting up camp at the corroboree site, Radcliffe-Brown immediately busied himself, in the manner of Haddon and Rivers, with the natives' string-games, which were "similar to cat's cradle". The expedition then settled down to its ethnographic investigations, which Mrs Bates describes as questioning the Aborigines "regarding genealogies and customs", and which Watson characterizes as the tabulation of "fact pertaining to the four class marriage system".[48] However, their labours were soon interrupted by a posse of white police seeking the perpetrators of some tribal killings. On being woken just before dawn by the sound of gunshots and galloping horses, Watson emerged from his tent to see a posse of policemen riding through the camp, firing their pistols at the native dogs, and swearing vividly. Almost to a man the natives were leaving, melting silently into the bush in the manner proverbial for Australian Aborigines. Watson noticed that Radcliffe-Brown was already standing at the entrance to his tent, with the flap closed behind him. When the officer in charge of the police spoke to him, Radcliffe-Brown listened to his tales about dangerous murderers, then let it be known that the raid had effectively ruined the work of the expedition. The police having departed, Radcliffe-Brown pulled back the flap of his tent and, as Watson tells the story, "out from the interior emerged two of the murderers, who had taken refuge with their white-man-friend, whom they declared was 'close up along-side-of-God' ".[49]

This turn of events precipitated the first serious rift between Radcliffe-Brown and Mrs Bates. Despite her pleasure at seeing Radcliffe-Brown protect two of her beloved natives from police injustice, she disagreed with him over the question of remaining at the corroboree site. In Radcliffe-Brown's opinion the natives would probably not return, so he decided to change his plans and make for Bernier and Dorre Islands, some thirty miles off the coast. On these islands the anthropologists would have large numbers of captive informants, in the form of venereally infected patients who had been confined to crude isolation hospitals. This contingency had evidently been pre-planned by Radcliffe-Brown, who had obtained permission to visit the islands from the proper governmental authority before leaving Perth.[50] According to Daisy Bates, however, the dispersed natives would return to finish their corroboree, and she therefore wished to remain at the site and complete her work. The upshot of this disagreement was that Radcliffe-Brown, Watson and Olsen left for the islands, leaving Mrs Bates to return to Perth.

Watson has described with frightening vividness, how patients were collected for the hospitals:

A man unqualified except by ruthlessness and daring, helped by one or two kindred spirits, toured the countryside, raided the native camps, and there, by brute force, "examined" the natives. Any that were obviously diseased or were suspected of the disease were seized upon. These, since their hands were so small as to slip through any pair of handcuffs, were chained together by their necks, and were marched through the bush, in the further search for syphilitics. When a sufficient number were judged to have been collected, the chained prisoners were marched to the coast, and there embarked on an ancient lugger to make the last sad stage of the journey.

These journeys, from start to finish often took weeks; often the patients died on the way. Flies buzzed about their suppurating sores; their chains were never removed. Men, women and children were mingled indiscriminately, and it would be a wonder if not all the survivors were thoroughly infected with all possible varieties of venereal ailment by the time of their arrival at their respective destinations.[51]

His description of the hospital on Bernier Island is equally chilling:

The hospital was a very simple building. It consisted of three walls made of tarred canvas and a corrugated iron roof. In it there were ten beds. In the beds were sick natives, broken and hopeless pieces of humanity who lay still all day and looked out across the bleak expanse of sand-dunes, under which they were destined to be buried, and thought regretfully of their beloved far-away bush. Some other fifteen, who were not considered well enough for hard work, hung about and did odd jobs and waited on those who lay in beds.[52]

The permanent white residents on the island were two in number. The young doctor in charge of the hospital was, as Watson graphically remarks, apparently "more interested . . . in spirochetes than in suffering men".[53] The other white was a "stockman", whose ostensible task was to tend the few sheep and cattle on the island, but whose real duty was to keep order amongst the Aboriginal patients, using force if necessary.[54] Towards the end of the expedition's stay, the doctor and stockmen took to stalking each other through the sand-dunes and exchanging rifle shots.

To Daisy Bates, who after holding out for a couple of months had eventually swallowed her pride and rejoined the expedition, we owe a memorable description of Radcliffe-Brown's ethnographic style:

[The natives] obligingly sang the songs of *woggura* and *wallardoo* – crow and eaglehawk – into Professor Ratcliffe-Brown's [sic] phonograph. He in return regaled them with *Peer Gynt* and *Tannhauser* and *Egmont*, to which they listened politely.

Despite such diversions, however, Mrs Bates overall evaluation, as expressed twenty-seven years after the episode in a summation of her life's work, was that life on the islands provided horrors of inhumanity which "unnerve me yet".[55] For the youthful Grant Watson, the stay on Bernier Island proved so unforgettable that he later wrote a novel, based largely on his experience of the doctor-stockman relationship, which purported to show how "on the outermost fringes of civilization, the bonds of restraint are likely to be loosed".[56] For Radcliffe-Brown, the experience provided an opportunity, as Watson recalls, to begin "enquiries regarding the four-class social organization of the aborigines".[57]

Lest it be thought that I am portraying Radcliffe-Brown as an insensitive monster, I should point out that in summing up their work together, Watson wrote:

He was invariably gentle and just towards the natives who were his study, and was regarded by them as, in truth, a being from another world – no white man, but as a black man resurrected from the happy hunting grounds of the dead, sent back to them to be their protector and their master-spirit. Although he treated these people as children, and to a certain extent, traded on their easy credulity, he never lacked in respect towards them; they were his charge and his concern . . . [58]

Moreover, it should be noted that, whatever Watson and Bates may have written later, the former did not allow the horrors of the hospitals to spoil a generally pleasant stay on the islands,[59] and the latter's official reports of her work disclose little of the revulsion which she was to express in retrospect.[60] The point I wish to emphasize is not (albeit a valid one) that Radcliffe-Brown failed, both in his published work and his surviving correspondence, to ever voice any kind of moral outrage at the condition of his ethnographic subjects. Rather it is that one has to search his writings with a fine-tooth comb to find any hints that his data on Australian social organization was largely extracted, not from healthy and functioning societies, but from the wretched remnants of an apparently dying people.

Thus, in his famous article on "Three Tribes of Western Australia", Radcliffe-Brown, in discussing the local organization of the Kariera, mentions that a man who has left the territory of his local group will often express a wish. to die and be buried in his own inherited hunting grounds.[61] The poignant circumstances under which this truth was almost certainly driven home to Radcliffe-Brown are nowhere made explicit. In fact, the article does not even refer to Bernier or Dorre Islands. Admittedly Radcliffe-Brown states at the beginning of the article that it was based exclusively on fieldwork done "during a journey through the country of the tribes referred to", which presumably took place during a phase of the expedition post-dating the sojourn on the islands. However, it seems apparent that Aboriginals from the general area inhabited by Radcliffe Brown's "three tribes" were incarcerated on Bernier, and in any case, each of the three tribes were coastal, the territories of two of them (the Kariera and the Ngaluma) actually embracing what are (by West Australian standards) fairly sizeable towns. Hence, I think we will be justified in assuming that the "Three Tribes" article was based on data collected from communities decimated by contact with white society, and in condemning Radcliffe-Brown for lack of candour about the conditions under which his fieldwork was performed.

Similarly, in the 1912 article on "Beliefs Concerning Childbirth", Radcliffe-Brown confines to a footnote the information that one of his Kariera informants, who had supplied data on totemic clan ceremonies, was unfortunately too old to take the anthropologist to see the ceremonial grounds, and constituted the last male survivor of his clan.[62] It is a bitter irony that the man who was to give to the anthropological world a celebrated presentation of the interlocking Australian complex of beautiful and symmetrical kinship systems, obtained his own empirical contributions to this presentation by piecing together the threads of a social fabric which had largely disintegrated. And once again this shortcoming can be related to Radcliffe-Brown's role as the first professional in British Social Anthropology. Being in process of creating the fantasy that indigenous societies always function in organic harmony, Radcliffe-Brown was evidently unwilling, in the context of a British empiricist value-system, to admit that his own experience of data collection demonstrated how insubstantial that fantasy was.

Partly because he had extracted from his hospitalized informants almost as much as he could towards the task of tabulating four-class systems, and partly because of mounting hostility between himself and Daisy Bates, Radcliffe-Brown decided, after a stay of nearly six months, to leave Bernier Island. Finally parting company with the expedition, Mrs Bates returned to Perth, while Radcliffe-Brown, Watson and Olsen set off up the Gascoyne River with the aim of interrogating nomadic aboriginal bands using the watercourse. After a journey lasting only a few weeks, the ethnographic trio returned to Carnarvon, and Watson said farewell to the expedition, the lure of European civilization having proved too strong for him. Radcliffe-Brown and Olsen then continued the expedition for another nine to twelve months, and while it seems certain that the former devoted a good deal of time to the social organization of the tribes between the Fortescue and the De Grey rivers, the exact nature and location of his operations during the remainder of this period is a matter for conjecture.

By July 1912, Radcliffe-Brown was on his way back to England and Daisy Bates again had reason to question his good faith. I have already mentioned that, prior to leaving for Australia, Radcliffe-Brown had read a chapter from Andrew Lang's copy of a projected book by Mrs Bates and suggested that she should shelve the question of publication until he had had a chance to suggest some revisions. After his arrival in Perth, the West Australian Government had given Radcliffe-Brown a typed copy of the complete work, on the understanding that he would edit it, and arrange publication. This Radcliffe-Brown had promised to do, although, following a difficulty over a stipulation that the publisher should provide several hundred free copies, the authorities later released him from this commitment. At any rate, when he left Australia in mid 1912, he failed to take the manuscript with him. It was therefore handed back to Daisy Bates, who found that it had been "mutilated beyond recovery".[63] Now according to Watson, Radcliffe-Brown regarded the contents of Mrs Bates's mind as "somewhat similar to the contents of a well-stored sewing basket, after half a dozen kittens had been playing there undisturbed for a few days".[64] Hence, taking the charitable view, it seems likely that Radcliffe-Brown's modifications represented an unfinished attempt to make Mrs Bates's work scientifically acceptable. Even on this interpretation, however, Radcliffe-Brown was guilty of impropriety. Having extensively altered the manuscript without consulting its author, and with apparent disregard for her own objectives in presenting the material, Radcliffe-Brown then added insult to injury by failing to see his self-initiated task through to completion. The situation was made even less tolerable for Mrs Bates by the death of Andrew Lang contemporaneously with Radcliffe-Brown's departure for England. Following Lang's demise, his executors released only those sections of Mrs Bates's manuscript which Lang had had typed and, despite Marett agreeing to take on the task of revision, Mrs Bates was unable to find a publisher, then, or at a later date.

Radcliffe-Brown, however, had apparently taken careful note of the contents, for on two subsequent occasions, Mrs Bates accused him of plagiarizing her. The more striking of these instances came during the 1914 British Association Meeting in Australia. Radcliffe-Brown having delivered a paper on the myths of the West Australian Aborigines, the chairman asked Mrs Bates whether she had any comments. Her reply was that, since "Mr Brown had given her notes so nicely, there was no occasion to add to them". The meeting "grimaced audibly", Mrs Bates later recalled, providing an incident which "I don't think Mr Brown will ever forget".[65]

THE EMERGENCE OF A THEORETICAL STANDPOINT 1912–1914

Following his return to England, Radcliffe-Brown began reworking his Andaman material, to convert his fellowship thesis into a full-length book. This process was affected by influences emanating from three sources: first and most important Rivers, with whom he had extensive and crucial correspondence; second the Durkheimian school of sociology; and third his experience of Australian ethnography.

Let us enter into this maze of interacting influences by the Durkheimian door. As I mentioned earlier in the present chapter, a letter written to Daisy Bates strongly suggests that by 1910, Radcliffe-Brown had been influenced by certain of Durkheim's contributions to the *Année Sociologique*, and that the British anthropologist's specific hypothesis about the possible evolutionary significance of the transposition of Australian Aboriginal section-names had been inspired by this source. In August 1912, however, we find him writing to Durkheim's follower Marcel Mauss that he is "somewhat disappointed" with Durkheim's recently published book *Les Formes Elémentaires de la Vie Religieuse*. Radcliffe-Brown avers that this work, which seeks the origins of religion in Australian totemism, demonstrates that Durkheim "has misunderstood the real nature of the Australian social organization". Nonetheless, Radcliffe-Brown emphasizes that he is "in complete agreement with the view of sociology" espoused in the *Année Sociologique*, describes himself as "the first person to expound those views in England", and laments the fact that the British generally ignore or misunderstand the work of Durkheim.[66]

In the second half of 1913, Radcliffe-Brown sent Durkheim a reprint of his article on "Three Tribes of Western Australia", which is critical of Durkheim's theory that the change from maternal to paternal descent of the totem provided the mechanism for evolutionary changes in Aboriginal systems of relationship.[67] Enclosed with the reprint was a letter (which has not come to light) in which Radcliffe-Brown apparently confided that, despite his differences with Durkheim on particular matters relating to the Australian Aborigines, his views concerning the general principles of the science of sociology were in agreement with those of the Frenchman. Replying to this letter in November 1913, Durkheim declared himself grateful for the opportunity of entering into direct relations with the young English anthropologist, and expressed his pleasure at learning of their agreement on matters of theoretical import. "Nothing", wrote Durkheim "could give me greater confidence in the method that I am trying to apply". With regard to Radcliffe-Brown's specific criticism of his theory about the evolution of Australian kinship, Durkheim was conciliatory, admitting that "The objection is a very strong one", but saying that, in order to ascertain whether he should totally abandon his previous explanation, he would have to "carry out a new study of the facts", which his heavy teaching load prevented him from doing.[68] Following this initial exchange, Radcliffe-Brown apparently sent Durkheim a copy of the programme for a series of lectures he was delivering at Birmingham. In response to this, Durkheim expressed his interest in the programme, and averred, "It constitutes one more proof of the understanding [*entente*] which exists between us about the general conception of our science."[69]

This brief interchange of letters seems to represent the totality of the direct contacts between the two men. Summing up the nature of their intellectual exchange, it would seem that Radcliffe-Brown first began reading Durkheim on technical matters relating to Australian totemism and kinship, that he initially gave considerable credence to Durkheim's hypothesis about the evolutionary efficacy of the change from maternal to paternal descent of the totem, but that, after testing this hypothesis in Western Australia, decided that the evidence was against it. To a young man who was in the process of establishing himself as the preeminent authority on the technicalities of Australian social organization, Durkheim's book *Les Formes Elémentaires* ... proved to be something of a let-down.[70] However, at the same time as he expressed this disappointment, Radcliffe-Brown was at pains to emphasize his concurrence with the view of sociology espoused in the *Année Sociologique*, and to depict himself as the first person in England to expound this view. Now the correspondence to which I have referred does not make clear the mode of explanation involved in this view of sociology. Let me therefore quote a clear exposition of it as applied to religious phenomena, which is due to Durkheim's follower and fellow contributor to the *Année Sociologique*, Henri Hubert:

Nous disons donc que toute explication des phénomènes religieux doit être cherchée dans la série même des phénomènes. Il faudra considérer, s'il agit d'un mythe, non pas l'idée problématique qui suggéra les images qui le composent à leur premier assembleur, mais, entre autres choses, les conditions de temps et de lieu, les circonstances qui le rappellent régulièrement, rituellement à la mémoire d'un group d'hommes associés et les gestes que leur commande cette pensée présente. S'il s'agit d'un rite, on considérera non pas l'intention de celui qui l'exécute, mais les effets, quels qu'ils soient, images suggérées, modifications de rapports et de qualités, qui le suivent nécessairement. Le premier résultat de pareilles observations sera de faire rattacher les faits particuliers à des faits plus généraux ... Mécanisme d'une part, effets produits ou fonction de l'autre, telles seront les bases de l'explication des faits religieux ... Il ne s'agit en somme que de retrouver dans les faits particuliers des formes très générales d'activité. On ne sort pas du connaissable.

The essence of the new approach to sociology, in other words, was that social phenomena such as myths and rites should not be explained in an evolutionary fashion, by speculating about the intellectual ideas which first gave rise to them; nor should they be explained psychologically, by invoking the overt motivations of individuals taking part in the social drama; rather the explanation should involve currently-operative social entities which have the same epistemological status as the phenomenon in question, and which will elucidate its function within the broader framework of the society. Now Radcliffe-Brown was to quote this passage with approval in the Preface which he added in 1932 to his book on *The Andaman Islanders*, and to state that "It was the method thus defined by Hubert that I attempted to apply to the beliefs and customs of the Andaman Islanders in the fifth and sixth chapters of this book."

Here then, would seem to be a clear statement of Radcliffe-Brown's indebtedness to the Durkheimian school, on just the point which constitutes the essence of what later came to be known as the structural-functional position. When he attempted to apply this mode of explanation, however, vestiges of the old evolutionary approach still remained. Specifically, in rewriting his Andaman data Radcliffe-Brown seems to have keep one eye on his recently acquired knowledge of Australian social organization, so that the former could be seen as an evolutionary precursor of the latter. In fact, the theory of ritual relations which he developed was apparently designed to be applicable, not only to the pre-totemic society of the Andamans, but also to the various forms of totemism in Australia. Briefly, this proto-Durkheimian theory runs as follows: [71]

For a social group such as a clan to be cohesive, it must be bound together by sentiments of solidarity among its members. Such sentiments can be sustained in existence, however, only if they are given collective expression by symbolic acts. These acts, if regularly performed, tend to become ritualized. Now the essence of an act of ritual is the conceptual juxtaposition of some familiar object with the notion being symbolized. In this way, the sentiment of group solidarity is generally expressed by ritualized collective behaviour involving an object which is taken to represent the group itself.

So far, says Radcliffe-Brown, he has merely restated Durkheim's theory of totemism in his own words. This theory is, he opines, valid but incomplete. It falls short of explaining why all over the world, in pre-totemic as well as in totemic societies, species of animals or plants should be chosen as the objects which symbolize social groups. This fact can be explained, according to Radcliffe-Brown, by the additional observation that, in all societies in which a special ritual relation is set up between social groups and species of animals and plants, the animals and plants in question are vital to the subsistence of the group.

In pre-totemic societies the symbolic relation between man and nature is a general one between the society as a whole, and the objects deemed sacred. In totemic societies, on the other hand, the social organism will be found to have segmented into discrete sub-entities, each of which will possess a special ritualized relation to one or more of the societies' objects of subsistence. Hence, using this theory, Radcliffe-Brown was able to encompass both differentiated and undifferentiated forms of social organization, and to thereby simultaneously account for the Australian and Andaman data.

It appears to be the received wisdom amongst anthropologists and historians of the behavioural sciences that the influence of Durkheim was crucial for the development of Radcliffe-Brown's structural-functional approach.[72] Nonetheless, it seems to me that a case can be made out for the assertion that the true source of this approach was less Durkheim than Rivers.

Two passages which are relevant to this case may be found in the surviving remnants of the correspondence which Radcliffe-Brown and Rivers carried on between about 1912 and 1914.[73] In total, these comprise eleven letters and one unattached postscript by Radcliffe-Brown, and two letters and one unattached fragment by Rivers. Despite the fact that Radcliffe-Brown's letters are for the most part quite lengthy and detailed, there are problems in evaluating the correspondence as a whole. For one thing, while Rivers's letters have dates (one of which seems to be incorrect), Radcliffe-Brown's letters, with only one exception, are undated. For another the preponderance of Radcliffe-Brownian letters means that one tends to obtain a very one-sided view of the dialogue. Moreover, it is obvious that even Radcliffe-Brown's letters by no means represent a complete set. Finally, both men tend to change their views somewhat in the course of the discussion. These factors combine to make it very difficult to be absolutely certain about the nature of all the issues raised in the correspondence, or even to decide the order in which the letters were written. Nonetheless, the surviving pieces of correspondence leave absolutely no doubt that the interchange was of seminal importance for the two men. Indeed, Radcliffe-Brown in particular seems to have used his mentor's criticisms as an anvil on which to beat his own theoretical views into shape, sometimes forming them in the same mould, more often adapting, modifying, reacting in opposition.

The first passage which appears to be relevant to Radcliffe-Brown's adoption of a synchronic mode of sociological explanation comes from a letter in which Radcliffe-Brown is replying to Rivers's criticisms of an interpretation which Radcliffe-Brown had produced of Andaman Island society. Rivers had evidently wished to tag certain Andamanese customs described by Radcliffe-Brown with the label "survivals". To this Radcliffe-Brown replied that the whole purpose of his interpretation was to demonstrate that the customs of the Andamanese "fulfil vitally important social functions at the present day, and that they are completely adapted to the present needs of the Andaman society". "If this be so", continued Radcliffe-Brown, "then it does not matter in the least ... whether the customs in question were invented by the Andamanese or were adopted by them after contact with some other race." Radcliffe-Brown was willing to admit that "historical" questions are worth pursuing; however, in his opinion "they do not ... affect the questions of causal relations in the present". While it is true that the customs of the Andamanese resemble those of other races, Radcliffe-Brown could not see that Rivers had any grounds for calling them "survivals", unless he could produce "some principles ... for distinguishing survivals from living institutions". Whilst in the Andaman Islands, Radcliffe-Brown had noted an occurence which might have appeared to the casual observer as a survival. However, Radcliffe-Brown, who had observed its origin, knew that it represented a case of independent invention:

The Andamanese have no corroboree, i.e. spectacular dance in which the dancers represent mythical or sacred beings. However, the corroboree has been invented in recent times by a medicine-man of the North Andaman, and his performance is described in the next batch of proofs that I shall send you. Here we have an individual invention which, if it were adopted as a regular institution, would give something like the Australian corroboree, only much less elaborate. Yet I fancy, if the sort of performance in question had been a regular institution, you would have been tempted to regard it as a survival.

If one wishes to know which customs are survivals and which are not, implies Radcliffe-Brown, one can do no better than to ask whether they contribute to social equilibrium:

I regard (with Durkheim) the customs of a society as serving to maintain a certain system of ideas and emotions which in its turn is what maintains the society in existence with its given structure and its given degree of cohesion. Any custom which does not serve to maintain this system is a survival, or in other words is entirely unnecessary and probably harmful.

Here then is a linking of Durkheim's name with the social equilibrium hypothesis, which, if read out of context, might suggest that it was the French sociologist who inspired Radcliffe-Brown's use of the hypothesis. However, as I hope my contextual account has made clear, Radcliffe-Brown actually seems to have invoked the hypothesis on this occasion because he wished to undermine Rivers's use of the concept of survivals, and to thereby attack his former mentor's recently acquired predilection for indulging in "historical" speculation.

A further passage which is relevant to Radcliffe-Brown's adoption of a synchronic mode of sociological explanation comes from a letter in which Radcliffe-Brown gives his reactions to Rivers's 1914 book on *Kinship and Social Organization*. In the main body of the letter, Radcliffe-Brown refers to the desirability of eventually writing down and publishing his own "general hypothesis as to nature of society and of social institutions". He then goes on to state that he does't "want to do this just yet, for many reasons, and after all there is a good deal of it in Durkheim". So it is evident that, in regard to his own general theory of society, Radcliffe-Brown was prepared to acknowledge that Durkheim had anticipated him to a considerable extent. However, when he comes to discuss the synchronic mode of explanation which later came to be identified with structural-functionalism, it is Rivers rather than Durkheim who is mentioned as having espoused this explanatory mode. In a postscript to the letter, Radcliffe-Brown suggests that, if *he* had written a book on kinship, he would have laid more stress on

... the rule of method that we should first of all seek the explanation of the system of relationship terms in the institutions actually existing in the society, and only when this fails should we resort to hypotheses as to the past. Perhaps you would not attribute quite the same importance to this rule that I do, but at any rate you do observe it to a great extent and this is what provides the great contrast between your method and Morgan's.

Here then, at just the time when Radcliffe-Brown's theoretical position was taking shape, we have him declaring that his former mentor has "to a great extent" observed the rule that explanations of social phenomena should be sought in "the institutions actually existing in the society", and that Rivers's observance of this rule provides the most significant difference between his work and the previous evolutionary speculations of Morgan. Considering that this declaration was made after Rivers had converted to diffusionism, and after he had begun to exhibit a predilection for producing speculative historical reconstructions, it is hardly surprising that Radcliffe-Brown set his declaration in the context of stressing that Rivers's latest book should have placed more emphasis upon this rule. Indeed, the above postscript could plausibly be interpreted as yet another example of a disciple taking sides on the issue of earlier versus later Rivers. For Radcliffe-Brown, it would seem, earlier Rivers had leaned strongly towards explaining social phenomena in terms of the institutions currently operating in society. The danger with later Rivers, implies Radcliffe-Brown, is that he is now less forthright about adopting this mode of explanation, and resorts too quickly to speculative hypotheses about the past.

It has been mentioned in the present chapter that, in the memo which he drew up preparatory to Radcliffe-Brown's field trip to Western Australia, Rivers had advanced the proto-functionalist hypothesis that an anthropologist can give a satisfactory account of marriage-regulation only if he undertakes an exhaustive investigation of the total culture.

In Chapter II, I described how, in a 1907 article on "The Marriage of Cousins in India", Rivers had entertained the hypothesis that cross-cousin marriage might provide the explanation for the special role of the mother's brother amongst the Todas. The same chapter also makes the point, by reference to Rivers's monograph on *The Todas*, that beneath the narrowly scientific exterior which early Rivers presented to his colleagues, there beat the heart of a humanist who was capable of painting an emotive and organic portrait of aboriginal society. And in Chapter V, I mentioned that, for the 1912 edition of the *Notes and Queries on Anthropology*, Rivers and Myres had contributed a number of sections advocating a remarkably prescient approach to social organization. Indeed, one passage in particular from Rivers's section on "Social Organization" reads like an incisive summary of the essence of structural-functionalism:

A full comprehension of the social organization of any people only becomes possible after the complete study of their institutions, and of the functions of their social groupings in the maintenance of social order, in the conduct of warfare, in the division of labour among the members of the community, and above all in the regulation of marriage.[74]

Does it not seem likely that Radcliffe-Brown's concern to arrive at "a full comprehension of the social organization" of aboriginal peoples by studying "the functions of their social groupings in the maintenance of social order" had its ultimate source in the teachings, writings and example of the man who introduced him to anthropology, and with whom he had friendly discussions extending over a period of ten years?[75]

As I have stated, the Rivers–Radcliffe-Brown correspondence seems to have been crucial for the emergence of the younger man's theoretical standpoint. Hence, even though the imperfect dating and incompleteness of the correspondence makes it well-nigh impossible to pin down all the issues raised therein, I could hardly proceed without looking a little more closely in this direction. Without claiming to be comprehensive, let me mention four important issues which are discussed in the correspondence and whose nature is tolerably clear.

Firstly, it is evident from several comments made by Radcliffe-Brown that he was ready to acknowledge the deficiencies arising from his earlier neglect of Rivers-style kinship investigations. For example, responding to some apparently unfavourable comments made by Rivers in respect of a draft of *The Andaman Islanders*, Radcliffe-Brown admits that he "did not get to the bottom of the Andaman system" of relationship, and confesses that he now feels "very dissatisfied" with his analysis. He states that he believes the system to be "pre-classificatory", but does not feel he possesses sufficient evidence to argue the point.[76] In a further letter, Radcliffe-Brown states, apparently in response to another criticism by Rivers, that his omission of the father and the daughter from his list of Andamanese relatives who greet one another by weeping, is "due to pure ignorance on my part". Confessing that he neglected to ask the requisite questions in the field, Radcliffe-Brown continues, "I now realize how important the matter really is, which I suppose I did not at the time."[77]

A second issue broached in the correspondence, concerns the efficacy of the diffusionistic approach to anthropology. Knowing that Rivers had converted to diffusionism in 1911, it will come as no surprise to learn that this issue does, in fact, loom very large in the dialogue. What may startle some people familiar with Radcliffe-Brown's later work is that, in attacking diffusionism, he supports what he calls the "psychological" approach to anthropology. Just what he meant by this may be illustrated by an example which he himself adduces in one of the letters. The S-shaped bow of the Andamanese is sometimes compared, for purposes of speculating about cultural diffusion, with a similarly shaped bow used in the New Hebrides. However, Radcliffe-Brown's study of the "static problems" connected with the Andaman bow shows that "it depends on making use of the principle that when a tree bends . . . in the course of its growth the wood of the concave part of the bend acquires great toughness and elasticity." So far as Radcliffe-Brown can ascertain, this is not the principle governing the Melanesian bow, and he therefore concludes that the two weapons are not strictly comparable.[78]

Hence, for Radcliffe-Brown, to adopt a "psychological" approach was to be neither Freudian nor reductionistic. Rather it was to invoke collectively-held principles, the operation of which affected the workings of the society in question. As the years wore on, Radcliffe-Brown was to drop his use of the word "psychological" in this sense, and to subsume the notion it stood for under the term "social structure".

A third and rather difficult issue raised in the correspondence is similarly relevant to the evolution of Radcliffe-Brown's "social structure" concept. Rivers claimed to believe that what he called "social organization" was so fundamental that a society could not exist in an intermediate state between two alternative forms of it. If two forms of social organization blended in a single society, then inevitably one would flourish and the other would wither, although the former could undergo profound modification in the process of triumphing over its competitor. For Australia, Rivers evidently believed that the totemic complex and the relationship complex represented two originally separate forms of social organization, which had come together as a result of cultural migrations. This mingling process, thought Rivers, had taken place in such a way that the relationship complex had become predominant, totemism persisting "perhaps only ... through its magico-religious functions".[79] Radcliffe-Brown, even more of a purist than Rivers about the ontological priority of social organization, objected to what he took to be Rivers's assumption that two different forms of social organization have co-existed side-by-side in Australia. The totemic clans and the relationship system are, he says, both part of the "social structure", and as such are inseparably bound up with each other.[80] However, later in the correspondence we find Radcliffe-Brown arguing for the adoption of a definition of totemism which would leave it open that there might be no essential connection between totemism (considered as a religious phenomenon) and any form of social structure.[81] The apparent turnabout can be explained by Radcliffe-Brown having read in the interim Durkheim's *Les Formes Élémentaires* .... This book evidently convinced him that, in order not to exclude Arunta totemism, which has no connection with the relationship system, one needs a broader definition of totemism than the one adopted by Durkheim. So that, while Radcliffe-Brown evidently still believed that social organization is primary and religious customs are secondary, he wanted a definition of totemism which did not *presuppose* this belief. Hence, it seems that Radcliffe-Brown's concept of social structure had its beginnings as a refined version of Rivers's notion of social organization, but that in defining his theoretical terms, Radcliffe-Brown was anxious not to allow the concept to slip in as part of the definition.

A fourth issue broached in the correspondence concerns the significance of the Aranda and Dieri tribes within the total pattern of Australian social organization. Radcliffe-Brown argues that the Dieri tribe will provide the key to many of the most perplexing puzzles of Australian sociology. The importance of this tribe lies, according to Radcliffe-Brown, in the fact that it possesses two sets of totems. One of these sets has patrilineal descent, and is very similar to the type of totems found in Western Australia, whilst the other set has matrilineal descent and resembles those of Eastern Australia. His "present working hypothesis", he says, "is that in Western Australia there has been a change from female to male descent of the totems, one of the most important factors tending to produce this change being the localization of the totemic cult".[82] Here we have an elaboration of the idea which had been expressed to Daisy Bates in 1910, and which was eventually to be rejected in his 1913 article on "Three Tribes of Western Australia". In the 1910 letter, Radcliffe-Brown had suggested that the transposition of section names might be explicable in terms of a change from matrilineal to patrilineal totemic descent. Now he goes one step further and suggests a mechanism for this change — the localization of the totemic cult. Such a localization might be expected to lead to totemic patrilineality, since the particular animal regarded as sacred would tend to become associated with the appropriate territorial hunting band, which typically have patrilineal descent of the marriage-classes.

According to Radcliffe-Brown then, the Dieri probably represents a tribe which, while retaining its original totemic organization with female descent, has also adopted localized patrilineal totemism from the west.[83] On this interpretation, he implies, Arunta totemism represents a late and somewhat aberrant development of the West Australian variety.[84] Lest Rivers should think that he is making diffusionistic assumptions, Radcliffe-Brown is careful to point out that his concept of the transmittal of totemic systems from one tribe to another does not involve a mechanical mixture of cultural traits in the manner assumed by diffusionists such as Graebner and Schmidt. Rather Radcliffe-Brown conceives of the West Australian form of totemism as being transmitted by "imitation", a process which Radcliffe-Brown evidently regards as more akin to organic intercommunion than to mechanical blending.[85] Before leaving Radcliffe-Brown's "working hypothesis" on the origin of West Australian totemism, I should mention that he states in one letter that he is not aware of any serious evidence in favour of the hypothesis. Rather he wishes to use it merely as a heuristic device, and to consciously leave open the possibility that the Eastern and Western types of totemism may have arisen independently of each other. Nonetheless, he says, "while I hold that these different forms of totemism *may* be *historically* independent, I hold very strongly that there is a close relation of *psychological* dependence between them".[86] Hence, by the time he wrote this letter to Rivers, Radcliffe-Brown had demoted hypotheses about the historical origins of social phenomena to the status of heuristic aids in an enterprise, the basic aim of which was already socio-structural.

By way of drawing together our account of the emergence of Radcliffe-Brown's theoretical position between 1912 and 1914, let us consider whether it was Rivers or Durkheim who provided the most important influence on Radcliffe-Brown during this formative period. The widespread belief that Radcliffe-Brown owed his version of social anthropology primarily to Durkheim would seem to derive largely from his monograph on *The Andaman Islanders*, and from his articles "On the Concept of Function in Social Science", and on "Religion and Society". Now it is true that, in each of these items, Radcliffe-Brown not only adopts an apparently Durkheimian mode of procedure, but also pays explicit tribute to the work of the French school of sociology. Nonetheless, a careful consideration of these items casts doubt upon the hypothesis that Durkheim had provided Radcliffe-Brown's primary inspiration in respect of either generalized theory or specific technicalities.

Consider first *The Andaman Islanders*. Certainly the 1932 Preface contains, as I have already mentioned, what appears to be a clear acknowledgement that the fifth and sixth chapters of the book are indebted to the Durkheimian method as defined by Hubert. However, this version of the Preface is in striking contrast with that included in the original 1922 edition of the book. Here Radcliffe-Brown does not even mention the Durkheimian school, and presents the same two chapters "as an example of the method which I believe to be fundamental in the science that has lately come to be known as social anthropology". Moreover, in the 1922 edition the book is given the subtitle "A Study in Social Anthropology", which is conspicuously absent in later editions. Finally in the 1922 (but not in the 1932 version), Radcliffe-Brown expresses the opinion that his preliminary training in anthropology under the Cantabridgean team of Haddon, Rivers and Duckworth had been "as thorough as possible", and thanks Haddon and Rivers for reading the proofs of the book and for making "many helpful suggestions". It seems clear then, that between 1922 and 1932, Radcliffe-Brown found it convenient to stop presenting his book as a case-study in the newly-christened discipline of "social anthropology", which Rivers and Haddon had been instrumental in creating, and to hitch his Andaman wagon to the Durkheimian school. The dropping of the earlier emphasis is understandable, even if it is not to be entirely condoned. In the interim between the writing of the two versions of the Preface, Rivers had died (which no doubt made the acknowledgement of his assistance less expedient), and the battle to establish social anthropology as a recognized discipline had been largely won. Radcliffe-Brown's motive for re-proclaiming the book as a Durkheimian production will be suggested later in the chapter, but the point which I wish to emphasize at this juncture is that Radcliffe-Brown's original presentation of his monograph seems to be historically more accurate. Certainly, when I first read the book immediately after having carried out an intensive study of the work of Rivers, what struck me most forcibly was the quantity and cogency of the indications that Rivers had been Radcliffe-Brown's mentor in both psychology and anthropology. I refer in particular to Radcliffe-Brown's repeated use of dichotomies which recall Rivers's protopathic-epicritic distinction. For example, consider the following passage, in which Radcliffe-Brown argues that mythology provides an appropriate vehicle for expressing the Andaman view of the world:

The Andamanese, like other savages, have not acquired the power of thinking abstractly. All their thought necessarily deals with concrete things. Now the story form provides a means of expressing concretely what could otherwise only be put in an abstract statement. (A large part of the interpretation of the legends, as here undertaken, consists in restating the content of the legends in abstract terms.) Moreover, even if the Andaman Islanders were capable of thinking abstractly, yet, since what they need to express are not thoughts so much as feelings (not intellectual so much as affective processes), they would still need a concrete form of expression. For it is a familiar fact that the concrete has a much greater power of . . . appealing to our feelings than has the abstract.[87]

The opposing of "savage" to civilized modes of thought was, of course, standard fare for all social anthropologists of the period. What gives this passage its distinctly River-like flavour is the way in which Radcliffe-Brown links this opposition both to the concrete-abstract dichotomy and to the distinction between "affective" and "intellectual" mental processes. Moreover, Radcliffe-Brown, like the later Rivers, reveals a tendency to reject rationality in favour of affectivity as the major determinant of indigenous social behaviour and belief.[88] In addition, he shares Rivers's view that the type of mental process which underlies aboriginal legends is akin to that which takes place during dreams, both types being fundamentally concrete and visual, rather than abstract and rational.[89] Finally, we should mention the theory of the arousal of the aesthetic emotions which Radcliffe-Brown briefly sketches in the fifth chapter. Like Rivers before him, Radcliffe-Brown here attributes great importance to the visual aspects of cognition, which he regards as closely bound up with the ability of the motor sense to directly modify affectual response. A particular form is perceived as beautiful because it induces the eye to move in a way which is "felt" as harmonious. Similarly, the aesthetic appreciation of music seems to be largely dependent upon one's ability to feel the music as movement, "the sounds appealing not to the ear only but to stored up unconscious motor memories". Finally, the aesthetic enjoyment gained from watching the rhythmic and harmonious movements of a dancer is "of similar nature to that obtained from the contemplation of beautiful shapes or listening to music".[90]

Thus, it seems that Radcliffe-Brown was implicitly assuming a dichotomy in which concrete, affective, pictorial and dreamlike forms of mental process were regarded as being interrelated and collectively opposed to abstract, rational, verbal and conscious forms of thought. The resemblance between this dichotomy and the protopathic-epicritic distinction is, I feel, sufficiently striking for us to infer direct influence on Rivers's part. But the most significant point to notice about *The Andaman Islanders* concerns the dedication, which was retained in all editions. It must be emphasized that Radcliffe-Brown dedicated his "work of apprenticeship" not to Durkheim, but to Haddon and Rivers, "to whose instruction and kind encouragement is due whatever value it may possess".

When we come to Radcliffe-Brown's 1935 article "On the Concept of Function in Social Science", it may likewise seem at first sight as though Durkheim's influence is indisputable.[91] In fact, having opened this article by describing the concept of function as "based upon an analogy between social life and organic life", Radcliffe-Brown then states that, as far as he is aware, "The first systematic formulation of the concept as applying to the strictly scientific study of society" occurs in Durkheim's 1895 book *Règles de la Methode Sociologique*. Durkheim's definition of function is referred to, and Radcliffe-Brown proceeds to give a generally sympathetic elaboration of it. But even though it would have to be conceded that the notion of function was crucially important in Radcliffe-Brown's own social theories, this article does *not* provide convincing proof of Radcliffe-Brown's intellectual debt to Durkheim. On the contrary, it seems likely that here Radcliffe-Brown was hitching his wagon to Durkheim in order to establish his own position in relation to American Cultural Anthropology. For this article, like the 1932 version of the Preface to *The Andaman Islanders*, was written during Radcliffe-Brown's controversial stay as Professor of Anthropology at the University of Chicago. And the article contains a number of pointed digs at American anthropologists like Robert Lowie, Ruth Benedict and Paul Radin. These anthropologists had evidently annoyed Radcliffe-Brown because their approach to the discipline seemed excessively piecemeal. Thus, Radcliffe-Brown refers disparagingly to Lowie's "shreds and patches" theory of culture. He also quotes with disapproval firstly Benedict's opinion that to analogize society to an organism represents a "superstition", and secondly Radin's statement that it is "crying for the moon" to attempt to arrive at systematically testable generalizations about society. As a great figure from the past who could be invoked in support of Radcliffe-Brown's stance against majority opinion in United States anthropology, Durkheim had his uses. For the French sociologist's pithy pronouncements about the functional and organic nature of society were admirably suited for adaptation as propaganda against the shreds and patches approach of the Americans.[92]

Radcliffe-Brown's 1945 article on "Religion and Society" similarly appears to provide firm evidence of the British anthropologist's intellectual debt to Durkheim. In this article, Radcliffe-Brown refers to Durkheim's *Les Formes Elémentaires* . . . as "a most important contribution" to "the general theory of the social function of religions", and opines that "Durkheim's major thesis as to the social function of the totemic rites is valid and only requires revision and correction in the light of the more extensive and more exact knowledge we now have".[93] This evaluation, which might also be taken as providing the explanation for the somewhat Durkheimian idiom of the final two chapters of *The Andaman Islanders*, makes it appear that Durkheim bequeathed to Radcliffe-Brown a generalized theoretical position which the latter found to be particularly helpful for handling the social aspects of religion. However, such an evaluation does not rule out the possibility that the path leading to Radcliffe-Brown's acceptance of this position had been prepared by the proto-structural-functional concerns of Rivers. And there can be no doubt that, in the case of Rivers, these concerns had been developed as a result of his investigations into kinship, which were also to form the major focus and contribution of Radcliffe-Brown's career. Furthermore, it appears that a good deal of what Radcliffe-Brown took from Durkheim came via Rivers. For example, it is known that Radcliffe-Brown learned of the appearance of *Les Formes Elémentaires* . . . through Rivers,[94] that Radcliffe-Brown discussed aspects of Durkheim and Mauss's essay on primitive classification in a letter to Rivers,[95] and that circa 1913, Radcliffe-Brown expressed his envy to Rivers on the occasion of the latter's having talked with Mauss.[96] Moreover, as Radcliffe-Brown's surviving correspondence makes clear, the ideas which he took from Durkheim were incorporated into his social theories only after lengthy discussions of their significance with Rivers.

In concluding this evaluation of the relative importance of Rivers and Durkheim in the emergence of Radcliffe-Brown's theoretical position, a number of points need to be made. Firstly, judging from the correspondence which has survived, direct communications between Durkheim and Radcliffe-Brown were few in number, brief, polite and rather formal. They contain the record of a fleeting and mutually congratulatory exchange between an eminent representative of the outgoing generation of French sociologists, and an up-and-coming member of the incoming generation of British anthropologists.[97] By way of contrast, the surviving correspondence between

Radcliffe-Brown and Rivers indicates that direct written communications between the two men were numerous, lengthy and attempted to deal with matters of theoretical import and difficulty. What is more, Radcliffe-Brown's side of the correspondence demonstrates that he was in process of shifting his theoretical position certainly during the course of, and probably as a result of, the running debates between the two men.

A further point to note is that communications between Radcliffe-Brown and Durkheim seem to have consisted only of written material and to have lasted less than six months. Radcliffe-Brown's interchanges with Rivers, on the other hand, involved verbal communication in addition to letters and extended over a full decade. Finally, knowing that Radcliffe-Brown was prone to "cultivate style" and affect the dress of a Paris *savant*, one cannot help wondering about the extent to which his endorsement of the Durkheimian school was symptomatic of snobbish Francophilia, rather than of genuine intellectual indebtedness.

The writings of the Durkheimian School, to be sure, contained a number of quotable passages about the sociological mode of explanation, the concept of function and the organic nature of society, and Radcliffe-Brown's later publications make significant use of such passages. However, it seems to me that this usage was less an indication of actual intellectual ancestry, than of Radcliffe-Brown treating the Durkheimian cause as a convenient instrument for getting at his enemies. Certainly, when I first came to scrutinize the work of Radcliffe-Brown, it seemed to me that my just-completed investigations of Rivers had prepared me well for what I was to find in the writings of his most prominent pupil. There did not, in other words, appear to be any sizeable lacunae in my understanding of Radcliffe-Brown's intellectual development, and especially not a lacuna which would have to be plugged by reference to the work of the French sociologist. That is to say, the essence of Radcliffe-Brown's structural-functionalism would seem to have derived from Rivers, and the writings of the Durkheimian school apparently played the comparatively minor roles of providing reinforcement for views which had originated elsewhere, and of acting as a source of pithy quotations.

AUSTRALIAN SOCIAL ORGANIZATION I, 1913–1923

Judging from his famous 1913 article on "Three Tribes of Western Australia", Radcliffe-Brown had evidently learned a lesson from the shortcomings of his Andaman experience and had used the genealogical method extensively in his

West Australian fieldwork. The article contains six "genealogical tables", and Radcliffe-Brown reveals that his debt to Rivers is not only methodological but also interpretational, by enumerating some abstract "laws" which, he says, are "expressed in a concrete form" in these tables.[98] Like Rivers, Radcliffe-Brown evidently regarded the genealogical method as uncovering the actual mental processes which natives use to operate their kinship systems. This may be seen from his description of what happens when a stranger comes to an Aboriginal encampment. The stranger is approached by a few of the males, who ask a question such as "Who is your father's father?" The discussion then proceeds, according to Radcliffe-Brown, "on genealogical lines", until all parties are satisfied of the exact relation of the stranger to each native present in the camp.[99]

In the "Three Tribes" article, Radcliffe-Brown uses the social organization of the Kariera people as his major "type" for purposes of classification. From the point of view of functioning as the taxonomic type of a four-class system, Kariera social organization has one obvious advantage over that of the Kamilaroi. As Withnell had pointed out in 1903, the totems of the West Australian tribes have nothing to do with the regulation of marriage. In other words, unlike the Kamilaroi marriage classes, those of the Kariera are not inextricably interwoven with the totemic system. However, the most important point for Radcliffe-Brown seems to have been the fact that the Kariera employ localized centres for the performance of totemic rituals. For reasons which I have briefly sketched in the immediately preceding section of this chapter, Radcliffe-Brown's interest in this aspect of Kariera social organization seems to have been that it promised to provide a suitably broad comparative context in which to locate the puzzling phenomena of Arunta totemism.

In the passages in the article which deal with marriage regulation, it is obvious that Radcliffe-Brown has chosen, not only to pick a hitherto obscure tribe as his major type, but also to abandon the number of classes as his fundamental taxonomic criterion. For example, he defines the Kariera type of marriage law ("Type I") in terms of marriage with the real or classificatory mother's brother's daughter.[100] However, he apparently does not intend this as an inclusive specification of the definition, for he also says that the "characteristic feature" of Type I is the fact that the term for mother's mother's brother is the same as that for father's father.[101] That is, he was pointing to what Rivers would have called a "kinship correspondence". In attempting to fathom the reason for Radcliffe-Brown's abandonment of the number of marriage-classes as his fundamental criterion for typology, a cynic might suggest that he simply wanted to ensure that his classification looked different from those of his predecessors. However, his main reason was probably that his notion of kinship as an extension of family relationships (which notion he apparently borrowed from Rivers, as did Malinowski), and his commitment to a quasi-Heraclitan philosophy, led to the downgrading of the importance of marriage-classes as such, and to the interpretation of kinship systems as a mode of systematically classifying kinsmen. In other words, he was focusing on the *process* of putting things into boxes, rather than on the boxes themselves.

This apparently novel interpretation of the Australian class systems was favourably cited by Rivers in his article on "Marriage" in James Hastings's *Encyclopaedia of Religion and Ethics*, published in 1916. Rivers stated that Australian social organization had until recently been supposed to be unique, but that Radcliffe-Brown had shown "that it is nothing more than a system-atization of the regulation of marriage by kinship which is generally associated with exogamous systems". N. W. Thomas, however, was angered by Rivers giving Radcliffe-Brown credit for priority in this interpretation. In March 1916, Thomas wrote to Rivers pointing out that, in his book on *Kinship Organizations and Group Marriage in Australia*, which had been published a decade earlier (and had been reviewed by Rivers at that time), he had stated that "The class systems are . . . simply a systematization of the terms of kinship in use under the two phratry system".[102] While I doubt that any plagiarism was involved in this instance, it is interesting to note that, having apparently been led by the writings of his most prominent pupil to make an inaccurate claim to priority on the latter's behalf, Rivers was then held accountable for his error by a member of the old guard of writers on the Australian Aborigines.

The question of Radcliffe-Brown's right to ethnographic priority regarding his material on Kariera social organization is one which it will fortunately be unnecessary for me to consider in any detail, since Rodney Needham has written a long and impressive piece addressing just this question.[103] In 1930, Radcliffe-Brown made the following claim in a footnote to one of his articles on Australian social organization:

The discovery of the Kariera system by myself in 1911 was the result of a definite search, on a surmise made before visiting Australia, but after a careful study of Australian data in 1909, that some such system might very well exist and that Western Australia would be a reasonable place in which to look for it.[104]

Needham has considered in detail the validity of a number of possible interpretations of this allegation, ranging from the strong interpretation that Radcliffe-Brown was claiming to have discovered the four-section system, to the weak interpretation that he was claiming merely to have discovered that one form of this system was in operation among a people bearing the name "Kariera". Making extensive use of Australian ethnographic material which predates Radcliffe-Brown's investigations, Needham demonstrates that Radcliffe-Brown's claim is without foundation over a wide range of possible interpretations. Moreover, Needham points out, and my own researches corroborate, that historically there is no evidence at all that Radcliffe-Brown ever expressed his alleged "surmise" about the Kariera type of system before visiting Australia. Rather, his retrospective claim about discovering the Kariera system seems to have been the product either of wishful reminiscing or of wilful fabrication.[105]

In the decade following the appearance of the "Three Tribes" article, Radcliffe-Brown consolidated his reputation in the area of Australian social organization by promulgating several further pieces on the subject. The year 1914 saw the publication of an article dealing with the relationship system of the Dieri tribe of South Australia. This article provides a notable example of a pupil using the master's tools to modify one of the master's conclusions. Having produced a tortuous argument to explain why the kinship term "nadada" is used for two different relatives, an argument which structurally is very reminiscent of Rivers's favoured mode of discourse circa 1914, Radcliffe-Brown accounts for this double usage by invoking a fictitious fraternal bond which the Dieri regard as connecting ego with the two relatives in question. In other words, Radcliffe-Brown explained what Rivers would have regarded as a kinship "correspondence" by an argument which, however similar in form to those deployed by Rivers, does not depend upon the postulation of an anomalous marriage.[106]

An article which Radcliffe-Brown published in 1918 under the title "Notes on the Social Organization of Australian Tribes, Part I", embodies a detailed, first-hand description of the social organization of eighteen tribes inhabiting the lower reaches of the Murray River. From our point of view, the most interesting thing about the article is Radcliffe-Brown's attempt to find traces of a dual division into two exogamous matrilineal moieties among the Nanuruku people. Knowing that the dual division is found in tribes higher up the river, Radcliffe-Brown infers its former existence among the Nanuruku from present kinship terminology. In so doing, he uses a diagram and a train of thought which are strikingly reminiscent of those employed in Rivers's discussion of the dual organization near the beginning of *The History of Melanesian Society.*[107]

Radcliffe-Brown's career having been disrupted by the war and ill-health, the second part of his "Notes on the Social Organization of Australian Tribes" did not appear in print until 1923. The referee for the sequel was Rivers, who recommended to the Royal Anthropological Institute that it should be published without any omissions or alterations. Rivers, writing less than three months before his death, also ventures the opinion that: "This is a continuation of a work of great value already published in the Journal and is an important contribution to our knowledge of Australian sociology."[108] If, after recalling his humiliating experience with the Ambrym system, one is tempted to conclude that the latter-day Rivers had lost his confidence and feel for kinship investigations, this conclusion would be supported by comparing the above opinion with the reality of Radcliffe-Brown's article. Apart from the fact that Part II deals with the social organization of tribes which inhabit an area geographically adjacent to that covered by Part I, the sequel does little to complement the undoubted contribution of its predecessor. Part II is much more scrappy and less well expressed than any of Radcliffe-Brown's previous anthropological publications. Radcliffe-Brown seems to have been unable to discover any overriding pattern in the social organizations of the tribes discussed. The characteristics which he singles out for comment seem random and unsystematic, and indeed he presents little evidence which would so much as justify his references to various social institutions as "systems".

Whatever the actual shortcomings of this later article, there can be no doubt that Rivers approved, not only of it, but also of Radcliffe-Brown's earlier efforts in the collection and analysis of Australian data. In an appendix to his book on *Social Organization*, published posthumously in 1926, Rivers describes the social organization of Australian tribes as being "of great theoretical importance", and makes a number of laudatory references to the work of Radcliffe-Brown, whom he obviously regards as the authority on the subject.[109]

A SOUTH AFRICAN INTERLUDE

During the latter half of the Great War, Radcliffe-Brown had served as Director of Education in Tonga. However, in 1919 he became ill and was invalided out to South Africa. In March 1920, Radcliffe-Brown wrote to Haddon that, although he had not yet fully recovered his health, he was keen to obtain the position of ethnologist at the Museum in Pretoria. Radcliffe-Brown therefore asked for a letter of recommendation and also suggested that Haddon write to

General J. C. Smuts, in an attempt to persuade the South African Prime Minister to inaugurate an Ethnographical Bureau for the purpose of performing an anthropological survey of the Union.[110]

Responding to Radcliffe-Brown's request, Haddon wrote to Smuts in April 1920. In support of the suggestion regarding the establishment of an Ethnographical Bureau, Haddon advanced the following consideration:

There is yet a great deal to learn concerning the intimate social structure of the family and of the clan and other groupings. Kinship terms and other details which are requisite for a thorough knowledge of any people should be collected. No one has studied the South African natives by modern methods of sociological research – more particularly by the genealogical method introduced by Dr Rivers of St Johns Cambridge; at all events nothing has been published as yet on these lines.

In the same letter Haddon also put in a good word for Radcliffe-Brown:

It so happens that Mr A. R. Brown is at the present time in Johannesburg ... He is a thoroughly well-trained ethnologist who received his preliminary training here under Dr Rivers and myself. Then he went as the Anthony Wilkin Student to the Andaman Islands, where he did excellent work and his book on the Andamanese is now going through the Cambridge University Press and will probably be the final word on the subject ... Since then he has studied natives in various parts of Australia, about whom he has published very valuable accounts, mainly sociological ... Thus you have on the spot the most brilliant and experienced of the younger students turned out by the Cambridge School of Ethnology, and I am sure that you could not get a more competent investigator from elsewhere.[111]

Smuts responded by writing a personal letter to Radcliffe-Brown, which read as follows:

Dear Mr Brown, I have received a letter from Mr Haddon of Christ's College about our ethnological work in South Africa and your special qualifications for such work. I have discussed the subject with Professor Beattie of the Cape Town University and shall be glad if you will communicate with him as the University has a scheme for taking up this work. Yrs sincerely, J. C. Smuts.[112]

Subsequent to this favourable communication from the South African Prime Minister, Radcliffe-Brown was appointed first to the position of museum ethnologist and then, in July 1921, to the foundation Chair of Social Anthropology at the University of Cape Town. Radcliffe-Brown's tenure of the chair did not constitute the most prolific phase of his career, but he was to publish one paper which has since been accepted by the anthropological world as a model analysis of the rights and duties of kinsmen. I refer to his 1924 article on "The Mother's Brother in South Africa",[113] the argument of which will be discussed in a subsequent section of the present chapter.

Throughout his sojourn in South Africa, it would seem that Radcliffe-Brown, as one of his anthropological colleagues later informed Haddon, "always rather hankered after Australia ... chiefly I think because he felt he hadn't finished the work there that he set out to do." [114] By late 1923, Radcliffe-Brown had evidently made up his mind to again shift his field of operations to the Antipodean continent. As he explained to Haddon in October of that year:

The real motive impelling me to wish to return to Australia is undoubtedly that in 1913, having thought of the whole matter very thoroughly for several months, I decided to give up the next eight or ten years to attempting the solution of a number of Australian problems which seemed to me of particular importance for the general theories of sociology. Having once made such a definite plan of life it is difficult to get away from it. [115]

AUSTRALIAN SOCIAL ORGANIZATION II, 1926–1931

Again and again in his correspondence from 1913 on up through the twenties, and especially in his letters to Rivers and Haddon, Radcliffe-Brown mentions that he is working up his material on Australian social organization. [116] In fact, it would take only a casual perusal of his surviving correspondence to convince one that this period of his career was sharply focused on the production of a major work on this topic. In 1925, the opportunity for which he had been waiting presented itself. The University of Sydney advertised a newly-founded Chair of Anthropology. A committee consisting of Elliot Smith, Haddon and J. T. Wilson, formerly Professor of Anatomy at Sydney, met in Haddon's house at Cambridge to recommend the most suitable candidate. Having considered a number of anthropologists likely to be available for the position, the Committee fixed on two former pupils of Rivers, namely Radcliffe-Brown and Hocart. Whether Haddon was supporting the genealogically-inclined Radcliffe-Brown and Elliot Smith was supporting the diffusionistic Hocart, as might have been expected at this time, I do not know. However, it is known that the Committee believed that if Hocart had been offered the Chair, he would have been unlikely to accept, "because he is of the opinion that he can do more useful work in anthropology in Ceylon". At any rate, the Committee concluded that the general academic qualifications of the two men were very nearly equal, but that "Mr Radcliffe-Brown's successful experience as a University teacher and the fact that he is anxious to continue the anthropological work which he began in Australia in 1910 weigh the balance in his favour". Hence, they recommended that Radcliffe-Brown be offered the Sydney Chair.[117]

Radcliffe-Brown took up the position early in 1926, and as he himself was later to claim, "spent five of the best years of my life in building up the Sydney Department".[118] These activities included the training of administrators for colonial New Guinea, the setting up of a research program in Australian Aboriginal studies and the establishment of the journal *Oceania*, with himself as the foundation editor.

During this period, Radcliffe-Brown's distaste for diffusionism, previously expressed privately in his pre-war letters to Rivers, and publicly in his 1923 Presidential Address to the Anthropology Section of the South African Association for the Advancement of Science, became progressively stronger and better known among his colleagues. Having been told by Haddon that Deacon had claimed allegiance to earlier rather than later Rivers, Radcliffe-Brown replied in the 1927 letter already quoted in Chapter VI, that he too was a disciple of earlier Rivers and that he had always deeply regretted the disagreement which arose between Rivers and himself "when Elliot Smith got hold of him". Radcliffe-Brown further stated that he was particularly annoyed at the way in which Elliot Smith and Perry had "been using Rivers's name for their own purposes". "I agree with you thoroughly in distrusting that school", said Radcliffe-Brown to Haddon.[119]

At the 1929 Pan Pacific Science Congress in Java, Radcliffe-Brown and Elliot Smith were both in attendance, and their differences must have been painfully obvious. Each man delivered a paper on totemism, but their approaches were radically divergent. Elliot Smith, needless to say, gave a diffusionistic analysis of the phenomenon, while Radcliffe-Brown took the sociological path.[120] Furthermore, Radcliffe-Brown took the opportunity of reading a second paper which argued that the structural-functional approach to culture was, from the point of view of applying anthropology to colonial administration, far superior to the historical-diffusionist interpretation.[121] As will be remembered from the chapter on the diffusion controversy, Elliot Smith had, for a number of years previously, been involved in a frustrating attempt to outmaneuvre his rivals and obtain money to finance ethnology at University College, so no doubt Radcliffe-Brown's use of the Java Congress to present this financially-consequential argument would have been particularly annoying to him.

After Radcliffe-Brown finally left Australia in 1931, Elliot Smith averred to the Australian politician Stanley Melbourne Bruce that the activities of the Sydney Department had been "disappointing in certain respects", but that the "recent change of personnel" had altered the Department's approach and thereby "eliminated the causes of the disappointment".[122] If the rest of the anthropological community had known about this privately expressed opinion of Elliot Smith, I have no doubt that the great majority of them would have regarded it as jaundiced at best. For apart from building up a flourishing department, which had attracted students from all over the English-speaking world, Radcliffe-Brown had published four influential articles on Australian social organization, which were featured one at a time in the inaugural issues of *Oceania*. Indeed cynics might have suspected that Radcliffe-Brown founded the journal primarily for the purpose of functioning as the vehicle for this definitive presentation of his work on Aboriginal society. When funds became short early in the thirties, Radcliffe-Brown threatened to discontinue publication of *Oceania*. However, it should be noted that this discontinuation was not planned to take effect until *after* the appearance of the fourth issue, containing the final article in the series.[123]

Radcliffe-Brown's articles, which were reissued as the famous 1931 monograph, embody the published culmination not merely of his Sydney sojourn, but indeed of his total career over the previous two decades. Certainly in terms of the number and variety of Australian tribes covered, the monograph is far more impressive than anything any other single person had done in one publication. Nonetheless, despite its revered place in the folklore of anthropology, the monograph is in several important respects less impressive on close inspection than it may seem at first sight. Theoretically it represents little or no advance on Radcliffe-Brown's previous contributions to the subject. The central theoretical notion is that of social structure, and it remains basically unchanged.

Moreover, very little of the empirical material in the monograph is original, despite the fact that Radcliffe-Brown obviously wants to leave his readers with the impression that much of it is his own work. A close study of the earlier writings on Australian social organization reveals that Radcliffe-Brown is noticeably grudging in dispensing plaudits to his predecessors, and always ready to denigrate them by pointing out minor faults. Although he acknowledges the existence of their work in bibliographies, and therefore cannot technically be accused of plagiarism, he is not at all specific about which particular points he extracted from whom. The most badly treated was R. H. Mathews, who had written some two hundred articles on the Australian Aborigines, of which over one hundred had dealt with social organization. A. P. Elkin, whose familiarity with the material was unmatched, lists no less than eleven achievements of Mathews,[124] most of which are used in

Radcliffe-Brown's monograph without any specific acknowledgement of
Mathews's priority. The unpublished field-notes of Daisy Bates, many of
which must have been accessible to Radcliffe-Brown, likewise get short shrift.
The monograph contains only one reference to her field-notes, which are
listed after a miniscule account of an unnamed tribe inhabiting a region
vaguely delineated as "eastward of Esperance". This account consists of only
three sentences, the second of which states that Mrs Bates had informed him
that the tribe is divided into totemic groups, and the third of which reads in
its entirety, "The real nature of these groups is unknown".[125]

   In a paper published at about the same time as the social organization
monograph, Radcliffe-Brown outlined a system of notation for expressing
relationships which he claimed to have been using to good effect in his
fieldwork for many years.[126] Since he does not footnote the inventors of any
previous notations, one is apparently meant to conclude that the notation
described was his own creation. However, as Rodney Needham has recently
pointed out,[127] Radcliffe-Brown's notation bears a number of striking resemblances to one described forty-seven years earlier in the Macfarlane paper
which I mentioned in Chapter I. Needham not only implies that Radcliffe-
Brown was plagiarizing Macfarlane, but goes so far as to doubt Radcliffe-
Brown's claim that he found his notation to be "of great use in fieldwork".[128]
Actually, a perusal of the field notebooks of Radcliffe-Brown, which survive
at Sydney University, removes all doubt on this latter score. Radcliffe-Brown
certainly did use this notation in the field, and used it extensively. Once
again, however, we are forced to the conclusion that Radcliffe-Brown was
guilty, at the very least, of lack of generosity in failing to acknowledge his
reliance upon the work of a predecessor.

   Radcliffe-Brown's shabby treatment of the people who had laid the
foundations for his own achievement was perhaps best summed up by one
of those most frequently wronged. In a letter to Haddon in 1921, Baldwin
Spencer wrote

I cannot quite make [Radcliffe-Brown] out. He seems so far as I can judge . . . to place
himself in opposition to anyone else and try to show that they are either wrong or have
presented things in the wrong way. I know of course only his Australian work which
is good so far as it goes but is rather written as if he were the great "Poo-Bah" without
sufficient regard to the work of men like Howitt.[129]

Baldwin Spencer himself, need I mention, was one of the "men like Howitt".
   To make an evaluation of the extent to which the 1931 monograph fulfilled Radcliffe-Brown's own ambitions in anthropology, let us now consider

his original goals in respect of the Australian data. In a letter to Rivers probably written early in 1914, Radcliffe-Brown had stated that he hoped "to work out ... the psychology of the Australian system of relationship".[130] A clue to what he meant by this may be found in another letter written to Rivers during the same period, where he states that he regards "the dual division as of fundamental importance", and that he is "more wedded than ever to my theory that the dual division is essentially a mode of organizing the 'oppositions' that arise in savage societies in connection with marriage, initiation etc".[131] The type of approach adumbrated here certainly is present in some of Radcliffe-Brown's later publications.[132] However, in the monograph, the analysis is harnessed to aims which are primarily taxonomic. Now as can be seen from his posthumously published *Natural Science of Society*, Radcliffe-Brown regarded the descriptive, taxonomic objective as a merely preliminary goal for a true science of social phenomena.[133] I would like to suggest that the ultimate aim of Radcliffe-Brown's social anthropology in general, and of his Australian investigations in particular, was an aetiological form of explanation using structural "oppositions" of the kind which Levi-Strauss has detected and praised in Radcliffe-Brown's work on totemism,[134] and which constitute the basis of the French anthropologist's own brand of "structuralism". That Radcliffe-Brown did not attempt this goal in his 1931 magnum opus, is an indication of the complexity of the Australian material, and of consequent curtailing of his scientific ambitions.

Radcliffe-Brown's desire to go beyond the taxonomic concerns of the 1931 monograph and to enter the realms of structural aetiology, may be seen from his surviving handwritten notebooks on social organization. One such notebook contains a detailed plan for what was evidently a projected major work on social theory.[135] Judging from this plan, he apparently intended to establish the proposition that "opposition is as fundamentally necessary to human society as solidarity". A chapter entitled "Social Statics" was to have included an important section on "The Social Organization of the Australian Aborigines". This section was to attempt a "general theory of kinship systems", which would evidently have been based on the general notion that "oppositions" are crucially important to sociology, and the specific notion that moieties provide a "means of organizing social opposition". A section entitled "On Opposition" would have discussed such topics as the oppositions resulting from marriage and initiation, the mode of organizing social opposition in Australia, and the mythical representation of this opposition in the symbolic figures of Eaglehawk and Crow. As things turned out, Radcliffe-Brown never wrote the projected book, and the only one of the above topics which he developed at any length was that involving the Eaglehawk and Crow symbols.[136] Nonetheless, a knowledge of these unfulfilled intentions of Radcliffe-Brown adds an extra dimension to our understanding of the place to be allotted to the 1931 monograph in his anthropological corpus. It was his major effort, but only by default.

But however much Radcliffe-Brown fell short of his own program, and whatever the morality of his bibliographical procedures, his presentation of Australian social organization was rapidly accepted as a classic in its field. In an article on "kinship" in the *Encyclopaedia of the Social Sciences*, published in 1932, the American ethnologist Robert Lowie refers several times to Radcliffe-Brown, and lists his 1930–1931 *Oceania* articles in the bibliography. Moreover (and this is especially significant for the development of a field undergoing professionalization), an American anthropological textbook by A. Goldenweiser published in 1937, includes a detailed discussion of Australian kinship systems which draws heavily on Radcliffe-Brown's account.[137] Even Elliot Smith, while attributing some "disappointing" aspects of the Sydney Department's work to Radcliffe-Brown's presence, had to acknowledge that the Department's investigations of the Australian Aborigines were "widely recognized by anthropologists in Europe and America" as having "yielded results of great scientific importance".[138] A more recent tribute has been paid by Meyer Fortes, who sees Radcliffe-Brown's monograph as providing "the generic paradigm of Australian social systems".[139]

After leaving Sydney, Radcliffe-Brown proceeded to Chairs in Chicago, Oxford and Alexandria and Visiting Professorships at Yenching and São Paulo. Although this period of his career is better known to most current anthropologists than the earlier phase which provides the primary focus for this chapter, although it saw no slackening of his department-building activities, and although it produced some notable publications, including the Introduction to *Kinship and Marriage in Africa*, it was, in respect of the narrowly technical task of analyzing and classifying systems for regulating marriage and descent, a rather pale reflection of the earlier phase of his career. Having pulled off what he and many others regarded as an Australian triumph, Radcliffe-Brown spent much of his subsequent career enjoying its renown, or attempting to repeat the *coup* in other regions. But this was to little avail. The Australian data had an apparent unity and symmetry unmatched by the kinship systems of any comparable area.

Radcliffe-Brown's monograph on Australian social organization must be regarded as representing the culmination of the dominant thrust of the programme of kinship studies which had emanated from earlier Rivers. For in contributing substantially to the task of clarifying the specifications of Australian kinship systems, Radcliffe-Brown was giving substance to the scientistic ideology which had been a feature of the writings, teachings and propagandizing of Rivers and Haddon. However, if Radcliffe-Brown had never gone beyond the technically impressive but essentially narrow concerns of the monograph, his career would never have become, as it did in fact become, a springboard for the future theorists of British Social Anthropology. The line of investigations which proved to be seminal in this regard, bore upon the broader and more humanly-involving topic of the rights and duties of kinsmen. And while this topic was not one which would necessarily have been suggested by the scientistic propaganda emanating from the Rivers—Haddon school, it was nonetheless the case that Radcliffe-Brown's approach to the topic also stemmed from Rivers.

THE RIGHTS AND DUTIES OF KINSMEN

As Fred Eggan has pointed out, Lewis Henry Morgan's pioneering investigations into kinship were deficient in one important respect. For Morgan had paid scant attention to the behaviour patterns which exist between specific relatives:

[Morgan] realized that kinship systems were real, and basic to the political and social organization, but he never probed deep enough to lay this foundation bare. If he had gone below the clan level to the world of actual kinship behaviour, he would have discovered that particular relatives had rights and obligations beyond inheritance and succession. Had he translated the speeches at his adoption [into the Hawk clan of the Seneca Tribe], detailing the rights and duties of relatives, he could have understood better the relations between terminology and behaviour, between household and lineage, and between lineage and clan.[140]

The essential steps towards remedying this deficiency in Morgan's analysis were to be taken by Rivers. As Radcliffe-Brown expressed it:

In his field work Rivers had discovered and revealed to others the importance of the investigation of the behaviour of relatives to one another as a means of understanding a system of kinship.[141]

As I have mentioned in Chapter II, Rivers had published material on the social functions of certain kinsmen soon after the Torres Straits expedition. By way of explaining the special role of the mother's brother in Mabuiag society, Rivers had suggested that it represented a survival of a period when descent was traced in the female line, at which time the mother's brother would have been regarded as a closer relative than the biological father. Later, as I have described, Rivers was to make some significant, although not totally decisive moves away from this typically nineteenth-century mode of explanation. In 1910, Rivers published an article entitled "The Father's Sister in Oceania". Focusing on the close relationship which exists between a person and his father's sister in communities with matrilineal descent, Rivers had considered a number of possible explanations for the special nature of this relationship. One of these possible explanations had rested on the postulate that the society in question had previously employed patrilineal descent. This postulate Rivers dismisses with the observation that it has been advanced "chiefly as a matter of form". The explanation to which he gives the most credence runs as follows. In any matrilineal society with a dual organization, the father's sister and her brother's child will be members of opposite moieties. These moieties often tend to be hostile to one another. On the island of Mota it is a function of the father's sister to act as custodian of the nail parings of her brother's child. Otherwise, the parings might be used by an enemy in rituals designed to inflict injury on the child. Rivers's suggestion is that when indigenes reach a stage of intellectual enlightenment such that they begin to recognize the kin relationship of the genetic father, the father's sister will be the relative entrusted with the task of seeing that the child comes to no harm through his nail parings falling into hostile hands. In other words, the special role of the father's sister originated in the necessity for promoting social harmony in view of the hostile situation existing between the child's moiety and that of its father. Whilst advancing this explanation, Rivers at one stage refers to Radcliffe-Brown, who had called his attention to an Australian Aboriginal correlation between the functions of certain kinsmen and their membership of different social divisions.[142]

Although Radcliffe-Brown's article on "The Mother's Brother in South Africa" nowhere footnotes Rivers, one could hardly wish for a more striking demonstration of Radcliffe-Brown's debt to his former teacher. As all anthropologists now know, thanks to Rivers and Radcliffe-Brown, the mother's brother in a patrilineal society and the father's sister in a matrilineal situation fulfill similar social roles, the fundamental reason being that in both cases the relative in question must belong to a different social group from ego. So the title of Radcliffe-Brown's article must have been intended to echo that of Rivers's earlier paper. But the most important resemblances are to be found in the nature of the problems tackled and the arguments adduced. In both cases, the problem for solution requires the explication of a special social relationship between a child and a sibling of one of the child's parents. Like Rivers, Radcliffe-Brown mentions, and then firmly rejects, a nineteenth-century style explanation in terms of a change in the line of descent. Like Rivers, the explanation which he endorses involves the observation that the societies in question embody a division of function between the social group to which the child belongs and the social group to which he does not. Like Rivers, Radcliffe-Brown relies on the postulate that the group to which the child does not belong is in some sense inimical to the interests of the child. But let us consider Radcliffe-Brown's explanation in more detail.

Radcliffe-Brown achieves his desired explanation by invoking a number of premises, which he refers to variously as "principles", "tendencies" or "formulae". These premises may be paraphrased as follows:

(1)   If one man stands in a particular social relation to another, he will regard himself as standing in the same general kind of relationship to the latter's brother; and similarly for a woman and her sister. (The "principle of the equivalence of brothers,")[143]

(2)   Where the classificatory system reaches a high degree of elaboration a person will tend to develop behaviour patterns in relation to the mother's brother and the father's sister which indicate that he regards the former as a sort of male mother, and the latter as a sort of female father.[144]

(3)   In a strongly patriarchal society, there will be a tendency for the father to demand respect and obedience, whereas the mother will be a source of tenderness and indulgence.[145]

(4)   In indigenous societies with male authority, any considerable degree of social familiarity will generally be permitted only between persons of the same sex.[146]

From these four premises, Radcliffe-Brown deduces that, in a strongly patriarchal indigenous society with a highly developed classificatory system, one would expect a boy to relate to his mother's brother with a higher degree of social familiarity than is acceptable in any relationship with a female. The anthropologist then points out that this behaviour pattern is precisely what is found among a number of societies with the requisite specifications. The analysis has a further bonus in that a different behaviour pattern, involving respect and obedience, is deducible for the father's sister. As Radcliffe-Brown is quick to remark, this deduction too is corroborated by observation. His claims to having brought to fruition an aspect of Rivers's programme for developing kinship studies have nowhere looked as firm. What more satisfying experience could a disciple have than to tackle a problem-area pioneered by one's master, to develop a more rigorous version of the master's mode of explanation and, finally, in a kind of casual *coup de grace*, to demonstrate that the solution to the problem which originally claimed the attention of the master is nothing more than a minor corollary of the current exercise.

Further on in the article, Radcliffe-Brown says that, in order to reach "a really final explanation", one must study the behaviour of a person, not just in relation to the mother's brother, but to all the other kinsmen on his mother's side.[147] Radcliffe-Brown then goes on to apply the notion of kinship "extensions", which as we learnt previously, also derived from Rivers. Thus, in this sense too, the "Mother's Brother" paper can be regarded as demonstrating Radcliffe-Brown's bona fides as a disciple of Rivers.

In his contributions to the 1912 edition of the *Notes and Queries on Anthropology*, Rivers had emphasized strongly the importance of collecting data on the rights and duties of one kinsman in relation to another. "Record fully any functions connected with ties of relationship" was his advice to the budding ethnographer. It will not generally be possible to obtain a complete list of these numerous and varied functions simply by asking directly for their enumeration. In fact, "it is necessary to cover the whole culture of the people" before the interlocking complex of relationship-governed duties and privileges can be recorded in full. So whenever a particular social phenomenon is being studied, special attention should be directed to the behaviour patterns of relatives. And the recommended procedure involves the prior collection of genealogies. Thus, in recording a rite of some kind, "the names of all participants should be obtained and their relationship to others taking part sought out in the pedigrees". Of particular importance are restrictions on the behaviour of relatives, which may be collectively designated as "customs of avoidance". Examples of such customs are "that one person may not say the name of [a particular relative], may not speak to him, or only from a distance, may not eat in his presence, may not pass him when he is sitting, may not take anything from above his head, may not eat anything which he has carried".[148]

That Radcliffe-Brown had received instruction of this kind from Rivers seems apparent. Whilst in the Andaman Islands, Radcliffe-Brown had noticed that "the parents of a man and the parents of his wife must avoid each other". On the other hand, he had also been told that "they will regularly send each other presents" as tokens of their "friendship".[149] It therefore occurred to him that customs of avoidance and relationships of friendship, which at first sight seem to be polar opposites, are actually two sides of the same coin. The problem, as Radcliffe-Brown formulates it, is to see how a relationship which, like the Andaman one, expresses both social disjunction and social conjunction, can be "given a stable, ordered form". Now social disjunction implies, according to Radcliffe-Brown, "divergence of interests and therefore the possibility of conflict and hostility". Social conjunction, on the other hand, requires the averting of strife. In order for the two to coexist in harmonious equilibrium, two divergent approaches are possible. One involves the observance of "a limitation of direct personal contact". In their most extreme form these limitations will entail "complete avoidance of any social contact" between the two relatives concerned. Such avoidance must not be interpreted as an expression of actual hostility. As Radcliffe-Brown expresses it:

One does of course, if one is wise, avoid having too much to do with one's enemies, but that is quite a different matter. I once asked an Australian native why he had to avoid his mother-in-law, and his reply was, 'Because she is my best friend in the world; she has given me my wife'. The mutual respect between son-in-law and parents-in-law is a mode of friendship. It prevents conflict that might arise through divergence of interest.[150]

The second approach involves the sublimation of serious hostility via the habitual display of "mutual disrespect and licence". One example of such display is the "joking relationship", in which one person is required or permitted to tease or make fun of a particular relative, "who in turn is required to take no offence".[151] Hence, the two apparently contradictory forms of behaviour are, on Radcliffe-Brown's account, both responses to the problem of preserving social harmony. As I have argued, Radcliffe-Brown's formulation of such problems in this manner, usually attributed solely to the influence of Durkheim, actually seems to have originated in the extrapolation of Rivers's concern with what the latter had called "the functions of . . . social groupings in the maintenance of social order". The upshot of Radcliffe-Brown's development of this concern was that kinship became more central to social anthropology than it would have done if kinship studies had remained stuck with simply trying to give rigorous descriptions of systems of relationship. For once the problem had been formulated in terms of showing how various social institutions serve to maintain the equilibrium of society, kinship, which permeates nearly all aspects of aboriginal behaviour, came to be seen as the thread which held the social fabric together.

*   *   *   *   *

In attempting to answer the question as to how Radcliffe-Brown assembled the elements of structural-functionalism, I have seriously considered only two candidates — Rivers and Durkheim — as possible influences upon him.[152] And my conclusion has been that, contrary to received opinion amongst modern anthropologists, it was Rivers rather than Durkheim who here provided the seminal contribution. Inasmuch as the writings of the Durkheimian school played a role, they seem to have reinforced the theoretical position which Radcliffe-Brown had already extrapolated from Rivers, and to have acted as a convenient bandwagon from which Radcliffe-Brown could launch campaigns against his opponents.

To sum up my discussion of Rivers's most famous disciple, let me review the ways in which the shape of Radcliffe-Brown's career was determined by his role as the first professional in British Social Anthropology. Clearly there are important senses in which his published work is more professional than that of his immediate contemporaries or predecessors. He did think more clearly, and wrote both more transparently and more economically than any of his rivals. He was more sensitive to the problem of defining terms in such a way that no theories were presupposed. He did succeed in establishing more academic departments, and in disseminating his theoretical views over a wider area of the earth's surface than any other anthropologist. No less than five of his most important academic posts were newly-created positions, a sure sign that the field was professionalizing and that he was in the vanguard of the movement. Despite an unpromising beginning, he was the first student from the Rivers—Haddon school to apply the genealogical method successfully. He did select, as the subjects of his personal field investigations, communities which, being regarded as the most "primitive" societies extant, were for that reason held to be the most fundamental for purposes of anthropological theory. He did attack, with considerable justification, the extreme diffusionists, whose conjectural excesses he saw as threatening the professional standing of anthropology as a scientific discipline. Finally, in choosing kinship studies as his main professional speciality, he did contribute to the development of one of the most technically impressive branches of anthropology.

It is all the more to be regretted then that his genuine standing as the first professional social anthropologist was diminished by his own egocentric perception of himself in that role. How much more impressive his career would have been if his early trumpeting of the scientific method in anthropology had not been largely bluff, if he had not been so quick to claim principles of low generality as scientific "laws", if his espousal of French sociology had not been rendered suspect by a snobbish Francophilia, and especially if he had given due credit to his predecessors in Australian ethnography. How unfortunate it was that, for Radcliffe-Brown, the realities of his pioneering professionalism were distorted by a spurious professional pose which made his scientific career into a continual game of intellectual one-upmanship.

But it would be a pity to end this chapter by condemning a talented anthropologist's admittedly controversial personality. What must be emphasized is that, when we consider Radcliffe-Brown's pivotally important career, we find ourselves dealing, not only with the professionalization of a disciple which aspired to be scientific, but also with the "scientization" of a disciple which was becoming professionalized.[153] For the two processes represent different sides of the same coin. Radcliffe-Brown's depiction of his discipline as "the natural science of society" represented a very useful stance for someone who was assuming the role of the first real professional in British Social Anthropology. But equally, the advocacy of an apparently rigorous method and the adoption of the technical modes of analysis which accurately mimicked esoteric puzzle-solving were important intellectual determinants of the formation of the first professionalized "closed-shop" in the discipline.

CHAPTER VIII

CONCLUSION

In focusing primarily upon the Ambrym episode and the career of Radcliffe-Brown, I have neglected other manifestations of Rivers's concern to develop the study of kinship. One of these had been C. G. and Brenda Seligman's 1911 ethnography on *The Veddas*, in which there are lengthy chapters on "Social Organization", "Family Life" and "Property and Inheritance". The first of these chapters begins with Vedda genealogies, and then proceeds to analyze the Vedda kinship system. In making explicit his indebtedness to his old Torres Straits colleague, C. G. Seligman explicitly thanks Rivers for the "unflagging interest" he has shown in the book, "the whole of which he has read in manuscript and discussed with us, to the very great advantage of the work".[1]

There were, of course, other people affiliated with the Cambridge school, who would have been in a position to contribute to the development of kinship studies, but who, for one reason or another, failed to do so. C. B. Humphreys was one who has been mentioned in this regard. Another was J. D. Newsom, a student of Rivers who was granted money from the Percy Sladen Trust Fund to make a field trip to New Caledonia. Newsom's ethnographic adventures, and with them the hope of a career in academic anthropology, came to a miserable end following illness in the field, shortage of funds ˆand the discovery that the indigenous culture he had been sent to investigate was largely inoperative due to the influence of missionaries.[2] As one of his relatives complained:

To my mind it seems incredible that he had to go to such a place to do his very first fieldwork. One has only to note the lack of any work relating to it to realize that from the anthropologist's viewpoint, it is hopeless.[3]

So it would seem that Rivers's judgement as director of his students' field investigations was hardly infallible.

Another episode illustrates even more graphically the way in which the qualities which normally made Rivers an effective anthropological mentor could sometimes backfire. In 1912, Rivers was visited at Cambridge by one Captain Grenville St John Orde Browne, a colonial officer stationed in British East Africa, who wanted some advice on ethnological matters. Rivers attempted to explain to him the efficacy of the genealogical method, but was informed by Orde Browne that the natives of Kenya do not make a point of remembering genealogies. To this Rivers replied that he was much surprised, and suggested further enquiries. Upon returning to East Africa Orde Browne discovered that, in spite of three years prior experience among the natives, he had been quite wrong in saying that they do not keep genealogies. "It is not easy at all to get the genealogies", Orde Browne informed Haddon, "but they do exist, and I have managed to get some fairly complete ones".[4] In August 1913, Orde Browne wrote a letter to Rivers, enclosing a sketch of a book he intended to write about some Kenyan tribes. "The subject is a very large one", wrote Orde Browne, "and I find myself bewildered with the attempt to divide it up in an intelligible way."[5] His sketch listed possible topics for sixteen chapters, of which the first four were to treat of historical, social, legal and ceremonial matters respectively, and the fifth was to deal with religion and magic. The specification for the second chapter read in full: "*Social*. The family, genealogy, marriage, the structure of society, with notes on possible changes past and future."[6] Rivers's reply bears quoting in some detail:

Dear Captain Orde Browne,

I am very glad to hear that you have been able to do so much since your return and are thinking of publishing your results in a book.

I hope very much that you will decide in favour of a strictly scientific rather than a popular account . . . The arrangement of such a book as you propose is, as I know well from my own experience, a matter of the greatest difficulty. My own feeling is that it is a mistake to use categories derived from our own way of looking at things, such as legal, social, moral and ceremonial, but rather to use as a means of classification categories which belong as much to native thought as to our own. After the historical account, I should give an account of social organization, including such topics as modes of social grouping, nature of social units, relationship, marriage, chieftainship and mode of government, dividing the chapters according to the amount of the material. It is then useful to have a chapter or chapters on periods of life, birth and childhood, which would include accounts of such things as circumcision. Death is usually sufficiently important and rich in material to have a chapter to itself. I think it is then best to go on to dances and technical subjects as you propose, but to include in the accounts of the latter anything of a ceremonial or magico-religious character which accompanies technical processes, such as house-building, war or agriculture. In these chapters and in those on death and childhood you will thus be continually giving the facts of the magico-religious culture, and then at the end you can have the chapter on magic and religion in which you coordinate these facts, adding any others, probably very few, which have escaped mention in the previous chapters . . .

I shall be very pleased at any time to look over chapters or special sections if you think my criticism will be of any use. I should be particularly interested in seeing your account of social groupings and relationship as these are subjects in which I might possibly be able to direct your attention to points on which further information might be sought. I suppose you have the new edition of "Anthropological Notes and Queries". I forget whether it was out when you were at home.

With best wishes for the book,

Yours sincerely,
W. H. R. Rivers.[7]

So, in Rivers's opinion, the book should be aimed at a specialized rather than a mass audience; it should make social organizaton, including particularly his own favoured interests of social groupings and relationship, the central theme; it should include chapters using the ontogenetic "periods of life" mode of presentation; and it should present the bulk of the data relating to magic and religion within chapters dealing with other topics. The best comment on the worth of this particular piece of advice was provided by the book which Orde Browne eventually published in 1925. Replete with pictures of chieftains, witch-doctors and warriors in full battle regalia, *The Vanishing Tribes of Kenya* is obviously aimed at a popular and not a professional audience. The only chapter presenting kinship material is a mere eight pages long and is, from the theoretical point of view, very weak indeed. Although there are two chapters dealing with "periods of life", Rivers is nowhere mentioned and his name is conspicuously absent from the list of people thanked in the Introduction. In fact, the only sure trace of Rivers comes near the beginning of the book. Here Orde Browne avers that when asking ethnographic questions it is best "to acknowledge the concrete outlook" of one's informants, and states that he "found it a great help to use a set of little cardboard figures, cut out and painted to represent the various members of a family; these could be moved about the table, so as to meet each other, give the customary greetings, quarrel, arrange a marriage and so forth".[8] One cannot help wondering whether the cardboard cut-outs were primarily for the benefit of the natives or for that of Orde Browne!

What the Orde Browne episode illustrates, apart from Rivers's donnish impracticality, is the esoteric nature of a genuinely scientific enterprise. No rank outsider, no matter how well-meaning, should, on the basis of a brief coaching session, be expected to acquire the outlook and expertise necessary for the successful performance of modern anthropological fieldwork and analysis. Assuming that the appropriate motivations and intellectual abilities are present, the only way to ensure that beginners become members of a mature discipline is to apprentice them, in a less than superficial sense, to a functioning practitioner. This was the situation for all the people I have

previously labelled as disciples of Rivers. It was unfortunately not the case
with Orde Browne.

Far more typical of the Rivers–Haddon school was Mrs Winifred Hoernle,
a faithful disciple whose name has until now been mentioned only in passing.
Writing to Rivers from the scene of her first field expedition, Miss Tucker (as
she then was) confided:

I feel I must ... tell you about my work for I have been feeling more and more that
without the genealogical method I should be quite lost. More and more things are
coming out and entirely by the use of this method. One bumps up against a new term
and can't fit it in any way and one goes home filled with depression, and then another
day from another source the explanation will come ... The whole intertribal intercourse
is very interesting and to me the whole system seems wonderfully well organized. If I
could only get to the bottom of the clan names and the family system of naming! Can
you give me any assistance? Do you think it is interesting and is there any hint you could
give me for getting further?[9]

In those final questions one may discern the essence of discipleship in the
Rivers–Haddon school.

A very individualistic product of Cambridge anthropology was that recent
guru of the counter-culture, Gregory Bateson, who had entered Cambridge
anthropology shortly after the demise of Rivers. Son of the famous geneticist
William Bateson, Gregory had been converted to anthropology by Haddon
who had, as Gregory relates, told him "in a railway train between Cambridge
and King's Lynn that he would train me and send me to New Guinea".[10]
Haddon having made good his promise to give Bateson an anthropological
education, the young man was awarded the Anthony Wilkin Studentship and
Haddon ensured the perpetuation of the Torres Straits tradition by decreeing
that his protégé's first field trip should be to the Sepik River.[11] Apart from
Haddon, the anthropologists who played the most seminal role in establishing
Bateson's early theoretical position were Radcliffe-Brown and Malinowski
who, on Bateson's own account, "influenced my ideas so profoundly that I
cannot point to any ideas and say that they are truly mine".[12]

Whilst on the Sepik River, Bateson met up with fellow anthropologists
Margaret Mead and Reo Fortune, who had previously come to the conclusion,
independently of each other, that Rivers "was the man under whom we
would like to have studied – a shared and impossible daydream, since he
had died in 1922".[13] Apart from becoming romantically entangled with
Mead, whom he later married, Bateson had many discussions with Mead and
Fortune, in the course of which, as he tells us, "my approach to anthropological problems had its origin".[14] Bateson's first book, *Naven*, which is

dedicated to Haddon, shows a spectrum of influences which mark it as a definite (albeit somewhat unconventional) product of the Rivers—Haddon school.[15] For example, in a chapter on "The Sociology of *Naven*", Bateson discusses two apparently contradictory recommendations about marriage amongst the Iatmul people. The first of these is that a man should marry his father's mother's brother's son's daughter. The second is that a man should marry his father's sister's daughter. After drawing a diagram to illustrate the first type of marriage, Bateson demonstrates that the second type of marriage can be slotted into the first in such a way that a man's wife can be his father's sister's daughter *at the same time as* she is his father's mother's brother's son's daughter. In fact, Bateson suggests in a footnote that the second type of marriage may have evolved out of the interaction of the first type of marriage with the practice of sister-exchange. The reasons which Bateson offers in support of this suggestion are that the kinship vocabulary allegedly indicates that the first type of marriage is older than the second type, and that the custom of exchanging women could have been "adopted from neighbouring peoples".[16] All in all the problematic, the approach, and the mode of discourse are strikingly reminiscent of those favoured by Rivers circa 1914. In fact, I think it no exaggeration to say that if this particular passage were to be inserted within Rivers's books on *Kinship and Social Organization* or *The History of Melanesian Society*, it would arouse no sense of disjunction or incongruity.

A further example of Bateson exhibiting the concerns of the Rivers—Haddon school comes in the chapter on "The Eidos of Iatmul Culture", where Bateson compares the Iatmul kinship system with the class systems of Australia. Having pointed out that both varieties of system are similar in that they put an emphasis upon the alternation of generations, Bateson also notes that there is a "conspicuous difference", in that the Australian systems are "closed", whereas the Iatmul system is not. Bateson then reveals that he believes (as did other members of the Rivers—Haddon circle) that the Australian systems are essentially inflexible, in that marriage arrangements are strictly determined by considerations of class. In Iatmul society, on the other hand, "the natives see their community, not as a closed system, but as an infinitely proliferating and ramifying stock". In speculating about the rationale lying behind this difference, Bateson then adopts an approach which is thoroughly reminiscent of Rivers. "In Australia," he writes, "classificatory kinship is really classificatory." Amongst the Iatmul, by contrast, kinship forms are assigned, not because the objective is that of classifying relatives, but rather "on a basis of *extension* from the family itself".[17] As I have mentioned elsewhere, this notion of kinship "extensions", which is found in the writings of earlier Rivers, had been picked up and developed both by Malinowski and Radcliffe-Brown, so Bateson could have acquired it from any or all of these three sources. But the wellspring of the notion would seem to have been Rivers.

A third example of Rivers's influence on Bateson concerns ethnographic method. While emphasizing that his approach to fieldwork had been so uncontrolled as to be almost chaotic, Bateson mentions that he nonetheless did collect genealogies and kinship terminology. What is more, he refers to these endeavours as "standard procedures",[18] which indicates the extent to which the genealogical method had, by the 1930s, become part and parcel of the British Social Anthropologists' field technique.

Finally we may mention that Bateson, for all the diversity and humanism of his interests, concluded the first edition of *Naven* with a plea for the scientization of Social Anthropology which recalls similar pleas by Rivers, Haddon and Radcliffe-Brown:

Our unscientific knowledge of the diverse facts of human nature is prodigious, and only when this knowledge has been set in a scientific framework shall we be able to hope for new ideas and theories.[19]

Certainly Bateson was no slavish follower of Rivers (or of anyone else). He was and is a stunningly original thinker and the sources upon which he draws are nothing if not eclectic. But in the formative period of his thought, which produced what was probably the most stimulating ethnography to come out of British Social Anthropology in the 1930s, he was, in many significant senses, a product of the Cambridge school. And, since such things matter in Cambridge, it should also be noted that like Rivers before him, his college affiliations were with St Johns.

A further product of the Rivers—Haddon approach to anthropology was the late Reo Fortune. As a young student of psychology in New Zealand, Fortune had been vastly impressed by the writings of Rivers, but like Bateson had arrived on the Cambridge scene too late to benefit from the tutelage of the master. In the preface to his first ethnographic work, *Sorcerers of Dobu*, Fortune states that he owes his spiritual initiation into anthropology mainly to the writings of Malinowski, Radcliffe-Brown, Rivers, Frazer and Haddon, "which, with others, I read at Cambridge under the careful eye of the Reader, Colonel T. C. Hodson". Certainly the influence of Malinowski bulks large in the conception, execution and presentation of Fortune's first field trip. Fortune went to Dobu, which is in the same archipelago of eastern New

Guinea as the Trobriand Islands, because he had been a great admirer of Malinowski's field work in the latter area, and "felt that, where so much had been done, accretion would be of most value". And Malinowski was to write a generous introduction to Fortune's book. In this introduction, Malinowski pays tribute to Fortune's ability to bring to life native fears, passions and feelings of communality which Malinowski had elsewhere depicted as being obscured by what he regarded as the sterile and dehumanizing "kinship algebra" of earlier Rivers. Moreover, Malinowski uses the introduction to get in some direct shots at Rivers by referring derogatively to the latter's "far-fetched" theory of anomalous marriages,[20] and to his notion of Melanesian "communism".[21] However, polemics aside, Fortune's book should actually be regarded as lying squarely on the line of descent which had emanated from the Rivers—Haddon school.

In his preface, Fortune draws the attention of the reader to five passages in the book which he "value[s] especially" because he regards them as being of "theoretical importance". Each of the passages in question is concerned with social organization, the topic which, as I have argued, had emerged as central to British Social Anthropology primarily because of the work of Rivers. The first, second and fourth of these passages deal specifically with a sociologically fundamental Dobuan institution called the *susu*, which consists of a man, his sister and her children. In discussing the social functions of the *susu*, therefore, Fortune is necessarily concerned with the duties and privileges of the mother's brother, and attempts to show how they contribute to the smooth operations of the society as a whole. As we have learnt, the general approach and the specific subject matter had been opened up by the work of Rivers, and honed to perfection by Radcliffe-Brown. So even though Fortune's locutions sometimes echo those of American rather than British anthropology,[22] I would argue that, historically speaking, the passages in question have their most substantive source in the work of the Cambridge school. The main point of the second passage is a terminological one. Whereas old-time anthropologists like Bachofen might have referred to the Dobuan situation as an instance of "mother-right", Fortune points out that such a label is inadequate. For while the Dobuans put primary stress upon the *susu* relationship, and secondary stress upon the relationship between a mother and her daughter, they also emphasize the relationship between a father and his son, or (more rarely) between a man and his father's sister. In other words, the term "mother-right" tends to obscure the finer details of the Dobuan situation. Having made this point, Fortune states that, at the inception of his fieldwork in Dobu, his outlook had been "bound by the rigidity of the old mother-right conception", and that this rigidity had been partly loosened by Malinowski's material from the Trobriands. Whatever Fortune believed about his own intellectual development, however, this acknowledgement of Malinowskian influence is historically misleading. For, of all the pioneers of British Social Anthropology, the one whose programme had been most clearly and unequivocally dedicated to using ethnographic data to tighten up the terminology of kinship had been Rivers, who had, in fact, singled out the term "mother-right" for critical scrutiny in Hasting's *Encyclopaedia of Religion and Ethics*.

Only the third of the five passages is suggestive of primarily Malinowskian influence. It consists of an appendix in which Fortune briefly compares the social organization of Dobu with that of the neighbouring culture of Basima. Here he emphasizes that, while the people of Basima resemble the Dobuans in being predominantly matrilineal and using the same relationship terminology, they differ in that they practise patrilocal residence. This difference can, according to Fortune, be correlated with the greater prevalence and effect-iveness of sorcery on Dobu. In thus attempting to use kinship material to illuminate variations in the nature and functions of magic, Fortune might be seen as following more closely in the footsteps of Malinowski than of any other British anthropologist. Nonetheless, for all Fortune's gratitude to Malinowski, and despite Malinowski's attempt to annex Fortune's "precise sociological analysis of the tribal organization of the Dobuans" to the cause of "good functional field-work",[23] the overall impression left by the five passages is that these parts of the book which Fortune himself judged to be its most valuable contributions to anthropological theory are, in fact, best regarded as inspired by the work of Rivers and his school.

*   *   *   *   *

The contents of this book may be summarized as follows. The real focus of the work is Rivers, and the way in which he and his students developed kinship studies, and made them into an integral part of the method and theory of British Social Anthropology. Before considering this topic, however, I devoted an introductory "Prologue" to previous work on kinship which either was or might have been utilized by Rivers and his school. Now I favour the view that Rivers's achievements in kinship studies were attained in almost total independence of his most plausible intellectual ancestor Morgan, and that the only disciple of Rivers who relied significantly upon nineteenth-century students of kinship was that master of imperfect acknowledgement,

Radcliffe-Brown. The historical evidence relating to this view is equivocal and I, therefore, presented and documented this introductory material quite fully so that readers would be in a position to come to their own decisions about its relevance to the work of the Rivers school. The justification for the Prologue's heavy emphasis upon Australian Aboriginal material is that, even though Rivers himself did not make much use of it, one could hardly understand the significance of the Ambrym episode, or judge the work of Radcliffe-Brown, without being familiar with the pioneering investigations of the Australian ethnographers. Some readers of pre-publication drafts of the present work have interpreted this emphasis as indicating excessive devotion to the narrow concerns of "kinship algebra". However, such an interpretation is uncharitable. The class systems of the Australian Aborigines are not, or at least were not regarded by the mainstream of early British Social Anthropologists, merely as complicated curiosities. As one recent exponent of the genre has expressed it, "To describe Aborigines without describing their classes would be like playing Hamlet without the Prince of Denmark."[24] For on this account, the classes have many interlocking functions in Aboriginal social organization and world-view. As well as playing a major role in the regulation of marriage and descent, the classes also invest religious symbols with meaning, ritual acts with purpose, and the cosmos with order.[25] And since the Australian material represented the most coherent large body of data on social organization accessible to British anthropology, it is not surprising that the class systems constituted the framework upon which many British Social Anthropologists chose to hang their facts. Indeed, as Kenelm Burridge has wisely said:

... few theories about the nature of man, society, and culture ... have not found a testing ground in Australian Aboriginal life, and few anthropologists staking a claim to theoretical significance have not tried their hands at unraveling the complexities it contains ... It was taken for granted and generally accepted – by Frazer and Durkheim among others ... – that Australian Aborigines were the "most primitive" representatives of man. Howitt, Spencer, and Durkheim himself revealed the Aboriginal as perhaps the most complicated representatives of man. It is this paradox that has kept Australian Aborigines at the center of anthropological intellectual life.[26]

In proceeding to discuss the career of Rivers, I place considerable emphasis on a psycho-physiological experiment which Rivers performed on his friend and colleague Henry Head. Although Rivers himself did not attempt to relate this experiment to his anthropological investigations, I used it to illuminate Rivers's distinction between protopathic and epicritic. For, as I have argued, this distinction helps one to understand not only Rivers's general attitude towards the study of "primitive" man, but also his specific invention, deployment and presentation of the genealogical method as a "concrete" tool for getting at "abstract" social organization. What is more, my analysis has revealed that the sub-conscious or semi-conscious harnessing of this distinction for anthropological purposes was not simply an idiosyncracy of Rivers. In fact, he seems to have transmitted it to Haddon, to Radcliffe-Brown (who used it extensively in *The Andaman Islanders*), to Perry, to Malinowski, and even to such a marginal figure as Orde Browne. Finally, Rivers's intellectual affinity with Elliot Smith seems to be at least partly explicable in terms of the latter's espousal of a kind of neurological analogue to the protopathic-epicritic distinction.

The other major point which emerges from my account of Rivers's early career is that, through his effective publicization of the genealogical method, through his analyses of the social organization of the Torres Strait islanders and the Todas, and through his brilliance in oral discussion, Rivers built up a formidable reputation for expertise in the technicalities of kinship. However, when he attempted to analyse the kinship systems of Pentecost and Ambrym, Rivers found himself hoist by his own petard. Sensing that the remarkable features of the Pentecost data indicated a theoretically interesting system of relationship, Rivers became increasingly frustrated at his repeated failures to lay bare the nature of the system. After attempting an analysis which involved particular forms of anomalous marriage, Rivers worked himself into a state of nervous anxiety, which was to be resolved only when he formulated a theory which purported to provide a general explanation of the peculiar forms of marriage. While Rivers himself seems to have been quite proud of this unified theory, his colleagues were profoundly unimpressed, regarding it as thoroughly implausible, if not downright crazy. Analyzing the Ambrym data after this harrowing experience, Rivers did not approach the task in a sanguine frame of mind and seems to have given up hope of uncovering a coherent "system" of relationship.

Rivers's unfortunate brush with the Pentecost system and his failure to come to grips with the Ambrym data coincided with and to some extent seems to have been causally related to, his conversion to diffusionism. For in effectively abandoning the cautious, analytic programme which had dominated the early phase of his anthropological career, and in espousing his speculative theory of anomalous marriages, Rivers unwittingly opened the floodgates to the outlandish hypotheses of diffusionism. The story of Rivers's deepening "conversion" is of course more complicated than this, and involved an intense three-way relationship between Rivers, Elliot Smith and Perry, which I have tried to explain in terms of a series of biographical accidents, a common devotion to an empiricist ideology and a constellation of shared personal and intellectual tendencies.

In emphasizing the difference between "earlier" and "later" Rivers, I hope it will not be thought that I have fixed upon something which is revelatory only of the personal and intellectual development of one individual human being. For while Rivers was unusual in having a scientific career which was sharply divided between a meticulous attention to technicalities and a predilection for extravagant speculation, this sort of split has wide significance in the social sciences. How often, in the analysis of human behaviour, do fashions oscillate between, on the one hand, an explicit adherence to a strict empirical methodology, a cautious devotion to the solving of only those problems which can be handled in strictly scientific terms; and, on the other hand, a willingness to "think-big", to refuse to be constrained by narrow specialism, to entertain hypotheses which are daring, or have implications for the nature of humanity in general? In other words, Rivers's career reproduces, in microcosm, a conflict which forms a recurrent theme in all the sciences of man.

Moreover, I must stress that the distinction between earlier and later Rivers, which I have used to lend structure to my historical material, was not something which I invented, but was originally drawn by Deacon in an attempt to specify his own intellectual ancestry, and was immediately taken up by Haddon and Radcliffe-Brown as a weapon to be used against Elliot Smith. In other words, the distinction was part of the official interpretation of the Cambridge approach to social anthropology in the years immediately following Rivers's death. Because my first major research project was to go through the Haddon Collection, which serves as a record of the beliefs and attitudes of the Cambridge school, this interpretation was the one which first came to my notice and which for a time I accepted as valid. Since unearthing more evidence and rethinking the matter, I now feel the official interpretation to be somewhat flawed, but nonetheless still find it useful as an ordering device.

Briefly, the authorized version of the school of earlier Rivers ran as follows: Rivers's first excursions into anthropology, in which he invented the genealogical method and used it to investigate preliterate social organization, were admirable and worthy of emulation. His later conversion to diffusionism represented a retrograde step, and threatened to negate the worth of his previous contributions. The diffusion controversy following Rivers's death in the early twenties, represented a conflict between the forces of good and evil.

The leader of the evil forces was Elliot Smith, a man given to twisting the teachings of later Rivers to his own advantage. Deacon's work on Ambrym represented a triumph for the approach of earlier Rivers, and any attempts by Elliot Smith to claim Deacon for the diffusionist cause were to be resolutely opposed. By the same token, Layard's investigations in the New Hebrides were to be judged a failure, and his suspected association with Elliot Smith and Perry rendered him unsuitable for the task of editing Deacon's manuscripts. Finally, Radcliffe-Brown's analysis of Australian social organization represented a masterly achievement, and a fitting vindication of the approach of earlier Rivers.

In sharp contrast to this, there was the interpretation of the extreme diffusionist school, adopted by those ethnological heretics Elliot Smith and Perry. On their account, Rivers's anthropological career was not to be regarded as divided into two clearly defined phases. Certainly his studies of diffusion after 1910 were more interesting than his investigations of social organization, but the former were in no way opposed to the latter. The diffusion controversy should indeed be interpreted as a conflict between the forces of light and darkness, but this time the evil forces were seen as those opposed to diffusionism. Some of the leading opponents of the truth, such as Haddon, had fallen into sin because of their unfaithfulness to the memory and intentions of Rivers. Haddon and his cohorts had no right to claim Deacon as a follower, because the young man had demonstrated an early allegiance to diffusionism, and his discovery of the Ambrym marriage-class system could be interpreted as lending support to the hypothesis of culture contact between the New Hebrides and Australia. Finally, even though the Sydney Anthropology Department's investigations of the Australian Aborigines were of "great scientific importance", Radcliffe-Brown's presence had been the occasion for activities which were "disappointing in certain respects".

Neither of these interpretations fully accords with the facts. What we require is a revised standard version of the Haddon–Radcliffe-Brown account. Haddon and Radcliffe-Brown were correct in regarding Rivers's anthropological career as proceeding in two clearly defined phases, and I share their strong preference for the earlier phase. Moreover, I agree with their condemnation of the later phase on the grounds that, despite Rivers's repeated assertions to the contrary, it effectively entailed an abandonment of his earlier aim of making anthropology scientific. However, I believe they tended to overrate Rivers's ability as an analyst of social organization. Both sides were surely being melodramatic in regarding the diffusion controversy as a clash between good and evil. A number of different parties were involved in the opposition to Elliot Smith and Perry, and each had their own reasons and motives, many of which had little to do with value judgements about what constituted good and bad scientific practice. However, the stance of the Royal Anthropological Institute, which served as the major institutional springboard for the attack on extreme diffusionism, seems to have been quite similar to that of Haddon. With regard to Deacon's Ambrym investigations, Haddon's evaluation seems closer to the truth than Elliot Smith's. Certainly Deacon had evinced some leanings towards diffusionistic speculation. More significantly, however, the young man had exhibited considerable facility in a type of quasi-puzzle-solving which he had learnt at Cambridge from a former pupil of Rivers, and which Deacon himself associated with "earlier Rivers". Furthermore, the solution which he obtained was judged by himself and by the rest of the Rivers—Haddon school as a discovery of crucial importance. Radcliffe-Brown's work did provide, with at least one important qualification, the culminating achievement of the Rivers—Haddon school. His 1931 monograph, plausibly described by a modern Cambridge anthropologist as "the generic paradigm of Australian social systems", provided a comprehensive taxonomy of the most intricately interwoven set of kinship data in existence. However, an important qualification must now be made. A large proportion of the material in Radcliffe-Brown's monograph does not represent his own work. In fact, much of the monograph should be interpreted as an imperfectly acknowledged compilation of the writings of previous amateur investigators. However, as I have argued in Chapter VII, Radcliffe-Brown's shabby treatment of these precursors stemmed from his warped perception of his role as the first professional in British anthropology, a role which had been created largely through the efforts of Rivers and Haddon.

It would, however, be unfair to end this summary of the doings of the Rivers—Haddon school on such a negative note. For the significance of Radcliffe-Brown's work extended far beyond the morality of his bibliographical procedures, and even beyond the comprehensive taxonomy of the *Oceania* monograph. If British Social Anthropology had devoted itself exclusively to "kinship algebra", it would rapidly have become stuck in a scientistic dead-end. For there was a limit to how far the world's kinship systems could be coherently analyzed and meaningfully classified. What Radcliffe-Brown's brilliantly constructed articles on the social functions of the rights and duties of kinsmen did was to open the discipline up to a broader, more organic and more humanistic style of analysis. And although some of Radcliffe-Brown's retrospective pronouncements imply that the wellspring of this new style of analysis had been Durkheim, our investigations indicate that, in fact, Radcliffe-Brown was exploring a line of investigation which once again had its most relevant source in Rivers. In developing this new style of analysis, Radcliffe-Brown continued to speak of it in terms of the scientistic ideology which he had inherited from Rivers. Nonetheless, there can be little doubt that it more closely resembled philosophy than science. For while some functional analyses are obviously better than others in that (for example) they are more cogently argued, no such analysis would ever be described by practitioners of the trade as indisputably "correct". In other words, rather than techniques which closely mimic scientific puzzle-solving, we are now talking about trains of argument which are judged to be cogent or otherwise simply in terms of the criteria of rational disputation. When social anthropologists *do* indulge in debate about the adequacy of a particular structural-functional account, the discussion will typically centre around the wisdom of applying key theoretical terms (such as "matrilineal", "patrilateral" or "cognatic") to specific situations. Thus, what we have are controversies which (to use Kuhn's characterization) commonly focus upon "claims, counter-claims and debates over fundamentals".

In short, the main thrust of this book has been to argue that the contributions of Rivers and his disciples to kinship studies were instrumental in bringing about the maturing of social anthropology as a quasi-scientific enterprise at Cambridge. The signs of this coming of age were numerous.

First, there were the institutional ones. Despite a singular lack of financial aid from the university, social anthropologists at Cambridge developed, under the guidance of Haddon and Rivers, into a surprisingly coherent and productive group. One symbol and cause of this coherence and productivity was the Anthony Wilkin Studentship which, being awarded to Radcliffe-Brown (twice), Armstrong, Barnard, Deacon and Bateson, did much to further the pursuit of fieldwork in the Rivers style. Another institutional sign was the rise of anthropological professionalism, first exemplified by Radcliffe-Brown.

Second, there was a methodological sign. I refer, of course, to the deployment and advocacy of the genealogical method, which served as a procedural guide and inspiration for the whole Rivers—Haddon school.

Finally and most importantly, there were two theoretical signs. The first of these involved the acknowledgement that procedures which accurately mimicked scientific puzzle-solving should be adopted as one of the central tools of kinship analysis. The best example of this was provided by the successful decipherment of the Ambrym system. In this case the procedures used by Deacon were instantly recognized by the Cambridge initiates as the sort of thing they had all been working towards. Here, however, is a problem. As his unfortunate encounter with the Ambrym data demonstrated, Rivers's reputation in this area of expertise was not fully deserved. Undoubtedly the techniques which Deacon, Barnard, Brenda Seligman and Radcliffe-Brown used to unravel kinship systems had some sort of a direct historical pedigree. However, that pedigree did not necessarily pass through Rivers. Rather, it more plausibly involved previous ethnographers, such as Howitt and Baldwin Spencer. Nonetheless, for purposes of judging scientific maturation, the crucial usage of something which resembled puzzle-solving techniques was not by part-time anthropologists like Howitt and Spencer, but by the Rivers—Haddon school. In the latter instance, these techniques were utilized, not simply as a means of ordering intransigent data, but as subjects which are worthy of serious critical discussion for their own sake. And ultimately, much of the credit for this must go to Rivers. For he was instrumental in creating the value system which led his disciples to hold such techniques in high esteem.

In some ways, the development of technical procedures by the Rivers school was imperfectly realized. For example, Rivers's theory of anomalous marriages should be regarded, not as a useful supplement to the genealogical method, but rather as a spurious perversion of legitimate analysis. Secondly, a consensus as to the most efficient techniques for representing and comparing kinship systems was only partially achieved. Layard's excellent diagrams of marriage-class systems came twenty years too late, then failed to gain wide acceptance. Finally, there was the reception (or rather the lack of one) accorded to Barnard's argument for the existence of a six-class system on Ambrym. Assuming that Haddon and Brenda Seligman read the thesis they were supposed to be supervising, it seems odd that they missed Barnard's clear statement of the discovery which, a few years later, they were to hail as crucially significant.

Nonetheless, the development of techniques which had (or appeared to have) only one right answer, the correctness of which would be endorsed by all the competent practitioners in the area, had a clearly-defined effect upon the sociological characteristics of the discipline. Social anthropology, and particularly its subdiscipline of kinship studies, became the preserve of the technically competent, who not only shared similar value-systems, ethnographic procedures and modes of explanation, but who also were capable of handling specific technicalities which facilitated a really firm consensus about the correctness or otherwise of suggested solutions. In this way, social anthropology followed its path to maturity, becoming in the process a more exclusive and an apparently more rigorous discipline than it had hitherto been.

The second theoretical sign was one which, under the auspices of Radcliffe-Brown and Malinowski, was to eventually become the trademark of British Social Anthropology. I refer to the recognition that the main business of a social anthropologist was to give a comprehensive, general account of the current workings of single societies and to the specific deployment of the concepts of "structure" and "function" to this end. The present work, which is concerned with the role of Cambridge anthropology in laying the foundations of British Social Anthropology, has confined itself to describing the beginnings of this style of analysis in the work of Rivers and its subsequent development by Radcliffe-Brown. To tell the complete story, which involves the work of Malinowski, his interactions with Radcliffe-Brown and the activities of younger social anthropologists who were the disciples of one or both of these two men, would take another book and I shall not be attempting this task here. However, I would like to sketch out the relationship between this new style of analysis and the process by which British Social Anthropology achieved maturity.

Although the mechanisms for achieving consensus about the quality of a particular structural-functional analysis were very different to those involved in procedures for which there was evidently only one right answer, the location of social anthropology within British academia ensured that the pattern of development appeared to be quite uniform. As Robert F. Murphy has argued, the academic set-up of British Social Anthropology was conducive to the discipline staying small, rigorous and exclusive. In the United States, where the system of academic anthropology is large, diffuse and eclectic, there are many professors within a single department and, as Murphy puts it, more "chiefs than Indians". The British university system, on the other hand, generally involves only one professorial chair per department, and the pay-scales are deliberately kept somewhat below a level which would make material affluence possible.

Under these circumstances, it is possible for a single man to determine the limits of debate within a department and for a small group of scholars to accomplish a similar conscription within an entire nation. This does not require a gerontocracy in which tyrannical old professors terrorize their juniors ... Rather, conformity is exercized within broad limits and defined not so much by the center of orthodoxy as by its limits, the point beyond which one becomes *outré* and "unprofessional". The very uncertainty of these limits provides the push toward the center.[27]

Such a set-up is, we might add, particularly well-suited to keeping a tight rein on a discipline in which there is plenty of room for disagreement about how comprehensive, cogent or elegant a particular structural-functional analysis might be. So whether social anthropologists are concerned with the efficacy of particular applications of structural-functionalism, or whether they are concerned with inherently more testable questions like "Does society X employ kinship system Y?", they are likely to conduct themselves in a superficially similar way. In fact, it is as though British Social Anthropology, having approached the maturity of a genuine scientific enterprise via its sub-discipline of kinship studies, has transferred to its more general analyses the form but not the substance of true scientific discourse.

* * * * *

Before bringing the book to a close, let us look at some aspects of the story which have been inadequately covered in the main body of the text.

Firstly, let us epitomize the impact of Rivers's personality and intellect upon his colleagues by focusing on two memorable tributes paid long after his death. One of these tributes, a gentle memory of Rivers's capacity for ethnographic empathy, was treasured by someone who would have had good cause to show resentment towards the man who abandoned him on an island inhabited by reputed cannibals. In his unpublished autobiography, John Layard casts his mind back fifty years, to the period which immediately preceded this abandonment. Whilst visiting south-east Australia during the British Association meeting, Layard went on a trip with Rivers and others to see an encampment of Aborigines. Although most of the details of the trip have slipped from memory, Layard does recall,

being impressed by the way that Rivers talked to them. They were of course clothed like white men, and were a tiny remnant living there. But Rivers touched and coaxed them as a mother would, and I loved him for it.[28]

Another moving tribute was paid by a fellow Johnian. The eminent psychologist F. C. Bartlett recalls that on Saturday 3rd June 1922 he had walked through St John's College on his way to play in a cricket match. In the process he met Rivers, who was out for a brisk jaunt along the Backs. The two men walked together to the college gate, and Bartlett recalls that Rivers seemed "cheerful, energetic and well". On Monday morning, Bartlett was again passing St Johns and noticed that the flag was flying at half-mast. He called at the Porter's Lodge and was told "Dr Rivers is dead". To let Bartlett continue the story of this fateful Whitsunday weekend:

Sightseers were everywhere among the Cambridge Colleges, gazing, joking, laughing;

the sun was brilliant; the spring colours were shining. To me, and to many more, it all seemed silly, irrelevant, far away: Rivers was dead.[29]

There seemed no sense in it, for Rivers who was my friend and counsellor had gone, and I should see him no more.[30]

But Bartlett's story was to have a strangely emotive sequel:

A fortnight or so later I met him again, for the last time. I was in the College Combination Room, at the end where the Council meetings are held. The table was set for a meeting. All the members of Council were there but one. There was one vacant chair. Then he came in, erect and quick as usual. He went to the empty chair and sat down. He had no face. Nobody else knew him, but I knew him. I tried to say "Rivers! It's Dr Rivers", and I couldn't utter a word. Then I woke up. I was in bed, at home. It was pitch dark. For what seemed like several minutes I was absolutely sure that he was there, in the deep darkness, close to me. It was a dream. We had talked many times about death. He had said that if he should die before me, as seemed likely, if he could he would try to get through to me . . .[31]

A further aspect of the story which needs to be discussed concerns the fate of kinship studies after Rivers and his immediate students. In one way, it might be said that Rivers and his little school led kinship studies into a scientistic dead-end. While considerable progress had been made towards the goals of developing a foolproof and thoroughly objective ethnographic method, of tightening up the terminological armoury of kinship analysis, and of creating techniques for the precise and unambiguous specification of kinship systems, all these goals ultimately proved to be utopian, given the current state of the art.

This is nicely illustrated by a consideration of a protracted technical debate about the nature of the kinship system employed by the Murngin people of the Northern Territory. The Murngin controversy sputtered into life in 1933 following an article by T. T. Webb which criticized accounts of the Murngin system which William Lloyd Warner had published in 1930 and 1931. The height of the controversy was reached during the 1950s, but in a paper published in 1967, J. A. Barnes judged that the issues involved had still not finally been settled.[32] In many ways this is surprising, since a considerable amount of detailed fieldwork and analysis has been carried out by a number of talented anthropologists in a direct attempt to resolve the controversy. A list of the participants in the debate reads like a roll call of big names in the discipline who have been concerned with Australian social organization. They include Lloyd Warner, Radcliffe-Brown, Barnes, G. P. Murdock, A. P. Elkin, R. M. Berndt, Lester Hiatt and Claude Levi-Strauss. Talent and effort notwithstanding, however, the pattern of the debate has not resembled that of the puzzle-solving which is found in the more developed sciences. The formidable technical apparatus involved in the debate has not functioned as a means of bringing the controversy to a swift resolution, such that all competent practitioners in the area would now agree that the correct puzzle-solution has been obtained. On the contrary, there would seem to be much evidence of what appears to be technical incompetence. Barnes, for example, claims that "a careful study of the literature on this controversy brings to light a remarkable number of obvious errors, statements that look wrong, and inconsistencies between different statements in books and articles by the same author".[33] In support of such a claim, Barnes mentions four separate instances in which writers on the Murngin use diagrams which distort or openly contradict information which is given in the text.[34] He also endorses R. L. Sharp's conclusion that what Lloyd Warner obviously regarded as objective information about the Murngin system, is actually an artefact of "the way in which Warner draws his chart", and of "the rectangular form he thinks it must have".[35] Finally, we should mention Barnes's conclusion that the use of a number of standard concepts from the terminological armoury of social anthropology has, in fact, confused rather than clarified the Murngin debate. Thus, for example, the incautious deployment of Radcliffe-Brown's unsatisfactory notion of a "descent line" has resulted in the reification of an entity which does not exist on the level of ethnographic reality[36] and Levi-Strauss and André Weil have caused confusion by sliding from one meaning of the term "class" to another.[37]

In conclusion then, it seems apparent from the pattern of the Murngin debate that earlier events such as Deacon's apparently unambiguous representation of the Ambrym system and Radcliffe-Brown's sorting out of the varieties of Australian social organization, which look at first sight as though they constitute genuine scientific puzzle-solutions, in fact, represent a kind of false dawn. There is a level upon which the Australian and Ambrym data can *appear* to have been accurately and unambiguously specified. However, it seems that when one looks a little more critically, problems begin to appear. Indeed, what has happened recently in respect of the Ambrym system would seem to provide positive proof that, despite appearances, Deacon's analysis did *not* constitute true scientific "puzzle-solving" in Kuhn's sense. In a 1970 article which I referred to in the first Note to Chapter III, Hal Scheffler argued that Deacon was wrong in interpreting the Ambrym system as involving marriage-classes and suggested instead that it "is nothing more than a simple system of kin classification which features certain unusual rules of terminological extension". Now, ten years after the event, there does not seem to be any firm consensus amongst kinship experts about who was right. So this challenge to Deacon's alleged puzzle-solution has so far proved to be, not a swift and conclusive victory or defeat for Scheffler, but only an indecisive skirmish, such as are not supposed to happen in a "normal" period of a mature scientific discipline.[38]

The conclusion that the apparent scientization of kinship studies by the school of earlier Rivers was actually a false dawn, is independently suggested by the fact that hyperdiffusionism was able to make decisive inroads into British anthropology. As Meyer Fortes has written:

Elliot Smith's fantastic doctrine of the origin of all civilization in Ancient Egypt and its distribution by the mysterious "Children of the Sun" could not have been foisted on a well-grounded scientific discipline.[39]

A consideration of the history of investigations into Australian social organization following the publication of Radcliffe-Brown's 1931 monograph similarly disconfirms the claim that the Rivers—Haddon school had given genuine scientific status to the study of kinship. During the 1930s, Radcliffe-Brown's demonstration that Australian Aboriginal kinship systems embody an incredibly complex set of variations around a few basic themes, and that these variations could be elegantly formalized and usefully compared, seems to have been widely admired in the discipline. However, it rapidly became apparent that the techniques which were useful for analyzing the Australian data, such as the summary statement of section-based prescriptions regarding marriage and descent, were inapplicable to the kinship systems found outside the Australian region. Moreover, the apparent precision of the Australian regulations seemed oddly irrelevant to the issues which began to emerge as central to the study of non-Australian systems. For example, anthropologists became interested in how a kinship system could be flexible enough to accommodate the ephemeral or ambiguous liaisons necessitated by the give-and-take of life in a real society. Given this type of problematic, the Aborigines depicted in Radcliffe-Brown's monograph seemed more like calculating machines than real people. Slowly, therefore, Australian Aboriginal society came to be regarded, not as prototypically "primitive", but as an aberrant adaptation to an abnormally harsh and arid natural environment. And the devotees of Australian kinship algebra were left to ply their strange trade in isolation from the mainstream of kinship studies.[40]

However, this situation was not to last indefinitely. As early as 1939, Phyllis Kaberry revealed, through a tabulation of "regular", "alternate" and "wrong" alliances, that in fact a sizable proportion of Australian marriages do not obey the sectional prescriptions.[41] But what can plausibly be regarded as the real turning point was not reached until 1965, with the publication of L. R. Hiatt's book *Kinship and Conflict*. In a foreword, J. A. Barnes praised Hiatt's discussion of Aboriginal marriage disputes as enabling the reader "to see in action social institutions that hitherto have usually been presented as lifeless sets of rules". According to Barnes, Hiatt's achievement was to present the Aboriginal marriage market

neither as a machine for smoothly circulating brides and generating social solidarity, nor as a social field divided tidily into two opposed moieties or into eight, sixteen or some other number of kin categories. Rather it is an arena in which every man has limited assets (principally nieces) with which to satisfy diverse claims on him for wives and to achieve certain objectives for himself (brides and allies) . . . At the same time women are not chattels in the market but have substantial autonomy . . .[42]

Moreover, Hiatt's analysis demonstrates that

although there is virtually complete consensus about the form of marriage prescribed, and although almost all disputes over women are argued in terms of these prescriptions, nevertheless the proportion of men . . . who are married in conformity with the rule is quite low . . . In fact there is not a single prescriptive rule but a hierarchy of rules.[43]

By such means, Barnes concludes, Hiatt's book "brings Australian ethnography firmly back into the mainstream of contemporary social inquiry". In an acknowledgement, Hiatt then reflects Barnes's praise back upon its originator, stating that it is Barnes himself who should be given credit for putting the Australian Aborigines back on centre-stage. Be that as it may, and whether people other than Hiatt or Barnes should also be given credit, the reinstatement of Australian Aboriginal society to theoretical significance seems real enough.

With regard to the main theme of this book, the moral of these changing estimates of the centrality of Australian social organization would seem to be as follows: In contributing to the exact specification of the marriage-class type of kinship system, Radcliffe-Brown *et al.* must be credited with a genuine and considerable achievement. For the societies concerned they did, in fact, succeed in delineating an idealized pattern of marriage and descent, against which all deviations, however numerous and however serious, can be measured. Certainly any current kinship theorist who has reaped the benefit of an additional half a century's data gathering and theoretical refinement will be able to find deficiencies in knowledge and injudicious usages of terminology. And as I have outlined, the whole presentation now looks far too stark, static and inflexible to cope with the complications and ambiguities of everyday life in a real society. But what cannot be denied is that, at the level at which they were operating, which is the level of idealized mental constructs which exist, certainly in the mind of the anthropologist, and hopefully also in the minds of the informants, they produced something which had the *appearance* of genuine scientific puzzle-solving. For in terms of technical accomplishments like diagrams and symbolic shorthand, in terms of narrowness of focus and the achieving of answers which a small group of practitioners would agree to pronounce either right or wrong, the kinship analyses which emanated from the school of earlier Rivers, filled the puzzle-solving bill very nicely.

So the current situation in kinship studies is that of an enterprise which once had an apparently solid and scientific achievement at an important period of its development, but which has now been forced, by the very complexity of the data, to renege on its programme of attempting to acquire scientific status. The sort of move which Barnes detects in Hiatt's book, in which the presentation of a lifeless set of rules is replaced by a complex description of day-to-day behaviour, can be regarded as the proverbial step backwards which must be taken before another forward step will become feasible.

Modern work on kinship often reflects this heritage of a partial and incomplete acquiring of scientific status. Consider, for example, the alternative ways in which general accounts of a society customarily open by laying out what purports to be the essential specifications of the society's kinship system. One popular approach is to give the specification very briefly and with apparent definiteness in the first few sentences ("Society X is matrilineal and patrilocal . . ."). One might speculate that the author here realizes that her/his anthropological colleagues regard kinship as important, but that, being unwilling or unable to enter into controversy over fine distinctions and points of detail, she/he has opted for sweeping the problem under the front door mat. Another approach is to open with a detailed discussion of a people's social organization, which will typically involve comparisons with the best known examples of aboriginal society (such as the Nuer, the Trobrianders or the Tallensi). The conclusions which result from such discussion are generally advanced with confidence which may seem to be born of certainty. However, when one looks at the nature of the discussion itself, it will commonly embody, not precise puzzle-solutions, but risky analogies, claims, answers to counter-claims and disputation over the appropriateness of applying particular terms in particular social situations. In other words, for all its assertive bravado, the discussion resembles more closely the inconclusive controversies of philosophy, rather than the decisive exchanges typical of a mature science. Nonetheless, it is to be hoped that, if the clear-minded and technically impressive approach of people like Harrison White is pushed a good deal further, the scientistic goals of the school of earlier Rivers will eventually become a reality.

The task of summing up the lasting intellectual and methodological heritage bequeathed by Rivers, would be facilitated if it were possible to depict his influence as spreading uniformly outwards from its Cambridge epicentre, like the ripples on a pond. Unfortunately, however, the reality was not as simple as this. To some extent, of course, the influence of an academic teacher does and must die with him. Inasmuch as Rivers's and Haddon's influence depended upon their ability and willingness to offer their students constructive criticism, to provide them with references and introductions, to get them jobs, to persuade publishers to accept their work, to nominate them to learned societies or to indulge in other string-pullings on a person-to-person basis, Rivers's early demise and Haddon's retirement naturally severed the most central of the threads which bound the Cambridge social anthropological network together. These functions were to some extent passed on to younger members of the school, although Radcliffe-Brown's peripatetic career, Deacon's untimely death, Armstrong's and Barnard's withdrawals from social anthropology and Layard's failure to secure an academic post, did not help in this regard.

One way in which the influence of an academic teacher does live on is, of course, through his publications. And here the direct influence of Rivers was and is considerable. In his 1914 book on *Kinship and Social Organization*, Rivers had argued against A. L. Kroeber's belief that relationship terminology is determined primarily by language and is reflective of psychology rather than of social realities.[44] This argument proved to be important in the transmission of Rivers's influence to the United States. For Robert Lowie gave the book an extended and more-than-favourable review in the *American Anthropologist*, concluding that Rivers had "definitely refuted Professor Kroeber's universal negative as to the sociological causation of kinship terminology", and demonstrated that, "in regions of Melanesia the nomenclature has been partly moulded by the custom of cross-cousin marriages".[45] At the same time, however, Lowie evinced deep-seated scepticism about Rivers's speculations regarding anomalous marriages.[46] In short, Lowie's intention in writing the review would seem to have been to promote what we have characterized as the approach of earlier Rivers, and to downgrade that of later Rivers.[47] And in view of Lowie's standing amongst American anthropologists, and the numerous citations of the review which appear in subsequent American work on kinship, it would seem that this intention was fulfilled.

Moreover, Kroeber himself was later to admit that he had been "intransigent" in his opposition to Rivers, and that it would have been better if he had argued that "as part of language, kin terms reflect unconscious logic and conceptual patterning *as well as* social institutions" (italics in original). And Kroeber went on to give a plausible exposition of the real issues which underlay his debate with Rivers:

Rivers began as a laboratory physiologist who pushed on to psychology and then to ethnology. He was accordingly seeking deterministic proofs as rigorous and definite as in the exact sciences . . . and he found them in the determination of kinship by social institutions . . . I came from humanistic literature, entered anthropology by the gate of linguistics, saw meaning in forms and their relations, but deeply distrusted a determinism that attributed specific, limited but sufficient causes to cultural phenomena.[48]

So, if Kroeber's assessment is given credence, Lowie's support for Rivers's position may be seen as an endorsement of Rivers's programme for giving anthropology the status of a science.

The direct influence of Rivers has not been extinguished, even yet. A perspicacious modern evaluation of anthropological theory detects three major "styles" in the study of kinship.[49] One of these is identified with Britain's Meyer Fortes, another with France's Lévi-Strauss and the final one with America's George Peter Murdock. Fortes and Murdock have explicitly acknowledged their debt to Rivers,[50] and some of Lévi-Strauss's most important work represents an extension of just those passages in Radcliffe-Brown which most clearly derive from Rivers.[51] Indeed, Lévi-Strauss himself in one place, attributes the origination of the "dualist theory" of structural oppositions to "Rivers and his school", and for that reason likens Rivers's role in anthropology to that of Galileo in physics. Since Rivers's time, says Lévi-Strauss in a somewhat overgenerous tribute, "no one has said anything not already anticipated by that great theoretician".[52]

H. W. Scheffler, by contrast, in an article published in 1966, implied that the contemporary Cambridge trio of Fortes, Goody and Leach are guilty of "ancestor worship", in that they credit Rivers with considerable perspicacity in conceptual and terminological matters relating to descent. According to Scheffler, Rivers's notion of descent is confused and outmoded, and he looks forward to the day when Rivers's "ghost may be laid to rest, no longer to trouble an anthropology which has outgrown the 'theoretical' basis of his terminological dogmas".[53] But even if Scheffler is right, there is little doubt that, however harmful, Rivers's influence lives on at his home university.

Despite a widespread lack of credence in Rivers's diffusionistic specula-
tions, no modern anthropologist would think of embarking upon a study of
either Melanesian kinship or the social organization of the Todas without first
familiarizing himself with the Cambridge don's work in those areas. R. and B.
Lane, who specialize in the New Hebrides, continue to widen and consolidate
Rivers's kinship trail in a manner which is very reminiscent of its pioneer.
And to take an example from the previous generation of anthropologists, A.
P. Elkin, who modified and extended Radcliffe-Brown's work on Australian
social organization, attributed his initial interest in the subject to a reading of
Rivers's exposition of the genealogical method in *The History of Melanesian
Society.*[54]

But if it can be said of Rivers that his direct influence has carried over into
the modern era, the same is doubly true of Radcliffe-Brown. The collection
of Radcliffe-Brown's papers entitled *Structure and Function in Primitive
Society* has been a popular textbook in most British and American anthropology departments over the past two or three decades, and selected articles
are also read in related fields such as sociology. Very often, when a modern
social anthropologist wants someone to argue against, he will look first to
Radcliffe-Brown, whose works now seem to epitomize the conventional
wisdom which the young progressive will wish to modify.[55] During his
five-year stay at the University of Chicago, Radcliffe-Brown profoundly
modified the course of American anthropology. In the introduction to a
farewell *Festschrift* which itself constitutes an impressive record of Radcliffe-
Brown's influence, Robert Redfield wrote that

Professor Radcliffe-Brown brought to this country a method for the study of society,
well defined and different enough from what prevailed here to require American anthropologists . . . to scrutinize their objectives, and to attend to new problems . . . Few . . .
have been entirely indifferent, and many have found it necessary to emphasize their
agreement, or disagreement, with his views. One could assemble a small anthology of
papers and chapters written recently each with an eye out to Radcliffe-Brown, the writer
feeling called upon to define or declare his position in a field in which Radcliffe-Brown
appears as leader, adversary, or challenger.[56]

An equally impressive tribute, also in the form of a farewell *Festschrift*, was
produced when Radcliffe-Brown retired from the Chair of Social Anthropology at Oxford in 1946. In the preface to this work, Meyer Fortes wrote
that many of the most important advances made in the study of kinship over
the past quarter of a century have been due to Radcliffe-Brown. Referring to
Radcliffe-Brown's "single-minded and detached devotion to the advancement
of social anthropology 'as a branch of natural science'", Fortes claimed that

he had "founded or revivified teaching and research in social anthropology in
all the five continents". "No living scholar has had so decisive an influence on
the development of social anthropology as A. R. Radcliffe-Brown," averred
Fortes. "As a teacher he is unrivalled; and his writings are ranked among the
classics of anthropology."[57] Finally, we may mention that, in a review of
Structure and Function in Primitive Society, the American sociologist
George Caspar Homans wrote that Radcliffe-Brown "has of course, been the
chief influence in social anthropology for at least a quarter of a century".
After itemizing various aspects of the theory of social structure developed by
Radcliffe-Brown, Homans opined, "No other anthropologist has done so
much. Surely this is the most important contribution to anthropology in our
time . . . "[58]

But however important the *direct* influence of Rivers and Radcliffe-Brown
may have been, it is the *indirect* influence of Rivers which I wish to emphasize
most strongly. For the contributions of Rivers, which have been thoroughly
digested and assimilated into British Social Anthropology, are no less real for
being almost invisible. The modern anthropologist who recognizes that he
cannot do all his research in a library, but must involve himself in participant
observation, probably attributes this innovation, if he attributes it at all,
to Malinowski. Little does he realize that Malinowski was extending and
publicizing the achievements and sentiments of the Torres Straits investigators, including and especially Rivers. The modern fieldworker who assumes
that his investigations can and should be carried out in a methodical fashion,
and who uses genealogies as a fundamental ethnographic tool, probably does
not realize the extent to which not only the procedure, but also its widespread
adoption, were due to the intellectual acuity and effective public relations
work of Rivers. The modern social theorist who assembles a comprehensively
organic account of how a society operates, would probably want to claim as
his main intellectual ancestors Radcliffe-Brown and/or Durkheim. Little does
he realize the important role played by Rivers in making the achievement
of Radcliffe-Brown possible. The modern academic anthropologist who, in
participating in a seminar, assumes that the careful analysis of kinship material
is germane to the understanding of social organization, probably has no idea
of the extent to which his value-system was created and transmitted by Rivers.
The modern anthropological educator who assumes that kinship studies
should be a compulsory strand at all levels of courses in his subject, probably
has only the vaguest idea about the historical pedigree of his assumption.
Little does he realize that, for British anthropology, the real milestones
were firstly Rivers's empirical discovery that kinship plays a crucial role in

aboriginal social organization and, secondly, Rivers's and Haddon's successful promotion of a scientistic ideology which pushed kinship studies to the centre of anthropological theory and practice. What I am saying, in short, is that all modern social anthropologists, whether they recognize the fact or not, are the intellectual and methodological heirs of Rivers.

In many ways, the story I have told is a strange one. Considering his insights and achievements, Rivers's personal perspective on kinship and marriage was a remarkably narrow one. As Raymond Firth has written:

... his treatment of the content of marriage was naive. Rivers remained all his life a bachelor, and his view of what marriage involved, at least as implied in his writings, was an extraordinarily limited one. He regarded it as an "institution", basic to social organization, and was aware of the rights and duties pertaining to spouses, and of the intricate social relationships involved in the bringing up of their children. But in his use of the concept of marriage in his theoretical constructions he focused almost entirely on its legalization of sex relations.[59]

What is more, Radcliffe-Brown, who presented a widely-acclaimed portrayal of the organic functioning of the Kariera marriage-class system, and who demonstrated his sensitivity to the rights and duties attaching to consanguineal and affinal links, had what seems to have been a thoroughly unsatisfactory marriage.[60]

On a more technical and less personal level, it also seems odd that Rivers could have built up such a reputation for expertise when he made no substantial contributions to Australian kinship theory and failed so badly in his self-imposed task of deciphering the Ambrym system of relationship. Similarly, it seems odd that Radcliffe-Brown, being possessed of an equally formidable reputation, and intellectual brilliance which could never be doubted, stooped to such shabby treatment of amateur Australian ethnographers in the process of putting together his otherwise most impressive acccount of Australian social organization.

But history can be both complicated and surprising, and for all its shortcomings, there can be little doubt that the Rivers—Haddon school was instrumental in laying the foundations of British Social Anthropology. In fact, I would go so far as to suggest that the seminal year for the discipline was not 1922, when *Argonauts of the Western Pacific* and *The Andaman Islanders* were published. Rather it was 1912, when the fourth edition of the *Notes and Queries on Anthropology* appeared, containing the brilliant contributions in which Rivers gives the first clear statement of what later came to be identified as the procedural and theoretical basis of British Social Anthropology.

To conclude, I can do no better than to quote from Sol Tax's remarkably perceptive 1935 summation of the history of research into social organization:

To most anthropologists today, Rivers is the founder of the modern study of social organization. Mrs Seligman is his direct disciple; Radcliffe-Brown, his pupil, owes to him his interest in kinship and to some extent its direction; he changed the views of Lowie and Kroeber in America; and the pupils of all of them in the British Commonwealth and in America are indirectly indebted to him. Only Malinowski in England (and not his pupils) was somewhat free from the point of view of Rivers, and, of course, his contributions, in both method and theory, also have some foundation in the work of Rivers.[61]

In fact, on Tax's account, it was Rivers who, "almost single-handed, made research into the social organization of tribes what it is today".[62]

NOTES AND REFERENCES

PREFACE

[1] In the period of history covered by the present work, the words most commonly used to describe the type of society studied by anthropologists were "primitive" and "savage". Since however, neither of these words can be used without strongly pejorative overtones, I have done my best to avoid them, substituting instead more emotionally neutral words like "aboriginal", "indigenous" and "preliterate". None of these words is perfectly suited to the job at hand and the result may sometimes come out sounding rather oddly. Nonetheless, I would rather be guilty of minor offences of usage than of encouraging Eurocentric prejudice.

[2] Peter Lawrence, "The Ethnographic Revolution", *Oceania* 45, 253–271 (1975).

[3] A recent work which makes a start in this direction is *Perspectives on the Emergence of Scientific Disciplines*, Gérard Lemaine, Roy MacLeod, Michael Mulkay and Peter Weingart (eds.), (The Hague and Chicago, 1977). From our point of view the most interesting contribution is Michael Worboy's study of British tropical medicine, a discipline which, largely because of its relationship to British imperialism, exhibited a maturation process which bore many similarities to that of British Social Anthropology.

[4] Jairus Banaji, "The Crisis of British Social Anthropology", *New Left Review* 64, 75 (Nov.–Dec. 1970).

[5] E. E. Evans-Pritchard's famous 1940 ethnography on *The Nuer*, for example, often regarded as the ultimate achievement of British Social Anthropology, presents the Nuer as a self-contained, static and harmoniously-operating group. However, it is evident from a number of things which Evans-Pritchard mentions in passing that, in fact, the Nuer interact so substantially with the neighbouring Dinka people that, instead of reifying "the Nuer" as a self-contained social entity, it may well have been more sensible to write a book about the Nuer-Dinka complex. Moreover, it also seems apparent from things he lets slip about Arab incursions into Nuerland, and the impact of Anglo-Egyptian colonialism, that the society may be undergoing permanent undirectional changes, and may embody elements which are essentially dysfunctional.

[6] Mead was at one stage married to Reo Fortune and, later, to Gregory Bateson. For a not-very-revealing account of these relationships and a retrospective look at her early work in cultural and social anthropology, see her autobiography, *Blackberry Winter* (New York, 1972). It must not be imagined, however, that all was roses between Mead and British anthropologists generally. As one of my referees wrote in response to an earlier draft of the present work, "She certainly hated and was warmly hated in turn by the majority of British Social Anthropologists of whom the outstanding instance was E. E. Evans-Pritchard. I knew Mead and at one point when I taught in England discussed this with her and it was people like Firth and the humane Fortes whom she could abide, if not feel intellectually warm toward."

7 Malinowski, article on "Culture" from the 1931 *Encyclopaedia of the Social Sciences*, p. 625. Quoted in Gregory Bateson, *Naven* (2nd edn., Stanford, 1958), p. 27.

8 Meyer Fortes has objected strenuously to my use of this phrase in such a context. However, I can see absolutely no reason why a phrase which social anthropologists themselves use in a wide variety of contexts should not be applied to the discipline itself. After all, for most young anthropologists, intensive fieldwork is (*inter alia*) an ordeal which must be gone through before their senior colleagues will regard them as having crossed the threshold into the profession. Or perhaps Professor Fortes thinks that social anthropologists are beyond the pale of human society?

9 J. H. M. Beattie, "Kinship and Social Anthropology", *Man* 64, 102 (1964); P. Rigby, *Cattle and Kinship Among the Gogo* (Cornell, 1969), p. 298 n.

10 Robin Fox, *Kinship and Marriage* (Penguin, Harmondsworth, 1967), p. 10.

11 M. Fortes, *Kinship and the Social Order* (Chicago, 1969), p. 12.

12 J. G. Frazer, "William Robertson Smith", in *The Gorgon's Head And Other Literary Pieces* (London, 1927), pp. 286, 287. The piece on Robertson Smith was originally published in 1894.

13 Barbara Freire-Marreco and John Linton Myres (eds.), *Notes and Queries on Anthropology* (4th edn., London, 1912), p. 250.

14 Ibid., pp. 252, 254.

15 Ibid., p. 255.

16 Ibid., pp. 254, 255.

17 Fortes, op. cit. (note 11), p. 219.

18 Ibid., p. 13.

19 An excellent introduction to Stocking's work is provided by the collection of his papers entitled *Race, Culture and Evolution* (Free Press, New York, 1968).

20 Ibid., p. 157.

21 I am not alone in using the word "school" to refer to the anthropological movement which emanated from Cambridge University. Meyer Fortes, for example, uses the word with a capital "S" in his *Social Anthropology at Cambridge since 1900* (Cambridge, 1953), pp. 16, 18, 45. See also G. Elliot Smith, letter to the editor of *The Times Literary Supplement* of 7 Oct. 1926; and C. Lévi-Strauss, *Structural Anthropology* (New York, 1967), p. 158.

22 A book which, like mine, attempts to give a realistic account of a specific British academic movement is Ernest Gellner's *Words and Things* (Pelican, Harmondsworth, 1968), which represents a critique of "Linguistic Philosophy". While the book is very amusing and in many ways informative, and while Gellner claims to be giving both a "logical" and "sociological" account of the movement (p. 18), it happens to be a fact that, as Gellner remarks, "the logic of the ideas [in Linguistic Philosophy] is in a sense also the sociology of the movement" (p. 179). For this reason the book is a lot less sociologically informative than one might have hoped. Nonetheless, for anyone interested in the dynamics of small, inbred intellectual movements, it might be an interesting exercise to read Gellner's book in parallel with mine.

23 Thomas S. Kuhn, "Reflections on My Critics", in I. Lakatos and A. Musgrave (eds.), *Criticism and the Growth of Knowledge* (Cambridge, first published 1970, reprinted with corrections 1974), pp. 237, 238.

24 Ibid., pp. 245–247, 254.

25 Ibid., p. 6.

[26] In his *Anthropologists and Anthropology* (Peregrine, 1975), for example, Adam Kuper uses 1922 as the "baseline" for his book, primarily because this was the year in which Malinowski and Radcliffe-Brown published their first major field-studies, and secondarily because this was also the year in which Rivers, "the greatest figure in the pre-functionalist generation", died. Kuper in fact goes so far as to say that 1922 was "the *annus mirabilis* of functionalism", and that when Malinowski and Radcliffe-Brown set British Social Anthropology going, "they had all the lonely certainty of prophets and seers" (pp. 9, 10).

CHAPTER I

[1] See for example Colin Rosser and Christopher Harris, *The Family and Social Change. A Study of Family and Kinship in a South Wales Town* (London, 1965).

[2] See for example Marvin Harris, *Cows, Pigs, Wars and Witches. The Riddles of Culture* (Glasgow, 1977). The entire book is relevant to the issue of aboriginal pragmatism, although an excellent sample of Harris's approach may be obtained from the section entitled "Mother Cow".

[3] Leslie A. White, "How Morgan Came to Write *Systems of Consanguinity and Affinity*", *Papers of the Michigan Academy of Science, Arts and Letters* 42 (1957). Carl Resek, *Lewis Henry Morgan: American Scholar* (Chicago, 1960).

[4] Quoted in Resek, ibid., p. 26.

[5] Quoted in Resek, ibid., p. 36.

[6] Quoted in White, op. cit. (note 3), p. 262.

[7] Ibid., pp. 262, 263.

[8] Resek, op. cit. (note 3), p. 78.

[9] Ibid., p. 97 ff.

[10] c.f. M. Harris, *The Rise of Anthropological Theory* (New York, 1968), p. 185.

[11] Resek, op. cit. (note 3), p. 98.

[12] Lewis Henry Morgan, *Ancient Society* (London, 1877), p. 62.

[13] *American [Whig] Review* 5 186 (1847). The same sentence occurs in Morgan's *League of the Iroquois*, (1962 Corinth Books reprint of original 1851 edn.), p. 82.

[14] See, for example, the first few pages of Chapter IV.

[15] A more detailed and technical discussion of classificatory kinship systems, in which ten "indicative features" are listed may be found in Morgan's *Systems of Consanguinity and Affinity* . . . (Washington, 1870), pp. 155–161.

[16] W. H. R. Rivers, *Kinship and Social Organization* (London, 1914), pp. 4, 5.

[17] J. G. Frazer, Introduction to R. R. Marett and T. K. Penniman (eds.), *Spencer's Last Journey* (Oxford, 1931), p. 9.

[18] Robin Fox, *Kinship and Marriage* (Penguin, Harmondsworth, 1967), p. 260.

[19] Ibid. Fox's account is written against the background of extensive debates, which occurred during the first half of the present century, about whether or not certain aboriginal peoples recognize a connection between copulation and pregnancy. For a polemical modern discussion of some of the issues involved in these debates, see Edmund Leach, "Virgin Birth", *Proc. Roy. Anthrop. Instit.* 1966, pp. 39–49. For a comprehensive general review of the debates up until 1936, see M. F. Ashley Montagu, *Coming into Being Among the Australian Aborigines* (London, 1937), Chaps. 1–10.

[20] A. R. Radcliffe-Brown, "On Social Structure", original 1940, reprinted in A. R. Radcliffe-Brown, *Structure and Function in Primitive Society* (New York, Free Press edn., 1965), p. 203.

[21] F. Engels, *Origin of the Family, Private Property and the State* (reprint of 4th edn., Moscow, 1952), p. 13. See also pp. 30–32.

[22] Specifically J. F. McLennan, John Lubbock, Andrew Lang and, to a lesser extent, E. B. Tylor, were perceived as hostile. Bernard J. Stern (ed.), "Selections from the Letters of Lorimer Fison and A. W. Howitt to Lewis Henry Morgan", *Am. Anthrop.* NS **32** (1930), passim.

[23] J. H. Morgan, 'Introduction' to Everyman's Library edn. of Sir Henry Maine, *Ancient Law* (London and New York, 1917), p. v.

[24] Sir Henry Maine, *Ancient Law* (London and New York, 1917. Originally published 1861), p. 74.

[25] Ibid., p. 88.

[26] Ibid., p. 91.

[27] Ibid., p. 99.

[28] Ibid., p. 100.

[29] John F. McLennan, *Primitive Marriage. An Inquiry into the Origin of The Form of Capture in Marriage Ceremonies* (Chicago and London, 1970. Originally published 1865), p. 5.

[30] Ibid., p. 6.

[31] Ibid., p. 17. The passage cited is actually a quotation from Lord Kame's *Sketches of the History of Man* (Edinburgh, 1807).

[32] Quoted in H. R. Hays, *From Ape to Angel. An Informal History of Social Anthropology* (New York, Capricorn edn., 1964), p. 45.

[33] Peter Rivière's 'Introduction' to John F. McLennan, *Primitive Marriage* (Chicago and London, 1970), p. xiii.

[34] W. Robertson Smith, *Kinship and Marriage in Early Arabia* (London, 1907. Originally published 1885), p. 27.

[35] Ibid., p. 30. See also E. L. Peters, article on 'William Robertson Smith' in the *International Encyclopaedia of the Social Sciences* (Macmillan and Free Press, 1968), p. 333.

[36] Robertson Smith, op. cit. (note 34), p. xi.

[37] Peters, op. cit. (note 35), p. 333.

[38] Ibid., p. 329.

[39] E. B. Tylor, *Researches Into The Early History of Mankind* (London, 1865). 1878 edn., p. 279. Quoted in M. Fortes, *Kinship and the Social Order* (Chicago, 1969), p. 12.

[40] *J. Anthrop. Inst.* **18**, 245–269 (1888).

[41] James Frazer, "William Robertson Smith", in Frazer, *The Gorgon's Head and Other Literary Pieces* (London, 1927), pp. 281, 282.

[42] Quoted in E. O. James, "Sir James George Frazer O. M., F. R. S., F. B. A.", *Man* **42**, 2 (1942).

[43] Quoted in Abram Kardiner and Edward Preble, *They Studied Man* (New York, 1963), p. 74.

[44] c.f. G. M. Young, *Victorian England: Portrait of An Age* (Oxford, 1960), pp. 149, 109, 74 ff, 69 n. 2.

[45] These two lines occur in the "Double Ballade of Primitive Man". In Andrew Lang, *XXXII Ballades in Blue China* (London, 1888), pp. 44–46. A footnote at the end of

the ballad reveals that the stanza in which the lines occur was written by "an eminent Anthropologist" [i.e., Tylor]. See also the article on Tylor by George W. Stocking Jnr in the *International Encyclopaedia of the Social Sciences* (New York, 1968).

[46] Quoted in Kardiner and Preble, op. cit. (note 43), p. 91.

[47] Bibliography of Tylor in *Anthropological Essays Presented to Edward Burnett Tylor in Honour of His 75th Birthday* (Oxford, 1907).

[48] R. R. Marett and T. K. Penniman (eds.), *Spencer's Scientific Correspondence With Sir J. G. Frazer and Others* (Oxford, 1932), p. 43.

[49] Edmund Leach, "Frazer and Malinowski", *Encounter* 25: 5, 30 (November, 1965). See also Edmund Leach, "Golden Bough or Gilded Twig?" *Daedalus* (Spring 1961), p. 376. The first-mentioned of these two articles sparked off a substantial and interesting debate. Ian Jarvie replied in defence of Frazer in *Encounter* of April 1966, and Leach replied to Jarvie in the May 1966 issue of the same periodical. All three items were then reprinted in *Current Anthrop.* 7: 5 (December 1966), together with further comments by a number of other contributors, and a final reply by Leach. While Leach ends up by conceding one or two points to his critics, his attack on Frazer's anthropological scholarship emerges, in my judgement, substantially intact.

[50] Fox, op. cit. (note 18), p. 195.

[51] Harrison C. White, *An Anatomy of Kinship. Mathematical Models For Structure of Cumulated Roles* (Englewood Cliffs, New Jersey, 1963). White's book also contains, in the form of appendices, two pioneering attempts, by André Weil and Robert R. Bush respectively, to apply mathematical methods to kinship systems of the Australian kind. Here, therefore, between the one set of covers is an interesting collection of mathematically sophisticated contributions towards a general theory of systems of relationship.

[52] For example, in his discussion of the Murngin system, White apparently obtains all his data from Lloyd Warner's 1937 book *A Black Civilization*, thereby ignoring a whole host of other investigators.

[53] White, op. cit. (note 51), pp. 51, 97. Ones mother's brother's child and ones father's sister's child are called "cross-cousins" because, in any unilineal system, these kinsmen will not be in one's descent group. In traversing the relationships which connect ego with the kinsmen in question, the lines of descent must be "crossed". The mother's brother's child may be labelled more precisely as the "matrilateral" variety of cross-cousin, and the father's sister's child as the "patrilateral" variety.

[54] Ibid., pp. 68, 145.

[55] Ibid., pp. 76, 109, 110.

[56] J. A. Barnes, *Inquest on the Murngin* (London, 1967), p. 11. For the proof that there are six distinct kinds of four-class system, see John G. Kemeny *et al.*, *Introduction to Finite Mathematics* (2nd edn., Englewood Cliffs, New Jersey, 1966), p. 432.

[57] J. A. Barnes, personal communication.

[58] Barnes, op. cit. (note 56).

[59] A precursor of this kind of schema was first developed by Howitt in 1888, adopted by Stirling in 1896, and by Spencer and Gillen in 1904. The slightly modified form represented by my Figure 1 was first used by Radcliffe-Brown, in 1910.

[60] In adding symbols for men and women to the schema, I am following a practice developed by John Layard in his book *Stone Men of Malekula* (Chatto and Windus, 1942). Layard, however, did not normally set out his diagrams like my Figure 2. As we

shall find out later in the book, he devised circular methods of representation which reflect very nicely the repetitive structure of marriage-class systems.

[61] See Barnes, op. cit. (note. 56), pp. 10, 11. Also Kenneth Maddock, *The Australian Aborigines. A Portrait of their Society* (Pelican, Harmondsworth, 1974), p. 74.

[62] Anthropology is sufficiently male-chauvinistic to always talk about men exchanging women, and never about women exchanging men. Which locution is the more appropriate in any particular instance would depend upon which sex plays the more active role in arranging marriages.

[63] See Barnes, op. cit. (note 56) pp. 10, 11. Also Maddock, op. cit. (note 61), p. 74.

During the early twentieth-century there was some debate about whether the allocation of children to marriage-classes in eight-class systems proceeds matrilineally or patrilineally. This will be mentioned in Chapter VII in my account of the development of Radcliffe-Brown's career. However, a more issue-oriented discussion of the same debate would seem to be appropriate at this point.

At the turn of the century, R. H. Mathews had described the marriage-class systems of a number of tribes from the Northern Territory. According to Mathews, the women in these tribes can be classified into two "cycles", descent from class to class within the cycles being determined matrilineally. In their 1904 book *The Northern Tribes of Central Australia*, Spencer and Gillen had discussed a Northern Territory tribe which they called the "Bingongina". They presented a table giving the class-governed regulations for marriage and descent among the Bingongina, and asserted that the tribe is divided into two moieties which the natives call "Wiliuku" and "Liaraku". In an article entitled "Matrilineal Descent, Northern Territory", published in the 1908 volume of *Man*, Mathews claimed that, while Spencer and Gillen's speculations for the Bingongina marriage-class system were very similar to data which he himself had reported, Spencer and Gillen had arranged their tabulation of the Bingongina classes in such a way as to imply that, within the so-called "moieties", descent took place patrilineally. Citing descent practices stemming from non-standard marriages, Matthews claimed that it is possible for Liaraku children to have Wiliuku fathers. Hence, it seemed clear to Mathews that, whatever Wiliuku and Liaraku represent, they can hardly be two independent, patrilineal moieties. "Consequently", Mathews concluded, "Spencer and Gillen have utterly failed . . . to prove descent through the men". A further article by Mathews, also published in 1908 (*Am. Anthrop.* NS 10, 88–102), discussed marriage and descent among the Arunta (or, as Mathews spelled the name, "Arranda"). In this article Mathews alleged that inquiries made by "a friend" in 1899 had revealed that the classes of the Arunta had "consolidated" since the Reverend Louis Schulze made his pioneering investigations one or two decades previously. Following this consolidation, all the women of the tribe could be placed in two cycles. (These cycles were presumably not given names by the Arunta, since Mathew labels them simply "A" and "B".) Within each of these alleged cycles, descent from class to class is traced via the women. Thus once again, Mathews was pushing a matrilineal interpretation of an eight-class system.

In April 1910, A. R. Radcliffe-Brown published a reply to Mathews called "Marriage and Descent in North Australia" (*Man* 10, 32). On this occasion Radcliffe-Brown argued that it makes no sense just to talk about "descent". Rather one has to talk about descent with respect to class, phratry or totem. And where four or more classes are involved, one must take irregular marriages into account in order to decide which line of descent is being followed. Using Arunta genealogies from articles by Mathews, Radcliffe-Brown arrived at what he called a "law", which states that the evidence of irregular marriages indicates that the Arunta count descent, as regards class, in the paternal line. In the June 1912 issue of *Man*, Mathews came back with a further article in which however he managed to ignore Radcliffe-Brown's main point about it not making sense to talk about descent in isolation from social units, and did little more than restate his former conclusion about descent in various Australian tribes. The last word in the dispute would seem to have been uttered by Radcliffe-Brown. In the August 1912 issue of *Man*, Radcliffe-Brown took Mathews to task for missing the point. Where a tribe is divided into four or eight classes, wrote Radcliffe-Brown, then as long as we consider only the classes, "and take note only of regular marriages, there can be no question as to whether descent is through the father or the mother. In every case it is through both". Where classes are grouped into moieties, it *does* make sense to talk about descent with respect to the moieties. Mathews apparently wishes to deny, said Radcliffe-Brown, that the named moieties reported by Spencer and Gillen really exist. But Radcliffe-Brown could see no reason for doubting the accuracy of Spencer and Gillen's fieldwork.

In view of the fact that, in this early debate, Radcliffe-Brown's patrilineal interpretation of the Arunta class system appeared to have won the day, it is interesting to note that currently accepted opinion endorses the matrilineal interpretation.

[64] This mode of presentation is borrowed from Barnes's article on "Genealogies" in A. L. Epstein (ed.), *The Craft of Social Anthropology* (London, 1967), pp. 126, 127. In this source Barnes states that his method of depicting class-systems is based upon the indigenous system of representation which Deacon recorded in Ambrym in 1927. However, in a recent communication with the author, Barnes described this method as "a simplified adaptation of Layard's circular diagrams". At any rate, the distinction is a fine one, since, as we shall learn in Chapter VI, Layard's circular diagrams would seem to have been created in the first instance as a means of systematizing the expositions of the Ambrym kinship system given by Deacon's informants.

One aspect of Barnes's mode of presentation which I have not borrowed is his numerical notation for the classes. Now, as Barnes demonstrates in *Inquest On the Murngin*, p. 15 ff, and as Maddock reiterates in his book on *The Australian Aborigines* (Pelican, Harmondsworth, 1974, p. 79 ff), this notation can be quite illuminating in many ways. However, for historical reasons it seemed sensible that I should stick to modes of presentation which were actually used by people who took part in the developments being recounted. Also I did not want to overwhelm my reader with too many alternative modes of presentation.

[65] A. W. Howitt, "Further Notes on the Australian Class Systems", *J. Anthrop. Inst.* 18, 44 (1888).

[66] As set out by Barnes op. cit. (note 56), p. 15.

[67] Barnes's article on "Genealogies" in A. L. Epstein (ed.), *The Craft of Social Anthropology* (London, 1967), p. 126.

[68] Fox, op. cit. (note 18), Chap. 7.

[69] E. B. Tylor, review of *Kamilaroi and Kurnai*, *The Academy*, 9 Apr. 1881, No. 466, p. 264.

[70] Lorimer Fison and A. W. Howitt, *Kamilaroi and Kurnai* (Melbourne, 1880), p. 37 fn.

[71] W. Ridley, "On the Kamilaroi Tribe of Australians and Their Dialect", *J. Ethnological Soc. Lond.* 4, 285–293 (1856).

[72] At one point (ibid., p. 289) Ridley refers to the "privileged class of ippai". One

suspects that his informant came from this class, and that this fact (assuming it was a fact) constituted the only sense in which Ridley would have been justified in labelling the class "privileged".

[73] According to Ridley (ibid., p. 288) an Ippai can sometimes marry an Ippata.

[74] Fison and Howitt, op. cit. (note 70), p. 48 n.

[75] W. Ridley, "Report on Australian Languages and Traditions", *J. Anthrop. Inst.* 2, 257–291 (1872).

[76] Ibid.

[77] Ibid.

[78] Fison, memoranda appended to paper on Australian kinship by Lewis Henry Morgan, *Proc. Amer. Acad. Arts Sci.* 8, 429–438 (1868–1873).

[79] Morgan, ibid., pp. 412–428.

[80] W. E. H. Stanner, article on Fison in *Australian Dictionary of Biography*, Vol. 4, 1851–1890 (Melbourne, 1972).

[81] Fison and Howitt, op. cit. (note 70), section entitled "Theory of the Kurnai System . . . ". In 1892, Fison wrote that the theory of the Kurnai system which he advanced in *Kamilaroi and Kurnai* is "not worth a rush", since further enquiry showed conclusively that the Kurnai arrived at their system "by a different road". (Quoted in J. G. Frazer, "Fison and Howitt", in Frazer, *The Gorgon's Head and Other Literary Pieces* (London, 1927), pp. 300, 301.

[82] Ibid., section on "Kamilaroi Marriage, Descent and Relationship . . . ".

[83] Ibid., p. 27.

[84] Ibid., p. 67.

[85] Ibid., p. 132.

[86] Lewis Henry Morgan, conclusion to *Ancient Society* (London, 1877).

[87] Fison and Howitt, op. cit. (note 70), p. 128.

[88] Ibid., pp. 33–40.

[89] Ibid., p. 203, pp. 103, 104.

[90] Tylor, op. cit. (note 69).

[91] Fison and Howitt, op. cit. (note 70), p. 179.

[92] A. W. Howitt and L. Fison, "From Mother-Right to Father-Right", *J. Anthrop. Inst.* 12, 33, 34 (1883). A. W. Howitt and L. Fison, "On the Deme and the Horde", *J. Anthrop. Inst.* 14, 142–169 (1885). See also letter from Howitt to Morgan dated 18 Aug. 1881, in B. J. Stern (ed.), "Selections from the Letters of Lorimer Fison and A. W. Howitt to Lewis Henry Morgan", *Am. Anthrop.* 32, 447 ff (1930). See also Howitt's reply to McLennan in *Nature*, 7 Sept. 1882, p. 452.

[93] A. W. Howitt, "Notes on the Australian Class Systems", *J. Anthrop. Inst.* 12 (1883). Surprisingly by 1904, Howitt had forgotten that he had put forward this theory, and attributed it to Frazer. Frazer later realized the error and corrected it. See J. G. Frazer, "Fison and Howitt", in Frazer, *The Gorgon's Head and Other Literary Pieces* (London, 1927), pp. 315, 316.

[94] A. W. Howitt, "Further Notes on the Australian Class Systems", *J. Anthrop. Inst.* 18, 41 ff (1888).

[95] A. W. Howitt, "The Dieri and Other Kindred Tribes of Central Australia", *J. Anthrop. Inst.* 20, 36, 37 (1891). See also Howitt, op. cit. (note 93), p. 499 fn.

[96] Howitt, op. cit. (note 94).

[97] Ibid., p. 44 ff.

98 Howitt, op. cit. (note 93), p. 510. Howitt, op. cit. (note 94), p. 31.

99 Howitt, op. cit. (note 94), p. 42.

100 Marett and Penniman, op. cit. (note 48), p. 108.

101 Louis Schulze, "The Aborigines of the Upper and Middle Finke River . . . ", *Trans. Roy. Soc. Sth. Aust.* 14, 223 ff (1891).

102 An almost complete bibliography of Mathews's publications up until 1904 is given in the *J. Roy. Soc. New Sth. Wales* 38, 376—381 (1904).

103 A. P. Elkin, "A. R. Radcliffe-Brown, 1880—1955", *Oceania* 26, 249, 250 (1956).

104 R. H. Mathews, "Divisions of Australian Tribes", *Proc. Am. Phil. Soc.* 37, 151—154 (1898).

105 The eight further articles are listed in the final article of the series: R. H. Mathews, "The Wombya Organization of the Australian Aborigines", *Am. Anthrop.* NS 2, 494—501 (1900).

106 R. H. Mathews, "The Origin, Organization and Ceremonies of the Australian Aborigines", *Am. Phil. Soc. Proc.* 39, Plate VIII (1900).

107 R. H. Mathews, "Social Organization of the Chingalee Tribe, Northern Australia", *Am. Anthrop.* NS 7, 301—304 (1905).

108 *Nature*, 9 May 1907, pp. 31—32; 28 Nov. 1907, pp. 80, 81.

109 Howitt's message was published in the *Revue des Etudes Ethnographiques et Sociologiques* for December 1908.

110 Howitt Collection, La Trobe Library, Melbourne.

111 R. H. Mathews, "The Totemistic System in Australia", *Am. Antiq.* 28, 147 (1906).

112 R. R. Marett, "Memoir", in Marett and Penniman, op. cit. (note 17), pp. 22, 23.

113 Ibid., p. 25. Hays, op. cit. (note 32), p. 91.

114 W. Baldwin Spencer (ed.), *Report on the Work of the Horn Scientific Expedition to Central Australia* (London, 1896), Part IV, "Anthropology" by E. C. Stirling, pp. 45, 47.

115 Marett and Penniman, op. cit. (note 17), p. 26.

116 G. Elliot Smith, review of *The Arunta* by Spencer and Gillen in *The Sunday Times*, 11 Dec. 1927.

117 Marett and Penniman, op. cit. (note 17), p. 30.

118 W. Baldwin Spencer and F. J. Gillen, *The Native Tribes of Central Australia* (London, 1899), pp. 56—58.

119 Ibid., pp. 60, 61, 71, tables facing pp. 67, 81.

120 Ibid., p. 56.

121 Ibid., p. 55.

122 Ibid., p. 70.

123 Ibid., pp. 55, 59 ff. See also W. Baldwin Spencer and F. J. Gillen, *The Northern Tribes of Central Australia* (London, 1904), pp. 70—77.

124 É. Durkheim, "Sur le Totemisme", *Année Sociologique* 5, 104, 105 ff (1900—1901).

125 Frazer, "The Origin of Totemism", Parts I and II, *Fortnightly Review* NS 65, 836 (Jan. to June 1899). These two articles, which aroused a storm of controversy in the decade following their publication, provide a good brief introduction to Frazer's views on totemism.

126 Marett and Penniman, op. cit. (note 48), passim.

127 Radcliffe-Brown. "Australian Social Organization", *Am. Anthrop.* NS 49, 154 (1947).

[128] N. W. Thomas, *Kinship Organizations and Group Marriage in Australia* (Cambridge, 1906), p. viii.

[129] Marett and Penniman, op. cit. (note 17), "Introduction" by J. G. Frazer, p. 1.

[130] John G. Withnell, "Marriage Rites and Relationships", *Science of Man* 6, 42 (1903). Quoted in Rodney Needham, *Remarks and Inventions: Skeptical Essays About Kinship* (London, 1974), pp. 141, 142.

[131] Robert H. Lowie, review of W. H. R. Rivers, *Kinship and Social Organization* in *Am. Anthrop.* NS 17, 329, 330 (1915).

[132] For an entertaining account of how this heavy-handedness was manifested in the medical profession, see Alex Comfort, *The Anxiety Makers* (Panther, 1968).

[133] In an article called "Science and Society in Nineteenth Century Anthropology", published in the 1974 volume of *History of Science*, Gay Weber sketches out a case for including professional affiliations within a generalized class-analysis of nineteenth-century anthropological evolutionism. See especially Weber, p. 281.

[134] For an excellent account of the anthropological significance of the Brixham Cave excavations, see Jacob Gruber, "Brixham Cave and the Antiquity of Man". In M. E. Spiro (ed.), *Context and Meaning in Cultural Anthropology* (New York, 1965).

[135] George W. Stocking Jnr., *Race, Culture, and Evolution. Essays in the History of Anthropology* (New York, 1968), pp. 105–106. For a more general statement of the case that nineteenth-century anthropology was dominated by the desire to dispense with God as an active historical agent, see Marvin Harris, *The Rise of Anthropological Theory. A History of Theories of Culture* (New York, 1968), especially pp. 55, 210–211.

CHAPTER II

[1] For a discussion of Malinowski's debt to, and divergence from Rivers, see the present work Chapter V, pp. 171–177. For a statement of the case for regarding Radcliffe-Brown as a disciple of Rivers, see ibid., Chapter VII, pp. 271–282.

[2] As an indication of Rivers's international standing, let me point out that in 1926, Margaret Mead, who had been educated as a disciple of Boas in America, and Reo Fortune, a young New Zealand psychologist who later became a noted anthropologist, discovered that they had independently concluded that Rivers "was the man under whom we would like to have studied – a shared and impossible daydream, since he had died in 1922". Mead, *Blackberry Winter* (New York, 1972), p. 158.

As an indication of his standing with his closest British colleague, let me point to the statements of Haddon which I have quoted in Chapter II, p. 67.

As an indication of his influence during the formative war years on one of British anthropology's young Turks, let me point to the fact that Malinowski's New Guinea diaries contain many references to Rivers, of which I have quoted the most pertinent in Chapter V, pp. 172, 173.

As an indication of his interdisciplinary standing in the United States, let me point out that, after Rivers's death, the American Ethnological Society and the Psychological and Anthropological Sections of the New York Academy of Sciences staged a "Rivers Memorial Meeting", at which a number of prominent personages paid tribute to Rivers's work in experimental psychology, ethnology and psychoanalysis.

[3] A. C. Haddon, "Report to the Percy Sladen Trustees on the Expedition to Papua", Haddon Collection, Envelope 25.

[4] Joseph Ben David and Randall Collins, "Social Factors in the Origins of a New Science: The Case of Psychology", *Am. Soc. Rev.* **31**, 451—456 (Aug. 1966).

Items giving biographical information about Rivers, and/or analysis of his work, are listed below in approximate order of usefulness:

Richard Slobodin, *W. H. R. Rivers* (New York, 1978), 295 pp. This book contains an assiduously researched "Life" of Rivers running to 85 pages, a series of evaluations of key aspects of Rivers's work, a representative selection of Rivers's writings, and a bibliography of works cited by Slobodin by and about Rivers.

Ethel S. Fegan, "Bibliography" [of Rivers], *Man* **61**, 100—104 (1922).

Charles S. Myers, "The Influence of the Late W. H. R. Rivers (President Elect of Section J) on the Development of Psychology in Great Britain". Address to Section J (Psychology) by Charles S. Myers, President of the Section. *Rep. Brit. Ass. Adv. Sci.* (1922), pp. 179—192.

Edmund R. Leach, "W. H. R. Rivers", *International Encyclopaedia of the Social Sciences* (New York, 1968), Vol. 13, pp. 526—528.

L. E. Shore, "W. H. R. Rivers", *The Eagle* [Magazine of St John's College Cambridge], 1922, pp. 2—12.

Arnold Bennett, "W. H. R. Rivers: Some Recollections", in Bennett, *Things That Have Interested Me* (2nd Ser., London, 1923), pp. 1—7.

Siegfried Sassoon, *Sherston's Progress* (London, 1936) Part I, pp. 13—89.

A. C. Haddon (a), "The Late Dr W. H. R. Rivers, F.R.S.", *Nature*, 17 June 1922, pp. 786—787.

A. C. Haddon (b), "William Halse Rivers Rivers . . .", *Man* **22**, 97—99 (1922).

Henry Head (a), "W. H. R. Rivers, M.D., D.Sc, F.R.S. An Appreciation", *Brit. Med. J.*, 17 June 1922, pp. 977, 978.

Henry Head (b), "Obituary for W. H. R. Rivers", *Proc. Roy. Soc. Ser. B*, **95**, xliii—xlvii (1924).

F. C. Bartlett (a), "William Halse Rivers Rivers . . .", *Man* **22**, 99—100 (1922).

F. C. B[artlett] (b), "W. H. R. Rivers", *The Eagle* [Magazine of St John's College Cambridge], 1922, pp. 12—14.

Frederic C. Barlett (c), "Cambridge, England — 1887—1937", *Am. J. Psych.* **50**, 102—107 (1937).

Frederic Bartlett (d), "W. H. R. Rivers", *The Eagle* [Magazine of St John's College Cambridge] **62**, 156—160 (1968).

Walter Langdon-Brown, *Thus We Are Men* (London, 1938), pp. 62—67.

H. D. S[kinner], "Obituary, Dr W. H. R. Rivers", *J. Polyn. Soc.* **31**, 87—88 (1922).

J. L. Myres, "W. H. R. Rivers", *J. Roy. Anthrop. Inst.* **53**, 14—17 (1923).

C. G. Seligman, "Dr. W. H. R. Rivers", pp. 162, 163 [source unidentified], Haddon Collection, Envelope 12081.

Morris Ginsberg, "The Sociological Work of the Late Dr W. H. R. Rivers", *Psyche* **5**, 33—52 (1924—25).

Anonymous obituary in *Brit. Med. J.*., 10 June 1922, pp. 936, 937.

Erwin H. Ackerknecht, "In Memory of William H. R. Rivers 1864—1922", *Bull. Hist. Med.* **11**, 478—481 (1942).

The Times, assorted items for 7 June, 14 June, 15 June, 16 June, 9 Sept. and 12 Sept. 1922.

Interesting biographical snippets about Rivers are also contained in the following:

T. H. Pear, "Some Early Relations Between English Ethnologists and Psychologists", *J. Roy. Anthrop. Inst.* 90, 227–237 (1960).

Siegfried Sassoon, *Siegfried's Journey 1916–1920* (London, 1945). See especially pp. 64, 98, 118 ff, 186.

D. E. Broadbent, "Frederic Charles Bartlett 1886–1969", *Biog. Mem. Fell. Roy. Soc.* 16, 1–4 (1970).

C. H. Rolph, *Kingsley. The Life, Letters and Diaries of Kingsley Martin* (London, 1973). See especially p. 88.

Bertrand Russell, *Sceptical Essays* (Unwin Paperbacks, 1977), p. 13.

Bertrand Russell, *The Autobiography of Bertrand Russell*, Vol. II, 1914–1944 (London, 1968), p. 115.

Bertrand Russell, "Science and Life", *The New Leader*, 3rd November 1922, p. 12.

For a descriptive account of Rivers's Cambridge as it was in the last few years before his death (and a mention of Rivers) see Kingsley Martin, *Father Figures. A First Volume of Autobiography 1897–1931* (London, 1966), Chaps. 5 and 6.

[5] Seligman, ibid.

[6] John Layard, *The Times* (non-Royal edition), 16 June 1922, p. 7.

[7] For reasons which, if they could be revealed, would be seen as perfectly understandable and proper, I am duty bound not to reveal the source of the suggestion, which was advanced as a clear and confident statement of fact, that Rivers was a closeted homosexual. Nonetheless, this information seems far too important for the understanding of Rivers's scientific career to be entirely ignored.

[8] John Layard, personal communication, 2 July 1973.

[9] Myers, op. cit. (note 4), p. 187.

[10] Shore, op. cit. (note 4), p. 9.

[11] Sassoon wrote two poems acknowledging his debt to Rivers – "To a Very Wise Man", which was included in the collection *Picture Show*, privately printed by the Cambridge University Press in 1919, and "Revisitation" (1934). The former poem begins:

> Fires in the dark you build; tall quivering flames
> In the huge midnight forest of the unknown.

In the latter poem, written twelve years after the death of Rivers, Sassoon states that he still feels Rivers's influence "undiminished", and "his life's work, in me and many, unfinished". Graves's acknowledgement occurs in his book *Poetic Unreason* (London, 1925), pp. 99–101, 127–131 and passim.

[12] Myers, op. cit. (note 4), p. 187.

[13] Shore, op. cit. (note 4), p. 10.

[14] Bennett, op. cit. (note 4), p. 1.

[15] Myers, op. cit. (note 4), p. 187.

[16] Bartlett (b), op. cit. (note 4), p. 14.

[17] Arthur Marwick, *The Deluge. British Society and the First World War* (London, 1965), p. 297.

[18] W. H. R. Rivers, *Instinct and the Unconscious* (Cambridge, 2nd edn. 1922), p. 12. See also W. H. R. Rivers, *Conflict and Dream* (London, 1923), pp. 94, 95.

19 G. Elliot Smith, Introduction to W. H. R. Rivers, *Psychology and Ethnology* (London, 1926), p. xii.

20 Head (a), op. cit. (note 4), p. 977.

21 Elliot Smith, op. cit. (note 19).

22 W. H. R. Rivers, Article on "Vision", in Edward Sharpey Schafer (ed.), *Textbook of Physiology*, Vol. 2 (New York, 1900).

23 Myers, op. cit. (note 4), pp. 181, 182.

24 W. H. R. Rivers, "General Account [of contributions to comparative psychology resulting from the Torres Straits expedition] and Observations on Vision etc." *J. Anthrop. Inst.* 29, 220 (1899).

25 W. H. R. Rivers and Henry Head, "A Human Experiment in Nerve Division", *Brain* 31, 324 (1908).

26 Ibid., p. 429 ff. For a slightly different account see W. H. R. Rivers, James Sherren and Henry Head, "The Afferent Nervous System Considered From A New Aspect", *Brain* 28, 104 (1905).

27 Rivers and Head, op. cit. (note 25), p. 345.

28 Gordon Holmes, obituary for Head in *Obituary Notices of Fellows of the Royal Society* 10 (Dec. 1941), p. 671.

29 W. H. R. Rivers, James Sherren and Henry Head, "The Afferent Nervous System Considered From a New Aspect", *Brain* 28, 102 (1905).

30 Rivers and Head, op. cit. (note 25), p. 342.

31 Ibid., p. 345.

32 Ibid., pp. 342, 343.

33 Ibid., pp. 412–419, 441 ff. Rivers, Sherren and Head, op. cit. (note 29), p. 105 ff.

34 Ibid., pp. 419–422. Rivers, Sherren and Head, op. cit. (note 29), p. 107 ff.

35 Ibid., pp. 442, 443.

36 Ibid., p. 448.

37 Ibid., pp. 388–392.

38 Rivers, Sherren and Head, op. cit. (note 29), pp. 112–114.

39 Ibid., p. 115.

40 W. H. R. Rivers, *Instinct and the Unconscious* (2nd edn., Cambridge, 1922), p. 148. See also Jonathan Miller, "The Dog Beneath the Skin", *The Listener*, 20 July 1972, p. 74.

41 Rivers and Head, op. cit. (note 25), pp. 405, 406.

42 Rivers, op. cit. (note 40), p. 27.

43 See Rivers, op. cit. (note 18), pp. 22–29, 31, 50, 51. See also W. H. R. Rivers, "Dreams and Primitive Culture", *Bull. John Rylands Library* 4, 393 (1918). For an indication of the way in which Rivers used the word "protopathic" in everyday conversation with his colleagues, see Pear, op. cit. (note 4), p. 228.

44 Gerald Geison, "Keith Lucas", in C. C. Gillispie (ed.), *Dictionary of Scientific Biography* (New York, 1973).

45 *Dictionary of National Biography* (1931–40), pp. 410, 411.

46 L. S. Hearnshaw, *A Short History of British Psychology 1840–1940*, p. 172. Myers, op. cit. (note 4), p. 181. Gerald Geison, "Michael Foster", in C. C. Gillispie (ed.), *Dictionary of Scientific Biography* (New York, 1972).

47 Rev. William Ridley, "On the Kamilaroi Tribe of Australians . . . ", *J. Ethnol. Soc. Lond.* 4, 287 (1856).

342 NOTES AND REFERENCES

[48] W. S. Lilly, "The New Naturalism", *Fortnightly Review* 38, 251, 252 (1885). The lines of poetry within the quotation come from Tennyson's "In Memoriam" CXVIII.

[49] Jonathan Miller, "The Dog Beneath the Skin", *The Listener*, 20 July 1972.

[50] That there was a rigid split in Rivers's psyche between the controlling forces of rationality and discrimination, on the one hand, and the suppressed forces of sensuality and emotion, on the other, was suggested to me by John Layard, oral communication, July 1972. Head (a), op. cit. (note 4), p. 977, describes Rivers in terms which suggest that, in later life, Rivers's emotions, while normally held under tight control, were capable of breaking through to the surface, especially if his canons of scientific discourse were violated: "He was endlessly patient with an honest expression of personal opinion. His charity was boundless; but unsuspecting persons who expressed some mischievous view were often startled by the vehemence of the reaction they evoked from this modest man of science." See also Myers, op. cit. (note 4), p. 187.

That Rivers suffered from some degree of sexual repression right up until the end of his life may be seen from *Conflict and Dream* (published posthumously in 1923). In this book he analyzes a number of his own dreams, but scrupulously avoids any dreams which involved sex conflicts, since "the analyzes would probably have been full of passages which a natural reticence would have driven me to withhold or garble" (p. 111).

[51] See, for example, Gerald Geison, "John Newport Langley", in C. C. Gillispie (ed.), *Dictionary of Scientific Biography* (New York, 1973).

[52] Head published two books of his own poetry, *Songs of La Mouche and Other Verses* (London, 1910) and *Destroyers and Other Verses* (Oxford, 1919). A critical discussion of Head's poetry by Frederick Peterson may be found in the *Charaka Club Proceedings, New York* 6, 108–113 (1925).

[53] Rivers and Head, op. cit. (note 25), pp. 405, 406.

[54] A. Hingston Quiggin, *Haddon the Head Hunter* (Cambridge, 1942), p. 81.

[55] Ibid., p. 97.

[56] Ibid., pp. 88, 89.

[57] Downie, *Frazer and the Golden Bough* (London, 1970), pp. 25, 112.

[58] Ibid., p. 112.

[59] The most detailed account of the Torres Straits expedition and what it meant to the men involved is contained in A. C. Haddon's *Headhunters, Black, White and Brown* (London, 1901). A brief but informative account, which places the expedition in the context of the history of British psychology, may be found in *A Short History of British Psychology 1840–1940*, by L. J. Hearnshaw (London, 1964), p. 172 ff. Further material about the expedition is given in the introductions and prefaces to the six volumes of the *Reports of the Cambridge Anthropological Expedition to Torres Straits* (Cambridge, 1901–1935), and in the biographies of Haddon, Rivers and Seligman in the *International Encyclopaedia of the Social Sciences* (New York, 1968).

[60] The occasion was a speech made after Haddon had been presented with the first Rivers Medal by the Royal Anthropological Institute on 27 Jan. 1925. Quoted in Quiggin, op. cit. (note 54), p. 97 n.

[61] A. H. Quiggin and E. S. Fegan, "Alfred Cort Haddon 1855–1940", *Man* 40, 98 (1940).

[62] G. Elliot Smith, Introduction to *Psychology and Ethnology* by W. H. R. Rivers (London, 1926), p. xi.

[63] Shore, op. cit. (note 4), p. 5.

[64] See, for example, *Reports of the Cambridge Anthropological Expedition to Torres Straits*, Vol. I (Cambridge, 1935), p. xii, and "A Genealogical Method of Collecting Social and Vital Statistics" by W. H. R. Rivers, *J. Anthrop. Inst.* **30**, 74 (1900).

[65] Head (a), op. cit. (note 4), p. 977.

[66] "Haddon's Private Journal for the 1898 Torres Straits Expedition", pp. 201, 202 (Haddon Collection, Envelope 1030).

[67] A letter from one Henry Jones to one I. E. Harting dated 19 Nov. 1889 (Haddon Collection, Envelope 21), reveals that Harting and Haddon were interested in cat's-cradles at this early date. Jones remarks that he "should like to know whether the natives of the Torres Straits have improved on our game, and should like to meet you and Professor Haddon to discuss and try it".

[68] Quoted in Quiggin and Fegan, op. cit. (note 61), p. 100.

[69] See, for example, letter from E. Hornbostel to Haddon dated 1st December 1922 (Haddon Collection, Envelope 24).

[70] Quoted in Quiggin and Fegan, op. cit. (note 61), p. 100.

[71] In a note to Rivers from Government House, Ootacamund, where Rivers apparently stayed during his fieldwork among the Todas, one Edgar Thurston writes "Your cat's-cradle performance is a treasured memory". The date on the note is 9th August 1905 (Haddon Collection, Envelope 12040).

[72] W. H. R. Rivers, review of *String Figures* by Caroline Jayne, *Folklore* **18** (1907).

[73] Haddon, op. cit. (note 66), p. 251.

[74] *Rep. Brit. Assoc. Advanc. Sci.* (1899), p. 879.

[75] *J. Anthrop. Inst.* **30** (1900). The same volume of the journal reveals that C. G. Seligman, McDougall and Wilkin were also elected as fellows of the Institute in 1900. Haddon, Ray and Myers had been fellows of the Institute since before the 1898 expedition.

[76] Haddon was already a member of the council. See ibid., pp. 6, 8, 10, 11.

[77] W. H. R. Rivers, "A Genealogical Method of Collecting Social and Vital Statistics", *J. Anthrop. Inst.* **30**, 82 (1900).

[78] Ibid., p. 76.

[79] The levirate is a practice requiring or permitting a man to marry the widow of his real or classificatory brother.

[80] Between 1877 and 1893 Galton had delivered over half-a-dozen addresses to the Anthropological Section (or, prior to 1884, to the Anthropological "Department") of the British Association, and each of these addresses had been concerned, in some way, with emphasizing the importance of quantification for the study of man.

[81] *Reports of the Cambridge Anthropological Expedition to Torres Straits*, Vol. 5 (Cambridge, 1904), p. 126.

[82] W. H. R. Rivers, "Primitive Colour Vision", *Popular Science Monthly* **59**, 48 and passim (1901).

[83] Miller, op. cit. (note 49), p. 74.

[84] See, for example, Rivers's article on "Methodology" in B. Freire-Marreco and J. L. Myres (eds.), *Notes and Queries on Anthropology*, 4th edn. (London 1912).

[85] W. H. R. Rivers, "Dreams and Primitive Culture", *Bull. John Rylands Library* **4**, 393 (1918).

[86] Ibid., pp. 393, 394.

[87] Elliot Smith's preface to *The Threshold of the Pacific* by C. E. Fox (London, 1924).

Elliot Smith quotes Fox as saying the he (Fox) had written some "chaffing rhymes" about the genealogical method for Rivers in 1908, and had later discovered that Rivers was keeping them in his study at Cambridge. Slobodin, op. cit. (note 4), having missed this reference, speculates (p. 44) that the author of the verse might have been William Sinker, the captain of the *Southern Cross*.

88 Haddon Collection, Envelope 12051.

89 *Reports of the Cambridge Anthropological Expedition to Torres Straits*, Vol. 6 (Cambridge, 1908), pp. 64, 65.

90 Ibid., p. 100.

91 Ibid., p. 169.

92 Ibid.

93 Freire-Marreco and Myres, op. cit. (note 84), p. 129.

94 *Reports of the Cambridge Anthropological Expedition to Torres Straits*, Vol. 5 (Cambridge, 1904), p. 139. Also op. cit. (note 89), p. 92.

95 W. H. R. Rivers, "On the Origins of the Classificatory System of Relationships", in *Anthropological Essays Presented to Edward Burnett Tylor* (Oxford, 1907), p. 312.

96 Op. cit. (note 89), p. 98.

97 Rivers, op. cit. (note 95), pp. 312, 313.

98 Ibid., pp. 313, 314.

99 Ibid., p. 320.

100 Ibid., pp. 321, 322.

101 Op. cit. (note 94). Rivers's section on "The Functions of Certain Kin" occurs within the chapter on kinship. He had previously published a summary report on this topic in the 1901 volume of *Man*.

102 Op. cit. (note 94), p. 146.

103 Ibid., p. 150.

104 Ibid., p. 149. In describing this explanation, and the previously mentioned one about the role of the mother's brother, as characteristic of the nineteenth-century, I do not intend the term "nineteenth-century" to be understood in a derogatory manner, as synonymous with "old-fashioned". That this type of explanation was, in fact, inferior to the type which the twentieth-century was to produce, even when both types are considered as historical products of the centuries in which they appeared, I would not deny for a moment. What I do wish to deny is that there is any necessary connection between theoretical novelty and theoretical merit – that there is any built-in law of improvement which automatically renders yesterday's mode of scientific explanation inferior to today's.

105 W. H. R. Rivers, "The Marriage of Cousins in India", *J. Roy. Asiatic Soc.* NS 39, 612 (1907).

106 Ibid., p. 623.

107 W. H. R. Rivers, *The Todas* (London, 1906), p. v.

108 Ibid., p. 11.

109 Ibid., p. 2.

110 Ibid., p. 483.

111 R. L. Rooksby, "W. H. R. Rivers and the Todas", *South Asia* 1, 113 (1971). This article, which I came across only during last-minute revisions to my book, covers a good deal of the ground traversed in the final section of the present chapter.

112 Rivers, op. cit. (note 107), pp. 494, 483.

113 M. B. Emeneau, "Language and Social Forms. A Study of Toda Kinship Terms and Dual Descent", in L. Spier, A. I. Hallowell and S. S. Newman (eds.), *Language, Culture and Personality* (Menasha, 1941), pp. 158, 159, 161.

114 Ira R. Buchler and Henry A. Selby, *Kinship and Social Organization* (New York, 1968), p. 221.

115 Rivers, op. cit. (note 107), pp. 488, 486, 487.

116 Lewis Henry Morgan, *Systems of Consanguinity and Affinity* ... (Washington, 1870), pp. 155–161.

117 *Man* 7, 90–92 (1907).

118 A. E. Crawley, "An Anthropologist Among The Todas", *Nature*, 14 Mar. 1907, pp. 462, 463.

119 Introduction to Rivers, *Kinship and Social Organization* (New York, 1968, reprint of 1914 original), p. 20.

120 Haddon, op. cit. (note 59), pp. 123, 124.

121 The passage in question is pp. 155–161. In the 1904 volume of the Torres Straits *Report*, Rivers cites this passage (and also *Ancient Society*, pp. 437–440) in a footnote.

122 See the dedication to John Layard's *Stone Men of Malekula* (London, 1942).

123 See for example Rivers, "Some Sociological Definitions", *Rep. Brit. Assoc. Adv. Sci.* (1907), pp. 653, 654.

124 Rivers, op. cit. (note 107), p. 466.

125 Ibid.

126 Reprinted in Slobodin (op. cit., note 4), pp. 187–193.

CHAPTER III

1 H. W. Scheffler, "Ambrym Revisited: A Preliminary Report", *Southwestern J. Anthrop.* **26**, 52–66 (1970). Scheffler's argument that the marriage-class interpretation of the Ambrym system represents a misconstrual of the data is of considerable theoretical interest, and, if my book had been intended as a contribution to social anthropology, I would have felt obliged to evaluate it. However, since the present work is being offered as a contribution to the *history* of the social sciences, since it appears that professional anthropologists are going to have a good deal more to say before one will be in a position to decide whether or not Scheffler is right, and since I am anxious to avoid the ultimate historical crime of forcing the past into false molds through too close attention to the opinions of the present day, I shall not be opening this particular can of worms. It should be mentioned, however, that in her doctoral thesis on "Kinship, Marriage and Ritual in North Ambrym" (University of Sydney, 1976), Mary Patterson argues, on the basis of extended fieldwork on Ambrym, that Scheffler's reinterpretation of the Ambrym kinship data is mistaken.

2 W. H. R. Rivers, "Unpublished Notes on Ambrim"; "Introduction", pp. 5–12, Haddon Collection, University Library Cambridge, Envelope 12000. Among Rivers's surviving correspondence (Haddon Collection, Envelope 12039) there is a letter which gives an idea of the close relationship which Rivers maintained between himself and a favourite informant like Temar. The letter, dated 1 Mar. 1915, is signed "William Ambrim in the Mission Station Tangoa", and presumably was authored by Temar. In very quaint English the writer thanks Rivers (and God) for sending "your love in the gift of watch".

[3] Ibid., p. 12.

[4] Ibid., p. 1.

[5] W. H. R. Rivers, *The History of Melanesian Society*, Vol. II (Cambridge, 1914), pp. 88, 89.

[6] Letter from Bernard Deacon to A. C. Haddon dated 15 Feb. 1927, Haddon Collection, University Library Cambridge, Envelope 16001.

[7] Here Radcliffe-Brown has a footnote to A. Bernard Deacon, "The Regulation of Marriage in Ambrym", *J. Roy. Anthrop. Inst.* 57, 333 ff (1927).

[8] A. R. Radcliffe-Brown, "A Further Note on Ambrym", *Man* 29, 50 (1929).

[9] See, in particular, W. H. R. Rivers, "Some Sociological Definitions", *Rep. Brit. Assoc. Adv. Sci.* (1907), pp. 653, 654. Also section entitled "Terminology of Social Organization" in the fourth edition of the *Notes and Queries on Anthropology*, which was authored by a committee of which Rivers was a member.

[10] W. H. R. Rivers, "The Father's Sister in Oceania", *Folklore* 21, 58, 59 (1910). See also Rivers op. cit. (note 5), pp. 92, 94. For an excellent discussion of the emergence of the concept of bilateral descent in Rivers's thought, see J. D. Freeman's article "On the Concept of the Kindred", *J. Roy. Anthrop. Inst.* 91, 195–198 (1961). Freeman argues that in regard to descent, the concept of bilaterality is not evident until quite late in Rivers's career.

[11] T. T. Barnard, "The Social Organization of Ambrim", *Man* 28, 133–137 (1928).

[12] Ibid., p. 136.

[13] In his Ph.D. thesis, Barnard calls the man "Lan". However, in his article on "The Social Organization of Ambrim" in *Man* 28 (1928), Barnard adopts the spelling "Lau", which is the one used by William Bowie in the letter where he tells Rivers that Temar's information about the *vantinbul* had been wrong (Haddon Collection, Envelope 12000).

[14] Quoted by Barnard, ibid., p. 135.

[15] In actual fact, however, the situation tends to be more complicated than this, since the membership of a given *vantinbul* can cut across the territorial boundaries which separate one village from another.

[16] Rivers, op. cit. (note 2), chapter on "Social Organization", pp. 2–7. See also Bowie's comments, which appear at the end of this chapter.

[17] W. H. R. Rivers, *Kinship and Social Organization* (New York, 1968 reprint of 1914 edn.), p. 57.

[18] Ibid., p. 57.

[19] Ibid., pp. 57, 58. See also W. H. R. Rivers, "Is Australian Culture Simple or Complex?" *Rep. Brit. Assoc. Adv. Sci.* (1914), pp. 529–530.

[20] W. H. R. Rivers, *The History of Melanesian Society*, Vol. I (Cambridge, 1914), p. 190.

[21] Ibid., p. 190.

[22] Ibid., p. 190.

[23] Rivers, op. cit. (note 5), pp. 74, 75.

[24] Ibid., p. 67.

[25] Brenda Z. Seligman, "Asymmetry in Descent, With Special Reference to Pentecost", *J. Roy. Anthrop. Inst.* 58, 533–558 (1928). Another disciple of Rivers, John Layard, favours a rather different marriage-class interpretation of data from Pentecost. Specifically, Layard points out (*Stone Men of Malekula*, p. 140 ff.) that a creation myth from south Pentecost seems to imply the present or former existence of a 232 type of

six-section system similar to the one which he had postulated as a first approximation to the system of Vao. (According to Layard this latter system resembles the Ambrym system except that descent within the moieties is patrilineal rather than matrilineal, and descent within the trisections is matrilineal rather than patrilineal.)

[26] Rivers, op. cit. (note 21).

[27] Seligman, op. cit. (note 25), p. 540.

[28] In an attempt to minimize the difference between the Pentecost system and the standard marriage-class systems of Australia, Seligman refers the reader to Radcliffe-Brown's 1913 article on "Three Tribes of Western Australia" (*J. Roy. Anthrop. Inst.* 43, 143—194 (1913)) where, to use Seligman's words, he demonstrates that "in the named classes of South-West Australia men are not free to marry any woman of the correct named class, but, within the class, marriage is regulated by consanguinity". (op. cit., note 25, p. 549) However, in the passage to which Seligman is apparently alluding, (p. 155), the prohibited marriages mentioned by Radcliffe-Brown are all with people who are separated from ego by two generations, and which would therefore, in most cases, be socially and physically impractical anyway. What I am saying is that a system of marriage regulations which neglected to automatically prohibit the widely forbidden alliances of a parent with its child, and of a man with a girl and her mother, would have seemed less plausible than one whose only crime was the failure to rule out marriages which, on practical grounds, could have been entered into not at all or only rarely.

[29] Rivers, op. cit. (note 23).

[30] Rivers, op. cit. (note 17), p. 58.

[31] Rivers, op. cit. (note 5), p. 89.

[32] Ibid., p. 187.

[33] The Crow and Omaha systems, of which Rivers would have been cognisant, constitute notable exceptions to this generalization.

[34] Rivers, op. cit. (note 17), pp. 56, 58.

[35] For a brief critical discussion of Kohler's essay, and a cursory mention of the anthropologists (including Rivers) who followed his lead, see A. R. Radcliffe-Brown's *Structure and Function in Primitive Society* (Free Press, New York, 1965), pp. 56—58.

[36] Cf. Rivers, op. cit. (note 17), p. 55.

[37] Ibid., p. 58.

[38] Ibid., p. 58.

[39] c.f. ibid., pp. 59, 60.

[40] Rivers, op. cit. (note 20), pp. 203, 204. C.f. Rivers, op. cit. (note 17), pp. 60, 61.

[41] Rivers, op. cit. (note 17), p. 61.

[42] Ibid., p. 62.

[43] Ibid., pp. 62, 63.

[44] Unpublished letter from E. Sapir to W. H. R. Rivers dated 7 Feb. 1917, Haddon Collection, Envelope 12022.

[45] Rivers, op. cit. (note 5), p. 57.

[46] Unpublished, untitled and undated typescript of a paper by W. H. R. Rivers, Haddon Collection, Envelope 12004. Since the paper is in a very rough and only partially corrected form, in quoting it I have taken a few liberties necessary to tidy up the English. However, I do not believe that I have altered Rivers's meaning in any way.

[47] Rivers, op. cit. (note 5), pp. 58—60.

[48] Ibid., pp. 60, 61.
[49] Ibid., p. 65.
[50] *Daily Telegraph* (Sydney, 27 Aug. 1914). See also *Rep. Brit. Assoc. Adv. Sci.* (1914), pp. 531, 532.
[51] Marginal annotation on preliminary typescript of this book, Oct. 1978.
[52] Rivers, op. cit. (note 4).
[53] Unpublished and undated typescript entitled "Marriage with the Wives of the Grandfather and Uncle" by W. H. R. Rivers, Haddon Collection, Envelope 12002.
[54] Ibid., p. 11.
[55] Ibid., p. 12.
[56] Unpublished and undated series of rough hand-written notes entitled "Ambrim Relationship", Haddon Collection, Envelope 12002.
[57] Reference to Figure 11 reveals that each of the women who would be involved in these three anomalous marriages do, in fact, belong to the section into which an Ambrym man is allowed to marry. However, one should not conclude from this that such marriages are actually practised. In fact, the orthodox form of alliance in the Ambrym system – marriage with the mother's brother's daughter's daughter – is considerably less anomalous than any of the above three unions, since it involves people who are separated by only one generation.
[58] Rivers, op. cit. (note 2), chapter on "Social Organization", p. 22.
[59] See ibid., p. 21.
[60] See, for example, the list of permitted marriages in ibid., chapter on "Marriage and Childbirth", p. 2.

CHAPTER IV

[1] W. H. R. Rivers, *Conflict and Dream* (London, 1923), p. 94.
[2] W. H. R. Rivers, "The Ethnological Analysis of Culture", *Rep. Brit. Assoc. Adv. Sci.* (1911), pp. 490–499. The word "conversion" is used by Rivers himself on p. 492 of this address.
[3] Ibid., p. 493.
[4] Ibid., p. 494.
[5] W. H. R. Rivers, *The History of Melanesian Society* (Cambridge, 1914) Vol. II, p. 2.
[6] See F. Boas, "On Alternating Sounds", *Amer. Anthrop.* II 47–53 (1889). For an illuminating analysis of this article and its place in the development of Boas's thought, see George W. Stocking Jr., *Race, Culture and Evolution* (New York, 1968), pp. 157–160.
[7] Rivers, op. cit. (note 5), Vol. I, p. 18.
[8] Note from Ray to Rivers dated 20 Mar. 1911, Haddon Collection, Envelope 12056.
[9] See, for example, Rivers, op. cit. (note 5), Vol. II, p. 173.
[10] A. C. Haddon, "The Percy Sladen Trust Expedition to Melanesia", *Nature* (27 Aug. 1908), p. 393.
[11] Ibid., p. 394.
[12] Ibid., p. 394.
[13] Ibid., p. 394.

[14] A. M. Hocart, "The Cult of the Dead in Eddystone of the Solomons", *J. Roy. Anthrop. Inst.* **52**, 71 (1922).

[15] Ibid., p. 72.

[16] Letter from Hocart to Rivers from Nanduri (Vanua Levu, Fiji), dated 27 Sept. 1912, Haddon Collection, Envelope 12019.

[17] A. Koestler, *The Case of the Midwife Toad* (Picador edn., London, 1975), pp. 30, 31.

[18] E. Dennert (1903), quoted in V. L. Kellog, *Darwinism Today* (New York, 1907), p. 6.

[19] Kellog, ibid., p. 4, 5.

[20] Ibid., p. 26.

[21] William Coleman, *Biology in the Nineteenth Century* (New York, 1971), pp. 165, 166.

[22] Quoted in C. P. Blacker, *Eugenics, Galton and After* (London, 1952), p. 258.

[23] Article on Galton by F. N. David in the *International Encyclopaedia of the Social Sciences* (New York, 1968).

[24] Blacker, op. cit. (note 22), pp. 258, 259.

[25] A. M. Hocart, review of *The History of Melanesian Society* by W. H. R. Rivers, *Man* **15**, 91 (1915). See also Elliot Smith's introduction to the discussion on megalithic monuments in *Rep. Brit. Assoc. Adv. Sci.* (1912), p. 607, where he attributes to the opponents of diffusionism the view that the builders of megaliths must have been motivated by an "inborn impulse".

[26] Arthur Koestler, *The Act of Creation* (Picador edn., London, 1975), p. 118. See also ibid. p. 169, 170 for an account of an earlier semiconscious vision which had helped Kekulé to arrive at his theory of molecular constitution.

[27] For the relevant extract from Poincaré's lecture, see ibid. pp. 114–116. See also ibid. pp. 164–166, 211. Poincaré's role in publicizing the creative uses of unconscious thought during the early years of the twentieth-century was pointed out to me by Meyer Fortes.

[28] Unpublished, untitled and undated typescript of a paper by W. H. R. Rivers, Haddon Collection, Envelope 12004. Since the paper is in a very rough and only partially corrected form, in quoting it I have taken a few liberties to tidy up the English. However I do not believe that I have altered Rivers's meaning in any way. For a later description of the two kinds of house found on Temotu, see Rivers, op. cit. (note 5), Vol. I, p. 223.

[29] Ibid. In his later work *Conflict and Dream* (London, 1923), the semi-comatose state following sleep is assigned an important role in psycho-analysis. In fact, at one point Rivers writes that "the general principle of interpretation upon which this book is based [is] that the thoughts present in the half-waking state following a dream provide a clue to the thoughts by which this dream has been determined . . . " (pp. 122, 123).

[30] Ibid.

[31] Rivers, op. cit. (note 1), p. 90.

[32] W. H. R. Rivers, *Instinct and the Unconscious* (Cambridge, 2nd edn., 1922), pp. 94, 95.

[33] W. H. R. Rivers, *Psychology and Ethnology* (London, 1926), pp. 38, 39. It may be relevant to mention that, shortly before leaving on the 1908 expedition, both Hocart and Rivers had contributed articles on perception to the *Brit. J. Psychol.*, of which Rivers was at that time an editor. Rivers's article, which was co-authored by G. Dawes Hicks, deals specifically with a variety of illusion. The fundamental conclusion to be

drawn from the paper is that the illusion in question, once acquired, persists in the absence of the bodily function which would have seemed to hold out the best hope of furnishing a physiological explanation for the illusion. It seems just possible that this negative result may have sensitized Rivers to the possibility that the immediate explanation of the illusions he witnessed on Eddystone Island would have to be sought in fields other than physiology, especially since he and Hocart would have been subjected to the same external stimuli as the other people in the house. And, if such stimuli were deemed incapable of providing the requisite explanation, then, assuming that deliberate trickery was not involved, there would remain only the internal recesses of the subconscious, which Rivers regarded as the repository of phantasms and dreams.

34 Rivers, op. cit. (note 33), p. 16.

35 Ibid., pp. 17, 18.

36 Graham Wallas, *Human Nature in Politics* (New York, 1921). Preface to 3rd edn. (1920), p. 5.

37 W. H. R. Rivers, *Conflict and Dream* (London, 1923), p. 62 ff.

38 Rivers, op. cit. (note 32), pp. 50, 51. For evidence of the fact that Rivers regarded individual instinctive tendencies as opposed to social forces of control, see pp. 115, 144, 145, 146, 157.

39 Ibid., pp. 93, 94.

40 Ibid., p. 99.

41 Another way of putting this point would be to say that Rivers, while never relinquishing the claim to be proceeding scientifically, was increasingly allowing his own subjective feelings to enter into the execution and interpretation of his fieldwork.

42 W. H. R. Rivers, *Social Organization* (New York, 1924), p. 108. Another account of the incident may be found in W. H. R. Rivers, *Psychology and Politics* (New York, 1923), pp. 36, 37.

43 W. H. R. Rivers, *History and Ethnology* (Helps for Students of History No. 48), (London, 1922), pp. 10, 13–24.

44 W. H. R. Rivers, "The Place of Evolution in Sociology". Undated and apparently unpublished typescript in the Haddon Collection, Envelope 12013.

45 Warren R. Dawson (ed.), *Sir Grafton Elliot Smith, a Biographical Record by his Colleagues* (London, 1938), pp. 21–23.

46 Records of admission held in St John's College Library, Cambridge.

47 Dawson, op. cit. (note 45), p. 128.

48 C. S. Myers, "On the Influence of the Late W. H. R. Rivers on the Development of Psychology in Great Britain", *Rep. Brit. Assoc. Adv. Sci.* (1922), p. 181. Elsewhere Rivers is described as having been invited to Cambridge in order to lecture on "the psychology of the senses". See, for example, Haddon's obituary for Rivers in *Nature* (17 June 1922).

49 Entry for Head in *Dictionary of National Biography*, 1931–40.

50 W. H. R. Rivers, *Psychology and Politics* (London, 1923), p. 126 fn., and Elliot Smith's Introduction to Rivers's *Psychology and Ethnology* (London, 1926), pp. xiii, xiv. In Dawson, op. cit. (note 45), W. J. Perry gives a somewhat different account, which does not mention Rivers.

51 *J. Roy. Anthrop. Inst.* 40, 540 (1910).

52 Dawson, op. cit. (note 45), p. 206, c.f. p. 51.

53 Ibid., pp. 51–53.

[54] *Rep. Brit. Assoc. Adv. Sci.* (1912), pp. 575, 576.

[55] Ibid., pp. 598, 599. For Rivers, degeneration was definable as the "disappearance of the useful". In an article in *The Sociological Review* for October 1913, he discusses the converse phenomenon of survival, which he defines as "the persistence of the useless".

[56] *Rep. Brit. Assoc. Adv. Sci.* (1912, 1913, 1914, 1915).

[57] Dawson, op. cit. (note 45), p. 54.

[58] Op. cit. (note 56).

[59] Rivers's papers, Haddon Collection, Envelope 12058.

[60] Dawson, op. cit. (note 45), p. 52.

[61] Ibid., p. 66.

[62] Ibid., pp. 63–65. Watson states (p. 62) that these events took place in Brisbane, but this must be a mistake, as Rivers says in his review of *The Migrations of Early Culture* (*J. Egypt. Archeol.* II, 256 (1915)) that Elliot Smith examined the mummy "during a visit to his old medical school", and Perry (Dawson, op. cit., note 45, p. 207) backs this up by the statement that the mummies were in the Macleay Museum, which he locates correctly at the University of Sydney. C.f. also Rivers, op. cit. (note 50), p. 127 ff.

[63] Obituary for Rivers by A. C. Haddon, *Nature*, 17 June 1922.

[64] See especially Rivers op. cit. (note 62).

[65] Haddon Collection, Envelope 12017.

[66] Dawson, op. cit. (note 45), p. 52. Also Elliot Smith's preface to C. E. Fox, *Threshold of the Pacific* (London, 1924), p. v.

[67] Elliot Smith, ibid., p. vi.

[68] J. W. Layard, personal communication, 7 Sept. 1972.

[69] J. W. Layard, personal interview, July 1972.

[70] Haddon Collection, Envelope 3.

[71] Dawson, op. cit. (note 45), p. 56.

[72] Ibid., p. 60. However it was Elliot Smith who first informed Rivers of the opportunities for work on psychoneuroses at the Maghull Hospital – see L. E. Shore's obituary for Rivers in *The Eagle* (1922), p. 9. See also T. H. Pear, "Some Early Relations Between English Ethnologists and Psychologists", *J. Roy. Anthrop. Inst.* 90, 231 (1960).

[73] Haddon Collection, Envelope 3053.

[74] Lest I be misunderstood, it should be remarked that Rivers's switch from evolutionism to diffusionism in no way involved a verbal renunciation of the genealogical method. On the contrary, Rivers tells us in the preface to *The History of Melanesian Society*, the book which embodies a record of his "conversion", that he hopes to demonstrate the correctness of his prior belief in "the fundamental importance to the science of Sociology of the method of counting relationships"; to show, in fact, "that systems of relationship are far more vitally important and their investigation far more fruitful than my utmost hopes had led me to anticipate". However, as I hope this chapter and the previous one have made clear, despite a continued verbal adherence to the goal of providing a scientific analysis of human culture, in fact the ethnological work which Rivers did after his conversion to diffusionism, when measured against the standard of his earlier achievements in anthropology, must be judged implausible and unduly speculative.

[75] Elliot Smith, op. cit. (note 66), p. vi.

[76] Rivers, op. cit. (note 5), p. 127.

[77] Dawson, op. cit. (note 45), p. 96.

[78] Ibid., p. 60.
[79] Rivers, op. cit. (note 1), p. 151 ff.
[80] Dawson, op. cit. (note 45), p. 208.
[81] W. H. R. Rivers, "The Psychological Factor", in W. H. R. Rivers (ed.), *Essays on the Depopulation of Melanesia* (Cambridge, 1922).
[82] Myers, op. cit. (note 48), p. 186.
[83] Dawson, op. cit. (note 45), p. 21.
[84] Ibid., p. 89.
[85] Elliot Smith, preface to Rivers, op. cit. (note 1), p. viii.
[86] Dawson, op. cit. (note 45), p. 71.
[87] Rivers, op. cit. (note 1), p. 10 n. See also p. viii.
[88] Pear, op. cit. (note 72), pp. 231, 232.
[89] Ibid., p. 232.
[90] Dawson, op. cit. (note 45), pp. 162–64, c.f. also pp. 71, 72.
[91] Ibid., pp. 172–76. Circa 1916, Rivers had been invited, apparently on Elliot Smith's initiative, to come to Manchester to discuss the possibility of becoming the Professor of Comparative Religion there. However, his war work on psychoneurosis evidently prevented this contingency – see L. E. Shore's obituary for Rivers in *The Eagle* (1922), p. 9.
[92] Ibid., p. 169.
[93] Ibid., p. 180.
[94] Ibid., p. 178.
[95] For an account of Elliot Smith's notion of "Human Biology", see ibid., pp. 89–95.
[96] W. H. R. Rivers, "The Unity of Anthropology", *J. Roy. Anthrop. Inst.* 52, 23 (1922).
[97] Archive A3, Part 2, Royal Anthropological Institute Library, London. See also *J. Roy. Anthrop. Inst.* Miscellanea, 1921–22.
[98] *The Sunday Times*, 11 Dec. 1927.
[99] Elliot Smith, letter to *The Times* of 27 Sept. 1926.
[100] Elliot Smith, "The People of Egypt", *Rep. Brit. Assoc. Adv. Sci.* (1910), p. 728.
[101] A synopsis of this lecture is given in *Nature*, 23 Feb. 1924, p. 291.
[102] Dawson, op. cit. (note 45), p. 105.
[103] G. Elliot Smith, "Notes on the Natural Subdivision of the Cerebral Hemisphere", *J. Anat. Phys.* 35, 431 (1901).
[104] Dawson, op. cit. (note 45), p. 191.
[105] G. Elliot Smith, Presidential Address to Section H, Anthropology, *Rep. Brit. Assoc. Adv. Sci.* (1912), pp. 582, 583.
[106] Ibid., p. 583.
[107] Ibid.
[108] G. Elliot Smith, "New Light on Vision", *Nature*, 31 May 1930, pp. 821, 822.
[109] G. Elliot Smith, "The Evolution of Mind", in George C. Campion and G. Elliot Smith, *The Neural Basis of Thought* (London, 1934), p. 30.
[110] Dawson, op. cit. (note 45), p. 191.
[111] See Elliot Smith, op. cit. (note 108), p. 824, and Elliot Smith, op. cit. (note 109), p. 37 ff.
[112] Rivers, op. cit. (note 32), pp. 27, 28.
[113] Dawson, op. cit. (note 45), p. 174.

114 Clayton Joel, "William James Perry 1887–1949", *Man* 50, 3 (1950). Meyer Fortes has written, in a marginal comment to the typescript of the present work, that he believes Perry to have been *related* to Rivers. However, apart from the fact that Perry sometimes begins his letters to Rivers by writing "Dear Uncle . . . ", the evidence seems to be against this belief. Certainly, as Rivers's biographer, Richard Slobodin has pointed out to me, Perry cannot have been an "actual" nephew of Rivers (in terms of our kinship system). Only one of Rivers's siblings, his brother Charles, was married; he had one child: a girl called Joan. Hence, Perry could not have been a consanguineal nephew of Rivers. Neither, since Perry did not marry Joan, could he have been a nephew in the affinal sense. It is still possible that Perry was a more distant kinsman of Rivers, but there does not seem to be any evidence for this. Perry's obituary in *The Times* for 4 May 1949 stresses his association with Rivers, but does not state that they were related. Moreover, Rivers's niece Joan talked to Professor Slobodin about Perry and Rivers without indicating any relationship between the two men (although Slobodin did not question her directly about this). Thus, in the absence of any supporting evidence, it would seem that the avuncular relationship implied by Perry's mode of addressing Rivers in letters must have had no biological or marital basis, but simply expressed the regard and affection of a younger man for his older mentor. This conclusion is decisively borne out by a recent letter from Mr. Clayton Joel, who writes:

> I can confirm, on the authority of Perry's daughter, that there was no family relationship between [Rivers and Perry]. During my close association with Perry over twenty years until his death in 1949, when Rivers's name frequently cropped up in conversation, he never, as far as I can recall, referred to the "relationship" . . . The use of the relationship terms was undoubtedly, as you surmised, an indication of their intellectual relationship which may have emerged some time after mid-1914, for in one of the few letters to Perry in which Rivers gives the year in his date, "June 18 1914", Perry was still "My dear Perry"; by April 1915 he was "My dear nephew".

115 Archives, Royal Anthropological Institute Library, London, A22.
116 W. J. Perry, "An Analysis of the Genealogical Tables Collected by Dr Richard Thurnwald in Buin", *Anthropos* 9, 801–811 (1914). Rivers refers to Perry's analysis in *The History of Melanesian Society*, Vol. II, pp. 28, 118.
117 Dawson, op. cit. (note 45), p. 161.
118 W. H. R. Rivers, *Psychology and Politics* (London, 1923), p. 122.
119 W. J. Perry, "On The Influence of Egyptian Civilization upon the World's Culture", *Rep. Brit. Assoc. Adv. Sci.* (1915), pp. 669, 670. Published in full in *Mem. and Proc. Manch. Lit. and Phil. Soc.* 60 (1915), pt. 1, pp. 1–36.
120 Rivers, op. cit. (note 118), pp. 118–121.
121 W. J. Perry, *The Megalithic Culture of Indonesia* (Manchester, 1918), p. ix.
122 Elliot Smith's preface to W. H. R. Rivers, *Medicine, Magic and Religion* (London, 1924), p. vii.
123 Letter from Perry to Rivers dated 27th May 1922, Haddon Collection, Envelope 12081.
124 Elliot Smith's preface to W. H. R. Rivers, *Social Organization* (New York, 1924), p. vi.
125 In a note to Rivers dated 25 Oct. 1915 (Haddon Collection, Envelope 12017), Perry talks about reading extracts for Rivers from a Dutch book.

[126] Obituary for Rivers by L. E. Shore, *The Eagle* (1922), pp. 7, 8.
[127] W. J. Perry, *The Children of the Sun* (London, 1923), pp. 476–78.
[128] Perry, op. cit. (note 123).
[129] Perry, op. cit. (note 127), p. 482 ff.
[130] Ibid., p. 485.
[131] Ibid., p. 477.
[132] Ibid., p. 484.
[133] Ibid., pp. 484, 485.
[134] Ibid., p. 485.
[135] Ibid., p. 479.
[136] Joel, op. cit. (note 114).
[137] R. L. Rooksby, "W. H. R. Rivers and the Todas", *South Asia* 1, 118 (1971).

CHAPTER V

[1] Warren R. Dawson (ed.), *Sir Grafton Elliot Smith. A Biographical Record by His Colleagues* (London, 1938), pp. 79, 80.
[2] Letter from Elliot Smith to Pitt-Rivers dated 30th August 1928, R.A.I. Archives, A58.
[3] R.A.I. Archives, A3, Part 2. See also *J. Roy. Anthrop. Inst.*, Miscellanea, 1922–27.
[4] Letter from Elliot Smith to John L. Myres dated 13 Dec. 1922, R.A.I. Archives, A58, Part 3.
[5] Ibid.
[6] Ibid.
[7] Letter from E. N. Fallaize to John L. Myres dated 18 Dec. 1922, R.A.I. Archives, A58, Part 3.
[8] Minutes of first meeting of "Joint Committee for Anthropological Research and Teaching", R.A.I. Archives, A58, Part 3.
[9] Letter from E. N. Fallaize to John L. Myres dated 30 May 1923, R.A.I. Archives, A58, Part 3.
[10] John L. Myres, memorandum entitled "The Relation of Anthropology to Other Subjects, With Special Reference to History, Geography and Economics", R.A.I. Archives, A58, Part 3.
[11] A. C. Haddon, "Migrations of Culture", *The Observer*, 22 June 1924.
[12] Dawson, op. cit. (note 1), p. 214.
[13] A. C. Haddon, "Pearls as Givers of Life", *Man* 24, 131 (1924).
[14] Haddon Collection, Envelope 5274.
[15] Letter from Elliot Smith to Haddon dated 16 Nov. 1924, Haddon Collection, Envelope 5274.
[16] Letter from Elliot Smith to Haddon dated 18 Nov. 1924, Haddon Collection, Envelope 5274.
[17] H. J. Fleure, obituary for Haddon in *Obituary Notices of Fellows of the Royal Society* 9, 451 (Jan. 1941).
[18] Letter from William Ridgeway to Haddon dated 10 Dec. 1924, Haddon Collection, Envelope 4.
[19] W. J. Perry, "Pearls and Pearl Shell in the Pacific", *Man* 25, 22 (1925).
[20] A. C. Haddon, "Pearls as Givers of Life", *Man* 25, 32 (1925).

21 *The Times*, 17 Jan. 1925.

22 Letter from E. N. Fallaize to John L. Myres dated 19 Jan. 1925, R.A.I. Archives, A58, Part 3.

23 Ibid.

24 *The Times*, 30 Jan. 1925.

25 Undated letter from Balfour to Fallaize, to which Fallaize replied on 11 Feb. 1925, R.A.I.Archives, A58, Part 3.

26 *The Times*, 23 Jan. 1925.

27 Letter from E. N. Fallaize to O. G. S. Crawford dated 11 Feb. 1925, R.A.I. Archives, A58, Part 3.

28 *Edinburgh Review*, Jan. 1924 and Apr. 1924.

29 Letter from O. G. S. Crawford to E. N. Fallaize dated 12 Feb. 1925, R.A.I. Archives, A58, Part 3.

30 *The Times Literary Supplement*, 11 June 1925.

31 Ibid.

32 *The Times Literary Supplement*, 18 June 1925.

33 Ibid.

34 *The Times Literary Supplement*, 25 June 1925.

35 In an interview with the author given in New Zealand in May 1976, C. E. Fox threw a little further light on the nature of his attitudes towards Rivers and Elliot Smith. After paying tribute to the personal and intellectual qualities of Rivers, Fox went on to indicate that he had some reservations about Elliot Smith, and said that, in his opinion, Rivers too was "not so sure" about the Australian anatomist.

36 Transcribed copy of letter from C. E. Fox to "The Reviewer of *The Threshold of the Pacific*", dated 25 Nov. 1925, Haddon Collection, Envelope 5363.

37 Letter of 13 Mar. 1980 from Paul Jorion to the author, following communications between Jorion and Mr. G. Phillips of *The Times* archives. In the doctoral dissertation upon which the present work is based, I wrongly inferred, from an ambiguous annotation by Haddon on a transcribed copy of the letter from Fox to his reviewer, that the reviewer was Colonel T. C. Hodson, who was shortly thereafter appointed to succeed Haddon as Reader in Ethnology at Cambridge. This led me, in the dissertation, to argue that Hodson's appointment was primarily motivated by the desire to stop the extreme diffusionists getting any sort of foothold in Cambridge Ethnology. Since, however, Jorion's industry and persistence has proved that Hodson was not the reviewer, and since, as will be argued shortly, it appears that Hodson was appointed to strengthen the Cambridge Department's claim to being an aid to imperialism, I have decided to drop this line of argument.

38 Letter from Elliot Smith to Haddon dated 5 Oct. 1926, Haddon Collection, Envelope 5274.

39 Rough draft of letter from Haddon to Radcliffe-Brown dated 26 Mar. 1927, Haddon Collection, Envelope 16002.

40 M. Mead, *Blackberry Winter* (New York, 1972), p. 159. See also Dawson op. cit. (note 1), pp. 77, 78.

41 Review of John Mathew's *Two Representative Tribe of Queensland*, Man **10**, 82 (1910).

42 B. Malinowski, *A Diary in the Strict Sense of the Term* (London, 1967), pp. 64, 65. The entry is actually dated 17 Jan. 1914, but this is obviously incorrect by a margin of one year.

[43] Ibid., pp. 65, 66.

[44] James Urry, "*Notes and Queries on Anthropology* and the Development of Field Methods in British Anthropology 1870–1920", *Proc. Roy. Anthrop. Inst.* (1972), p. 52.

[45] B. Malinowski, *Coral Gardens and Their Magic* (London, 1935), p. 326.

[46] Letter from Malinowski to Haddon dated 25 May 1916, Haddon Collection, Envelope 7.

[47] B. Malinowski, "Ethnology and the Study of Society", *Economica* 2, 218 (1922).

[48] B. Malinowski, *Argonauts of the Western Pacific* (New York, 1961, original edn., 1922), p. 15.

[49] Ibid., p. 5.

[50] B. Malinowski, *Myth in Primitive Psychology* (New York, 1926), pp. 92, 93.

[51] Raymond Firth, *Man and Culture* (New York, 1957), p. 6.

[52] Ibid. For a review of Malinowski's field diaries which draws some interesting parallels between Malinowski and Joseph Conrad, see George W. Stocking Jr., "Empathy and Antipathy in the Heart of Darkness", *J. Hist. Behav. Sci.* 4, 189–194 (1968).

[53] Meyer Fortes, *Kinship and the Social Order* (Chicago, 1969), p. 5.

[54] B. Malinowski, "Kinship", *Man* 30, 17 (1930).

[55] A. C. Haddon (ed.), *Reports of the Cambridge Anthropological Expedition to Torres Straits* 5 (1904). See Rivers's partly hypothetical sketch of the way a member of the Mabuiag community becomes familiar with the kinship system (pp. 140–142).

[56] B. Freire-Marreco and J. L. Myres (eds.), *Notes and Queries on Anthropology* (4th edn., London, 1912). See for example the section on "Social Organization".

[57] In A. C. Seward (ed.), *Science and the Nation* (Cambridge, 1917).

[58] From the Special Foreword to the third edition of *The Sexual Life of Savages* (London, 1932).

[59] John L. Myres, "A Geographical View of the Historical Method in Ethnology", *The Geographical Teacher* 13 (1925–1926).

[60] Ibid.

[61] Ibid.

[62] W. J. Perry, "Professor Myres and the Historical Method", *The Geographical Teacher* (1925).

[63] John L. Myres, "Reply to Mr Perry", *The Geographical Teacher* (1925).

[64] Letter from L. H. Dudley Buxton to Haddon dated 15 Mar. 1925, Haddon Collection, Envelope 5274.

[65] Letter from Mrs. Winifred Hoernle to Haddon dated 28 Apr. 1926, Haddon Collection, Envelope 9. In the same letter Mrs Hoernle talks about a well-known physical anthropologist who for our purposes had better remain nameless: "Professor [X] is a great trial in many ways, for he is a keen Elliot Smith man and is more keen than thorough. He starts all sorts of hair-brained [sic] theories without any basis or practically none, and of course he captures the popular imagination with the result that one is kept busy trying to check students from doing the same thing."

[66] Cambridge University Archives, "General Board of Studies", p. 36.

[67] Ibid., ("Private Uncorrected Minutes for Members of the General Board of Studies Only", 12 May 1926).

[68] Cambridge University Archives ("Private Uncorrected Minutes for Members of the General Board of Studies", p. 40, 21 July 1926). One of the two candidates interviewed was presumably Hodson. The identity of the second interviewee is not recorded.

[69] Personal communication with W. E. Armstrong, 19 Apr. 1973.

[70] Op. cit. (note 66), p. 20.

[71] Envelope 4019 in the Haddon Collection contains information regarding a special course of lectures for Indian Civil Service probationers given by Haddon in 1910 and 1911.

[72] Rep. Brit. Assoc. Adv. Sci. (1911), pp. 509, 510.

[73] Annotation in Haddon's handwriting on Fox, op. cit. (note 36).

[74] The Times Literary Supplement, 30 Sept. 1926.

[75] The Times Literary Supplement, 7 Oct. 1926.

[76] Letter from Elliot Smith to Haddon dated 1 Oct. 1926, Haddon Collection, Envelope 5274.

[77] Rough draft of a letter from Haddon to Elliot Smith dated 3 Oct. 1926, Haddon Collection, Envelope 5274.

[78] Letter from Elliot Smith to Haddon dated 5 Oct. 1926, Haddon Collection, Envelope 5274.

[79] Letter from Elliot Smith to E. E. Embree dated 31 Jan. 1927, Rockefeller Foundation Archives 401D.

[80] The year of publication of Tylor's Primitive Culture.

[81] Letter from Elliot Smith to C. J. Herrick dated 13 Feb. 1927, Rockefeller Foundation Archives, "401AD University College". Herrick, an eminent neurologist, was apparently acting for the Rockefeller Foundation during a visit to London.

[82] Letter from Elliot Smith to Embree dated 19 Feb. 1927, Rockefeller Foundation Archives, "401AD University College — Anthropology 1924, 1926–27 (No funds granted)".

[83] Ibid.

[84] Elliot Smith to Herrick, op. cit. (note 81).

[85] Elliot Smith to Embree, op. cit. (note 82). It was in fact on the basis of this policy that University College had created a Readership in Cultural Anthropology in 1922, which position Elliot Smith had originally tried to persuade Rivers to accept. (See Chapter IV, p. 146).

[86] Letter from E. E. Embree to Elliot Smith dated 23 Feb. 1927, Rockefeller Foundation Archives, "401AD".

[87] Letter from Elliot Smith to E. E. Embree dated 14 Mar. 1927, Rockefeller Foundation Archives, "401 AD". I could find no record in these archives of any Rockefeller grant earmarked for Malinowski at this time. Nonetheless he did benefit from a general grant which the Memorial provided for the London School of Economics.

[88] Letter from Elliot Smith to Embree dated 18 June 1927, Rockefeller Foundation Archives, "401AD".

[89] Letter from Dr Alan Gregg to Elliot Smith dated 20 June 1927, Rockefeller Foundation Archives, "401AD".

[90] G. Elliot Smith, Bronislaw Malinowski, Herbert J. Spinden and A. Goldenweiser, Culture: The Diffusion Controversy (London, Psyche Miniatures, 1928), p. 9.

[91] Ibid., p. 29.

[92] Ibid., p. 42.

[93] Ibid., p. 45.

[94] Ibid., p. 54.

[95] Ibid., p. 50, 51.

[96] Ibid., p. 92.

[97] Ibid., p. 94.

[98] Ibid., pp. 95–98.

[99] R.A.I. Archives, A24 (Rivers Memorial Fund Proceedings).

[100] R.A.I. Archives, A10, Part 4.

[101] Op. Cit. (note 99).

[102] Minutes of the R.A.I. "Appeal and Research Committee", 25 Oct. 1927, R.A.I. Archives, A58, Part 3. The "Appeal and Research Committee" was a subsidiary of the Joint Committee.

[103] This correspondence consisted of a letter from officials of the Melanesian Mission in the 8 June issue of *The Times*, and a letter by Keith, Westermarck and Pitt-Rivers in the 16 June issue.

[104] Letter from Fallaize to Myres date 26 June 1928, R.A.I. Archives, A58, Part 3.

[105] Minutes of the R.A.I. Appeal Committee Meeting, 3 July 1928, R.A.I. Archives, A58, Part 3.

[106] Letter from Fallaize to Myres dated 13 Aug. 1928 and letter from Myres to Fallaize 18 Aug. 1928, R.A.I. Archives, A58, Part 3.

[107] Letter from Elliot Smith to Pitt-Rivers dated 30 Aug. 1928, R.A.I. Archives, A58, Part 3.

[108] Ibid.

[109] Ibid.

[110] Ibid.

[111] Ibid.

[112] Letter from Keith to Fallaize dated 28 Aug. 1928, R.A.I. Archives, A58, Part 3.

[113] Letter from Fallaize to Keith dated 30 Aug. 1928, R.A.I. Archives, A58, Part 3.

[114] Letter from Fallaize to Myres dated 30 Aug. 1928, R.A.I. Archives, A58, Part 3.

[115] Letter from Fallaize to Perry dated 19 Sept. 1928, R.A.I. Archives, A58, Part 3.

[116] Letter from Perry to Fallaize dated 23 Sept. 1928, R.A.I. Archives, A58, Part 3.

[117] Letter from Fallaize to Elliot Smith dated 25 Sept. 1928, R.A.I. Archives, A58, Part 3.

[118] Letter from Fallaize to Myres dated 8 Nov. 1928, R.A.I. Archives, A58, Part 3.

[119] Screed headed "Royal Anthropological Institute Appeal", R.A.I. Archives, A58, Part 3.

[120] Letter from C. G. Seligman to Fallaize dated 7 Jan. 1929, R.A.I. Archives, A58, Part 3. The "highly qualified man" working in the Sudan was presumably E. E. Evans-Pritchard, then engaged upon his investigations of the Azande.

[121] Letter from Elliot Smith to Fallaize dated 9 Jan. 1929, R.A.I. Archives, A58, Part 3.

[122] Screed headed "Draft of Anthropological Research Fund Appeal", R.A.I. Archives, A58, Part 3.

[123] Screed headed "Suggestion as the Basis for Discussion of an Appeal for Funds for Anthropological Research", R.A.I. Archives, A58, Part 3.

[124] Letter from Fallaize to Elliot Smith dated 31 Jan. 1929, R.A.I. Archives, A58, Part 3.

[125] Letter from Elliot Smith to Fallaize dated 1 Feb. 1929, R.A.I. Archives, A58, Part 3.

[126] Letter from Myres to Fallaize dated 6 Mar. 1929, letter from Fallaize to Myres dated 8 Mar. 1929, and letter from Ormsby Gore to Fallaize dated 11 Apr. 1929, R.A.I. Archives, A58, Part 3.

[127] Index to *The Times*, 1929.

[128] Circular letter by Fallaize dated 1 May 1928, R.A.I. Archives, A58, Part 3.

[129] Sheet of paper headed "Replies to Enquiries as to the Establishment of Anthropological Union under the International Research Council", R.A.I. Archives, A58, Part 3.

[130] Letter from Elliot Smith to Fallaize dated 10 May 1928, R.A.I. Archives, A58, Part 3.

[131] Letter from Perry to Fallaize dated 14 May 1928, R.A.I. Archives, A58, Part 3.

[132] Lothian Collection, Edinburgh.

[133] Letter from C. G. Seligman to the Trustees of the Laura Spelman Rockefeller Memorial dated 1 July 1925, letter from C. G. Seligman to Dr B. Ruml dated 3 July 1925, letter from Dr B. Ruml to C. G. Seligman dated 31 July 1925, letter from C. G. Seligman to Dr B. Ruml dated 23 Oct. 1925, and letter from E. N. Fallaize to Dr B. Ruml dated 6 Nov. 1925, Rockefeller Foundation Archives, Laura Spelman Rockefeller Memorial, "Royal Anthropological Institute 1924–30".

[134] Letter from Fallaize to George E. Vincent, President of the Rockefeller Foundation, dated 30 Jan. 1929, Rockefeller Foundation Archives, Laura Spelman Rockefeller Memorial, "Royal Anthropological Institute 1924–30".

[135] Inter-office correspondence between E. E. Day and G. E. Vincent dated 27 Feb. 1929, Rockefeller Foundation Archives, Laura Spelman Rockefeller Memorial, "Royal Anthropological Institute 1924–30".

[136] Annotation on letter from E. E. Day to Elton Mayo dated 8 Mar. 1929, Rockefeller Foundation Archives, Laura Spelman Rockefeller Memorial, "Royal Anthropological Institute 1924–30".

[137] Letter from E. E. Day to Fallaize dated 3 Apr. 1929, Rockefeller Foundation Archives, Laura Spelman Rockefeller Memorial, "Royal Anthropological Institute 1924–30".

[138] Letter from G. E. Vincent to Fallaize dated 23 May 1929, Rockefeller Foundation Archives, Laura Spelman Rockefeller Memorial, "Royal Anthropological Institute 1924–30".

[139] Letter from Hocart to Haddon dated 23 June, Haddon Collection, Envelope 4. Although the year is not given in the date on the letter, one can be reasonably confident from a knowledge of the dates of Hocart's fieldwork that the year was indeed 1929.

[140] Excerpt from dairy of J. Van Sickle headed "Paris, October 6th 1930", Rockefeller Foundation Archives, Laura Spelman Rockefeller Memorial, "Royal Anthropological Institute 1924–30".

[141] The suggestion that Elliot Smith should represent the Royal Anthropological Institute at this Congress was made by Pitt-Rivers, who seems to have been more favourably inclined to Elliot Smith than most other members of the Institute. See letter from Pitt-Rivers to Myres dated 27 Aug. 1928, R.A.I. Archives, A58, Part 3.

[142] R.A.I. Archives, A24, Judging from the handwriting, the author of these retrospective "Proceedings" was J. L. Myres.

[143] Ibid.

[144] Letter from E. E. Day to J. Van Sickle dated 17 July 1931, Rockefeller Foundation Archives, "401S Royal Anthropological Institute 1931–33, 1937–38".

[145] In addition to his apparently negative reaction to Keith's version of the Institute's appeal for funds, Elliot Smith had earlier crossed swords with Keith over the evidence

relating to the so-called "Piltdown Man". See the correspondence in *Nature* 92 (Sept. 1913 – Feb. 1914).

[146] R.A.I. Archives, A23.

[147] Dawson op. cit. (note 1), p. 85. This source states that, on Elliot Smith's recollection, the term "human biology" emerged in the course of discussion with E. E. Embree following Elliot Smith's trip to Australia in 1932. However, this date must be wrong, since the term was in currency before 1932.

[148] Rockefeller Foundation Archives, "401S Royal Anthropological Institute 1931–33, 1937–38".

[149] Fortes, "Discussion" of Glyn Daniel's paper on "Elliot Smith, Egypt and Diffusionism", in Lord S. Zuckerman (ed.), *The Concepts of Human Evolution* (Academic Press, 1973), p. 431.

[150] Young, in Zuckerman, ibid., p. 167.

[151] This article appears in James Hasting's *Encyclopaedia of Religion and Ethics* (Edinburgh, 1913). In the 1930 volume of *Man* (p. 20 fn), Malinowski described the article as "excellent".

[152] Letter from Myres to Fallaize dated 25 Sept. 1928, R.A.I. Archives, A58, Part 3.

CHAPTER VI

[1] W. H. R. Rivers, *The History of Melanesian Society* (Cambridge, 1914) Vol. I, p. 1.

[2] C. E. Fox, *The Threshold of the Pacific* (London, 1924), p. vi.

[3] W. H. R. Rivers, "The Unity of Anthropology", *J. Roy. Anthrop. Inst.* 52, 19 (1922).

[4] Letter from Fred. G. Bowie of Tangoa, Santo, New Hebrides, to Rivers dated 6 Oct. 1920, Haddon Collection, Envelope 12081.

[5] Letter from Fred. G. Bowie to Humphreys (then apparently in Sydney) dated 6 Oct. 1920, Haddon Collection, Envelope 12081.

[6] Bowie, op. cit. (note 4).

[7] Letter from Fred. G. Bowie written in Aberdeen Scotland, to Rivers dated 9 May 1922, Haddon Collection, Envelope 12081.

[8] C. B. Humphreys, *The Southern New Hebridge – An Ethnological Record* (Cambridge University Press, 1926), p. x.

[9] Ibid.

[10] Ibid.

[11] Haddon Collection, Envelope 4.

[12] John Layard, personal communication. Something of the flavour of the Heretics Society may be gleaned from Kingsley Martin's book *Father Figures* (London, 1966). Martin writes that the object of the Society was "to take the place of compulsory chapel. Why should not students discuss philosophy seriously instead of singing hymns and listening to sermons?" (p. 108). Martin describes how Lytton Strachey read a paper at the Society which "discussed the proper attitude to sex and had the great advantage from our point of view of breaking all conventions about the value of 'the bawdy'" (p. 102). He also gives a memorable pen-portrait of C. K. Ogden (pp. 105–108), and describes him as the "creator" of the Society.

[13] Layard, ibid.

[14] John Layard, *Stone Men of Malekula* (London, 1942), p. xvii.

15 A. C. Haddon, "Report to the Percy Sladen Trustees on the Expedition to Papua", Haddon Collection, Envelope 25. Ironically Haddon himself was eventually able to arrange a survey cruise to New Guinea in 1914. Whilst in the Mailu area, he met up with Malinowski, then pursuing his first, tentative ethnographic expedition, which was later followed by the Polish emigre's now famous intensive fieldwork in the Trobriands.

16 One gathers from Malinowski's diary (B. Malinowski, *A Diary in the Strict Sense of the Term*, London, 1967) that he did not live among the native huts at all during his first expedition to New Guinea, lasting from August 1914 to March 1915. Indeed the first diary entry which records the pitching of his tent in a native village is 13 Dec. 1917 (Malinowski, ibid., p. 150 ff), during his third expedition. This would have been more than two years after Layard "went native" on Atchin. However, Malinowski's diary scarcely covers his second expedition at all, and one may infer from other sources that he must have lived in his tent for a considerable period of time during this expedition, which lasted from May 1915 to May 1916. For example, *Argonauts of the Western Pacific* contains a photograph of Malinowski's tent pitched in the village of Omarakana, where Malinowski worked for part of his second expedition; and, in a letter written to Haddon from Samarai on 15 Oct. 1915 (Haddon Collection, Envelope 7), Malinowski, after bemoaning the standard of his ethnography during the first expedition, states that he is now "living right among the natives in a village, since beginning of July".

17 John Layard, personal communication, July 1973.

18 W. E. Armstrong, personal communication, Apr. 1973.

19 Actually Armstrong refers to his closed class systems with a descent interval of three generations as "twelve-class" systems. This apparent terminological confusion is due to the fact that Armstrong is regarding brothers and sisters as belonging to separate classes, rather than to the same class. When this difference from usual anthropological terminology is acknowledged, as Armstrong himself does, the twelve classes of his closed systems may be seen as corresponding to what are normally called the six classes of the Ambrym system.

20 W. E. Armstrong, *Rossel Island* (Cambridge, 1928), p. 248.

21 Armstrong's first diagram looks as follows:

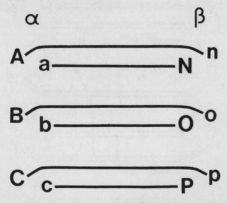

α and β are the two matrilineal moieties. A, B, C etc. represent successive generations, capital letters indicating males and small letters females. Horizontal lines indicate marriage.

When the marriage lines are drawn double, to conform with current practice, lines indicating siblingship and descent are included, and four rather than three successive generations are depicted, Armstrong's diagram becomes:

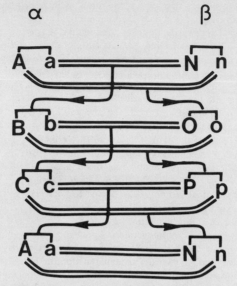

Now the actual Ambrym system may be represented by the following diagram, which is equivalent to Figure 10.

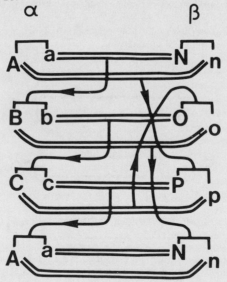

A comparison of the latter two diagrams makes the two systems *appear* to be quite similar. As Professor J. A Barnes has pointed out to me, this apparent similarity may have no real structural significance, and probably represents nothing more than an arte-fact of the convention used in drawing the diagrams. Nonetheless, it is worth remarking firstly that the convention used in drawing the diagrams was deployed by Armstrong (and was presumably taught to his pupils), and secondly that Deacon tended to concep-tualize kinship systems in pictorial, diagrammatic terms.

[22] Armstrong, op. cit. (note 20), pp. 255, 246.

[23] T. T. Barnard, personal communication, Apr. 1973.

[24] T. T. Barnard, "The Social Organization of Ambrim", *Man* 28, 134 (Aug. 1928).

[25] Ibid.

[26] Barnard, op. cit. (note 23).

[27] Haddon Collection, Envelope 6.

[28] Barnard, op. cit. (note 24).

[29] Barnard, op. cit. (note 23).

[30] Ibid.

[31] Barnard, op. cit. (note 24).

[32] Ibid.

[33] T. T. Barnard, "The Regulation of Marriage in the New Hebrides . . ." (Cambridge University Ph.D. Thesis, 1924), Chap. VI, p. 2.

[34] Ibid., Chap. VI, p. 23.

[35] Ibid.

[36] Ibid., pp. 23, 24.

[37] Barnard, op. cit. (note 23).

[38] Ibid.

[39] Barnard, op. cit (note 33), Chap. VI, p. 34.

[40] Barnard, op. cit. (note 24), p. 135. C.f. Barnard, op. cit. (note 33), Chap. VI, p. 22.

[41] Barnard, op. cit. (note 33), Chap. VI, p. 36; Chap. VI, Appendix B, p. 1.

[42] For example, Barnard, op. cit. (note 23). See also letter from Barnard to Mrs Rishbeth (Kathleen Haddon) dated 31 Oct. 1954 (Haddon Collection, Envelope 12001). My use of the word "mere" in connection with "deduction" is, I feel, appropriate in reference to the Britanically empirical context in which Barnard worked.

[43] Barnard, op. cit. (note 23).

[44] Letter from Barnard to Mrs Rishbeth dated 31 Oct. 1954, Haddon Collection, En-velope 12001.

[45] John Layard, personal communication, 1972. Envelope 16003 of the Haddon Collec-tion contains a letter to Haddon from the missionary at whose home Deacon died, dated 17 Oct. 1927. From this one gathers that Haddon had written asking whether Deacon had in fact died of blackwater fever.

[46] Haddon's preface to *Malekula — A Vanishing People in the New Hebrides* by A. Bernard Deacon, p. xiv.

[47] Undated letter from Deacon to Haddon written at Bushman's Bay, N. E. Malekula, Haddon Collection, Envelope 16005.

[48] Letter from Deacon to Haddon written at South West Bay, Malekula, 15 Feb. 1927, Haddon Collection, Envelope 16001. Also quoted in Haddon, op. cit. (note 46).

[49] From box of Deacon's papers held by Edmund Leach, Mar. 1980. I am indebted to

Paul Jorion for pointing out the existence of these papers, and for sending me photo-copies of them.

[50] Letter from Edmund Leach to Paul Jorion dated 14 Mar. 1980.

[51] Haddon, op. cit. (note 46), p. xv.

[52] Deacon's article on "The Kakihan Society of Ceram . . ." reveals Patasiwa and Patalima to be the names of two groups of inhabitants of the western district of Ceram. The article further states that the religious and social system embodied in the cult practised by the ruling elite of the Patasiwa presents an association of cultural elements characteristic of Perry's "Archaic Civilization", and that this elite may possibly con-stitute "the most definite example in Indonesia today" of the "Children of the Sun". While representing a considerable concession to Perry's views, this opinion is based upon alleged cultural convergences, rather than on the kind of socio-structural evidence which would be necessary to warrant labelling Patasiwa and Patalima a "Dual Organization". Hence Deacon's exclamation mark.

[53] Haddon Collection, Envelope 16014.

[54] Barnard, op. cit. (note 23).

[55] Haddon, op. cit. (note 46), p. xvi.

[56] Haddon, ibid., p. xvi, and Layard's "Supplementary Preface", included in some copies of Deacon's *Malekula* . . . Haddon's account does imply that he had known about South West Bay only because of Layard's fieldwork there. A letter from Layard to Haddon dated 3 May 1934 (Haddon Collection, Envelope 16012) also discussed this matter, with Layard refusing to relinquish his claim to having directed Deacon's atten-tion to South West Bay.

[57] Haddon Collection, Envelope 16002.

[58] Letter from Deacon to Armstrong dated 4 Nov. 1925, R.A.I. Manuscripts, MS 91. The R.A.I. Manuscripts also contain (MS 98) an undated rough draft by Deacon of what appears to be a developed version of ideas mentioned in this letter. The rough draft is notable for its attempt, possibly under the influence of Armstrong, to explain the development of a Melanesian grading system less in terms of cultural transmission, than by recourse to purely economic factors.

[59] Letter from Deacon to Haddon dated 16 Jan. 1926, Haddon Collection, Envelope 16009.

[60] Deacon, ibid. I have been unable to ascertain the identity of Rorsali.

[61] Notes found amongst Deacon's papers indicate that, as well as being familiar with the eight-class systems of the Arunta and Warramunga, Deacon interpreted the Dieri system as possessing eight classes (although these classes are not named). Now, as I have pointed out in Chapter I, the Arunta and Warramunga systems both have matrilineal periodicities of four. And the Dieri system likewise has a matrilineal periodicity of four when it is interpreted as Deacon does. Since Deacon's time, however, eight-class systems with matri-periodicities different from four have been suggested. Although I have not seen Marcel Granet's *Catégories matrimoniales et relations de proximité dans la Chine ancienne* (Paris, 1939), the work is said to postulate the existence of an eight-class 244 system in China. And according to J. A. Barnes, Trobriand marriage has recently been analyzed in terms of an eight-class 224 system.

[62] Letter from Haddon to Deacon dated 20 May 1926, in box of Deacon's papers held by Edmund Leach, Mar. 1980. The letters from Haddon in this box, copies of which were kindly sent to me by Paul Jorion, deal with the early part of Deacon's fieldwork,

for which I have unfortunately been unable to locate Deacon's side of the correspondence. (The letters from Deacon which I *have* tracked down, and which I use extensively in the present chapter, were written mainly during the latter part of his fieldwork, for which, ironically, Haddon's side of the correspondence does *not* seem to have survived.)

[63] *The Historical Register of the University of Cambridge Supplement, 1921–30* (Cambridge University Press, 1932), p. 319.

[64] Letter from Haddon to Deacon dated 2 Aug. 1926, in box of Deacon's papers held by Edmund Leach, Mar. 1980.

[65] Landtman's monograph on the Kiwai was not to be published until 1927. For a discussion of the place of the ethnographic achievements of Landtman and his fellow Finn Rafael Karsten in the development of intensive fieldwork in British Social Anthropology, see George W. Stocking, "Clio's Fancy: Documents to Pique the Historical Imagination", *History of Anthropology Newsletter* Vol. VI, No. 2 (1979), pp. 9–12.

[66] R.A.I. Archives, MS 91 (Copied extracts from Deacon's letters, South West Bay, June 1926).

[67] Ibid.

[68] Letter from Deacon to Armstrong, May 1926, Haddon Collection, Envelope 16006.

[69] Copy of letter from Bernard Deacon to his father, headed South West Bay, May 1926, Haddon Collection.

[70] Deacon, op. cit. (note 66).

[71] Ibid.

[72] R.A.I. Archives, MS 91. (Copied extracts from Deacon's letters, 1926, this extract from Lambumbu.)

[73] R.A.I. Archives, MS 91. (Copied extracts from Deacon's letters, 1926, this extract apparently from Lambumbu.)

[74] Ibid.

[75] Ibid.

[76] Ibid.

[77] Elliot Smith would not have liked to have been linked by implication to Griffith Taylor in this way. In *Nature* No. 2834, Vol. 113 (1924), p. 291, Elliot Smith refers derogatorily to Griffith Taylor's work, which he apparently regards as naively deterministic in regard to geographical factors. He implies that Taylor's "Isothermal zones" have had very little effect on "human structure", and says "Such speculations have done immense harm in impeding serious research".

[78] R.A.I. Archives, MS 91. (Copied extracts from Deacon's letters, 1926, this extract apparently from Lambumbu.)

[79] Letter from Deacon to Haddon written at Lambumbu, Oct. 1926, Haddon Collection, Envelope 16006.

[80] Ibid.

[81] Ibid.

[82] Ibid.

[83] R.A.I. Archives, MS 91. (Copied extracts from Deacon's letters, this extract written from Bushman's Bay, 29 Oct. 1926.) Haddon may have had this passage in mind when he wrote in the preface to Deacon's *Malekula*, "I have not thought it necessary to transcribe a good deal of what Deacon wrote in his letters to various friends, as had he lived he might have expressed himself differently."

[84] Ibid.

[85] Letter from Deacon to Haddon labelled "South West Bay, Februray 15th 1927", Haddon Collection, Envelope 16001.

[86] Undated letter from Deacon to Haddon, written from Bushman's Bay, N.E. Malekula, Haddon Collection, Envelope 16005.

[87] In a letter to Haddon written from South West Bay and dated 15 Feb. 1927 (Haddon Collection, Envelope 16001), Deacon, who had just finished his six week stint on Ambrym, writes that he had sent out a "first report (very brief)" of his Ambrym work to Radcliffe-Brown, and had already received a laudatory reply in "the last mail". This should be compared with a letter to Haddon dated 1 Mar. 1927 (Haddon Collection, Envelope 16001), in which Radcliffe-Brown writes that Deacon had sent him "some little time ago" a "detailed account of the class system he has discovered in Ambrym". It is possible that Deacon notified Radcliffe-Brown of his discovery at an even earlier date than the one (or ones) which might be inferred from these letters, for in another letter which Deacon's mother later quoted to Haddon, and which she claims was headed "Feb 4th 1926 Balap, S. W. Ambrym" (the year should certainly be 1927) Deacon refers to the Ambrym system and says that he is cheered by "Browne's letter", since it confirms his own views on the importance of the discovery (Haddon Collection, Envelope 16003). Whatever the interpretation to be placed on this piece of evidence, it is also debatable whether the "first", "very brief" report mentioned in the 15 Feb. letter to Haddon refers to the notes which eventually became the published paper or not. Haddon states in his introduction to the paper that Deacon sent "a brief account" of his Ambrym work to Armstrong, Radcliffe-Brown and Haddon himself, and "later" wrote the paper which "fully proves and documents his independent discovery". However, in a letter to Haddon dated 2 May 1927 (Haddon Collection, Envelope 25), Radcliffe-Brown writes that "Deacon sent me only one portion of his notes, dealing with the kinship organization of Ambrym . . . Beyond this I have nothing except five geometrical figures which he collected in Ambrym". This is supported by a further letter to Haddon dated 25 May 1926 (obviously should be 1927), in which Radcliffe-Brown writes, "I am sending you all the MS notes that I have received from Deacon. Apart from a few Ambrym geometrical figures they consist of a brief description of the Ambrym system of kinship and marriage. It is this I consider so important as to be worth publishing as soon as possible" (Haddon Collection, Envelope 16002).

[88] Actually descent in Buin is matrilineal — see Chapter III, p. 110.

[89] See Chapter III, p. 102.

[90] A. Bernard Deacon, "The Regulation of Marriage in Ambrym", *J. Roy. Anthrop. Inst.* 57, 326, 327 (1927).

[91] Ibid., p. 327.

[92] Ibid., p. 329.

[93] For the sake of making Figures 18 and 19 compatible with Figure 20, I have used letters different from those employed by Deacon.

[94] Deacon says "the children of" the married couples, but this is obviously a mistake.

[95] For his exposition of the standard six-section system, Layard chooses to use data from the Ranon district of Ambrym (*Stone Men of Malekula*, p. 121 ff). The only major difference between the Ranon system and the Balap system is that, in the former, the society is regarded as being divided into two matrilineal moieties called "*batutun*", whereas in the latter, the division into matrilineal moieties is (to quote Deacon) "absent,

or only slightly developed". For this reason, Layard depicts his annulus as circularly bisected, in contrast to the non-bisected annulus of my Figure 22.

[96] Undated letter from Deacon to Haddon written at Bushman's Bay, N.E. Malekula, Haddon Collection, Envelope 16005. Quoted in Deacon, op. cit. (note 90), p. 329 fn.

[97] Deacon, op. cit. (note 90), p. 332.

[98] Ibid., p. 334.

[99] Ibid., Introduction by Haddon, p. 325.

[100] Letter from B. Seligman to Haddon dated 27 Sept. 1927, Haddon Collection, Envelope 16002.

[101] Review of Deacon's *Malekula* by Layard in *Nature*, 15 Sept. 1934.

[102] Layard, op. cit. (note 14), p. xxii.

[103] Ibid., p. 47.

[104] T. T. Barnard, personal communication, Apr. 1973.

[105] Barnard, op. cit (note 24), p. 133.

[106] A. R. Radcliffe-Brown, "The Regulation of Marriage in Ambrym", *J. Roy. Anthrop. Inst.* 57, 348 (1927).

[107] Letter from Radcliffe-Brown to Haddon dated 1 Mar. 1927, Haddon Collection, Envelope 16001.

[108] Quoted in letter from Deacon to Haddon dated 15 Feb. 1927, Haddon Collection, Envelope 16001.

[109] Radcliffe-Brown, op. cit. (note 106), p. 343.

[110] Layard, op. cit. (note 14), p. xxii.

[111] Letter from B. Seligman to Haddon dated 27 Sept. 1927, Haddon Colleciton, Envelope 16002.

[112] Letter from B. Seligman to Haddon dated 11 Jan. 1928, Haddon Collection, Envelope 16002.

[113] Letter from Felix Speiser to Haddon dated 19 Apr. 1928, Haddon Collection, Envelope 16002.

[114] Seligman, op. cit. (note 112).

[115] Letter from A. R. Radcliffe-Brown to Haddon dated 11 Jan. 1930, Haddon Collection, Envelope 5416.

[116] Letter from Deacon to his mother, quoted in her letter to Haddon dated 29 Apr. 1928, Haddon Collection, Envelope 16003.

[117] Letter from Deacon to Haddon dated 15th Feb. 1927, Haddon Collection, Envelope 16001.

[118] This, as will be evident from the account given in Chapter III, is incorrect. Rivers questioned his Ambrym informant on the island of Tangoa.

[119] Deacon, op. cit. (note 90), p. 327.

[120] Letter from Deacon to his mother, quoted in her letter to Haddon dated 29 Apr. 1928, Haddon Collection, Envelope 16003.

[121] Undated letter from Deacon to Haddon written from Bushman's Bay, N.E. Malekula, Haddon Collection, Envelope 16005.

[122] Rodney Needham has convincingly called into question Radcliffe-Brown's good faith in making this claim. See Chapter 3 of Needham's *Remarks and Inventions – Skeptical Essays About Kinship* (London, 1974).

[123] Radcliffe-Brown, op. cit. (note 106), p. 343.

[124] R.A.I. Archives, MS 91. (Copied extracts from Deacon's letters, 1926; undated extract, apparently from Lambumbu).

[125] Letter from Deacon to Haddon dated 15 Feb. 1927, Haddon Collection, Envelope 16001.

[126] Assuming that Deacon here does mean "paper" and not "thesis", he must have been referring to an unpublished paper, for Barnard at this time had not published any of his results.

[127] Undated letter from Deacon to Haddon written at Bushman's Bay, N.E. Malekula, Haddon Collection, Envelope 16005.

[128] Barnard, op. cit. (note 24), p. 133.

[129] Ibid., p. 135.

[130] Barnard, op. cit. (note 23).

[131] Letter from Radcliffe-Brown to Haddon dated 29 July 1927, Haddon Collection, Envelope 16002. An extract from Deacon's letter to Radcliffe-Brown is contained in the R.A.I. Archives, MS 98.

[132] Letter from Radcliffe Brown to Haddon dated 28 Apr. 1931, Haddon Collection, Envelope 16001.

[133] Ibid.

[134] The female member of the missionary couple with whom Deacon stayed at South West Bay died in June 1927, which added to the confusion about what happened to Deacon's effects. In a letter to Haddon dated 28 April 1931 (Haddon Collection, Envelope 16001), Radcliffe-Brown writes that when the male missionary left South West Bay (presumably after the death of his wife), "there were vast masses of paper scattered about, some of which were destroyed by the people who succeeded him".

[135] Rough draft of a paper from Haddon to Mrs Emily Deacon, dated 21 March 1927, Haddon Collection, Envelope 16003. There can be no doubt that Haddon, in expressing this hope, was not simply being considerate to the bereaved mother of a former student. In a letter to Bernard Deacon dated 20 May 1926 (from box of Deacon's papers held by Edmund Leach), Haddon had advised Deacon, who was still in his early twenties, to take up a lectureship at the University of Sydney, adding: "After you have had experience in teaching you would have a very strong claim for anything that might be going in England."

[136] Letter from Mrs Emily Deacon (Bernard Deacon's mother) to Haddon dated 29 Mar. 1927, Haddon Collection, Envelope 16003.

[137] Quoted in rough draft of postscript dated 31 Mar. 1927 to letter dated 26 Mar. 1927 from Haddon to Radcliffe-Brown, Haddon Collection, Envelope 16002.

[138] Emily Deacon, op. cit. (note 136).

[139] Letter from Mrs Emily Deacon to Haddon dated 25 Mar. 1927, Haddon Collection, Envelope 16003.

[140] Rough draft of a letter from Haddon to Radcliffe-Brown dated 26 Mar. 1927, Haddon Collection, Envelope 16002.

[141] Ibid.

[142] Ibid.

[143] Rough draft of postscript dated 31 Mar. 1927 to rough draft of letter dated 26 Mar. 1927 from Haddon to Radcliffe-Brown, Haddon Collection, Envelope 16002.

[144] Letter from Radcliffe-Brown to Haddon dated 9 May 1927, Haddon Collection, Envelope 25.

[145] Letter (presumably to Haddon) from Ewan Corlette dated 6 Dec. 1927, Haddon Collection, Envelope 16003.

[146] *J. Roy. Anthrop. Inst.* 57, Miscellanea (1927).

[147] Note from Elliot Smith to Haddon dated 12 Dec. 1927, Haddon Collection, Envelope 16002.

[148] Envelope 16012 of the Haddon Collection contains a series of letters relating to this matter. The "Supplementary Preface" in its published form was simply headed "Note", and was inserted immediately after Wedgwood's "Introduction", with which it took issue on a number of points. Layard was also permitted to insert a "List of Errata Occurring in References to Mr Layard's Work", and a series of errata and corrigenda which were interleaved at appropriate places in the text. Despite Haddon and the publishers agreeing to the insertion of this material, I have come across some copies of the book which do not, in fact, contain it.

[149] Haddon's letters to Deacon (in box of Deacon's papers held by Edmund Leach) make evident the influence of Haddon in persuading Radcliffe-Brown that Deacon should be hired as a lecturer. In a letter dated 3 Mar. 1926 Haddon writes: "Radcliffe-Brown is arriving this month ... I have much to say to him about future developments in Australia. I know about the Rockefeller schemes for Australia and possibly some extension might be made to Melanesia." Later letters by Haddon make it clear that his plans for an Australian-based study of Melanesia involve the lectureship in Social Anthropology at the University of Sydney, and that for this position he recommends Deacon:

> I have seen a good deal of A. Radcliffe-Brown and have told him about you and shown him your Folklore paper ... If he can manage it I feel sure that he will offer you the Lectureship in the Univ. of Sydney when you go to S. from the New Hebrides ... I feel certain that you and he would form a strong and harmonious team [9 Apr. 1926].

> Brown will at first devote himself to research in Australia and this will take several years and he proposes to leave Melanesia etc. to the lecturer ... I have very little doubt that Brown would do his best to appoint you − if you care to apply. He is a "strong" man and would probably get his own way ... I think you might do much worse than settle in Sydney for a time and continue your Melanesian researches ... [20 May 1926].

CHAPTER VII

[1] A. R. Radcliffe-Brown, "The Study of Kinship Systems", original 1941, reprinted in Radcliffe-Brown, *Structure and Function in Primitive Society* (New York, 1965), p. 50.

Raymond Firth, "Alfred Reginald Radcliffe-Brown 1881−1955", *Proc. Brit. Acad.* 42 (1956).

Fred Eggan and Lloyd Warner, "Alfred Reginald Radcliffe-Brown 1881−1955", *Am. Anthrop.* 58 (1956).

Letter from Radcliffe-Brown to Rev. W. A. Goodwin dated 9 Jan. 1922, Haddon Collection, Envelope 4.

[2] A. R. Radcliffe-Brown, "The Methods of Ethnology and Social Anthropology", original 1923, reprinted in M. N. Srinivas (ed.), *Method in Social Anthropology* (Chicago, 1958), p. 22.

Letter from Radcliffe-Brown to Mauss dated 6 Aug. 1912. Quoted in Steven Lukes, *Émile Durkheim. His Life and Work* (London, 1973), p. 527.

A. R. Radcliffe-Brown, *Structure and Function in Primitive Society* (Free Press, 1965), pp. 123 ff, 178 ff.

A. R. Radcliffe-Brown, 1932 Preface to *The Andaman Islanders* (Free Press, 1964), p. viii.

A. R. Radcliffe-Brown, *The Social Organization of Australian Tribes*, Oceania Monograph No. 1 (1931), p. 15, n. 5.

Fragment headed "Aranda Totemism" found in Radcliffe-Brown's personal copy of the above monograph, Rare Book Room, Fisher Library, University of Sydney.

A. R. Radcliffe-Brown, "Australian Social Organization", *Am. Anthrop.* NS 49, 151–154 (1947).

[3] *J. Roy. Anthrop. Inst.* **12** (1882).

[4] Sir Richard Temple, obituary for E. H. Man, *Man* **30**, 9 (1930).

[5] Letter from Temple to Haddon dated 16 Mar. 1906, Haddon Collection, Envelope 8.

[6] Letter from Radcliffe-Brown to Haddon dated 10 Aug. 1906, Haddon Collection, Envelope 8.

[7] Letter from Radcliffe-Brown to Haddon written circa 26 Aug. 1906, Haddon Collection, Envelope 8.

[8] Ibid.

[9] Ibid.

[10] A. R. Radcliffe-Brown, *The Andaman Islanders* (1964, Free Press reprint of 1922 Cambridge University Press edn.), p. 82 n. See also p. 69 n., p. 322 n.

[11] Ibid., p. 72 n.

[12] *J. Roy. Anthrop. Inst.* **12**, 421–425 (1882).

[13] A. R. Radcliffe-Brown, 1932 Preface to *The Andaman Islanders* (Free Press edn., 1964).

[14] A. R. Radcliffe-Brown, "The Religion of the Andaman Islanders", *Folklore* **XX**, 257–271 (1909).

[15] W. Schmidt, "Pulaga, the Supreme Being of the Andamanese", *Man* **10**, 2 (1910).

[16] A. R. Radcliffe-Brown, "Pulaga – A Reply to Father Schmidt", *Man* **10**, 17 (1910).

[17] A. Lang, "Pulaga", *Man* **10**, 30 (1910).

[18] Sir Richard Temple, Obituary for E. H. Man, *Man* **30**, 9 (1930).

[19] M. Harris, *The Rise of Anthropological Theory* (New York, 1968), p. 391.

[20] H. R. Hays, *From Ape to Angel* (Capricorn edn., New York, 1964), p. 134.

[21] E. L. Grant Watson, *But to What Purpose* (London, 1946), pp. 83, 84.

[22] Ibid., p. 83.

[23] M. Mead, letter to Ruth Benedict dated 18 Oct. 1928. Quoted in Margaret Mead, *Writings of Ruth Benedict. An Anthropologist At Work* (New York, 1966), p. 310.

[24] Ruth Benedict, letter to Margaret Mead dated 28 Dec. 1932. Quoted in Mead, ibid., p. 327. For other comments revelatory of Radcliffe-Brown's personality, see Mead, ibid., pp. 309, 326–328, 333–335, 433.

[25] A. P. Elkin, "A. R. Radcliffe-Brown, 1880–1955", *Oceania* **XXVI**, 243 (June 1956).

[26] Firth, op. cit. (note 1), p. 296.

[27] Ibid., p. 290.

[28] M. N. Srinivas, "Introduction" to *Method in Social Anthropology. Selected Essays By A. R. Radcliffe-Brown* (Chicago, 1958), p. xviii. Meyer Fortes informs me that Radcliffe-Brown "never said" that Kropotkin was his neighbour in Birmingham, but claimed to have met Kropotkin in Kent while on holiday there. For an article which argues that Kropotkin was an important early influence on Radcliffe-Brown's anthropology, see Richard J. Perry, "Radcliffe-Brown and Kropotkin: The Heritage of Anarchism in British Social Anthropology", *Kroeber Anthropological Society Papers* Nos. 51 and 52 (Berkeley, 1978), pp. 61–65. Perry, who rather astoundingly does not refer to the passage from Srinivas cited above, bases his argument on purely circumstantial evidence.

[29] A. R. Radcliffe-Brown, "Marriage and Descent in North Australia", *Man* 10, 32 (1910). Further discussion of the subject occurs in articles by Mathews and Radcliffe-Brown in the 1912 volume of *Man*.

[30] Letter from Radcliffe-Brown to "The Secretary of the Anthropological Board" dated 4 Nov. 1909, Haddon Collection, Envelope 8.

[31] Haddon Collection, Envelope 12013.

[32] Grant Watson, op. cit. (note 21), p. 84.

[33] Ibid., pp. 84, 85.

[34] Undated letter from Radcliffe-Brown to Daisy Bates beginning "Mr Marett has handed to me a letter which you wrote to him on the subject of an ethnological expedition to West Australia", J. S. Battye Library of West Australian History, Perth.

[35] Ibid.

[36] Elizabeth Salter, *Daisy Bates* (New York, 1972), p. 135.

[37] Undated letter from Radcliffe-Brown to Daisy Bates beginning "I shall be unable to sail from England until July 28th . . . ", J. S. Battye Library of West Australian History, Perth.

[38] Ibid.

[39] For an interesting discussion of this article and Radcliffe-Brown's use of it see J. G. Peristiany, "Durkheim's Letter to Radcliffe-Brown", in K. H. Wolff, *Émile Durkheim 1858–1917* (Ohio, 1960), pp. 317–324.

[40] A. R. Radcliffe-Brown, "Three Tribes of Western Australia", *J. Roy. Anthrop. Inst.* 43, 193–194 (1913).

[41] Radcliffe-Brown, op. cit. (note 34).

[42] Radcliffe-Brown, op. cit. (note 37).

[43] A. R. Radcliffe-Brown, "Australian Social Organization", *Am. Anthrop.* NS 49, 153 (1947).

[44] Radcliffe-Brown, op. cit. (note 37).

[45] The *West Australian*, 10 Sept. 1910. (Clipping in Haddon Collection, Envelope 8.)

[46] My account of the 1910–1912 West Australian expedition is based mainly on the relevant chapters in E. L. Grant Watson's autobiography, op. cit. (note 21). A further eyewitness description of the expedition is given in Daisy Bates, *The Passing of the Aborigines. A Lifetime Spent Among the Natives of Australia* (London, 1938), Chapter IX. Secondary accounts, which like mine are based mainly upon Watson, are given in Salter, op. cit. (note 36); Rodney Needham, *Remarks and Inventions. Skeptical Essays About Kinship* (London, 1974); and Adam Kuper, *Anthropologists and Anthropology: The British School 1922–1972* (London, 1973).

[47] Grant Watson, op. cit. (note 21), pp. 105, 106.

48 Bates, op. cit. (note 46), p. 95. Grant Watson, op. cit. (note 21), p. 109.

49 Ibid., p. 110.

50 Letter from Radcliffe-Brown to [The Chief Protector of Aborigines?] dated 3 Oct. 1910, J. S. Battye Library of West Australian History, Perth.

51 Grant Watson, op. cit. (note 21), p. 112.

52 E. L. Grant Watson, *Where Bonds Are Loosed* (New York, 1918), pp. 31, 32. In *But to What Purpose* (p. 113), Grant Watson describes this book, his first novel, as depicting the situation on Bernier Island "with little deviation from the actual events".

53 Grant Watson, op. cit. (note 21), p. 113.

54 Ibid., p. 114.

55 Bates, op. cit. (note 46), p. 101.

56 Grant Watson, op. cit. (note 21), p. 113.

57 Ibid.

58 Ibid., p. 85.

59 Ibid., pp. 115, 116.

60 Salter, op. cit. (note 36), p. 145.

61 Radcliffe-Brown, op. cit. (note 40), p. 146.

62 A. R. Radcliffe-Brown, "Beliefs Concerning Childbirth in Some Australian Tribes", *Man* 12, 96 (1912).

63 Letter from Daisy Bates to Rev. John Mathew. Quoted in Salter, op. cit. (note 36), p. 147.

64 Grant Watson, op. cit. (note 21), p. 105.

65 Salter, op. cit. (note 36), p. 176.

66 Letter from Radcliffe-Brown to Mauss dated 6 Aug. 1912, in possession of Raymond Aron. Quoted in Steven Lukes, *Émile Durkheim. His Life and Works* (London, 1973), pp. 527, 528.

67 See Radcliffe-Brown, op. cit. (note 40).

68 Letter from Durkheim to Radcliffe-Brown dated 9 Nov. 1913. Reproduced in Peristiany, op. cit. (note 39), pp. 317, 318. The original had been preserved by Radcliffe-Brown in his annotated copy of Durkheim's *Le Suicide*. In fact Durkheim never did "carry out a new study of the facts", because the First World War, which disrupted and almost destroyed the Durkheimian school of sociology, was to break out in less than a year, and Durkheim himself was to die before the hostilities had run their course.

69 Letter from Durkheim to Radcliffe-Brown dated 12 Jan. 1914. From Radcliffe-Brown's papers at the Oxford Univeristy Institute of Social Anthropology. Quoted in Lukes, op. cit. (note 66) p. 528 n.

70 In other places, however, when Radcliffe-Brown considers the book as presenting a generalized theoretical position, he evaluates it in a much more favourable light. See for example his 1945 article "Religion and Society", reprinted in Radcliffe-Brown, *Structure and Function in Primitive Society* (New York, 1965), pp. 153–177.

71 A. R. Radcliffe-Brown, "The Sociological Theory of Totemism", originally 1929, reprinted in Radcliffe-Brown, *Structure and Function in Primitive Society* (New York, 1965), p. 124 ff. See also Radcliffe-Brown, "The Methods of Ethnology and Social Anthropology", original 1923, reprinted in M. N. Srinivas (ed.), *Method in Social Anthropology* (Chicago, 1958), pp. 20, 21. See also undated letter from Radcliffe-Brown to Rivers beginning "If the point is of interest to you . . . ", Haddon Collection, Envelope 12027.

[72] See for example Marvin Harris, *The Rise of Anthropological Theory* (New York, 1968), p. 515 ff.

[73] The passages in question, which are discussed and quoted in the immediately ensuing text, come from the following two sources: Undated latter from Radcliffe-Brown to Rivers beginning "Many thanks for your criticisms on the proofs . . . ", Haddon Collection, Envelope 12058. Undated letter from Radcliffe-Brown to Rivers beginning "I am very sorry to hear that you are laid up in hospital . . . ", Haddon Collection, Envelope 12062.

[74] B. Freire-Marreco and J. L. Myres (eds.), *Notes and Queries on Anthropology* (4th edn., London, 1912), p. 143.

[75] A. R. Radcliffe-Brown, "The Study of Kinship Systems" (1941). Reprinted in Radcliffe-Brown, *Structure and Function in Primitive Society* (Free Press paperback, 1965), p. 51.

[76] Letter from Radcliffe-Brown to Rivers dated 18 Oct. 1913, Haddon Collection, Envelope 12039.

[77] Undated letter from Radcliffe-Brown to Rivers beginning "Many thanks for your criticisms on the proofs . . . ", Haddon Collection, Envelope 12058.

[78] Ibid.

[79] Unattached fragment by Rivers beginning "Social Organization is so fundamental . . . ", Haddon Collection, Envelope 12027.

[80] Undated letter from Radcliffe-Brown to Rivers beginning "Many thanks for your paper. With the greater part of it I most heartily agree". Haddon Collection, Envelope 12027.

[81] Undated letter from Radcliffe-Brown to Rivers beginning "Many thanks for your letter. I am sorry that my notes on Totemism . . . ", Haddon Collection, Envelope 12062.

[82] Undated letter from Radcliffe-Brown to Rivers beginning "I should have greatly liked to have a talk with Mauss . . . ", Haddon Collection, Envelope 12027.

[83] Ibid.

[84] Undated letter from Radcliffe-Brown to Rivers beginning "There is a good deal more in Siebert's paper . . . ", Haddon Collection, Envelope 12027. See also Radcliffe-Brown, "Notes on Totemism in Eastern Australia", *J. Roy. Anthrop. Inst.* 59, 411 ff (1929).

[85] Undated letter from Radcliffe-Brown to Rivers beginning, "If the point is of interest to you . . . ", Haddon Collection, Envelope 12027.

[86] Radcliffe-Brown, op. cit. (note 81). Emphasis in original.

[87] Radcliffe-Brown, op. cit. (note 10), p. 393.

[88] Ibid., pp. 245, 257, 309, 232–234.

[89] Ibid., pp. 397, 167, 304.

[90] Ibid., p. 250.

[91] For a secondary source which uses this article to argue that Radcliffe-Brown's concept of function is heavily derivative upon that of Durkheim, see Harry Alpert, *Émile Durkheim and his Sociology* (New York, 1961), pp. 104–108.

[92] Another possible reason why Radcliffe-Brown hitched his wagon to Durkheim at this time might be concerned with the intellectual climate at the University of Chicago. As George Stocking has pointed out in his booklet *Anthropology at Chicago: Tradition, Discipline, Department* (University of Chicago, 1979), p. 29:

Debate on the nature of social science was part of the crackling intellectual milieu at the University in the mid-1930s. President Hutchins' neo-Thomist protégé Mortimer Adler, who was causing some to worry that students might convert to Catholicism, argued that "systematic social science" must be grounded in the categories of Aristotelian psychology. In response, Radcliffe-Brown gave a valedictory seminar in the spring of 1937, in which he defended the possibility of a "theoretical natural science of society" which "was in no sense a psychology".

The fact that Durkheim had taken an avowedly anti-psychological line may therefore have provided Radcliffe-Brown with a further motive for wishing to claim intellectual ancestry from the French sociologist.

[93] A. R. Radcliffe-Brown, *Structure and Function in Primitive Society* (New York, 1965), pp. 164–166. Radcliffe-Brown had outlined some of these necessary revisions and corrections to Durkheim's thesis in his 1929 article on "The Sociological Theory of Totemism". See ibid., p. 123 ff.

[94] Radcliffe-Brown to Rivers, op. cit. (note 84).

[95] Radcliffe-Brown, op. cit. (note 81).

[96] Radcliffe-Brown, op. cit. (note 82).

[97] Peristiany, op. cit. (note 39), p. 319.

[98] Radcliffe-Brown, op. cit. (note 40), p. 154. Strictly speaking Radcliffe-Brown's "genealogical tables" are not genealogies in Rivers's sense, since they do not include proper names.

[99] Ibid., p. 151.

[100] Ibid., p. 190.

[101] Ibid., p. 191.

[102] Letter from N. W. Thomas to Rivers dated 14 Apr. 1916, Haddon Collection, Envelope 12022.

[103] Rodney Needham, "Surmise, Discovery and Rhetoric". In Needham, op. cit. (note 46). Whilst the subject under consideration is that of priority, I should mention that, although there is no disputing Needham's priority in publishing his sceptical attack on Radcliffe-Brown's claim to having "discovered the Kariera system", I did not in fact derive my own very similar views on this matter from Needham. On the contrary, I had arrived independently at these views before Derek Freeman drew my attention to Needham's account late in 1974.

[104] A. R. Radcliffe-Brown, "The Social Organization of Australian Tribes", *Oceania* 1, p. 46, n. 5 (1930).

[105] A spirited but I think unconvincing rejoinder to Needham's attack on Radcliffe-Brown is given in Fred Eggan's "Aboriginal Sins", *The Times Literary Supplement* (13 Dec. 1974), pp. 1402, 1403. Eggan argues that, in speaking of "the Kariera system", Radcliffe-Brown was not referring, as Needham assumes, simply to the four sections and their associated marriage regulations. On the contrary, writes Eggan, Radcliffe-Brown considered that the Kariera system included many other social phenomena as well, including "the local groupings, the residence patterns, the division of labour, the totemic cults, and the nature of the tribal integration". Now it is true that Radcliffe-Brown regarded kinship systems as fulfilling many more social functions than just the regulation of marriage. Howeve, the fact remains that, in claiming to have made his "discovery", Radcliffe-Brown strongly implies that the entity which he allegedly discovered is nothing

more nor less than the Kariera method of regulating marriage. In the penultimate paragraph before the citation of the footnote in which the claim is made, the topic under discussion is marriage regulation. And immediately after citing the footnote, the text states that the Kariera system is "based on" cross-cousin marriage.

A second point made by Eggan is that, if Needham had bothered to look up the verb "to discover" in the *Shorter Oxford English Dictionary*, "he would have learnt that the meaning he provides is numbered eight in a list of ten; and that to uncover, or expose to view, or make known, or exhibit, or explore are all possible or acceptable meanings". However, Eggan conveniently neglects to discuss the context in which Radcliffe-Brown uses the word. For Radcliffe-Brown claims that his "discovery" was made as the result of a "search", which had been inspired by a previous "surmise" that such a system "might" exist somewhere within an area comprising over a million square miles. This context makes it clear that, whatever the possible meanings of "discover", the meaning provided by Needham is far and away the most appropriate one for the usage in question.

Eggan concludes his rejoinder with some uncharitably simplistic inferences about Needham's motive for attacking Radcliffe-Brown. According to Eggan, Needham has long borne Radcliffe-Brown a grudge as the result of an incident which occurred in the King's Arms Hotel at Oxford about a quarter of a century before. On this occasion, Radcliffe-Brown treated the young Needham's knowledge of Chinese calligraphy with disdain. These events, on Eggan's account, "led to detailed investigations of Radcliffe-Brown's discoveries and pronouncements, which called into question his status as a scholar and as a person". "It seems clear", concludes Eggan, "that the events in the King's Arms have powerfully influenced [Needham's] behaviour and scholarly judgement".

As a counterbalance to Eggan's article, I would like to refer the reader to Frederick G. G. Rose's *Classification of Kin, Age Structure and Marriage Amongst the Groote Eylandt Aborigines* (Berlin, 1960), pp. 4–5, 160–165. Rose, who himself carried out extensive fieldwork among the Australian Aborigines, reveals himself to be extremely sceptical about the worth of Radcliffe-Brown's Australian results, and of the claims made about how these results were obtained. It is also worth noting that in *An Anatomy of Kinship* (Englewood Cliffs, New Jersey, 1963), p. 95, Harrison White refers to the clarity of Radcliffe-Brown's presentation of the Kariera system as being "suspiciously perfect".

[106] A. R. Brown, "The Relationship System of the Dieri Tribe", *Man* 14, 33 (1914).

[107] A. R. Brown, "Notes on the Social Organization of Australian Tribes, Part I", *J. Roy. Anthrop. Inst.* 48, 245, 246 (1918). W. H. R. Rivers, *The History of Melanesian Society*, Vol. I (Cambridge, 1914), p. 17.

[108] W. H. R. Rivers, Referee's report dated 8 Mar. 1922, R.A.I. Archives, A9, Supplement.

[109] W. H. R. Rivers, *Social Organization* (London, 1926), p. 195 ff.

[110] Letter from Radcliffe-Brown to Haddon dated 13 Mar. 1920, Haddon Collection, Envelope 8.

[111] Letter from Haddon to the Rt. Hon. Lt. Gen. J. C. Smuts, L.L.D., Pretoria, Haddon Collection, Envelope 8. The same envelope also contains a letter by Haddon recommending Radcliffe-Brown for the position of Ethnologist in the Museum of Pretoria.

[112] Quoted in Firth, op. cit. (note 1), p. 293.

[113] A. R. Radcliffe-Brown, "The Mother's Brother in South Africa", original 1924,

reprinted in Radcliffe-Brown, *Structure and Function in Primitive Society* (New York, 1965).

114 Letter from Winnie Hoernle to Haddon dated 3 Feb. 1926, Haddon Collection, Envelope 9.

115 Letter from Radcliffe-Brown to Haddon dated 22 Oct. 1923, Haddon Collection, Envelope 8.

116 See, for example:

(a) Undated letter from Radcliffe-Brown to Rivers beginning "In explaining the Dieri system of social organization . . . ", Haddon Collection, Envelope 12027.

(b) Letter from Radcliffe-Brown to Haddon dated 27 June 1921, Haddon Collection, Envelope 4.

(c) Letter from Radcliffe-Brown to Haddon dated 12 Nov. 1921, Haddon Collection, Envelope 4.

(d) Letter from Radcliffe-Brown to Rivers dated 20 Feb. 1922, Haddon Collection, Envelope 12081.

(e) Letter from Radcliffe-Brown to Haddon dated 6 Mar. 1922, Haddon Collection, Envelope 4.

(f) Letter from Radcliffe-Brown to Haddon dated 18 Dec. 1922, Haddon Collection, Envelope 4.

Only at the beginning of his 1918 article (Radcliffe-Brown, op. cit. note 107, p. 222) does Radcliffe-Brown exhibit any lack of resolution in his ultimate goal of producing a major work on Australian social organization.

117 Copy of a "Report to the Vice-Chancellor by the Advisory Committee on the Selection of a Professor of Anthropology in the University of Sydney", Cambridge, 14 Sept. 1925, Rockefeller Foundation Archives, 401D "University of Sydney, Anthropology, 1924–26".

118 Letter from Radcliffe-Brown to E. E. Day of the Rockefeller Foundation dated 3 Oct. 1932, Rockefeller Foundation Archives, 410D "Australian National Research Council 1932".

119 Letter from Radcliffe-Brown to Haddon dated 9 May 1927, Haddon Collection, Envelope 25.

120 G. Elliot Smith, "The Problem of Totemism", A. R. Radcliffe-Brown, "The Sociological Theory of Totemism", *Proceedings of the Fourth Pacific Science Congress* (Java, 1929).

121 A. R. Radcliffe-Brown, "Historical and Functional Interpretations of Culture in Relation to the Practical Application of Anthropology to Native Peoples" (Abstract), *Proceedings of the Fourth Pacific Science Congress* (Java, 1929).

122 Copy of letter from Elliot Smith to Stanley M. Bruce dated 13 Oct. 1932, Rockefeller Foundation Archives, 410D "Australian National Research Council 1932". Bruce, a former Prime Minister of Australia, was at this time "Minister Without Portfolio" for the Australian Government in London.

123 Letter from Radcliffe-Brown to Dr Mason of the Rockefeller Foundation dated 17 Nov. 1930, Rockefeller Foundation Archives, 410 D "Australian National Research Council 1930".

124 Elkin, op. cit. (note 25), pp. 249, 250.

125 A. R. Radcliffe-Brown, *The Social Organization of Australian Tribes* (Oceania Monograph No. 1, Melbourne, 1931), p. 221. C.f. Needham, op. cit. (note 46), p. 153.

126 A. R. Radcliffe-Brown, "A System of Notation for Relationships", *Man* **30**, 93 (1930).
127 Rodney Needham, *Rethinking Kinship and Marriage* (London, 1971), pp. xxii–xxv.
128 Ibid., p. xxviii.
129 Letter from Spencer to Haddon dated 15 Oct. 1921, Haddon Collection, Envelope 4.
130 Undated letter from Radcliffe-Brown to Rivers beginning "I am very sorry to hear that you are laid up in hospital . . . ", Haddon Collection, Envelope 12062.
131 Undated letter from Radcliffe-Brown to Rivers beginning "I am glad that you are pleased with the M.S. which you kindly returned to me . . . ", Haddon Collection, Envelope 12027.
132 See, for example, Radcliffe-Brown, "The Comparative Method in Social Anthropology", *J. Roy. Anthrop. Inst.* 81 (1951).
133 A. R. Radcliffe-Brown, *A Natural Science of Society* (Glencoe, 1957), pp. 32, 33.
134 C. Lévi-Strauss, *Totemism* (Boston, 1963), pp. 83–91.
135 A. R. Radcliffe-Brown, manuscript notebook E5 on Australian social organization, Department of Anthropology, University of Sydney.
136 A. R. Radcliffe-Brown, "The Comparative Method in Social Anthropology", *J. Roy. Anthrop. Inst.* 81 (1951).
137 A. Goldenweiser, *Anthropology* (New York, 1937), pp. 338–350.
138 Elliot Smith, op. cit. (note 122).
139 Meyer Fortes, *Kinship and the Social Order* (Chicago, 1969), p. 45.
140 Fred Eggan, "Lewis H. Morgan in Kinship Perspective", in G. E. Dole and R. L. Carneiro (eds.), *Essays in the Science of Culture* (New York, 1960), p. 185. Actually it should be mentioned that Morgan's *Systems of Consanguinity* . . . (Washington, 1870), p. 158, does contain a promising but very brief passage on the social functions of the mother's brother.
141 Radcliffe-Brown, op. cit. (note 75), p. 51.
142 W. H. R. Rivers, "The Father's Sister in Oceania", *Folklore* **21**, 55 (1910). For a discussion by Rivers of the social functions of the mother's brother, see his "Survival in Sociology", *Sociological Review* **6**, 293–305 (1913).
143 Radcliffe-Brown, op. cit. (note 113), p. 18.
144 Ibid., p. 19.
145 Ibid., p. 20.
146 Ibid.
147 Ibid., p. 24.
148 Freire-Marreco and Myres, op. cit. (note 74), pp. 153, 154.
149 A. R. Radcliffe-Brown, "A Further Note on Joking Relationships" (1949), reprinted in Radcliffe-Brown, *Structure and Function in Primitive Society* (Free Press paperback, 1965), p. 106.
150 A. R. Radcliffe-Brown, "On Joking Relationships" (1940), reprinted in ibid., p. 92.
151 Ibid., p. 90.
152 Another possible influence upon Radcliffe-Brown might be Lewis Henry Morgan. Meyer Fortes, who now owns what used to be Radcliffe-Brown's personal copy of Morgan's *Ancient Society*, claims in *Kinship and the Social Order* (Chicago, 1969), p. 5, that "one need only turn the pages and note the passages he [Radcliffe-Brown] marked to realize how closely he had read it and how he had penetrated to what was fundamental

in Morgan's work". My attempts to pursue this matter further (whilst doing research at Cambridge during the summer of 1972) were not helped by the fact that, when I politely requested permission to look at the aforesaid copy of Morgan's book, my request was greeted with the bluntest of refusals. And since my own investigations of the fairly extensive correspondence which has survived from the period when Radcliffe-Brown's theoretical position was taking shape reveal little to suggest that Morgan's work provided a consequential part of Radcliffe-Brown's intellectual ancestry, I have given little credence to the hypothesis of Morganian influence.

[153] This way of expressing the matter was suggested to me by a paper on "Professionalization and the History of Australian Biology", which was read by Lyndsay Farrall at the University of New South Wales on 12 June 1980.

CHAPTER VIII

[1] C. G. Seligman and Brenda Z. Seligman, *The Veddas* (Cambridge, 1911), p. xi.

[2] Letter from E. L. Newsom to J. Knox-Shaw dated 4 Nov. [1921?]. Letter from J. D. Newsom to J. Knox-Shaw dated 11 Nov. 1921. Both letters in Haddon Collection, Envelope 12081.

[3] E. L. Newsom, ibid.

[4] Letter from G. St. J. Orde Browne to Haddon dated 8 Feb. 1913, Haddon Collection, Envelope 24.

[5] Letter from G. St. J. Orde Browne to Rivers dated 24 Aug. 1913. Haddon Collection, Envelope 12065.

[6] Sketch accompanying ibid.

[7] Undated letter from Rivers to Orde Browne, Haddon Collection, Envelope 12065.

[8] G. St. J. Orde Browne, *The Vanishing Tribes of Kenya* (London, 1925), p. 8.

[9] Undated letter from Winifred Tucker to Rivers written at "Sandvorthein [?] Near Walfisch Bay", Haddon Collection, Envelope 12064.

[10] Gregory Bateson, "Foreword" to *Naven* (originally published 1936, second edition, Stanford, 1958), p. ix.

[11] Gregory Bateson, "Social Structure of the Iatmul People of the Sepik River", *Oceania* 2, 245, 246 (1932).

[12] Ibid.

[13] Margaret Mead, *Blackberry Winter* (New York, 1972), p. 158.

[14] Bateson, op. cit. (note 10), p. x.

[15] I owe this point to Edmund Leach, personal communication.

[16] Bateson, op. cit. (note 10), p. 90.

[17] Ibid., p. 249.

[18] Ibid., p. 257.

[19] Ibid., p. 279.

[20] R. F. Fortune, *Sorcerers of Dobu* (London, 1932), p. xxiii.

[21] Ibid., p. xxvii.

[22] The fifth passage, for example, occurs as the summation of a chapter with the neo-Boasian title: "The Individual in the Social Pattern".

[23] Fortune, op. cit. (note 20), p. xviii.

[24] Kenneth Maddock, *The Australian Aborigines. A Portrait of Their Society* (Penguin, Harmondsworth, 1974), p. 72.

[25] Ibid., Chapter 4.

[26] Kenelm Burridge, *Encountering Aborigines* (Pergamon Press, Oxford, 1973), p. 238.

[27] Robert F. Murphy, *The Dialectics of Social Life: Alarms and Excursions in Anthropological Theory* (Basic Books, 1971), p. 21. Pages 20–23 of Murphy's book contain a number of brilliantly expressed insights into the nature of British Social Anthropology.

[28] John Layard, *The Story of My Life* Part IV (begun March 1964), p. 22. Photocopy of typescript kindly supplied by the author's son, P. R. G. Layard. The site of the Aboriginal encampment is in some doubt. Layard states that the Aborigines "lived near the River Darling in Victoria". However, the River Darling is located in New South Wales and southern Queensland, so Layard must have misremembered either the name of the river, or the name of the State.

[29] F. C. Bartlett, "Cambridge, England: 1887–1937", *Am. J. Psychol.* 50, 107 (1937).

[30] F. C. Bartlett, *The Eagle* (Magazine of St John's College) 62 (1968), p. 160.

[31] Ibid. My attention was drawn to this passage by J. A. Barnes.

[32] J. A. Barnes, "Inquest on the Murngin", *Roy. Anthrop. Inst. Occas. Paper* 26 (London, 1967), p. 1. Barnes's paper is recommended as providing an excellent summary, evaluation and bibliography of this difficult controversy.

[33] Ibid., p. 2.

[34] Ibid., p. 45.

[35] Ibid., p. 43.

[36] Ibid., pp. 31, 32.

[37] Ibid., p. 19.

[38] It might be suggested that Scheffler's revaluation of kinship studies via componential analysis represents such a drastic revision of the previous approach that it in fact constitutes what Kuhn would call a "paradigm shift". On this interpretation, the protracted and indecisive nature of the skirmish would be understandable, since it would represent part of a "scientific revolution" in kinship studies, in which fundamental assumptions and modes of explanation are up for grabs. This interpretation is supported by the observation that something which closely resembles what Kuhn depicts as the "incommensurability" of different paradigms is often in evidence when devotees of componential analysis attempt to engage more traditional anthropologists in debate. Under such circumstances, a good deal of mutual incomprehension occurs, with people talking "through" instead of to each other. However, it seems to me that, in the final analysis, Scheffler's revaluation of Deacon looks more like a small-scale clash between purported puzzle-solutions, rather than a clash between anything as metaphysically consequential as two distinct paradigms.

[39] M. Fortes, *Social Anthropology at Cambridge Since 1900* (Cambridge University Press Inaugural Lecture, 1953), p. 14.

[40] C.f. J. A. Barnes, "Foreword" to L. R. Hiatt, *Kinship and Conflict* (Canberra, 1965), p. viii.

[41] Phyllis Kaberry, *Aboriginal Woman. Sacred and Profane* (London, 1939), p. 115 ff.

[42] Barnes, op. cit. (note 40), p. x.

[43] Ibid.

[44] For an account of the issues involved in the Rivers-Kroeber debate see A. R. Radcliffe-Brown, *Structure and Function in Primitive Society* (Free Press, 1965), pp. 59–62.

[45] Robert Lowie, "Review of *Kinship and Social Organization* by Rivers", *Am. Anthrop.* NS 17, 339 (1915).

[46] Ibid., pp. 332–334.

[47] Lowie gives a similarly weighted evaluation of Rivers's anthropological career in his *The History of Ethnological Theory* (New York, 1937), pp. 169–176.

[48] A. L. Kroeber, *The Nature of Culture* (Chicago, 1952), pp. 172, 173.

[49] J. A. Barnes, *Three Styles in the Study of Kinship* (University of California Press, 1971).

[50] Meyer Fortes, *Kinship and the Social Order* (Chicago, 1969), p. 9 ff. George Peter Murdock, "Anthropology's Mythology", The Huxley Memorial Lecture 1971, *Proc. Roy. Anthrop. Inst.* (1971), p. 17.

[51] For example, the Lévi-Straussian account of totemism is partly based upon an extension of Radcliffe-Brown's analysis of the symbolic significance of Eaglehawk and Crow among the Australian Aborigines. This analysis itself relies upon a structural dichotomy of the type invoked by Rivers. See C. Lévi-Strauss, *Totemism* (Boston, 1963), p. 83 ff.

[52] C. Lévi-Strauss, "Do Dual Organizations Exist?" in Lévi-Strauss, *Structural Anthropology* (Anchor, 1967), pp. 158, 159, 160 fn.

[53] H. W. Scheffler, "Ancestor Worship in Anthropology . . . ", *Current Anthropology* 7, 543 (1966).

[54] Elkin in conversation, 1974.

[55] Cf. John Beattie: "Modern social anthropologists frequently refer to Radcliffe-Brown, but often as not they do so only to point out how wrong he was." From Timothy Raison (ed.), *The Founding Fathers of Social Science* (Penguin, Harmondsworth, 1969), p. 178.

[56] Robert Redfield, "Introduction" to Fred Eggan (ed.), *Social Anthropology of North American Tribes* (Chicago, 1937), pp. vii, viii.

[57] Meyer Fortes, "Preface" to Meyer Fortes (ed.), *Social Structure. Studies Presented to A. R. Radcliffe-Brown* (New York, 1963), pp. vii, v.

[58] George Caspar Homans, writing in the *American Anthropologist*, date unknown. (Quoted on the cover of the 1965 Free Press paperback edition of *Structure and Function in Primitive Society*.)

[59] Raymond Firth, "Introduction" to reprint of Rivers, *Kinship and Social Organization* (London, 1968), pp. 21, 22.

[60] John Layard in conversation, 1973.

[61] Sol Tax, "From Lafitau to Radcliffe-Brown. A Short History of the Study of Social Organization". In F. Eggan (ed.), *Social Anthropology of North American Tribes* (Chicago, 1937), pp. 471, 472. Originally written as Part I of Tax's Ph.D. dissertation, University of Chicago, 1935.

[62] Ibid., p. 472.

INDEX OF NAMES

INDEX OF SUBJECTS

387